Working with Economics

Seventh Edition

a Canadian Framework

Working with

Economics

Seventh Edition

a Canadian Framework

H. Richard Hird

Durham College

PEARSON

Prentice Hall

Toronto

To Nancy, Matthew, and Heather

National Library of Canada Cataloguing in Publication

Hird, H. Richard
  Working with economics : a Canadian framework / H. Richard
Hird. — 7th ed.

Includes index.

ISBN 0-13-121923-5

1. Economics. 2. Canada—Economic conditions. 3. Canada—Economic policy. I. Title.

HB171.5.H57 2005   330   C2003-904829-2

0-13-121923-5

Vice President, Editorial Director: Michael J. Young
Senior Acquisitions Editor: Gary Bennett
Marketing Manager: Steve McGill
Associate Editor: Stephen Broadbent
Production Editor: Jennifer Handel
Copy Editor: Kelli Howey
Proofreader: Nancy Carroll
Production Coordinator: Andrea Falkenberg
Permissions: Nicola Winstanley
Page Layout: Nelson Gonzalez
Art Director: Mary Opper
Interior and Cover Design: Anthony Leung
Cover Image: Ken Davies/Masterfile

Statistics Canada information is used with the permission of the Minister of Industry, as Minister responsible for Statistics Canada. Information on the availability of the wide range of data from Statistics Canada can be obtained from Statistics Canada's Regional Offices, its World Wide Web site at http://www.statcan.ca, and its toll-free access number 1-800-263-1136. The Statistics Canada CANSIM II database can be accessed at http://cansim2.statcan.ca/cgi-win/CNSMCGI.EXE.

3 4 5   09 08 07 06 05

Printed and bound in Canada.

Brief Contents

Contents

Preface

Welcome to the seventh edition of *Working with Economics.* Although I was happy with the first edition, it is my belief that each subsequent edition has been an improvement on the previous one. With each new edition changes have been introduced: new Everyday Economics readings have been added; topics in the text have been updated; new topics have been introduced; international comparisons have been added; and references to websites have been inserted. Thanks to the suggestions from my colleagues at Durham College and from the reviewers of the text, this edition is no exception.

Organization and Approach

Many students are formally exposed to the study of economics in an introductory course. Only a small percentage of students who enrol in an introductory principles course proceed with further study. The introductory economics course must, therefore, not only familiarize students with economic principles, but also provide them with an appreciation of the major economic issues in our society, such as unemployment and inflation, as well as with programs and regulations created to deal with these issues.

This textbook is intended for an introductory college course in economics. It was written with three assumptions in mind. First, an introductory course need not cover all topics in the field of economics but rather should emphasize basic principles. Many existing texts are too large and cover topics rarely discussed in an introductory course. Although sometimes interesting, these topics are best left to an intermediate or more advanced course. This textbook excludes such topics but provides the student with the basic tools necessary to analyze most economic issues.

The second assumption is that students learn best by doing rather than simply by reading. Understanding economics is not easy, and most students must work at it. This textbook emphasizes an applied approach by including review questions throughout each chapter. If students can master these questions, they are well prepared to move on to the next topic. More questions are provided at the end of each chapter, and these can be used to introduce classroom discussion about economic principles. In the seventh edition, we have provided even more review questions.

Third, students gain a better understanding of economic principles when they can apply them to everyday events. All chapters contain boxed readings called "Everyday Economics." This special material can provide the basis for interesting classroom discussion relating the theoretical with the practical. The issues dealt with in these sections are meant to highlight the theoretical concepts contained in the chapter without affecting the continuity of the text itself.

Changes to the Seventh Edition

The following changes have been made to the seventh edition.

- A new feature called Core Concept Building was added to help students make connections between important concepts. Topic areas in economics are often interrelated, and this feature offers useful cues to other areas of the text, where students can refresh their knowledge of important prerequisite concepts before tackling a new chapter.
- New Everyday Economics readings have been added on softwood lumber, costs in the software industry, equalization payments, immigration, and price fixing.
- More questions have been added to the Everyday Economics readings, the Questions for Review and Discussion, and the Test Bank for instructors.
- The data in each chapter have been updated, as have the Everyday Economics readings and the International Comparisons.
- The Glossary has been inserted back into the text. Since students rely on the Glossary when studying for tests and exams, it is necessary that it be close at hand.

Pedagogical Features

This textbook contains several features aimed at improving the student's understanding of economic principles. These are as follows:

- Chapters begin with the objectives, key terms, and core concepts clearly stated. This material clarifies the pedagogical goals within the chapter and relates the chapters to each other.
- A definition for each key term appears in the margin adjacent to its first appearance. The key terms are also defined in the Glossary near the back of the book. The margin definitions provide an explanation on first reading of the material; the Glossary offers a summary and quick reference.
- Questions for review are interspersed throughout each chapter at the end of the text sections. By attempting to answer these questions, students will be able to immediately check their comprehension of new material.
- Questions are included in the boxed Everyday Economics features to promote further exploration of the topic.

- A Summary near the end of each chapter briefly restates the main points.
- Questions for Review and Discussion appear at the end of each chapter. They help students reinforce their understanding of the content.
- An annotated list of Suggested Readings and Selected Websites at the end of each chapter will help students who want to pursue particular topics.

Student Resource CD

Interactive Graphics Exercises

Many of the graphs and diagrams used in the study of economics have an implicit, dynamic "before and after" dimension: for example, the supply curve has one position before the imposition of an excise tax and another position after the tax has been imposed on the manufacturer. Similarly, the shape and position of the production-possibilities curve also changes after a change in the amount of available resources.

Traditional textbooks do their best to represent these dynamics. Devices such as arrows and subscripted curve names (such as S_1 and S_2) try to convey the change in position. To students studying economics for the first time these conventions may not always appear obvious. Interactive Graphics provides hands-on, visually oriented activities for students to truly immerse themselves in the key dynamics of the models being studied. Students will need some knowledge of Excel software. For those students unfamiliar with the software, an introduction on the CD provides some basic instructions. The Interactive Graphics exercises are indicated within the text with a (Interactive Graphics) symbol; the exercises themselves are contained on the accompanying CD.

Additional Resources

The CD also contains an electronic version of the Glossary for easy reference, as well as four appendices pertaining to specific topics in the text. The appendices are referenced in their appropriate sections of the text.

Instructor Supplement

An Instructors Resource CD-ROM has been specially created for this edition, which provides a convenient, single source location for the following:

1. *Instructor's Manual.* Provided in MS Word and PDF formats, each chapter of this manual contains lecture suggestions, a list of possible class activities or assignments, and answers to all questions in the textbook.

2. *PowerPoint Transparencies*—The IRCD also contains PowerPoint Transparencies of most of the figures and tables in the textbook.

3. *Pearson TestGen*—The Pearson TestGen is a special computerized version of the Test Item File that enables instructors to view and edit the existing questions, add questions, generate tests, and print the tests in a variety of formats. Powerful search and sort functions make it easy to locate questions and arrange them in any order desired. TestGen also enables instructors to administer tests on a local area network, have the tests graded electronically, and have the results prepared in electronic or printed reports. The Pearson TestGen is compatible with IBM or Macintosh systems.

Acknowledgements

No textbook is written without the assistance of others. My wife, Nancy, and my children, Matthew and Heather, did not complain about the time allocated to the rewriting of this textbook; they fully appreciate the concept of opportunity cost. I am also grateful for the assistance provided by the reviewers of the first six editions of this text. Their suggestions are an integral part of the book's success and acceptance in educational institutions. I appreciate the comments from my colleagues at Durham College who have used the book in their classes.

In addition, I would like to thank the following people who offered formal reviews for this edition: James Herbert (Red River College), Keith Jensen (Malaspina University-College), Mike Katz (Humber College), Hafiz Rahman (University-College of the Cariboo), Kevin Richter (Douglas College), James Seldon (University-College of the Cariboo), and Stuart J. Wilson (University of Regina).

I would also like to acknowledge the assistance that I was given by the staff at Pearson Education Canada, especially Gary Bennett (Senior Acquisitions Editor), Stephen Broadbent (Associate Editor), Jennifer Handel (Production Editor), and Kelli Howey (Copy Editor).

I hope that you will find this text extremely useful in explaining economic concepts. If you have any comments, I would be delighted to hear from you. I can be reached at **webinfo.pubcanada@pearsoned.com.**

Rick Hird

Introductory Concepts

Key Terms

scarcity
opportunity cost
production-possibilities curve
law of diminishing returns
free-market approach
command approach
positive relationship
inverse relationship

Core Concept Building

This chapter introduces two of the most important concepts in economics: opportunity cost and the law of diminishing returns. Ensure that you have a good understanding of these concepts before you proceed to the next chapter. You will encounter the concept of opportunity cost again in Chapters 9, 11, and 14. The law of diminishing returns will again appear in Chapters 11 and 14.

Chapter Objectives

After successfully completing this chapter, you will be able to:

- relate the concept of scarcity to the science of economics
- understand what is meant by the term "resource"
- differentiate between direct and opportunity costs
- use the concept of opportunity cost in your everyday life, and relate it to the allocation of Canada's resources
- construct a production-possibilities curve and identify the assumptions under which the curve is drawn
- define the law of diminishing returns, using an example of conditions under which it would apply
- understand the differences between the two basic approaches to economic decision making: the free-market approach and the command approach
- understand why it is necessary to make certain assumptions when developing economic theories
- identify and present in graphic form positive and inverse relationships between two variables

THE COD FISHERY

In recent years one of the best examples of scarcity and the need for decision making regarding the use of scarce resources has been the depletion of the Northern Cod fish stocks in the Atlantic Ocean. The Northern Cod is a population of cod located on the eastern shores of Newfoundland and Labrador north of St. John's. It is one of 11 cod stocks in the Atlantic region. For centuries Europeans, North Americans, and others have fished for Northern Cod. The cod fishery was the economic foundation for settlements in Newfoundland and Labrador.

From 1850 to 1950, the annual average catch was 250 000 tonnes. During the 1960s the size of the annual catch increased, reaching a peak of 800 000 tonnes in 1968. Unfortunately, the stock of fish was not large enough to support these levels. In 1977, Canada declared a 320-km management zone for the fish stocks and restricted the amount that could be caught each year. In 1991, the federal government set a limit of 120 000 tonnes on the catch of Northern Cod. In 1992, the federal government closed the Northern Cod fishery; it closed other fisheries in 1993. Cod fishing has never been fully shut down in the Atlantic region; however, restrictions have been placed on the size of the catch.

In 1999, the federal government reopened the Northern Cod fishery with a limit of 7000 tonnes. The rationale behind the reopening of the fishery was to gather scientific information on the size of the cod stocks. Based on new information, the federal government ordered a halt to cod fishing off the northeastern part of Newfoundland and Labrador and in the Gulf of St. Lawrence. Fishing for cod off the southeast coast of Newfoundland and Labrador is permitted.

The following table shows the cod landings in tonnes in the Atlantic region for the years 1989 and 2001. Note that the decline in the landings is attributed mainly to the restrictions placed on the northern cod catch.

Atlantic Coast commercial landings: cod, in tonnes, 1989 and 2001

	1989	2001
Newfoundland and Labrador	262 083	23 707
Prince Edward Island	4 729	803
Nova Scotia	122 860	10 527
New Brunswick	10 490	1 258
Quebec	25 927	4 031
Total	426 089	40 325

SOURCE: Fisheries and Oceans Canada, www.dfo-mpo.gc.ca (December 2002). Reproduced with the permission of Her Majesty the Queen of England in Right of Canada, 2003.

This reading on cod stocks introduces the concept of *scarcity*, an important concept in the study of economics. If cod stocks were abundant, would much time and effort be put into managing them? No—it is because cod is available only in a limited supply that a decision must be made on the use of this resource. Chapter 1 explains that economics is a study of how decisions are made regarding the use of scarce resources. As you read the chapter, think about who should make the decision on the use of the cod resource.

What Is Economics?

Why is it so difficult to find a job? Why is Canadian money worth less than American money? Should governments in Canada enact more strict pollution-control legislation? Why are there differences between the wages paid to men and those paid to women? Why do many athletes earn more than the prime minister of Canada? Should medical care be provided free of charge to all residents of this country?

These are some of the questions that concern Canadians. To many of us, they may seem unrelated, yet the answers to all of them fall within the subject matter of economics. An adequate understanding of economic issues is becoming more and more essential to everyday living. This book is an introduction to the science of economics: it helps provide the information and skills that will enable you to answer the questions raised above, and many others as well.

The dictionary defines economics as the science that deals with the production, distribution, and use of goods, money, natural resources, and services. But this definition does not provide a real understanding of the subject. One important element of economics is missing from the definition. If it were not for the concept of *scarcity*, there would be no need to study economics. As a starting point for our definition, let us discuss scarcity.

Scarcity

The dictionary tells us that **scarcity** is "an insufficient amount or supply." In economic terms, anything that has a limited supply is referred to as scarce. As a result, almost everything is scarce because very few things are available in unlimited quantities. The only items that cannot be considered scarce are air and sunshine—at certain times of the year. If there is only a limited amount of a commodity, then a decision has to be made as to how that commodity will be used.

On an individual basis, time and money are always scarce commodities. There are only 24 hours in a day. Regardless of how many things we plan to do each day, we are restricted by the number of hours available. For example, time has to be set aside for sleeping, eating, studying, and recreation. A decision has to be made about how best to use the time available. Also, not many of us have an unlimited supply of dollars on hand. Because the amount of money that we possess is limited, we must decide how to allocate it among various purchases. It is only when things are not limited in supply that we do not have to make such decisions.

People who are in business also have to deal with scarcity. Farmers are restricted by the amount of land available and must decide what crops they

In economics, the term scarcity refers to anything that is available only in a limited supply.

are going to grow. Store owners have a limited amount of space to use, which means they must make decisions about what products they will or will not stock on their shelves. Manufacturers must decide what products they will produce with a given quantity of machines and equipment. Again, the fact of scarcity requires that decisions be made.

On a much larger scale, it can be said that Canada has a limited amount of *resources*. The dictionary defines a resource as something that a country or state can use to its advantage. Resources are used to produce goods and services, and can be classified into three groups: *land, labour,* and *capital.*

When we refer to *land* as a resource, we mean more than the ten million square kilometres that comprise Canada's land mass. We include such natural resources as minerals, wild animals, vegetation, and water. Canada is the world's largest producer of asbestos, zinc, silver, and nickel. It is the second-largest producer of potash, gypsum, molybdenum, and sulphur, and is a major producer of uranium, titanium, aluminum, cobalt, gold, lead, copper, iron, and platinum. Our country also has abundant oil and natural gas reserves. Wild animals form the basis of our fur and hunting industries. Most of the world's stock of woodland caribou, mountain sheep, wolves, grizzly bears, and wolverines is found in Canada. One form of vegetation—trees—covers about 4.5 million square kilometres. This resource enables Canada's lumber, newsprint, and pulp-and-paper industries. As mentioned above, water is also a resource. The minerals and vegetation that are present under water make up part of the resource that we refer to as land. Tonnes of fish are taken annually from Canadian waters. Although Canada's land resources are extensive, they still have their limitations and decisions must be made regarding their use.

The population of Canada forms the basis of our *labour* resource. Canada's population in 2003 was approximately 32 million people. Our population is continuing to grow, but not at the rate that it has in the past. The reason for the slower rate of growth is that the fertility rate in Canada has been declining. In 1959 there were an average of 3.9 births per woman. In 2000, the national fertility rate was 1.49. Only in the Northwest Territories did the number of births increase in the year 2000 from the previous year. Even though women are having fewer children, our population is still growing because of the large number of women who are in their child-bearing years. A steady flow of immigrants is also responsible for increases in the population of Canada.

Statistics Canada also calculates the number of births per 1000 people. As would be expected, the decline in the fertility rate is accompanied by a decline in the birth rate. Canada's birth rate has fallen from 26.91 births per 1000 people in 1946 to 10.6 in 2002. Table 1.1 presents the number of births per 1000 population for Canada, the provinces, and the territories for 2002–2003. Similar to data for fertility rates, the lowest birth rate was in Newfoundland and Labrador and the highest birth rate per 1000 people was in Nunavut.

Table 1.1 *Birth rate per 1000 population, Canada and the provinces/territories, 2002–2003*

Newfoundland and Labrador	8.8
Prince Edward Island	9.9
Nova Scotia	9.4
New Brunswick	9.4
Quebec	9.7
Ontario	11.0
Manitoba	12.1
Saskatchewan	12.0
Alberta	12.3
British Columbia	9.8
Yukon	11.3
Northwest Territories	14.8
Nunavut	25.2
Canada	10.6

SOURCE: Adapted from the Statistics Canada CANSIM database, Tables 051-0001 and 051-0004.

A comparison of data on population density for 2000 and the birth rate for selected countries is presented in International Comparisons 1.1. The data were collected by the Organization for Economic Cooperation and Development (OECD) (accessed at http://www.statcan.ca in January 2003).

As well as growing, the Canadian population is also aging. In 1971, people aged 65 and over comprised 8.2 percent of the population. By 2002, this figure had risen to 12.7 percent, and by the year 2026 it is projected to be 18.8 percent. Elderly individuals are not expected to be part of our labour resource. The population of Canada by province for 2002 is listed in Table 1.2.

International Comparisons 1.1

Total fertility rates for selected countries, 2003

Country	Children born/ woman	Country	Children born/ woman
United States	2.07	Ethiopia	5.55
Mexico	2.53	Somalia	6.98
United Kingdom	1.66	Greece	1.35
South Africa	2.24	Italy	1.26
Israel	2.5	Pakistan	4.1
Germany	1.37	Nigeria	5.4
Barbados	1.65	Netherlands	1.65
France	1.85	China	1.7
Dominican Republic	2.92	Argentina	2.28
Philippines	3.29	Senegal	4.93
Saudi Arabia	6.15	Yemen	6.82
Syria	3.72	Chad	6.44

SOURCE: www.cia.gov/cia/publications/factbook.

Table 1.2 *Population of Canada by province and territory, 2002*

	THOUSANDS
Newfoundland and Labrador	531.6
Prince Edward Island	139.9
Nova Scotia	944.8
New Brunswick	756.7
Quebec	7 455.2
Ontario	12 068.3
Manitoba	1 150.8
Saskatchewan	1 011.8
Alberta	3 113.6
British Columbia	4 141.3
Yukon	29.9
Northwest Territories	41.4
Nunavut	28.7
Canada	31 414.0

SOURCE: Adapted from the Statistics Canada CANSIM database, Table 051-0001.

Our *labour* resource includes more than just the number of people in Canada. It refers to the variety of skills, level of education, and technical training of the Canadian population. Those people who are working and those who are willing to work are all included in the labour force.

Capital resources, which form the third classification, refer to manufactured items that are used to produce goods and services. Buildings, factories, equipment, computers, tools, lathes, drill presses, forklift trucks, and conveyor belts are examples of capital resources. Also included under the heading of capital resources are steel and paper mills, nuclear and hydroelectric power plants, train stations, and airports. Transportation vehicles such as trucks, railway cars, buses, and airplanes are further examples of capital.

Despite the abundance of these various resources, Canada still has a limited amount of each. These limitations require that Canadians decide how best to use our available resources. What products will we produce? What services will we provide? How will these goods and services be produced? Who will receive these goods and services? These are just some of the decisions that must be made as a result of the limits on productive resources.

Whenever a resource is scarce or available only in limited supply in relation to the demand for it, a decision must be made about how the resource will be used. *Economics is the study of how we make decisions regarding the use of our scarce resources.*

EVERYDAY ECONOMICS 1.1

Water: A Scarce Resource?

It may seem unbelievable to suggest that Canada could face a water shortage. Canada has 14 percent of the world's lakes and 9 percent of the world's river flow, serving less than one percent of the world's population. More than seven percent of our country is covered with water. The Great Lakes contain 22 800 cubic kilometres of water, or about 18 percent of the fresh water on this planet. Lake Superior is the world's largest freshwater lake. Canada has 244 000 kilometres of coastline, the longest in the world.

Despite these impressive statistics, Canada may soon be facing a water crisis. Why is this so? Much of the problem in Canada centres on matching the demand for water with the available supply. On average, each Canadian uses 7100 litres of water a day—taking into account household, industrial, and agricultural use. The demand for water by Canadians is quite high. In fact, we are the second-highest water users in the world, following only the Americans. Apart from needing water to drink, Canadians also require a great deal of water for our modern conveniences. For example, one flush of a toilet uses 23 litres of water; a shower uses about 25 litres a minute; a dishwasher uses about 65 litres; an automatic clothes washer uses 230 litres; and a garden hose uses 1500 litres or more per hour.

In addition to our domestic use of water, industry and agriculture require water. Examples of industrial and agricultural uses for water include the following:

- Producing one tonne of steel can consume 280 tonnes of water.
- Manufacturing an automobile uses 50 times the car's weight in water.
- Producing one kilogram of steak can require up to 20 500 litres of water.

The demand for water clearly exists. But what about the supply? The opening paragraph in this Everyday Economics feature suggests that the supply of water in Canada is extensive; however, this fact must be examined in more detail. Sixty percent of Canada's water flows north, but most of Canada's population lives in the south, close to the U.S. border. Much of the water is not accessible to our population.

Over the next 50 years, global warming and climatic change will threaten Canada's freshwater fisheries and the state of our drinking water. Warm spells have resulted in the thinning and receding of glaciers in the Rockies; glaciers represent the source of most of western Canada's drinking water. Lower water levels are having an impact on shipping in the Great Lakes. In addition to global warming, Canada's water supply is being affected by acid rain, human and livestock wastes, increased ultraviolet radiation, and airborne toxins.

A number of Canadian companies want the right to export Canadian water to other countries, particularly the United States. One proposal is to ship Lake Superior water by tanker across the border. Another proposal involves exporting the water from interior Newfoundland and Labrador lakes. A third proposal would ship pure British Columbia mountain water to California. Thus far, all the proposals for exporting water have been rejected by the provincial governments involved. Should water be treated with respect to trade the way we treat other resources, such as trees, minerals, animals, and fish? Will Canada be forced to sell its fresh water to other countries?

It can be argued that water in its natural state is defined under trade agreements (NAFTA and the World Trade Organization) as a tradable commodity. A counter-argument can also be made; that is, trade agreements govern the rules of trade but do not force countries to trade. If Canada does not want to sell its fresh water, the decision does not violate any trade agreement. A ban on water sales could be justified under environmental protection considerations.

The Constitution of Canada assigns the responsibility for the management of Canada's water resources to both the federal and provincial governments. The federal government decided not to put an outright ban on water exports. If some provinces started exporting bulk water, water would become a tradable commodity and would be subject to the provisions of NAFTA. In 1999 the federal government asked the provinces to place a moratorium on water exports until an agreement prohibiting the bulk export of water can be reached. The federal government has also approached the United States to request that the International Joint Commission study the impact of bulk water removal on lakes.

Water is a scarce resource even for Canadians. The fact of its scarcity is forcing us to make decisions regarding the use of this valuable resource.

More information on water-related issues can be found at the following websites:

www.ijc.org The website for the International Joint Commission (Canada and the United States) on water usage and water pollution.

www.ec.gc.ca/water/index.htm The website for Environment Canada. It provides information on water policy and legislation, water management, water treaties, and some interesting water facts.

www.statcan.ca The website for Statistics Canada. Information is available on the elevation and the area of lakes, on the length and the drainage areas of rivers, and on the dimensions of the Great Lakes.

Questions

1. Money is required to ensure an adequate supply of fresh water: to clean up the lakes; to irrigate farmland; and to repair water distribution systems. Discuss the opportunity cost associated with spending money on water.

2. Do some Canadian industries rely more heavily on the availability of a water resource than others? Explain.
3. The water crisis is worse in the western United States than in Canada. In your opinion, could the fact that Canada has more fresh water than the United States be a source of conflict between the two nations?
4. Can you suggest ways that Canadians could reduce their demand for water?
5. Canadians use more water on average than do residents of warmer climates. Why is this so?
6. What impact might the "greenhouse effect" have on the problem of an inadequate water supply?

Direct Costs/Opportunity Costs

The process of decision making involves costs, which can be divided into two groups: direct costs and opportunity costs. *Direct costs* can be defined as the out-of-pocket expenses that are required to do something. For instance, deciding to attend college involves certain expenses, such as paying for tuition, books, and supplies. Living away from home makes room and board an expense, too. Transportation is also a major cost of attending college. These are all direct costs. However, possibly the biggest expense of the decision to attend college is not a direct cost. The biggest expense is the salary, or income, that you could have earned had you not decided to further your education. The income thus sacrificed has to be considered as part of the expense of a college education and is referred to as *opportunity cost*.

Every time you spend money you incur not only a direct cost but also an opportunity cost as well! Consider another example: assume that you saved $8000 and decided to spend this money on a car. What is the opportunity cost of this decision? If the money were to be deposited in a savings account at a bank, it could earn interest. The opportunity that was sacrificed was the chance to earn interest on the $8000 had it been deposited in a bank account. The opportunity cost is the value of the lost alternative—the interest. If the interest rate paid on a savings account were 5 percent per year, you would have sacrificed $400 a year by withdrawing $8000 from the bank. The opportunity cost of this decision is $400 a year, or the opportunity that was sacrificed. The total cost of the car would be the sum of the direct and opportunity costs—$8400. Every decision carries with it an opportunity cost, since in order to do one thing, something else must be sacrificed.

There are opportunity costs involved in making decisions regarding Canada's scarce resources. If we decide to construct a housing development on good agricultural land, we have to give up the farm produce that could have been grown on the land. The opportunity cost of the housing development is the value of the farm produce that was sacrificed. If someone decides to accept a job as an electrician, he or she cannot be an accountant or a computer programmer at the same time. The opportunity cost of being an electrician is the earnings that were forgone by not working at another occupation. There are also opportunity costs associated with machines and other capital resources. If a wood lathe is used to make salad bowls, it cannot be used to make table legs at the same time.

There is an opportunity cost associated with every decision. This cost is present because resources are scarce; when a decision is made regarding resource use, something has to be sacrificed. Thus, **opportunity cost** is defined as the value of the best possible alternative that is sacrificed when resources are allocated to a specific use.

In reality, every time a decision is made to put a resource to a certain use, several other options have to be sacrificed. If $8000 is withdrawn from a bank in order to purchase a car, the money cannot be used to take a vacation, buy a swimming pool, put a down payment on a house, or earn interest on an investment. If all of these options must be sacrificed, what is the opportunity cost of purchasing a car? *The opportunity cost is the value of the best possible alternative that is given up.* In this example, therefore, the opportunity cost is the lost interest that would have been earned had this money been invested.

Opportunity costs **represent the value of the best possible alternative that is given up in the decision to use a resource.**

R E V I E W

1.1 Why is scarcity so important to the study of economics?

1.2 What is the opportunity cost of going to a movie the night before an economics exam?

EVERYDAY ECONOMICS 1.2

The Costs of College Attendance

As mentioned on page 9, there are opportunity costs associated with attending college. Not everyone will have the same opportunity costs, because tuition costs, job opportunities, travel costs, and other expenses differ for each person. Nonetheless, the process of determining the opportunity costs associated with attending college can be reviewed. The example in this reading will relate to the opportunity costs associated with a student enrolling in a business program in an Ontario college of applied arts and technology in the academic year 2003–04. The resources used by an individual to attend college are money and time. There are opportunity costs linked to the use of each resource.

The opportunity costs associated with the use of one's money to attend college are discussed first. The monetary costs associated with attending college are:

- *Tuition, books, and incidentals:* It is estimated that these expenses are $3000 per year.
- *Travel expenses:* Even if one did not attend college, there would be travel expenses incurred in looking for a job, or travelling to a job. The only travel expenses included in this calculation would be those over and above normal travel expenses such as would occur if one moved to another city to go to school. Assume these expenses are $400 per academic year.
- *Room and board:* Whether one attends college or not, there are room and board expenses. In this calculation only the additional room and board expenses associated with attending college are included. Assume these are $600 per academic year.

The total amount of the above items is $4000. Thus, the direct costs of attending college are $4000 per academic year. What is the opportunity cost associated with this use of one's money? The opportunity cost is the value of the next-best alternative that was sacrificed in order to go to college. This money could have been invested in the stock market or mutual funds, or it could have been deposited in the bank. Assume that an interest rate of 4 percent could have been earned on the $4000 had it been placed in a bank. The lost interest, or opportunity cost, is $4000 × 0.04 = $160. The money could have earned $160 in interest for one year. Using the money for college meant a sacrifice of $160 in interest.

Attending college also takes time. An individual's time also has a value associated with it. Assume that a student sacrificed a 40-hour-per-week job at the minimum-wage rate (assume $7.00 per hour). If the academic year is 8 months (approximately 32 weeks), the lost income is approximately 40 x $7.00 x 32 weeks, or $8960. By attending college the student sacrificed $8960 in income (not taking into consideration any paycheque deductions). A student may not sacrifice this amount by going to college if the student acquires a part-time job during the academic year. The amount sacrificed could also be higher if the student quit a better-paying job in order to return to school. Further, if the student had remained employed and not attended college, there may have been promotional opportunities that would have increased the wage rate.

In order to determine the total cost of attending college for an academic year, the opportunity costs must be added to the direct costs.

direct costs = $4000
opportunity costs = $160 + $8960 = $9120
total cost = $4000 + $9120 = $13 120

Since there are opportunity costs associated with college attendance, is a college education not worthwhile? First, you cannot escape opportunity costs. Whether one attends college or uses time and money in other ways, opportunity costs are present. Second, the answer to the question about the value of a college education is beyond the scope of this reading. To answer that question, the benefits, monetary and otherwise, of a college education must be added up. These benefits will accrue for many years. The benefits need to be compared with the costs of attending college. In order to compare benefits and costs that can occur at different points in time, the present value of both the benefits and the costs must be determined (see the section on capital in Chapter 14).

Questions

1. Would the opportunity costs of attending college vary according to an individual's age? Explain.
2. Can the value of a college education be determined by focusing on the costs? Explain.
3. Would the opportunity costs of attending college vary depending on the program selected? Explain.
4. Would all of the costs and benefits of attending college be monetary? Discuss.

Production-Possibilities Curves

The production-
possibilities curve
**represents the maximum
amount of two products
that can be produced using
all available resources
efficiently.**

The choices that Canadians have to make about the use of scarce resources, and the associated opportunity costs, can be depicted by a **production-possibilities curve**. This curve will be introduced using a simple society as an example. Assume that this society can produce only two products—an agricultural product, corn, and a hunting product, spears. If every individual concentrates on the production of corn, the group could produce 100 bushels of corn from the available land each year. On the other hand, if everyone uses all of the available materials to make spears, the group could manufacture 27 spears in one year. If both corn and spears were produced in the same year, lesser amounts of the two products would be available: the more spears produced, the more corn would have to be given up. Land and labour previously used to produce corn would be turned over to the production of spears. An increase in the production of corn, on the other hand, would require the use of some land, labour, and materials that were previously used to make spears. Various combinations of corn and spears could be produced. Five of these combinations are given in Table 1.3.

This table indicates five of the options that are available to the society under discussion. As the amount of corn produced increases, the number of spears decreases. There is an inverse relationship between the two products: when one goes up, the other goes down.

The information from Table 1.3 is plotted on a graph in Figure 1.1. Joining the points plotted on the graph creates a line called the production-possibilities curve. This curve shows all the possible combinations of corn and spears that can be produced by this simple society in one year. In order to draw this curve, it is assumed that all of the resources available to this society (land, people, tools, and equipment) are being used in the most efficient way. If resources are not being used efficiently (for example,

Table 1.3 *Alternative combinations of corn and spears that could be produced in one year*

OPTION	CORN (BUSHELS)	SPEARS
A	0	27
B	20	25
C	50	19
D	85	10
E	100	0

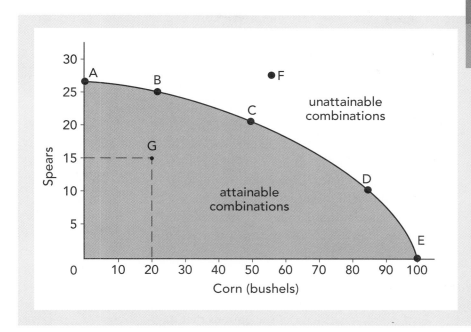

Figure 1.1

The production-possibilities curve

The possible combinations of spears and corn are represented by the curve. The combinations to the left of the curve (e.g., **G** in the shaded area) are attainable, while those to the right of the curve (e.g., **F**) are not.

if some workers are unemployed), the level of production of corn and spears would be less than the optimum. The level of production resulting from such an inefficient use of resources can be represented by a point to the left of the curve. This point is indicated as G in Figure 1.1. At G, 15 spears and 20 bushels of corn are produced—well below capacity because, according to Table 1.3, 25 spears can be produced along with 20 bushels of corn. Any combination of corn and spears to the left of the production-possibilities boundary represents an inefficient use of available resources.

What about combinations to the right of the production-possibilities curve, as indicated by point F in Figure 1.1? This combination of corn and spears is currently unattainable since the production-possibilities curve shows the maximum amount of these two products that can be made using available resources.

Will the combination of corn and spears as indicated by point F ever be attainable? Yes; this society will not always be limited to the choices on the present production-possibilities curve. Over time, the ability to produce both corn and spears is likely to increase. Any increase in the amount of available resources will permit the increased production of both commodities. For example, as the population increases, more workers would be available to work both in the corn fields and in spear manufacturing. More corn and spears could be produced, causing the options listed in Table 1.3 to change. Increases in the amounts of corn and spears that can be produced will cause the production-possibilities curve to shift to the right (see Figure 1.2).

Increases in production will also occur if a new method of producing either product is developed. For example, a new way to plant corn may be discovered that increases its yield. This would also cause a change in the options presented in Table 1.3 and, therefore, in the production-possibilities curve. The effect of this change is shown in Figure 1.3. In the diagram, the maximum amount of corn attainable from available resources is now 120 bushels, whereas previously it was only 100 bushels. The maximum number of spears that could be produced has not changed and remains at 27. Any change in production methods or technology will cause the production-possibilities curve to shift to a new position.

The concept of opportunity cost can be applied to the production-possibilities curve. In order to produce more spears, a certain amount of corn will have to be sacrificed. Assume that this society is producing the combination of corn and spears indicated by option D in Table 1.3. If the society decided to shift production to option C, an additional nine spears could be produced. In order to make nine additional spears, 35 bushels of corn have to be given up. The 35 bushels of corn could be referred to as the opportunity cost of producing the additional spears.

Figure 1.2

Effect of a population increase on the production-possibilities curve

The increase in population permits more of both spears and corn to be produced. The shaded area shows the newly attainable combinations of spears and corn.

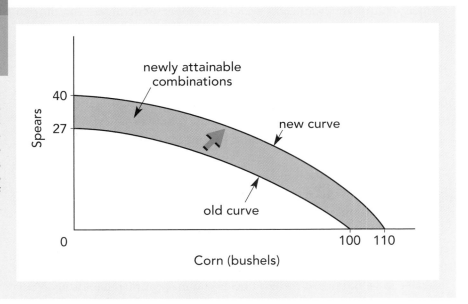

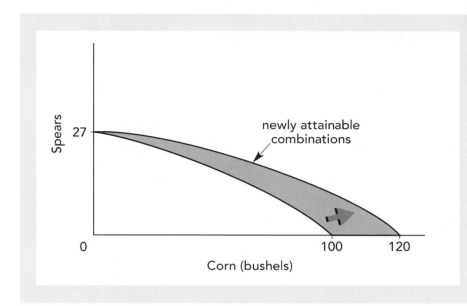

Figure 1.3

Effect of technological change on the production-possibilities curve

A change in the technology of corn production allows more of both spears and corn to be produced (unless only spears are produced). The newly attainable combinations are represented by the shaded area.

Is the concept of the production-possibilities curve relevant for a complex country like Canada? The answer is yes. Canadians have to decide among thousands of goods and services, not just two. We have a wide variety of resources and must decide how these resources are to be employed. Canadians also have a series of production possibilities, whereas our numerical example was limited to only two products—corn and spears. Further, the graph that was used to plot the various options is limited to two dimensions—vertical and horizontal. If we were to draw a production-possibilities curve for Canada, we would require more than two axes, since our choices would not be limited to two products. Changes in Canada's production possibilities can also take place if more resources become available or if new technology is developed to make better use of existing resources.

The choices that Canadians are faced with are almost endless. Farmers must decide which crop to plant for the next year. Businesses must decide which product line to pursue. Homemakers must decide how to best utilize a limited amount of money while trying to provide for their families. For each of these decisions, the concept of a production-possibilities curve could be used to map out the various options.

Canada's production-possibilities curve shows the maximum amount of goods and services available to Canadians. It is a reflection of our potential standard of living. In order to improve our standard of living, it is necessary to shift Canada's production-possibilities curve to the right. This can be accomplished by increasing the amount of resources available to produce goods and services. The most likely resources that can be increased are labour and capital. Improvements in the quality of these resources will also allow the production of goods and services to increase. Government expenditures on education are aimed at improving the quality of our labour resource. Improvements in capital equipment and technological change also permit production to expand. In order to encourage technological improvements, governments in Canada have assisted in financing industrial research and development. The choices available to Canadians can also be expanded through foreign trade. A discussion of the impact of foreign trade on the standard of living in Canada appears in Chapter 9.

The shape of the production-possibilities curve is significant when analyzing the ability of the simple society to trade off spears for more corn, and vice versa. If it is desirable to give up some spears in order to produce more corn, the society will discover that more and more spears have to be sacrificed for the same amount of corn. For example, if this society were producing at option A (27 spears; 0 corn) in Table 1.3, the sacrifice of two spears would enable corn production to increase by 20 bushels—option B. On the other hand, if the society were producing at option D (10 spears; 85 bushels of corn) and decided to increase corn production, the sacrifice in terms of spears would be much greater. At point D, 10 spears would have to be given up in order to acquire 15 more bushels of corn. The opportunity cost of acquiring more corn increases as the amount of corn produced increases. Why is this so?

The reason is that different resources in different quantities are used in the production of each product. The production of spears requires mainly labour, while the production of corn requires mainly land. Furthermore, not all of the same resource is of identical quality. Some people are good spear makers, others are not. Some land is good agricultural land, some is not. Any attempt to increase corn production will necessitate the use of land that is less suited for corn production. More and more spears must be given up in order to acquire more food.

The differences in resource quantity and quality partially account for the shape of the production-possibilities curve. Another factor influencing the shape of the curve is the law of diminishing returns.

The Law of Diminishing Returns

The simple society in our example faces several constraints in its attempt to produce more corn and more spears. The resources available to it, mainly labour and land, are limited. As the population increases, it will be necessary to produce more food. With more workers, the ability of this society to supply food should increase, but the gains in food production will be limited by the amount of land available. The amount of land is a fixed resource not subject to change, while population is not a fixed resource and is subject to change. Eventually, a point will be reached beyond which the addition of more workers adds very little to the total output of food.

This analysis also applies to complex societies like Canada. Our country has a limited amount of land available for food production; as our population increases, more food will be required. Our ability to produce food will be constrained by the amount of land available. Even though one resource (the number of workers) may be increasing, another resource (land) remains fixed. Eventually, the increases in food production that can be achieved by the addition of more workers to the land will start to decline. Each successive worker will contribute less food to the total amount produced because he or she has less and less land to work with.

This important economic principle is known as the **law of diminishing returns**. It applies when one resource used in the production of a commodity remains fixed. When other resources (workers) are combined with the fixed resource (land), total production will increase. A point will be reached, however, beyond which the increases in total production associated with the increases in other resources become smaller and smaller.

When a fixed resource is combined with increasing amounts of a variable resource, the law of diminishing returns states that increases in total output will eventually become smaller and smaller.

The law of diminishing returns applies as well to a business firm. Assume that a company has rented a building in order to manufacture chairs. In this case, the building is the fixed resource and cannot be changed. Chair production could increase by employing more workers and more machines. Yet the ability of the company to increase chair production is restricted by the size of the building. Even though more workers are hired, increases to the number of chairs produced by increasing the labour resource in this way will eventually begin to decline.

The law of diminishing returns states that when increasing amounts of a variable resource are added to a fixed resource, the increases in total output will eventually become smaller and smaller. The presence of the law of diminishing returns influences the shape of the production-possibilities curve. In our example, as more and more workers begin to produce corn, a point will be reached at which the additional corn produced by adding one more worker is less than the additional corn provided by the previous worker. This causes the production-possibilities curve to bow in as more corn is produced. The law of diminishing returns is an important concept in the study of economics. Its impact on a company's production costs will be discussed in Chapter 11.

REVIEW

1.7 What condition has to be present for the law of diminishing returns to have any impact on the production of goods and services?

1.8 Determine the effects of change in the availability of fixed or variable resources on output.

EVERYDAY ECONOMICS 1.3

The Theories of Thomas Malthus

The idea of diminishing returns was first introduced by an English clergyman and economist, Thomas Robert Malthus (1766–1834). He lived in England during the time of the Industrial Revolution and witnessed its effects. Machinery was beginning to displace many qualified craftsmen from jobs, and unemployment was a serious problem. Many people had come to the conclusion that England was overpopulated.

Despite the reports of misery created by technological change, many believed that society would eventually progress to a point at which everyone would live in happiness and comparative leisure. In fact, technological change had improved the lot of many people. Malthus believed that these forecasts of happiness and leisure were wrong, and in 1798 he published his *Essay on the Principle of Population*. Malthus based his pessimism on two assumptions: first, that food was necessary to human existence, and second, that sexual passion between males and females was necessary and would remain so, and people would, consequently, continue to reproduce and increase the population.

Malthus argued that the population of the world would increase faster than the ability of the world to produce food. The world's population would increase in a geometric progression (1, 2, 4, 8, 16, 32, 64...) whereas food production, at the very best, could increase only at an arithmetic rate (1, 2, 3, 4, 5...). The end result is too many people and too little food.

In order to prove his point, Malthus used the example of North America, where the population had doubled over a period of 25 years. This was his estimate of how quickly the population would increase on a worldwide basis if it remained unchecked. However, he did not expect this population expansion actually to take place, because there are certain checks that prevent the population from increasing at this rate. These checks include war, disease, and famine. Nonetheless, he believed that population increases would continue to outstrip food production.

Malthus had several proposals to improve the situation. He advocated moral restraint in the form of later marriages and smaller families. He was also opposed to giving any type of relief to the poor. If they were kept alive by charity, they would continue to propagate and make conditions worse. In a sense, charity, according to Malthus, was cruelty in disguise. Malthus would, however, give charity to those who were poor because of some undeserved calamity. These came to be known as the "deserving poor."

The ability of population increases to surpass food production was the basis for the law of diminishing returns. There was no question that a given piece of land would yield more produce with the application of fertilizer and the use of more labour. There comes a point, however, beyond which it does not pay to add any more fertilizer or labour to the land. Additional increments of fertilizer and labour will not bring about corresponding increases in production. In fact, a point may be reached beyond which additional workers may even reduce production.

Some changes in the world have clearly delayed the confirmation of Malthus' predictions. For example, family size has decreased and birth control has become more prevalent. In industrialized countries, people are marrying at a later age. Advances in technology have increased the agricultural yield per hectare and have improved the world's ability to produce food.

Are Malthus' theories dead or are they still alive? The world's population in April 2000 was approximately 6.06 billion persons and is growing at about 1.3 percent per year. Eighty percent of the world's population lives in the less developed regions and 20 percent in the more developed regions. The population growth rate is 1.8 percent in the less developed regions and 0.4 percent in the more developed regions. It is expected that the population of the world will be 9.4 billion persons by the year 2050.

The world's population is growing, but at a slower rate than in previous years. The decline in the fertility rate in less developed countries has been the main reason for the slower increases in the world's population. Declines in the fertility rate have occurred in Bangladesh, India, Pakistan, Turkey, Myanmar, and Kenya as well as other nations. The fertility rate has remained high in sub-Saharan Africa, where it is more than six births per woman in 17 countries. A higher mortality rate resulting from war and the spread of AIDS has also contributed to the slower rate of growth in population.

What is happening to food production? World food output is increasing ahead of population growth. For the period 1951–92, there was a 30-percent increase in food production per capita. This increase in food production occurred in spite of the fact that farmers in many countries are paid to keep their land out of production. Also, much of the world's grain output is fed to livestock instead of humans. Danish economist Ester Boserup argues that increases in the population actually force communities to abandon inefficient agricultural methods and increase food output. It is difficult to

▶

predict whether these increases in food production will continue, as usable crop land is reaching its limit and the world fish catch is levelling off.

Rather than a problem of production, there is a problem of distribution. The poor in many countries cannot afford to buy food. In Africa, the high population growth rate has not been matched by increases in food production. The problems related to food production in Africa have been exacerbated by droughts, wars, and government intervention in agriculture.

Questions

1. Relate Malthus' ideas on population to the law of diminishing returns.

2. There is some evidence that increased educational levels among women are associated with declining fertility rates in many countries. Why do you think this may be the case? (Hint: consider the concept of opportunity cost.)

3. Worldwide there has been a tendency for people to move from rural areas to the cities. By the end of the century it is expected that one-half of the world's population will live in urban areas. What will this development do to Malthus' predictions?

4. In many African countries, governments have followed policies that keep food prices low. How do you think African farmers would react to low food prices? (Hint: again consider the concept of opportunity cost.)

International Comparisons 1.2

The world's most populous nations, 2003 (population in millions)

China	1290.6	Russia	144.7
India	1054.8	Bangladesh	134.6
United States	282.0	Nigeria	131.8
Indonesia	233.3	Japan	127.1
Brazil	176.9	Mexico	104.3
Pakistan	149.4		

SOURCE: http://www.geohive.com (January 2003).

Economic Systems

The production-possibilities curve outlines all of the possible combinations that are available in the production of goods and services. The problem facing every society is which combination to select. How does a group of individuals make decisions about the use of scarce resources? In the terms of our example, which option from Table 1.3 should this society select? There are basically two approaches that may be followed in economic decision making: the **free-market approach** and the **command approach.** These approaches to economic decision making will be discussed under resource ownership and the decision process.

Resource Ownership

In a free-market system, the nation's productive resources are privately owned by individuals and businesses. Farmers own their land, businesses own their factories and equipment, individuals own their homes, and so on. The free-market system is based on private ownership of property. In contrast, the command approach requires public, not private, ownership of all resources. Land, labour, and capital are all jointly owned and not possessed by any one individual or business.

In Canada we have a combination of these two approaches. The majority of our resources are owned privately. However, a substantial portion of our resources are publicly owned. Examples of publicly owned resources include parks, government office buildings, electricity-generating stations, military equipment, and certain educational institutions. In addition, Crown corporations such as Canada Post Corporation and the Canadian Broadcasting Corporation own some of our nation's resources.

The Decision Process

In a free-market economy, the decisions of individuals and businesses determine how our resources are to be used. Consumers are the major determinant of resource use. If they continue to purchase a certain product or service, resources will be allocated to the production of that item. If consumers stop purchasing a certain product, the resources used in its production will go elsewhere.

In a command system, decisions are more centralized and not left up to individuals. Since individuals do not own the resources, it is difficult for them to decide on resource use. Decisions must be made by a group of individuals with official status. Such a group must determine what goods and services will be produced and who will receive them.

The free-market approach **in economic decision making is based on private ownership of property and resources.**
The command approach **describes a situation in which resources—land, labour, and capital—are jointly or publicly owned.**

International Comparisons 1.3

Economic freedom rankings, 2001

Country	Rank	Country	Rank
Hong Kong	1	Germany	15
Singapore	2	France	38
United States	3	Greece	45
United Kingdom	3	India	73
New Zealand	5	Sri Lanka	77
Switzerland	6	Poland	89
Ireland	6	Bulgaria	97
Canada	6	China	101
Australia	9	Bangladesh	107
Netherlands	10	Iran	109
Finland	11	Romania	114
Iceland	12	Russia	116
Denmark	12	Myanmar	122

SOURCE: www.freetheworld.com (October 2003). Reprinted with the permission of The Fraser Institute.

Again, in Canada we have a combination of these approaches. *Basically, individuals make decisions regarding privately owned resources and government makes decisions regarding publicly owned resources.* Governments may also make decisions regarding the use of privately owned resources. For example, certain provinces have enacted rent-control legislation that limits the amount that a landlord can charge for rental accommodation. Also, minimum-wage laws require that employers provide a certain minimum wage per hour to every worker, and municipal zoning regulations put restrictions on land use.

No country in the world adopts either of these approaches to decision making exclusively. Countries where the free-market approach predominates, such as the United States, are referred to as *capitalist*. Even in capitalist countries, the government plays a significant role in economic decision making. For example, in the United States the government operates the post office, the airports, the military, and many other services.

Canada's Political Parties

A political party is an organization whose aim is to form the government of Canada or of a province through the electoral process. Once in control of government, the party can decide what public policy on various matters will be. In deciding upon public policy, the party will be presenting its ideas on how economic decisions should be carried out.

Political parties are divided in their approach about how economic decisions should be made. Some parties are strong proponents of the free-market system and allocate only a small role to government. Others believe that the free-market system needs to be modified by government policies. Still others advocate the elimination of the free-market system.

In Canada, two political parties have dominated the scene since Confederation: the Liberals and the Progressive Conservatives. The approaches of each party do not vary significantly. Both parties see a role for government in our economy, but see private enterprise as having the major decision-making role. Where the two parties differ is in the areas of leadership and specific issues. Personalities play a large role in political activity and the personality and image of one party's leader may be the reason for its public acceptance. On such issues as energy prices, constitutional reform, and economic policy, the two parties may differ on a pragmatic, but not an ideological, basis.

The New Democratic Party (NDP) does differ ideologically from the other two. This party has its roots in the Co-operative Commonwealth Federation (CCF), which had a philosophy counter to the free-market approach. The NDP sees a more important role for government in economic decision making than do the Liberal or Progressive Conservative parties. The NDP, like the CCF, is a socialist party, but recently has been trying to broaden its appeal to voters by relaxing its socialist stand on some issues.

In the last 20 years, several new political parties have entered candidates in federal and provincial elections. The Reform Party, with its roots in western Canada, was a proponent of individual enterprise and initiative. According to the party literature, the main focus of government should be to create an environment where individual initiative can survive. On March 25, 2000, the Reform Party members voted to adopt the constitution of the Canadian Reform Conservative Alliance; the new party is commonly referred to as the Canadian Alliance. In October 2003, the Canadian Alliance and the Progressive Conservative Party agreed to merge into the Conservative Party. The Bloc Québécois' ultimate goal is the separation of Quebec from the rest of Canada. Until that happens, the Bloc wants more provincial control over such areas as health care and immigration.

Other federal political parties registered with Elections Canada include the Marxist-Leninist Party of Canada, the Canadian Action Party, the Communist Party of Canada, the Marijuana Party, the Natural Law Party, and the Green Party of Canada. The following parties are eligible for registration: the Christian Heritage Party, the National Alternative Party of Canada, and the Ontario Party of Canada. There are several other non-registered political parties at both the federal and provincial levels.

Questions

1. Draw a line, labelling the free-market approach at the right-hand side and the command approach at the left-hand side. Situate each of Canada's major political parties on the line in accordance with their views on economic decision making.

2. What political party holds power in your province? What are its views on economic decision making?

Countries that stress the command approach are referred to as *socialist* or *communist.* In socialist countries, the ownership of the nation's productive resources is in public hands. In communist countries, private ownership of property is not permitted. In communist nations such as China, however, private ownership has not been completely eliminated. Some small farms and businesses are privately owned and the decision on what to produce is made by the individual owner.

All countries combine the free-market and command approaches to economic decision making. Therefore, we can say that all countries have *mixed economies,* even though the nature of the mix between free-market and command decisions varies by country.

R E V I E W

1.9 How do the free-market and command systems vary in the area of resource ownership?

Economics as a Science

Economics is a science. A dictionary definition states that science is the body of knowledge and theory dealing with things in nature and the universe, and with the forces that create, shape, and form them. Science is based on facts that are obtained from careful study of experiments. Economics fits this definition. There is a major difference, however, between the science of economics and other sciences such as chemistry and physics. In chemistry, most of the environmental conditions can be controlled during the experiment. That is, in the process of conducting an experiment, the scientist can control the air temperature, the amount of solution, the filtration process, and so on. Since economic experiments must be conducted in the course of everyday events, this type of precision and control is impossible. Economic experiments are conducted under conditions that cannot be easily controlled. In our economic environment, changes are taking place each day that will influence the results of experimentation.

For example, assume that a company wanted to determine how consumers would react to lower prices for its products. It could set up an experiment whereby it systematically lowered prices and recorded the sales at each price. If sales increased after a price reduction, the company could assume that there is a relationship between the number of sales and prices. This assumption may not be correct, however. At the same time that the company lowered prices, people's incomes may have increased, their tastes may have altered, or the prices of other products may have changed. Any or all of these adjustments could have resulted in higher sales. The company may believe that lower prices increase sales, yet it cannot be sure unless it takes other factors into consideration. Unlike an experiment in chemistry, it is not possible for the company to control all the external factors that could influence the economic experiment.

In order to avoid this problem of a changing environment in the study of economics, we assume that all external factors affecting the outcome of an economic experiment remain constant and do not influence the results. If the company wants to determine how sales are going to be affected by lower prices, it will have to assume for practical purposes that all other factors remain constant. Although this assumption is unrealistic, it aids in the understanding of possible economic consequences of certain actions. Therefore, just as in scientific experiments, it will be necessary throughout this text to assume that factors surrounding economic issues are remaining constant.

The science of economics concerns individuals and their behaviour regarding the use of scarce resources. The physical sciences are concerned with atoms, molecules, bacteria, and so on. A major difference between the sciences that study human behaviour and those that study the physical relationships in the universe is the fact that individuals are not pre-programmed. They have free will. Although economists assume that individuals act rationally, they may not always do so. The ability of individuals to change their behaviour makes predictions in economics more difficult than in the physical sciences.

The science of economics and the physical sciences also differ in the role that *values,* or moral judgments, play in scientific reasoning. The physical sciences do not categorize facts as either "good" or "bad." The physical scientist is, hopefully, an impartial observer of the facts. For example, when two chemicals are combined, the result is simply observed. No value judgment is made. The economist is not as likely to be free from making value judgments while conducting research. As a member of society, the economist is rarely indifferent about the results of research. In fact, one's values may guide the type of research undertaken. If an economist is concerned about the fairness in the differences in pay between men and women, his or her research may reflect this concern.

The fact that moral judgments and values can influence economic investigations impacts on the role the economist plays in society. This role is discussed in the next section.

The Role of the Economist

What use do economists make of their understanding of decision making in society? What role do they play in society? Are they asked to design public policy? Are they asked to comment on public policy? Not everyone agrees on the role that should be assigned to economists in our society.

The differences in points of view with respect to the role of economists can be traced to the differences between positive and normative statements. Positive statements are statements about "what is," while normative statements are statements about what "ought to be." How do we judge whether a statement is right or wrong? Positive statements are judged by their accuracy in describing events. They are tested by conducting studies to determine if they are valid. For example, with respect to a minimum-wage rate increase, a positive statement may be that a minimum-wage rate increase results in unemployment for some members of the labour force. This statement can be tested to determine if it is correct. Further, the statement does not imply that the increase in the minimum wage rate is "good" or "bad." Some economists prefer that their role be one of making positive or *value-free* statements about public policy.

In response to an increase in the minimum-wage rate, other economists may state that the rate should increase believing it to be a means of improving the lot of the working poor. Economists in this instance play a role in the decision-making process. Their values have influenced their position on government policy. If the minimum-wage rate increases, some people will become unemployed. Others will get an hourly wage rate increase and, assuming they work as many hours as previously, will bring home more money. The minimum-wage rate increase will make some people better off while making others worse off. Is there a role for the economist in assessing the benefits and the losses associated with a minimum-wage rate increase? If the benefits outweigh the losses, should the increase go ahead? What if the benefits equal the losses? Should those who benefit from a change in government policy help compensate those who lose as a result of the change in policy? The economist can play a role in answering these questions by helping to measure benefits and losses.

The answers to these questions involve value judgments. Should the answers be provided, and the decisions made, by economists? Economists are members of society and should be able to express an opinion on government policy. Once value judgments enter into a statement, the individual is acting more like a policy maker than a scientist.

The positive and normative aspects of economics cannot be separated in all instances. Economists must select certain areas to research in order to develop theory. The selection of research topics is often influenced by the issues that one believes to be important and by one's values. It is also possible that values could influence the interpretation of research results.

The role of the economist in society is not clear. There is certainly a role for the economist in the development of economic theory. Is there also a role for the economist as a policy maker? When you are discussing economic issues such as freer trade and the distribution of income in society as you read this text, identify whether you are making positive or normative statements. Are your statements reflecting the theory or your values?

An Introduction to Graphs

It may appear strange to be beginning an economics textbook with a discussion of graphs. Yet graphs provide us with a useful aid in explaining economic concepts. If you are not familiar with graphs, it would be advantageous to read this section and attempt the exercises. Even if you are comfortable with the use of graphs, it may be wise to review the concepts presented in this section. The material is sufficient for understanding any graph used throughout the book.

Graphs are simply a visual way of communicating information in a manner that assists in the presentation of economic theories. The statement that a picture is worth a thousand words applies very well to graphs. Graphs represent a relationship between two sets of figures and can be drawn only if the background information is available.

A graph consists of two numbered lines, or *axes,* that intersect at a 90-degree angle. The intersection point is called the *origin.* It has the numerical value of zero and is the starting point for all measurements. It is possible to measure two variables on a graph. For convenience, the axes are labelled *x* and *y.* Positive and negative values of *x* and *y* are measured as shown in Figure 1.4. The following two examples will demonstrate the use of graphs.

Example Number 1: Positive Relationships

Suppose that Mason's Department Store decided to collect information on the number of umbrellas sold in relation to the amount of rainfall in the area to better understand the factors that influence umbrella sales. Assume that the store collected the information shown in Table 1.4 for the months from April to October.

Upon reviewing the information, the store could determine that in the months when the rainfall was highest, the number of umbrellas sold was

Figure 1.4

Axes of a graph

The axes (X and Y) of a graph intersect at the origin (O).

Figure 1.4 Axes of a graph. The axes (X and Y) of a graph intersect at the origin (O).

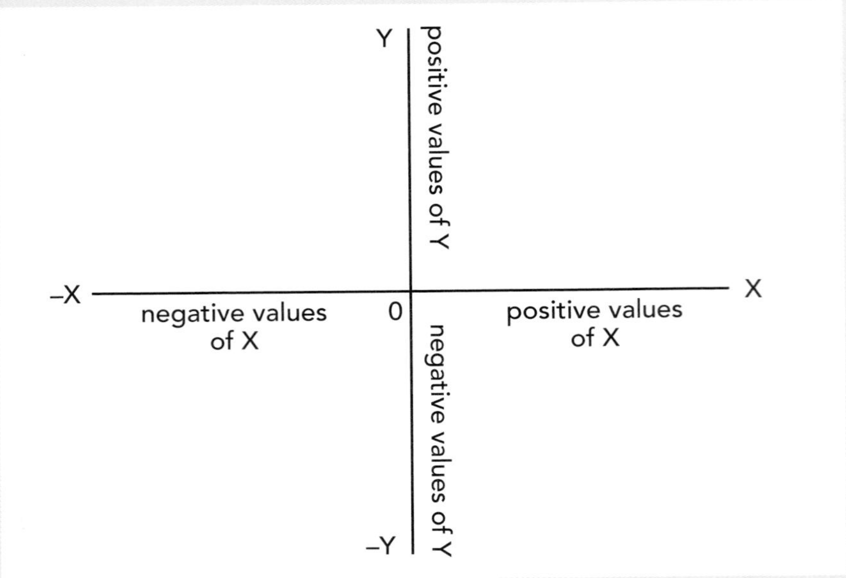

Table 1.4 *Relationship between centimetres of rainfall and umbrellas sold*

MONTH	CENTIMETRES OF RAINFALL	NUMBER OF UMBRELLAS SOLD
April	5.0	25
May	3.0	20
June	2.0	10
July	1.0	5
August	2.5	15
September	0.5	3
October	1.5	7

A positive relationship is one in which an increase or a decrease in one variable results in a corresponding increase or decrease in the other variable.

also highest. In the month of September, when the amount of rainfall was lowest (0.5 cm), the lowest number of umbrellas (three) was sold. The relationship between the amount of rainfall and the number of umbrellas sold is referred to as a **positive relationship**. In other words, as the value of one increases, the value of the other increases. Conversely, as the value of one decreases, the corresponding value of the other decreases.

This information collected by the store can be depicted on a graph. In Figure 1.5, the number of umbrellas sold is measured along the vertical axis and the centimetres of rainfall are measured along the horizontal axis.

The information in the table is plotted in Figure 1.5 by recording the data for each month separately. For example, in the month of April, there were five centimetres of rainfall and 25 umbrellas were sold. This point, shown as April in Figure 1.5, was obtained by first measuring along the horizontal axis to the point referring to five centimetres of rainfall. From this point, locate the point on the vertical (or y) axis that corresponds to 25 umbrellas sold. Repeat this procedure for each of the remaining months. Once all the points are plotted, they can be connected as shown in the diagram. The line that is drawn on the graph represents the relationship between umbrellas sold and centimetres of rainfall. There is a positive relationship between these variables. Any line or graph that proceeds away from the origin into the positive quadrant represents a *positive relationship* between the variables measured on the axes.

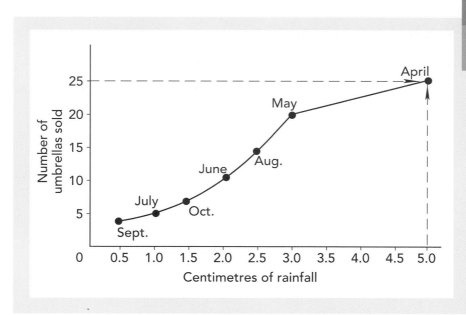

Figure 1.5

Graphical representation of a positive relationship

A positive relationship is indicated by an upward-sloping curve away from the origin.

Example Number 2: Inverse Relationships

Suppose that Mason's Department Store wanted to find out how the price of bicycles affected bicycle sales. Assume that the store varied the price on a certain type of bicycle and recorded the sales at these prices.

As shown in Table 1.5, when the price of bicycles decreased the number of bicycles sold increased. This is referred to as an **inverse relationship**.

The graphical presentation of an inverse relationship is shown in Figure 1.6. The price of the bicycles is measured along the vertical axis and the number of bicycles sold along the horizontal axis. When the information from the table is plotted and the points joined, the line slopes down to the right. Any line on any graph that slopes down to the right indicates that an *inverse relationship* exists between the two variables being measured.

You will note that the line drawn in Figure 1.6 is a straight line. For many of the graphs throughout this textbook, a straight line will be used as a matter of convenience. In reality, the relationship between any two variables can seldom be represented by a straight line.

A graph is simply a visual presentation of the relationship between two variables. Graphs do not exist without numerical information. They are constructed from this available information. In order to construct the graph, some numerical information had to be collected beforehand.

> **In an** inverse relationship, **an increase in the value of one variable results in a corresponding decrease in the value of the other.**

Table 1.5 *Relationship between number of bicycles sold and the price of the bicycles*

PRICE	NUMBER OF BICYCLES SOLD
$200	10
$190	15
$180	20
$170	25
$160	30

Figure 1.6

Graphical representation of an inverse relationship

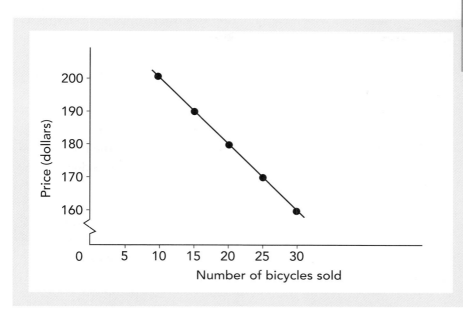

Graphical representation of an inverse relationship.

REVIEW

1.10 Draw a graph to indicate each of the following relationships. In each instance, make up your own numbers and put them in the form of a table before drawing the graph. Be sure to label your axes. Plot:

a) the relationship between the number of litres of gasoline used and the number of kilometres driven;

b) the relationship between an individual's age and height; and

c) the relationship between the number of potatoes and the number of carrots that can be grown on the same plot of land.

Summary

The key word in the study of economics is scarcity. Since resources are available only in limited quantities, decisions must be made regarding their use. Economics is concerned with how these decisions are made. An opportunity cost is associated with each decision. It refers to the value of the best alternative that is sacrificed when resources are allocated to a specific use.

The production-possibilities curve allows us to put these decisions into perspective. The curve shows the maximum possible combinations of two items that can be produced using all available resources. The citizens of a country must select which combination is most acceptable or desirable. Any change in a country's resources or a change in technology will change the combinations of items that can be provided. This is shown graphically as a shift in the production-possibilities curve.

Like other peoples, Canadians must make decisions regarding the use of scarce resources. We allocate our resources through a combination of individual and government decisions. Some of our resources are privately owned, and owners must decide how they will be used. For example, each individual is free to decide what type of job he or she would like to pursue. Government also commands control over some of our resources, and uses them to provide such services as hospitals, schools, and defence.

Economics is a science. As in other sciences, economists are interested in conducting experiments and developing theories. The difference between economics (a social science) and the physical sciences is that external factors influencing experiments are more difficult to control in economics; experiments cannot be done under controlled conditions in a laboratory. The theories developed from these experiments must take these external factors into consideration. For purposes of explanation and demonstration, economic theories are usually stated with the assumption that all other factors remain unchanged.

Questions for Review and Discussion

1. Almost everything in this world is scarce. Can you list some items that are not scarce (available in unlimited quantities)?
2. Classify the following resources as either labour, land, or capital:
   a) grain elevator
   b) waiter
   c) screwdriver
   d) natural gas
   e) electrician
   f) railway car
   g) trees
3. Identify the economic resources that are available in your community. Classify these resources as land, labour, or capital.
4. List the resources that are required to make a hamburger and have it served at your favourite restaurant. Classify these resources as land, labour, or capital.
5. Consider the resources available to Japan. Why do the Japanese emphasize education and training?
6. If something could be obtained without giving up anything, is there an opportunity cost? Explain.
7. Is a free sample of cheese handed out in your local supermarket actually free in economic terms? Is it possible for some things to be free

from the point of view of the individual, but not from the point of view of society? Explain.

8. The Canadian government spends money on military equipment. What is the opportunity cost of this spending?

9. Some politicians argue that health care should be free for all Canadians. Can health care ever be free? Explain your answer.

10. The time required to travel from Toronto to Montreal by airplane is one hour at a cost of $200. The time required to drive from Toronto to Montreal by car is five hours at a cost of $50. Which method is cheaper for someone who values his/her time at a) $10 per hour; b) $40 per hour?

11. In 1990, it was decided that the 1996 Summer Olympics would be held in Atlanta, Georgia. The city of Toronto and other levels of government had worked for three years putting together Toronto's application for these games. On September 18, 1990, there were 40 representatives from Canada in Tokyo, Japan to hear the decision of the Olympic Committee as to the 1996 site. What was the opportunity cost associated with Toronto's bid to host the 1996 games? What would have been the opportunity cost of hosting the Olympics had Toronto's bid been successful?

12. For how long should you continue to look for a lost $20 bill?

13. In many nations the military is composed of volunteers. Often the military has a greater proportion of volunteers from the less wealthy segments of society than from the more wealthy segments. Can the concept of opportunity costs be used to explain this situation? Explain.

14. At a vegetable-canning plant several varieties of vegetables are processed and put in cans, although only one type of vegetable can be processed at a time. Explain how the concept of opportunity cost would apply to this plant.

15. The citizens of country AAA are able to produce only two products: X and Y. The country has resources that are suitable only for the production of product X and other resources capable of producing only product Y. Labour (workers) can produce both products. The following table indicates the daily production of both X and Y based on the number of workers allocated to that product.

X		Y	
NO. OF WORKERS	DAILY PRODUCTION	NO. OF WORKERS	DAILY PRODUCTION
0	0	0	0
1	4	1	10
2	10	2	30
3	18	3	60
4	30	4	100
5	50	5	130
6	75	6	145
7	85	7	150
8	90	8	152

    a) Construct a production-possibilities curve for the products X and Y.

    b) At what point does diminishing returns set in for product X? for product Y?

16. Assume that a country had only two products it could produce: bananas and radios. Draw a production-possibilities curve showing the various combinations in the production of these two products that are available to this country. Show what the impact on the production-possibilities curve would be if the population of this country increased.

17. The Pinetree Furniture Company produces two products: pine tables and pine cupboards. The company employs ten carpenters in its factory. Each carpenter can work on only one product at a time. Pinetree management has calculated that the company's daily production of furniture has to be one of the following options:

OPTION	TABLES	CUPBOARDS
A	8	0
B	6	1
C	4	2
D	2	3
E	0	4

Plot a production-possibilities curve for the Pinetree Furniture Company. What is significant about the shape of the curve? Would you expect many production-possibilities curves to look like this? Why or why not?

18. Draw a production-possibilities curve showing the various combinations of televisions and video-cassette recorders that can be produced by an electronics company. Show the impact on the production-possibilities curve of a technological breakthrough in the production of television receivers.

19. The Espanola Manufacturing Company produces only metal chairs. Some chairs are sprayed with red paint, and the remainder are sprayed with green paint.
    a) Draw a production-possibilities curve for the Espanola Manufacturing Company. Would this curve be similar to the curve drawn for corn and spears? Explain.
    b) If the Espanola Manufacturing Company were not producing at capacity and an order arrived for 100 red chairs, what would be the opportunity cost associated with filling this order?

20. *The law of diminishing returns states that because resources are not of equal quality the production-possibilities curve has a shape concave to the origin.* Evaluate this statement.

21. Classify the following countries as capitalist, socialist, or communist:
    a) Great Britain
    b) Cuba
    c) Sweden
    d) Japan
    e) Poland
    f) France

22. List two services provided by each level of government—federal, provincial, and municipal—in Canada. Do any of these services compete with services being offered by privately owned businesses in your community?

23. Explain why economics cannot be considered as a science in the same category as physics and chemistry. What implications does this have for economic experiments and the theories derived from these experiments?

24. Discuss the impact of Canada's aging population on the country's labour force.

Suggested Readings

Cork, David, with Susan Lightstone. *The Pig and the Python: How to Prosper from the Aging Baby Boom.* Toronto: Stoddart, 1996. The authors focus on the financial implications of the aging of a large segment of our population.

Foot, David, with Daniel Stoffman. *Boom, Bust & Echo 2000. Profiting from the Demographic Shift in the New Millennium.* Toronto: Stoddart, 1998. The authors discuss the implications of the shifts in the age distribution of the population on marketing, investments, house prices, and other aspects of our lives.

George, M.V., Shirley Loh, Ravi B.P. Verma, and Y. Eddward Shin. Population Projections for Canada, Provinces and Territories 2000–2026. Ottawa: Statistics Canada, March 2001.

Harris, Catherine. *Canada's Resource Industries.* Toronto: Canadian Foundation for Economic Education, 1995. This booklet has a short chapter on each of Canada's resource industries.

O'Rourke, P.J. *All the Trouble in the World: The Lighter Side of Overpopulation, Famine, Ecological Disaster, Ethnic Hatred, Plague, Poverty.* New York: The Atlantic Monthly Press, 1994. As the subtitle indicates, this book presents a lighter look at some of the issues that have been discussed in this chapter.

Report on the Demographic Situation in Canada 2001: Current Demographic Analysis. Ottawa: Statistics Canada, July 2002. An annual publication with information on births, deaths, immigration, and migration.

Wong, Jan. *Red China Blues.* Toronto: Doubleday, 1996. A very good account of life under a command system.

Selected Websites

www.census.gov/cgi-bin/ipc/popclockw This site provides an up-to-the-minute estimate of the world's population. The site has links to the U.S. Bureau of the Census' International Data Base on population statistics for 227 countries and areas around the world.

www.dayof6billion.org This site is presented by Population Action International and focuses on October 12, 1999, the day the world reached a population of six billion.

www.statcan.ca The website for Statistics Canada contains information on Canada's labour and land resources.

www.nrcan.gc.ca The website for Natural Resources Canada provides data on Canada's forests.

www.cfee.org The Canadian Foundation for Economic Education (CFEE) is a non-profit educational organization that attempts to increase awareness and understanding of economic matters.

www.economist.com The website for *The Economist* contains articles from the well-known magazine.

www.elections.ca The website for Elections Canada contains information on Canadian political parties.

http://home.ican.net/~alexg/can.html This site contains information on lesser-known political parties in Canada.

The Operation of a Market

Key Terms

market
demand
supply
change in demand
change in quantity demanded
change in supply
change in quantity supplied
equilibrium price
price system
elasticity

Core Concept Building

This chapter introduces the concepts of demand and supply and the setting of prices. There is an old saying that if you can teach a parrot to say "demand and supply," then you have an economist. Demand and supply are extremely important and appear again in Chapters 3, 6, 7, 9, 12, 13, and 14. Also, ensure that you fully understand price elasticity of demand, a concept that appears again in Chapters 3, 8, 12, 13, and 14.

Chapter Objectives

After successfully completing this chapter, you will be able to:

- define the concept of a market
- understand that the law of demand shows an inverse relationship between price and quantity and that the law of supply shows a positive relationship between the same variables
- graphically show the impact on price and quantity of changes in demand and supply
- differentiate between a change in quantity demanded (supplied) and a change in demand (supply)
- explain the interaction of demand and supply in the marketplace
- graphically show the determination of price in the marketplace
- relate the concept of a market to real-world markets such as the stock and futures markets
- understand the concept of price elasticity and recognize its determinants
- use the formula for determining price elasticity and the total revenue approach for elasticity in relating to real-world market conditions
- understand the concepts of income elasticity and price cross-elasticity

DUTCH AUCTION

It is stated in this chapter that a market is where buyers and sellers get together in order to exchange a product or service and to establish a price. One type of market that many of us are familiar with is an auction. We have probably seen antique auctions, car auctions, farm auctions, art auctions, or auctions of property. In each of these auctions, potential buyers constantly bid up the price that the item will be sold for. Eventually, the selling price is reached.

Not all auctions, however, are conducted in this manner. In situations where the auction must be conducted quickly, it may be beneficial to operate the auction in reverse—that is, to start at a high price and to have the price steadily drop. This is known as a "Dutch auction," one example of which is the flower auction conducted by the Ontario Flower Growers Co-operative. Flower growers bring their flowers to the auction in order to sell them to retail florists. The auction begins early in the morning and must be conducted quickly so that retailers can transport the flowers back to their shops.

Retailers bid on flowers offered for sale by the growers. The starting price is set on a large clock—as the second hand of the clock moves, the price begins to fall. The amount that the price drops each second depends on the type of flower or plant being auctioned and the original starting price. For some items the price may drop by $1 a second, while for others the price may drop by only 10 cents a second. When a retail florist or wholesaler believes that the price has dropped far enough, he or she can press a button in order to stop the clock. At this point a sale is made. A flower grower can also stop the clock if he or she feels that the price is falling too low.

The website for the Ontario Flower Growers is **www.ontarioflowers.com**. Links to other sites with examples of the use of clocks can be found at the site of a company that makes the clocks: **www.oes-inc.com**.

One approach to economic decision making is the free-market system. This chapter discusses the operation of such a system, including concepts of supply and demand.

What Is a Market?

A market describes the interaction of buyers and sellers for the purpose of making an exchange of goods or services and establishing a price for them.

The local farmers' market in your area provides a good example of how a **market** works. It is normally located in a historic part of the community and is the focal point for the exchange of farm produce. The central location of the market has advantages for both buyers and sellers: shoppers are exposed to a wide variety of farm products of differing qualities, and farmers save time and energy in selling their produce by reaching many potential customers at one location.

Apart from bringing the buyers and sellers of farm products together, the market performs another function. It establishes a price at which the products will be sold. The determination of a price, as will be pointed out in this chapter, is the most important aspect of a market.

An antique auction also provides a good example of how a market operates. Periodically, buyers and sellers of antiques are brought together through the notice of an auction. Unlike other markets, where the price may be set by the seller, at an auction the buyer actively participates in the determination of a price. Antiques are offered for sale and the bids of buyers determine the ultimate price. The more buyers at the auction, and the more money they have to spend, the higher the prices will be. Buyers are not, however, solely responsible for determining the price. Sellers at an auction may influence the price by establishing a minimum below which they will not sell the antique article. This is one example of how the price is set. Regardless of how the price is determined, each market establishes a price and provides for an exchange of goods and services.

Markets exist for any commodity or service that has a price. It is easy to understand the concept of markets, but often difficult to identify the actual market. For example, where is the market for rare coins? Since these coins are bought and sold a market must exist, but its location is probably scattered all over the globe. In fact, there are many products sold in an international market. As Canadians, we know that not all of our food is grown locally; some food items (e.g., oranges, bananas) come from a variety of foreign countries. For these products, Canadians are buyers in the international marketplace. Canadian manufacturers, such as those producing steel and paper, often seek customers outside of Canada, and therefore are suppliers to international markets.

A **market**, therefore, is the interaction of buyers and sellers for the purpose of making an exchange, which establishes a price for the goods or services exchanged.

> A market is the interaction of buyers and sellers for the purpose of making an exchange.

Markets do not need money in order to operate, although money is used as a medium of exchange in most markets. Prior to the introduction of money, exchange was carried on through a system of trading goods and services. This is referred to as *barter,* and is better suited to a more primitive economy than a modern industrialized one. Under a barter system, individuals need to have something to trade. Many people in today's society do not produce anything tangible to trade. For example, after a day's work, an office worker does not have anything tangible to offer in the marketplace. During the day, the worker may process hundreds of paper forms, but cannot take the forms home to trade for other products. Money solves this problem by providing something of value in return for the worker's services. This money can then be exchanged by the worker for goods and services.

Trades are difficult to make in the barter system. In order to complete a trade, a buyer of a certain product has to locate a seller interested in what he or she has to offer. Money again solves the problem. Since money is acceptable to both buyers and sellers, the exchange of goods and services is facilitated. The barter system, although inefficient, is not dead. It is still used in many parts of the world and appears to be making a comeback in industrialized countries. Rapidly rising prices and a desire to lessen the burden of personal income tax have resulted in the increased use of barter. Professional people and store owners appear to be best suited for participating in this type of exchange, since they have a service or a product that may be attractive to others. For example, an electrician may do some electrical work on his or her dentist's house in exchange for a certain amount of dental care. Since no records are kept, nor money transferred, the services will not be recorded as income for either the electrician or the dentist.

In order to analyze the operation of a market in more detail, it is necessary to review the actions of buyers and sellers separately. The buyers' side of the market is referred to as the *demand* side. In other words, buyers have a certain **demand,** or desire, for various goods and services. This demand is represented by the quantity of goods and services that they are willing and able to purchase. The sellers' side of the market is referred to as the *supply* side. It represents the quantity of goods and services that sellers are willing and able to **supply,** or offer, to the market.

> The market for any good or service is divided into two sections: the demand side, representing those who are willing to purchase the product; and the supply side, representing those who are willing to sell the product.

The Concept of Demand

You may have heard the expression "The consumer is king." This reference to royalty implies that consumers have the power to decide what products are supplied to the market simply by making their preferences known to manufacturers. Consumer preferences are transferred to the market in terms of the goods and services that they buy. If they continue to buy a certain product, it will continue to be produced. On the other hand, if they do not purchase a product in sufficient quantity it will disappear from the market.

In actual fact, the consumer is not king. The decision about which products will be offered for sale is made jointly by the consumer and the supplier. Nonetheless, *consumer demand* and changes in this demand are an important aspect of any market. In circumstances where consumer demand has changed, the nature of the market changes as well. The automobile market provides a good example. The large increase in gasoline prices in the

1970s has changed driving habits. The demand for small, fuel-efficient cars increased, while the demand for "gas-guzzlers" decreased. These changes in demand forced automobile manufacturers to increase the production of smaller and more fuel-efficient cars. Large gasoline price increases have dampened the demand for the popular sports utility vehicles (SUVs).

Factors Affecting Demand

Many factors can cause consumer demand for a product to change. These can be summarized as follows:

Price: The fact that stores hold "clearance sales" attests to the importance of price to the consumer. Under normal circumstances, a person will buy a larger quantity of a product if the price is low. A lower price allows the consumer to buy more. Also, a lower price enables the consumer to substitute the lower-priced product for a more expensive alternative.

Change in the price of substitute products: Since a number of products are fairly close substitutes for each other, changes in the price of one product will likely influence the demand for another; for example, in the past sharp increases in the price of coffee have convinced some consumers to drink more tea and less coffee. Wrapping paper provides another example: as the price of gift bags dropped, they became more attractive substitutes for conventional wrapping paper.

Change in the price of complementary products: The demand for a product is also influenced by any changes in the price of a complementary product. A complementary product is one that is used in conjunction with the product in question. As the price of gasoline increased, the demand for big cars declined. When mortgage interest rates increase, the number of houses that consumers buy declines.

Incomes: Changes in the general level of income have an effect on product demand. Under most circumstances, the more money consumers have to spend, the greater the demand for the product. This is shown in the increased demand for luxury items such as backyard swimming pools and foreign vacations. The demand for luxury products has increased as the level of consumer income in Canada has increased. In periods when the real incomes of Canadians decline, the demand for luxury items declines as well. This relationship, however, does not hold for all products. If a product is seen as cheap or inferior, consumers may purchase less of it as their incomes increase and be forced to buy more of it when their incomes decrease. For example, as a person's income increases he or she may eat less hamburger and more steak; when income declines, hamburger outsells steak.

Tastes and preferences: Individual tastes, preferences, and needs also influence demand. A major influence on individual tastes is advertising. Manufacturers have resorted to advertising in various media in order to maintain or increase the demand for their products. If consumers are constantly exposed to a certain brand through advertising, their purchase choices are likely to be affected. Advertising is not always aimed at persuading the consumer to buy the product. A certain amount of advertising simply provides information, which is especially true of government service ads.

Some industries do a more effective job of influencing consumer tastes than others. The fashion industry has been successful at constantly changing styles in apparel and footwear. These changes convince consumers that their present wardrobe is not satisfactory, creating a demand for new lines of clothes.

Consumer preferences may also be altered by receiving more information about a product. In the area of nutrition, medical research continually provides more data on the harmful effects of various food additives. For example, red dye and nitrites have been linked to cancer. The importance of consumer information has made such an impact that the federal government has established the Department of Consumer and Corporate Affairs in order to provide more information on product safety and quality. This department has also enacted legislation to eliminate misleading advertising.

Expectations of future prices: If consumers believe that the price of a product will increase in the near future, they are likely to buy more of the product in the present. In the past, the expectation of rapidly rising house and mortgage costs increased the demand for houses. With housing being the important consumer item that it is, buyers were eager to purchase houses at the lowest possible price. The expectation of future prices has also influenced the gold and silver markets and the stock markets. Rapidly rising prices led to the belief that prices would continue to rise. On the other hand, if people expect prices to be lower in the near future, they will postpone purchases until a later date.

Number and characteristics of buyers: As the population increases, the demand for most products increases as well. There is a greater need for food, clothing, housing, and so on. For certain products, it is not only the number of potential buyers but also the characteristics of those buyers that are important. For example, the age of the population affects product purchases. The greater the number of young people, the greater milk sales will be. The age of our population also influences the sales of running shoes, CDs and cassettes, home video equipment, houses, toys, and other such items.

Expectations of future incomes: Individuals' expectations about their future incomes also affect their purchases. For example, if someone expects to be on strike in the near future, they may postpone purchases until the strike is settled.

The factors discussed above do not remain constant. They are continually changing and continually altering the demand for products. These changes complicate the analysis of demand. The effect of a change in any one of these factors on product demand is difficult to determine when several other factors are changing at the same time. In order to simplify the analysis of demand we assume that all factors influencing demand, other than price, remain constant. It is as if the analysis of demand refers to one specific moment in time, before any changes can take place. After reviewing the reaction of consumers to price changes, we can relax this assumption and see how demand responds to other changes.

Consumer Response to Price Changes

How do consumers respond to changes in the price of a product? Under most circumstances, they will buy more of a product if the price is low and less of it if the price is high. When the price of a product increases, less of the product can be purchased with the current level of income. Also, when the price of a product increases, consumers may substitute another, cheaper, product for it. The inverse relationship between the price of a product and the quantity of the product demanded can be presented by means of a *demand schedule.*

In order to better analyze the changes on the demand side of the market, let us derive a demand schedule for submarine sandwiches. This schedule is shown in Table 2.1. It indicates the number of sandwiches that would be demanded in your town at various prices during one week. The table shows an *inverse relationship* between the price and the quantity demanded.

Table 2.1 *Demand schedule for sandwiches*

PRICE OF SANDWICH	QUANTITY DEMANDED IN ONE WEEK
$2.90	500
$3.00	450
$3.10	400
$3.20	350
$3.30	300

If the price of sandwiches were $2.90, consumers would be willing to buy 500 in a week; if the price were $3.30, consumers would want to purchase only 300.

The information in this table is presented in graphical form in Figure 2.1. In the graph, price is presented on the vertical axis and the number of sandwiches demanded per week is shown on the horizontal axis. After plotting the relationships from Table 2.1 and connecting the points, we can see that the graph shows a line representing an inverse relationship between the price and the quantity demanded. In Figure 2.1, this curve is labelled D^1 and is known as a *demand curve*. Remember, the demand curve does not provide any more information about the consumer demand for sandwiches than the demand schedule does, since it is derived from the schedule. The demand curve will, however, facilitate our future discussions of demand.

The inverse relationship between price and quantity demanded is referred to as *the law of downward-sloping demand*. This means that consumers are willing and able to buy more of the product the lower the price, and less of the product the higher the price. When the price of sandwiches changes, the quantity of sandwiches demanded changes as well, but the demand curve itself does not.

Figure 2.1

The demand curve

The inverse relationship between the price and the quantity demanded is represented by a downward-sloping curve.

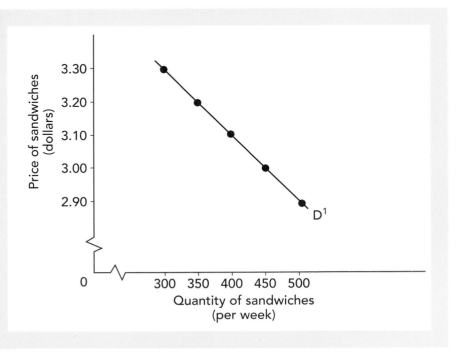

Changes in Demand

Consumer demand for a product is not likely to stay constant over time. The factors that influence consumer demand are always changing. For example, individual tastes do not remain the same. The demand for submarine sandwiches may decline, while the demand for another type of fast food increases. Changes in consumer incomes will also affect the demand for sandwiches. During the summer, when students are working and earning money, the demand for submarine sandwiches will likely be higher than in other months. Changes in the price of other fast foods will also affect the demand. If the price of hamburgers increases, the number of sandwiches demanded at submarine shops may increase as people substitute sandwiches for hamburgers. The demand schedule derived for sandwiches in Table 2.1 would no longer be applicable if any of these changes were to take place. We were able to compile this table only under the assumption that everything else stayed the same. Assume that the price of hamburgers has changed and that a new demand schedule for submarine sandwiches has to be drawn up. This schedule is presented in Table 2.2. After an increase in the price of hamburgers, consumers would be willing to buy 600 sandwiches at a price of $2.90. At all other prices, consumers would be willing to buy more sandwiches. How will a change in the demand schedule affect the demand curve?

Figure 2.2 translates the new demand schedule into a new demand curve (D^2). An increase in the price of hamburgers has resulted in a shift to the right of the demand curve for sandwiches. This is called an *increase in demand*. In other words, consumers are willing to buy more sandwiches at the same price than they were prior to the change in the price of hamburgers. Other changes in the submarine-sandwich market may cause the demand curve to shift to the left.

If consumer tastes change and consumers are less eager to purchase sandwiches, the demand curve for sandwiches would move to the left. In this

Table 2.2 *Demand schedule for sandwiches (after an increase in the price of hamburgers)*

PRICE OF SANDWICH	QUANTITY DEMANDED LAST WEEK	QUANTITY DEMANDED THIS WEEK
$2.90	500	600
$3.00	450	550
$3.10	400	500
$3.20	350	450
$3.30	300	400

Figure 2.2

A shift in the demand curve

An increase in the price of a substitute product has shifted the demand curve to the right. More sandwiches will be demanded, regardless of the price, than previously.

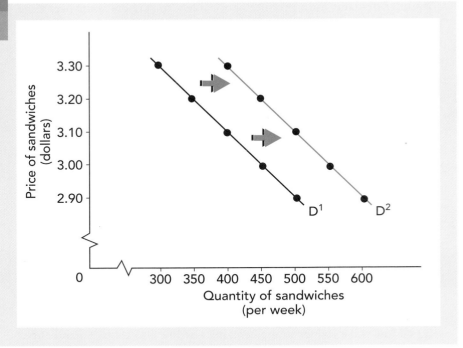

A change in demand is a response to a change in a factor previously held constant.

A change in the quantity demanded is a response to a change in the price of a product or service.

situation, regardless of the price, consumers would buy fewer sandwiches. A shift to the left in the demand curve is called a *decrease in demand*. In fact, any time there is a change in one of the factors held constant when drawing the curve, the demand curve for a product shifts. This shift is referred to as a *change in demand* and must be distinguished from a *change in the quantity demanded*. The latter occurs in response to a change in the price of the product. In order to determine consumer reaction to a change in the price of submarine sandwiches we do not draw a new curve, but refer to a new point on the existing curve corresponding to the new price. That is, a **change in demand** occurs when one of the constant factors changes and results in a shift of the demand curve. In contrast, a **change in the quantity demanded** occurs in response to a change in the price of the product and is shown by moving along the demand curve. A diagram representing the change in demand and the change in quantity demanded appears in Figure 2.3.

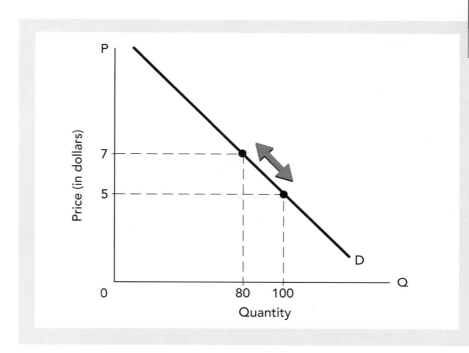

Figure 2.3a

Change in quantity demand

A change in the quantity demanded results in movement along existing demand curves.

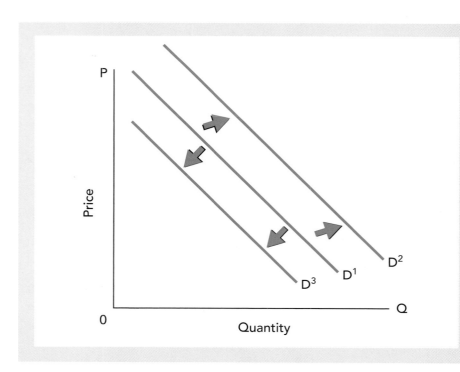

Figure 2.3b

Change in demand

A change in demand results in a shift of the entire demand curve.

REVIEW

2.1 For each of the following changes show the effect on the respective demand curve. Draw a separate graph for each answer, being sure to label your axes:

a) the effect of an increase in the price of tea on the demand for coffee;

b) the effect of a decrease in consumer incomes on the demand for new cars;

c) the effect of an advertising campaign by Coke on the demand for Coke;

d) the effect of an advertising campaign by Coke on the demand for Pepsi;

e) the effect of a shoe price increase on the demand for shoes.

2.2 View the impact of price changes for complementary products on the demand for sandwiches.

EVERYDAY ECONOMICS 2.1

Get Crackin'

The average Canadian eats almost 200 eggs per year. The demand for eggs, like the demand for all products, depends on a number of factors. Some of the influences on the demand for eggs are discussed below.

Tastes and preferences: The demand for eggs depends heavily on consumer attitudes toward eggs. This attitude is influenced by health and diet considerations and by the advertising and promotion of eggs. Concerns over cholesterol previously tempered the demand for eggs, while the popularity in recent years of protein-rich diets has increased the demand for eggs. Changes in the breeding of laying hens and improvements in feed have changed the nutritional composition of eggs. The Canadian Egg Marketing Agency (CEMA) reports that the average egg today contains 22 percent less fat and 31 percent less cholesterol than the average egg produced prior to 1989.

The advertising of eggs is conducted by both the Canadian Egg Marketing Agency and by provincial egg marketing boards. The advertising of eggs included the "Get Crackin'" and "Eggs Instead" promotions. The most recent promotion is "Eggs, Grade A Goodness." CEMA also makes information available on the nutritional value of eggs. For example, eggs contain the nine essential amino acids and are a good source of protein. Eggs also contain vitamins A, D, and E, among others. The promotion of eggs is aimed at changing consumer attitudes toward the product.

Consumer preference for eggs increases at Easter. Eggs are seen as a symbol of the start of life. The popularity of eggs decorated by Ukrainian folk artists will also influence the demand for eggs. To meet the demand for egg decoration, CEMA published a booklet entitled "Brunch with Eggs, Paint with Eggs," providing recipes and egg-decorating ideas.

Consumer incomes: As per capita incomes increase, individuals have more money to spend on eggs. Do they buy more eggs or other foods when their incomes increase? The research is inconclusive; however, there is some evidence that increases in income may lead to a slight reduction in egg consumption.

Prices of other products: Products such as cereal are substitutes for eggs. Changes in the price of cereal can influence egg consumption. Changes in cereal advertising expenditures also influence the demand for eggs. Changes in the price of complementary products such as bacon can also influence the demand for eggs.

Population: The overall demand for eggs is influenced by changes in the Canadian population. An increase in the population shifts the demand curve for eggs to the right.

Questions

1. Can you list any factors other than those mentioned above that influence the demand for eggs?
2. Would an increase in egg prices result in a shift of the demand curve for eggs to the left? Explain.
3. Using a graph in your answer, show the impact of egg imports from the United States on the demand for Canadian-produced eggs.
4. Why is it necessary for an agency such as CEMA to promote egg consumption? Is it possible for the promotion of eggs to be undertaken by individual farmers?

The Concept of Supply

Changes are also taking place constantly on the supply side of the market: the number and variety of products available to consumers is constantly increasing. For example, the kinds of cellular phones offered in the marketplace have increased rapidly in recent years. There has also been an increase in the number of fast-food outlets available to consumers. On the other hand, some items have disappeared from the marketplace, or are in the process of disappearing: high gasoline prices have reduced the average size of the cars on our roads, and radial tires have replaced bias-ply tires on automobiles. The introduction of the ball-point pen has almost eliminated the use of fountain pens.

Factors Affecting Supply

There are several factors affecting the supply side of the market:

Price: The higher the price that a supplier can receive for a product, the more of the product the supplier will offer to the market. When the price is high, the time and effort involved in supplying the product become more worthwhile. The opportunity cost of not providing the product is also greater when the price is higher. That is, when the price is high, the amount of money given up by not supplying the product is greater. At low prices, the time and cost involved in supplying a good or service may be too great in relation to the reward (the price). For example, when the price of pork increases, farmers are encouraged to increase their stock of pigs. It becomes worthwhile to spend more time and money raising pigs. Therefore, with the higher prices, there will be more pork offered to consumers in the marketplace. On the other hand, when pork prices fall, some farmers may reduce their stock of pigs. The end result is that less pork is sent to the marketplace.

Production costs: Supplying a product to the market involves many expenses, including raw materials, transportation, rent, wages, salaries, energy, machines and equipment, interest payments on loans, and taxes. A change in any of these costs influences the supply of a product. If the wages paid to employees increase, the cost of supplying the product will increase. The supplier may be willing to supply the product after granting a wage increase only if a higher price for the product is received.

Technological change: Businesses employ both workers and machines to produce their products. Changes in the type of machinery or equipment available could influence the supply of the product to the market. Improvements in equipment are referred to as technological changes. The impact that these changes can have on supply can again be shown with reference to farming. The development of pesticides reduced the damage to crops by insects and increased the yield that farmers could expect from a given acreage. Irradiation and genetic modification have also had an impact on the supply of food.

The development of computer technology has changed the production techniques of many businesses. The introduction of word processors has revolutionized office procedures. The new equipment has increased the demand for certain office skills, while reducing the demand for others. There is more need for people with a knowledge of computers and their capabilities, and less need for outdated skills in areas such as manual inventory control. Computer technology has also introduced robots on the production lines of certain manufacturing companies.

Government regulation: The supply of a product or service to the market is often influenced by government regulations. Some products and services are illegal. Provincial governments regulate the amount of certain agricultural products that can be produced. Municipal governments can regulate supply through zoning by-laws and by prohibiting certain types of businesses to operate within their boundaries.

Psychology of owner: Although it is assumed that all suppliers are in business to make a great deal of money, there may be other reasons. Some individuals may be in business in order to be their own boss, or to reduce their taxable income. Any change in the psychological aspects of business will ultimately affect supply.

Weather conditions: For agricultural products in particular, weather conditions have an important influence on supply. Extremely wet or dry conditions may reduce the volume of farm output and ultimately affect market conditions.

The approach to the analysis of the supply side of the market is the same as for demand. It is difficult to analyze the supply side of the market when everything is changing. Therefore, it is assumed that all factors influencing supply, other than price, remain constant. The reaction of suppliers to changes in the price of the product will be analyzed first.

Supplier Response to Price Changes

The quantity supplied of a product to the market increases when the price of the product is higher. The additional costs of supplying more of the product to the market begin to increase beyond a certain level of output. Since costs increase, a higher price must be obtained in order for the supply to be increased. In the case of submarine sandwiches, the supplier's costs will increase if more sandwiches are to be provided beyond a certain number. These costs could include storage and refrigeration capacity, restaurant seating space, and the supplier's time.

The *positive relationship* between the price of sandwiches and the quantity supplied can be represented in a supply schedule (Table 2.3). The schedule assumes that all other factors influencing supply (e.g., rental costs, workers' wages, the price of buns, etc.) remain constant. At a price of $2.90,

Table 2.3 *Supply schedule of sandwiches*

PRICE PER SANDWICH	QUANTITY SUPPLIED IN ONE WEEK
$2.90	300
$3.00	350
$3.10	400
$3.20	450
$3.30	500

submarine-store owners are willing to supply only 300 sandwiches per week; if the price increased to $3.30, 500 sandwiches would be provided.

The supply schedule can be depicted in graphic terms, as in Figure 2.4. The price of sandwiches is represented on the vertical axis, and the quantity of sandwiches on the horizontal axis. By plotting the points and joining them a line is formed, indicating the positive relationship between the two variables. This upward-sloping line, designated by S^1, is called the *supply curve.* With all the other factors that influence supply remaining constant, an increase in the price of sandwiches will lead to an increase in the quantity supplied. A decrease in the price will lead to a decrease in the quantity supplied.

Changes in Supply

The supply of a product to the market will change over time because of changes in the factors that influence that supply. For example, an increase in the rent that a store has to pay will affect supply. It will result in a change to the supply schedule, because submarine-shop owners will want a higher price for sandwiches. The supply schedule in Table 2.3 is now obsolete, and a new schedule is required. Assuming that rent increases apply to all suppliers, a new schedule is presented in Table 2.4 and translated into a graph

Figure 2.4

The supply curve

The positive relationship between the price and the quantity supplied represented by an upward-sloping curve.

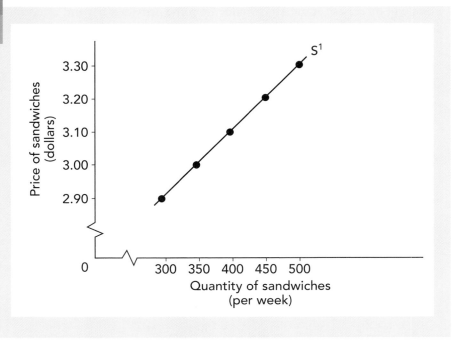

Table 2.4 *Supply schedule of sandwiches (after the increase in rent)*

PRICE PER SANDWICH	QUANTITY SUPPLIED IN ONE WEEK
$3.00	300
$3.10	350
$3.20	400
$3.30	450
$3.40	500

in Figure 2.5. Under the new conditions, suppliers would supply 300 sandwiches at a new price of $3.00 per sandwich. Similar price increases would be necessary for other quantities.

The new supply curve is represented by S^2. A change in rent has shifted the supply curve to the left. Proprietors are willing to supply only the same number of sandwiches at a higher price. Another way to say this is that for the same price, suppliers will put fewer sandwiches on the market after the

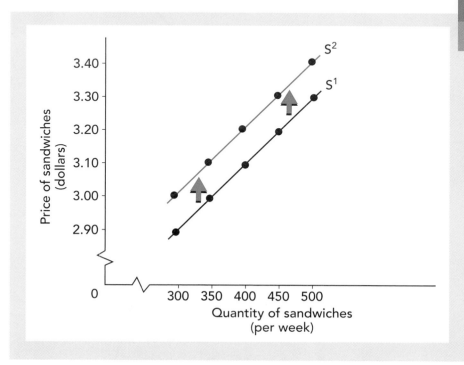

Figure 2.5

A shift in the supply curve

An increase in production costs results in a shift of the supply curve to the left. The same number of sandwiches will only be supplied to the market at a higher price.

increase in rent. This is referred to as a *decrease in supply.* In contrast, any change that will lower costs results in a move of the supply curve to the right. This is an *increase in supply.* Any change in a constant factor, such as production costs, will cause the supply curve to shift. This circumstance is referred to as a *change in supply* and must be distinguished from a *change in the quantity supplied.* The latter occurs in response to a change in the price of the product. In order to determine supplier reaction to a change in the price of submarine sandwiches, we do not draw a new curve, but refer to a new point on the existing curve corresponding to the new price. That is, a **change in supply** occurs when one of the constant factors changes; this results in a shift of the supply curve. In contrast, a **change in quantity supplied** occurs when the price of the product changes, and is shown by a movement along the existing supply curve. A diagram representing the change in supply and the change in quantity supplied appears in Figure 2.6.

A **change in supply** is a response to a change in a factor previously held constant.

A **change in quantity supplied** is a response to change in the price of the product or service.

Figure 2.6a

Change in quantity supplied

A change in the quantity supplied results in a movement along an existing supply curve.

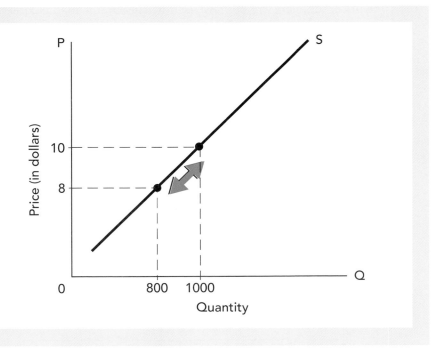

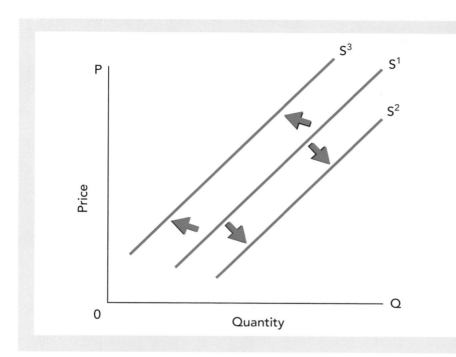

Figure 2.6b

Change in supply

A change in supply results in a shift of the entire supply curve.

REVIEW

2.3 Using your knowledge of supply curves, show the impact of the following changes on the respective supply curves:

a) an increase in construction workers' wages on the supply curve for new houses;

b) the development of a new pesticide on the supply curve for wheat;

c) the effect of a drought on the supply curve for corn; and

d) the effect of an increase in the price of shoes on the supply of shoes.

2.4 View the impact of changes in the costs of production on the supply of sandwiches.

The Supply of Oil

One of the most pressing problems facing Canada in recent years has been the use and supply of energy. The energy crisis began in 1973 after the Arab–Israeli conflict. At that time, the Organization of Petroleum Exporting Countries (OPEC) reduced the supply of oil and drastically increased the price. (The OPEC nations are Algeria, Indonesia, Iran, Iraq, Kuwait, Libya, Nigeria, Qatar, Saudi Arabia, the United Arab Emirates, and Venezuela.) This move produced greater concern in Western industrialized countries regarding the possibility of oil shortages in the future.

At the time of the OPEC price increase, the Canadian government had been following a policy of low oil prices, which were substantially below world oil prices. The result of these low prices was a reduction in the amount of money being spent on oil exploration. Because the return on their investment was low, oil companies were investing in other countries where the return was greater.

The federal and provincial governments both realized that Canada's oil-pricing policy would have to change. If the supply of oil in Canada were to increase, prices would have to start increasing toward the world level. The higher oil prices stimulated exploration in the Arctic and off the shores of the Atlantic provinces. Development continued in the oil sands of Alberta.

The higher prices for oil were necessary in order to increase the supply and to assist Canada in becoming more self-sufficient in energy. Higher oil prices, however, had a different impact on the demand side of the market. Consumers were forced to adapt to higher prices for energy and did so by decreasing the quantity of oil demanded. By the early 1980s, the world found itself facing an oil surplus. Oil prices have fluctuated over the years. Iraq's takeover of Kuwait in the summer of 1990 resulted in a sharp increase in oil prices. As the threat of war escalated, the price of a barrel of oil increased. Oil prices declined during the war once a Coalition victory seemed certain. Oil prices increase when the OPEC nations agree to limit the supply of oil and fall when the agreement falls apart.

What do low oil prices mean for Canada? Cheaper gasoline and lower home-heating costs are welcomed by consumers and by businesses such as airlines, which are major consumers of energy. For example, Air Canada estimates that a $1 increase in the price of a barrel of oil results in an increase of $17 in pre-tax operating costs. Producers of oil are not as happy. If low oil prices do not make oil exploration and production feasible, companies will close down and jobs will be lost. The impact of low oil prices is not felt equally across Canada. Alberta, Saskatchewan, the Atlantic provinces, and the Arctic will suffer the most. The livelihood of many communities depends on continued oil exploration and production. It is also less likely that Canada will become self-sufficient in energy with low oil prices continuing on the market.

Further information on the topic of oil supplies can be obtained from the Canadian Centre for Energy Information or at its website: **www.centreforenergy.com**. Additional information on world energy supplies—oil, natural gas, coal, hydro, and nuclear—can be found at the website for the International Energy Agency: **www.iea.org**.

Questions

1. Draw a supply curve for oil in Canada. From the point of view of the Canadian economy, why may it be necessary for oil prices to increase?

2. What will be the effect of higher oil prices on the demand side of the market?

3. As the price of oil increases, what will be the impact on other sources of energy such as electricity and solar power?

4. In your opinion, should the federal government become involved in the exploration for and the production of oil?

5. Why would exploration costs increase as the search for oil continues?

Are Gasoline Prices Too Low?

Canadians depend a great deal on fossil fuels. We live in a cold climate and we need fuel to heat our homes. Canada is a large country and we need fuel for the transportation of individuals and products. Because of our dependence on fossil fuels, Canadians are very concerned about increases in energy prices.

An argument can be made that the current price of gasoline does not reflect the true cost of gasoline usage in our society. It can be argued that there are hidden costs to the use of gasoline, such as the health and environmental costs associated with an increase in the use of fossil fuels. Also, governments are forced to provide the infrastructure that is required for our economy to operate on fossil fuels (e.g., highways). A 1998 report by the International Centre for Technological Assessment quantified the added costs associated with the use of gasoline-powered automobiles. The unaccounted-for costs were as much as $1.7 trillion annually. In order for the price of gasoline to fully reflect these costs, it would be ten times the current price. The estimated price per litre of gasoline in Canada needed to reflect the total cost of gasoline usage is $5.40.

Does it matter if we are paying too little for gasoline? A low price results in overuse. We live in large houses. We drive SUVs and other large vehicles. The demand for fossil fuels is there but the supply is dwindling and non-renewable. There are numerous estimates concerning the world's supply of oil. Since new oil reserves are still being discovered, the estimates are not necessarily accurate. Nonetheless, one estimate has world oil production peaking by as early as 2007. Another estimate states that, by 2040, world output may be less than one-half of today's output.

Energy is needed not only for automobiles. Farmers need fuel for farm machinery. The fishing industry needs fuel for boats. Airplanes need fossil fuels. We also need fossil fuels for medicine, paint, plastics, fertilizers, and pesticides. The relationship between the demand and the supply for fossil fuels will certainly lead to future price increases. Should prices increase now as a means of forcing us to conserve this resource?

Questions

1. Is the demand for fossil fuels likely to increase?
2. Will a high price for gasoline force us to look for substitutes?
3. Gasoline prices are increasing and so is the demand for SUVs. Explain this apparent contradiction.
4. What impact would higher prices for gasoline have on the demand for houses in the suburbs of major Canadian cities? Explain.

The Interaction of Demand and Supply

The primary function of a market is to bring buyers and sellers together in order to establish a price and to make an exchange. Now that they have been discussed separately, it is time to join the demand and supply sides of the market. This is done in Table 2.5 and Figure 2.7, using the demand and supply curves previously developed for submarine sandwiches. The demand and supply curves on the same graph represent the market for that particular product or service. We can use these curves to show how

Table 2.5 *Comparison of demand and supply schedules for sandwiches*

PRICE	QUANTITY DEMANDED	QUANTITY SUPPLIED	PRICE CHANGE
$2.90	500	300	↑
$3.00	450	350	↑
$3.10	400	400	no change
$3.20	350	450	↓
$3.30	300	500	↓

Figure 2.7

Equilibrium

The intersection of the demand and the supply curves for a product. At equilibrium there is no tendency for the price or quantity of sandwiches to change.

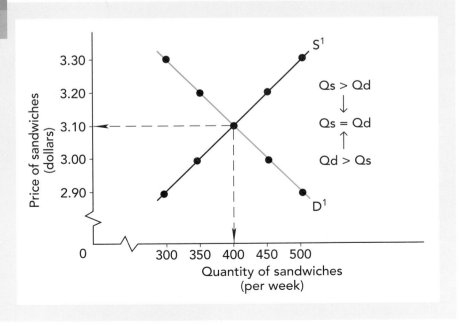

the buyers and sellers in a market get together in order to establish the price and quantity exchanged.

Suppose that the suppliers of sandwiches decided to sell sandwiches for $3.30. At this price, they are willing to supply 500 sandwiches per week. How would consumers react to this price for subs? According to Table 2.5, consumers would be willing to buy only 300 sandwiches a week at that price. As a result, suppliers would find that they could not sell all of their sandwiches. One possible solution would be to lower the price. Suppose that the price was dropped to $3.20. Consumers would be willing to buy an additional 50 sandwiches a week. Suppliers, on the other hand, would reduce the number of sandwiches that they were prepared to make. The lower price would still leave proprietors with a surplus of 100 sandwiches. In fact, until the price drops to $3.10, there will be a surplus of sandwiches. At $3.10, the quantity of sandwiches demanded is just equal to the quantity of sandwiches supplied. Therefore, there is no reason for the price to change.

What would happen if suppliers started selling sandwiches for $2.90? At this price, they would be willing to supply 300 sandwiches, but the consumer demand would total 500 sandwiches per week. Consumers would be willing to purchase more sandwiches than are available at that price. There is a shortage of sandwiches. Suppliers would be willing to supply more sandwiches, but only at a higher price. The price of subs will continue to rise until it reaches $3.10. At this price, the quantity of submarine sandwiches demanded is equal to the quantity supplied. Since there is no tendency for the $3.10 price to change, it is referred to as an **equilibrium price**. This equilibrium price is determined by the intersection of the demand and supply curves for a product. If the price of the product is not at the equilibrium level, it will constantly be moving toward equilibrium. The only stable price in a market is the equilibrium price.

Prices change as they move toward equilibrium. They also change when changes take place in the factors that affect the demand and supply sides of the market. For example, what effect does an increase in the price of hamburgers have on the price of submarine sandwiches? It increases the demand for sandwiches, a substitute product; this is shown in Figure 2.8. An increase in the price of hamburgers shifts the demand curve for sandwiches to D^2. The new demand curve now intersects the supply curve at the new equilibrium price of $3.20. The increased demand for sandwiches forces up the price under the existing supply conditions.

It should also be noted that at this new price, more sandwiches are purchased (450 compared to 400 before demand increased). Is this a contradiction of the law of downward-sloping demand? How can the price of sandwiches increase, and the quantity purchased increase as well? This is only

The equilibrium price is the price at which the quantity demanded of a product is equal to the quantity supplied.

Figure 2.8

A new equilibrium position
(shift in the demand curve)

A shift in the demand
curve to the right
results in a higher
equilibrium price and
quantity.

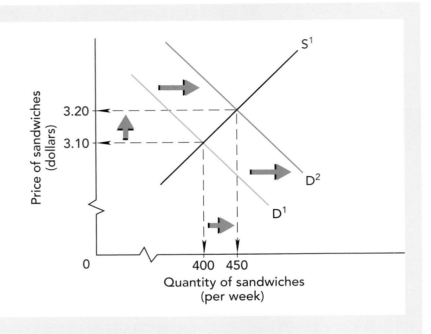

an apparent contradiction. It was stated earlier that—all things remaining
the same—any increase in price would decrease the quantity demanded.
However, not all things have remained the same. The price of hamburgers
has increased, and as a result consumers must reassess their demand for
submarine sandwiches. The new conditions have convinced them to purchase more sandwiches than before. Under the new conditions represented
by D^2 in Figure 2.8, consumers will still purchase fewer sandwiches if the
price goes above $3.20 and more sandwiches if it falls below $3.20. That is,
the law of downward-sloping demand applies to the new curve D^2, just as
it did with the previous curve D^1.

How will changes in supply affect the price? Suppose that the price of
butter used in the sandwiches increases. Suppliers are going to ask a higher
price for the same number of sandwiches. This is represented in Figure 2.9
as a shift in the supply curve to S^2. The new supply curve intersects demand
at a higher equilibrium price ($3.15). In this case, fewer sandwiches (375)
are purchased by consumers than before the shift in supply. A decrease in
supply (shift of the supply curve to the left) results in a higher price and a
lower quantity exchanged under constant-demand conditions.

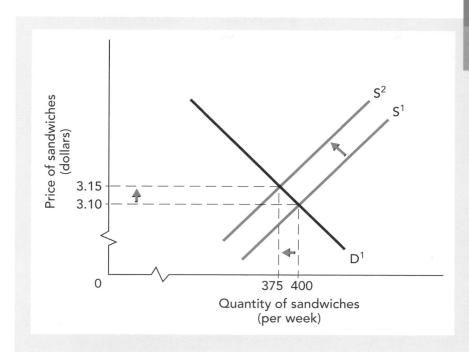

Figure 2.9

A new equilibrium position (shift in the supply curve)

A shift in the supply curve to the left results in a higher equilibrium price and a lower equilibrium quantity.

R E V I E W

2.5 Using your knowledge of both demand and supply curves, show the impact of the following:
   a) an increase in consumer incomes on the price of restaurant meals;
   b) an increase in the price of steel on the price of new cars;
   c) a decrease in the price of tea on the price of coffee;
   d) the development of new pesticides on the price of corn; and
   e) the expectation of future price increases on the present price of houses.

2.6 Discover how equilibrium price and quantity vary with changes in demand and supply curves.

A Market for Organs?

Numerous articles have appeared in Canadian newspapers over the last few years about the shortage of human organs for transplants. Radio advertisements urge Canadians to sign the donor pledge portion of their driver's licence. According to reports, Canada has one of the worst organ-donation rates in the western world. In recent years, the number of individuals waiting for donations has increased while the number of transplants has decreased. This shortage has occurred in spite of medical and technological advances.

Organ transplants can actually save money in the delivery of health care. It is estimated that follow-up treatment for a kidney transplant costs about $50 000 over a five-year period. Five years of dialysis for those who do not receive a transplant costs approximately $250 000. Thus, a financial argument, as well as a health argument, can be made for increasing the number of transplants.

Blame for the lack of donor organs has been placed on the health-care system. There is not a coordinated organ-retrieval program. Analysts point to Canada's donation rate of 14.1 donors per million population and compare it to Spain's rate of 26.8 per million. In Spain each hospital is responsible for the coordination of donors and those needing transplants. Apart from some reorganization in the health-care system, could the marketplace help with the shortage of organs in Canada?

What if potential donors were paid for their organs? Would the free-market system save the lives of many who are waiting for transplants? The marketplace is used to provide other necessities of life such as food and shelter. We do not wait for food donations in order to eat. Turning over organ donations to the marketplace may reduce the shortage of donor organs. Would an individual sign a donor card for a cash payment right now? The organ would be donated only after the person's death. The price to be paid for various organs would depend on demand and supply.

Questions

1. In your opinion, why is it currently illegal to pay for organ donations?
2. Discuss the advantages and disadvantages of a market for organs.

Speculators

According to the dictionary, one of the several definitions for speculation is an investment involving high risk but also possible high profits. To *speculate* means, among other things, to arrive at a conclusion without knowing the complete set of facts. A speculator is one who speculates. In which markets do speculators operate? What impact do speculators have on these markets?

To some people, speculators are a destabilizing influence on a market. They purchase a product with the expectation that the price of the product will increase. When the price increases, the speculator sells. If many speculators sell, the price drops. Do the actions of speculators cause fluctuations in the price of products? It may be that speculators stabilize rather than destabilize markets. We will use the market for wheat, where the supply changes throughout the year, as an example of the price stabilization effects of speculators.

The price of wheat fluctuates throughout the year. The price reaches its lowest point at harvest time, when the supply of wheat is abundant. The price is highest just prior to harvest, when the supply is at its lowest. How will speculators act in the market for wheat? They know the price will increase after harvest, so they buy wheat when the price is low. They sell when the price increases just before harvest. The buying of wheat by speculators increases the price at harvest time. Thus, the price does not fall as much as it would without speculators. As the next harvest approaches speculators sell wheat, driving down the price from what it otherwise would be. The price does increase as much with speculators in the market. Thus, speculators can have a stabilizing influence on the price. Price fluctuations can be minimized, or reduced, in a market where speculators operate.

Questions

1. Can you think of other markets where speculators operate?
2. In the above example, the supply of wheat changed throughout the year. What would the impact of speculators be on a market where the supply is relatively fixed, such as art or houses?

The Operation of a Free-Market System

The markets described in this chapter accomplish two things in our economy. They coordinate the exchange of goods and services by bringing buyers and sellers together, and they establish market prices. It is the system of prices that emerges from the various markets that makes effective the free-market approach to economic decision making.

You will recall from Chapter 1 that Canadians have to decide how to use the scarce resources that they have available. What products and services are these resources going to produce? Who will receive these products and services when they are available? The **price system** is the technique by which all of these questions are answered.

Resources will be allocated to the production of those products and services that provide the greatest return to the owner of the resource. Individuals seek out jobs that pay the highest salary. Others use their capital in the most profitable manner. They rent their buildings under circumstances that provide the highest return. The complete system of prices, rents, wages, and interest organizes economic activity. Price changes also assist in the necessary adjustments that have to be made in any economy. If there is a shortage of a product, the price will rise until the shortage is effectively eliminated. Surpluses are eliminated through price reductions.

How will the various commodities be produced? Resources will be combined in such a manner that the good or service can be produced at the lowest possible price. When competition is present, suppliers are forced to

The **price system** is the technique by which scarce resources are allocated to the production of those products and services that provide the greatest return to the resource owner. In this way, the system of prices, rents, wages, and interest organizes economic activity.

offer their goods or services at a competitive price. Consumers purchase more at lower prices, so suppliers need to be concerned about price increases.

Who will receive the goods and services that are produced? The items produced will be distributed to those who are willing and able to pay for them. Individuals will use their limited incomes to purchase those products that have a high priority for them. Therefore, the products that are produced and purchased will be items that consumers want. These wants are made known by purchases.

The price system has two distinct advantages in allocating resources. First, it is *efficient.* It allows thousands of individuals to cooperate in making economic decisions. These people do not necessarily know each other or have the same attitudes and beliefs. Each individual is making decisions based on prices and price changes. The price system permits a great deal of individual freedom in the decision-making process. Actions of individuals on what job to take and what product to buy are all voluntary. Prices do not tell people what to do, yet they do influence their decisions and induce them to act in a certain way.

Second, the price system *transmits information* to buyers and sellers. The price differences among products assist consumers in allocating their limited income to various purchases. When prices decrease, consumers are able to purchase more of the product with the same amount of income. Price changes also provide information to suppliers. Higher prices identify products that may be profitable to produce. Competition from other suppliers forces businesses to be price-conscious. They are encouraged to adopt the least costly and most efficient means of production.

If the price system is prevented from operating, information is not being transferred to buyers and sellers. As a result, these participants in the market are not able to make knowledgeable decisions about product choices. Under such circumstances, shortages and surpluses tend to persist. For example, when prices are not allowed to increase (possibly due to government regulations) in response to a shortage, suppliers are not encouraged to put more of the product on the market. In countries where the price system does not organize economic activity, shortages and surpluses tend to be persistent problems.

Our knowledge of the free-market system provides insight into the concept of *value.* What is the value of a diamond ring? a new car? a compact disc? a glass of water? The only indicator of value that we have is the price established for these products in the marketplace. If a diamond ring costs $1000, then its value is said to be $1000. The same applies to all other products.

Using this definition of value, it follows that a diamond ring has more value than a glass of water. Yet, we can survive without diamond rings, but we cannot survive without water. Surely water has more value than a diamond ring. Why is the price of water not higher than that of diamonds? The answer lies in the concept of relative scarcity. Although there is a tremendous demand for water, there is also a great supply. The demand for diamonds is less than the demand for water, but the supply of diamonds is relatively more scarce than the supply of water. The interaction of demand and supply therefore results in a higher price for diamonds than for water.

Elasticity

Price Elasticity of Demand

The *law of downward-sloping demand* states that, all other factors remaining constant, the quantity demanded of a product increases as the price falls. However, price changes for different products affect consumers in different ways. For example, a 10-cent increase in the price of milk is not likely to have a significant impact on the quantity of milk that consumers buy. For many families, especially those with small children, milk is a necessity. They will continue to buy milk even at higher prices. In contrast, a 10-cent increase in the price of a chocolate bar may greatly reduce the number of chocolate bars that consumers are willing to buy. Since chocolate bars are not a necessity, some consumers may be reluctant to pay the higher price. The demand curves for both milk and chocolate bars are downward-sloping, but their shapes are different. The exact shape of the demand curve and consumer response to price changes are of great concern to those on the supply side of the market—the manufacturers and retailers. The different responses of quantity demanded to price changes are shown in Figure 2.10.

The demand curve for milk is D^1, while D^2 represents the demand curve for chocolate bars. A reduction in the price from P_0 to P_1 causes a greater increase in the quantity demanded in the case of D^2 as opposed to D^1. The price reduction increased the quantity demanded from Q_0 to Q_2 in the case of D^2, but only from Q_0 to Q_1 in the case of D^1. Although both demand curves show an inverse relationship between price and quantity demanded, the nature of the relationship is different.

In order to measure the extent to which the quantity demanded of a product responds to a change in price, economists have developed the concept of price elasticity. **Price elasticity of demand** measures the responsiveness of quantity demanded to a change in price. An *elastic demand* is one

Price elasticity of demand **measures the extent to which the quantity of a product demanded responds to a change in price.**

Figure 2.10

Price elasticities of demand

A drop in price from P_0 to P_1 brings about a greater change in the quantity demanded for D^2 than D^1. The demand for products with elastic demand curves responds more to price changes than it does for products with inelastic demand curves.

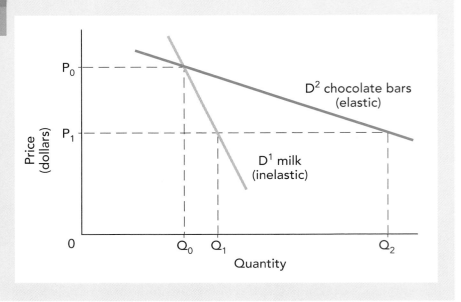

in which a price change brings about a greater than proportional change in the quantity that consumers demand. A small increase in the price of chocolate bars is likely to have a large impact on the number of bars sold. In cases where the quantity of a product demanded does not vary a great deal with the price, it is considered an *inelastic demand.* Milk has an inelastic demand curve, since price changes appear to have little effect on the quantity of milk sold. The determination of whether a product has an elastic or inelastic demand is made through the use of a formula:

price elasticity of demand coefficient (E_d) $= \dfrac{\text{percentage change in quantity demanded } (Q_d)}{\text{percentage change in price (P)}}$

$$E_d = \frac{\%\Delta Q_d}{\%\Delta P} \text{ (where } \Delta = \text{ change in)}$$

For example, if a 10-percent cut in the price brought about a 20-percent increase in the quantity demanded, the elasticity coefficient would be:

$$E_d = \frac{\%\Delta Q_d}{\%\Delta P} = \frac{20}{10} = 2.0$$

The negative sign associated with the decrease in price is often ignored in the calculation of price elasticity of demand.

If, on the other hand, the same price cut encouraged only a 1-percent increase in quantity demanded, the elasticity coefficient would be:

$$E_d = \frac{\%\Delta Q_d}{\%\Delta P} = \frac{1}{10} = 0.10$$

If the elasticity coefficient (E_d) is greater than one, the demand is said to be elastic. If the coefficient is less than one, the demand is inelastic. Finally, if the elasticity coefficient equals one, the demand is said to be unitary elastic.

Some characteristics of a product that help to determine whether it has an elastic or inelastic demand are:

Luxury or necessity: Generally, items that are necessities have an inelastic demand. Consumers have to buy them regardless of the price. Conversely, luxuries have an elastic demand. Food and clothing are necessities, while event tickets and DVD players are luxuries.

The number of close substitutes: The more close substitutes a product has, the more elastic its demand. If the price increases, the consumer has several alternatives to turn to. There are many restaurants in the larger Canadian cities. The demand facing any one restaurant is likely to be elastic, as the consumer has many alternatives. Conversely, if a product has few substitutes, its demand is usually inelastic. Milk is a product with very few substitutes. There are also few substitutes for the services of a dentist. The demand for dental care is inelastic. The demand for the services of a certain dentist is likely, however, to be elastic.

Percentage of budget spent on the product: If a product takes up only a small fraction of a consumer's budget, price changes are not likely to have a great impact on quantity demanded. As a result, the demand for the product will be inelastic. An example of such a product is pepper. Products that comprise a large percentage of one's budget have an elastic demand. Changes in the prices of these products will force a reaction on the part of many people. For example, rent comprises a large portion of the budget. An increase in rent may result in a search for alternative accommodation.

Length of time since price change: The consumer is unlikely to significantly alter the quantity of a product purchased immediately after a price change. There may be no close substitutes available in the marketplace at the time the price change is introduced. As time passes, however, substitutes become available and the consumer has occasion to adjust his or her buying patterns.

Therefore, over a longer period of time, the demand for a product is likely to be more elastic.

For example, the quantity demanded for oil did not change much in the short run after the significant increases in oil prices during the 1970s. People were still driving big cars. They had not done a good job of insulating their houses. They still commuted long distances to work. Given time, they would adjust to price increases by purchasing smaller, more fuel-efficient cars, insulating their houses, and moving closer to work. Over a long period of time the demand for oil is more elastic than it is over a short period of time.

It should be noted that a product need not possess all of the above characteristics in order to be classified as having either an elastic or inelastic demand. For example, it has been determined that cigarettes have no substitutes according to cigarette smokers, and this is the main reason for their inelastic demand. Yet it can be argued that cigarettes are not a necessity and, in some cases, comprise more than a small percentage of one's income. One of the above characteristics may be sufficient to determine the elasticity of demand for a product or service.

REVIEW

interactive graphics

2.7 Assuming that income and all other conditions remain the same, state whether the demand for the following items is elastic or inelastic. Give your reasons.
   a) gasoline   d) restaurant meals
   b) salt   e) milk
   c) cigarettes f) newspapers

Total Revenue Approach to Price Elasticity of Demand

The concept of price elasticity of demand can also be discussed in terms of any change in the total amount of money people spend on a product when the price changes. The amount of money people spend on a product is referred to as *total revenue* (TR) and is calculated by multiplying the price by the quantity demanded.

$$TR = P \times Q_d$$

If the demand for a product is elastic, any decrease in price will increase total revenue; conversely, any increase in price will decrease total revenue.

elastic: when P↑, TR↓
when P↓, TR↑

If the demand for a product is inelastic, any decrease in price will cause total revenue to fall, and any increase in price will cause total revenue to increase.

inelastic: when P↓, TR↓
when P↑, TR↑

Finally, when the elasticity of demand is unitary, any change in price leaves total revenue unchanged.

unitary elastic: when P↑ or P↓
TR remains the same

The total revenue approach to elasticity has important consequences for business. For example, it is known that a lower price will increase the quantity demanded of a product, but will the price decrease increase the revenue that the store receives from selling the product? This depends on the elasticity of demand. If the demand for a product is inelastic, the store owner would be reluctant to lower the price, even if more of the product could be sold. Why? For an inelastic demand, any drop in price will be accompanied by a decrease in total revenue. If a product has an inelastic demand, consumers do not respond significantly to price changes. It is unlikely, then, that store owners would have sales on goods with an inelastic demand (such as cigarettes).

Conversely, where a product with an elastic demand is involved, sales may be more commonplace. Any decrease in price should generate additional revenue. Automobile manufacturers regularly have sales on cars with the hope of stimulating sales.

REVIEW

2.8 Why does total revenue (TR) decline when there is a price increase for a product with an elastic demand?

2.9 If your local bus company were losing money and decided to increase fares, what is the company's view of the elasticity of demand for its products?

Differing Price Elasticities for the Same Product

It is technically incorrect to state that the demand for a product is inelastic or elastic. This is true only within a certain price range. Within another price range, the coefficient of elasticity is likely to change.

In order to prove this point, refer to Figure 2.11. The demand curve in this case is a straight line, so that a five-cent change in the price of the product will bring about a 10-unit change in the quantity demanded. The *elasticity coefficient* in the range $0.55–$0.60 is less than one, or inelastic. The elasticity coefficient in the price range $1.95–$2.00 is greater than one, or elastic. The elasticity of demand becomes greater as the price rises.

A good example of how price ranges can affect elasticity is gasoline. In recent years the price of gasoline has been steadily increasing. At lower prices for gasoline, the demand appeared to be relatively inelastic. Even when price increases did occur, people still drove big cars and drove at high speeds. Now that gasoline prices have increased substantially people are making changes in the amount of gasoline they consume, including driving more fuel-efficient cars. Where possible, they are making greater use of public transportation and carpooling.

The elasticity of demand for a product also increases over time. Substitutes are developed and become more readily available. This results in a more elastic demand for the product. Often price increases encour-

Figure 2.11

Price elasticity for various sections of the demand curve

The elasticity of demand varies within different price ranges for the same product. At higher prices, the elasticity of demand becomes more elastic.

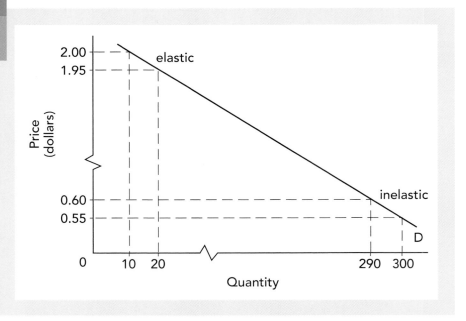

age the development of substitute or competing products. This takes time, but as more substitute products come onto the market, the price elasticity of demand increases. For example, higher energy costs have stimulated an interest in the development of new energy sources. As these new sources appear on the market, the price elasticity of demand for home-heating oil increases. The elasticity of demand also increases over time because it often takes consumers a while to adjust to the higher prices.

REVIEW

2.10 Why does the price elasticity of the demand coefficient increase over time?

2.11 Explain how price elasticity of demand can vary for the same product.

Special Cases of Price Elasticity of Demand

The general principle of demand states that as the price of the product falls the quantity demanded of that product increases. When the price rises, the quantity demanded decreases. The degree to which quantity demanded reacts to a change in price is a measure of the price elasticity of demand. There are two special cases of a demand curve where the price and quantity demanded are not inversely related.

In Figure 2.12a, the demand curve is horizontal. At the set price P_1, the quantity demanded is unlimited. The price elasticity of demand coefficient (E_d) in this case is 8** (undefined).

Although situations similar to this one are limited in the real world, there are applications of such a demand curve, known as a *perfectly elastic demand curve*. In Chapter 12, the discussion of perfectly competitive pricing employs such a demand curve. Another real-world example of a perfectly elastic demand curve occurred during the 1950s and 1960s in the United States in relation to gold. It was illegal for U.S. citizens to possess gold, and they were required to sell their gold to the government at $35 an ounce. The government agreed to purchase an unlimited amount of gold at this price.

In Figure 2.12b, a vertical demand curve is shown. A certain quantity (Q_1) of this product is demanded and any price will be paid to acquire that amount. The price elasticity of demand coefficient is zero and is referred to as *perfectly inelastic*. Such a curve may reflect the demand for a necessary drug or medicine. A person may require a certain amount of this medicine and would be willing to pay any price in order to acquire it.

Figure 2.12a

Perfectly elastic demand curve

A horizontal demand curve implies that at price P_1 an unlimited quantity of this product would be demanded.

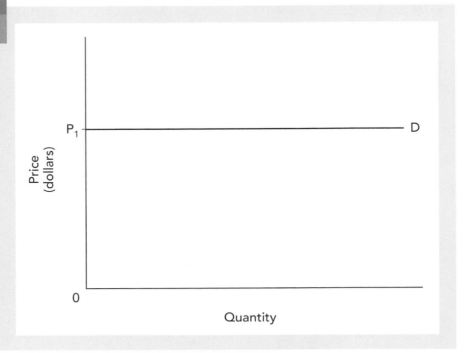

Figure 2.12b

Perfectly inelastic demand curve

A vertical demand curve implies that an unlimited price would be paid for a set quantity (Q_1) of this product.

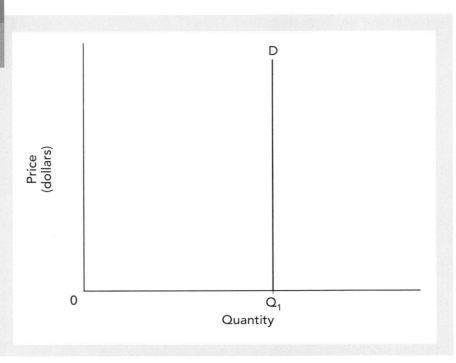

Price Elasticity of Supply

Since suppliers also differ in their capacity to respond to price changes, the concept of price elasticity can also be applied to the supply curve. The terminology used in discussing supply price elasticity is similar to that of demand. If a supplier is able to adjust supply readily when the price changes, the supply is referred to as elastic. If the quantity supplied does not respond to price changes, supply is said to be inelastic.

The numerical determination of supply elasticity is as follows:

$$\text{price elasticity of supply coefficient } (E_s) = \frac{\text{percentage change in quantity supplied}(Q_s)}{\text{percentage change in price (P)}}$$

$$E_s = \frac{\%\Delta Q_s}{\%\Delta P}$$

If the coefficient is greater than one, supply is *elastic*; if less than one, it is *inelastic*; and finally, if the coefficient is equal to one, the supply is *unitary elastic.*

What are the major factors determining the price elasticity of supply?

Time: The primary determinant of supply elasticity is time. For a single moment in time, supply is fixed and cannot be adjusted to price fluctuations. The longer the time allowed to adjust to price changes, the more it is likely that existing firms will be able to increase production. They will be able to attract the necessary resources in order to increase output. Also, the longer the time allowed for adjustment, the more new firms will be able to enter the industry in response to a price increase.

Consider a farmer bringing fresh produce to market. The supply of produce is fixed for that day. This can be represented by curve S^1 in Figure 2.13. The curve S^1 is perfectly inelastic, and the price elasticity coefficient of supply is zero. Over a period of time the farmer will be able to adjust the supply that he or she brings to market depending on the price obtainable for that produce. If the price of a certain product increases, the farmer will likely grow more of that product in the future. The supply curve over a longer period of time is represented by curve S^2 in Figure 2.13. The supply curve S^2 shows a greater ability to respond to price changes than does S^1, and is therefore more elastic.

Ability to store product: Some products such as food items are perishable and cannot be stored for long periods of time. Since the items cannot be kept off the market until the price rises, their elasticity of supply is inelastic. Regardless of the price, they must be sold. This also applies to products

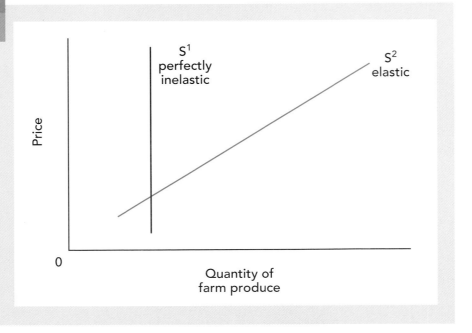

that are expensive to store. For example, if a product requires extensive refrigeration, it is not likely to be stored indefinitely. The elasticity of supply for products that can be stored will be more elastic.

Ability to substitute during production: The ability of suppliers to react to price changes also depends on whether or not production can be easily shifted to an alternative product. Automobile manufacturers may be able to switch production levels between two similar types of cars. However, they may not find it so easy to switch from producing large cars to producing small cars. If the switch from one product to another is relatively easy, the supply elasticity is likely to be elastic. If the switch is not easily made, or cannot be made quickly, then the elasticity of supply will be inelastic.

R E V I E W

2.12 Why is the primary determinant of price elasticity of supply the time period being considered?

2.13 Explain the effect of variation in the price elasticity of supply on the response of quantity supplied to price changes.

Other Types of Elasticity

We have calculated elasticity values based on changes in the price of a product and the resulting impact on the quantity demanded or supplied. Economists also rely on other elasticity measures when analyzing markets.

Income elasticity measures the responsiveness of the change in quantity demanded to changing income levels. How is the quantity demanded of a product affected when incomes increase or decrease? If more of a product is purchased when incomes increase, the product is a normal good and has a positive value for income elasticity. If a product has a negative value for income elasticity, increases in income result in less of the product being purchased. Products with negative income elasticities are called *inferior goods*. They are not inferior in the sense of quality, rather in that consumers switch to other products when their incomes increase. As a student with a limited income, your diet may lack variety. You may choose to consume more of certain foods because they are less expensive. When your income increases, you may switch from buying these foods to buying others that cost a little more. Finally, products with income elasticities close to zero are necessities. Their consumption is not affected by income levels.

Economists are also interested in the impact that changes in the price of one product have on the quantity demanded of another product. This is referred to as *cross-elasticity of demand*. By calculating cross-elasticities, economists can better identify substitute and complementary products. If the value of cross-elasticity is positive, the two products are substitutes. That is, increases in the price of product A lead to increases in the quantity demanded of product B. If increases in the price of product A lead to reductions in the quantity demanded of product B, the two products are complementary. For complementary products, the value of cross-elasticity is negative. Values of cross-elasticity close to zero indicate a lack of association between the products.

Advertising elasticity of demand measures the degree of responsiveness of demand to changes in the level of advertising. Numerically, it is determined by the proportionate change in quantity demanded divided by the proportionate change in the expenditure on advertising. Firms and organizations that are advertising their products hope that the advertising elasticity of demand is positive.

A *research elasticity of supply* measures the degree of responsiveness of the supply of a product to changes in the dollar value of research undertaken to produce the product. In a manner similar to other elasticities, the research elasticity of supply is determined by dividing the proportionate change in the quantity supplied by the proportionate change in the amount of money spent on research.

Summary

Markets serve two functions in our economy. They are the focal point for exchanges of goods and services, and they establish prices. The system of prices determined in the various markets is a key component of a free-market system.

The market for any good or service is divided into two sections. The demand side of the market represents those who are willing to purchase the product. The supply side represents those who are willing to sell the product. Through the interaction of both sides, exchanges take place and prices are established.

The prices and quantities exchanged in each market are constantly moving toward a stable position called equilibrium. If the quantity that people are willing to buy at a certain price does not match the quantity supplied at that price, then adjustments begin to take place. The price either rises or falls, signalling changes on both sides of the market. Equilibrium is attained when the quantity demanded of a product at a certain price is equal to the quantity supplied at that price. This equilibrium position may, however, be only temporary. A change in any one of several factors will cause the market to seek out a new equilibrium.

An important concept in the study of markets is that of price elasticity. This measures the response of buyers and sellers to price changes. If consumers do not react very much to price changes in terms of the amount of a product purchased, the demand for the product is said to be inelastic. In contrast, if consumers react significantly to price changes, then the demand is said to be elastic. The same terminology applies to the supply side of the market.

There is a market for any commodity or service that has a price. In some instances the price is referred to by another name, such as rent, interest, or wages.

The free-market system of economic decision making is composed of thousands of operating markets. The markets described in this chapter operate free from government intervention. In reality, very few markets operate without some form of government intervention, and the rationale behind this intervention is presented in the following chapter.

Questions for Review and Discussion

1. Information on the quantity demanded and the quantity supplied for a particular product is listed below. Graph the information and from the curves estimate the equilibrium price and quantity.

PRICE	QUANTITY DEMANDED	QUANTITY SUPPLIED
$10	125	45
$20	100	70
$30	80	85
$40	65	105
$50	40	140

2. How would an increase in the price of beef affect the demand for beef? How would it affect the supply?

3. "Higher prices for houses will cause the demand for houses to decline. This will eventually result in lower prices for houses." Comment on the validity of this statement.

4. It has been stated that the consumer is king. What does this statement mean when referring to the operation of a market?

5. In 2001, 2000 units of a commodity were purchased at a price of $3.00 per unit. In 2004, 3000 units were purchased at a price of $4.00. Does this contradict the law of downward-sloping demand? Explain.

6. Draw a demand curve for wanting and having children. What factors would cause the demand curve to shift?

7. Why do motels and hotels lower their rates in the off-season and raise their rates in the peak season?

8. Which of the following would lead to an increase in the current demand for beef?
   a) higher pork prices
   b) higher consumer incomes
   c) higher prices for cattle feed
   d) a decrease in beef prices

9. "We cannot allow gasoline prices to rise too high, because gasoline is an essential product." Comment on this statement using your knowledge of demand and supply.

10. Although higher prices are not welcomed by consumers, they are good for producers. Some communities depend on high prices for the natural resources located in their vicinity. Name some communities that depend on:
    a) high oil prices
    b) high lumber prices
    c) high iron-ore prices
    d) high nickel prices
    e) high fish prices

11. Donor organs for transplants are in short supply. What would happen to the supply of organs if donors were paid in advance for their body parts?

12. Draw the supply curve for a limited-edition print or plate. What is the elasticity of supply for such an item?

13. What would happen to the price of a product if there were a simultaneous increase in both the demand and the supply? Explain, using a graph in your answer.

14. Why do sellers lower the price when there is a surplus? Why do buyers bid up the price when there is a shortage?

15. Using demand and supply curves in your answer, show the impact of the following:
    a) an increase in wood prices on the market for new houses;
    b) a decrease in the incomes of consumers on the market for new clothes;
    c) an increase in printers' salaries on the market for textbooks;
    d) an increase in the price of butter on the market for margarine;
    e) a hot dry summer on the market for corn;
    f) a new advertising campaign by the Turkey Marketing Board on the market for turkeys;
    g) an increase in the price of new cars on the market for used cars; and
    h) an increase in interest rates on the market for new cars.

16. In the 1970s a severe frost hit Brazil and damaged much of the country's coffee crop. Since Brazil is one of the world's leading coffee producers, what impact might this frost have had on world coffee prices? Use demand and supply curves in your answer.

17. Using your knowledge of demand and supply, explain why parking garages in the downtown core of Canadian cities have several levels, whereas in the suburbs parking lots tend to be only one level.

18. The disappearance of anchovies off the coast of Peru in 1972 caused a scramble for protein-rich substitutes, notably soybeans. Because soybeans are used in cattle feed, higher soybean prices eventually were translated into higher cattle prices. Use demand and supply diagrams to illustrate what happened in the anchovy, soybean, and cattle markets. Indicate which curves shifted in each instance and show the effects on the equilibrium price and quantity in each market.

19. In July 1993, an explosion destroyed the Japanese plant that was the world's largest supplier of memory-chip resin. The day before the explosion, memory chips for computers could be purchased for $40. Shortly after the explosion, the price had increased to $90. Using demand and supply curves, show the impact of this explosion on the memory-chip market as well as on the market for computers.

20. If the demand for many farm products is inelastic, why would a bad crop be to the advantage of farmers? Use demand and supply curves in your answer.

21. In the discussion of price elasticity of demand, it was shown that changes in total revenue could shed some more light on the question of demand elasticity. Why will a review of total revenue, similar to that used for demand, not work with the concept of elasticity of supply?

22. For each of the following goods and services, state whether the demand would be elastic or inelastic:
    a) postal service
    b) soft drinks
    c) theatre tickets
    d) textbooks
    e) houses
    f) home computers

23. Fire destroyed one-half of the trees on a certain tract of land in New Brunswick. The remaining lumber was worth more than the value of the trees before the fire. What does this say about the elasticity of demand for lumber?

24. In order to reduce the cost of medicare to the public, it has been suggested that individuals pay one dollar for each visit to the doctor. Discuss the impact of this user fee on the demand for medical services. Refer to the price elasticity of demand in your answer.

25. The cost of mailing a letter is constantly increasing. Postage is now subject to the GST. In your opinion, is the demand for stamps elastic or inelastic? Explain.

26. In March 1990, McDonald's Restaurants announced a reduction of up to 30 percent in the price of hamburgers and other items. A McDonald's spokesperson stated that although the lower prices will pinch profits, the increase in customers will ultimately compensate for the decline in earnings. What is McDonald's view of the price elasticity of demand for its food? Do you think that this view is correct? Explain.

27. A study on the advertising elasticity of demand for eggs for the period 1985 to 1997 determined the value to be 0.034. Interpret this value.

28. Provide examples of products with the following characteristics:
    a) positive cross-elasticities (two products); and,
    b) negative income elasticity.

29. Scalpers hawk their tickets outside theatres, sporting events, and concerts. Using demand and supply curves, discuss the market scalpers participate in. Address the following issues in your answer:
    — The price elasticity of demand.
    — The price elasticity of supply.
    — What happens to the price of concert tickets as the start of the concert nears?
    — Do scalpers exist only in markets where the supply is limited? Explain.

Suggested Readings

Parkin, Michael, and Robin Bade. *Economics: Canada and the Global Environment.* Fifth Edition. Don Mills: Pearson Education Canada, 2003. This 1000-page text is the fifth edition of a popular introductory Canadian text.

Heyne, Paul, and John P. Palmer. *The Economic Way of Thinking.* First Canadian Edition. Scarborough: Prentice-Hall, 1999. This is a Canadian edition of a popular introductory economics text in the United States. The text uses graphs sparingly.

Selected Websites

www.opec.org The website for the Organization of Petroleum and Exporting Countries. Information is provided on the history of OPEC, a list of member countries, general information about OPEC, FAQs, and an article on why we pay so much for gasoline from OPEC's point of view.

www.canadaegg.ca This is the website for the Canadian Egg Marketing Agency (CEMA). The site contains producer price lists, cost of production values, breaker prices, imports, and the inter-provincial movement of eggs.

The Role of Government in a Market Economy

Key Terms

invisible hand
natural monopoly
third-party effects
unmet public goods
privatization
price ceiling
price floor
excise tax

Chapter Objectives

After successfully completing this chapter, you will be able to:

- appreciate the advantages and shortcomings of the free-market system
- describe in your own words the concept behind Adam Smith's "invisible hand"
- understand the rationale behind government intervention in the free-market system
- graph the impact of price ceilings, price floors, and excise taxes on various markets

Core Concept Building

In Chapter 2, you learned how a market operates through the interaction of buyers and sellers. Since markets do not always operate in a manner that is acceptable to everyone, governments intervene in the marketplace on a regular basis. This chapter discusses the reasons for government intervention and introduces two forms of government activity in the market: price ceilings and price floors. You will meet these forms of government intervention again in Chapters 8, 12, and 14.

MINIMUM WAGE AND POVERTY

The introduction of a minimum wage is an example of a price floor in the market for workers. At the present time, all ten provinces as well as the federal government in Canada have minimum-wage legislation. There are several reasons for introducing a minimum wage into the labour market. One objective is to help reduce the level of poverty among the working poor. For some workers, an increase in the minimum wage will increase their hourly wage rate and their income.

Does the minimum wage reduce the level of poverty? There is strong evidence to suggest that it does not. First, low hourly wages are only one cause of poverty. Other factors contributing to poverty include unemployment, low hours of work, a large number of family members, and the health of family members. The minimum hourly wage rate cannot be raised high enough to solve all of these problems.

A second criticism of using the minimum wage to fight poverty is that increases in the legal minimum wage result in unemployment for some workers. Since the minimum wage is a price floor, it will create a surplus of labour in the market. Employers will want to hire fewer workers if they are forced to pay higher wages, and yet at higher wages more workers will be willing to offer their services. Any program that increases the level of unemployment cannot be considered an anti-poverty device.

Third, in most provinces there are certain groups of employees (such as some farm workers and domestic servants) who are exempt from minimum-wage coverage. For these workers, increases in the minimum wage are irrelevant and do not aid their financial situation.

Fourth, in order to be an effective anti-poverty device the minimum wage should permanently redistribute income among wage earners; that is, minimum wage increases should narrow the wage differentials between low- and high-wage workers. Studies have shown that an increase in the minimum wage is effective in reducing wage differentials for only a short period of time. Within a year, previous wage differentials among workers are usually restored.

Finally, it is important to have an understanding of the characteristics of workers who earn the minimum wage. A survey of low-wage workers has shown that women and young people are most heavily represented in this wage group. Many of these individuals would be better off working at the minimum wage than not working at all. That is, if they were not working they might not qualify for public assistance, and the benefits received by those who qualify would not be as much as their earnings at the minimum wage. Increases in the minimum wage are not beneficial to these individuals if employment opportunities are reduced.

The following websites contain articles discussing the impact of the minimum wage rate:

www-hoover.stanford.edu/pubaffairs/we/ current/macurdy_1199.html
www.ccsd.ca
www.caledoninst.org

A list of the current and proposed minimum wage rates in Canada can be found at the Human Resources Development Canada website:

http://labour-travail.hrdc-drhc.gc.ca

Government and the Free Market

In Chapter 2, we discussed how a free-market system works and explained that price changes are the vehicle by which the market system operates. Not only do price changes provide information and incentives to the marketplace, they also determine the distribution of products in our industrial society. Now let us look at how and why government becomes involved in the operations of the market.

The Writings of Adam Smith

The advantages of the free-market system were first highlighted by Adam Smith, a Scottish philosopher, in 1776. In his book *An Inquiry into the Nature and Causes of the Wealth of Nations* (usually referred to as *The Wealth of Nations*), Smith stressed the advantages to society of *individual self-interest* and decision making. He believed that the free-market system would channel selfish, egoistic motives toward the betterment of society. In his words, each producer

> intends only his own security; and by directing that industry in such a manner as its produce may be of the greatest value, he intends only his own gain, and he is in this, as in many other cases, led by an invisible hand to promote an end which was no part of his intention. Nor is it always the worse for the society that it was not a part of it. By pursuing his own interest he frequently promotes that of society more effectually than when he really intends to promote it. I have never known much good done by those who affected to trade for the public good. It is an affectation, indeed, not very common among merchants, and very few words need be employed in dissuading them from it. (p. 423)

Smith believed that society would be better off if everyone pursued his or her own self-interests and was not concerned about the effects of their actions on society. He felt that self-interest promotes the public good more than actions that are intended only for the betterment of society. He thought that it was as if an "**invisible hand**" directed the affairs of individuals toward a common goal.

How can Adam Smith's philosophy, written more than 200 years ago, be related to the twenty-first century? What are the consequences of an individual seeking to acquire wealth in today's society? In order to answer these questions, it is best to review the means by which you could become wealthy. You could win a lottery, marry into a wealthy family, inherit a fortune, or start your own business. Of these, starting your own business is the most common approach and has the greatest impact on the economy.

Philosopher Adam Smith introduced the term "invisible hand" to describe the effect that a free-market economic system has of directing the self-interests of individuals toward a common goal.

If you were to start a business, which one would you choose? This is a difficult question to answer. There are thousands of small businesses operating in Canada today. To be successful, you will have to provide a product or a service that consumers want. If people buy your product in sufficient quantities you will be able to earn a living. Both parties are happy—consumers receive a product they want, and you succeed in making money. In this way, you are improving not only your own welfare but also that of your customers. When deciding to start a business, you do so with a great deal of uncertainty and you take a risk in assuming that people will want whatever you have to offer. You may guess wrong and not make a success of your endeavour; thousands of small businesses fail each year for this reason. The fact that you have started a business does not guarantee success, because not enough consumers may want your product. If you cannot increase consumer welfare, your individual welfare does not increase.

If you succeed, your success is likely to attract the attention of others: it will attract competition! If you can make money, why can't they? In order to continue to sell your product or service, it will be necessary to make it more attractive than the product or service that the competition provides. This can be done by either lowering prices or by improving the quality of your good or service. Regardless of which option you choose, the consumer will benefit, because competition ultimately benefits the consumer.

This sequence of events has so far been undertaken without any government involvement. You are not told what business to enter, how to make your product, or what price to charge. Yet, through the pursuit of your own selfish interests, a product or service is provided and distributed to consumers. Just as you are successful in your business, others will be successful in their business pursuits if they satisfy consumer wants. The pursuit of individual self-interest through the free-market system results in the needs of the consumer being fulfilled. In economic terms, we say that the free market will tend to allocate resources (land, labour, materials) to their most efficient use. Adam Smith believed that any interference with the free-market system could have only negative consequences for society.

> *No regulation of commerce can increase the quantity of industry in any society beyond what its capital can maintain. It can only divert a part of it into a direction into which it might not otherwise have gone; and it is by no means certain that this artificial direction is likely to be more advantageous to the society than that into which it would have gone of its own accord.* (p. 421)

Smith assumed that consumers know what they want and will spend their money accordingly.

The free-market system guarantees a great deal of individual freedom, allowing people to be guided by their own self-interest and to do things that maximize their own satisfaction. Many believe that having freedom in economic matters is essential to having freedom in political matters.

REVIEW

3.1 What did Adam Smith mean by the term "invisible hand"?

3.2 Is there any significance in the fact that the United States became an independent country in 1776, the same year that *The Wealth of Nations* was published? On what principles was the United States established?

Possible Shortcomings of the Free-Market System

Even though the free-market system is efficient at satisfying consumer needs, it does have some shortcomings as an economic system. These deficiencies have led to some government involvement in the economy.

Market Imperfections

The free-market system described in Chapter 2 was a perfect system. In reality, however, there are certain imperfections that impede the operation of a market. We will review two of these imperfections.

Information

The theoretical explanation of the free-market system assumes that buyers and sellers have adequate information with which to make decisions. In reality, however, *satisfactory information* is not always available. Consumers may not know where they can find products that they are looking for and they may not know the price differences among different suppliers. Buyers also may not be aware of any differences in product quality. If suppliers have difficulty obtaining information, they may not know the best way to reach potential customers. They may not know where to find competent employees or what wage to pay them. For both consumers and producers, information is often inadequate.

Advertising helps to fill this information gap. Through advertising, suppliers are able to provide information to potential buyers, and consumers can find out more about the product, including the price. Advertising is influenced by economic conditions so that it more closely meets the needs of consumers. For example, fast-food restaurants provide nutritional information about their products in response to consumer demand for such information. Automobile manufacturers provide information on the number of kilometres per litre one can expect when driving their cars.

However, advertising does not completely close the information gap. More often than not, advertising is meant to persuade rather than to inform. Government has intervened in the workings of the market system in order to improve the information available to both the consumer and the supplier. It has also made illegal misleading advertising. Government regulations insist on certain labelling, especially in the area of food packaging. Food products are required to have a list of their ingredients on the package, in the order of their importance. Consumers often lack information in other areas as well. For example, they may not know whether standards of cleanliness are maintained in restaurant kitchens. For this reason, the government has introduced *health standards* for eating establishments. New home buyers cannot be sure how their home was constructed; government building codes are designed for consumer protection in this area. Perhaps you could think of other areas in which government has intervened in order to improve information in the marketplace. In Canada, many of these regulations and others are administered by Industry Canada. This federal government department works in conjunction with other federal departments and with provincial consumer affairs departments to increase consumer information and protection.

Information is also inadequate in the labour market. Job seekers may not know where available jobs can be found; employers may not know where to find employees with the necessary skills. Within the free-market system, individuals have taken some steps to improve this situation. Private placement agencies have been established in order to assist in the matching of workers and jobs. However, many of these agencies operate in specialized job markets only; for example, the fields of accounting, secretarial, engineering, and data processing. For most occupations and skills, no specialized job-finding assistance is provided. In order to fill the information gap, the federal government operates a network of Human Resources Centres of Canada (HRCCs) across the country. These centres provide job information and employment counselling services. Information on job opportunities across the country is made available at each centre. Employers can also use the services of the HRCC in their search for qualified workers.

Competition

A second type of imperfection in the marketplace is the lack of effective competition. If the market system is working as it should, new firms will set up in industries that are profitable. The resulting competition will improve the quality of the product or service and help to keep prices down. The entry of new companies in the ballpoint-pen market helped lower the price from its original $12.95 in the 1940s to what it is today. New firms have also had a restraining effect on prices in the cellular phone and running-shoe markets. What would happen if new firms were prevented from entering the industry? There would be less competition. There would be higher prices and less of the product available. Quality might also deteriorate.

Competition in the marketplace can be restricted in several ways. Firms may get together in order to fix prices. Some companies may sell their products at a loss for a short period of time with the sole purpose of eliminating competitors. Manufacturers may refuse to sell to retailers who do not charge a set price for the product. All of these practices, and others that intentionally limit competition, are illegal in Canada under the Competition Act. This act will be discussed in more detail in Chapter 13.

Despite the advantages of competition, it may be more efficient in some industries to have a single supplier of the product or service. For example, imagine the difficulties of having competing telephone companies in the same town. You would be required to keep several telephones in your house in order to be able to phone whomever you wish. There would be a great deal of duplication in setting up telephone lines, switchboards, and so on. Similarly, how many companies would be required to effectively provide sewer and water services to a municipality? It would be inefficient to have more than one. In situations like these, referred to as **natural monopolies,** the government either provides the service or regulates the company that does provide the service. The regulation of natural monopolies is another role that government plays in the market system. A more detailed discussion of natural monopolies appears in Chapter 13.

Natural monopolies are those industries in which it is more efficient to have only one company or supplier of a product or service.

REVIEW

3.3 Provide an example of a government service whose purpose is to provide more information to the consumer.

3.4 What do we mean by a natural monopoly?

Third-Party Effects

Market transactions benefit two parties—the buyer receives a desired good and the seller receives money. In many transactions, however, these are not the only parties to be affected. *A third party may be affected in either a negative or a positive manner.*

A transaction between a buyer and a seller may also have an impact on others, creating either positive or negative third-party effects.

Let us first discuss possible negative **third-party effects**. Consider the case of a paper mill. In the process of making paper, the mill may pollute the air and the water in the surrounding area. The mill will continue to pollute as long as it is cheaper simply to dump the waste than to dispose of it in any other way. Because the paper mill faces competition from other manufacturers it has to be concerned about costs, and will not be inclined to install pollution-control equipment. Higher costs mean higher prices. The paper mill would prefer not to raise the price of paper, because such a move would turn away customers.

There are additional costs to making paper not contained in the price of the paper. These are third-party, or external, costs that people in the surrounding area will suffer, such as ill health due to the pollution. Fish in the river will no longer be fit to eat. Acid rain may destroy some of the surrounding lakes and cropland.

In a free-market system, there would be no need for the paper mill to take steps to solve its pollution problem. The company is free to make paper the way it wants to. Governments believe that they have a responsibility to intervene, since not all of the costs associated with making paper are being considered. In the case of the paper mill, the government could force the mill to install pollution-control devices, or it could tax the mill in order to pay for pollution cleanup. Either way, the negative effects of paper-making on the third party would be reduced. The effect of government intervention on the price of paper is shown in Figure 3.1.

Government action, either in the form of a tax or the requirement to install new equipment, would cause the supply curve for paper to shift to the left (S^2) because of increased costs. This results in a higher equilibrium price in the market (P_2). The higher price would then reflect the total cost of providing this product. Pollution has negative third-party effects because its costs spill over to a third party.

Transactions between buyers and sellers may also have positive third-party effects. Assume that influenza vaccinations were being offered in the free market for a price. Those people who were concerned about their health and could afford it would probably get the necessary vaccinations. They would purchase the vaccination from a doctor or health clinic. In this transaction, both parties benefit. The doctor is paid for services and the consumer receives immunization against the ailment. Because influenza is a contagious disease, this transaction also benefits others. Those who come into contact with the immunized person now run a smaller risk of getting the flu. Many people benefit from this type of transaction, and it would be beneficial to society if more vaccinations could be provided. In this situation, a government may step in to ensure that more of this service is pro-

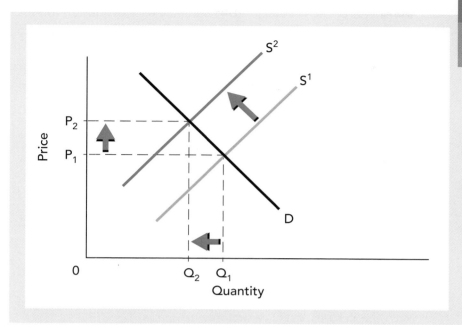

Figure 3.1

Government reaction to negative third-party effects

In order to account for third-party costs, the government undertakes action to decrease the supply of the product. This increases the equilibrium price and decreases the equilibrium quantity.

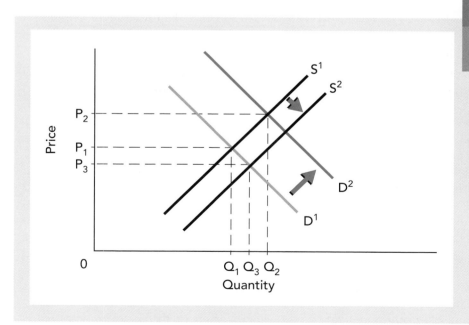

Figure 3.2

Government reaction to positive third-party effects

In order to account for third-party benefits, the government undertakes to increase the demand for or increase the supply of this product.

vided. This intervention may be accomplished by using tax dollars to subsidize the doctor or the health clinic. The impact of such subsidization is shown in Figure 3.2. The supply curve has shifted from S^1 to S^2. The price of influenza vaccinations has decreased from P_1 to P_3. Another option would be to pay for the vaccination on behalf of those who could not afford it. The effect of this on the influenza vaccination market is also shown in Figure 3.2. If the original price were P_1 in the market and the government assisted consumers in the purchase of this product, then the demand for vaccinations would increase. This would cause the demand curve to shift to D^2 and increase the equilibrium price to P_2. The new price would better represent the value of the service to society. Influenza vaccinations are referred to as a positive third-party effect because their benefits spill over to a third party.

REVIEW

3.5 Define third-party effects.
3.6 Why does government feel it is necessary to intervene in the market when the third-party effects are present?

EVERYDAY ECONOMICS 3.1

Education Vouchers

The positive third-party effects associated with an educated population suggest that government should play a role in providing this service to Canadians. However, the role played by government is open to discussion. Currently, elementary and secondary schools in each province are publicly owned. The provincial government sets the curriculum for each grade. Privately operated schools co-exist with publicly owned schools and must adhere to a designated curriculum. Does the government need to operate the schools? Does the government need to set the curriculum for each grade?

Individuals do not wear the same style in clothing nor do they eat the same type of food. There is a variety of automobiles on the market because individuals have different needs and tastes with respect to transportation. Is it reasonable to expect that one standard school curriculum would meet the needs of all Canadian children? Should parents have a choice in selecting the type of education for their children?

Many parents would like more control over the school curriculum. How can this be accomplished? One option would be for governments to get out of the education business. Government could legislate that children up to a certain age must be enrolled in school but leave the provision of that education up to the marketplace. Critics of this option argue that not everyone can afford to send their children to school and that for some of those individuals government financial assistance is required.

An improvement on the above proposal would be to allow privately owned companies to operate the schools but governments would provide parents with education vouchers. These vouchers would be for a certain amount of money, for example $10 000, to be used for spending on education. Parents could use the voucher to pay tuition at a privately owned and operated school. If the parents selected a school where tuition exceeded the amount of the voucher, it would be the parents' responsibility to pay the difference. In the current educational market, some parents already pay an additional amount of money to send their children to privately operated schools.

In order for the voucher system to work, governments would not set a standard curriculum for each grade. Each school would be free to design its own curriculum. Some schools may put more emphasis on science than others. Some schools may stress the arts while others stress athletics. Parents would select the school that best meets the needs of their child. The voucher system would result in competition among schools, as parents would want to send their children to the best school. Pressure would be put on all the schools to raise standards in order to attract students.

Questions

1. Do you see any additional advantages associated with a voucher system? Do you see any disadvantages?
2. Are there any geographic locations where a voucher system is likely to work better than in other geographic locations? Explain.
3. An argument can be made that government should be involved in education because of third-party effects. Does this argument include the construction and operation of schools? Explain.

Unmet Public Goods

The market system may not be able to provide a number of goods and services that are important to society—such as national defence, police protection, and municipal water supply and sewage treatment. This is because the benefits from these services are spread over such a large segment of the population that it is difficult to charge a fee for their use based on the benefits received. It may not even be possible to determine who receives the benefits. It is also difficult to divide these services up into units that can be sold in the marketplace. In the case of national defence, it would be impossible to charge each individual who benefits from the service. It is more efficient to have a government provide the service and pay for it from general tax revenue. If national defence were left up to the free market, only certain individuals would decide to purchase the service. Those who chose not to purchase the service would still benefit, since it would be difficult for the military to protect only those who had purchased the national defence service; if everyone benefits, then everyone should pay for it.

It is not necessary that government should own and operate all such services defined under the heading of **unmet public goods**. In many situations, it may be more efficient to contract out the service to private companies. Regardless of whether the service is government-run or contracted out, the government cannot rely on the free market to provide the

Unmet public goods describes those goods and services not provided by the free-market system due to the difficulty of charging a fee to the beneficiaries of the good or service.

service, because it may not be profitable for a private company to do so. Government has played a role in the free market by directing some of our resources toward the provision of these kinds of services.

REVIEW

3.7 Roads and sidewalks have been categorized as unmet public goods. Why?

3.8 Does a lighthouse qualify as an unmet public good? Explain.

EVERYDAY ECONOMICS 3.2

Privatization

Encouraged by the success of **privatization** efforts (the transfer of control of a company from government to private ownership) in countries such as Britain and France, the federal government sold a number of Crown corporations to private interests in the latter half of the 1980s. Since that time many Crown corporations have been sold by the federal government to private interests. Provincial governments have also privatized government-operated businesses such as liquor stores, electricity, and ambulances. Municipal governments have privatized garbage collection.

What is the rationale behind the selling of Crown corporations? Some argue that the rationale lay in the free-market ideology, which states that government should not compete in the private sector. That is, why should the government own a company that makes airplanes? Can this type of manufacturing not be done in the private sector? Others have argued that the motive for privatization is profit. The money received for Crown corporations can be used to help pay off the government debt. A third possible rationale, and the one adhered to by the federal government, is that private ownership will make Crown corporations more efficient and competitive. If Crown corporations were freed from government policy decisions that often are politically motivated, they would be more efficient.

Privatization of a Crown corporation is not easy. Apart from the legal and accounting difficulties, the concerns of those who have a strong interest in retaining the Crown corporation have to be addressed before the privatization can be called a success. The interests of four groups have to be taken care of while the privatization is being carried out. These groups are the employees of the Crown corporation, the workforce, the people who benefit from the program or company, and the legislators who must be ready to face complaints when the Crown corporation is being sold. Privatization is not so much an economic issue as it is a political issue. If the concerns of these groups can be addressed, the privatization effort will run more smoothly. For example, in order to address the concerns of the workforce, workers could be offered shares in the new private corporation. By offering shares to the workers, the shares would initially be more widely dispersed and not be held by a few individuals or groups.

From 1992–2002, privatization worldwide has raised more than $600 million for governments. Since many of the privatized companies were forced to compete with private-sector businesses, they have become more cost-effective and efficient and, in many instances, can provide better service than the pre-privatized operation. The privatized company tends to increase investment in the firm and also tends to increase production levels. The following is a website that focuses on the issues of privatization: follows.

www.privatization.org
The website for the Reason Public Policy Institute providing information on contracting out, privatization, and public/private partnerships.

Questions

1. Can you suggest some Crown corporations that you would not want the government to sell to private interests? What is your rationale? Is it economic or political?

2. Do you believe that giving shares to workers would reduce their concerns about privatization?

3. In December 1993, the Liberal government reversed the former Conservative government's policy and decided not to privatize Toronto's Pearson International Airport. How would a private company operate an international airport?

4. Should government-run liquor stores be sold to private interests? Should governments operate liquor stores? Discuss.

5. Does government need to own and operate the business in order to influence the operation? Explain.

Distribution of Income

One of the main advantages of the free-market system is competition. In a free-market system, there is competition not only among businesses, but also among individuals. In the pursuit of earning an income, individuals compete with each other for jobs. Because not all jobs pay the same wage, there will be differences in individual incomes. Some workers earn more money because they are more highly skilled, have more initiative, or live in an area of low employment. Some workers earn less, or are unable to find a job. In fact, the reasons for differences in incomes are numerous, and are discussed in more detail in Chapter 14.

In a free-market system, some people may not be able to compete. For example, many elderly people may not be able to compete with younger people for certain jobs, especially those requiring heavy manual labour or new technological skills. Some disabled persons may not be able to participate in the labour force at all. If a person is not able to compete in a free-market system, he or she will not be able to earn an income. Because our society has a conscience about these matters, government has intervened in the free market in order to achieve a more equitable distribution of income. Many *social welfare programs* have been put into effect. These include assistance for the elderly and the disabled, employment insurance, and financial assistance to single parents. In order to help finance these and other government programs, the government has introduced a *progressive income tax.* This type of tax requires that an individual pay taxes in relation to personal income. Someone with a higher income will pay a higher percentage of their income in taxes. The rationale behind our income tax system is presented in Chapter 4.

The extent of income differentials in Canada is presented in Table 3.1. In 2000, 27.6 percent of individual Canadians earned less than $10 000 per year. At the other end of the income scale, 10.0 percent of Canadians earned $60 000 or more per year. Significant sex differentials appear when reviewing the figures in Table 3.1. The average income in 2000 for a man was $36 865, and for a woman it was $22 885. A greater percentage of men than women are in the higher-income brackets. The data, however, should not be seen as evidence that women are always discriminated against in terms of income. There may be other reasons for the higher percentage of women in the lower-income categories. For example, a higher percentage of women work part time. Also, on average, women have not been in the labour force as long as men because of family responsibilities. This lower seniority in the workplace may result in lower incomes. A more detailed discussion of male/female wage differences appears in Chapter 14.

Income differentials also exist when comparing family incomes. The data in Table 3.2 refer to the percentage distribution of families by income group for 2000. In that year, 4.4 percent of all families in Canada had incomes less than $10 000. Another 6.7 percent of families had incomes between $10 000 and $19 999. At the other end of the income scale,

Table 3.1 *Percentage distribution of individual incomes by income groups and sex, Canada, 2000*

| | PERCENTAGE | | |
INCOME GROUP	MALE	FEMALE	TOTAL
Under $10 000	21.6	33.3	27.6
$10 000–19 999	16.6	25.1	21.0
$20 000–29 999	14.5	15.3	14.9
$30 000–39 999	13.7	11.3	12.4
$40 000–49 999	10.6	6.4	8.5
$50 000–59 999	7.6	3.7	5.6
$60 000 and above	15.4	4.9	10.0
Total	100.0	100.0	100.0
Average income	$36 865	$22 885	$29 769
Median income	$29 276	$17 122	$22 120

SOURCE: Adapted from the Statistics Canada CANSIM database, Tables 202-0201 and 202-0401.

Table 3.2 *Percentage distribution of families by income group, Canada, 2000*

INCOME GROUP	PERCENTAGE
Under $10 000	4.4
$10 000–19 999	6.7
$20 000–29 999	10.8
$30 000–39 999	11.4
$40 000–49 999	11.2
$50 000–59 999	10.4
$60 000–69 999	9.5
$70 000–79 999	8.0
$80 000–89 999	6.4
$90 000–99 999	5.0
$100 000 and over	16.2
Total	100.0
Average income	$66 160
Median income	$55 016

SOURCE: Adapted from the Statistics Canada CANSIM database, Tables 202-0101 and 202-0201.

16.2 percent of families had incomes of $100 000 per year and above. These wide differences in income prompt government to intervene in the free-market system in order to redistribute income. Despite government initiatives in this area, Tables 3.1 and 3.2 point out that income differentials continue to exist.

The existence of income differentials in Canada would not be a serious problem if every Canadian earned enough money to meet his or her basic needs. This, however, is not the case and many Canadians are forced to live in a state of poverty. What exactly do we mean by poverty? Several organizations in Canada have derived a definition of poverty in terms of a *minimum income necessary* for an individual or family. When annual income falls below this income standard it can be said that the person is living in poverty. One set of income standards is the low-income cut-off (LICO) prepared by Statistics Canada. The LICOs represent levels of gross income where people spend a disproportionate amount of their income on food, shelter, and clothing. It is estimated that the average Canadian family spends 44 percent of its after-tax income on those three items; the LICO is set at an income level where the family spends 64 percent of its income on food, shelter, and clothing. LICOs are not the only measure of poverty in Canada. They are, however, widely accepted and perform a useful task in identifying Canadians with low incomes. The LICOs for various family and community sizes are presented in Table 3.3. The LICO procedure established a poverty line of $19 261 for a single person living in a community with 500 000 or more people in 2002. According to Table 3.1, 48.6 percent of individuals had an income of less than $20 000 in 2000. According to Table 3.2, 11.1 percent of all families had incomes less than $20 000 in 2000. From the information provided in Table 3.2, it is more difficult to establish what proportion of families fall below the poverty line, because family size is not given in the table. The LICO for a family of three in a large community is $29 944. We can see that approximately 22 percent of families had an annual income of less than $30 000 in 2000. The income standard developed by the council is a national figure and should provide an adequate income in all areas of the country. The actual income necessary to escape poverty will vary by province and by region within a province. The poverty line will also be affected by health considerations in the family unit.

In May 2003, Human Resources Development Canada introduced a new indicator of poverty in Canada called the *market basket measure*. The basket of goods and services is based on the requirements of a family of four (two adults, a 13-year old boy, and a 9-year old girl). The cost of this basket of goods is determined for 48 locations across Canada. The indicator of poverty is an income that is too low to purchase this basket of goods in a specific city or rural area. Based on this measure, the income required

Table 3.3 *Statistics Canada's Low-Income Cut-Offs, by Family Size and Community Size, 2002*

FAMILY SIZE	COMMUNITY SIZE (POPULATION)				
	500 000+	100 000–499 999	30 000–99 999	LESS THAN 30 000	RURAL AREAS
1	$19 261	$16 521	$16 407	$15 267	$13 311
2	$24 077	$20 651	$20 508	$19 083	$16 639
3	$29 944	$25 684	$25 505	$23 732	$20 694
4	$36 247	$31 090	$30 875	$28 729	$25 050
5	$40 518	$34 754	$34 512	$32 113	$28 002
6	$44 789	$38 418	$38 150	$35 498	$30 954
7+	$49 060	$42 080	$41 788	$38 882	$33 907

SOURCE: www.ccsd.ca/factsheets/fs_lic02.htm. Reprinted with the permission of the Canadian Council on Social Development.

in Vancouver in the year 2000 was $27 791, while in Montreal it was $22 441.

Incomes also vary across the various regions of Canada. Table 3.4 shows the average individual and family income for the provinces in 2000. Incomes are highest in the Northwest Territories. In general, family incomes were lower in the Atlantic provinces and higher in Ontario and the western provinces of Alberta and British Columbia. The presence of regional income differences has prompted the federal government to transfer tax dollars in the form of equalization payments to the lower-income provinces and to undertake economic development projects in these provinces.

To what extent should governments intervene in the marketplace to alter the distribution of income? Faced with large debt, governments across Canada need to answer this question. Social-welfare spending accounts for the largest portion of all federal government spending and approximately one-fifth of all provincial and local government spending. Any attempt to reduce the public debt must address the amount of money spent on social welfare.

Table 3.4 *Average individual and family incomes by province and territory, 2000*

PROVINCE/ TERRITORY	AVERAGE INDIVIDUAL INCOME ($)	AVERAGE FAMILY INCOME ($)
Newfoundland and Labrador	22 620	49 679
Prince Edward Island	23 709	53 958
Nova Scotia	25 297	54 786
New Brunswick	24 091	52 704
Quebec	27 939	61 733
Ontario	32 865	73 849
Manitoba	26 416	59 005
Saskatchewan	25 811	57 005
Alberta	31 350	71 339
British Columbia	29 613	64 821
Yukon	31 917	69 564
Northwest Territories	35 012	75 102
Nunavut	26 924	52 624

SOURCE: Adapted from the Statistics Canada CANSIM database, Tables 202-0201 and 202-0401.

International Comparisons 3.1

Percentage of population below the national poverty line

Algeria	22.6	Jamaica	18.7
Argentina	17.6	Morocco	19.0
Bangladesh	35.6	Nigeria	34.1
Cambodia	36.1	Peru	49.0
Dominican Republic	20.6	Philippines	36.8
Honduras	53.0	Sri Lanka	25.0
India	35.0	Tanzania	41.6
Indonesia	27.1	Thailand	13.1
Ivory Coast	36.8	Zambia	86.0

SOURCE: World Bank Online by World Bank. © 2003 by World Bank. Reproduced with permission of World Bank in the format textbook via Copyright Clearance Center.

Economic Stabilization

The market system is characterized by fluctuations in economic activity. Periods of rapid economic growth, high levels of employment, and rising prices give way to a reduction in economic activity and rising levels of unemployment. At a later date, the economy begins to grow and employment levels rise. Classical economists believed these fluctuations in economic activity were temporary and the free-market system would make adjustments to return to a period of more stable economic activity. The Great Depression of the 1930s changed the attitude of many policy-makers about the ability of the market system to get itself back on track. The 1930s were characterized by very high levels of unemployment and, until the advent of the Second World War, a slowdown in economic activity.

When economic conditions did not improve during the 1930s, governments became more interested in the writings of English economist John Maynard Keynes. Keynes argued that in order to ensure stability in the economy, governments had to intervene. To correct periods of slow economic growth and high unemployment, governments were advised to increase their own spending on goods and services, even if it meant borrowing the money, and to decrease the amount of tax collected. A decrease in taxes would encourage spending as disposable incomes increased. If the market system was not ensuring an adequate level of spending to give everyone a job, the government should intervene. In times of economic expansion, Keynes advised governments to increase the level of taxation and to decrease the level of government spending; the increased tax revenues received by government should be used to pay down any existing government debt. A reduction in the amount of debt would put governments in a better position to borrow when another economic downturn occurred.

The advent of the Second World War made it necessary for governments to increase their spending. The increase in expenditures aimed at supporting the military helped reduce the high levels of unemployment. Thus, after the war, the Government of Canada issued a statement that it would assume responsibility for economic stabilization. That is, it would be responsible for ensuring high levels of employment, relatively stable prices, and an acceptable level of economic growth.

The adjustment of government spending and tax policy to economic conditions is known as *fiscal policy*. This topic is covered in more detail in Chapters 6 and 8. The Canadian government, through the Bank of Canada, also uses changes in the money supply to influence the level of economic activity. This policy is referred to as *monetary policy* and is discussed in Chapter 7.

Impact of Government Intervention

We have discussed the operations and results of the free-market system. It is important to determine the effect of government involvement on these results. Using the demand and supply analysis developed in Chapter 2, it is possible to analyze the impact of government intervention in the marketplace.

Price Ceilings

In certain situations, the government may not approve of the price established in the product market. Government officials may believe that the equilibrium price is too high. It may be that many people feel that they cannot afford to buy the product. In these situations, the government may legislate a price lower than the one established in the marketplace. This legal maximum price for a product is referred to as a **price ceiling**. It would

A price ceiling is a government-imposed maximum price.

be illegal to sell the product at a price in excess of the maximum price. Price ceilings have been introduced in Canada on apartment rents and oil prices. The impact of such a decision is shown in Figure 3.3. P_0 is the market price. Government may decide to set the maximum price that can be charged for the product at P_c. At this price the quantity demanded increases to Q_d and the quantity supplied drops to Q_s. This results in a shortage of the product $(Q_d - Q_s)$.

When shortages exist in the free-market system, the price increases and the shortage is eliminated. With government price ceilings in effect, it is illegal to raise the price above P_c. The shortage remains and government must find another way to eliminate it. Somehow either the demand curve or the supply curve will have to shift in order to establish a new equilibrium price at P_c. One possible way is for the government to offer a *subsidy* to the producers of the product. This would shift the supply curve to the right, with more of the product being offered on the market.

When controls are established, the allocation function of the free-market system is destroyed. An equilibrium situation in terms of price and quantity cannot be attained without further government involvement.

Figure 3.3

Price ceiling

The imposition of a price ceiling (P_c) results in a shortage of the product $(Q_d - Q_s)$.

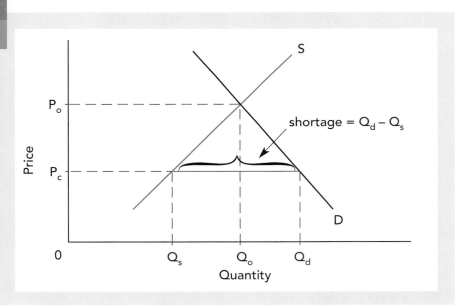

R E V I E W

3.10 Using demand and supply curves, show the impact of the government imposing a price ceiling on bread.

3.11 Learn whether a surplus or shortage results when a price ceiling for sandwiches is imposed.

EVERYDAY ECONOMICS 3.3

Medicare

Should health care be privately or publicly funded? That is, should individuals pay for health care as they would pay for food and clothing, or should health care be paid for by the state through tax dollars? In Canada, there is a combination of private and public health care. Visits to the chiropractor, the physiotherapist, and the naturopath are paid for by the patient or by the patient's insurance company. Visits to a medical doctor are paid for by a publicly funded health system. Why do governments intervene directly in the delivery of health care when they do not intervene directly in the provision of other essential items such as food and shelter?

There are positive third-party effects associated with the provision of health care. Disease is less likely to spread if everyone in the community is guaranteed at least a certain level of care. There is also a concern for individuals who, because of low incomes, are not able to afford adequate health care. A concern that low-income persons may not be able to afford adequate health care has prompted governments to keep the price of health care low. Extra billing by doctors was banned. The price of going to the doctor was reduced to zero. In effect, governments have introduced price ceilings on health care. Price ceilings result in shortages, and governments are faced with the problem of rationing health care. If there is a shortage of health-care services, how do governments decide who gets treatment? Should the decision on treatment be made by the

government? the doctor? the insurance company?

In many situations rationing is accomplished by a waiting list. Rationing also may be addressed by denying treatment to certain groups of individuals (for example, individuals who want medical treatment for cosmetic reasons). In other countries, rationing has taken the form of restricting intensive-care units to the elderly or denying liver transplants to alcoholics. Regardless of the manner by which rationing is undertaken, some form of rationing must be introduced.

If patients cannot receive a service (for example, an MRI scan) within a reasonable amount of time from the publicly funded service, should they be able to purchase the service from a private clinic? Should the government reimburse them for the amount paid to the private clinic? More Canadians each year are opting to go to private clinics for an MRI scan, at a cost of $500 to $800, rather than wait for an available opportunity at the local hospital. The waiting time for an MRI can be as long as five months at a hospital. Other Canadians have opted to obtain an MRI scan in the United States, where the price is $465 (U.S.). If individuals are allowed to pay for MRI scans and other services, is this a form of rationing? If so, is it an acceptable form of rationing?

Among the suggestions made on how to ration scarce health-care services in Canada are the following:

- introduce user fees for non–life threatening situations

- introduce an annual health-insurance premium so that individuals recognize that health care is not free. Higher premiums could be charged to smokers, drug addicts, alcoholics, or other groups.
- restrict the number of medical tests prescribed by doctors
- provide each individual with a voucher representing a certain amount of money for medical services. Once this money is spent, the individual is responsible for paying for extra health-care services.
- increase government spending on health care (a suggestion made by the Romanow report on

the future of health care in Canada, November 2002).

Questions

1. If health-care services are to be rationed, who makes the rationing decision?
2. Should individuals be permitted to spend money on the type of health-care services they want?
3. Will an aging population force governments to change the manner in which health care is delivered? Discuss.

Price Floors

A price floor is a government-imposed minimum price.

In contrast to a situation where a price ceiling is imposed, the government may feel that the market equilibrium price for a product is too low. This is quite often the case with agricultural products. If the equilibrium price is too low, a **price floor,** or minimum price, could be legislated, making it illegal to sell the product at a price below the legal minimum price. The effect of a price floor on the market is shown in Figure 3.4. The market equilibrium price is shown as P_0 and the price floor as P_f. At P_f the quantity demanded is Q_d and the quantity supplied is Q_s. There is a *surplus* of the commodity on the market; that is, Q_s is greater than Q_d. If this price floor were established in the egg market, there would be a surplus of eggs.

In a free-market situation, a surplus would be disposed of by lowering the price. With a price floor, however, a lower price is out of the question. Another way must be found to rid the market of the surplus. That is, something has to happen in this market to shift either the demand or supply curve so that a new equilibrium price is found at P_f. One method may be to restrict the amount of the product that can be produced. For example, in terms of egg production, farmers could be limited in the number of hens they are allowed to have. This would shift the supply curve to the left. Another solution would be to try to shift the demand curve to the right. One way in which the demand curve may be shifted is through advertising. Regardless of which alternative is chosen, the government becomes further involved in regulating market conditions. The imposition of a price floor results in a disequilibrium situation (i.e., a surplus) and the government has to intervene further in order to restore the balance.

Figure 3.4

Price floor

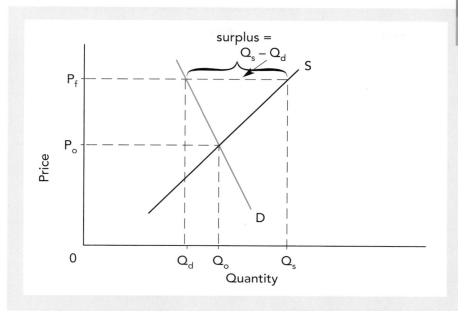

The imposition of a price floor (P_f) results in surplus of the product ($Q_s - Q_d$).

R E V I E W

3.12 Using demand and supply curves, show the impact of government imposing a price floor on the market for wheat.

3.13 Learn whether a surplus or shortage results when a price floor for sandwiches is imposed.

Excise Taxes

Excise taxes are extra costs imposed by government on the sale of particular commodities. These taxes may be used as a revenue source for government, or as a means of curbing the use of a particular commodity. For example, the excise tax on liquor and tobacco is a *source of revenue* for government, while the tax on air conditioners in automobiles is meant to reduce the sales of air conditioners, for environmental reasons. The manufacturer is required to pay the tax and to submit it to the appropriate government agency.

An excise tax is one levied by government on the suppliers of certain products.

Pareto Efficiency and the Minimum Wage

Vilfredo Pareto (1848–1923) was an Italian economist and sociologist who made important contributions to the theory of welfare economics. Originally trained as an engineer, Pareto used his knowledge of mathematics to develop economic theories of income distribution. His first book, *Cours d'economie politique*, included a mathematical formula that attempted to prove that the distribution of incomes and wealth in society is not random and that a consistent pattern of income and wealth distribution exists throughout the world.

It was Pareto's view that the well-being of a society is maximized when that society's resources are distributed in such a manner that it is not possible to make someone better off without decreasing another person's well-being. This is referred to as a *Pareto optimum* situation. Pareto argued that for society to reach this maximum there must be no third-party effects, perfect competition in markets, and excludability in the consumption of goods and services. Excludability is said to occur if the benefits of consumption accrue only to the person doing the consuming. Since these conditions are not likely to exist in all markets, can governments intervene in the free market in order to improve the overall welfare of society?

If it is possible to improve the well-being of some individuals while not decreasing the well-being of other individuals, then ideally government should proceed with that initiative. If someone could be made better off only at the expense of others, the rationale for government intervention is a little more complicated. For example, suppose government attempts to redistribute income by taking income away from some individuals and transferring it to others. What if the gains made by some individuals as a result of government involvement outweigh the losses incurred by others? If this situation results, the overall level of welfare in society will increase. Is it the role of government to improve the overall level of welfare in society?

We have seen that increases in the minimum wage rate increase the hourly wage rate for some employees while eliminating employment—or at least reducing hours of work—for other individuals. Some individuals are made better off at the expense of others.

Prior to discussing the merits of the minimum wage rate and answering the questions listed below, it would be beneficial to review the reading at the beginning of the chapter on the minimum wage rate. The reading lists a number of websites that contain articles on the impact of the minimum wage rate.

Questions

1. Should governments use minimum wage rates as a tool to increase society's overall level of welfare?
2. How do you measure the benefits received by those whose wage rate has increased and compare them to the costs incurred by those whose employment is eliminated or whose hours of work are reduced?
3. Approximately one-half of the minimum-wage earners in Canada are between 15 and 19 years of age. Would this influence the minimum wage rate set by governments in Canada? Explain.
4. In Canada the minimum wage rate represents about 34 percent of the average wage paid to a full-time, full-year worker. In Japan the ratio is 24 percent, and in Denmark it is 57 percent. Should Canadian governments refer to minimum wage rates in other nations when setting the minimum wage rate? Explain.

The effect of an excise tax on a market can be shown in Figure 3.5. Assume that the government decides to impose an excise tax of one dollar on each baseball hat that is produced. The equilibrium retail price for baseball hats prior to the imposition of the tax was five dollars per hat.

The impact of the excise tax will be to shift the supply curve upward by the amount of the tax. The supply curve shifts because the cost of producing the hats has gone up. In this case, the supply curve shifts vertically by one dollar. Suppliers will now want to receive one dollar more per hat than they had been receiving prior to the tax. What will happen to the price? More than likely, the price will increase, but by how much? Initially, suppliers may respond to the tax by raising the price of baseball hats to six dollars each. At six dollars, however, only Q_1 hats are wanted by consumers even though suppliers are still supplying Q_0 to the market. This surplus will force the price down to $5.60, the new market equilibrium price.

At this new price, Q_e baseball hats will be exchanged in the market. At this price, the quantity of hats demanded equals the quantity of hats supplied. The effect of the tax has been to raise the price of baseball hats. The price, however, has not risen by the full amount of the tax, but only by 60 cents. Since the supplier must still forward one dollar to the government from each hat sold, the consumer is paying 60 cents of the tax.

Figure 3.5

The effect of an excise tax

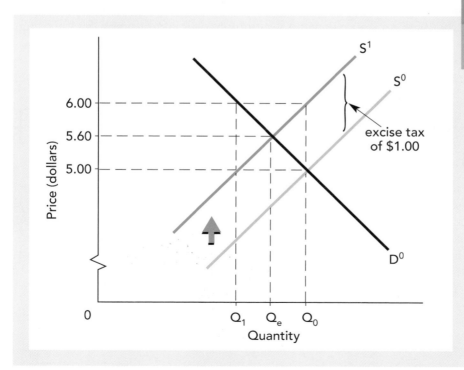

The imposition of an excise tax increases the equilibrium price of the product ($5.60) and reduces the equilibrium quantity (Q_e).

Part of the burden of paying for the tax has been shifted to the consumer. The ultimate burden of the excise tax is referred to as the *incidence* of the tax. In our example, the incidence of the tax is that the consumer pays 60 percent and the supplier 40 percent. Tax incidence varies by product. The price elasticities of demand and supply are major determinants of the incidence of a tax. For example, if the price elasticity of demand is inelastic, it is probable that the consumer will bear the greatest burden when an excise tax is imposed. If the demand for a product is inelastic, consumers will not decrease the quantity demanded a great deal when the price increases. If consumers continue to purchase the product in spite of the price increase, it will be easier for the supplier to shift the major burden of the tax to the consumers. If the demand for a product is elastic, suppliers will assume the greatest burden of an excise tax. Consumers will respond to price increases by reducing significantly the quantity demanded, and therefore suppliers will be reluctant to raise the price when an excise tax is imposed on their product.

On what products would the government impose an excise tax? The answer depends on the objective behind the tax. If the objective is to raise revenue, then a product with an inelastic demand (e.g., tobacco, liquor) will be chosen. Even after the imposition of the tax, consumers will continue to buy the product. If the objective was to discourage consumption, then a product with an elastic demand would be chosen. An example of a product with an elastic demand is automobile air conditioners. By imposing an excise tax on this product, the government hopes to decrease the number purchased and, ultimately, to save energy.

EVERYDAY ECONOMICS 3.5

Excise Taxes in Canada

Excise taxes at the federal government level in Canada are included in two pieces of legislation: The Excise Act and the Excise Tax Act. Excise duties are imposed under the Excise Act and excise taxes are imposed under the Excise Tax Act. Excise duties apply to domestic alcohol and tobacco products only, whereas excise taxes apply to various domestic and imported products. A further difference is that excise duties are more closely related to the production process and are paid at various stages of production. In contrast, excise taxes are paid at the end of the month following sales of the product.

Federal excise tax rates for 2002 are listed below:

Gasoline (motor and aviation)	10 cents/litre
Diesel and aviation fuel	4 cents/litre
Cigarettes	25.875 cents/5 cig.
Manufactured tobacco	$35.65/kg
Cigars	greater of 6.5¢ per cigar and 65% ad valorum
Tobacco sticks	3.965 cents/stick
Wine	
– alcohol 1.2% or less	2.05 cents/litre
– alcohol 1.2% to 7%	24.59 cents/litre
– alcohol over 7%	51.22 cents/litre
Automobile air conditioners	$100/unit
Jewellery	10 percent
Watches, clocks	10 percent

Federal excise duties for 2002 are as follows:

Distilled spirits	$11.066/L alc.
Mixed beverages (up to 7% alcohol)	24.59 cents/litre
Beer	
– up to 1.2% alcohol	$ 2.591/hL
– 1.2% to 2.5% alcohol	$13.9909/hL
– over 2.5% alcohol	$27.985/hL
Cigarettes	
– up to 1361 g/1000	$27.475/1000
– over 1361 g/1000	$29.374/1000
Cigars	$14.786/1000
Manufactured tobacco	$18.333/kg
Raw leaf tobacco	$1.572/kg
Tobacco sticks	$18.333/1000

SOURCE: Karin Treff and David B. Perry, *Finances of the Nation 2002* (Toronto: Canadian Tax Foundation 2002), p. 5:12.

There is a certain amount of controversy surrounding the imposition of excise taxes. If some luxury items are singled out for taxation purposes, why are not all luxury items taxed? For example, jewellery is taxed, but fur coats are not. Also, tobacco products are subject to both excise duties and excise taxes. Is it necessary to have double taxation on these products?

Questions

1. In your opinion, why are watches subject to excise tax?
2. Why does the government concentrate on tobacco products for both excise duties and excise taxes? Do they want people to refrain from smoking? Relate your answer to the concept of elasticity.
3. In the case of jewellery, who is likely to bear the greater burden of the excise tax, the consumer or the producer? Why?

Review

3.14 Using demand and supply curves, show the effect of government imposing a 50-cent excise tax on each ticket to a rock concert.

3.15 Learn about the effect on the price of sandwiches, and the quantity sold, when an excise tax is imposed.

Summary

The free-market approach to economic decision making has several advantages. First, there is a great deal of individual freedom in the decision-making process. Second, the free-market approach is efficient at allocating resources to various uses. This efficiency is achieved through the price system. Changes in prices act as signals to buyers and sellers and direct their behaviour. Third, the competition among sellers inherent in a free-market system provides for lower prices and better quality products.

Government becomes involved in the operations of the market due to certain shortcomings in a free-market system. First, markets are not always perfect in their operation. Buyers and sellers often do not have adequate information with which to make decisions. As well, competition may be circumvented by companies getting together to set prices and divide up the market. In other situations, competition in an industry may not be the ideal competitive situation; it may make more sense to have only one seller.

Second, transactions between two parties may affect a third party. Negative third-party effects are costs imposed on a third party, while positive third-party effects are benefits provided to a third party.

Third, the free-market system may not provide certain services that society considers important (unmet public goods). These services are not provided by the free market because it is difficult for companies to charge people individually or directly for the benefits that they receive from a service. An example is police protection.

Fourth, incomes may not be distributed equitably in a free-market system. Those individuals who cannot compete in the marketplace will earn little or no income. Our social conscience dictates that this situation is not acceptable.

Finally, the free-market system is not immune to fluctuations in the level of economic activity.

As a result of these market imperfections, governments intervene in our free-market system. Examples of this intervention include the imposition of price ceilings, price floors, and excise taxes.

Questions for Review and Discussion

1. For each of the following activities that have a significant amount of government involvement, identify the economic rationale for government participation.
   a) Canada Post
   b) police departments
   c) Canadian Broadcasting Corporation
   d) highways
   e) employment insurance

2. One reason for the strong participation of government in education is the presence of third-party effects. Identify these third-party effects.

3. Are some goods and services better able to be provided by government than by private companies? Explain your answer.

4. If competition is good for the consumer, why is it illegal in Canada to set up your own post office? Is there any competition for Canada Post?

5. Discuss the consequences of government imposing stringent pollution controls on paper mills. In your answer, you should consider the competition that paper mills face.

6. Why do local governments run the fire department? Does it have anything to do with third-party effects? Could fire protection be offered adequately by the free market?

7. What is the connection between positive third-party effects and unmet public goods?

8. Income differentials are one reason for government intervention in the free-market system. Would it be good for Canada if everyone earned the same level of income?

9. Much of the criticism of capitalism is that, if left unchecked, it will tend to concentrate economic power in too few hands. Do you agree? Why is this considered to be a negative aspect of capitalism?

10. In the former Soviet Union privately owned farms accounted for only 3 percent of the cropland and yet produced 27 percent of the country's food. Why do you believe this happened?

11. Should the responsibility for the poor be turned over to concerned citizens, charitable organizations, and churches and not be the responsibility of the government? Discuss this possibility.

12. Is there justification for natural monopolies in areas such as electricity and telephones? Would opening up the market to competition improve the variety and quality of service?

13. In many formerly socialist nations, food prices were kept low by the government. What impact did this have on the food supply? What action was the government then forced to take?

14. One of the responsibilities of the price system is to allocate resources to various uses. Why might the price system not be an efficient allocator of resources when third-party effects are present?

15. Public goods are defined as those goods or services for which it is not possible to exclude anyone from using the good or service whether they pay for it or not. Which of the following are public goods?
    a) North American air defence system
    b) public school
    c) Banff National Park
    d) fire department
    e) tickets to BC Lions football games

16. If people cannot be excluded from using a service, is the incentive to provide the service reduced? Explain.

17. The National Hockey League has teams in both Canada and the United States. Some Canadian teams in the league have a small population base from which to draw spectators. Some of these teams are requesting that their host cities build newer, more modern arenas in order to attract more spectators to hockey games. Should local taxpayers finance the new arenas? Who benefits the most from public expenditures on new arenas?

18. One reason that we have rent controls is that there are more tenants than landlords. Does this statement make sense?

19. In most provinces, the practice of extra-billing by doctors above the specified fees has been banned. What impact will this ban have on the supply of medical services in Canada?

20. In most provinces, there is a price ceiling on college tuition. With a price ceiling in effect, how are places at a college rationed to those who want them?

21. Governments are allowing law schools to charge whatever tuition is deemed appropriate. Tuition is increasing at many schools. Discuss the pros and cons of increasing tuition for law school.

22. Price floors tend to result in surpluses. With a given supply curve would you get a larger surplus by putting a price floor on a product with an elastic or an inelastic demand? Use a graph in your answer.

23. Draw two graphs with similar supply curves. On one graph draw a relatively inelastic demand curve, and on the other a relatively elastic demand curve. Assume a similar excise tax is imposed on each product. Under what circumstances is the price increase greater? Why?

24. In some respects, a subsidy can be considered the opposite of an excise tax. Using demand and supply curves, show the effect on the Canadian book market of the government offering the publishers a subsidy of 50 cents per book.

25. An OECD study stated that there are hidden costs associated with our reliance on the automobile. Name some negative third-party effects associated with automobiles.

26. Most analysts agree that there are positive third-party effects associated with health care. Does the existence of positive third-party effects imply that government should build and maintain hospitals?

Suggested Readings

Block, Walter E., Ed. *Economics and the Environment: A Reconciliation.* Vancouver: The Fraser Institute, 1990.

Poverty Profile 1999. Ottawa: National Council of Welfare, 2002. This annual publication discusses trends, sources of income for poor Canadians, and characteristics of Canadians deemed to be living in poverty.

Rydenfelt, Sven. *A Pattern for Failure: Socialist Economies in Crisis.* New York: Harcourt Brace Jovanovich, 1984. Although the material in this book is dated, the book contains a very good description of the problems of socialism.

Sarlo, Christopher A. *Poverty in Canada.* Vancouver: The Fraser Institute, 1992. This 200-page book discusses the definition and measurement of poverty in Canada.

Smith, Adam. *An Inquiry into the Nature and Causes of the Wealth of Nations.* 1776.

Welfare Incomes 2000 and 2001. Ottawa: National Council of Welfare, Spring 2002. This annual publication discusses trends, sources of income for poor Canadians, and characteristics of Canadians deemed to be living in poverty.

Selected Websites

www.ccsd.ca This is the site for the Canadian Council on Social Development. Information is provided on publications and on poverty levels by province.

www.fee.org The Foundation for Economic Education website. This is a free-market research group. Information is available on seminars and publications.

www.fraserinstitute.ca The Fraser Institute site. A public policy research organization based in Vancouver that focuses on free markets, private property rights, individual responsibility, and limited government.

www.caledoninst.org The Caledon Institute of Social Policy conducts social policy research and analysis. The institute develops proposals for the reform of social policy.

www.cato.org The Cato Institute is a nonpartisan policy research foundation based in Washington, D.C. The institute promotes policy options that are consistent with the principles of limited government and individual liberty.

www.blupete.com A website listing biographies of several economists.

www.mises.org The site for the Ludwig Von Mises Institute. This organization promotes free-market principles and states as one of its goals the restoration of theory in social science.

http://cato.org/pubs/pas/pa-274.html The link to an article entitled "How Rent Control Drives out Affordable Housing."

www.prospect.org/issue_pages The online home of *American Prospect* magazine.

http://cfc-efc.ca/docs/ccsd/00000324.htm This website compares poverty levels in Canada with those in other countries.

www.ncwcnbes.net The site for the National Council of Welfare—a citizens' advisory body to the Minister of Human Resources Development Canada on matters of concern to low-income Canadians.

Government in Canada

Key Terms

federalist system
Wagner's law of increasing state activity
direct tax
indirect tax
indexing
benefits-received approach
ability-to-pay approach
progressive tax
proportional tax
regressive tax
marginal tax rate
equalization payments
stabilization payments
gross public debt
net debt
gross domestic product (GDP)

Chapter Objectives

After successfully completing this chapter, you will be able to:

- appreciate the different responsibilities of the federal and provincial governments
- explain the reasons for the growth in government spending
- relate which taxes are collected by each level of government
- differentiate between the benefits-received and ability-to-pay approaches to tax equity
- differentiate between progressive, proportional, and regressive tax systems
- calculate marginal tax rates using your own figures

Core Concept Building

Every textbook on economics refers to the government and its activities with respect to the economy. This chapter distinguishes between the levels of government in Canada and introduces the progressive income tax, a concept that appears again in Chapters 8 and 14.

THE REAL PROPERTY TAX

The Constitution of Canada gives the provinces the right to levy direct taxes. The provinces in turn have empowered municipalities to impose certain types of direct taxes, including the real property tax. The real property tax is one of the oldest taxes in Canada. It is levied on the owners of property based on some measure of the value of the property.

Essentially, the tax base for the real property tax is the land and the things that are permanently attached to the land. Each province, however, varies in the scope of items that are taxed. All provinces include the land and the buildings in the tax base; some include machinery and equipment on the land in the tax base. Provinces differ in the tax treatment of mines, railways, oil and gas wells, and public utility distribution systems. All jurisdictions provide some exemptions from property tax. For example, churches and cemeteries are exempt in all provinces. Colleges and universities are also exempt in most jurisdictions. The tax rate, or mill rate, is usually expressed in dollars (or mills) per $1000 of assessed value. Different mill rates may apply to different types of property.

Assessment refers to the valuation of property for tax purposes. All provinces assess real property at some percentage of its market value. Provinces differ in the frequency of assessment, the base year used for assessment, and valuation methods. The responsibility for assessment also varies between provinces. Assessment is a provincial responsibility in Prince Edward Island, Nova Scotia, and New Brunswick. In Ontario, Saskatchewan, and British Columbia, the responsibility for assessment lies with a provincial corporation or independent assessment body. In Newfoundland and Labrador and Manitoba, municipalities and the province share assessment responsibilities. In Alberta and Quebec, assessment is a local responsibility.

What are the advantages of taxing real property from a municipality's point of view? The tax base is easy to find. It may be easier for a taxpayer to hide income from the tax collector than to hide real property. It is easy to determine the jurisdiction levying the tax. The tax is relatively inexpensive to collect on the part of the municipality. Finally, the assessed value of property (the tax base) remains relatively stable and may not fluctuate as much as incomes. It is true that market values of property do fluctuate; however, the assessed values do not change as often because of the administrative difficulty of changing assessed values on a regular basis.

Why impose a tax on real property? First, it is a charge for services provided by the municipality to property owners (e.g., garbage collection). The benefits that one gets from owning property are enhanced by the services provided by the municipality. A residence that is provided with sewers, road access, and fire protection is worth more than a residence that does not have access to these services. Residences that are provided with these services have a greater market value than others. Thus, it can be argued that the municipality has increased property values by providing services. A link can be established between the provision of services and the market value of property in the municipality. Market values for property can be used as a basis for municipal taxation.

Second, it is a charge for the services provided by the municipality that are available to everyone in the municipality (e.g., parks or education). For the latter services it would be difficult to charge residents of the municipality for the benefits they receive. It may be possible to charge someone for the amount of water use, but how do you charge someone for the benefit they receive from having a park in their community? Even though an individual may never use the park, he or she may receive "spillover" benefits from someone else using the park. For example, if a park with a baseball diamond provides a place for young people to participate in sports, these young people may be less likely to get into trouble. Since it would be difficult to assign individual benefits received to these services, the municipality levies a tax on the entire community.

In Chapter 3, the concept of tax incidence was introduced. The incidence of tax is the final resting place of the tax burden; that is, who ultimately pays the tax? The real property tax is a direct tax, meaning that it is imposed on the person expected to pay the tax. In the case of an owner-occupied dwelling, the owner bears the entire burden of the tax and cannot pass the tax on to others. Landlords and businesses also are subject to property tax. Landlords charge higher rates to tenants when they are subject to property tax. Businesses try to pass on the property tax to customers in the form of higher prices. Therefore, the real property tax is a direct tax only for owner-occupied residences.

The concept of elasticity is related to that of tax incidence. It was pointed out in Chapter 3 that in cases of an inelastic demand, such as the demand for cigarettes, the main burden of paying the excise tax is passed on to the consumer. The elasticity of property taxes refers to the degree to which property taxes can be passed on to others (for example, landlords charging higher rents to tenants). The ability of landlords to pass on the property tax to tenants depends on the demand and supply for rental units. The price elasticity of rental housing will be low if tenants do not have many housing alternatives. If the quantity of rental units demanded is greater than the quantity supplied at the present time, the price elasticity associated with rental units is likely to be low. It will also be low if the quantity of houses supplied is not increasing as quickly as the quantity demanded. A shortage of houses limits the housing options for tenants of apartments. The availability of mortgage funds may also limit the options of renters and keep the price elasticity low. With a low price elasticity of demand, the burden of a property tax can be passed more readily to tenants.

Constitutional Framework

Canada has a **federalist system** of government, which means that two levels of government—central and provincial—have jurisdiction over each citizen. On matters affecting the entire country, the federal (central) government has authority, while provincial governments have responsibility for their own smaller geographic areas. The powers and responsibilities of each level of government are outlined in the Constitution Act, which was originally the British North America (BNA) Act. The BNA Act, originally enacted in Great Britain, was patriated and renamed the Constitution Act, 1867. On April 17, 1982, the Constitution Act, 1982 was proclaimed and amended at a special ceremony in Ottawa. It contains the Charter of Rights and Freedoms.

At the time of Confederation (1867), it was the intention to create a powerful central, or federal, government in Canada. This level of government was awarded the major responsibilities of the time, as well as author-

A federalist system of government is one in which two levels of government have jurisdiction over each citizen.

ity over major revenue sources. Matters of war, foreign relations, foreign trade, customs duties, and the postal service are under the jurisdiction of the federal government. It is also responsible for such matters as the regulation of trade and commerce; navigation and shipping; penitentiaries; weights and measures; currency and coinage; and banking. Any residual powers not specifically granted to the provinces were also given to the federal government. Section 91 of the Constitution Act, 1867, allows this level of government "to make Laws for the Peace, Order, and good Government of Canada, in relation to all Matters not coming within the Classes of Subjects by this Act assigned exclusively to the Legislatures of the Provinces." In order to match these responsibilities with financial authority, unlimited taxing power was given to the federal government.

To the provincial governments were allocated matters of more direct local importance. Provincial responsibilities are outlined in Sections 92 and 93 of the Constitution Act, 1867. Provinces are responsible for hospitals; the licensing of businesses; the management and sale of public lands; and local works. In Section 93 of the legislation, provinces also were awarded responsibility for education. As these matters were seen as having less importance at the time of Confederation, provinces were given less command over revenue sources than was the federal government. Provincial governments were restricted to the collection of direct taxes; that is, taxes on the people who should pay them. In 1867 many of the provincial responsibilities were relatively unimportant, but in the early twenty-first century they are of major importance. Hospitals and education, for example, now comprise a large portion of total government spending.

We described Canada's system of government as federalist. In fact, it is probably best described as quasi-federalist. The jurisdictions of the federal and provincial governments are not totally separate. The federal government has the power to interfere with, or *check,* the authority of the provinces. For example, under Section 95 of the Constitution Act, 1867, the provinces are awarded responsibility for agriculture and for immigration. The same section of the act also gives the federal government the power to legislate in these areas, and states that provincial legislation cannot conflict with that of the federal government concerning these matters. In providing the federal government with the authority to make laws regarding the peace, order, and good government of the country, Section 91 of the Constitution Act, 1867 made it possible for the federal government to intervene in traditionally provincial matters, such as natural resources.

It was difficult for the architects of the constitution to foresee the situation in Canada more than 100 years later. The division of powers outlined in the legislation has resulted in some confusion and overlap. There are areas of responsibility in which both the federal and provincial governments have authority. This overlapping has also occurred in the field of taxation, which is discussed later in this chapter. Difficulties arise because matters awarded to provincial government jurisdiction in 1867 have increased in importance, while some matters awarded to federal government control have decreased in relative importance. The changes in these areas have not been matched with changes in the ability of the provinces to collect revenue. The federal government still has unlimited taxing power, while the provinces are restricted to collecting only direct taxes.

The Meech Lake Accord, signed by all ten provincial premiers and the federal government, was an attempt to change some of the constitutional arrangements between the federal and provincial governments. The Accord, however, was not passed by all provincial legislatures and it expired on June 23, 1990. On September 25, 1991 the federal government introduced new proposals, which were eventually rejected in a nationwide referendum in October 1992.

Government in Canada: Structure and Employment

The federal government governs the entire population of Canada. It is referred to as *bicameral,* meaning that it is comprised of two chambers. The House of Commons has 301 seats; members of the House are elected by the Canadian population. The Senate has 105 seats; members of the Senate are appointed by the political party with a majority of seats in the House of Commons. The constitutional head of the government of Canada is the Queen, whose representative in Canada is the Governor General. There are ten provinces in Canada and three territories. The territories have no powers granted to them under the constitution and are, to a great extent, controlled by the federal government. All provinces are *unicameral*; that is, there is only one legislative chamber. The Queen is represented in each province by the Lieutenant Governor. In the territories, the task of the Lieutenant Governor is performed by the Commissioner, who reports to the federal Minister of Indian and Northern Affairs.

Canada also has a variety of local governments, including municipal boards, school and other boards, agencies, and commissions. Local governments are not mentioned in the Constitution. They are creations of the province in which they are located and thus vary greatly in terms of structure and responsibilities. Municipal governments are elected and are headed by a mayor, reeve, chairperson, or warden. School-board officials are elected as well and are usually independent from the municipality in terms of administration and financing. School boards do not levy taxes but request a certain amount of money collected from property taxes.

The public sector is an important source of employment for Canadians. Public-sector employees include teachers, firefighters, police, health inspectors, immigration and customs officers, and so on. The number of public-sector employees at all levels of government declined in the late 1990s as governments cut back in the provision of services and privatized other functions: public-sector employment declined by almost 6 percent from 1995 to 1998. Table 4.1 lists public-sector employment for the various levels of government for 2001.

Government Spending by Function

Federal

The importance of various government responsibilities can be assessed by reviewing data on government spending. Information on federal government spending is presented in Table 4.2. The largest component of government spending is social services, which include old age security, the

Table 4.1 *Public-sector employment, Canada, 2001*

PROVINCE/TERRITORY	TOTAL
Newfoundland and Labrador	55 561
Prince Edward Island	15 800
Nova Scotia	102 354
New Brunswick	79 117
Quebec	692 447
Ontario	977 265
Manitoba	142 884
Saskatchewan	115 723
Alberta	268 683
British Columbia	357 760
Yukon	4 950
Northwest Territories	6 998
Nunavut	4 967
Outside Canada	3 095
Total	2 828 222

SOURCE: Compiled from tables in Karin Treff and David B. Perry, *Finances of the Nation 2002* (Toronto: Canadian Tax Foundation, 2003) p. 5.

Table 4.2 *Federal expenditure on a financial management basis,*
fiscal year 2001–2002ª

FUNCTION	MILLIONS OF DOLLARS	PERCENTAGE OF TOTAL
Social services	71 326	38.5
Debt charges	28 354	15.3
Protection of persons and property	19 866	10.7
Resource conservation and industrial development	6 494	3.5
General services	6 126	3.3
Education	4 726	2.6
Foreign affairs and international assistance	4 308	2.3
Recreation and culture	3 238	1.7
Labour, employment, and immigration	2 517	1.4
Research establishments	2 421	1.3
Health	2 154	1.2
Transportation and communications	2 077	1.1
Housing	1 911	1.0
Environment	1 412	0.8
Regional planning and development	447	0.2
Other	27 934	15.1
Total gross general expenditure	185 311	100.0

ªStatistics Canada revised estimate.
SOURCE: Karin Treff and David B. Perry, *Finances of the Nation 2002* (Toronto: Canadian Tax Foundation, 2003), p. A:9.

child tax benefit program, employment insurance, social welfare assistance programs, veterans' benefits, and expenditures on Indian and Inuit affairs programs. A major program under the heading of social services is employment insurance.

More than $11 billion was spent on employment insurance benefits and administration in 2001–2002. The Employment Insurance program is financed by both employer and employee contributions. Individuals who have been terminated or who have been temporarily laid off are eligible for employment insurance benefits. Special benefits are also available for women on maternity leave, individuals on parental and adoption leave, and individuals who are ill and not able to work. Special regulations under employment insurance provide assistance for self-employed fishers.

The Canada Pension Plan, a pension plan financed by employee contributions, is another program under social services. Coverage under the Canada Pension Plan is compulsory for most employees and self-employed persons. Under Old Age Security, individuals who are 65 years of age and meet the residency requirement receive $442.66 per month as of January 1, 2002. The Guaranteed Income Supplement (GIS) is available to low-income Old Age Security recipients. In 2002 the maximum GIS payment to an individual was $526.08.

The second largest expenditure for the federal government is debt charges. The public debt refers to all costs relating to unmatured debt, as well as annual amortization of bond discounts, premiums and commissions, servicing of the public debt, and costs of issuing new loans. Unmatured debt consists of marketable bonds, Canada Savings Bonds, Canada Pension Plan investment fund, treasury bills, and notes and loans payable in foreign currency. A more detailed discussion of Canada's debt appears later in this chapter.

Provincial and Local

The main areas of provincial government spending are health, education, social welfare, and payments on the provincial debt (see Table 4.3). Spending on health programs accounts for approximately one-third of provincial government expenditure. The health services provided by the provinces fall into three categories: public-health services, hospital insurance, and medical care. Public-health services encompass a wide range of activities, including programs for mental health, occupational health, disease control, maternal and child care, cancer treatment, and diagnostic laboratory services, among others. All provinces have hospital-care insurance systems partly financed by the federal government. The insurance covers services in hospitals, including accommodation and meals. Provinces also have medical-care insurance plans that are partly funded by the federal government. In order to receive federal government assistance for health care, provinces must comply with certain guidelines.

Five provinces and the territories finance their share of the costs of the provincial health insurance plans from general taxation; two provinces (Alberta and British Columbia) levy premiums, augmented by general taxation; and Manitoba, Ontario, and Quebec levy a payroll tax on employers, augmented by general taxation.

The second most important provincial program is education. All provinces look after elementary and secondary education, although policies and programs

Table 4.3 *Provincial government expenditure on a financial-management basis, fiscal year 2001–2002*

FUNCTION	MILLIONS OF DOLLARS	PERCENTAGE OF TOTAL
Health	74 550	33.0
Education	54 205	24.0
Social services	38 594	17.1
Debt charges	25 244	11.2
Resource conservation and industrial development	9 093	4.0
Transportation and communications	8 657	3.8
Protection	8 091	3.6
General services	3 842	1.7
Transfers to local governments	1 337	0.6
Other	2 209	1.0
Total expenditure	225 822	100.0

SOURCE: Karin Treff and David B. Perry, *Finances of the Nation 2002* (Toronto: Canadian Tax Foundation, 2003), p. A:12.

may vary by province. Assistance is also provided by provinces to local (municipal) governments for capital expenditures related to education.

Social-welfare programs account for approximately 17 percent of provincial government spending. These programs are operated in cooperation with the federal government, and in some cases with the municipal governments. The Canada Assistance Plan coordinates welfare spending in each province.

Provincial governments also borrow money. In 2001 the provinces owed more than $241 billion. The provinces also guarantee debt for government businesses.

A word should be said about municipal government spending. The authority of local governments to spend money comes from the provincial legislature. In other words, local governments can undertake spending only in areas approved by the provincial government. The main area of local government spending is education, which accounted for approximately 40 percent of total spending in 2001 (see Table 4.4). Other important services include maintenance of roads, protection of persons and property, environmental programs, recreation and culture, and social services. Local governments also borrow money; 3.8 percent of local government expenditure was debt-related in 2001.

Table 4.4 *Local government expenditure on a financial-management basis, 2001*

FUNCTION	MILLIONS OF DOLLARS	PERCENTAGE OF TOTAL
Education	33 139.7	40.5
Transportation and communications	10 306.1	12.6
Protection of persons and property	7 282.4	8.9
Environment	6 934.1	8.5
Social services	6 019.6	7.4
Recreation and culture	5 529.7	6.8
General services	5 008.2	6.1
Debt charges	3 107.4	3.8
Health	1 061.2	1.3
Other	3 365.2	4.1
Total expenditure	81 753.6	100.0

SOURCE: Karin Treff and David B. Perry, *Finances of the Nation 2002* (Toronto: Canadian Tax Foundation, 2003), p. A:14.

R E V I E W

4.1 What is a federalist system of government?

4.2 Which level of government in Canada has the primary responsibility for (a) education, (b) hospitals, (c) national defence, and (d) banking?

4.3 In what areas do federal and provincial government spending overlap?

The Growth of Government Spending

In Canada, government expenditures tend to rise in relation to the overall level of economic activity. Government spending on goods and services accounts for approximately one-fifth of Canada's total spending. In addition, money is redistributed by government throughout the country in the form of *transfer payments. These are monies paid out by government to individuals and other levels of government where no service was performed for the money. These payments include such items as unemployment compensation and pensions.*

Prior to 1930, government spending, including transfer payments, had risen to almost 17 percent of total spending in the economy. By 1992, this had increased to more than 51 percent. As a result of concern over government spending, this percentage fell to 39.7 percent in 2001. In other words, two-fifths of total spending in Canada is actively controlled by government. The figures do not take into consideration the maze of rules set up by government for regulating business activity.

Theories about why government is playing an increasingly greater role in the economy have been around for a long time. One of the earliest theories was proposed by a German economist, Adolph Wagner, in 1883. **Wagner's law of increasing state activity** postulated that government expenditures could be expected to grow at a faster rate than the total output of goods and services in industrialized economies. One reason was that the complexities of economic development would require the establishment of a centralized authority. Increased frictions between individuals as a result of greater urbanization would necessitate more money being spent on law and order. Wagner believed that government would also become involved in trying to correct market imperfections and in financing large-capital projects. Finally, he believed that cultural and welfare expenditures were luxury items, and as the level of national income grew more money would be allocated to these services.

In general, Wagner's theory seems to hold for Canada. Our transition from a rural to an urban country has made government more prominent. People in the cities require more services than do people in rural areas. Governments normally provide the following services in urban areas: water and sewers, garbage pick-up, sidewalks, street lights, and transportation services.

Increases in the amount of goods and services produced in Canada have also been accompanied by increases in social-welfare payments. Canadians appear to have a strong social conscience and have become more concerned about those who are less fortunate. Social-welfare expenditures now represent the biggest category of federal government spending, as well as approximately one-fifth of all provincial government expenditure. These expenditures cover such programs as pensions, disability and unemployment compensation, and general welfare assistance.

Wagner was also correct about the increasing complexities of economic development. The rapid pace of technological change is constantly altering the types of products available, as well as the production process itself. These changes require a skilled and trained labour force that is able to undertake research and development and to maintain and service new equipment. Government has become increasingly involved in the education

Adolph Wagner's law of increasing state activity postulates that in industrialized economies government spending can be expected to grow at a faster rate than the total output of goods and services.

process, particularly at the post-secondary level, in order to provide this labour force. Advances in technology can also create an increased demand for services that government traditionally supplies. For example, increased air travel has created a demand for improved airport capacity.

Wagner's theory helps to explain much of the increase in government spending. Yet there are still other factors to consider. One of the most significant is the political process itself. In order to get elected, candidates are likely to promise certain services that will be provided once they are in office. Following through on promises costs money—the more promises that are made, the more money is required to carry them out. Once in office, politicians are concerned with re-election, and government programs already in existence tend to continue. Since these programs benefit certain segments of the population, the elimination or reduction of programs may lose potential voter support. The rising cost of government is sustained because of a reluctance to reduce or eliminate certain programs that are no longer necessary.

Another reason for increased government spending is *military conflict*. During a war, government spending has to increase, yet it may not come down to previous levels once the war is over. Changes in spending as a result of war form part of a theory on government spending put forth by Alan Peacock and Jack Wiseman. They believe that the level of government spending depends on what taxpayers believe to be an acceptable level of taxation. In the event of war, when funds are needed, the concept of an acceptable level of taxation increases. Peacock and Wiseman believe that after a war the acceptable level of taxation remains above its pre-war level, and government continues to collect more money in taxes. The Peacock-Wiseman hypothesis, however, cannot really be proven in the case of Canada. In 1939, prior to the Second World War, government spending represented 21.4 percent of total spending in Canada. This increased to 50.5 percent of total spending in 1944, during the war. Yet by 1950, it represented only 22.1 percent of total spending in Canada. Wars cause changes in government involvement in the economy, but whether these changes are permanent is not clear.

An increase in government spending may result from the increase in tax revenue that government is receiving. With a progressive income tax structure (discussed later in this chapter), the percentage of income that an individual pays in taxes increases as the level of income increases. As Canada's production of goods and services rises, so do incomes; thus, government receives more money from income tax revenue. With more money available to spend, governments spend more. A trend of rising prices also helps tax revenues to increase, since income increases are often linked to price increases.

Finally, the nature of government services itself can lead to increased costs and increased government spending. Productivity increases have been harder to achieve in providing government services than in the provision of goods and services in the private sector. Productivity can be defined as the amount of work accomplished per person. If productivity increases match wage increases, then costs and prices do not have to increase. In the public sector, there is little incentive to increase productivity. The services provided by government are not in competition with those provided in the private sector, and the lack of competition means that government can be less cost-conscious in providing its services. Also, for some of the services provided by government, productivity increases are harder to come by—for example, health inspectors and immigration officers. In fact, several reports of the auditor general have criticized the federal government for a lack of concern over steps to reduce government expenses.

REVIEW

4.4 Explain Wagner's theory of increases in government spending. Does it apply to government spending in Canada?

4.5 How does the political nature of our government affect its level of spending?

International Comparisons 4.1

Government expenditures on goods and services as a percentage of GDP, 2000

Country	Percentage	Country	Percentage
Argentina	17.0	Brazil	26.8
Canada	20.3	Germany	32.7
France	46.2	United Kingdom	36.0
United States	19.2	Japan	23.2
China	10.9	Mexico	16.0
Australia	23.5	Chile	21.9
Greece	30.7	Pakistan	23.1
India	16.7	Israel	46.3
Italy	41.9	Netherlands	45.9
Poland	34.6	Russian Federation	22.9

Sources of Government Revenue

Constitutional Authority

The taxation powers of the various levels of government are contained in the Constitution Act, 1867. The act gave unlimited taxing powers to the federal government while restricting the provincial governments to collecting only direct taxes. The administrative arrangements of the tax determine whether it is a direct or an indirect tax. A **direct tax** is a tax imposed on the person who is intended to pay the tax. For example, an income tax is a direct tax since the individual receiving the income is expected to pay the tax. An **indirect tax,** on the other hand, is one that is levied against one person in the expectation that it will be paid by another person. An excise tax is an example of an indirect tax. It is levied on the supplier of a product, yet it is expected that the supplier will try to pay for the tax by charging a higher price to the consumer for the product. In 1867, direct taxes were not very common and so were given to the provinces as a source of revenue. The majority of government revenue at that time came from two indirect taxes: excise taxes and customs duties. These taxes became the responsibility of the federal government.

Today there are myriad direct and indirect taxes at both the federal and provincial levels of government. The conditions of the Constitution Act, 1867 have been altered through federal/provincial tax-sharing arrangements. Municipal-government tax responsibilities, not mentioned in the constitution, have also complicated the tax picture. Municipalities receive their taxing authority from their respective provincial governments.

> A direct tax is one imposed on the individual who should pay the tax, whereas an indirect tax is one levied against one individual in the expectation that it will be paid by another individual.

Federal

Sources of federal-government revenue are listed in Table 4.5. The *personal income tax* accounts for about 46 percent of all revenue. This tax applies to all individuals living in Canada. Tax is payable on all sources of income, whether earned in Canada or not. Individuals may receive income in various ways. Some earn income through employment; others earn income from investments; and others earn income from government assistance such as employment insurance. All sources of income are taxable, even though they may be taxed at slightly different rates.

Corporation income tax provided the government with more than $24 billion of revenue in 2002. Corporation tax rates vary depending on the type of business and the ownership. The basic federal tax on corporate income in a province is 25 percent. There is also a 4-percent surtax on all corporate income tax payable. A lower rate of tax (12 percent) is levied on

Table 4.5 *Federal revenue on a financial-management basis, fiscal year 2002 estimate*

SOURCE	MILLIONS OF DOLLARS	PERCENTAGE OF TOTAL
Income taxes		
personal income	89 715	46.5
corporate income	24 992	12.9
on payments to non-residents	4 038	2.1
Consumption taxes		
general sales	28 238	14.6
gasoline and automotive fuel	4 855	2.5
alcohol and tobacco	3 441	1.8
customs duties	2 979	1.5
other	426	0.2
Health and social insurance		
contributions	21 780	11.3
Investment income	6 682	3.5
Sales of goods and services	4 290	2.2
Miscellaneous taxes	482	0.2
Other revenue	1 138	0.6
Total revenue	193 056	99.9

SOURCE: Karin Treff and David B. Perry, *Finances of the Nation 2002* (Toronto: Canadian Tax Foundation, 2003), p. A:9.

small-business income earned by Canadian-controlled private corporations. Manufacturing and processing operations have a tax rate of 21 percent. For the particulars of these programs, reference has to be made to the Income Tax Act.

Other federal government taxes include *excise taxes* and *customs duties*. Excise taxes are levied on certain items classified as luxuries. The tax may be on an *ad valorem* basis (e.g., 10 percent), or on a specific basis (e.g., three cents per item). A list of federal excise taxes was presented in Chapter 3. Customs duties, or tariffs, are applied in conjunction with the World Trade Organization (WTO) and the North American Free Trade Agreement (NAFTA), discussed in more detail in Chapter 9.

The federal government also receives 18 percent of its revenue from non-tax sources. These include social insurance contributions, profits earned by Crown agencies, interest on loans, and bank interest. Also included is revenue from licences, fees, and proceeds from the operation of the Royal Canadian Mint.

Provincial and Local

Provinces receive about 70 percent of their revenue from taxes, while the remaining portion is divided among non-tax sources and transfers from the federal government.

Personal income tax provides the main source of revenue for the provinces (see Table 4.6). All provinces, except Quebec, have agreed to let the federal government collect provincial personal income tax. Provinces and territories calculate provincial or territorial tax as a percentage of federally defined taxable income rather than as a percentage of federal tax as was formerly the case.

Provinces also levy a corporation income tax. All provinces except Alberta, Ontario, and Quebec allow the federal government to collect corporation income tax. Corporations are subject to provincial income tax if they have a permanent establishment in the province. Corporate tax rates also vary from one province to another.

A major source of provincial government revenue is the retail sales tax. All provinces except Alberta have such a tax, although Alberta has a sales tax on hotel and motel accommodation. Each province sets its own retail sales

Table 4.6 *Provincial revenue on a financial-management basis, fiscal year 2001–2002*

SOURCE	MILLIONS OF DOLLARS	PERCENTAGE OF TOTAL
Personal income tax	52 082	22.7
Consumption taxes	49 021	21.4
Transfers from federal government	34 790	15.2
Investment income	23 106	10.1
Sales of goods and services	20 139	8.8
Miscellaneous taxes	14 548	6.3
Corporation income tax	13 907	6.1
Health and social insurance levies	10 217	4.6
Property and related taxes	8 450	3.7
Other	2 863	1.2
Total revenue	229 123	100.1

SOURCE: Karin Treff and David B. Perry, *Finances of the Nation 2002* (Toronto: Canadian Tax Foundation, 2003), p. A:12.

tax rate. Provinces also vary in the exemptions allowed from retail sales tax. The retail sales tax itself may vary depending on the item being taxed. For example, in several provinces alcoholic beverages are subject to higher taxes than other goods. Sales tax rates range from a high of 10 percent in Prince Edward Island to a low of 6 percent in Saskatchewan (see Table 4.7).

Provinces also receive revenue from excise taxes on alcohol, tobacco, and gasoline. In 2000–2001, the provinces received more than $7 billion in revenue from gasoline excise taxes and $3.4 billion in excise taxes on alcohol and tobacco. Specialty taxes exist in only certain provinces. These include amusement taxes, pari-mutual betting taxes, and land transfer and land speculation taxes.

Local governments also levy taxes and receive transfers of money from the other levels of government. The major source of tax revenue for local governments is the property tax, which accounts for approximately one-half of local government revenue (see Table 4.8). Transfers from other levels of government represent approximately 20 percent of local government revenue.

Table 4.7 *Provincial sales tax rates, 2002*

Newfoundland and Labrador	8%
Prince Edward Island	10%
Nova Scotia	8%
New Brunswick	8%
Quebec	7.5%
Ontario	8%
Manitoba	7%
Saskatchewan	6%
British Columbia	7.5%

SOURCE: Karin Treff and David B. Perry, *Finances of the Nation 2002* (Toronto: Canadian Tax Foundation, 2003), p. 5:6.

REVIEW

4.6 Define what is meant by direct taxation.

4.7 In what areas do federal and provincial government taxes overlap?

Table 4.8 *Local government revenue on a financial-management basis, 2001*

SOURCE	MILLIONS OF DOLLARS	PERCENTAGE OF TOTAL
Property and related taxes	32 490.9	40.1
Transfers from other governments	32 353.9	40.0
Sales of goods and services	12 192.4	15.1
Investment income	2 352.4	2.9
Miscellaneous taxes	559.1	0.7
Other	849.3	1.1
Total revenue	80 798.0	99.9

SOURCE: Karin Treff and David B. Perry, *Finances of the Nation 2002* (Toronto: Canadian Tax Foundation, 2003), p. A:14.

EVERYDAY ECONOMICS 4.1

Government Profits from Inflation

Inflation is defined as an increase in the overall level of prices. Because some government taxes are assessed on a percentage basis, the revenue collected from taxation increases as prices increase. For example, the provincial retail sales tax, applicable in all provinces except Alberta, is a percentage of the retail selling price. When prices are increasing, the money that consumers pay in retail sales tax is also increasing. Certain excise taxes are also levied on a percentage basis. Government revenue, therefore, increases along with inflation.

The most celebrated example of government profiting from inflation concerns the personal income tax. In Canada the personal income tax is a progressive tax. As one's income increases, a higher percentage of income is paid in income tax. In a period of rising prices, individual incomes are likely to increase as well. Many workers, particularly those who are members of trade unions, want to ensure that their wage increases keep up with price increases. As wages and incomes increase, individuals move into higher tax brackets and pay a greater percentage of their income in taxes. Some

of the gain from a wage increase is thus taken away. In fact, if wage increases only keep pace with inflation, the individual could be worse off than before, since a greater percentage of the individual's income is now paid in taxes.

In 1973—under public pressure to do something about inflation—the federal government introduced **indexing** (which involves making adjustments to taxes or payments according to changes in the rate of inflation) of the personal income tax. Indexing took the form of adjustments to the personal exemptions and the tax brackets. In order to adjust for price increases, personal exemptions were increased annually in line with inflation. For example, the basic personal amount used to calculate tax credits, which was $6066 in 1989, was increased to $6169 in 1990 as a result of indexing.

The indexing of personal income tax has been a benefit to the individual but a cost to government. Tax revenues are lower than they would have been without indexing. Some provincial governments also receive less revenue, since their personal income tax is based on a percentage of the federally defined taxable income. The loss of revenue from indexing is a major concern to government. The federal government in the 1980s considered the idea of removing indexing entirely from personal income taxes, but strong public reaction delayed the move. Apart from the personal gain that indexing provides, the public favours its maintenance in order to control the possibility of government profiting from inflation. If indexing were removed from the tax system, government tax revenues would increase right along with rising prices. The indexing factor for each year

is equal to the year-over-year increases in the Consumer Price Index (see Chapter 5) for the year ending September 30.

Questions

1. Why does government tax revenue increase in times of inflation under a progressive income tax structure?
2. Do you think that indexing helps control government spending?

Theory of Taxation

There is a saying that there are only two things in life that are certain: death and taxes. It appears as if taxes have been around forever. The Bible tells stories of taxes and tax collection. In Britain, public reaction to taxes led to the signing of the Magna Carta more than 700 years ago. The English tax on tea helped fuel a revolt in the colonies that led to the creation of the United States of America. Taxes are also part of Canadian history, and responsibility for taxes was written into the British North America Act, 1867.

Taxes are imposed in order to provide revenue for government, and also to influence economic conditions. Two of the major principles of taxation are maintenance of social justice and consistency with economic objectives.

Social Justice

Taxes should be *equitable*, or fair. The Royal Commission on Taxation in Canada during the 1960s concluded that the primary objective of any tax should be *equity*. Although this is not in dispute, the problem remains in defining what equity or fairness means. One approach to defining equity is to insist that all individuals who are in similar circumstances pay the same amount of tax. For example, all those who earn $40 000 per year should pay the same amount of income tax. All those who smoke one package of cigarettes per day should pay the same tax on cigarettes. Treating like people in a similar manner is referred to as *horizontal equity*. There is basically no argument over this approach.

The problem in terms of equity arises where individuals in different circumstances are concerned. In order to be fair, how do you treat individuals who have different amounts of wealth, income, and children? How should people in unlike circumstances be taxed in order to be fair? This is the problem of vertical equity.

There are two approaches to vertical equity: benefits received and ability-to-pay. The **benefits-received approach** proposes that people be taxed on the basis of the benefits that they receive from government programs. Those who benefit most from government spending should pay more taxes. Although this proposal appears equitable, two problems are associated with it. First, it is very difficult to determine who receives the benefits from various government programs. For example, who receives the benefit from a government-provided modern highway system? The benefits are spread out among many people. Those who use the highway obviously benefit. If food and other products travel by truck, then store owners and consumers also benefit from faster service. Those who live in residential areas of the city may benefit from less traffic and less pollution in their neighbourhood. Pedestrians may benefit because there is less traffic on residential streets. If people are to be taxed on the benefits they receive, it must first be determined who receives the benefit. In addition, the amount of the benefits has to be decided.

The second difficulty with the benefits-received approach relates to the composition of government spending. The biggest expenditure from the point of view of the federal government is social welfare. These expenditures go to those individuals who are not as fortunate as others, and who may not be able to provide for themselves. It is unreasonable to expect these individuals to pay for the benefits that they receive.

These problems with the benefits-received approach do not mean that this approach is useless. For some taxes, the benefits-received principle may be the most practical and equitable principle. A tax on airplane tickets forces those who use the airports to pay for their maintenance. Gasoline excise taxes help pay for the roads and are paid by those who use the roads. The more one drives, the more gasoline is used, and the more tax is paid.

The alternate approach to vertical equity is to tax individuals on their **ability to pay** taxes. Those with a greater ability to pay should pay more in taxes. How is ability to pay determined? This is where problems with this approach arise. Some economists argue that a person's wealth is the best measure of ability to pay. Personal wealth includes real estate, stocks, bonds, paintings, bank accounts, and so on. Others believe that the best measure of ability to pay is income. This represents the flow of money coming to an individual in a given year. Finally, ability to pay could be measured on the basis of expenditure. The more money that one spends, the more one should be able to pay taxes. Individual spending can be related to standard of living, and a higher standard of living represents a greater ability to pay taxes.

In Canada, all three approaches to ability to pay are used for taxation purposes. Federal and provincial governments tax corporation and individual income. Municipalities tax property, which is an indicator of wealth. Provinces impose retail sales taxes on consumer purchases. The major source of tax revenue, however, comes from income. Approximately 46 percent of federal government revenue and one-quarter of provincial government revenue come from personal income taxes. Corporation income taxes contribute another 13 percent and 6 percent, respectively.

Even though income taxes provide the greatest source of revenue for government, there is still discussion about how income should be taxed. It is agreed that those with higher incomes should pay more tax, but how much more? There can be several relationships between one's income and the percentage of income paid in taxes. If the percentage of income paid in taxes rises along with income, it is referred to as a **progressive tax.** If the percentage paid in taxes remains the same regardless of the level of income, it is a **proportional tax.** Finally, if the percentage paid in taxes declines as income increases, it is called a **regressive tax.** Regardless of which approach to taxation is used, individuals with more income will pay more in income taxes.

In Canada, the progressive form of taxation is used on income. It is believed that this type of tax is best suited for extracting an equal sacrifice from each individual. Even though someone with a higher income pays more in taxes than someone with a low income, the sacrifice that each has to make in paying taxes is thought to be the same. The proportional and regressive approaches do not accomplish this. In the proportional approach, individuals in low-income groups will make a greater sacrifice in paying their taxes because the money they pay in taxes means more to them than the amount paid by higher-income groups. With the regressive approach, the low-income individual pays a higher percentage of income in taxes and thus is making more of a sacrifice than someone in a higher-income tax group.

A regressive tax does not necessarily mean that low-income people pay more taxes; they just pay a higher percentage of their income in taxes. For example, assume that someone earning $50 000 per year pays 10 percent of his or her income in taxes, and someone earning $10 000 per year pays 20 percent of his or her income in taxes. The amount of money paid in taxes is $5000 and $2000, respectively. The higher-income person pays more tax, but the lower-income person pays a higher proportion of tax on that lower income. Thus, even under a regressive approach the taxation principle of ability to pay could still hold.

A **progressive approach** to taxation is one in which the percentage of income an individual pays in taxes increases as the individual's level of income increases.

A **proportional tax** is one in which the percentage of income paid in taxes remains constant regardless of an individual's level of income, whereas a **regressive tax** describes one in which the percentage of income paid in taxes decreases as the level of income increases.

Flat Tax: Fair or Foul?

Many people argue that the current income tax system is unnecessarily complicated. There are different tax rates for different types of income. There are deductions, exemptions, and tax credits that appear to benefit one group of taxpayers more than another group. For example, it can be argued that deductions for registered retirement savings plans (RRSPs) benefit high-income Canadians more than low-income Canadians. High-income Canadians are more likely to have money to put into an RRSP, and also receive a larger tax benefit than low-income persons should they both contribute the same amount to an RRSP. Over the years, various groups and individuals have proposed replacing the current tax structure with a single rate, or flat tax. That is, one income tax rate, for example 15 percent, would apply to all income. Under a flat-tax system, it is proposed that there be no exemptions, deductions, or tax credits.

There are several merits to a flat tax. First, it is easy to understand. If Canadian citizens can understand the tax, they are more likely to support it. Second, it is easy to calculate the amount of taxes owed. There would be less need for tax lawyers, tax accountants, and tax planners because filing an income tax form would be easier. The services of these trained individuals could be put to a more productive use in society. Third, a flat tax would eliminate the disincentive effects of high marginal tax rates. Under a progressive income tax system, marginal tax rates, or the taxes paid on another dollar of income, can be quite high. A high marginal tax rate discourages risk taking and hard work.

Finally, there might be less tax evasion if paying taxes were less onerous and less costly.

On the other hand, concern has been expressed that a flat tax would benefit high-income earners more than low-income earners. This view focuses on the burden of paying the tax. For example, if all taxpayers paid 10 percent of their income in taxes, the burden would be greater on low-income individuals. The loss in purchasing power resulting from taking away 10 percent of one's income places a greater burden on low-income persons than on high-income persons. Low-income individuals need the money to buy essential items. High-income individuals have enough money to purchase the essentials, and then some. To address this concern most proposals for a flat tax set an income cut-off below which no tax is paid. A flat tax could also be made more progressive by expanding the tax base. That is, all sources of income would receive the same tax treatment. Dividends, which are currently taxed in a different manner, would be subject to the same tax treatment as other income. Expanding the tax base could get complicated as companies might attempt to reward employees by means other than income. Alberta uses a flat tax, single-rate system; the rate is 10 percent of taxable income.

Questions

1. In your opinion, is a flat tax a fair tax?
2. Is there a problem with taxing dividends in a manner similar to other income?
3. Is taxing interest earned from a savings account a form of double taxation? If so, should double taxation be permitted?

When taxes are referred to as *progressive, regressive,* or *proportional* they are not always based on income, but the actual amount of the tax is related to income. For example, the municipal property tax is often called a regressive tax, even though it is not based on income. Individuals who live in the same type of house on the same amount of property pay the same amount of property tax. The individuals who live in these houses may not earn the same income; if this is the case, the low-income person will be paying a greater proportion of his or her income in taxes. This tax is not based on income but on *wealth.* The fact that two individuals have similar real estate wealth indicates that they should pay the same amount of tax in order to preserve horizontal equity.

Consistency with Economic Objectives

The imposition of taxes has economic consequences. As discussed in following chapters, taxes can be used by government to control price increases and unemployment. Tax increases tend to reduce spending and increase unemployment. When spending is reduced, price increases are also lower. The level of taxation has implications for the economy. Taxation changes therefore have to be in tune with economic objectives.

Government tax policy also has to be consistent with a desire for economic development. If it is desirable to see the petroleum industry expand in Canada, it may be necessary to give it a tax break not given to other sectors. If it is desirable to promote the Canadian publishing industry, the sales tax on books could be reduced or eliminated. Government has certain objectives for the economy, and taxation policy should be consistent with these objectives.

Government tax policy can also be used to influence the allocation of resources. If government does not want consumers to purchase air conditioners for automobiles, then it can put an excise tax on this product. If government would like consumers to drink Canadian wine as opposed to imported wine, the excise tax policy could reflect this objective. The tax on imported wine could be increased, while the tax on domestic wine could be eliminated or reduced.

REVIEW

4.8 What is the difference between vertical equity and horizontal equity?

4.9 For what type of taxes is the benefits-received approach most appropriate?

4.10 What is the difference between a progressive and a regressive tax?

Marginal Tax Rates

One of the most important aspects of a progressive income tax system is that of **marginal tax rates** (rates that define the percentage of any additional income that is paid in taxes). The word "marginal" is used regularly in the study of economics and means extra or additional. The marginal tax rate is the extra income tax paid in relation to an increase in income. An example will best serve our purpose here. The following table outlines a hypothetical progressive income tax structure.

TAXABLE INCOME	TAX RATE (PERCENT)	TAXES PAID	MARGINAL TAX RATE (PERCENT)
$10 000	10	$1 000	
			25
$15 000	15	$2 250	
			35
$20 000	20	$4 000	

In the above example, an individual earning $10 000 per year would pay $1000 in tax for that year. If that individual's income increased to $15 000 per year, $2250 would be paid in taxes. The individual's income, which increased by $5000, resulted in an increase in taxes paid of $1250. Twenty-five percent of the increase in income was paid in taxes. This is the marginal tax rate. For an increase in income from $15 000 to $20 000, an additional $1750 is paid in taxes. This represents a marginal tax rate of 35 percent.

How is it possible to have a marginal tax rate of 35 percent when someone is only in a 20-percent tax bracket? The answer is that when your income increases from $15 000 to $20 000, the 20-percent tax rate applies not only to the increase in income, but also to the $15 000 that you were already earning. You end up paying extra taxes on the money that you earned prior to your increase in income.

Combined (federal and provincial) marginal tax rates for personal income tax for selected taxable incomes are shown below by province for the year 2002.

	COMBINED MARGINAL TAX RATES % FOR MINIMUM NET INCOMES OF		
	$10 000	$50 000	$100 000
Newfoundland and Labrador	24.7	38.2	45.6
Prince Edward Island	14.9	35.8	44.4
Nova Scotia	14.9	37.0	44.3
New Brunswick	14.9	36.8	42.5
Quebec	27.1	38.4	45.7
Ontario	14.9	31.2	43.4
Manitoba	26.0	37.4	43.4
Saskatchewan	25.4	35.3	41.5
Alberta	14.9	32.0	36.0
British Columbia	20.5	31.2	40.7
Yukon	—	31.7	38.0
Northwest Territories	—	31.9	37.7
Nunavut	—	29.0	35.0

SOURCE: Karin Treff and David B. Perry, *Finances of the Nation 2002* (Toronto: Canadian Tax Foundation, 2003), p. 3:21.

For a net income of $10 000 per year, marginal tax rates range from 14.9 percent in several provinces to 27.1 percent in Quebec. For a net income of $100 000, marginal tax rates range from 35.0 percent in Nunavut to 45.7 percent in Quebec.

Questions

1. Calculate the marginal tax rates from the following example.

Taxable Income	Tax rate (percent)
$20 000	25
$30 000	30
$40 000	35

2. Under a progressive income tax structure, what effect may marginal tax rates have on an

individual's willingness to take on a second job or to work overtime?

3. What is the marginal tax rate under a proportional income tax structure?

4. As an aid to understanding marginal tax rates, obtain a copy of the general tax guide from Canada Customs and Revenue Agency. Refer to the tax tables at the back of the guide and calculate a couple of marginal tax rates.

5. Using the information provided, compare the marginal and average tax rates for the provinces. If you were the minister of finance, how would you establish tax rates for the various income levels?

interactive graphics

Federal/Provincial Financial Arrangements

Canada's system of government divides responsibilities among the federal and provincial levels of government. The authors of the BNA Act could not foresee some of the problems that these divided jurisdictions would create. Shortly after the act came into effect, the provinces complained that their revenue sources were inadequate. The federal government then agreed to make annual payments to the provinces based on their population.

There have always been differences in provincial abilities to collect tax revenue. Some provinces have a good tax base, while others are not so fortunate. Ontario, British Columbia, and Alberta have high per-capita incomes and a good industrial base. Prince Edward Island and Newfoundland and Labrador, however, have lower per-capita incomes and less-diversified economies. It is more difficult for the latter provinces to provide the same level of public service as the others.

The federal government, also in need of revenue, introduced additional taxes. A major characteristic of the Canadian taxation scene is the overlapping of taxes. Both levels of government have personal and corporate income taxes, as well as various excise taxes. This leads to duplication in administration as well as to the possibility of high tax rates.

The present system may also lead to a conflict in taxation policies. One level of government may pursue a policy of increasing taxes, while the other level of government may introduce completely opposite measures. For example, in order to stimulate the economy, the federal government may reduce personal income taxes, while the provinces are increasing taxes in order to finance new programs.

These difficulties have led to the signing of several federal/provincial taxation arrangements. The first was introduced during the Second World War, and provided for the provinces to rent their personal and corporation tax powers to the federal government. In return, the provinces received annual rental payments. The tax rental agreements, which lasted from 1941 to 1957, were replaced by tax-sharing arrangements. The major change introduced into the new agreement was that the provinces would receive a percentage of the revenue collected by the federal government instead of a lump-sum payment.

A variety of financial arrangements have existed between the two levels of government. The present system is referred to as *established program financing*. This arrangement centres on hospital insurance, medicare, and post-secondary education. Under established program financing, the federal government gives a province a percentage of personal and corporate income tax revenue plus a cash payment.

The federal government also makes equalization and stabilization payments to some provinces. **Equalization payments** are payments to provinces to ensure that the province can provide a reasonable level of public services without resorting to extremely high levels of taxation in order to get the money for these services. They are unconditional grants given to some of the provinces. In 2000–2001, the Department of Finance determined that all provinces needed minimum revenues of $5869 per person to pay for public services.

Stabilization payments are meant to ensure that provincial taxation revenues do not decline substantially from one year to the next. The federal government also provides statutory subsidies to the provinces.

Federal transfers as a percentage of provincial government revenue are shown in Table 4.9.

Equalization payments are payments to provinces to ensure that the province can provide a reasonable level of public services without resorting to extremely high levels of taxation in order to get the money for these services.

Stabilization payments are meant to ensure that provincial taxation revenues do not decline substantially from one year to the next.

Table 4.9 *Federal transfers as a percentage of provincial/
territorial revenue, fiscal year ending March 31, 2003*

	FEDERAL TRANSFERS		PROVINCIAL/ TERRITORIAL REVENUE FROM OWN SOURCES
	GENERAL PURPOSE	SPECIFIC PURPOSE	
Newfoundland and Labrador	32.9	9.7	57.4
Prince Edward Island	26.3	11.5	62.1
Nova Scotia	24.9	11.2	63.9
New Brunswick	24.8	14.1	61.1
Quebec	11.1	6.7	82.2
Ontario	—	12.3	87.7
Manitoba	21.3	12.7	66.0
Saskatchewan	8.7	12.6	78.6
Alberta	—	7.1	92.9
British Columbia	—	12.2	87.8
Yukon	65.4	4.1	30.5
Northwest Territories	45.2	6.4	48.4
Nunavut	84.9	6.6	8.5

SOURCE: Provincial budgets for 2000–1 in Karin Treff and David B. Perry, *Finances of the Nation 2002* (Toronto: Canadian Tax Foundation, 2003), p. 8:5.

EVERYDAY ECONOMICS 4.4

Equalization: Helping Hand or Welfare Trap?

Equalization payments are enshrined in the Canadian Constitution. Section 36(2) of the Charter of Rights and Freedoms states that

Parliament and the Government of Canada are committed to the principle of making equalization payments to ensure that provincial governments have sufficient revenues to provide reasonably comparable levels of public service at reasonably comparable levels of taxation.

The right to equalization payments is written into the Constitution, but the method of calculating the payment is not. The formula used to calculate the size of the payment can be altered.

Equalization payments were introduced in 1957. The intention was to bring the per-capita tax revenues of all provinces up to the levels of Ontario and British Columbia, the two wealthiest provinces. The per-capita tax revenue in each province had to be at least equal to the average of the ten provinces. Later the definition of the national average was changed to be the average of five designated provinces: Quebec, Ontario, Saskatchewan, Manitoba, and British Columbia. All provinces except Ontario have received equalization payments in the past. In most years, equalization payments are made to all provinces except Ontario, Alberta, and British Columbia.

In spite of the good intentions attached to equalization payments, some analysts question their long-term impact on the recipient provinces. If a province's revenue from its own sources increases, the size of the equalization payment is reduced. Does this discourage provinces from making changes to their economies? Since equalization payments make up a large portion of the total government revenue in some provinces (e.g., in Newfoundland and Labrador it is about 33 percent), provinces may not want to risk losing these funds.

Some researchers argue that provinces in receipt of equalization payments have higher tax rates and thus discourage outside investment. Higher tax rates in recipient provinces also encourage entrepreneurs to move to provinces with lower tax rates. The current formula for establishing the size of the equalization payment is based on tax revenue, not tax rates. Thus, income tax rates, capital taxes, retail sales taxes, and fuel taxes are all higher in the recipient provinces. Other researchers argue that the receipt of equalization money allows a province to maintain a larger than needed bureaucracy. Are politicians and bureaucrats more likely to spend money wisely when it has been received from their constituents rather than from somewhere else?

Equalization payments are not the only source of money transfer between the provinces. Money is redistributed among the provinces through Canada Health and Social Transfers (CHST), and through Employment Insurance (EI). The latter program pays money to individuals and not to governments.

Questions

1. In your opinion, should equalization payments be part of the Canadian Constitution?
2. The original proposal to transfer wealth among provinces suggested that the transfers be to individuals in the recipient provinces, not governments. How would such a proposal work?
3. Can you suggest an alternative way to redistribute money in Canada? Or, should we redistribute money among provinces?

Government Borrowing

The major alternative to taxation as a source of government revenue is borrowing. Paying taxes is compulsory, whereas lending money to the various governments in Canada is voluntary. All levels of government in Canada borrow money in order to pay for expenditures. Government borrowing is done by selling various types of securities to the public. These securities can be of varying maturities, ranging from a couple of months in the case of treasury bills (see Chapter 7) to longer-term government bonds. In 2001, the federal government borrowed $89 billion through treasury bills and $295 billion through marketable bonds.

Who buys Canadian government securities? Canadian chartered banks are the biggest buyers of new government bonds. Other buyers include pension funds, mutual funds, individual Canadians, foreigners, life insurance companies, provincial governments, other financial institutions, and the Bank of Canada. The share of government bonds purchased by the Bank of Canada has decreased in recent years because the Bank of Canada wants to restrict the growth of the money supply. A discussion of Bank of

Canada purchases of government bonds appears in Chapter 7. Foreign borrowings amounted to $33 billion in 2001.

The trends in government borrowing are displayed in Figure 4.1. **Gross public debt** refers to unmatured bonds, treasury bills, and notes as well as other liabilities including annuity insurance, pension accounts, and other special accounts. **Net debt** is gross debt minus recorded assets. Figure 4.1 shows the net debt as a percentage of gross domestic product (GDP) for the years from 1981 to 2001. The term **gross domestic product (GDP)**, discussed more fully in Chapter 5, represents the value of all the goods and services produced in Canada in a given year. In 1995 and 1996, gross public debt represented the entire amount of goods and services produced in Canada in those years. Canadian governments owed an amount of money almost equivalent to the amount of income earned by all Canadians in those years. Net debt as a percentage of GDP declined from 1947 to 1975; from 1975 on net debt continued to increase as a percentage of GDP, reaching a peak in 1996 of 102.1 percent of GDP. Thereafter, net debt as a percentage of GDP started to decline.

The federal government's debt represents the largest government debt in Canada. The federal government's unmatured debt was $16.97 billion in

Gross public debt is the combination of unmatured bonds, treasury bills, and notes as well as other liabilities.

Net debt is gross debt minus recorded assets.

Gross domestic product (GDP) is the value of all goods and services produced in a country in a given year.

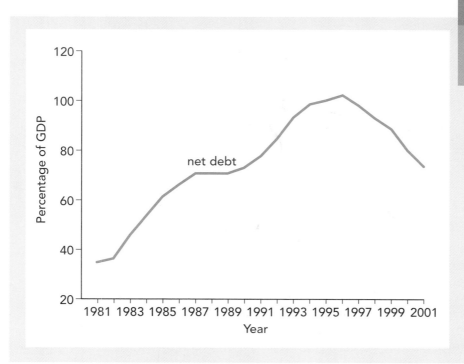

Figure 4.1

Total government net debt as a percentage of GDP, Canada, 1981–2001

SOURCE: Karin Treff and David B. Perry, *Finances of the Nation 2002* (Toronto: Canadian Tax Foundation, 2003), p. 5.

1961–62. It increased steadily until 1996–97, when it reached $476.85 billion. In 1998, the federal government started to reduce the amount of unmatured debt, and by 2001 the amount of unmatured debt had fallen to $446.40 billion.

The major source of provincial government borrowing has been in the form of bonds and debentures issued to the general public and to the Canada Pension Plan Investment Fund. The second source of borrowing is from non-residents of Canada. Since provinces cannot borrow from the Bank of Canada, much of their borrowing has to be done from individuals outside the country. Local governments are generally limited to borrowing only for capital expenditures, and they borrow through the sale of debentures to banks, trust and insurance companies, private lenders, and government agencies.

Why does government borrow money rather than collect it through taxes? The answer to this question lies mainly in the nature of the political process. Voters can see how much government is costing them when paying taxes. They have no idea, however, of what borrowing is undertaken and how much the borrowing costs, although this information is available. Most citizens are not as concerned about high levels of government borrowing as they are about high levels of taxation, which has a more direct impact on them as individuals. Through borrowing, government can carry on programs that would be possible only with excessively high levels of taxation.

The government may also borrow money for large *capital expenditures* such as electric power stations and airports. These projects are too costly to be paid for out of current tax revenue. Since the power station and the airport will be in operation for a number of years, they can be financed over a number of years through borrowing.

EVERYDAY ECONOMICS 4.5

G-20

On September 25, 1999, a new international forum was created for finance ministers and central bankers representing 19 countries, the European Union, and the Bretton Woods Institutions (i.e., the International Monetary Fund and the World Bank). This forum is referred to as the Group of Twenty (G-20). Its mandate is to promote discussion and review policy issues with respect to international financial stability. Member countries are Argentina, Australia, Brazil, Canada, China, France, Germany, India, Indonesia, Italy, Japan, Korea, Mexico, Russia, Saudi Arabia, South Africa, Turkey, the United Kingdom, the United States, and the European Union. Representatives from the

International Monetary Fund and the World Bank will participate in the discussions. The first chairman of the forum was Paul Martin, Canada's minister of finance at that time. The G-20 does not have a permanent secretariat. The country of the chairman (initially Canada) will provide administrative support to the forum. Meetings are to be held annually.

Canada is a member of the group of industrialized countries referred to as the G-7, which meets regularly to discuss international economic issues. Emerging economies were not represented in the G-7, so it was deemed necessary to expand the consultation group to include them, especially since events like the Asian financial crisis of the 1990s impacted financial markets in the developed countries as well as in the less-developed countries.

One issue the G-20 is addressing is that of a nation's external debt. The size and composition of the external debt can influence the ability of a country to weather international financial crises. Excessive debt can result in an international lack of confidence in a country's ability to pay off the debt. The lack of confidence may manifest itself in an unwillingness of lenders to lend to countries with excessive debt levels, or to lend to them only at relatively high interest rates. The repayment schedule of the debt is also important because a country may be faced with heavy debt payments within a relatively short period of time. The G-20 is hoping to assist countries with their debt management so that they do not suffer a financial crisis as a result of an international event. Countries are being encouraged not to build up an excessive amount of short-term debt in relation to their foreign-exchange reserves.

What is being done to assist with debt management? Lines of credit are being set up with private lenders to provide an alternate source of borrowing, should a country's regular source of borrowed funds dry up. Bonds are also being issued that tie debt repayment to variables that influence a country's ability to pay, such as the prices of a country's exports. The G-20 countries are also concerned about excessive debt in the private sector. There are proposals to strengthen the financial sector's regulation and supervision. If countries can develop an efficient domestic capital market, there will be less need to borrow externally. It is also proposed that governments not provide guarantees for foreign borrowing by private-sector firms. Topics under consideration for the G-20 change constantly. Among the topics for the 2003 meetings in Mexico are financing for developing countries and combatting terrorist financing.

Questions

1. Countries are discouraged from amassing a large amount of external debt mainly because of fluctuations in foreign-exchange rates. How would a nation's debt be affected by a decline in the foreign-exchange value of its currency?
2. Why do nations borrow from individuals and institutions in foreign countries?
3. The G-20 has no secretariat to enforce group decisions; it is primarily a discussion forum. How much influence will these discussions have on the policies of a participating nation?

Summary

Because Canadians are governed by a federalist system of government, more than one level of government exerts influence over the day-to-day lives of individuals. The powers of the federal and provincial government are outlined in Canada's constitution. The federal government was awarded the major responsibilities given to government at the time of Confederation,

1867. Along with these responsibilities, the federal government was given unlimited taxing power. The provinces were awarded lesser responsibilities and were given the authority to collect only direct taxes.

In terms of expenditure, the federal government spends about 30 percent of its budget on social services such as employment insurance and old age pensions. The second largest expenditure item is interest and service charges on the public debt. The major component of provincial government spending is health care, followed by education. The major components of municipal government spending are transportation and communications.

Both the federal and provincial governments obtain revenue from a variety of taxes. The personal income tax, levied by both governments, is the major source of tax revenue. Each level of government also imposes corporate income taxes and excise taxes.

A main objective of any tax is that it be equitable or fair. This objective of tax equity is not in dispute; however, the definition of an equitable tax is still in question. It is agreed that all individuals in similar circumstances should pay the same amount of money in taxes. It is not agreed, however, how individuals in different circumstances should be treated. One approach is to tax individuals on the basis of the benefits that they receive from government programs. For some programs, such as highways and airports, the benefits-received approach to tax equity is acceptable. It is not acceptable for other programs, particularly those in the social-services area.

The ability-to-pay principle is the alternative approach to vertical equity. It proposes taxing people on their ability to pay taxes. The measure of ability to pay could be income, wealth, or expenditure. The level of taxation could be on a progressive, proportional, or regressive basis. Canada's income tax is on a progressive basis: those with a higher income pay a higher percentage of their income in taxes.

Questions for Review and Discussion

1. Do you think that the federal government should be responsible for hospitals so that the same level of medical care is provided in each province? Discuss.
2. The biggest area of federal government spending is social services. Should the federal government turn over some social services to the private sector in order to reduce the size of the federal debt?
3. In 1867 the responsibilities deemed to be most important were given to the federal government. Are those responsibilities the most important today in terms of government spending?

4. Explain the differences between the Wagner and Peacock-Wiseman hypotheses regarding government spending.

5. Government involvement in the Canadian economy has increased substantially in the last 20 years. Do any of the reasons discussed in this chapter apply to this growth in government spending?

6. In Ontario and in the western provinces, the GST is calculated on the retail price. In Quebec and the eastern provinces, the GST is calculated on the retail price plus the PST. What difference do these two approaches have on GST revenue?

7. The town of Whitby, Ontario wants minor sports organizations to pay increased fees for the use of town baseball diamonds and soccer fields. Is this an example of the benefits-received approach to taxation? Are the recipients of the benefits easily identified in this situation?

8. In your opinion, should personal income tax rates be applied to individual or to family income? In other words, should all family members have their income lumped together for taxation purposes? Discuss.

9. The main objective behind Canada's personal income tax is that it be equitable or fair. What problems would arise if many individuals believed the current personal income tax system to be unfair?

10. Which do you believe is the most equitable income tax structure for Canada: progressive, proportional, or regressive? Explain.

11. In your opinion, what are the disadvantages of a proportional income tax system?

12. Canada has opted for a progressive income tax system as the most equitable approach to income taxation. Can you think of any negative aspects of a progressive income tax system?

13. Having corporations pay income tax does not make sense. Corporation profits should be taxed only when paid out to individuals as dividends. Discuss these statements.

14. Define marginal tax rates. Make up your own numerical example to show how marginal tax rates affect taxes paid under a progressive tax system when an individual's income increases.

15. Could higher marginal tax rates in one province cause its citizens to move to another province? To another country?

16. Explain why individuals with higher marginal tax rates are more likely to hire the services of a professional tax adviser.

17. The federal government has changed some tax deductions to tax credits. Research the difference between a tax deduction and a tax credit. Explain why tax deductions benefit high income earners more than low income earners. How does a switch to tax credits help correct this inequity?

18. The following taxable incomes and corresponding taxes were selected from the *1994 Income Tax Guide.* Calculate the marginal tax rate for a) an increase in income from $20 000 to $25 000; and b) an increase in income from $45 000 to $50 000.

TAXABLE INCOME	FEDERAL TAX	FEDERAL SIN TAX	PROVINCIAL TAX
$20 000	$3 401	$102	$1972.60
$25 000	$4 251	$128	$2465.60
$45 000	$9 038	$271	$5242.60
$50 000	$10 338	$310	$6095.90

Suggested Reading

Allan, Charles M. *The Theory of Taxation.* Middlesex: Penguin Books, 1971. This 200-page book provides a good discussion of the benefits-received and ability-to-pay approaches to taxation.

Selected Websites

www.ctf.ca The website for the Canadian Tax Foundation. *Finances of the Nation 2002* can be obtained on this website.

www.fin.gc.ca The website for the federal department of finance.

www.publicdebt.treas.gov/bpd/bpdfaq.htm This site contains answers to frequently asked questions about public debt. While the site is U.S.–based, the concepts are relevant to Canada. The site is maintained by the Bureau of the Public Debt and provides access to data on the debt as well.

www.brillig.com/debt_clock A daily update on the size of the U.S. debt.

www.hacienda.gob.mx/g20-2003 The official webpage for the G-20.

www.bondcan.com This site has links to the Bank of Canada, Statistics Canada, and federal and provincial finance departments. A good glossary of financial terms is also available.

CHAPTER 5

Economic Indicators

Key Terms

macroeconomics
gross domestic product (GDP)
Labour Force Survey
participation rate
employment rate
unemployment rate
underemployment
hidden unemployed
demand-deficient unemployment
frictional unemployment
seasonal unemployment
structural unemployment
insurance-induced unemployment
natural rate of unemployment
Consumer Price Index
demand-pull inflation
cost-push inflation
hyperinflation
National Accounts
circular flow of money
investment
net domestic product
personal income
personal disposable income
real GDP

Chapter Objectives

After successfully completing this chapter, you will be able to:

- define the participation rate and the unemployment rate as they appear in the Labour Force Survey
- understand exactly what the unemployment rate measures
- explain the five types of unemployment
- describe the composition of the Consumer Price Index
- explain the causes of inflation
- relate the problems of inflation to the Canadian economy
- calculate items in the National Accounts
- explain why the level of GDP cannot be associated with social welfare

Core Concept Building

This chapter begins a discussion of macroeconomics by focusing on three concerns for any country: unemployment, price increases, and the level of business activity. These issues are dealt with extensively in Chapters 6, 7, and 8.

BIGGER MAY NOT BE BETTER

Economists spend much time measuring and analyzing economic growth. The main indicator of growth used around the world is gross domestic product (GDP). A growing economy is associated with an improved standard of living. A growing economy provides jobs. Economic growth is measured by the amount of spending being undertaken in the economy. That is, more spending is associated with a growing economy.

All spending is included when measuring economic growth. Governments, businesses, and consumers spend money. Foreigners also buy Canadian products. The biggest component of spending is consumption, or consumer spending. Purchasing a hamburger or a pizza is consumption. Buying a new car is consumption. Buying new clothes is consumption.

If we are buying more and the economy is growing, is our standard of living improving? Can economic growth be "bad" for us? We need to ask if more consumption is positive. Environmentalists may consider growth to be bad. They might argue that more spending leads to more pollution and to a depletion of our natural resources, and that spending money on pesticides and herbicides may eventually prove to be harmful to our health. Economic growth may have negative consequences for others. Some individuals who prefer life in a small town may not welcome a housing boom in their town in spite of the jobs and increases in income that go along with it. Is more traffic congestion an improvement in our standard of living?

All consumer spending is listed as consumption, yet not all consumer spending is pleasurable. Spending more on car insurance, or car repairs, or a lawyer to represent you in traffic court may not be pleasurable but it increases consumption and is associated with growth. Money that one spends on burning gasoline while waiting on the expressway in a traffic jam results in an increase in consumption. Is that activity pleasurable? People consume food, alcohol, and tobacco and then spend money in an effort to stop spending money on these items. Not all spending leads to an increase in our well-being.

It is recognized that not all increases in GDP are associated with increases in the standard of living. One attempt to improve on an economic growth measurement related more to our standard of living is the genuine progress indicator (GPI). The GPI adds the contributions of housework and volunteer work to GDP. It subtracts such factors as crime, family breakdown, and pollution from GDP in an attempt to more accurately reflect economic progress.

More information on the shortcomings of our current measure of growth can be found at the following website: **www.rprogress.org/projects/gpi/**

Definition of Macroeconomics

Macroeconomics is the area of economics concerned with the overall view of an economy, rather than with individual markets.

Macroeconomics is the area of economic analysis concerned with the overall view of an economy rather than with individual markets. In Canada, macroeconomics analyzes the effects of all markets acting together. The issues that will be important in this section include those affecting all Canadians: employment, inflation, and the level of business activity.

This chapter reviews some of the sources of information that are available to assist our understanding of Canadian macroeconomic issues. These are the Labour Force Survey, the Consumer Price Index, and the National Accounts. All three sources are tracked by Statistics Canada.

Employment and Unemployment

The Labour Force Survey measures the number of employed and unemployed persons in Canada on a monthly basis. An employed person is one who had a job during the reference month for the survey. An unemployed person is one who did not have a job but looked for a job. Together the employed and the unemployed make up the labour force. The employment rate measures the number of employed as a percentage of the population. The unemployment rate measures the unemployed as a percentage of the labour force.

Unemployed individuals are a concern for Canada. If people are not working, then Canada is not using its resources efficiently. It means that Canada is producing a quantity of goods and services that falls inside its production-possibilities curve. The Labour Force Survey thus provides an indication of our underutilized resources.

Unemployment is also a concern on an individual basis. When a worker is unemployed his or her income is reduced, making it more difficult to support himself or herself or a family. People also like to feel that they are contributing to their society. Unemployment removes this sense of satisfaction. If high levels of unemployment persist, social unrest can result.

Inflation

The Consumer Price Index (CPI) measures the level of change in retail prices in Canada each month. Inflation means an increase in the general level of retail prices. Therefore, the Consumer Price Index is regarded as a measure of inflation. The problems of inflation are many and affect different individuals in different ways. Price increases hurt those persons who are on fixed incomes—for example pensioners, who have no other means of obtaining income. Rising prices favour people who have borrowed money and do not favour those who have lent money. The money that is paid back at a future date after a period of rising prices will buy fewer goods and services than the amount that was initially borrowed could have bought. The borrower is, therefore, in an advantageous situation. Canada's position in world markets is also hurt by increasing prices. If products made in Canada become too expensive, foreign buyers will look elsewhere. Canada is a country that relies heavily on foreign trade, and remaining competitive in foreign markets is a major concern.

Another disadvantage of inflation is that the rate of price increases may get higher and higher, and become more difficult to control. Rapidly rising prices destroy the purchasing power of incomes. This forces workers to demand higher wages in order to keep up with the cost of living. If companies are forced to pay higher wages, they will likely raise the price of their product. This could set off another round of *wage and price increases.* If price increases continue for any period of time, an *inflationary psychology* may develop in the population. People begin to react as if they expect prices to continue to rise. They spend now, before the prices go even higher. The increased demand puts further upward pressure on prices. As prices increase, the purchasing power of money decreases, and if price increases are not constrained the value of the currency is destroyed.

The presence of inflation in the economy also creates uncertainty about the future. The rate of inflation is rarely predictable. Without a degree of predictability about future prices, it is difficult to plan. In order to protect themselves from rising prices, households and businesses engage in speculative activity (such as buying real estate with the expectation that prices will rise) rather than becoming engaged in more productive endeavours (such as providing money for capital purchases that would benefit the economy). Periods of inflation are accompanied by rising interest rates, because savers want to be compensated for the uncertainty surrounding future rates of inflation.

Level of Business Activity

The National Accounts measure the overall level of business activity in Canada. The most common statistic in the National Accounts is **gross domestic product (GDP)**. This is a measure of the market value of final goods and services produced in Canada in a given period of time. GDP figures are produced on both a quarterly and an annual basis. "Final" goods and services are those purchased by their final user as finished, in contrast to those goods that are used as "inputs" in the production of other goods.

Why is it necessary to measure the level of business activity? The information tabulated in the National Accounts gives an indication of the *standard of living* in Canada. If the amount of goods and services produced is constantly increasing, then Canadian incomes are rising. Increases in incomes are associated with improvements in living standards.

Increases in the statistical measure of gross domestic product and the other tabulations of the National Accounts are, however, not synonymous with improved living standards. It is necessary to relate increases in GDP to increases in our population. Our standard of living will be improving only

> Gross domestic product (GDP) **represents the value of all final goods and services produced in a country in a given year.**

as long as GDP is increasing at a faster rate than the population. Also, GDP increases have to be compared to price increases. The real value of any increase in GDP may be eroded by rapidly rising prices.

The information available in the National Accounts has more uses than simply defining our standard of living. Businesses use the information for *forecasting market conditions* and for making decisions. If the forecast is that the level of business activity will decline, many businesses can expect a slump in sales and need to manage their affairs accordingly. Governments use GDP and other National Accounts figures to judge the success of their various programs. Many government programs are aimed at stimulating business activity and the success of the program is measured in terms of the changes in such tabulations as gross domestic product.

The terms *recession* and *depression* are defined by reference to changes in GDP. A recession is described as a drop in economic activity whereby GDP, adjusted for price increases, declines for two successive quarters. A depression is a more exaggerated slowdown in economic activity.

In this chapter, we will discuss the Labour Force Survey, the Consumer Price Index, and the National Accounts separately. In our economy, however, GDP, employment, and price level are closely related. For example, if the level of GDP is falling, unemployment is likely to be increasing. When business sales are low, companies will not need as many employees. The level of business activity may also affect prices. When activity is low, prices may fall as a result of special clearance sales and discounts. When business activity is great, prices may rise due to the increased demand for goods and services.

The Labour Force Survey

The **Labour Force Survey** is compiled monthly and is based on a survey of approximately 50 000 households across Canada. The survey excludes residents of the Yukon, Nunavut, and the Northwest Territories, persons living on Indian reserves, inmates of institutions, and full-time members of the armed forces. It was first introduced in Canada in 1945 in order to obtain more accurate information about unemployed persons. In January 1976, a revised survey was introduced in order to collect more data. The Labour Force Survey is a compilation of these data concerning the composition and characteristics of the various labour-force groups.

Selected households remain on the survey for six months, with one-sixth of the households being replaced each month. The interviewer gathers information on each member of the household 15 years of age and

The Labour Force Survey **provides a monthly measure of the number of unemployed in Canada. This measure provides an indication of the country's economic condition.**

over, in order to determine labour-force behaviour during a reference week. Each individual in the survey population is put into one of three categories based on work-related activities during the reference week. These categories are:

Employed: Any person who did any work for pay or profit during the reference week. Also included are unpaid family workers in a family farm or business. This category includes individuals who were on vacation, on strike, or on sick leave during the reference week.

Unemployed: Any person who, during the reference week, was without work, had actively looked for work in the last four weeks, and was available for work. An unemployed person has an immediate interest in finding work, and would be available if suitable work were found. Also unemployed are those who are not actively seeking work but who are on temporary layoff and those who will have a new job to start in the next four weeks.

Not in labour force: Any person who, during the reference week of the survey, was without work, yet not looking for work.

A number of definitions are derived from this categorization of the population. The labour force is defined as the number of persons who are either employed or unemployed. In other words, the labour force is comprised of individuals who are working or looking for work. Those individuals not in the labour force are neither working nor looking for work, and include students, retired persons, and homemakers (the Labour Force Survey does not include work done around the house in "work").

The **participation rate** is defined as the percentage of those people surveyed who are in the labour force. It is a measure of the proportion of the working-age population that is employed or seeking work. The calculation of the participation rate is shown in the formula below, and data on Canada's participation rates are shown in Tables 5.1 and 5.2.

The percentage of the population that is employed or actively seeking employment makes up the participation rate.

$$\text{participation rate} = \frac{\text{labour force}}{\text{population (15 years +)}}$$

Table 5.1 *Participation rates, employment rates, and unemployment rates by age and sex, Canada, 2002*

	PARTICIPATION RATE (%)	EMPLOYMENT RATE (%)	UNEMPLOYMENT RATE(%)
Both sexes	66.9	61.8	7.7
15–24 years	66.3	57.3	13.6
25–44 years	86.8	80.8	7.0
45–64 years	71.7	67.6	5.8
65 years+	6.7	6.5	3.1
Men	73.3	67.4	8.1
15–24 years	67.7	57.3	15.3
25–44 years	92.4	85.7	7.3
45–64 years	79.4	74.6	6.1
65 years+	10.5	10.2	2.9
Women	60.7	56.4	7.1
15–24 years	64.9	57.2	11.8
25–44 years	81.2	75.8	6.7
45–64 years	64.2	60.7	5.5
65 years+	3.7	3.6	3.6

SOURCE: Adapted from the Statistics Canada CANSIM database, Table 282-0002.

Table 5.2 *Participation rates, employment rates, and unemployment rates by province, Canada, 2002*

	PARTICIPATION RATE (%)	EMPLOYMENT RATE (%)	UNEMPLOYMENT RATE(%)
Newfoundland and Labrador	58.6	48.7	16.9
Prince Edward Island	68.2	60.0	12.1
Nova Scotia	62.8	56.7	9.7
New Brunswick	63.5	56.9	10.4
Quebec	65.1	59.5	8.6
Ontario	67.8	63.0	7.1
Manitoba	69.2	65.6	5.2
Saskatchewan	67.3	63.5	5.7
Alberta	73.0	69.1	5.3
British Columbia	64.9	59.4	8.5
Canada	66.9	61.8	7.7

SOURCE: Adapted from the Statistics Canada CANSIM database, Table 282-0002.

As shown in the tables, the participation rate for Canada was 66.9 percent in 2002. There are some definite differences in the rate when analyzed by sex, age, and province. Men have traditionally had a higher participation rate than women. Men 25–44 years of age and over have the highest participation rate (92.4 percent), and women 65 years and over the lowest (3.7 percent). Provincial participation rates range from a high of 73.0 percent in Alberta to a low of 58.6 percent in Newfoundland and Labrador. The long-term trend in participation rates has been stable for middle-aged men, declining for younger and older persons, and increasing for women.

These trends are influenced by several variables, which include family size and income, level of education, and general economic conditions. For example, the presence of improved educational opportunities has resulted in a lowering of the participation rate for younger individuals. People are staying in school longer. The declining participation rate of older workers can, in part, be attributed to the higher levels of income and the more lucrative social benefits available. Elderly individuals can more easily afford to retire from the labour force at an earlier age. The state of the economy can also influence participation rates. If unemployment is high, other family members may enter the labour force to look for a job, while some individuals may become discouraged about job prospects and leave the labour force. The participation rate for men has been on the decline. As mentioned above, the presence of improved educational opportunities has resulted in more young men staying in school. The high unemployment rate for young men, especially for those individuals without a high-school diploma, has encouraged many men to return to school.

Men are retiring earlier. During the late 1970s and mid 1980s the median retirement age was close to 65 years. By 2000, the median age for those retiring had dropped to 61.0 years. The Canada Pension Plan allows individuals to retire at 60 years of age. Company pension plans have lowered the age at which an individual can retire with a full pension. Unfortunately, in recent years some men have not retired voluntarily. The downsizing of companies during the 1990s forced some men to accept early retirement arrangements. Men are also living longer. The aging of the male population lowers the participation rate, as older men are less likely to be in the labour force.

Two additional reasons have been given for the decline in the male participation rate. Some men have become discouraged about the lack of job prospects and have withdrawn from the labour force. Others are staying home to raise a family. Though the number of families with stay-at-home parents has fallen overall, 110 700 Canadian men identified themselves as stay-at-home dads in 2002.

The most noticeable trend in participation rates has been the increase in the participation of women. In 1953, the participation rate for women was approximately 25 percent, and by 1990 was approaching 60 percent. In 2002, 46 percent of the labour force was female, compared to 35 percent in 1971. What factors accounted for this increase? Reasons for the higher labour-force participation of women include the following: a higher level of education among women; a higher opportunity cost of not working; the fact that family sizes are getting smaller; and the advances in household technology that have reduced the time necessary to complete household chores. There has also been an increase in the number of white-collar and part-time jobs that are more attractive to women. Economic and financial conditions have also made it necessary for some women to seek employment. Rising prices and unemployment among other family members have forced women to work outside of the home in order to supplement the family income. Attitudes about women's roles have been changing, as is evident in women's increased involvement in the workforce.

Greater government activity in the labour market has improved the attractiveness of employment for women. This government involvement includes the passage of equal-pay and affirmative-action legislation, maternity-leave provisions, and changes to employment insurance. The latter changes have made it easier for people to receive employment-insurance benefits when they are out of a job. There is also increased pressure on government to provide more subsidized daycare. Changes in legislation may have made it easier for women to enter the labour force, yet these changes would not likely have occurred without the increased labour-force participation of women that was already taking place. Greater participation of women in the labour force has also brought changes in the negotiating of collective agreements between unions and management. Changes have been negotiated in pension plans, maternity-leave provisions, and in other conditions of employment.

In addition to the participation rate, the Labour Force Survey allows Statistics Canada to calculate the **employment rate,** or the employment-to-population ratio. In 2002, the employment rate was 61.8 percent. The rate varied by province (refer to Table 5.2), ranging from a low in Newfoundland and Labrador (48.7 percent) to a high in Alberta (69.1 percent).

The employment rate **is the employment-to-population ratio.**

Employment in Canada has been on the increase since the end of the Second World War. Shortly after the war approximately 5 million Canadians were employed; by the year 2002, this number had risen to about 17 million. The growth in employment has not, however, been steady. A growth rate in employment of 3.6 percent in the 1970s dropped to 1.8 percent in the 1980s and to only 1 percent in the 1990s.

Part of the increase in employment is due to the increase in the number of working-age people. Canada's population has increased since the Second World War. However, the employment numbers have increased at a faster rate than the number of working-age people. The employment rate has been on an upward trend since 1960, mainly because of the increase in the employment of women. It reached a peak in 1989 at 64.2 percent, before falling to just under 60 percent for most of the 1990s. Because of strong economic conditions, the employment rate has increased to more than 61 percent in the first few years of this century.

Canada has experienced many changes in the composition of employment over the last 50 years. The most significant change has been the shift in employment away from goods-producing industries toward service-producing industries. The 2001 Census of Canada indicated that 74.4 percent of individuals in the employed labour force work in the service-producing sector, while 25.6 percent work in the goods-producing sector. In the service-producing sector more jobs are in retail trade than in any other sector of the economy.

There have also been shifts in the occupational composition of Canada's labour force. In 1948, only 10.9 percent of all workers were classified as managerial or professional. By 1998, one-third of all workers were in this category. Conversely, in 1948 more than one-quarter of all workers were employed as agricultural, fishing, logging, and trapping workers (i.e., primary workers). By 1998, the proportion of all workers listed as primary workers had fallen to just over 4 percent. Other changes in employment include the growing importance of part-time and non-permanent work, the trend to multiple jobholding, and the increase in self-employment.

The percentage of the labour force that is not employed yet is seeking employment comprises the unemployment rate.

The **unemployment rate** is defined as the percentage of the labour force that is not working, yet is looking for work. The unemployed are those who were without work but actively looked for work in the last four weeks. To be classified as unemployed, an individual must be available for work. Also classified as unemployed are individuals who are on layoff and available for work even though they may not actively be looking for work. Individuals who are waiting to start a new job but are available for work now are also deemed to be unemployed. The calculation of the unemployment rate is given below and data on the rate are presented in Tables 5.1 and 5.2.

$$\text{unemployment rate} = \frac{\text{unemployed}}{\text{labour force}}$$

As shown in the tables, the unemployment rate also varies by age, sex, and province. The overall unemployment rate for Canada in 2002 was 7.7 percent. There is a significant difference in the unemployment rates when ages are compared. The unemployment rate for those in the 15–24 year age group was 13.6 percent, while for the older age groups it was much lower. On a provincial basis, Manitoba had the lowest unemployment rate in 2002 and Newfoundland and Labrador had the highest.

Figure 5.1 shows the unemployment rates for Canada from 1966 to 2002. The trend over this 33-year period has been for unemployment rates to increase. In 1966, the unemployment rate was only 3.4 percent of the labour force. By 1983, the unemployment rate had reached 11.8 percent. The rate increased in the early 1990s but declined as the decade progressed. The reasons for this trend are varied and include changes in the composition of our labour force, changes in the employment-insurance program, changes in oil prices, changes in technology, and changes in the pattern of world trade. A more detailed discussion of the changes in unemployment rates appears in Chapter 8.

The participation, employment and unemployment rates for 2002 for selected metropolitan areas are presented in Table 5.3. Calgary had the highest participation rate at 75.8 percent, while Chicoutimi-Jonquière had the lowest at 60.0 percent. Calgary also had the highest employment rate while Chicoutimi-Jonquière had the lowest. Edmonton had the lowest unemployment rate at 5.1 percent, while Chicoutimi-Jonquière had the highest unemployment rate at 11.5 percent.

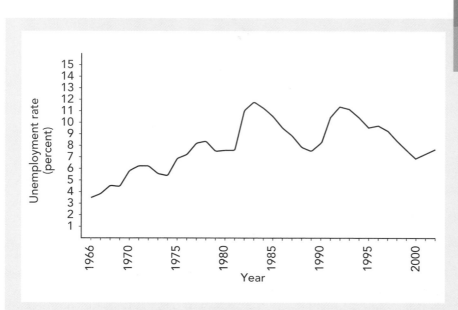

Figure 5.1

Unemployment rates (percent), Canada, 1966–2002

SOURCE: Adapted from the Statistics Canada CANSIM database, Series v2461224 and from the Statistics Canada publication *Historical Statistics of Canada*, Catalogue 11-516, 1983, Series D233.

Table 5.3 *Participation rates, unemployment rates, and employment rates for selected metropolitan areas, 2000*

METROPOLITAN AREA	PARTICIPATION RATE (%)	UNEMPLOYMENT RATE (%)	EMPLOYMENT RATE (%)
St. John's	67.6	8.9	61.6
Halifax	69.9	7.5	64.6
Saint John	66.8	8.2	61.3
Chicoutimi-Jonquière	60.0	11.5	53.1
Québec	66.9	6.3	62.7
Sherbrooke	65.5	7.7	60.4
Trois-Rivières	61.2	9.9	55.1
Montréal	67.4	8.4	61.7
Ottawa-Hull	69.8	7.2	64.7
Oshawa	69.6	6.7	64.9
Toronto	69.9	7.4	64.8
Hamilton	66.8	6.8	62.3
St. Catharines–Niagara	64.1	7.2	59.5
Kitchener-Waterloo	69.3	5.7	65.4
London	66.8	7.0	62.2
Windsor	67.8	8.3	62.2
Sudbury	63.1	9.0	57.4
Thunder Bay	64.5	6.6	60.3
Winnipeg	71.2	5.3	67.4
Regina	73.1	5.4	69.1
Saskatoon	69.6	6.1	65.4
Calgary	75.8	5.8	71.5
Edmonton	71.5	5.1	67.9
Vancouver	67.0	7.8	61.7
Victoria	62.7	7.1	58.3

SOURCE: Adapted from the Statistics Canada CANSIM database, Table 282-0053.

Although the Labour Force Survey provides monthly data on Canada's unemployment rate, there are still some questions that have to be answered before Canada's unemployment situation can be accurately assessed. The survey provides information on the number of unemployed, but not on the number of *job vacancies*. That is, the solution to the unemployment problem depends on the number of job vacancies available. If there are no jobs available, then jobs will have to be created. If jobs are available, then a way will have to be found to match the unemployed workers to the available opportunities.

The definition of unemployment used by the Labour Force Survey does not take into consideration **underemployment,** the situation in which individuals are employed, but not at a job that fully utilizes their skills. For example, a qualified plumber may accept a job delivering pizza if no other jobs are available. In terms of the Labour Force Survey, this person is employed, since she or he is working. However, this worker is not as productive as she or he could be. Individuals are also underemployed if they are working fewer hours a week than they want to work.

The survey categorizes an individual as unemployed if that person was looking for a job during the reference week. Although the survey questionnaire asks what the person has done to find a job, there is no indication of how hard the person looked for work. Some unemployed workers may have put a great deal of effort into finding a job, while others may have simply gone through the motions. Undoubtedly, unemployment means real financial hardship for some people. The higher the unemployment rate, the greater the degree of financial problems. The survey, however, does not measure the financial hardship suffered by unemployed persons. Some unemployed persons may have a separate source of income or have a spouse who is employed. In order to get a picture of economic hardship in Canada, Labour Force Survey data need to be combined with other data on incomes.

One criticism of the Labour Force Survey is its inability to identify the "hidden unemployed" or "discouraged searchers." These persons are interested in employment, but are not actively seeking a job because they believe that a suitable job is not available. Rather than being tabulated as unemployed, they are deemed by the Survey to be not in the labour force. In order to estimate the degree of **hidden unemployment,** Statistics Canada carries out a special survey in March of each year in conjunction with the monthly Labour Force Survey. Since March is normally a period of high unemployment, the maximum number of discouraged searchers is likely to show up at this time. Statistics Canada also publishes each month, as part of the labour force data, estimates of the number of people who have looked for work in the last six months, not just the last four weeks.

According to Statistics Canada, the number of discouraged searchers is decreasing. Some are opting for early retirement and others are returning to school. Statistics Canada is also classifying more individuals as unemployed rather than as not in the labour force. These are individuals who are waiting to be recalled to a job or are expecting to start a new job in the near future. Recent studies on the characteristics of discouraged searchers

Underemployment **is the term used to describe a situation in which individuals are employed but not at jobs that fully utilize their skills.**

The hidden unemployed **are those members of the population who are not actively seeking a job because they do not believe there are suitable jobs available.**

indicate that they are older and better educated than they were previously. The majority of discouraged searchers in Canada live in Quebec and the Atlantic provinces.

Some individuals are working part time but would prefer full-time employment. When surveyed, these individuals are classified as employed because they are working. There is a measure of hidden unemployment in this classification because these individuals are not working as many hours as they would like and are not contributing fully to the Canadian economy. Evidence suggests that women make up the majority of involuntary part-time workers, because they account for almost 70 percent of all part-time workers.

When the unemployment-rate statistics are released every month, two sets of figures are given. The actual unemployment rate and the *seasonally adjusted unemployment rate* are provided. The actual rate is the unemployment rate derived from survey statistics. The seasonally adjusted rate adjusts the actual rate to account for seasonal fluctuations. It takes into consideration the fact that unemployment is normally higher in the winter months than in the summer. The seasonally adjusted rate is used for month-to-month comparisons of the unemployment situation, and for revealing the underlying trend in the unemployment statistics.

The unemployment rates in selected countries are presented in International Comparisons 5.1.

International Comparisons 5.1

Unemployment Rates, 2002

Australia	6.3%	Germany	9.8%
Austria	4.8%	Hungary	5.8%
Bulgaria	18.0%	Ireland	4.3%
Canada	7.6%	Israel	10.4%
Chile	9.2%	Italy	9.1%
Colombia	17.4%	Japan	5.4%
Costa Rica	6.3%	Malaysia	3.8%
Czech Republic	9.8%	Peru	9.4%
Dominican Republic	14.5%	Philippines	10.2%
Finland	8.5%	United Kingdom	5.2%
France	9.1%	United States	5.8%

SOURCE: www.cia.gov/publications/factbook.

Unemployment Rates: A Canada–United States Comparison

Until the recession years of the early 1980s, the unemployment rate in Canada was similar to that in the United States. Since that time, the Canadian unemployment rate has consistently exceeded the rate in the United States. Even during the economic expansion of the late 1980s the Canadian unemployment rate was almost 3 percent higher. During the 1990s, it was approximately 4 percent higher. In 2002, Canada's unemployment rate was about 1.9 percent higher than the rate in the United States. There has been some discussion among economists as to the reason, or reasons, for this difference. Some of the suggested reasons are presented here.

In Canada, there are relatively fewer jobs in relation to the population. In other words, the number of people working as a percentage of the population was slightly lower in Canada. The Canadian employment insurance system is more generous than the arrangement in the United States. In Canada, one needs to work fewer weeks in order to collect employment insurance for more weeks. Seventy-two percent of the unemployed in Canada receive unemployment benefits, compared to 34 percent in the United States. The presence of these benefits in Canada may help explain why Canadians spend more time looking for work than Americans. If you continue to look for work, you are deemed to be unemployed. If you stop looking for work, you are not in the labour force and are not counted as unemployed.

Part of the difference in unemployment rates is due to the manner in which unemployment is measured. In Canada, casual job seekers are listed as unemployed. In the United States, one must be actively seeking work to be counted as unemployed. The higher degree of unionization of the labour force in Canada may also be a factor. Approximately 38 percent of Canadian workers are unionized compared to 16 percent in the United States. If unions are successful in pushing up the cost of hiring workers through higher wages and benefits, there will be fewer workers hired. Finally, the minimum wage is higher in Canadian provinces than in the states south of the border.

Questions

1. Would Canada's relatively greater reliance on resource industries help explain part of the difference in Canada–U.S. unemployment rates?
2. Why, in your opinion, does Canada have a higher percentage of workers in unions than does the United States?
3. Why would higher minimum wages in Canada result in a higher unemployment rate?
4. Explain how a more generous employment insurance program in Canada might lead to a higher unemployment rate.

Types of Unemployment

Demand-Deficient Unemployment

Employers want to hire workers to produce the products that they are selling. If employers are having difficulty selling their products, then they will not need to hire as many workers. A decrease in the level of spending by consumers will result in reduced sales for businesses. If consumers are not spending money on goods and services, employers will not need to hire workers. This results in unemployment. Lack of aggregate demand for products in the economy results in **demand-deficient unemployment.**

Demand-deficient unemployment **results from a lack of overall spending in the economy.**

Frictional Unemployment

Under all types of economic conditions, there will always be individuals who are in between jobs or who are just entering the labour force. These individuals are classified as being frictionally unemployed. In most cases, the unemployment is of short duration and the individual is expected to find a job relatively quickly. **Frictional unemployment** is peculiar in that it tends to be higher when economic conditions are good. When the aggregate demand for goods and services is high and jobs are plentiful, individuals are more willing to leave one job and look for a better one. When the aggregate demand is low and jobs are scarce, workers are less willing to leave one job voluntarily in order to begin searching for another.

Short-term unemployment on the part of individuals who have voluntarily left one job and are in the process of looking for another is termed frictional unemployment.

Frictional unemployment has also been referred to as *job-search unemployment.* It takes time to search for a job, and during this time one continues to be unemployed. Why does it take time to find a job when vacancies exist for which unemployed workers are qualified? Workers often possess very little information about where the jobs are that can utilize their skills. It is unlikely that unemployed people will apply to every employer with a suitable vacancy. It also takes time to acquire information about the job market. Finally, there are certain costs associated with the job search, including transportation and buying newspapers to read the help-wanted advertisements.

Seasonal Unemployment

Some jobs are very seasonal in nature. Employment in many areas of construction, recreation, tourism, and agriculture is available only in the warmer months of the year. For many workers in these industries, alternative employment opportunities may not be available during the winter. Ski instructors, on the other hand, may be employed during the winter months but unemployed for the rest of the year. In both cases, such workers experience **seasonal unemployment.**

Seasonal unemployment **results from the seasonal nature of some industries, such as agriculture, construction, tourism, and recreation.**

Structural unemployment **results from a mismatching of the demand for, and the supply of, workers on an occupational or geographic basis.**

Structural Unemployment

Structural unemployment results from a mismatching of workers and jobs, rather than from a shortage of jobs. This mismatching has two dimensions: occupational and geographic. In some instances, jobs are available yet the unemployed individuals do not have the necessary skills to fill the available jobs. The *occupational dimension* of structural unemployment results from a change in the consumer demand for goods and services as well as from changes in technology. As consumers' spending patterns change, some jobs are eliminated. Changes in methods of production or technology have also reduced the demand for certain types of workers. For example, the growth of computer technology has drastically altered the types of office jobs available.

The *geographic dimension* of structural unemployment means that unemployed workers may have the skills to fill the job vacancies, but the jobs are in another area of the country. There may be unemployed welders in Halifax and a shortage of welders in Edmonton. The solution to the geographic element of structural unemployment is to improve the matching process by increasing worker mobility from place to place.

Insurance-Induced Unemployment

Changes to the Unemployment Insurance Act in 1971 (currently Employment Insurance) affected Canada's employment rate. These changes, which made employment insurance easier to collect while at the same time increasing the available benefits, have tended to increase the unemployment rate by generating **insurance-induced unemployment.** For certain groups of individuals, weekly employment-insurance benefits may be more attractive than regular employment. Although technically a person has to be actively seeking work in order to be classified as unemployed and to qualify for insurance benefits, these circumstances may not be revealed by the Labour Force Survey. In other words, someone may be classified as unemployed on the survey, although he or she is not actively seeking work.

Insurance-induced unemployment **is caused by the level of employment-insurance benefits, which makes looking for work unattractive.**

Natural Rate of Unemployment

The unemployment rate that is present when the economy is operating at full capacity is referred to as the **natural rate of unemployment.** Economists believe that the labour market will always experience some unemployment because of frictional, seasonal, and structural factors. If the only unemployment persisting in the economy is a result of frictional, seasonal, and structural reasons, the economy is said to be operating at full employment.

What is the natural rate of unemployment? There is not a specific level of unemployment that economists designate as the natural rate. The natural rate of unemployment changes as economic conditions change. There is no consensus among economists about what unemployment rate should be designated as the natural rate, but estimates have ranged between 6 and 9

The natural rate of unemployment **is the unemployment rate present when the economy is operating at full capacity.**

percent. There is agreement, however, that the natural rate of unemployment is increasing. Reasons for the increase include the demographic shifts in the labour force, technological change, and the changes taking place in the economy due to deregulation and foreign competition.

REVIEW

5.1 Are students classified as being unemployed according to the Labour Force Survey? Why or why not?

5.2 What is the difference between the participation rate and the unemployment rate?

5.3 How does structural unemployment differ from demand-deficient unemployment?

5.4 Welcome to the Labour Force Game: discover how changes in labour-force conditions affect participation and unemployment rates in the city of Robota.

interactive graphics

EVERYDAY ECONOMICS 5.2

Employment Insurance and the Unemployment Rate

Canada's employment insurance program provides monetary benefits to persons who cease to be employed. Those eligible to collect benefits are persons who have been terminated or laid off from their job, who are not able to work because of illness, or who qualify for maternity benefits. In order to qualify, a person must have been employed and have made contributions to the employment insurance fund. The contributions are automatically deducted from earnings at the person's place of employment. The benefits that one receives when unemployed depend on the amount of contributions that were made. The program is based not on need but solely on contributions. Wealthy and low-income individuals are both eligible for employment insurance benefits under the same conditions.

Although the program is referred to as insurance, it differs from a typical insurance scheme. First, the program is compulsory, not voluntary. Only certain categories of workers (e.g., the self-employed) are not required to make contributions to the employment insurance fund. If the program were voluntary, many people would refuse to participate. If these people became unemployed, they might seek financial assistance from government in the form of welfare. The inevitability of many people receiving some type of public assistance once unemployed made the compulsory aspect of the program more practical. Second, until recently the contributions to the fund were insufficient to meet the benefits that were paid out. The federal government had to subsidize the program out of general tax revenue in order to make up the deficit.

There is some evidence that the program has had an impact on the unemployment rate. The program may increase job turnover, as the opportunity cost of leaving one job in order to search for another is reduced (however, in 1993 job quitters were disqualified from receiving benefits). Others may voluntarily remain unemployed for longer periods if financial assistance is still available. They may conduct a job search with less intensity and be willing to accept only high-paying jobs. They may not be willing to incur the cost and trouble of retraining in order to acquire new skills. The existence of employment insurance benefits may also encourage some individuals to enter the labour force because they are attracted by the possibility of receiving benefits if they lose their job.

Since the availability of employment insurance benefits makes leisure cheaper, some individuals who want more leisure may cut back on their job search while receiving benefits. This decision to get more leisure involves certain costs. First, there is the cost of finding a new job when the benefits run out. Some time must be spent in a job search, and this will cut into the leisure time. The length of the job search will depend not only on the individual's skill and experience, but also on the labour market conditions at the time. The second cost of accepting benefits is the waiting period that must be served before benefits commence.

In order to continue receiving benefits, an unemployed person must be actively seeking work. The individual has to prove to officials at Human Resources Development Canada that a job search did take place. The need to document job-search activities cuts into leisure time and is a third cost involved in deciding to accept employment insurance benefits.

A 1986 provincial royal commission in Newfoundland reported that employment insurance was harmful to the work ethic. The commission noted that employment insurance benefits account for approximately 8 percent of personal income in Newfoundland, compared with 2 percent in the rest of Canada. The employment insurance program is regarded as an income supplement and not as temporary income assistance between jobs. The commission suggested that employment insurance be retained in the province strictly as an insurance scheme, and that a guaranteed annual income program be established for which everyone is eligible.

The Commission of Inquiry on Employment Insurance (Forget Commission) also submitted its report in 1986. The report contained 53 recommendations for changes in the employment insurance legislation and other human resource development programs. The report recommended the introduction of an earnings supplementation program while phasing out the regionally extended benefits and fishing benefits. The problems with the current employment insurance legislation are addressed in the report. The report's first recommendation, however, is that Canada should give a high priority to economic growth rather than focus on restructuring the employment insurance program. A growing economy would create more employment opportunities for Canadians.

In the 1990s, changes were made to Canada's employment insurance legislation. Government contributions to employment insurance ended. Employers and employees now contribute all the money. The government redirected employment insurance money away from low unemployment areas to job-training programs. It is also harder to qualify for employment insurance in low-unemployment areas. The benefits for new parents and older workers increased.

In 1996, the Unemployment Insurance Act was changed to the Employment Insurance Act. The stated goal of the new legislation is to encourage people to return to the job market and the workplace. The legislation still provides for temporary income support but has placed an increased emphasis on active re-employment measures.

Benefits are now based on hours of work rather than weeks of employment. The minimum number of hours needed to qualify for benefits ranges from 420 to 700 hours in the previous year. New entrants to the labour force need 910 hours of work to qualify for benefits. Provision was also made for those receiving employment insurance benefits to earn some income without a reduction in benefits.

Questions

1. What groups of workers would be most likely to take advantage of the availability of employment insurance in order to have more leisure time?

2. Do you think that wealthy individuals should be able to collect employment insurance benefits? Discuss.

3. What effect would employment insurance have on the mobility of workers across the country?

4. Is it possible that Canada's Employment Insurance program could help prevent increases in the unemployment rate? Explain.

5. Do you think the presence of employment insurance benefits could lead to an increase in wage rates? Explain.

Consumer Price Index

The Consumer Price Index (CPI) lists the ratio of current prices of consumer products to the prices of those products in a base year. The percentage change in this index from year to year is referred to as the rate of inflation.

Inflation can be defined as a general increase in the level of prices. In Canada, the rate of inflation is measured by the percentage change in the **Consumer Price Index (CPI)**. The CPI is a monthly survey of retail prices undertaken by Statistics Canada. Starting in 1995, the survey expanded to cover both urban and rural centres. Six hundred consumer items are surveyed in the categories of food, clothing, transportation, health and personal care, housing, recreation and reading, and tobacco and alcohol. Some specific items included in the survey are restaurant meals, eyeglasses, cross-country skis, floor wax, movie tickets, interest payments on a mortgage, and gasoline. As some items are more important than others in a person's budget, those items are assigned more importance in calculating the index.

Monthly retail price increases are published in the form of an index. In order to calculate the index, prices in a selected year are given a value of 100.0 and prices in subsequent years are related to base-year prices. The formula for calculating the index is as follows:

$$\frac{\text{price level in current year}}{\text{price level in base year}} \times 100.0 = \text{CPI current year}$$

For example, assume that in 1992 the price of a movie ticket was $5.00 and by 2004 it had risen to $10.00. Calculation of an index for this item would be:

$$\frac{\$10.00}{\$5.00} \times 100.0 = 200.0$$

In other words, this shows that the price of movie tickets increased by 100 percent from 1992 to 2004.

The CPI keeps track of changes in retail prices of goods and services typically purchased by consumers. Since these goods and services change over time, the CPI must regularly update the "basket" of goods and services surveyed. With an increasing number of two-wage-earner families, more

money is now being spent in restaurants. With more leisure time available, more money is being spent on recreational activities and equipment.
New products such as low-fat foods and video camcorders are being introduced in the marketplace. These changes are identified through a survey of
family expenditures. Once the results of the survey are known, items surveyed by the CPI are adjusted. From 1990 to 1994 the basket of goods
and services identified by the 1986 family expenditure survey was used in
calculating the CPI. Beginning in January 1995, a new grouping of goods
and services was introduced based on a 1992 family expenditure survey.

The group of consumer items and their weightings in the Consumer
Price Index are presented in Table 5.4. The weighting refers to the importance of that item in the basket of goods and services, and determines the
degree of influence exerted by the price change of that basic grouping on the
aggregate index. As shown in the table, prices had increased 19.0 percent
from 1992 to 2002. All items, however, have not increased by the same
amount. Transportation prices increased by 34.4 percent over this period,
while clothing and footwear prices increased by only 5.2 percent.

In Table 5.5, the CPI data are provided for 18 Canadian cities for
2002. It should be pointed out that these data do not allow for comparisons
of the cost of living between cities. The figures simply refer to how much
prices have increased in each city from 1992. For example, in Toronto the
CPI was 120.6 and in Regina it was 124.6. This can be interpreted by stating that prices have increased 20.6 percent in Toronto and 24.6 percent

Table 5.4 *Consumer Price Index (2002) and relative weights for various groups, Canada (1992 = 100.0)*

GROUP	CPI	RELATIVE WEIGHTS (%)
Shelter	113.8	27.9
Household operations and furnishings	113.8	10.0
Food	120.3	18.0
Transportation	134.4	18.3
Clothing and footwear	105.2	6.6
Recreation, reading, and education	126.3	10.4
Tobacco and alcohol	123.6	4.5
Health and personal care	115.5	4.3
All items	119.0	100.00

SOURCE: Adapted from the Statistics Canada CANSIM database, Table 326-0002.

Table 5.5 *Consumer Price Index for selected Canadian cities, 2002 (1992 = 100.0)*

St. John's	117.3	Winnipeg	123.3
Charlottetown/Summerside	117.1	Regina	124.6
Halifax	119.1	Saskatoon	123.1
Saint John	118.2	Edmonton	121.9
Quebec City	116.2	Calgary	125.8
Montreal	115.7	Vancouver	118.6
Ottawa	121.9	Victoria	117.4
Toronto	120.6	Whitehorse	117.7
Thunder Bay	119.3	Yellowknife	116.3

SOURCE: Adapted from the Statistics Canada CANSIM database, Table 326-0001 and 326-0002.

in Regina since 1992. It is impossible to compare the cost of living between these cities because there is no information presented on the actual prices in each city in 1992.

The rate of inflation is calculated on the basis of increases in the CPI from year to year. Rates of inflation for Canada for selected years are presented in Figure 5.2. The figure shows that the rate of inflation was in double figures in the mid-1970s and early 1980s. The rates of inflation in

Figure 5.2

Annual average increase in the CPI, 1970–2002

SOURCE: Adapted from the Statistics Canada CANSIM database, Table 326–0002.

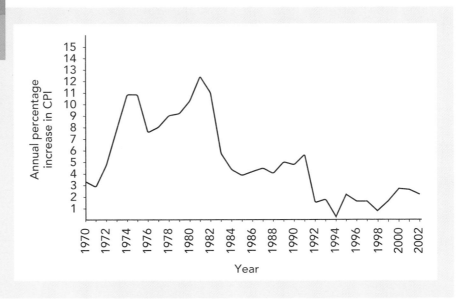

1984 and 1985 returned to the level of the 1960s and early 1970s. During the 1990s the rate of inflation has remained at relatively low levels.

It should be pointed out that the CPI is a retail price index and not a cost-of-living index. It is impossible to calculate a cost-of-living index because each individual has a different pattern of spending. A different cost-of-living index would be needed for each person. Certain individuals may not purchase all of the items included in the index, or purchase of the items in the ratio of assigned weights given in Table 5.4. The items that a retired individual would spend money on differ from those of a family of four or of a student attending college. The CPI simply relates the changes in retail prices of a certain basket of consumer goods. In actual practice, however, the CPI is often referred to as a cost-of-living index since no cost-of-living index is available.

The Consumer Price Index may also be an imperfect measure of the changes in the cost of living due to the presence of measurement biases. A quality bias exists if the prices used to construct the CPI are not adjusted for changes in the quality of products. A 2004-model automobile costs more than an older model but the 2004 model is a better car. Second, a commodity substitution bias exists because the weights used in the index are not kept up to date. Out-of-date weights do not take into consideration the ability of consumers to substitute one commodity for another as prices increase. A new-goods bias exists if the prices of new products change at a different rate from those included in the basket of goods surveyed. Finally, an outlet-substitution bias can exist if there are shifts in the market shares of different types of retailers. That is, consumers may switch their purchases to "no-frills" warehouses and away from traditional retailers in response to price increases.

The inflation rates for various countries are presented in International Comparisons 5.2. The Consumer Price Index is not the only price index calculated by Statistics Canada. There are also indexes on industrial product prices, raw material prices, machine and equipment prices, new-housing prices, non-residential building construction prices, farm input prices, farm product prices, and prices related to the items in the National Accounts. The Bank of Canada also publishes variations of the CPI. The Core CPI is the CPI excluding its eight most volatile components in terms of price changes as well as the effect of changes in indirect taxes on the remaining components. The most volatile components are fruit, vegetables, gasoline, fuel oil, natural gas, mortgage interest, inter-city transportation, and tobacco products. When the most volatile components of the index are removed, the trend in price changes can be better detected.

REVIEW

5.5   How would you interpret a CPI for Canada of 300.0?

5.6   What could you say about a CPI for Vancouver of 118.6 compared to a CPI for Montreal of 115.7 for the same month?

5.7   Why is it not correct to call the CPI a cost-of-living index?

International Comparisons 5.2

Inflation rates (percent), 2002

Canada	2.2	Mexico	6.4
United States	1.6	Australia	2.8
Japan	−0.9	South Korea	2.8
New Zealand	2.7	Austria	1.8
Belgium	1.7	Czech Republic	0.6
Denmark	2.3	Finland	1.9
France	1.8	Germany	1.3
Greece	3.6	Hungary	5.3
Iceland	5.2	Ireland	4.6
Italy	2.4	Jamaica	7.0
Netherlands	3.4	Norway	1.3
Poland	1.9	Portugal	3.7
Spain	3.0	Sweden	2.2
Switzerland	0.5	United Kingdom	2.1
India	5.4	Brazil	8.3

SOURCE: www.cia.gov/cia/publications/factbook.

Causes of Inflation

In order to understand why prices increase, it is necessary to understand how a market operates. This topic was discussed in Chapter 2. In order for a price to increase, either demand has to increase or supply has to decrease. Each of these causes will be considered separately.

Demand-Pull Inflation

Increases in the demand for a product result in price increases, assuming that nothing else has changed (see Chapter 2). The increased demand could result from a number of factors, including increased incomes and changing expectations about future prices. If consumers expect prices to increase in the future, they will purchase the necessary goods and services right now. The increased demand pushes up today's prices. If individuals are increasing their demands for all goods and services, then the overall level of prices will increase, causing **demand-pull inflation.**

Demand-pull inflation **describes the increase in the general level of prices that occurs when the aggregate demand for goods and services exceeds the supply.**

Cost-Push Inflation

Anything that causes supply to decrease will result in higher prices, or **cost-push inflation.** With reference to Chapter 2, this includes anything that will shift the supply curve to the left. Factors causing the supply curve to shift in this manner include wage increases, tax increases, raw-material and energy-price increases, and increased borrowing charges. For example, energy costs have been increasing since the mid-1970s and have put significant upward pressure on the cost of manufactured products.

Cost-push inflation **describes increases in the general price levels resulting from firms passing on their cost increases to consumers in the form of higher prices.**

In practice, it is difficult to separate demand-pull and cost-push influences on prices. They are often interrelated. For example, if the demand for products increases, higher prices will result. Price increases will lead to demands for higher wages, which will push up costs and eventually increase prices. The higher wages received by workers may lead to increased demands for goods and services and this will increase prices. The sequence could continue to repeat itself.

One indicator used by economists to distinguish between demand-pull and cost-push inflation is corporate profits in the manufacturing and commodity-producing industries. These industries are the most sensitive to changes in the business cycle. In times of demand-pull inflation, profit margins tend to widen; during times of cost-push inflation, they tend to narrow. Cost-push inflation is usually preceded by demand-pull inflation. Some economists argue that cost-push inflation does not really identify a cause of inflation. Rather, cost-push pressures are a matter of timing. After demand pressures have increased product prices, the prices for resources used to make the products increase.

Hyperinflation

If rising prices remain unchecked, **hyperinflation** (the term used to describe a very rapid increase in the level of prices that leads to a lack of public confidence in the currency) could result. This term refers to a situation of rapidly escalating prices. In fact, prices in a situation of hyperinflation are increasing so quickly that the value of the country's currency is eroded and the currency becomes useless. Imagine a situation in Canada in which prices increase to a level of 100 times what they are today. The real value of one Canadian dollar in terms of the amount of goods it could purchase would be equivalent to one cent prior to the price increases.

Although these figures seem impossible, there have been several cases of hyperinflation. The most celebrated case is that of Germany in the years after the First World War. Inflation in that country started to escalate in 1919, when prices tripled. By November 1923, prices were 1 422 900 000 000 times what they were before the First World War (in 1914). Clearly, the German currency had become useless. On November 20, 1923, Germany introduced a new currency. The exchange rate was a trillion units of the old currency to one unit of the new currency.

In recent years, several countries have experienced hyperinflation. In Israel, prices increased 191 percent in 1983, 445 percent in 1984, and approximately 404 percent in 1985. In Argentina, price increases were even higher over those years. In 1983 prices increased by 433 percent, in 1984 by 688 percent, and in 1985 by 771 percent. In 1985, the 10 000-peso note in Argentina had the purchasing power of one cent in Canadian money. Inflation continued, and in 1989 Argentina experienced an inflation rate of 3079 percent. After experiencing 328-percent inflation in 1983, and 2700-percent inflation in 1984, Bolivia had an inflation rate of 11 894 percent in 1985. Prices were climbing

hourly. Since Bolivia had its money printed outside the country, it cost more than 1000 pesos to print a 1000-peso note. In order to purchase a television set with 1000-peso notes, the consumer needed almost 31 kg of money.

In response to persistent inflation, Mexico removed three zeros from its currency. A 1000-peso coin became a 1-peso coin on January 1, 1993. Prices of goods and services, bank accounts, and salaries were denominated in new pesos. In July 1993, Brazil also chopped three zeros off the cruzeiro and in 1995 Poland chopped four zeros off the zloty. In 1993 inflation in the Ukraine was 5000 percent. The wartime economy in the former Yugoslavia in 1993–1995 resulted in hyperinflation. It is estimated that the rate of inflation in Yugoslavia in that period was 5 quadrillion percent. Many Yugoslavs refused to accept the Yugoslav currency (dinars) and the German Deutschmark (DM) effectively became the currency in Yugoslavia. The rapid depreciation in the value of the dinar in light of rising prices is shown below.

November 12, 1993: 1 DM = 1 million dinars
November 30, 1993: 1 DM = 37 million dinars
December 11, 1993: 1 DM = 800 million dinars
December 31, 1993: 1 DM = 3 trillion dinars
January 4, 1994: 1 DM = 6 trillion dinars

How does hyperinflation occur? The main ingredient in all cases is the printing of too much money by the country's central bank. If the amount of goods and services available to be purchased does not increase in the same proportion as the increases in the money supply, then prices will increase. More and more money is made available to buy the same amount of goods. The faster the money supply is increased, the faster prices rise. As consumers see prices rising quickly, they react accordingly. They buy goods and services now, before the prices increase even further. This increased demand, as a result of the expectation of higher prices, also pushes up prices.

Questions

1. In times of hyperinflation, would an individual want to hold his or her wealth in cash?
2. What would happen to the purchasing power of pension income or savings during a period of rapidly rising prices?
3. Could hyperinflation lead to social unrest in the country? Why?
4. Will the present Canadian dollar be worthless someday? If that happens, what will Canadians use for money?
5. In times of hyperinflation, who is forced to sacrifice more—the borrower of money or the lender of money? Why?
6. Why does hyperinflation often occur in countries that are involved in a military conflict?

REVIEW

5.8 Using the graphs, observe the effects of hyperinflation in various countries.

The National Accounts

Since Canada's economy has to grow in order to meet the demands of an increasing population, a measure of economic growth is seen as a valuable piece of information. Economic growth takes place whenever a country continues to produce more goods and services. This increase in production is seen as necessary in order to increase standards of living and to provide employment for an expanding population. In Canada, the **National Accounts** is a series of data prepared by Statistics Canada in order to measure economic growth. It is probably best to visualize the National Accounts in terms of a **circular flow of money** diagram like the one presented in Figure 5.3.

This diagram represents the flow of money in the Canadian economy. In our diagram we will assume that the Canadian economy is composed of only two sectors: businesses and households. The direction of the money flow is indicated by the arrows. In order to produce goods and services, businesses have to purchase resources. The money paid out for these resources in the form of wages, rent, interest, and so on is indicated in the lower loop of the diagram. This money finds its way to households. In turn, households spend money on goods and services produced by the business sector. This is shown in the upper loop of the diagram (the product markets).

The National Accounts are data compiled by Statistics Canada that measure the overall level of business activity in Canada.

The directional flow of money in the economy from the business sector to households and back is called the circular flow of money.

Money circulates from businesses to households and back to businesses. In the product markets, households demand products while businesses supply them. In the resource markets, businesses demand resources that are supplied by households (e.g., labour).

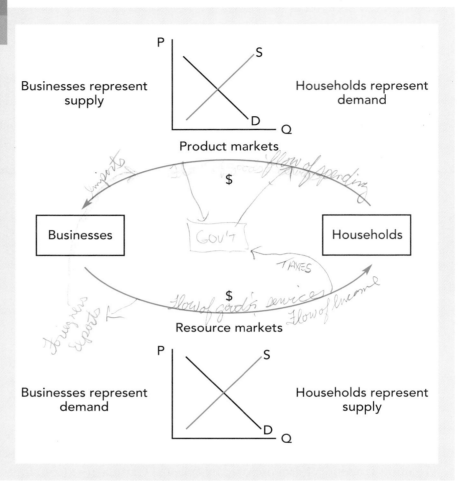

Businesses represent supply

Households represent demand

Product markets

Businesses

Households

Product markets

$

GOV'T

TAXES

$

Resource markets

Businesses represent demand

Households represent supply

Households spend money on a variety of items including clothes, food, housing, entertainment, and the like. The prices of these products are determined in the product markets. In these markets, households represent the demand side of the market and businesses represent the supply side.

Businesses must purchase certain resources in order to provide these goods and services. They need workers, raw materials, machinery, and buildings, as well as other resources. The lower loop of the diagram represents the resource markets. Businesses represent the demand for resources, while households supply these resources.

The circular flow diagram can be used to measure the level of economic activity in two ways. One measure, referred to as the *expenditure approach,* involves determining the amount of money that households spend on goods and services. This would entail adding up all the money that circulates in the upper loop of Figure 5.3. By adding up the dollar value of all consumer purchases, we would have an indication of the level of economic activity.

A second approach to measuring economic activity would be to determine the amount of money businesses pay out for the services they require. This is shown in the lower loop of the diagram and is called the *income approach.* The value arrived at in both approaches is gross domestic product (GDP).

The measuring rod used in each approach is money. That is, GDP is measured in dollars. In order to calculate GDP, we need to add up all of the items that consumers purchase. Yet how could we add T-shirts and tea bags? The only way to do this is to reduce everything to dollars and cents. Therefore, in order for an item to be included in the National Accounts, it must have a price.

Expenditure Approach to Gross Domestic Product

One way of measuring the level of economic activity in Canada would be to add up the total amount of spending during a calendar year. This expenditure approach, determining the total amount spent, and the resulting dollar value give the gross domestic product (GDP). In order to determine the total level of spending in the Canadian economy, it is necessary to include other groups that spend money besides households. These are businesses, government, and buyers from foreign countries (who buy our exports). Businesses make purchases from other businesses for such things as machinery, equipment, and new buildings. This type of spending is referred to as **investment**. Government purchases certain goods and services as well, ranging from the purchase of new fighter aircraft to the hiring of someone to cut the lawn on Parliament Hill. Government also undertakes investment spending. The construction of a nuclear power plant, an airport, and a government office complex are examples of investment spending by government.

Exports are also an important component of gross domestic product. Foreigners buy many products made in Canada. For example, most Canadian-made automobiles are produced for the U.S. market. Canadians also sell products such as wheat and paper products to residents of other countries. Gross domestic product is the total dollar value of these various types of spending and is calculated as follows:

Investment describes business spending on machines and equipment, new residential construction, and any change in inventories.

$$GDP = C + Ig + G + X - M \text{ (see Figure 5.4) where}$$

C = consumption spending by households on goods and services

Ig = gross investment by business and government, which includes the purchase of machines and equipment, new housing constructed, and any change in inventories

G = government purchases of goods and services

X = exports (foreign purchases of Canadian goods and services)

M = imports (Canadian purchases of foreign goods and services).

Why is it necessary to subtract the amount of money that Canadians spend on imports when calculating GDP? Money spent on imports is not returned to Canadian businesses. In turn, this money is not available to be paid out to Canadian households. The money spent on imported products such as Japanese cars, French wine, and Florida oranges can be said to leave the circular flow of money in Canada.

Figure 5.4

The National Accounts

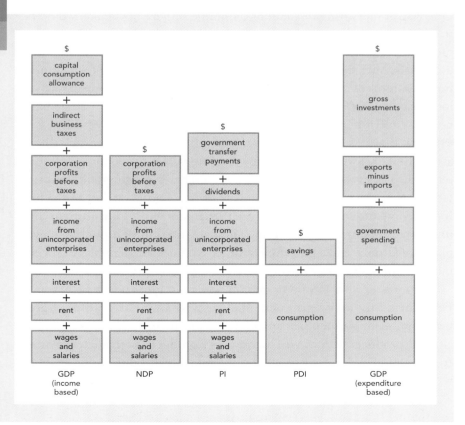

Gross investment is the term used to represent spending on manufactured resources in our economy. This type of spending is undertaken by both business and government. In the National Accounts it is divided into two groups: gross fixed capital formation, and value of physical changes in inventories. *Gross fixed capital formation* is composed mainly of residential and non-residential construction as well as purchases of machinery and equipment. *Inventory changes* are added to the investment calculation because it is necessary to record goods that were produced in a given year yet not sold in that year. If gross domestic product is to be an accurate measure of the level of economic activity, then products that remain on the shelves at the end of the year have to be included in GDP since they represent production in that calendar year.

During the process of producing goods and services, some physical deterioration of machinery and equipment takes place. This physical deterioration, or *depreciation,* of equipment is shown as *capital consumption allowance* in the National Accounts. If the dollar value attached to the capital consumption allowance is subtracted from gross investment, the resulting figure is net investment.

net investment = gross investment − capital consumption allowance

Not all spending by businesses is included in gross domestic product. Spending on intermediate goods is not included. The definition of intermediate goods can best be explained using an example. In order to build a car, automobile manufacturers must purchase a variety of materials, such as steel and plastic, from suppliers. The cost of these materials is included in the price of the car. If spending by business on steel and plastic were included in gross domestic product, as well as spending by the consumer when buying the car, double counting would take place. The price of the car includes the value of the steel, plastic, and other materials that have been purchased in order to make the car. Only spending on final goods and services is included in the calculation of GDP.

It is also necessary to clarify the government component of GDP. Government spending can be divided into two groups. The first group represents government spending on goods and services. All levels of government are involved in these purchases of machinery, paper, typewriters, landscape services, and so on. The second group is composed of *transfer payments.* These are government expenditures for which a service was not provided. Money is taken from one segment of the population in taxes and transferred to another segment of the population. Examples of government transfer payments are old-age pensions and general welfare assistance. Only those expenditures made on goods and services are included in the calculation of GDP.

Gross domestic product is not the only indicator of economic activity calculated via the expenditure approach. Statistics Canada also calculates *gross national expenditure* (GNE). The components of GNE are similar to GDP, with one difference. Gross domestic product (expenditure-based) can be defined as the value of all final goods and services produced *in Canada* in a given year, whereas gross national expenditure is the value of all final goods and services produced *by residents of Canada* in a given year.

Gross domestic product, then, is concerned with the economic activity undertaken in Canada, regardless of whether or not it is done by residents of Canada. Gross national expenditure is concerned with the economic activity of residents of Canada, even if they worked outside the country.

Income Approach to Gross Domestic Product

An alternative approach to measuring the level of business activity in Canada would be to determine the amount of money that circulates through the lower loop of the circular flow of money diagram (Figure 5.3). This includes business expenses for such items as rent, wages, and interest. Profits are also included in this flow, as they eventually end up in households and are spent on consumer goods and services. Profits can be considered as payment for that resource which represents the productivity of the owner. The lower-loop approach to economic activity is referred to as gross domestic product (GDP) and is calculated as follows:

GDP = wages and salaries
+ interest
+ rent
+ corporation profits before taxes
+ income from unincorporated enterprises
+ indirect taxes
+ capital consumption allowance

Included in our calculation of GDP is a dollar value for capital consumption allowance. In the process of producing goods and services, a certain amount of machinery and equipment was used up. This represents a cost to business, since this machinery will eventually have to be replaced.

Corporation profits can be divided into 1) corporation dividends, 2) corporation income taxes, and 3) undistributed corporation profits. The corporation profit figure, which includes corporation income taxes, is used in calculating GDP. Derivations of this figure are used in calculating other items in the National Accounts.

Not all the expenses of businesses are included in the calculation of GDP. Purchases from other businesses are excluded, and only the value added at each stage of production is considered. For example, if a shoemaker buys the leather for a pair of shoes for $40 and sells the shoes for $60, only the $20 that was added to the value by the shoemaker is included in GDP. The other $40 would have been included in GDP on behalf of the company that sold the leather to the shoemaker.

As shown in Tables 5.6 and 5.7, the dollar value of GDP is the same whether it is arrived at through the income approach or the expenditure approach. This result occurs because of the nature of the circular flow diagram on which these calculations are based. All of the money spent on goods and services ends up in the business sector of our economy. The business sector has to do something with this money, so it is paid out to individuals in the form of wages, rent, and interest. If profits, which are also returned to households, are added to the other expenses of business, then the dollar value of GDP is the same regardless of the approach used.

GDP (expenditure based) = GDP (income based)

Statistics Canada also used the income approach to calculate *gross national product* (GNP).[1] The components of GNP are similar to those of GDP, with one difference. As with GNE discussed earlier, GNP represents the value of all final goods and services produced by residents of Canada in a given year. Gross domestic product (income-based) represents the value of all final goods and services produced *in Canada* in a given year. If a

Table 5.6 *Gross domestic product, expenditure basis, Canada, 2002*

	$ (MILLIONS)
Personal expenditure on consumer goods and services	651 192
Government current expenditure on goods and services	214 174
Government investment	29 233
Business investment	197 507
Inventory charge	2 672
Exports of goods and services	470 114
Imports of goods and services	−423 096
Statistical discrepancy	372
Gross domestic product at market prices	1 142 123

SOURCE: Adapted from the Statistics Canada CANSIM database, Table 380–0002.

Table 5.7 *Gross domestic product, income basis, Canada, 2002*

	$ (MILLIONS)
Wages, salaries	595 267
Corporation profits before taxes	125 507
Interest and investment income	49 666
Accrued net farm income	2 119
Unincorporated business income	71 894
Government-enterprise profits	10 845
Taxes less subsidies on factors of production	53 152
Inventory valuation adjustment	−3 044
Net domestic product at basic prices	905 406
Indirect taxes less subsidies	84 448
Capital consumption allowance	152 642
Statistical discrepancy	−373
Gross domestic product at market prices	1 142 123

SOURCE: Adapted from the Statistics Canada CANSIM database, Table 380–0001.

Canadian citizen living in Windsor, Ontario, works every day in Detroit, Michigan, USA, then that person's income would be included in GNP but not in GDP. Conversely, if someone living in Detroit works in Windsor each day, that person's earnings are included in Canadian GDP but not in Canadian GNP. Since the dollar value of gross domestic product is the same regardless of the approach used (income or expenditure), the dollar values of GNE and GNP are also the same.[1]

In 1986, Statistics Canada switched from reporting GNP as the main indicator of economic activity in Canada to reporting GDP. Statistics Canada will continue to compute GNP figures; however, emphasis will be put on GDP as an economic indicator.

Gross domestic product is normally greater than gross national product, primarily because a large percentage of Canadian business is foreign-owned. The profits earned by foreign owners of Canadian businesses would be included in GDP because they were earned in Canada, but they would not be included in GNP. The annual changes in these two measures do not vary greatly. Since this is the case, both measures can be used to indicate changes in the level of economic activity.

---

[1] GNP is also referred to *as gross national income* (GNI).

The value of GDP provides a broad indication of the level of economic activity in Canada. For some uses, the aggregate figures may not be appropriate. Therefore, Statistics Canada manipulates the information collected in the National Accounts and, in addition to GDP, provides the information discussed below (see Figure 5.4).

Net domestic product (NDP): In order to calculate **net domestic product,** the dollar values of the capital consumption allowance and indirect business taxes are subtracted from the value of gross domestic product.

$$\text{NDP} = \text{GDP} - \text{capital consumption allowance} - \text{indirect business taxes}$$

Personal income (PI): **Personal income** equals NDP minus corporation income taxes and undistributed corporation profits, while adding government transfer payments. Transfer payments are moneys paid out to individuals for which no product or service was provided (e.g., old-age pensions).

$$\text{PI} = \text{NDP} - \text{corporation income taxes} - \text{undistributed corporation profits} + \text{government transfer payments}$$

Personal disposable income (PDI): **Personal disposable income** equals PI minus personal income taxes. PDI can also be considered as the total of household consumption plus household savings.

$$\text{PDI} = \text{PI} - \text{personal income tax}$$

The annual percentage changes in GDP for the years 1961 to 2000 are presented in Figure 5.5. The annual percentage increases have been as high as 19.4 percent (1974) and as low as 0.8 percent (1991).

Net domestic product (NDP) is the value of final goods and services produced in a country in a given year, minus an allowance for capital consumption and indirect business taxes.

Personal income (PI) is the total of consumption spending and savings in the economy.

Personal disposable income (PDI) is the level of personal income that remains after income taxes have been paid.

REVIEW

5.9 Why are government transfer payments not included in the calculation of gross domestic product?

5.10 Why are changes in inventories included in the calculation of GDP?

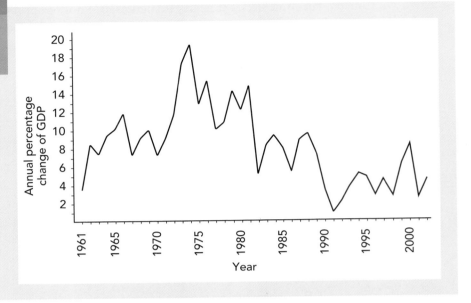

Figure 5.5

Annual percentage changes in gross domestic product, Canada, 1961–2002

SOURCE: Adapted from the Statistics Canada CANSIM database, Table 379-0017.

International Comparisons 5.3

Annual percentage change in GDP, 2002

Canada	3.4	Mexico	1.0
United States	4.2	Australia	3.6
Japan	−0.3	South Korea	6.2
New Zealand	2.5	Austria	0.6
Belgium	0.6	Russia	4.2
Denmark	1.8	Finland	1.1
France	1.0	Germany	0.4
Greece	4.3	Hungary	3.2
China	8.0	Ireland	5.2
Italy	0.4	India	4.3
Netherlands	0.3	Norway	1.6
Poland	1.3	Portugal	0.8
Spain	2.0	Sweden	1.8
Switzerland	0.0	United Kingdom	1.6
Zimbabwe	−12.1	Uruguay	−10.5

SOURCE: www.cia.gov/cia/publications/factbook.

Numerical Calculation of the National Accounts

In order to better understand the National Accounts, the following exercise is provided. Using the following information and referring to Figure 5.4, calculate GDP, NDP, PI, and PDI.

ITEM	$ (MILLION)
Consumption	75
Corporation dividends	15
Capital consumption allowance	15
Exports	15
Government expenditure on goods and services	25
Government transfer payments	5
Housing constructed	20
Imports	10
Income from unincorporated enterprises	25
Interest	10
Machinery and equipment manufactured	20
Net change in inventories	+10
Rent	15
Savings	25
Taxes: corporation income	10
personal income	15
indirect business	5
Undistributed corporation profits	15
Wages and salaries	45

The easiest calculations to make from these data are personal disposable income (PDI) and personal income (PI).

$$PDI = C + S$$
$$= 75 + 25$$
$$= 100$$

$$PI = PDI + \text{personal income tax}$$
$$= 100 + 15$$
$$= 115$$

It is possible to calculate gross domestic product if we calculate gross investment first.

$$
\begin{aligned}
\text{gross investment} = &\ \text{new housing constructed} \\
&+ \text{net change in inventories} \\
&+ \text{machinery and equipment} \\
&\quad \text{manufactured} \\
= &\ 20 + 10 + 20 \\
= &\ 50
\end{aligned}
$$

$$
\begin{aligned}
GDP &= C + Ig + G + (X - M) \\
&= 75 + 50 + 25 + (15 - 10) \\
&= 155
\end{aligned}
$$

$$
\begin{aligned}
NDP &= GDP - \text{indirect business taxes} \\
&\qquad - \text{capital consumption allowance} \\
&= 155 - 5 - 15 \\
&= 135
\end{aligned}
$$

An alternate approach is to calculate GDP from the income approach. All the components of GDP, except for corporation profits before taxes, are readily available from the list. Corporation profits before taxes can be determined as follows:

$$
\begin{aligned}
\text{corporation profits before} & \\
\text{taxes} = &\ \text{corporation dividends} \\
&+ \text{corporation income tax} \\
&+ \text{undistributed corporation profits} \\
= &\ 15 + 10 + 15 \\
= &\ 40
\end{aligned}
$$

$$
\begin{aligned}
GDP = &\ \text{wages and salaries} \\
&+ \text{interest} \\
&+ \text{rent} \\
&+ \text{income from unincorporated} \\
&\quad \text{enterprises} \\
&+ \text{corporation profits before taxes} \\
&+ \text{indirect business taxes} \\
&+ \text{capital consumption allowance} \\
= &\ 45 + 10 + 15 + 25 + 40 + 5 + 15 \\
= &\ 155
\end{aligned}
$$

The value of GDP is the same regardless of which approach is used.

Relationship of GDP to Social and Economic Welfare

Gross domestic product is a measure of the dollar value of final goods and services produced in Canada in a given year. The change in GDP from year to year is an indicator of the amount of economic growth in our country. If our economy is growing and producing more, it is assumed that our standard of living is improving as well. However, increases in GDP do not always represent improvements in our welfare. Some of the reasons why changes in GDP cannot be automatically associated with changes in the standard of living are:

Effect of price increases: Since GDP is arrived at by using market prices, the value of GDP will increase each year simply because of inflation. In order to determine whether more goods and services have actually been produced, it is necessary to adjust the dollar value of GDP in order to account for price increases. The resulting figure is referred to as **real GDP** and is expressed in constant, or 1986, dollars.

The impact of price increases on GDP is shown in Figure 5.6. In all years, the dollar-value growth in GDP was greater than the real growth in GDP. For example, in 1982 GDP increased by 5.2 percent over the 1981 level of GDP in current-dollar terms. Yet real GDP, or GDP in constant (1986) dollars, actually fell by 3.2 percent from the previous year. Even in years when the economy is growing, inflation can distort the GDP figures. In 1975, the current dollar value of GDP increased by 12.8 percent over 1974, whereas the constant (1986) dollar value increased by only 2.6 percent. In 1991, a 0.8 percent increase in current dollar GDP in 1991 was actually a decline of 1.8 percent in constant dollar GDP.

Effect of population size: Each year it is likely that GDP will increase. It is also likely that the population of Canada will increase. In order to determine if Canadians are better off from year to year, GDP has to be calculated on a per-capita basis. This is done by dividing the dollar value of real GDP by the population. If this figure increases from year to year, it means that there are more goods and services per person than there were the year before. GDP per-capita figures for various countries are presented in International Comparisons 5.4.

Need for a market price: If a good or a service does not have a market price, it is not included in GDP. If you purchase tomatoes at a vegetable market, the value of the tomatoes is included in GDP. If you grow tomatoes in your own garden for your own use, they are not included in GDP. The reason is that the tomatoes from your garden do not have a market price, whereas the other tomatoes do. If GDP is to accurately measure production,

> **Real GDP refers to the level of gross domestic product adjusted for increases in the average price level.**

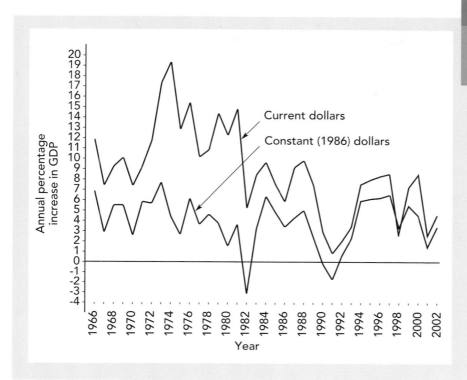

Figure 5.6

Gross domestic product annual percentage change in current and constant dollars, 1966–2002

SOURCE: Adapted from the Statistics Canada CANSIM database, Tables 379-0017 and 379-0008.

all tomatoes grown in Canada should be included. Yet, it is possible to include in the calculation of GDP only those goods and services that have a market price.

If Canadians start to do things for themselves—paint their own houses, fix their own cars, grow their own food, and sew their own clothes—the value of GDP will decrease. If Canadians begin to trade goods and services instead of purchasing them, GDP will again decrease.

Underground economy: Canada's GDP would be higher than reported if all financial transactions between individuals were recorded. Many financial transactions are not recorded in order to avoid paying both sales and income taxes. The existence of unreported financial activity is referred to as the *underground economy.* If Statistics Canada has no record of these transactions, the transactions cannot be included in GDP. Studies estimate the size of the underground economy ranges from 3.5 percent of GDP to 20 percent.

It is difficult for transactions to go unrecorded in areas of the economy such as paying utilities, purchasing transportation and financial services, and interest on consumer debt. It is easier for underground activities to exist in areas such as child care, tips, professional services, and residential construction, to name a few.

International Comparisons 5.4

GDP per capita in U.S. dollars (purchasing power parity), 2002

India	2 540	Italy	25 000
Mexico	9 000	Ireland	30 500
United States	37 600	Israel	19 000
Switzerland	31 700	Soth Korea	19 400
Norway	31 800	Greece	19 000
Denmark	29 000	Haiti	1 700
Hong Kong	26 000	Poland	9 500
Japan	28 000	Russia	9 300
Canada	29 400	Jamaica	3 900
France	25 700	China	4 400
Netherlands	26 900	Syria	3 500
Germany	26 600	Pakistan	2 100
Australia	27 000	Bangladesh	1 700
United Kingdom	25 300	North Korea	1 000
Sweden	25 400	Somalia	550

SOURCE: www.cia.gov/cia/publications/factbook.

EVERYDAY ECONOMICS 5.5

The Trillion-Dollar Club

Until the year 2000, only ten countries had GDPs in excess of one trillion Canadian dollars ($1 000 000 000 000). In 2000, Mexico and Canada joined the trillion-dollar GDP group. In 1942 Canada's GDP was $10 billion, and in 1971 it was $100 billion. It took only 29 years to grow from $100 billion to $1000 billion in the year 2000.

There are two ways to look at a nation's GDP. It can be viewed from the income approach as the total amount of income earned in the country in a calendar year. Those countries in the trillion-dollar club have generated more than one trillion dollars of income in a year. GDP can also be seen as the total amount of spending taking place in a country in a calendar year. In order for a nation's GDP to reach the trillion-dollar mark, total spending must increase.

The ability of a nation's GDP to reach this level depends on a number of factors. The population of the country is a major factor in determining the level of GDP. It is more likely that China and India will be members of the trillion-dollar club than Iceland and Bermuda. Since GDP is measured in current prices, the prices of goods and services produced in a country will affect the level of GDP. Nations that are primarily agrarian will be less likely to achieve high levels of GDP than more industrialized countries.

Finally, the productivity of the workforce will have an impact on incomes. If workers are more productive, their incomes will be higher.

The influences on GDP and the changes in GDP are discussed in the following chapters. A list of countries with the highest estimated GDPs in terms of Canadian dollars is presented below. The data represent trillions of Canadian dollars.

United States	11.224	United Kingdom	1.621
China	6.034	Italy	1.582
Japan	3.662	Brazil	1.502
India	2.428	Russia	1.482
Germany	2.346	Mexico	1.047
France	1.643	Canada	1.006

Questions

1. On the basis of the above data, does Canada have the 12th highest standard of living in the world? Explain.
2. Canada's economy is 100 times the level in 1942. Explain the role played by inflation in reaching the trillion-dollar mark for GDP.

Types of goods produced: Gross domestic product measures the dollar value of goods and services, not the type of goods and services. Some goods and services may be questionable in terms of the benefits that they provide. Nonetheless, all products that have a price are included. The dollar value of all items—guns, chocolate bars, houses, clothes, and so on—are all lumped together in order to arrive at a total figure.

Illegal items: Illegal goods and services are not included in the calculation of GDP. Although they are not included in GDP, these items increase the welfare of those who purchase them.

Pollution: It is possible that GDP may increase from year to year. However, it is also possible that increased production is accompanied by more pollution.

Leisure: The calculation of GDP does not consider how hard Canadians have to work to achieve a certain level of output of goods and services. If the number of paid holidays and vacations in Canada increased, it is likely that GDP figures would be lower, since fewer goods and services would be produced. Would this indicate that Canadians are not as well off? No; increased leisure time is a benefit that does not show up in GDP.

Improved product quality: GDP simply measures the value of goods and services produced. No attempt is made to account for changes in the quality of products. Improvements in quality lead to a better standard of living.

Distribution of income: As GDP increases, it is assumed that the population is better off. The GDP figure, however, does not state how this increased production and income is distributed among the population. It is possible that the increases go to only a small segment of the total population. The vast majority of Canadians may not be any better off.

R E V I E W

5.11 Why is it necessary to calculate real GDP? Per-capita GDP?

5.12 If you fix your own car, is the service included in GDP? Why or why not?

5.13 Use the following data to calculate GDP, NDP, PI, and PDI.

ITEM	$ BILLION	ITEM	$ BILLION
Consumption	50	Interest	5
Corporation dividends	2	Machinery and equipment manufactured	10
Capital consumption allowance	10	Net change in inventories	− 5
Exports	25	Rent	10
Government expenditure on goods and services	30	Savings	15
Government transfer payments	4	Taxes: corporation income	5
		personal income	21
Housing constructed	15	indirect business	5
Imports	20	Undistributed corporation profits	3
Income from unincorporated enterprises	25	Wages and salaries	40

Summary

Three issues that are important to all Canadians are unemployment, inflation, and the level of business activity. An unemployed person is someone who is out of work and looking for a job. The unemployment rate in Canada is measured monthly through the Labour Force Survey. The number of unemployed persons as a percentage of the labour force is called the unemployment rate.

The participation rate is also calculated by the Labour Force Survey. This measures the percentage of the Canadian population who are in the labour force. The most noticeable trend in participation rates has been the increase in the women's rate. This increase is a result of several factors, including smaller family sizes, higher levels of education, advancements in household technology, and changing attitudes about women's involvement in the labour force.

Inflation is defined as a general increase in the level of prices. In Canada, the rate of inflation is measured using the Consumer Price Index, and is calculated on the basis of annual increases in this index. The prices of several hundred consumer items are recorded in the index on a monthly basis. The items are weighted depending on their importance in the consumer budget. It should be remembered that the index is simply a measure of changes in retail prices, not a measure of cost-of-living changes.

The level of business activity in Canada is measured by the National Accounts. The most common statistic in the National Accounts is gross domestic product (GDP), which measures the value of final goods and ser- vices produced in Canada in a given year and is also used as an indicator of the total income earned by Canadians.

Even though GDP is a measure of the level of business activity, it is not necessarily useful as a measure of social welfare. The calculation of GDP does not take into consideration the type or quality of goods produced, how hard Canadians have to work to produce those goods, the negative third-party costs of production (such as pollution), how the increased income is distributed, or illegal goods and services.

Questions for Review and Discussion

1. Do you think that the unemployment rate is a good indicator of the economic hardship that Canadians are facing?
2. Is there any connection between the participation rate and the unem- ployment rate for various sex and age groups? What about rates for individual provinces?
3. Why is it that the seasonally adjusted level of unemployment is some- times rising when the actual number of unemployed is falling?
4. Is it possible for the unemployment rate and the employment rate to increase at the same time? Explain.
5. Identify the type of unemployment associated with each of the fol- lowing situations.
   a) John has recently graduated from college and is looking for a job.
   b) Lois is a landscape gardener and is having trouble finding employ- ment in the winter months.
   c) Although construction activity is up in other Canadian cities, a construction worker cannot find employment in his home town.
   d) As a result of a decline in sales, automobile manufacturers have ter- minated the employment of hundreds of workers.
6. Identify the type of unemployment exhibited in the following situations.
   a) Kristen quit her job as a hairdresser to look for a better position.
   b) Fred has recently retired.
   c) Matt is a ski instructor in the winter but is seeking summer employ- ment.
   d) As a result of the slowdown in the growth of GDP, Ivan has been laid off by his employer.

7. A small mining town in northern Manitoba has a population of 6000, of which 1000 are under the age of 15. Five hundred residents in the town are retired and another 300 parents do not work outside the home. Currently, 200 residents are out of work and looking for a job. The remainder of the labour force is employed.

    For this town, calculate:
   a) the labour force participation rate;
   b) the unemployment rate;
   c) the employment rate.

8. "The impact of inflation is not felt equally by all Canadians." Explain this statement.

9. Which of the following activities would lead to higher prices in Canada?
   a) more women entering the labour force;
   b) more workers joining labour unions;
   c) OPEC setting a higher price for a barrel of oil; or
   d) the federal government purchasing new aircraft.

10. The following information represents the Consumer Price Index for a hypothetical country for the years 2000 to 2003. Calculate the rate of inflation for the years for which the data are available.

YEAR	CPI	RATE OF INFLATION
2000	101.2	
2001	103.4	
2002	110.9	
2003	112.7	

11. Determine whether each of the following is included in GDP:
   a) the purchase of building materials by a contractor for the construction of a house;
   b) the purchase of building materials by you for the construction of your own house;
   c) the sale of vegetables at a local fruit and vegetable stand;
   d) growing vegetables in your garden for your own use;
   e) the distribution of holiday-season food hampers by the Salvation Army; and
   f) a ride on the roller coaster at a local carnival.

12. Why are the services performed by volunteers not included in the calculation of GDP? Should the work of volunteers be recognized in the National Accounts?

13. It has been argued that the government should provide a pension for homemakers. Why might it be difficult to introduce this proposal? Should the value of housework and the raising of children be included in GDP?

14. Why does a kilogram of beef add more to GDP than a kilogram of potatoes?

15. Why might changes in GDP, when measured in current prices, be a misleading statistic?

16. Some air pollution is the by-product of producing paper. The value of the paper is included in GDP but the air pollution is not. If steps are taken to clean up the pollution, will GDP increase?

17. Why do we include only final goods, and not intermediate goods, in the calculation of GDP?

18. Identify each of the following as either a final good or an intermediate good:
    a) a bar of cold-rolled steel
    b) a bag of fertilizer
    c) a pair of shoes
    d) a bag of flour
    e) a baseball glove

19. From the following sets of data, calculate GDP, NDP, PI, and PDI. Treat A and B as separate problems. Fill in the blanks where necessary.

ITEM	A $	B $
Change in business inventories	+8	−4
Consumption	−	33
Corporation profits after tax	9	−
Corporation profits before tax	−	10
Capital consumption allowance	7	−
Dividends	5	2
Exports	−	10
Government expenditure on goods and services	36	15
Government transfer payments	3	4
Gross investment	−	22
Housing constructed	20	10
Income from unincorporated enterprises	27	−
Interest	15	8
Imports	−	12
Machines and equipment manufactured	14	16
Net investment	−	18
Rent	9	7
Savings	29	17
Taxes, corporation income	10	3
indirect	4	3
personal income	35	−
Undistributed corporation profits	−	−
Wages and salaries	55	25

20. Identify under which category of gross domestic product (GDP) the following items should be included.
    a) John buys a new lawn mower that was made in Canada.
    b) John buys a new lawn mower that was made in Japan.
    c) The city of Windsor, Ontario hires a contractor to build a new bridge.
    d) Ford Motor Company expands its factory in Oakville, Ontario.
    e) A Saskatchewan wheat farmer buys a new tractor that was made in Canada.
    f) A Manitoba wheat farmer buys a used tractor from a neighbouring farmer.
    g) A Japanese company buys lumber from a mill in British Columbia.
    h) The federal government buys a helicopter that was made in France.
    i) Allan, Lois, and their children dine out at a restaurant in Massey, Ontario.
    j) Stephanie buys shares in Bell Canada.
21. Would the legalization of marijuana increase the value of GDP? Explain.
22. Why does the federal government calculate GDP? Why would private individuals and companies be interested in this information?
23. Why does GDP not measure all the goods and services produced in Canada in a given year?

Suggested Readings

Grant, John. *Handbook of Economic Indicators.* Toronto: University of Toronto Press, 1992. This book originated as a handbook for internal use in Wood Gundy's economics department. It provides a good discussion of all the economic data that are available on the Canadian economy.

Smith, Larry. *Canada's Charitable Economy: Its Role and Contribution.* Toronto: Canadian Foundation for Economic Education, 1992.

Selected Websites

www.hrdc-drhc.gc.ca This is the website for Human Resources Development Canada. Information is provided on the department's programs, particularly about employment insurance. Links are provided to other sites.

www.oecd.org The website for the Organisation for Economic Co-operation and Development. Twenty-nine countries including Canada are members of the OECD. This site contains economic data on the member countries.

http://stats.bls.gov This site contains information and studies on the Consumer Price Index by the U.S. Bureau of Labor Statistics (BLS) and provides links to other sources on U.S. and international economic conditions. A variety of statistics made available by the Bureau of Labor Statistics (BLS) in the United States are available at this site.

www.statcan.ca The website for Statistics Canada. Data are available on the Canadian economy.

http://economics.about.com The site provides information and articles on a wide variety of economic topics. A very good glossary is available at this site.

Determination of National Income

Key Terms

equilibrium GDP
aggregate demand
disposable income
dissaving
average propensity to consume
average propensity to save
marginal propensity to consume
marginal propensity to save
aggregate supply
paradox of thrift
expenditure multiplier
tax multiplier
balanced-budget multiplier
foreign-trade multiplier
full-employment level of GDP
recessionary gap
inflationary gap
Say's Law
Keynesian economics

Chapter Objectives

After successfully completing this chapter, you will be able to:

- explain equilibrium GDP using the circular-flow approach
- explain the paradox of thrift
- use the multiplier formulas to calculate changes in equilibrium GDP
- explain the fiscal-policy changes necessary to reach equilibrium GDP
- define the recessionary and inflationary gaps
- briefly describe theories of business cycles

Core Concept Building

You will draw on the concepts of demand and supply in this chapter to discuss the concept of an equilibrium level of economic activity. Pay close attention to the multipliers—the multiplier impact of spending lies behind the discussion of monetary and fiscal policies in Chapters 7 and 8.

TRENDS IN LABOUR'S SHARE

As pointed out in Chapter 5, the largest component of GDP calculated via the income approach is wages and salaries. The percentage of total income (GDP) that is labour income is referred to as *labour's share*. The estimates of labour's share come from T4 forms submitted to Canada Customs and Revenue Agency. Included in the definition of labour income are cash compensation, the value of stock options, and the value of taxable fringe benefits such as personal use of a company car or membership in a country club. All individuals who receive a wage or salary are lumped together under the factor of production we refer to as labour. This grouping includes a wide range of skills, from professionals to unskilled workers.

In 2002, wages and salaries represented 52 percent of GDP. Since 1947, labour's share of total income has fluctuated between 49 percent and 59 percent of GDP. Labour income has kept pace with inflation and with increases in labour productivity.

As workers became more productive, their wages increased to reflect the increase in productivity. If their wages did not keep up with increases in productivity, their share of total income would have decreased while the employers' share increased.

Interestingly, labour's share of total income increases during recessionary periods. In a recession, output decreases and the unemployment rate increases. As output falls, firms first reduce the hours of their workforce as opposed to laying off and terminating workers. Since output is reduced, the productivity of the workers is also reduced. However, if the workers remain employed, they continue to earn an income in spite of production cutbacks. Also, labour's share of total income may not decline because it is not easy to reduce the wage rate of workers when output drops off. Minimum-wage laws and collective agreements prohibit the employer from lowering wage rates below a certain level.

Gross Domestic Product

In Chapter 5, the calculation of Canada's National Accounts was reviewed. The most commonly used component of these accounts is gross domestic product (GDP), which refers to the value of goods and services produced in Canada in a given year.

The concept of GDP was first introduced with the aid of a circular flow diagram. Money circulates from the business sector to the household sector in the form of wages, salaries, rent, interest, and profits. This money then returns to the business sector when households purchase goods and services. We measured GDP by the flow of money in the circular flow diagram. If the level of GDP is to change, the flow of money, or the amount of spending in our economy, must change. This chapter discusses the reasons for changes in the level of GDP.

Household Savings and Investment

One way for the amount of spending to change would be for households to increase the amount of money that they save. Households save money by not spending it on goods and services. Savings can be put in a bank or other financial institution, or simply kept at home in a cookie jar. If household savings increase, then the amount of money sent to the business sector in the circular flow (the upper loop in Figure 6.1) would be reduced. Businesses react by cutting back on production and forwarding less money to households in the form of wages, interest, and rent. This reduces the flow of money in the lower loop of the circular flow diagram. Since the flow of money is reduced, the level of GDP is also reduced.

The amount of money in the circular flow would increase if businesses decided to increase their level of investment (spending on machinery and equipment). This increase in spending would increase payments to other businesses, which would, in turn, increase their payments to households. As households receive more income, their spending is likely to increase. As the total level of spending increases, so does the level of GDP.

Figure 6.1

The circular flow of money

Savings, taxes, and imports represent leakages from the circular flow of money, while investment, government spending, and exports represent injections.

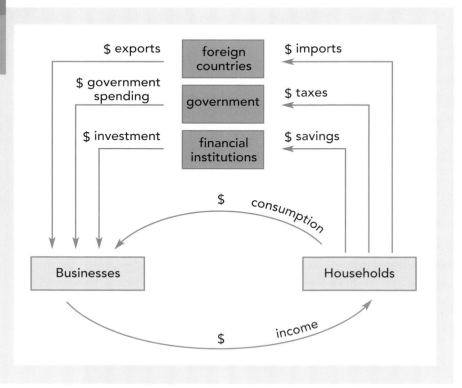

The procedure of saving money results in a reduction of money in the circular flow, while business investment results in an increase of money in the circular flow. If the overall level of savings is greater than the level of investment, GDP will decrease. If investment exceeds savings, GDP will increase. Finally, if the levels of savings and investment are equal, then the level of GDP will not change. This is referred to as **equilibrium GDP** (see Figure 6.2). When the amount of money leaving the circular flow is equal to the amount entering the circular flow, the result is an equilibrium, or stable, level of business activity. The term *equilibrium,* first introduced in Chapter 2, refers to a balanced or unchanging position.

The level of GDP will always be moving toward the equilibrium level. That is, it will always move toward a situation where the amount of money leaving the circular flow is equal to the amount of money coming in. For example, increased savings by households will reduce the flow of income going to the business sector. In turn, businesses will cut back production and lay off workers. The loss of employment reduces the flow of money back to households. With less money available, households will cut back on their spending. With less spending on goods and services, business spending (investment) will also decrease. With less investment, GDP will fall. As

GDP is said to be at an equilibrium, or stable, level when savings equals investment.

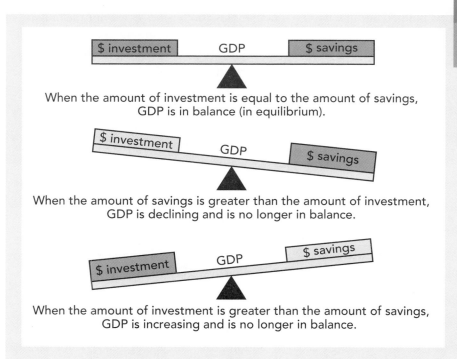

Figure 6.2

Equilibrium GDP

Only when investment ($) is equal to savings ($) is the economy in equilibrium.

GDP drops, households will not be able to save as much, since their incomes will be lower. This process will continue until a new equilibrium level of GDP is reached. This new level, lower than the original level, will be attained when the level of savings and investment are again equal.

A point of confusion for students of economics is the source of *investment funds* for business. Where do businesses get the money to spend on machines and equipment? Investment funds can come from one of four sources. First, businesses could use some of their income from sales to purchase new machines from other businesses. Second, they could borrow the money from a bank or other financial institution. Since banks are recipients of household savings, it is quite likely that household savings will be lent out to businesses for investment purposes (see Figure 6.1). Savings are taken out of the circular flow and put into financial institutions. When businesses borrow money from these institutions, the money finds its way back into the circular flow. Businesses also borrow money directly from the public by issuing bonds. Third, businesses issue shares in their corporations in order to raise money for investment. Fourth, some investment may come into Canada from outside the country. Decisions by Japanese automobile manufacturers to locate in Canada are examples of this type of investment.

The Government and Foreign-Trade Sectors

As pointed out in Chapter 5, households and businesses are not the only two participants in the Canadian economy. The government and foreign-trade sectors also have to be considered. Government spending is similar to business investment in its influence on the level of economic activity. Government spends money on equipment and services, and this money (which is paid out to Canadian businesses) will eventually find its way into Canadian households. In order to finance their spending, the various levels of government impose taxes. *Taxation removes money from the circular flow, and government spending puts it back in.*

Sales of goods and services to foreign countries, called *exports,* have the same effect on the level of GDP as do investment and government spending. Foreign purchases represent income for Canadian businesses. Canadian purchases of foreign products, on the other hand, represent a drain on the circular flow of money. These purchases, referred to as *imports,* result in money being paid to foreign businesses rather than to our own. *Exports cause GDP to increase while imports cause GDP to decrease.*

When the total amount of money injected into the circular flow (investment, government spending, and exports) exceeds the leakages from the circular flow (savings, taxation, and imports), the level of GDP will increase. There will be more money circulating in our economy. When the opposite occurs, the level of GDP will decrease. Under circumstances in which the amount of money injected equals the leakages, the level of GDP is in equilibrium.

Condition for equilibrium GDP:

$$\text{injections (\$)} = \text{leakages (\$)}$$

$$\begin{matrix} \text{investment (I)} + \text{government} \\ \text{spending (G)} + \text{exports (E)} \end{matrix} = \begin{matrix} \text{savings (S)} + \text{taxes (T)} + \\ \text{imports (M)} \end{matrix}$$

Changes in the level of GDP are also associated with changes in the level of unemployment and inflation. When the level of GDP is increasing, spending is up, jobs are being created, and the unemployment rate is likely to be low. However, when spending is high, the increased demand for goods and services puts pressure on prices, so inflation is likely to result.

We have discovered that whenever the level of spending in the economy changes, the level of GDP changes. What causes spending to change? This question can best be answered by analyzing each of the spending components of the economy separately.

R E V I E W

6.1 Why do we say that the economy, in terms of GDP, is in equilibrium when savings equals investment? *(ONLY IN BARE BONE ECONOMY)*

6.2 Why does the level of GDP always move toward an equilibrium level?

Components of Aggregate Demand

The total level of spending in the Canadian economy is composed of consumption, investment, government spending, and the difference between exports and imports. The total level of spending is referred to as the **aggregate demand** for goods and services produced in Canada.

Consumption

The level of household spending on goods and services is referred to as *consumption.* Some of the factors influencing the level of consumption expenditures are:

Disposable income: Possibly the most important determinant of the level of household spending is the level of **disposable income.** This is the income that remains in the household after taxes have been paid. There is clearly a

Aggregate demand is the total demand for goods and services in the economy, including consumption, investment, government spending, and the difference between exports and imports.

Disposable income is the income that remains in the household after taxes have been paid.

positive relationship between disposable income and consumption. As disposable income increases, consumption will increase as well.

Interest rates: In order to spend, it may be necessary for some people to borrow money. The decision on whether or not to borrow money often depends on the cost of borrowing. If borrowing costs (interest rates) are high, then spending will probably be reduced. When interest rates are high, households are also encouraged to save money because the return (the interest rate) they get for leaving money in a bank or other financial institution is also high. When interest rates are low, the cost of borrowing is less and the opportunity cost of not saving is also less. Therefore, at low interest rates, consumer spending usually increases.

Wealth: In addition to income, the level of accumulated wealth also influences consumption expenditures. Whereas income can be seen as a flow of money, wealth is seen as a stock or accumulation of money or assets. Wealth can be accumulated and held in many forms: real estate, savings accounts, gold, paintings, and other forms of valuable goods. The greater the accumulation of wealth the greater the ability to spend, and the higher the level of consumption.

Expectations: A major determinant of household spending is expectation about future prices and future levels of income. If consumers expect prices to increase in the future, they may purchase products now in order to get the product at a lower price. Expectations of future income will also affect spending. If there is a possibility of losing your job, or experiencing a lay-off in the near future, you are likely to cut back on your spending and increase your savings. These expectations will cause the total level of consumption to drop.

Psychological: A whole range of psychological factors influences spending. Some families may want to purchase "status" items in order to "keep up with the Joneses." Others may be content with purchasing essential items. Variations in individual tastes and preferences, and in individual motives toward spending, affect consumption. Advertising attempts to persuade households to alter, or maintain, their consumption habits.

New products: As new products come onto the market, spending patterns may change. The introduction of new products (such as cellular phones) may change household preferences and alter expenditure plans. The introduction of these products may convince consumers that a change in their lifestyle is required; the money needed to pay for these products may be taken out of savings rather than transferred from other purchases.

Distribution of income: The overall level of consumption in the economy may also be influenced by the distribution of income among households. Whereas high-income families are able to save, poorer families are not able to afford that luxury. Any shift in the distribution of income away from high-income households to low-income households may increase the total level of consumption. Certain government transfer programs redistribute income in favour of lower-income groups (see Chapter 4) and thus influence the overall level of consumption.

Prices: Prices and price changes are likely to influence the level of consumer spending. It is difficult to assess the effect that price changes will have on spending, since other factors are also involved in the decision to spend money. In some cases, households may cut back in response to price increases. In other cases, they may increase present spending, if it is expected that prices will rise even higher.

Demographic factors: Several demographic factors are bound to influence consumption. These include age, sex, race, family size, level of education, occupation, and location of residence.

Of the factors listed above, it is believed that *disposable income* is the most important. We will, therefore, concentrate on the positive relationship between *consumption* and *income.*

The Consumption Schedule

Table 6.1 presents various levels of disposable income, consumption, and savings for similar-sized families. These figures are arbitrary and are meant to serve only as examples. The table shows positive relationships between the levels of consumption and of disposable income. As the level of income increases, the level of consumption increases as well. Savings are also positively related to disposable income. In this particular example, a hypothetical family of four would break even with an income of $40 000 per year. At this level of disposable income, the family is consuming $40 000 worth of goods and services and saving nothing. At levels of disposable income below $40 000, families are in fact "**dissaving**" (that is, their spending, or consumption, is greater than their disposable income). The money needed to pay for this spending must come out of accumulated savings or else must be borrowed. In these situations, the level of consumption exceeds the level of disposable income. Positive savings levels appear at incomes above $40 000 per year. For example, at a disposable income of $50 000, this family manages to save $5000 per year.

Dissaving occurs when spending is greater than disposable income.

Table 6.1 *Levels of disposable income, consumption, and savings for hypothetical families of four*

DISPOSABLE INCOME $/YEAR	CONSUMPTION $	SAVINGS $	APC	APS	MPC	MPS
20 000	26 000	–6 000	1.3	–0.3		
					0.8	0.2
30 000	34 000	–4 000	1.13	–0.13		
					0.6	0.4
40 000	40 000	0	1.0	0		
					0.5	0.5
50 000	45 000	5 000	0.9	0.1		
					0.3	0.7
60 000	48 000	12 000	0.8	0.2		

APC = average propensity to consume
APS = average propensity to save
MPC = marginal propensity to consume
MPS = marginal propensity to save

The average propensity to consume (APC) **represents the ratio of consumption to income (or gross domestic product).**

The average propensity to save (APS) **represents the ratio of savings to income (or gross domestic product).**

From the table, it is possible to calculate two additional statistics that relate consumption to income. The **average propensity to consume (APC)** is the ratio of total consumption to total income. For example, the average propensity to consume (APC) for a family earning $50 000 per year is 0.9. This family is spending $45 000 per year, or 90 percent of its income. The **average propensity to save (APS)** is the ratio of savings to disposable income. Since there are only two things that can be done with one's income—to consume it and/or to save it—the average propensity to save (APS) for a family earning $50 000 per year is 0.1, or 10 percent.

$$\text{average propensity to consume (APC)} = \frac{\text{consumption}}{\text{disposable income}}$$

$$\text{average propensity to save (APS)} = \frac{\text{savings}}{\text{disposable income}}$$

$$APC + APS = 1.0$$

More important than the concept of average propensities is the concept of *marginal propensities,* which refers to the change in consumption resulting from a change in disposable income. According to Table 6.1, a family of four with an income of $40 000 per year has a **marginal propensity to consume (MPC)** of 0.5. The calculation can be made by looking at what would happen to consumption if a family's income increased from $40 000 to $50 000 per year. Consumption would increase from $40 000 to

The marginal propensity to consume (MPC) **represents the proportion of any increase in income that is used for consumption.**

$45 000, representing an increase in consumption of $5000 per year. Fifty percent of the increase in disposable income went for consumption spending. The **marginal propensity to save (MPS)** relates changes in the level of savings to the changes in the level of income.

marginal propensity to consume (MPC)   = $\dfrac{\text{change in consumption}}{\text{change in income}}$

marginal propensity to save (MPS)   = $\dfrac{\text{change in savings}}{\text{change in income}}$

By definition,

$$MPC \ + \ MPS \ = \ 1.0$$

As indicated in Table 6.1, it is expected that the MPC would decline as the level of income increases. Those families in the higher income brackets can afford the luxury of saving more of any increase in income. Those in the lower income categories may need to consume almost all of any increase in income and can afford to save very little. Empirical studies have shown that although the MPC is slightly lower for higher-income Canadians, the difference in MPCs between income groups is not very great. Several studies have estimated the MPC for Canadians. The value of the MPC for Canada for the years 1961–1985 was estimated by Statistics Canada to be 0.77.

> The marginal propensity to save (MPS) relates changes in the level of savings to the changes in the level of income.

R E V I E W

6.3 Discuss five factors that influence the level of consumer spending.

6.4 If your disposable income went up by $6000 per year and you increased your spending by $4000, what would be your marginal propensity to consume? To save?

EVERYDAY ECONOMICS 6.1

Saving

Saving has both a positive and a negative impact on the economy. On the positive side, savings provide a pool of money that can be lent for investment. Most Canadians put their savings in the bank, and the bank lends out the money to businesses. Normally, the larger the available pool of money, the lower the interest rate. Thus, when Canadians save, they are helping to lower interest rates. On the negative side, saving is the opposite of consumption. When Canadians save, they are not spending. When they are not spending, they are not creating employment opportunities.

Private saving in Canada is approximately 15 percent of GDP. Americans, on average, save less than 4 percent of their disposable income. Although the figures are not directly comparable, they do point to the fact that personal saving is higher in Canada than in the United States. Why is the level of saving high in Canada relative to the United States?

Some analysts have concluded that the higher rate of unemployment in Canada encouraged more precautionary savings on the part of Canadians. The high rate of inflation at the time convinced consumers to postpone spending. The high interest rates paid on savings accounts also encouraged people to save money. Although this seems like a logical response to the situation, Americans did not react in the same manner to their high rates of inflation and high interest rates. Why are Canadians and Americans different in terms of saving money?

Part of the answer lies in the differing income-tax regulations in each country. During the 1970s, Canada introduced several incentives for savings in the Income Tax Act. These included the Registered Retirement Savings Plan (RRSP) and the Registered Home Ownership Savings Plan (RHOSP). Both plans enabled individuals to reduce the amount of tax payable if savings were deposited to one of these registered plans. Another change to Canada's Income Tax Act allowed Canadians to earn a certain amount of interest on their savings before the interest became taxable.

By contrast, the American income-tax system was, until recently, geared more toward spending. For example, Americans were allowed to deduct the interest charges on mortgages, bank cards, other general-purpose credit cards, and charge accounts from their taxable income. Now, only the interest payments on mortgages are tax-deductible. Residents of the U.S. can now reduce their taxable income by putting money into Individual Retirement Accounts. These accounts, which are similar to Canadian RRSPs, encourage savings.

Another reason for the higher level of savings in Canada may be the approach to paying for social services like medical care. In Canada, a higher percentage of medical costs are paid for out of tax dollars than in the United States. Medical care is basically a private expense in the United States. Since Canadians have already paid for these services through taxes, they can afford the luxury of saving more of their after-tax income.

Higher levels of savings in Canada have been attributed to the fact that real interest rates have been higher in Canada than in the U.S. Real interest rates are determined by subtracting the rate of inflation from the nominal, or actual, rate of interest.

During the 1990s the savings rate in Canada declined. What accounted for the decrease in the savings rate during a decade when inflation was held in check? Accompanying a moderate rate of inflation during the 1990s was a very small increase in wage rates. Real income (income after the impact of inflation is taken into consideration) had almost no growth. The tax burden on Canadians did grow, however, and hindered the ability to save.

Savings also differ considerably between province and territory in Canada. Savings as a percentage of personal disposable income are the lowest in British Columbia, Saskatchewan, and Alberta, and the highest in the Yukon and the Northwest Territories. What accounts for the differences in savings rates? Do higher-income provinces have higher savings rates? The answer is no. Higher-income provinces such as Alberta and British Columbia have low savings rates, and some lower-income provinces such as Prince Edward Island and Newfoundland have savings rates above the Canadian average.

It is possible that demographics play a role in savings rates between provinces. For example, a province such as British Columbia attracts a large number of retired individuals who may have lower savings rates than younger Canadians. This explanation, however, needs further study. A discussion of the reasons behind provincial savings rates is complicated by the fact that provincial savings rates are not stable.

Questions

1. What group of Canadians would benefit most from RRSP plans? Why?
2. Why would Americans have been more willing to borrow money in the past for consumer purchases than Canadians?
3. What would be the effect on the economy if the government took steps to encourage more Canadian savings?
4. Saving provides money for investment. If saving is at a low level, companies must rely on borrowing foreign funds for investment. Foreign funding of U.S. investment has increased to 5 percent of GDP in 2002. Are there any concerns associated with an increased reliance on foreign funds for investment? Explain.

Investment

Investment is defined as business or government purchases of machines and equipment, new-housing construction, and any change in business inventories. It is the most volatile component of GDP and is also the most difficult to predict. There are two major reasons for this. First, many investment decisions are based on business expectations about the future. Quite often these expectations are subjective in nature and open to change. Second, there are several variables that influence the level of investment spending. Changes in any of these variables alter investment spending. These variables are:

The interest rate: In order to purchase new equipment many businesses are forced to borrow money. High borrowing costs, or interest rates, are likely to discourage borrowing and, therefore, to reduce the level of investment spending. Some equipment purchases may be regarded as only marginally profitable, and if interest rates are too high these projects will be abandoned. On the other hand, lower interest rates may encourage spending on projects that were not feasible at the higher interest rates.

Innovation and changes in technology: As new products are developed, companies may want to purchase them in order to improve the efficiency of their operation. For example, the introduction of the laptop computer, the personal computer, and word-processing equipment has revolutionized office procedures. In order to be able to compete, companies are forced continually to update their equipment and methods of operation. Many companies are now investing in e-commerce. Investments in telecommunications and computer manufacturing have shown significant increases.

Government policy and taxes: Many government policies affect business spending. For example, rent controls may reduce the number of new apartment buildings being constructed. An excise tax on a product, which increases the price, will influence consumer demand and, ultimately, business investment. Changes in the Income Tax Act may change the conditions under which businesses can depreciate capital purchases. The switch from the Foreign Investment Review Agency (FIRA) to Investment Canada has changed the image of Canada from a foreign investor's point of view. Whereas FIRA was seen as a hindrance to foreign investment, Investment Canada encourages foreign investment. These decisions and others will have an impact on investment. The philosophy of the political party in power can also influence investment. Investors may be more willing to spend money if the government in power leans toward the free-market approach rather than one advocating government control in order to solve economic problems.

Expectations: Expectations about the future business environment influence spending. Changes in the level of sales, profits, and GDP affect business expectations about the future. For example, if GDP were forecasted to increase significantly, companies would expect their sales to increase. If sales are expected to increase, investment will increase. Conversely, expectations about depressed economic conditions will reduce the level of investment.

Replacements: In the process of producing goods and services, some equipment will wear out and have to be replaced. The spending required to replace this equipment is investment. Some economists believe that spending on replacement equipment is the major reason for the fluctuations in investment and ultimately in GDP.

Cost of capital goods: As with the purchase of any product, the price is also important. Price increases would tend to discourage the purchase of new equipment.

Gross domestic product: When GDP increases, it is an indication that the total level of income in the economy is increasing. If total income is increasing, spending is increasing, and companies will need to buy more equipment in order to be able to keep up with the increased demand. Investment spending will be required unless business already has unused productive capacity.

The New Economy

Much has been written in recent years about the changes taking place in our economy. To many individuals the change in our economy is so major that the term "New Economy" has been coined to describe it. What is the nature of this change and what is the New Economy?

The New Economy is described as the shift from a manufacturing-based economy to an economy based on services and technology. The New Economy is knowledge-based. That is, much of the wealth created in the future will be based on knowledge rather than the ownership of land or capital. There will be less demand for lower-skilled jobs and more demand for those workers with specific skills. People will work less with their hands and more with their brains. Most jobs will require some computer skills, and change will be occurring at such a rapid pace that life-long learning and upgrading will be necessary.

Typical of the changes in the workplace that are taking place are the changes experienced on the production line. For many years, jobs on the assembly line did not require a great deal of education. Factory employees operated various types of manufacturing equipment to produce a product and quality checks were done at the end of the line. Those products not up to standards were sent to a repair facility to be fixed before being shipped to the customer.

Beginning in the 1970s, more automation was introduced on the factory floor. More automation meant better-quality products, less delay, lower costs, and more profit. Advances in technology now enable companies to ship more products with fewer employees. For those employees who remain on the factory floor, the skills required for their jobs have changed. New terminology—such as CAD/CAM, just-in-time inventory, computer-integrated manufacturing, and process simulation—is in common usage in the production process. Quality checks are made throughout the manufacturing process, not only at the end.

The New Economy will also be characterized by increased competition. More competition will come from improvements in transportation and communications, deregulation of industry, privatization of government-owned enterprises, and increased globalization that comes with lower trade barriers and less restrictive foreign-investment rules. It is now possible to transfer large amounts of money around the globe in a very short period of time. Countries must provide an attractive environment for investors, or money will go elsewhere. The increased international mobility of money will also spur competition.

Questions

1. Can you provide an example of an industry that has changed in order to adapt to the New Economy?
2. Firms will be investing in humans as well as machinery and equipment in the New Economy. Discuss this statement.
3. How can Canada provide an environment that is favourable to foreign investors?

Government and Foreign Trade

The third component of aggregate demand is government spending. In order to carry out its mandate, government spends money on goods and services in a manner similar to any other business. The variables that influence the level of government spending were discussed in Chapter 4. The final component of aggregate demand is the difference between exports and imports. The factors that influence Canada's foreign trade will be discussed in detail in Chapter 9.

Aggregate Demand Curve

In Chapter 2, we learned that a demand curve for a specific product or service is drawn with the price of the product or service on the vertical axis and the quantity on the horizontal axis. We can draw a demand curve for all products in much the same manner. The aggregate demand curve (AD) is shown in Figure 6.3. On the vertical axis the price level for all products is measured. On the horizontal axis is real gross domestic product (RGDP).

Why use real gross domestic product instead of quantity on the horizontal axis? Actually, RGDP is a measure of quantity. As stated in Chapter 5, GDP is a measure of the flow of money from the business sector in our economy to the household sector. It is a measure of the total amount of income earned in our economy in a given year. It is also a measure of the total amount of goods and services produced. Since we cannot add up bushels of apples, tonnes of steel, houses sold, lawns cut, and so on, we convert all these products and services to money. Adding them up in money

Figure 6.3

Aggregate demand and aggregate supply

The aggregate demand curve (AD) shows an inverse relationship between the price level and RGDP, whereas the aggregate supply curve shows a positive relationship.

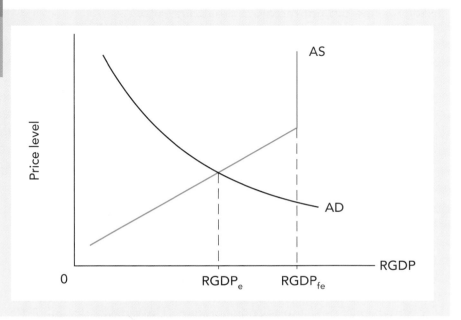

terms provides us with GDP. Because GDP is a measure of production, it can be used as a measure of quantity in deriving the aggregate demand curve.

Because price increases alone can result in an increase in GDP, an adjustment for price increases is necessary so that GDP will adequately reflect the amount of goods and services produced. Adjusting GDP for price increases gives us real gross domestic product (RGDP).

Why does the aggregate demand curve slope down to the right? Economists believe that there are two factors influencing the slope of the curve: the wealth effect and the substitution effect. Individuals hold their wealth in bonds, in shares, in bank accounts, and so on. When prices increase (everything else remaining the same), an individual's real wealth decreases. That is, the purchasing power of the accumulated wealth declines. Economists argue that when this occurs people will try to restore their real wealth by increasing their saving and reducing their demand for goods and services.

The substitution effect is related to the impact of interest-rate increases on consumption. As the price level rises, interest rates increase (this process will be explained more fully in later chapters). When interest rates increase, individuals cut back on spending and increase saving. They postpone their spending until a later date. Economists state that individuals are substituting future consumption for present consumption.

The aggregate demand curve (AD) is similar to the individual demand curves introduced earlier. As the price level increases, the quantity of goods and services demanded, represented by RGDP, decreases. As the price level falls, RGDP increases. Individual demand curves shift when one of the factors influencing demand, other than the price, changes. Similarly, the aggregate demand curve will shift when one of the components of aggregate demand changes. For example, if businesses decide to increase the level of investment spending, then the AD curve will shift to the right. If consumers decide to increase the amount of their savings, the AD curve will shift to the left.

Aggregate Supply

In order to discuss the concept of equilibrium gross domestic product, it is necessary to introduce the concept of **aggregate supply**. Aggregate supply represents the summation of all the individual supply curves in the economy. The aggregate supply curve (AS) is shown in Figure 6.3. The aggregate supply curve shows the relationship between the price level and the GDP supplied when the money wage rate and the prices of other resources remain constant. It bears a resemblance to the market supply curves introduced in Chapter 2. The price level is measured on the vertical axis. The

Aggregate supply is the total production of goods and services available in the economy over a certain period of time.

horizontal axis measures quantity in terms of real gross domestic product (RGDP). In a fashion similar to individual market supply curves, the aggregate supply curve (AS) shows a positive relationship between price and quantity supply. As the price level increases, the quantity of goods and services produced increases as well. The AS curve, however, does not continue to increase indefinitely. There is a physical limit to the amount of goods and services that Canadians can produce. This maximum is shown in Figure 6.3 as $RGDP_{fe}$, which represents the production of goods and services that would be possible if all available resources were fully employed. $RGDP_{fe}$ refers to the full employment level of real gross domestic product. You will recall from Chapter 5 that full employment in the economy means that the unemployment that does exist is due to frictional, seasonal, and structural factors. In other words, the economy is operating at its natural rate of unemployment.

Apart from price change, what determines the level of aggregate supply in our economy? It is primarily determined by the quantity and quality of resources available. An introduction to Canada's resources was presented in the first chapter of this text. *The more resources (land, labour, and capital) available to Canadians, the greater the amount of goods and services produced.*

The quantity and quality of land will determine Canada's ability to supply goods and services (the definition of this resource is in Chapter 1). Land means more than square kilometres; it includes such natural resources as minerals, wild animals, vegetation, and water.

Human resources are also necessary for production. Increases in the population will normally lead to increases in the labour force. Changes in labour-force participation rates, such as those discussed in Chapter 5, may also increase the size of the labour force.

The productivity of our resources also influences production levels. If members of Canada's labour force receive better instruction, better training, and better education, they will be more productive. If management techniques are updated and improved, increases in productivity will occur. Improvements in technology will also result in increased production.

If businesses invest in new factories, machinery, and equipment, our capital resources will increase. If businesses fail to invest, then our capital resources may be reduced as existing machinery and equipment wears out. Business investment not only represents a major component of aggregate demand, but also has a significant impact on aggregate supply.

Government regulation may influence aggregate supply as well. Many Canadian industries are strictly controlled by government in terms of the number of companies allowed to operate in the industry. Examples of such industries are telephone, cable television, and natural gas. In agriculture, the number of producers of eggs, chickens, tobacco, milk, and turkeys is also restricted by marketing boards. Alternatively, government may also act in order to increase aggregate supply. Tax changes may make it more attractive for businesses to increase production. Government promotions like those being undertaken by Investment Canada may encourage more foreign companies to locate in Canada.

Equilibrium Gross Domestic Product

Equilibrium in an individual market is achieved at the price level at which the quantity demanded and the quantity supplied are equal. A similar situation occurs with aggregate demand and aggregate supply. The level of RGDP at which they are equal is referred to as equilibrium RGDP (RGDP$_e$ in Figure 6.3). At this level of economic activity there is no need for RGDP to change. The amount of goods and services demanded will be equal to the amount of goods and services supplied. Once achieved, the equilibrium level of RGDP will change only when either AD or AS changes.

If RGDP is not at equilibrium, how does it get there? Assume that the price level was at P_1. At this price level, aggregate demand (AD) is greater than aggregate supply (AS) (see Figure 6.4). In this situation, inventories

Figure 6.4

Equilibrium real gross domestic product

Equilibrium real gross domestic product occurs where the aggregate demand and aggregate supply curves intersect.

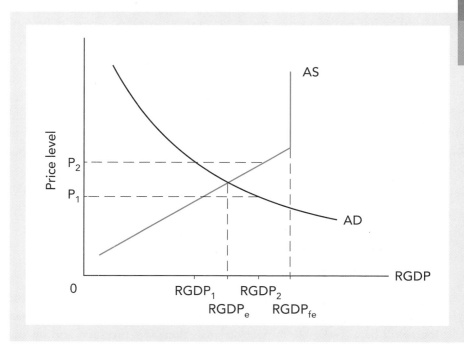

would be depleted and suppliers would need to increase production in order to meet the demand. As new employees are hired and new machinery put into use, production levels will increase. Real gross domestic product will increase. For a price level at P_2 the level of aggregate supply is greater than the level of aggregate demand. Inventories would begin to accumulate. Companies would cut back on production and lay off employees. The level of gross domestic product would decline. Only at a level of RGDP where AS and AD are equal ($RGDP_e$) would the economy be in equilibrium. That is, only at this level of economic activity would the total level of spending and the total level of production remain the same.

How does the equilibrium level of RGDP change? Anything that would cause aggregate demand or aggregate supply to change would change the equilibrium level of RGDP. For example, if consumers decide to increase their spending on goods and services, the AD curve will shift to the right. At the present level of equilibrium, $RGDP_1$, the aggregate demand now exceeds aggregate supply. This circumstance will cause production to increase and the RGDP to rise until it reaches $RGDP_2$. Conversely, a drop in aggregate demand caused by a decline in investment would shift the AD curve to the left. This would cause the level of equilibrium RGDP to decline.

Paradox of Thrift

The paradox of thrift **states that an increase in the level of savings in the economy can lead to lower levels of income and ultimately to lower levels of savings.**

An interesting aspect of the consequences of saving is the **paradox of thrift.** According to the dictionary, a paradox is "a statement that appears to be contradictory, but in fact may be true." The contradiction in relation to savings is that by attempting to save more, we may end up saving less. The result would be a lower level of equilibrium RGDP. As RGDP moved toward this new equilibrium level, the total income earned in Canada would begin to decline. Some people would be able to work only part time, some would experience layoffs, and others would simply lose their jobs. As the level of income in Canada fell, the ability of Canadians to save money would fall as well.

In terms of the circular flow of money diagram (Figure 6.1), when households decide to increase their savings less money will circulate to the business sector. In turn, businesses pay out less money to households in the form of wages, rent, interest, and profits. With a reduced level of income, households will not be able to save as much. As a result, the total level of savings would be reduced.

The paradox of thrift applies only if a significant number of people decide to increase their savings. If only a few people decide to save more, then there will be a negligible impact on gross domestic product, and on the total level of savings. It should be noted that not everyone will suffer a reduced level of savings. Some individuals may not suffer a drop in income when the level of gross domestic product declines. Government employees are an example of people whose incomes do not depend on the level of business activity or, more specifically, on the sales and profits of their company.

R E V I E W

6.5   Why is RGDP a better indicator of the amount of goods and services produced than GDP?

6.6   What factors might cause the aggregate demand curve to shift to the right?

6.7   If AS is greater than AD at the current level of RGDP, will the level of RGDP move toward equilibrium? Explain.

6.8   In your own words explain the paradox of thrift.

6.9   Welcome to the Aggregate Demand Game: determine how news items affect aggregate demand.

The Multiplier

What impact do changes in aggregate demand have on GDP? Any increase in aggregate demand will cause GDP to increase because GDP is a measure of the total level of spending in the economy. By how much will the level of GDP increase? Surprisingly, the level of GDP increases by more than the initial increase in aggregate demand.

The Expenditure Multiplier

Assume that you decide to spend $1000 on some new audio equipment. What is the impact on GDP? Your initial spending will cause GDP to increase by $1000. Your spending also represents income to the owner of the audio shop. The owner may spend some of that money on other purchases. The amount that the owner spends depends on his or her marginal propensity to consume (MPC). Another person will be the recipient of this spending and will, in turn, spend part of what he or she receives. Every time that spending takes place, GDP increases. In fact, your decision to spend $1000 has started a chain reaction that results in an increase in the level of GDP of more than $1000. How much more? The ultimate impact on GDP can be shown as follows:

$$\Delta \text{ GDP} = \$1000$$
$$+ (\text{MPC}) \times \$1000$$
$$+ (\text{MPC})\ (\text{MPC}) \times \$1000$$
$$+ (\text{MPC})\ (\text{MPC})\ (\text{MPC}) \times \$1000$$
$$+ \ldots\ldots\ldots\ldots$$

This formula assumes that everyone has exactly the same MPC, and spends the same percentage of any increase in income. It is possible to add up these expenditures using a short mathematical formula. This formula is known as the *sum of a geometric progression.* Assume that the MPC is equal to 0.8.

$$\Delta \text{ GDP} = \Delta \text{ AD} \times \frac{1}{1 - \text{MPC}} \quad \text{(where } \Delta \text{ means "change in")}$$

$$\Delta \text{ GDP} = \$1000 \times \frac{1}{1 - 0.8}$$

$$\Delta \text{ GDP} = \$1000 \times \frac{1}{0.2}$$

$$\Delta \text{ GDP} = \$1000 \times 5$$

$$\Delta \text{ GDP} = \$5000$$

Your initial decision to spend $1000 could have the effect of increasing the level of GDP by $5000, since GDP measures the total amount of spending in our economy. This is referred to as the **expenditure multiplier.** The change in spending (Δ AD) is multiplied by an amount 1/(1 – MPC) in order to determine the final effect on GDP. The formula used above is referred to as *the multiplier formula.*

The multiplier formula can also be used when a decrease in spending or in aggregate demand occurs. The impact of a decrease in consumer spending of $7000 on GDP is shown as follows:

$$\Delta \text{ GDP} = \Delta \text{ AD} \times \frac{1}{1 - \text{MPC}}$$

$$\Delta \text{ GDP} = -\$7000 \times \frac{1}{1 - 0.8}$$

$$\Delta \text{ GDP} = -\$7000 \times \frac{1}{0.2}$$

$$\Delta \text{ GDP} = -\$7000 \times 5$$

$$\Delta \text{ GDP} = -\$35\ 000$$

The expenditure multiplier **is the amount by which a change in aggregate demand is multiplied in order to determine the change in GDP.**

A cut in consumer spending of $7000 led to a decrease in GDP of $35 000. When consumers reduce their spending, less money circulates in the business sector. Less money is then paid out in wages and salaries, and then a further reduction in spending takes place. Ultimately, GDP is reduced by $35 000. This example used a MPC of 0.8. If another MPC were used the reduction in GDP would be different. For example, if the MPC were 0.75, then the reduction in GDP would have been $28 000.

REVIEW

6.10 What would be the impact on GDP if consumer spending increased by $1000 and the MPC were 0.75? What would your answer be if the MPC were 0.50?

6.11 What would be the effect on GDP if the business sector decided to increase its spending by $20 million? Assume an MPC of 0.75.

6.12 The multiplier concept works in reverse as well. A decrease in spending will cause GDP to fall by a multiple amount. Can you explain why?

6.13 Examine how an initial change in aggregate demand combined with consumers' marginal propensity to consume affects GDP, as predicted by the expenditure multiplier.

The Tax Multiplier

Government tax changes have a multiple effect on GDP. If government lowers the rate of tax, consumers and businesses have more money to spend; this increased spending has a multiple effect on GDP. The effect resulting from the **tax multiplier** is slightly different from the one shown by the expenditure multiplier. Some of the reduction in taxes will not be spent by households, but will be saved. Therefore, the initial increase in spending resulting from a tax reduction will not be equal to the initial reduction in taxes. Since a reduction in taxes affects savings, tax changes do not have the same impact on GDP as do changes in government or other spending. When taxes are increased, some of the money paid in taxes will come out of savings. For example, what would be the effect of a $20-million tax reduction on the level of GDP? Assume that the MPC is 0.75. If $20 million is returned to the public in the form of tax reductions, $5 million will be saved and $15 million will be spent. The effect of an increase of $15 million in spending on GDP is as follows:

> The **tax multiplier** is the amount by which any change in the level of taxation must be multiplied in order to determine the impact on GDP.

$$
\begin{aligned}
\Delta \text{ GDP} = \ & \$15 \\
+ \ & \text{MPC} \times \$15 \\
+ \ & (\text{MPC})\,(\text{MPC}) \times \$15 \\
+ \ & (\text{MPC})\,(\text{MPC})\,(\text{MPC}) \times \$15 \\
+ \ & \ldots\ldots\ldots
\end{aligned}
$$

Again, this can be added up by the use of a formula. The formula is:

$$\Delta\,GDP = -\left[\Delta\,taxes \times \frac{MPC}{1 - MPC}\right]$$

$$\Delta\,GDP = -\left[-\$20 \times \frac{0.75}{1 - 0.75}\right]$$

$$\Delta\,GDP = -\left[-\$20 \times \frac{0.75}{0.25}\right]$$

$$\Delta\,GDP = -[-\$20 \times 3]$$

$$\Delta\,GDP = -[-\$60\ million]$$

$$\Delta\,GDP = +\ \$60\ million$$

The reduction in tax revenues of $20 million had a positive effect of $60 million on GDP. If government had increased the level of taxes rather than decreased them, GDP would decline. The same formula would be used to determine the impact of a tax increase. The formula used to calculate the effect of a tax change on GNP is called the tax multiplier formula.

REVIEW

6.14 What is the impact on GDP of a $10-million increase in taxes? Assume that the MPC is 0.8.

6.15 Which has more impact on the economy—a $20-million increase in government spending or a $20-million decrease in taxes? Use the expenditure and tax multipliers in your answer.

Balanced-Budget Multiplier

Often, government increases in tax revenues are used to finance increases in government spending. Increases in taxes tend to decrease the level of GDP, while government spending tends to increase the level of GDP. In order to determine the combined effect of these measures, assume that the government increased taxes by $10 million and then spent the $10 million on job-creation programs. If the MPC is 0.8, the impact will be as follows:

$$\Delta\,GDP = -\left[\Delta\,taxes \times \frac{MPC}{1 - MPC}\right]$$

$$\Delta\,GDP = -\left[\$10 \times \frac{0.8}{1 - 0.8}\right]$$

$$\Delta\ GDP\ =\ -\left[\ \$10\ \times\ \frac{0.8}{0.2}\ \right]$$

$$\Delta\ GDP\ =\ -\ [\$10\ \times\ 4]$$

$$\Delta\ GDP\ =\ -\ \$40$$

The impact of government spending is then as follows:

$$\Delta\ GDP\ =\ \Delta\ spending\ \times\ \frac{1}{1\ -\ MPC}$$

$$\Delta\ GDP\ =\ \$10\ \times\ \frac{1}{1\ -\ 0.8}$$

$$\Delta\ GDP\ =\ \$10\ \times\ \frac{1}{0.2}$$

$$\Delta\ GDP\ =\ \$10\ \times\ 5$$

$$\Delta\ GDP\ =\ \$50$$

The increase in taxes had the effect of reducing GDP by $40 million. The subsequent increase in spending had the effect of increasing GDP by $50 million. The net effect on GDP is, therefore, an increase of $10 million. This is referred to as the **balanced-budget multiplier,** since the increase in taxes and the increase in government spending were the same amount. The government has balanced the books and GDP has increased by $10 million. Therefore, if the government is interested in stimulating the economy, a greater stimulus is provided by government spending rather than by reducing taxes.

> The balanced-budget multiplier **is the amount by which an equal increase in taxes and in government spending increases GDP.**

When taxes are paid, some of the money comes from a reduction in savings. The government then spends this money along with the money that households would have spent yet gave up in taxes. The government is spending your potential savings. When taxes are reduced, the opposite occurs. Not all of the additional money that households receive from tax deductions will be spent. Some of it will find its way into savings.

Government policy that changes expenditures and taxation in order to influence the level of economic activity in Canada is referred to as *fiscal policy.* At the federal government level, fiscal policy is the responsibility of the Department of Finance.

R E V I E W

6.16 What is the net effect on GDP of government increasing taxes and spending by $50 million? Assume that the MPC is 0.5.

Foreign-Trade Multiplier

The *expenditure*, or *spending, multiplier* $\frac{1}{(1 - MPC)}$ is the number that any change in spending is multiplied by in order to determine the ultimate effect on GDP. Our previous discussion of the multiplier omitted the impact of exports and imports on the level of GDP. Canada, however, is a major participant in international trade and so it is necessary to discuss this impact. This discussion will require an adjustment to the expenditure multiplier formula.

In our earlier discussion of the multiplier, we assumed that an individual had only two choices in handling money. It could be spent (consumed) or saved. Any increase in income had to be allocated to these choices. International trade is a third element involved in the allocation of money. Households can spend some of their income on imports. This money acts as a leakage in the circular flow. Money spent on imports is not returned to Canadian businesses and is not paid out in wages, rent, or interest to Canadian households. The spending of money on imports reduces the impact of the spending multiplier on GDP. A numerical example will help in the explanation.

Assume MPC = 0.8, MPS = 0.2, Δ AD = \$100.

$$\Delta \text{ GDP} = \Delta \text{ AD} \times \frac{1}{1 - \text{MPC}}$$

$$\Delta \text{ GDP} = \$100 \times \frac{1}{1 - 0.8}$$

$$\Delta \text{ GDP} = \$100 \times \frac{1}{0.2}$$

$$\Delta \text{ GDP} = \$100 \times 5$$

$$\Delta \text{ GDP} = \$500$$

Without taking into consideration the foreign-trade sector, an increase in spending of \$100 leads to a \$500 increase in GDP. Now let us introduce international trade into our models. If one's income can now be spent on imports, the concept of marginal propensity to import (MPM) has to be introduced.

$$\text{marginal propensity to import (MPM)} = \frac{\Delta \text{ imports}}{\Delta \text{ income}}$$

Previously,

MPC + MPS = 1

Now,

MPC + MPS + MPM = 1

The introduction of MPM has reduced the value of MPC because some of the money previously spent on domestic items is now spent on imports. Making changes to our example, assume

$$MPC = 0.6, \ MPS = 0.2, \ and, \ MPM = 0.2$$

Now,

$$\Delta GDP = \$100 \times \frac{1}{1 - 0.6}$$

$$\Delta GDP = \$100 \times \frac{1}{0.4}$$

$$\Delta GDP = \$100 \times 2.5$$

$$\Delta GDP = \$250$$

When international trade is inserted into the model, the resulting increase in GDP is only $250. Therefore, the multiplier effect on total spending when using the **foreign-trade multiplier** (the amount by which a change in aggregate demand is multiplied to determine the change in GDP while taking into account the impact of foreign trade) is not as great as it was without taking into consideration international trade.

The amount by which a change in aggregate demand is multiplied in order to determine the change in GDP, taking into account the impact of foreign trade, is the foreign-trade multiplier.

The multiplier $\frac{1}{1 - MPC}$

can be rewritten $\frac{1}{MPS + MPM}$

since,

$$MPC + MPS + MPM = 1.$$

Full-Employment GDP

The level of aggregate demand in the economy required to ensure that everyone who wants to work can work is called full-employment GDP. As shown in Figure 6.4, it may be possible for the equilibrium level of GDP ($RGDP_e$) to be less than the **full employment level of GDP** ($RGDP_{fe}$). If this situation exists, then all of the resources available to Canadians are not being fully utilized. Some land and equipment remains idle while some workers remain unemployed. Because full employment is a desirable objective, it is necessary to increase the level of aggregate demand so that equilibrium GDP will occur at a full-employment level. The AD curve must shift to the right in order to intersect the AS curve at $RGDP_{fe}$. The amount

The level of aggregate demand in the economy required to ensure that everyone who wants employment has a job is the full-employment level of GDP.

that aggregate demand has to increase in order to raise equilibrium GDP to a full-employment level is referred to as the **recessionary gap.**[1]

We can use the expenditure multiplier in order to measure the size of the recessionary gap. Assume that the equilibrium level of GDP is $400 billion and that $RGDP_{fe}$ is $450 billion. In other words, if $RGDP_e$ were $450 billion, there would be enough spending in the economy to provide everyone with a job. Under these conditions, what increase in aggregate demand is necessary in order to achieve full employment? If it is desirable to increase the level of GDP by $50 billion, the expenditure-multiplier formula can be used to determine the necessary increase in aggregate demand.

$$\Delta \text{ GDP} = \Delta \text{ AD} \times \frac{1}{1 - \text{MPC}} \quad (\text{assume MPC} = 0.75)$$

$$\$50 = \Delta \text{ AD} \times \frac{1}{1 - 0.75}$$

$$\$50 = \Delta \text{ AD} \times \frac{1}{0.25}$$

$$\$50 = \Delta \text{ AD} \times 4$$

$$\$12.5 = \Delta \text{ AD}$$

An increase in aggregate demand of $12.5 billion is sufficient to raise the equilibrium level of GDP from $400 billion to $450 billion. The size of the recessionary gap is therefore $12.5 billion.

What reduction in taxes would accomplish the same thing? Using the tax-multiplier formula, we can show that a $16.67-billion reduction in taxes will result in an increase in GDP of $50 billion. Remember that a greater reduction in taxes than an increase in spending is necessary to bring about the same increase in GDP. Some of the tax reduction will be saved and thus will not circulate in the economy.

$$\Delta \text{ GDP} = - \left[\Delta \text{ taxes} \times \frac{\text{MPC}}{1 - \text{MPC}} \right]$$

$$\$50 = - \left[\Delta \text{ taxes} \times \frac{0.75}{1 - 0.75} \right]$$

$$\$50 = - \left[\Delta \text{ taxes} \times \frac{0.75}{0.25} \right]$$

---

[1] The presence of a recessionary gap does not necessarily imply that the country is experiencing a recession.

$$\$50 \;=\; -\;[\Delta \text{ taxes} \times 3]$$

$$\frac{\$50}{3} \;=\; -\;\Delta \text{ taxes}$$

$$-\$16.67 \;=\; \Delta \text{ taxes}$$

If it is possible for Canadians not to be spending enough money in order to guarantee full employment, is it possible for them to spend too much? Yes, it is possible. If the limit on aggregate supply has been reached, then any further increases in aggregate demand will not increase the amount of goods and services produced. The increases in aggregate demand at this point will only lead to price increases. Once full employment has been reached, increases in aggregate demand will not cause RGDP to increase but will cause the current dollar value of GDP to go up. In order to reduce these inflationary pressures, it would be necessary for the level of aggregate demand to decrease. The reduction in aggregate demand necessary to reduce the level of aggregate demand and still maintain full employment is referred to as the **inflationary gap**. The inflationary gap could be eliminated through either a reduction in spending or an increase in taxes.

Say's Law and John Maynard Keynes

Prior to the 1930s, economists tended to accept the writings on economics of a French economist, J. B. Say. **Say's Law** stated that supply creates its own demand. The process of producing goods and services resulted in incomes being paid out to those who contributed to the production process. Say held that this income would always be sufficient to buy what was produced. The theory relied on the flexibility of wages and prices. That is, if there was an oversupply of products, prices would fall and stimulate the consumption of these products. Say's Law also assumed that there were no household savings because households spent, or consumed, all of their income. The consequence of Say's Law was that there would be no involuntary unemployment. A person was out of work only if he or she chose to be.

The Great Depression of the 1930s pointed out the weakness of Say's Law. Levels of production fell and unemployment rose dramatically. The automatic correction of Say's Law did not take place. During the 1930s, the writings of a British economist, John Maynard Keynes, began to receive more acceptance. In fact, his book *The General Theory of Employment, Interest and Money* has been referred to as the most influential book of the twentieth century.

It was Keynes' view that the demand for goods and services had to be maintained in order to keep the economy out of a recession. If households decide to save more money, they will spend less and the overall demand

The decrease in the level of aggregate demand required to bring the equilibrium level of GDP down to the full-employment level of GDP is referred to as the inflationary gap.

Say's Law states that the supply of products creates its own demand, since all production creates income for households that can be spent on goods and services.

Keynesian economic theory proposes that government take an active role in the economy, increasing government spending in order to support the demand for goods and services and, therefore, to preserve employment.

for goods and services will be lower. If this demand is not sufficient to provide everyone with a job, it is the responsibility of the government to provide the necessary spending. *Keynes believed that government should take an active role in economic matters.*

The advent of the Second World War gave support to Keynes' ideas. The need for massive government spending in the war effort stimulated the economy and reduced the level of unemployment that had prevailed throughout much of the 1930s. After the war, many Western governments assumed the responsibility for overall economic conditions in their countries and adopted many of the teachings of Keynes. The economic theories presented in this chapter are often referred to as **Keynesian economics.**

> ## REVIEW
>
> 6.17 Will increases in government spending be sufficient to provide everybody with a job? In your answer consider the types of unemployment discussed in Chapter 5.

The Business Cycle

You have surmised from the material in the two previous chapters that the level of GDP is not constant. Decreases in GDP are accompanied by decreases in employment levels and lower rates of inflation. Increases in GDP are accompanied by increases in employment and rising prices. Economists who track changes in GDP look for discernable patterns in the way that GDP changes. They measure the time from the beginning of a period of economic expansion to the start of a slowdown in economic activity. They also measure the amount of time before the economy picks up again. The term "business cycle" has been attached to these changes in economic activity. In addition to measuring the time between noticeable changes, economists are interested in the causes of the cyclical behaviour in the economy.

This section will discuss the theories associated with the business cycle. All theories recognize that random external shocks to the economy such as wars, climatic change, disease, and so on can interfere with the economy. The first three theories associate business cycles with changes in the total amount of spending in the economy.

Keynesian theory: Expectations are the key component of the Keynesian theory and the cause of economic fluctuations. If business firms expect sales to increase, the demand for machinery and equipment will increase.

The increased investment will have a multiplier effect on the economy. Poor expectations about the future result in a drop in investment spending and the multiplier works in the opposite direction. Keynes believed that expectations about future profits are volatile and can change even as a result of rumours about tax changes, inventions, political change, and so on.

Monetary theory: This theory of the business cycle states that changes in the money supply (defined in Chapter 7) are the source of fluctuations in economic activity. The rate of change in the money supply is the important factor. An increase in the rate of growth in the money supply provides an impetus for economic expansion, while a slowdown in the rate of growth in the money supply is accompanied by a slowdown in the economy. Increases in the rate of growth of the money supply result in lower interest rates. Spending is sensitive to changes in the interest rates. When interest rates decrease, investment and consumption spending increase. The increases in investment and consumption have a multiplier effect on the level of GDP.

Rational expectations theories: A rational expectation is a forecast based on all of the available information. These theories are based on the assumption that the impulse that changes economic conditions is the unanticipated change in total spending. A larger than anticipated increase in the total demand for goods and services will result in an economic expansion, while a smaller than anticipated increase will result in a decrease in the level of GDP. Proponents of rational expectation theory argue that when changes in total spending are accurately forecast, money wage rates are adjusted to lessen the impact of any change in spending. For example, if total spending is expected to grow, workers will demand higher wage rates. Any price increases that accompany the increase in total spending will be matched by an increase in the wage rate to leave the "real" wage rate the same. If the spending level was not anticipated and the wage rate did not change, increases in the price level would decrease the "real" wage rate.

Real business cycle theory: This theory regards changes in productivity as the source of economic change. Changes in productivity are brought about mainly by technological change. The pace of technological change can vary and, as it does, the economy experiences fluctuations. Rapid productivity growth is associated with an economic expansion, while any decrease in productivity brings about a recession.

Agricultural theories: Earlier economists trying to understand business cycles focused on the main industry at the time, agriculture. These theories are related to factors that cause fluctuations in the harvest. One such theory proposed a link between sunspots that appeared approximately every ten years and fluctuations in the harvest.

Psychological theories: If individuals act in a way that "follows the crowd," there will be an impact on the economy. For example, if many people believe that prices on the stock exchange will increase in the near future, they will begin to purchase shares. The mass purchase of shares will cause prices to increase. If many individuals are pessimistic about economic conditions and stop spending, the economy will experience a downturn.

Political theories: It is possible that major political changes such as a revolution can bring about significant changes in the economy. Canada's economy was influenced by such political events as the Oka crisis and the referenda in Quebec. A major tax change or trade agreement may also bring about major change in the economy.

Underconsumption theories: If the economy is expanding, the production of goods and services may be increasing more rapidly than the consumption of goods and services. It is possible that not all of the goods and services produced will be consumed, resulting in an accumulation of inventories. As inventories build up, production cutbacks and layoffs occur. Why is there a discrepancy between production and consumption?

Underconsumption theories argue that the discrepancy is due to the unequal distribution of income. Higher-income persons do not consume all of their income, while lower-income individuals do not have enough income to meet their needs.

Investment theories: Savings are at the heart of these theories. Savings accumulate when no immediate investment opportunities are present. Savings continue to accumulate until investment opportunities appear. The accumulated savings provide a pool of funds from which firms can borrow in order to finance investment opportunities. As firms invest, the economy grows by a multiplied amount. As the pool of savings dries up, investment decreases. As investment decreases, the economy slows down.

EVERYDAY ECONOMICS 6.3

The Great Depression

The year 1999 marked the 70th anniversary of the Great Depression. The depression years were characterized by declining levels of economic activity, by a high unemployment rate, and by the inability of government to take the proper corrective action.

The Great Depression is said to have started on October 29, 1929, known as "Black Tuesday." On this day, stock prices declined drastically on the New York Stock Exchange. The drop in stock prices did not cause the depression to occur, but presaged the downward trend in economic conditions.

The years leading up to 1929 were good from an economic point of view. In 1927, real GNP grew by 9.5 percent in Canada; in 1928, it grew by 9.1 percent. The unemployment rate in those years was estimated to be only 2 or 3 percent of the labour force. By 1933, real GNP in Canada had declined by 30 percent. In fact, it was to take 10 years before the level of real GNP regained the 1929 level. The unemployment situation was drastic. In 1933, the unemployment rate had increased to an estimated 19 percent of the labour force. This figure is only an estimate and many believe that it is too low.

Initial government attempts to deal with the situation were not successful. The government did not initiate spending increases to make up for the decline in spending on the part of consumers, businesses, and foreigners. One attempt by government to solve the crisis was to increase the tariff (tax) on imported products. If imported products became more expensive, consumers would be forced to buy Canadian products and thus preserve Canadian jobs. This approach had two problems. First, if Canadians did not purchase foreign products, foreigners did not have the money to purchase Canadian products. Second, other countries reacted to high tariffs by increasing their own tariff rates. This tended to reduce international trade and prolong the depression by decreasing the level of spending around the world.

Increases in spending were necessary to lift the Western industrialized countries out of the economic doldrums. These increases were proposed by Keynes. It was his belief that government should initiate these spending increases, even if it meant that government had to go into debt in order to get the money. Keynes' ideas received increased support during the Second World War, when the spending necessary for the war effort stimulated economic activity and reduced the levels of unemployment.

Has Canada experienced a repeat of the 1930s depression? Canada has not had another depression, but there have been a number of recessions. What is the difference between a recession and a depression? The former term is associated with a period of negative economic growth. That is, if real GDP declines in two consecutive quarters, the economy is said to be in a recession. In recent times, Canada experienced recessions in 1981–82 and again in 1990–91.

There is no technical definition of a depression. Economists describe a depression as a prolonged and severe recession. Apart from the depression of the 1930s, the only other depression to hit Canada occurred between 1873 and 1879.

Questions

1. In light of your knowledge of GDP and its determinants, what policies would you have introduced in order to solve the economic crisis of the Great Depression?
2. Do you believe that a repetition of the depression conditions is possible in Canada?
3. Should governments in Canada maintain a high level of spending in order to prevent recessions? Explain.

Summary

When GDP is in equilibrium, the level of business activity is steady and unchanging. Equilibrium occurs when the leakages from the circular flow of money are equal to the additions to the circular flow. When the additions are greater than the leakages, GDP starts to increase. When the leakages exceed the additions, GDP begins to decline.

In order to analyze why the level of business activity fluctuates, it is necessary to study the components of business activity. Consumption is the spending by households on goods and services. Investment is the spending by businesses on capital equipment, and includes residential construction and any change in inventories. Government spending on goods and services is also included in national income accounting. Finally, the foreign-trade aspect of our economy, imports and exports, also influences the level of business activity. Changes in any of these components bring about changes in the level of GDP.

The paradox of thrift points out a possible contradiction of savings. If enough people decided to increase their savings, the level of spending in the economy would fall. With reduced spending, less income is earned, the ability to save declines, and savings fall.

Every time that spending increases, GDP increases. The total impact of any increase in spending on GDP is determined by use of the multiplier. There is a difference in impact on GDP when comparing expenditure changes and tax changes. The difference results from the influence that tax changes have on savings. Part of any increase in taxes is financed through savings, while part of any tax reduction finds its way into savings.

A stable level of business activity (equilibrium GDP) is not necessarily an ideal situation. In certain instances, the level of total spending in the economy may not be enough to provide everyone with a job. The economy may not be at a full-employment level of GDP. The amount that spending has to increase in order to achieve full employment is known as the deflationary gap. When there is too much spending, prices start to rise. The inflationary gap indicates how much total spending exceeds the amount of spending necessary for full employment.

The discussion of macroeconomics contained in this chapter is known as Keynesian economics. It was Keynes' view that the demand for goods and services had to be maintained in order to keep the economy out of a recession. If the total demand was not sufficient, Keynes believed that government should take an active role in influencing economic conditions.

Questions for Review and Discussion

1. How could consumer expectations about future price levels affect the level of GDP? (Hint: think of the effect on consumption.)
2. The development of new products influences consumer spending. Can you list three new products that have altered consumer spending?
3. What determines the level of savings in Canada each year?
4. Complete the following table.

DISPOSABLE INCOME ($)	CONSUMPTION ($)	SAVING ($)	APC	APS	MPC	MPS
30 000	29 000					
40 000	37 000					
50 000	44 000					
60 000	50 000					
70 000	54 000					

5. Savings can have both negative and positive consequences for the Canadian economy. Discuss the potential consequences associated with an increased desire on the part of Canadians to save.

6. How is it possible for people to have negative savings?

7. Why must the MPC and the MPS always add up to the total of one?

8. Does advertising affect the overall level of consumption in Canada or simply influence the consumer's choice? Can you think of an advertisement that has resulted in an increase in your spending?

9. How might you react to an increase of $2000 in your income? What is your marginal propensity to consume (MPC)?

10. Capital goods such as machinery and equipment wear out. Could the replacement of these goods result in a change in economic conditions? Explain.

11. How do technological advances such as robotics in the automotive industry and laser printers in the publishing industry affect GDP? (Hint: think of their impact on investment.)

12. What factors cause the equilibrium level of GDP to change?

13. Using the appropriate multiplier formula, determine the impact of the following:
   a) an increase in investment spending of $200 million on the level of GDP (MPC = 0.8)
   b) an increase in savings by Canadians of $50 million on GDP (MPC = 0.9)
   c) a decrease in taxes of $3 billion on GDP (MPC = 0.75)
   d) an increase in government spending of $15 million on GDP (MPC = 0.75)

14. What change in taxes is necessary in order to eliminate an inflationary gap of $10 billion (MPC = 0.8)?

15. What increase in government spending is necessary in order to increase the level of GDP by $20 billion (MPC = 0.9)?

16. What is the balanced-budget multiplier? Use a numerical example in your answer (MPC = 0.8).

17. In order to assist the Canadian mining industry, the government could change the income-tax rules that mining companies must abide by. Discuss the impact on our economy of a tax change that allows mining companies to depreciate new equipment more rapidly.

18. In a recession, government should not undertake any unnecessary expenditures. Comment on this statement.

19. How would you use a combination of government spending and taxation to improve our current economic situation?

20. Is the equilibrium level of GDP necessarily an ideal economic situation?

21. What is the connection between J. M. Keynes and Say's Law?

Suggested Readings

Berton, Pierre. *The Great Depression 1929–1939.* Toronto: McClelland & Stewart, 1990. A good account of government attempts to deal with the economic downturn of the 1930s. The book also relates world events to the Canadian experience.

Parkin, Michael, and Robin Bade. *Economics: Canada and the Global Environment.* Fifth Edition. Don Mills: Pearson Education Canada, 2003. This 900-page text is the fifth edition of a popular introductory Canadian text.

Rabbior, Gary. "The 'Macro' Economy: An Introduction to How It Works." Canadian Foundation for Economic Education Insight #2, November 1989. The diagram approach in this 15-page pamphlet is a good supplement to the material in this chapter.

Rabbior, Gary. "The Canadian Economy: The Big Picture." Toronto: Canadian Foundation for Economic Education, 1993. This 26-page supplement uses flow charts to discuss macroeconomic concepts.

Selected Websites

www.fin.gc.ca The Department of Finance website. Information is available on Canadian savings and investment.

www.ccra-adrc.gc.ca The website for Canada Customs and Revenue Agency (formerly Revenue Canada).

www.cabe.ca The website for the Canadian Association for Business Economics. Information is available on membership and publications.

http://ideas.uqam.ca/QMRBC/index.html The Quantitative Macroeconomics and Real Business Cycle website provides links to data, articles, and other sources on business-cycle topics.

www.tcb-indicators.org The Conference Board's business cycle indicators.

www.britannica.com The *Encyclopaedia Britannica* provides a very good summary of the business cycle.

http://homepage.newschool.edu/het The History of Economic Thought website. Biographies are available on many economists including J. M. Keynes.

http://encarta.msn.com The Encarta Encyclopaedia has a good summary of the business cycle.

Money and the Canadian Banking System

Key Terms

barter
legal tender
fiat money
Gresham's Law
chartered bank
deposit insurance
branch banking
unit banking
trust company
caisse populaire
credit union
liquid assets
crude-quantity theory of money
Fisher equation of exchange
treasury bills
bank rate
open-market operations

Chapter Objectives

After successfully completing this chapter, you will be able to:

- discuss the shortcomings of a barter system
- explain the functions of money
- explain how, and under what conditions, banks can create money
- use the money-supply expansion formula
- define the Canadian money supply
- explain the various demands for money
- describe how interest rates are determined
- outline the responsibilities of the Bank of Canada
- describe the various tools of monetary policy
- explain why the money supply would be increased or decreased
- explain the relationship between the money supply and the interest rate

Core Concept Building

The money creation activities of chartered banks are key to this chapter. The discussion of money creation is followed by a discussion of the role of the Bank of Canada in regulating the money supply. Activities taken by the Bank of Canada to regulate the money supply and ultimately the level of economic activity are referred to as *monetary policy*. The role of the Bank of Canada is also discussed in Chapters 8 and 9.

ICELAND: A CASHLESS SOCIETY?

The use of credit and debit cards is more extensive in Iceland than in any other country. In 2000, Visa claimed that it had 314 000 cards in circulation among a population of 275 000. Visa also claims that its cards are accepted by 99 percent of the retailers in Iceland. Even hot dog stands accept payment by credit card. Debit cards are used for very small payments as well, such as the purchase of an apple.

Very little cash circulates in the economy. Less than 10 percent of all transactions are made with cash. In some European countries the proportion of all transactions using cash is 80 percent. The number of cheques written by Icelanders in the year 2000 was only 20 percent of the number of cheques written in 1993. In May 2000, Iceland introduced a cash card that could be inserted into vending machines and parking meters.

In some other nations, the move to a cashless society has met with more resistance from the general public and from merchants. Why have Icelanders almost entirely adopted plastic when others have not? One explanation is that Icelanders readily adapt to new technology. Internet and mobile phone use is higher in Iceland than in many other countries. Sixty percent of homes in Iceland are connected to the Internet and more than 35 percent of the population has shopped online. Iceland is a small, homogeneous society and the lack of diversity may assist in the acceptance of this innovation. For historical reasons, residents of other countries may want to accept only cash. Finally, fraud is almost non-existent in Iceland. In Iceland, fraud is present in only 0.0003 percent of all transactions. In some situations the requirement to provide a personal identification number or sign for a credit card purchase has been abolished.

What Is Money?

The Barter System

Barter **is the process by which goods or services are exchanged without the use of money.**

The importance of money in our economy can best be explained by imagining an economic system without it. Even if money did not exist, exchanges would still take place between individuals by trade, or **barter**. Barter systems are still in use today; however, there are several problems in using a barter system extensively in our advanced economy.

Exchanges that take place through barter necessitate a coincidence of wants. That is, if you have an item to trade you have to find someone willing to sell the item that you desire. With luck, this person will be willing to accept whatever you have to trade. For example, assume that you need a radio and all that you have to offer is a bicycle. You need to locate someone who is willing to exchange a radio for your bicycle. This may not be easy to do. Divisibility is also a problem with barter. It is not possible to divide many items up into smaller units. Someone may be willing to trade only part of a radio for your bicycle. How will the radio be divided? Since this is very difficult, it is likely that the exchange will not take place.

A barter system functions more effectively in a less-industrialized economy than ours. In an industrialized economy, individuals normally work for someone else and simply add to the company's total production. After a week of inserting windshields on new cars, what does the individual have to trade? He cannot use the windshields for barter. In less-industrialized countries, workers are more likely to be self-employed. The fruits of their labours will be some agricultural product or another product that they have made—a vase, a knife, or whatever. They can take these products and exchange them for others. In order for barter to take place in the Canadian economy, individuals must be self-employed or have some item to offer for exchange. *In a modern economy, money serves as a medium of exchange.* Workers are willing to offer their services to an employer in exchange for money. Store owners are willing to accept money for the goods and services that they sell. Individuals are willing to accept money in exchange because they know that others will also accept money.

It is difficult to express values or prices in a barter system. With no common denominator, there can be as many prices for one item as there are articles for trade. For example, one sheep may trade for three bushels of wheat, or four chickens, or five bushels of corn, or two goats, or three vases, or whatever else anyone is willing to trade. Also to be considered in setting a price is the quality of merchandise. If one sheep is to be traded for four chickens, how much do the chickens have to weigh? How much does the sheep have to weigh? *In the Canadian economy, money acts as the common denominator, or the unit of account.* Prices and values are expressed in terms of the same unit. Regardless of what item is for sale, it will have a money price stated in terms of Canadian dollars.

Our industrialized Canadian economy also involves a substantial amount of borrowing. Consumers and businesses borrow in order to pay for current expenses. How would loan repayment take place in a barter system? Each time a loan is undertaken, specific instructions would have to be set out as to the type of repayment. For example, if I borrowed two sheep in order to complete a transaction, would I have to pay back two sheep? What about interest payments on the loan? Money facilitates the borrowing process and becomes a standard for deferred payments. In addition to simplifying debt repayment, future payments for such matters as salaries, rental payments, and dividends payable are specified in money.

Finally, how does an individual accumulate wealth without money? Wealth would have to be accumulated in physical items. Storage could be a problem if wealthy items are bulky. It is also important that wealth be kept in the form of a durable commodity. It would be unwise to store wealth in a commodity that was sensitive to temperature, or that deteriorated after being kept in storage for a long time. In our economy, money performs the function of being a store of wealth, as well as a medium of exchange, a unit of account, and a standard for deferred payments.

The barter system, however, is not dead. It is used more extensively in less-developed countries than in Canada. It is gaining favour in our country as well. In order to avoid paying income and sales taxes, individuals have sometimes resorted to barter. If individuals simply exchange services, and do not exchange money, no tax is paid. Finally, in industrialized countries there have been situations in which people have lost faith in the current value of money and have resorted to barter.

The History of Money

Since the barter system has its drawbacks, societies have adopted the use of money. One of the first forms of money was cattle. In fact, the Latin word for money, *pecunia*, is derived from the word *pecus,* meaning herd of cattle or sheep. The English word *pecuniary* (relating to, or consisting of money) has these Latin origins. Cattle were used as money because they had value. Cows could be used for food and the skins could be used for clothing. Since they had value, people were willing to accept cattle in exchange for a good or a service. Cattle skins themselves were also used as money, as were other types of livestock, especially sheep.

Legal tender is that part of the money supply that is acceptable for purchases and for repayment of debt.

In addition to livestock, grains (especially corn and wheat) have been used as currency. In fact, in some American states legislation was enacted that made corn **legal tender**, or money. The advantage of grain over livestock was that it was easier to divide into small amounts. In ancient Rome, Greece, and Egypt, human beings were sometimes used as money. Slaves were exchanged, with the stronger ones being of greater value.

One difficulty (apart from the moral issues) in using cattle, sheep, and even human beings as money is that these are not standard items. Not all humans are the same. Not all cattle are the same. There was a time when it was required that taxes be paid in cattle. Individuals would keep old and undernourished animals available for the tax collector, while keeping the healthy animals for themselves. Additional problems arose in the use of cattle and grain as money. Cattle need constant care and feeding. Grain tends to deteriorate over time and requires extensive storage space.

Various minerals have also been used as money. Many minerals—diamonds, gold, silver, copper—had ornamental value and were often used in jewellery. Since jewellery contained precious minerals, it also circulated as money. Again, as long as something is perceived to have value it can perform the main function of money: it can be used in exchanges. Minerals such as copper, gold, and silver were used to make practical items such as utensils, as well as for monetary purposes. The precious metals themselves also circulated as money; however, there were problems connected with weighing metals to determine exact amounts.

The problem of weighing was partly solved through the introduction of coins. The coins, made out of various metals, were stamped with the weight of the metal in them. This was supposed to eliminate the weighing of the coins. However, since pieces of the coins were often clipped (or trimmed) off, weighing them was still necessary. Clipping coins was done with the objective of acquiring enough metal to make a new coin without significantly diminishing the value of the original coins. Scales and measures were as important to earlier businesses as a cash register is today. At times, coins were stamped with a replica of the monarch's head in order to give them some official status.

Since anyone could make a coin, there were often thousands of different coins in circulation. Yet it was difficult to determine how much precious metal was present in each coin. With so many coins in circulation, no one was sure about the value of a particular coin that they might be offered in exchange. The coins in use today are referred to as "token money." The metallic value of the coin is less than the face value (the purchasing power) of the coin. Other items that have been used as money throughout history include playing cards, books, tobacco, and beaver skins. Aboriginal peoples in North America often used beads, or "wampum."

Paper money came into existence because those who began to accumulate money wanted a safe place to store it. Some types of money, such as gold, were very heavy to carry around. The discovery of a safe place to store money was the beginning of banking. People obtained a receipt for the money they stored in a vault. When it was necessary to get the money for a transaction, the receipt would be turned in at the vault, or bank. After a while, the receipts began to circulate in the economy just as money would. This was the beginning of paper money. People would accept receipts as money because they believed that the receipts, or paper money, were backed by "real money." They believed that the paper money had value. *Today, people accept paper money as money because they believe it has value.*

Our paper money circulates because of people's faith in it. There is no gold backing up our paper money. The term used to describe our paper currency is **fiat money**. It is money because it has been declared to be money and it is accepted as such. A fiat is an order or a decree.

If a commodity is to circulate as money (as paper currency does), it must have certain characteristics. It must be:

Fiat money is the currency issued by a government or a bank that is not matched by holdings of gold or other securities.

- *Durable:* If money is to change hands often during exchanges, it must be sturdy.
- *Portable:* Money has to be carried around in order to make exchanges, so it cannot be too heavy or cumbersome.
- *Divisible:* Since not every product has the same price, money must be divisible into smaller amounts.
- *Recognizable and readily accepted:* If it is not accepted by the population, the item will cease to function as money.
- *Not easily copied:* The ease of manufacturing counterfeit money would destroy the value of the commodity as money.
- *Face value greater than actual value:* If the metallic value of a coin is greater than the face value of the coin, it will not circulate as money. For example, pre-1967 Canadian silver dollars do not circulate as money because the value of the silver in the coin exceeds one dollar. The same rule applies to paper currency.

REVIEW

7.1 Why did coins replace other forms of money?

7.2 What is the most important characteristic of anything that continues to circulate as money?

Definition of Money in Canada

The most recognizable form of money in Canada is *paper currency,* which is issued by the Bank of Canada. These paper notes are referred to as legal tender, and must be accepted as a medium of exchange and for the payment of debts. *There is no gold or precious metal behind the issuing of paper money.* As long as Canadians are willing to accept Bank of Canada notes in exchange for goods and services, the notes will continue to circulate as money. This points out one of the major characteristics of any commodity that circulates as money: it must be perceived as having value. If Canadians did not believe these notes had value, they would not accept them.

The federal government in Canada also operates a mint that produces coins, which circulate as money. The value of the metal in the coin is less than its face value, but the coins are still accepted as money. Interestingly, if the face value of the coin was less than the value of its metal content, it is unlikely that the coin would circulate as money. People would tend to hoard the coins and not use them as currency. For example, if the value of the silver contained in a nickel was greater than five cents, people would not spend their nickels. By spending a nickel they would receive only five cents worth of product and would be giving up more than five cents worth of silver. Thomas Gresham formulated a hypothesis to describe the practice of hoarding money that has an actual value greater than the face value. Known as **Gresham's Law,** it states that bad money forces good money out of circulation.

Gresham's Law **states that bad money forces good money out of circulation.**

One final form of money in Canada is *bank deposits,* especially chequing deposits. It is possible to purchase goods and services with a cheque. Therefore, the cheque is a medium of exchange and performs a monetary function. Other bank deposits are not strictly money, but are close to it. For example, you cannot spend money directly from your savings account if it does not have chequing privileges, yet it is a simple process to withdraw this money and spend it.

The Bank of Canada is concerned with the amount of money in Canada at any given time. In order to determine this amount, a definition of the money supply is necessary. This definition reflects the total purchasing power available in the country at any given time. Included in the Bank of Canada definition are coins and paper currency in circulation, plus chartered bank deposits. Only coins and currency in circulation are counted as money. When coins and currency are put into a bank, they no longer are referred to as money. The deposit that was created becomes part of the money supply.

The inclusion of bank deposits in the money supply creates some problems because not all bank deposits are the same. Some deposits are *demand deposits* in that the depositor can get his or her money back on demand. These deposits have chequing privileges and may pay no interest on the money in the deposit. Savings deposits, on the other hand, usually pay interest. Savings deposits are referred to as *notice deposits,* because the depositor may be required to give notice before withdrawing money. A true savings account does not have chequing privileges. At most banks, a combination of these two accounts is available.

The existence of several types of deposits makes the definition of the money supply complicated. Demand deposits are very close to currency, since cheques can be written against the money in these deposits. Also, the money in the deposit can be obtained on demand. Savings accounts without chequing privileges are not as close to our definition of money, because they are not readily spendable. Yet these accounts are very liquid and can be converted into money quite readily either by withdrawing cash from the account or by accessing the account via a debit card. In order to accommodate the various types of deposits, the Bank of Canada has developed several definitions of the money supply. These definitions are presented in Table 7.1. All of the definitions refer to deposits at chartered banks and not to deposits at any other type of deposit-accepting institution. In this chapter, the money supply definition Gross M1 will be used in all the examples.

Table 7.1 *The Canadian money supply, January 2003*

		$ (MILLIONS)
Currency outside banks		39 247
Gross M1	Currency plus personal chequing accounts and current accounts	139 112
M2	M1 plus personal savings and personal notice deposits	567 350
M3	M2 plus non-personal term deposits and foreign-currency deposits of residents booked in Canada	761 151

SOURCE: www.bank-banque-canada.ca (March 2003). Published with the permission of the Bank of Canada.

R E V I E W

7.3 Why are there several definitions of the Canadian money supply?
7.4 Why are bank deposits included in the money supply?
7.5 Study how changes in the demand for money and in the money supply impact together on the equilibrium interest rate.

interactive
graphics

EVERYDAY ECONOMICS 7.1

Debit Cards and Electronic Cash Cards

Canadians are very familiar with credit cards. When using a credit card to make a purchase, the purchaser is provided with an instant loan. The credit card is not money, but represents instant access to money. We have also become familiar with debit cards. When using a debit card to make a purchase, the money is taken immediately out of one's bank account. If the bank account does not contain sufficient funds, the purchase does not take place. Debit cards are not money but provide instant access to your money.

Both cards require authorization. That is, before a credit card can be used, it must be determined that the person's credit limit has not been overextended. Before a debit card can be used, it must be determined that there are sufficient funds in one's bank account. In order to be able to authorize the use of these cards, a communication system through telephone lines must be established.

In the future, Canadians will become familiar with electronic cash cards. Money will be transferred from your bank account to a chip on the card. When you make a purchase, money is transferred from your cash card to the merchant's cash card. It will also be possible to have individuals transfer money between themselves using cash cards in a way similar to that in which currency is exchanged today. No authorization is needed to use cash cards. The money on the cash card has already been withdrawn from a bank account. Since authorization is unnecessary, costs are reduced. When the money on your card's chip has been spent, you walk into your bank and say "Fill'er up."

Questions

1. Are cash cards money?
2. In your opinion, will carrying cash cards be safer than carrying currency?

Canadian Chartered Banks

By far the largest financial institutions in Canada are the **chartered banks**. They are referred to as chartered banks since they operate under a charter granted by the Parliament of Canada. The chartered banks are privately owned companies whose purpose is to make a profit for shareholders. Bank profits are earned by charging a fee for financial services and by charging interest on loans. Banks accept deposits from individuals, businesses, and government, and lend the money to these same groups. The difference between the rate of interest paid to depositors and the rate of interest received on loans represents profits for the bank.

Chartered bank is the term used to describe a financial institution operating under the authority of Parliament that accepts deposits and lends money to businesses, government, and households.

Types of Deposits

Individuals have a number of choices when depositing their money in a bank. These choices consist of the various types of deposits available. The most popular type of deposit is the personal savings deposit (see Table 7.2).

Chartered banks offer a variety of deposits and products to their customers. Some of these deposits are described below in general terms. Banks will offer variations of these deposits. For example, special accounts may be available to seniors or youth.

Chequing account: This account is a demand deposit (your money is available to you on demand) and is intended for day-to-day banking transactions such as paying bills. The account often carries a monthly fee and pays a low (or no) rate of interest.

Savings account: This account pays the depositor a higher rate of interest than the chequing account and is intended for short-term savings.

Term deposits: The depositor leaves the money with the bank for a fixed amount of time. The rate of interest is higher than on a savings account because the bank knows that it will have the depositor's money for a certain amount of time. Term deposits may be turned into cash before the maturity date; however, the depositor sacrifices some interest if the deposit is

Table 7.2 *Selected assets and liabilities of Canadian chartered banks, January 2003*

ASSETS	$ (MILLIONS)
Bank of Canada deposits, notes, and coin	4 172
Treasury bills	25 967
Government of Canada direct and guaranteed bonds	71 130
Call and short loans	617
Selected short-term assets	31 323
Non-mortgage loans	352 503
Mortgages	334 482
Canadian securities	93 911

LIABILITIES	$ (MILLIONS)
Canadian-dollar deposits:	
personal savings deposits	373 545
non-personal term and notice deposits	180 563
demand deposits	100 743
Government of Canada	2 263
Bankers' acceptances	39 664

SOURCE: www.bank-banque-canada.ca (March 2003). Published with the permission of the Bank of Canada.

cashed in prior to maturity. Term deposits range from one day to five years in length and the minimum investment is usually $1000.

Guaranteed investment certificates: The bank's highest rate of interest is paid on guaranteed investment certificates (GICs). Money is deposited with the bank for a fixed term with the minimum investment $5000. Most GICs are not cashable prior to maturity. Although most GICs have a fixed interest rate for the term of the investment, some banks are now offering variable-rate GICs.

Mutual funds: Chartered banks also offer a variety of mutual funds. Some funds invest in treasury bills, others in mortgages, and still others in shares. The degree of risk and the rate of return vary with the type of fund.

In general, if a depositor is willing to leave his or her money in the bank for an extended period of time, the bank will pay a higher interest rate on the deposit. Also, if a depositor is willing to give the bank a larger sum of money, the bank will pay a higher rate of interest. If you deposit $50 in the bank and declare that you want access to your money on demand, you

International Comparisons 7.1

Worldwide ranking of banks by asset size, 2001

Rank	Bank	Country	Assets ($millions CDN)
1	Mizuho Financial Group	Japan	1 876 772
2	Citigroup	United States	1 674 750
3	Sumitomo Mitsui Banking Corp.	Japan	1 338 400
4	Deutsche Bank	Germany	1 288 926
5	Mitsubishi Tokyo Financial Group	Japan	1 196 957
6	UBS	Switzerland	1 190 158
7	BNP Paribas	France	1 158 483
8	HSBC Holdings	United Kingdom	1 109 196
9	JP Morgan Chase & Co.	United States	1 104 726
10	HypoVereinsbank	Germany	1 022 146
48	Royal Bank of Canada	Canada	351 052
56	Canadian Imperial Bank of Commerce	Canada	280 447
57	Toronto-Dominion Bank	Canada	279 788
58	Scotiabank	Canada	276 182
66	Bank of Montreal	Canada	232 362
130	Desjardins Group	Canada	80 503
144	National Bank	Canada	72 447

SOURCE: Adapted from the Canadian Bankers Association, www.cba.ca/en/content/stats/bankrankings02eng.pdf (Nov 7, 2003).

will get a lower rate of interest than you would get by depositing $50 000 in the bank and stating that you do not need the money for five years.

Money may also be placed into a demand deposit. With such a deposit, the individual can get back his or her money on demand. Usually no interest is paid on demand deposits. The advantage of the deposit is that chequing privileges accompany it. There are no chequing privileges with a true savings account or with fixed-term deposits. As mentioned, combinations of these types of deposits are also available.

> R E V I E W
>
> 7.6 Explain why banks may want to keep higher reserves for demand
> deposits as opposed to personal savings deposits.

The assets of Canada's domestic and foreign banks are listed in Table 7.3.

Table 7.3 *Total assets of domestic and foreign banks, January 2003*

BANK	TOTAL ASSETS $ (MILLIONS)	PERCENTAGE
RBC Financial Group	390 319.9	22.44
CIBC	283 054.4	16.28
TD Bank Financial Group	311 438.2	17.91
Scotiabank	289 587.8	16.65
BMO Financial Group	254 606.0	14.64
National Bank of Canada	73 125.2	4.20
Laurentian Bank of Canada	18 582.3	1.07
Canadian Western Bank	3 924.3	0.23
Total 8 Domestic Banks	1 624 638.1	93.42
Other Domestic Banks[1]	3 852.5	0.22
Foreign Banks	110 542.0	6.36
Total	1 739 032.6	100.00

[1] Other domestic banks include Manulife Bank of Canada, Citizens Bank of Canada, Bank West, CS Altema Bank, Pacific and Western Bank of Canada, and President's Choice Financial. First Nations Bank is included with Toronto Dominion Bank.

SOURCE: Canadian Bankers Association website, www.cba.ca (April 2003).

EVERYDAY ECONOMICS 7.2

Can Banks Go Bankrupt?

Canadians have faith in their banking system. Prior to 1985, the last bank collapse in Canada was that of the Home Bank of Canada in 1923. Since that time, other banks that were in financial difficulty have merged with a larger bank—preventing any loss of confidence on the part of the Canadian public. But the confidence that Canadians have in

their banks was shaken in September 1985, when two banks based in Western Canada—the Canadian Commercial Bank and the Northland Bank—were declared no longer to be viable financial institutions. The liquidation of the Canadian Commercial Bank proceeded immediately. The Northland Bank was given time to reorganize or amalgamate with another bank. Eventually the Northland Bank failed as well.

What circumstances would lead to a bank going out of business? In the case of the Canadian Commercial Bank (CCB), it was a combination of factors. The bank conducted most of its business in Western Canada, and the economy in that part of Canada was having trouble recovering from the recession of the early 1980s. Real-estate prices had dropped substantially. In some areas, house prices had dropped by 25 percent or more. People were walking away from houses rather than paying off a mortgage on an inflated house price. Farmers were receiving low prices for their products. The oil and gas industry was still suffering from the federal government's National Energy Program (1980), lower world oil prices, and high interest rates. Many of the loans made by the Canadian Commercial Bank were not being paid back because of the poor economic conditions.

The situation at the CCB was aggravated because of the loans made by a subsidiary bank in California. The Westland Bank had made a large number of loans to oil and gas drilling companies in the southwestern part of the United States. Low oil prices discouraged drilling and made many of these loans non-performing. (A loan is referred to as non-performing when payments are not being made to the bank by the borrower; neither the principal nor interest is being paid.) Non-performing loans had reached 10.2 percent of eligible assets by January 31, 1985—an unacceptably high level.

Apart from the depressed economy, poor management at the bank was also cited as a reason for its downfall. The CCB had too many loans in the energy and real-estate areas. The bank was also criticized for not making adequate loss provisions on major problem loans. Banks set aside a certain amount of money in order to cover non-performing loans. This money is referred to as a *loan-loss provision*. A House of Commons committee report accused the bank of questionable accounting practices, inadequate disclosure of its financial position, and poor supervision.

In spite of the difficulties that the CCB was facing, the Bank of Canada continued to lend money to the bank. A total of $1.316 billion was loaned to the Canadian Commercial Bank by the Bank of Canada. The Bank of Canada was later repaid as the assets of the bank were liquidated.

Prior to the collapse of the Canadian Commercial Bank, the federal government had tried to save it. In March 1985, the federal government arranged a $255-million bail-out package to prevent the CCB from folding. The federal government, the government of Alberta, and the main Canadian chartered banks contributed this money. The news of the bail-out package, however, had a negative impact on bank confidence. Depositors began to withdraw their money. In order to remain in business, a bank must be able to attract money from depositors.

Why did the federal government want to assist the CCB financially so that it could remain in business? Since the bank is a private company, why not let the shareholders take financial responsibility? The federal government was concerned about a drop in confidence in the Canadian banking system. If the CCB failed, would depositors take their money out of other small banks, most of them located in Western Canada, as well? If depositors were not able to get their money back, more bankruptcies could result. Experience has shown that some banks that are in financial trouble can be saved. The Continental Illinois National Bank and Trust Company of Chicago, the eighth largest bank in the United States, survived under even more difficult circumstances. There was also political motivation associated with the decision to assist the Canadian Commercial Bank. The Progressive Conservative government had received strong support from Western Canada in the 1984 federal election. Western Canada had desperately wanted to establish a banking industry in order to escape the domination of the eastern financial institutions. The federal government was compelled to help out.

The financial problems at the CCB caused further trouble for the Northland Bank. This bank

▶

also had an alarming percentage of bad loans. When word got out that the Northland was in trouble, depositors began removing their money. The Bank of Canada advanced $510 million to the Northland Bank in order to keep it afloat, but the federal government would not arrange any further bail-out packages for the bank. Since no other bank wanted to take over the Northland, it also collapsed.

Questions

1. The CCB was Canada's tenth largest chartered bank. The Northland was the eleventh largest. Together their assets represented 1 percent of bank assets in Canada. Why were these banks, based in Western Canada, more likely to fail than the larger banks?

2. Depositors at banks are insured up to $60 000 by the Canada Deposit Insurance Corporation. The federal government introduced legislation to compensate depositors for uninsured deposits. Why would the federal government do this?

3. The Canadian Commercial Bank offered slightly higher interest rates on deposits than did other banks. As a result, it continued to attract some depositors in spite of its financial trouble. How much risk should depositors have to take when putting their money into a bank?

4. Would the collapse of these two banks affect other small Canadian banks?

Deposit Insurance

If chartered banks can lend out most of the money deposited in savings deposits, will there be any money in the bank when you want to withdraw your money? In most cases, the answer is yes. As some people are withdrawing their money, others are depositing money; therefore, the banks do not have to keep a high percentage of deposits at the bank. The banking system in Canada is based on the trust that individuals have in being able to get their money back at any time. If everyone showed up at the bank at the same time to get their money, there would be insufficient funds to pay off all the depositors.

In order to provide some protection for depositors, the Canada Deposit Insurance Corporation (CDIC) was established in 1967 by an Act of Parliament. The purpose of the corporation is to provide **deposit insurance** for depositors in case of the insolvency of a bank or other financial institution. The CDIC requires memberships by banks, trust companies, and mortgage loan companies. Only the deposits with member institutions are insured.

It is not necessary for a depositor to apply for deposit insurance. The depositor is covered automatically if his or her money is deposited in a member institution. The maximum amount of insurance is $60 000 for each person, regardless of the number of deposit accounts that each individual has. The $60 000 amount applies to the combined total of principal and interest. That is, if a $60 000 deposit earned $3000 in interest by

Deposit insurance is insurance on the deposit liabilities of chartered banks and other financial institutions.

the time the institution became insolvent, the depositor would receive only $60 000 from the CDIC.

Deposit insurance covers demand deposits, savings and chequing accounts, guaranteed investment certificates (GICs), and term deposits that are redeemable within five years after the date of deposit. There are a number of deposits that are not covered, including pooled funds, mortgage and real-estate investments, foreign-currency deposits, and stocks and bonds. Money in registered retirement savings plans (RRSPs) is covered separately. These plans have insurance coverage up to $60 000 if the money is deposited in an account eligible for insurance, such as a personal savings account. RRSPs based on stocks, bonds, and mortgages are not covered under the insurance plan. If a depositor has $60 000 in an RRSP and another $60 000 in a savings account, both amounts are covered.

Various government bodies have been reviewing the role of the CDIC and deposit insurance in Canada. One recommendation is to limit CDIC coverage on deposits over $30 000. Making the customer more responsible for his or her funds is referred to as *co-insurance*. Another proposal is to have the CDIC borrow money from capital markets and not the government. At the time of writing, neither proposal had been adopted.

The Bank Act

The Bank Act is federal government legislation that regulates the banking industry in Canada. The act describes the procedure that banks must follow in order to become incorporated. The act also outlines some of the arrangements that must exist between the bank's shareholders, directors, and management. It determines the services that banks may provide to the public and sets controls on the banks, such as the legal reserve requirement. Under the 1967 Bank Act, chartered banks were required to keep reserves equal to 4 percent of their Canadian-dollar term-and-notice deposits and 12 percent of their Canadian-dollar demand deposits.

The Bank Act in Canada has an interesting feature. Every ten years the act has to be reviewed and enacted again. This provides an opportunity for officials to review Canada's financial system in light of possible changes in economic conditions. The changes to the 1967 Bank Act were not made until November 1980. At that time, the Banks and Banking Law Revisions Act was passed.

The main thrust of this legislation was to increase competition among Canadian banks. One such change is the acceptance of subsidiaries of foreign banks locating in Canada. In previous banking legislation, even foreign ownership of Canadian banks was restricted. A single non-resident could own no more than 10 percent of the bank's outstanding voting shares. Prior to 1980 some foreign banks were established in Canada, but only on a limited basis. The local offices of foreign banks made business loans but were not allowed to accept deposits. With the legislative change, foreign banks are now allowed to conduct business in a manner similar to Canadian banks.

Although foreign-controlled banks are allowed to operate in Canada, they are subject to certain restrictions. Foreign bank subsidiaries must get a licence from the Minister of Finance before they can begin operating. This licence comes up for renewal once a year for the first five years and every three years thereafter. Foreign-owned banks are also restricted in terms of the assets and the number of branches that they may have. For example, no foreign bank will be allowed to open more than one branch without the consent of the Minister of Finance. Some of the concessions to foreign-banking interests were made in the new legislation because of the Canadian banking industry's involvement in foreign countries.

Changes to the Bank Act were passed in 1992 as part of the government's financial reform package. The changes allowed banks, trust companies, insurance companies, and brokerage firms to protect their core business while allowing some cross-over into each other's areas of business. Banks are permitted to own trust and insurance companies. Reserve requirements for bank deposits were phased out over a two-year period. Currently, there is no legal reserve requirement for chartered banks.

Canada versus the United States: Banking

Branch banking is a system of banking in which a commercial bank is permitted to operate branches of the main bank.

Unit banking is the system in which commercial banks are either not permitted to operate branches or permitted to operate only a limited number.

The system of banking in Canada is referred to as **branch banking**. There are eight domestic chartered banks operating in Canada. The changes to the Bank Act 1980 permitted foreign banks to operate in Canada. Foreign banks are not, however, allowed to establish the extensive system of branches that Canadian-owned banks have. In the United States, there is a **unit-banking system.** In that country, there are no banks with offices all across the country. Some banks are regulated by federal law and others are regulated by state law. Some states allow branches; others do not. Where branches are allowed, they are usually within a restricted area. For example, in some states, a bank may not have a branch farther away than 25 miles (40 km) from the head office. In comparison to Canada's small number of chartered banks, there are in excess of 13 000 commercial banks in the United States.

There are a number of advantages to each system. A bank that has a number of branches spread over a wide area is likely to be more stable than a bank with only one office, because it will have more diversified assets and liabilities. Funds can be transferred between branches to accounts where they are needed the most. If each bank branch is independent, it is likely that the majority of its loans are in one area or are concentrated in certain industries. This can be more risky from the point of view of bank stability.

Branch banks may be better able to respond to the loan demands of large borrowers due to the ease of transferring assets from other branches. A large bank may be able to open a branch in a location that would not be feasible for a one-office bank.

The main advantage of a unit-banking system is that it protects against the centralization of financial power. In Canada, the head offices of chartered banks are located mainly in Toronto and Montreal. If the United States had adopted a branch-banking policy, the head offices of the major banks would probably be located in the eastern cities of New York, Boston, and Philadelphia. As it is now, major banking centres are spread all across the United States. A further argument for unit banking is that each bank has a big stake in its community and will thus be better able to respond to local needs. In recent years the United States has moved toward more branch banking.

Deposit-Accepting Institutions

Although they are the largest financial intermediaries in terms of total assets, chartered banks are not the only deposit-accepting institutions in Canada. Other institutions have been set up for specific purposes. These include trust companies, mortgage loan companies, caisses populaires and credit unions, and government savings institutions.

Trust Companies

Trust companies were established to act as trustees for property interests and to conduct other confidential business. The most important sources of funds for trust companies are estates, trusts, and agency accounts. *Estates* are usually established under wills and are administered for a fee according to the instructions contained in the will. *Trust funds* are assets for which the trust company assumes a responsibility during the lifetime of the beneficiary. The most important category of trusts is *pension funds*. Also, *agency funds* are administered by trust companies under the orders of clients. The trust company acts as an agent for the client in the area of investments. Trust companies obtain other funds from the public in the form of deposit accounts and investment certificates, and by the sale of share capital. Term deposits and guaranteed investment certificates comprise

A **trust company** is a financial institution that acts as a trustee for property interests and conducts other confidential business.

the bulk of trust-company liabilities. Demand and savings deposits are also available. The amount of a company's deposits and certificates is limited to 20 times its shareholders' equity. Trust companies are required to maintain reserves in cash, in deposits with other institutions (e.g., chartered banks), and in short-term government securities equal to 20 percent of their deposits and borrowed funds coming due in less than 100 days. The main assets of trust companies are *mortgage loans.* They also invest in government securities.

Caisses Populaires and Credit Unions

A caisse populaire is a financial institution that is usually organized on the basis of Roman Catholic parish boundaries and that receives funds by selling shares and accepting deposits from members.

Similarly, a credit union sells shares and accepts members' deposits. These institutions are oriented toward consumer lending.

Caisses populaires and **credit unions** were established in order to enable groups of individuals to combine their savings, and thus to provide loans to members at relatively low interest rates. They receive their funds by selling shares and accepting deposits from members. Credit-union shares are similar to non-chequing savings deposits in a bank. Their deposits are similar to a bank's current account. The shares in a caisse populaire resemble term deposits at trust companies. Their deposits are similar to chequing savings deposits at chartered banks. Caisses populaires were founded in 1900 in Quebec. They are organized on a territorial basis, usually consisting of parish boundaries of the Roman Catholic Church. Caisses populaires stress the advantages of thrift. Credit unions, on the other hand, stress the availability of credit, and are oriented toward consumer lending. Credit unions are often established along occupational or industrial lines.

The difference in orientation between these institutions is also reflected in a difference in their assets. Caisses populaires have a larger percentage of *residential mortgages* than do credit unions. They are also larger purchasers of bonds issued by municipalities and school boards. Credit unions have a greater percentage of their assets in *consumer loans.* They also have a higher loan-to-deposit ratio than do caisses populaires.

Other Institutions

The major sources of funds for *mortgage loan companies* are term deposits and debentures. Debentures are usually one to five years in length. Most of the assets of mortgage loan companies are in residential mortgages. There is a close association between trust companies and mortgage loan companies, with one being the other's parent or subsidiary.

Alberta treasury branches were started in 1938 in order to provide financial services to communities that were too small to warrant a chartered-bank branch. The treasury branches are still primarily located in rural Alberta. These institutions accept demand, term, and savings deposits and issue guaranteed investment certificates. Any profit earned by the treasury branches is split with the government of Alberta. It is expected that Alberta treasury branches will be privatized in the near future.

REVIEW

7.7 What are the major differences between chartered banks and other deposit-accepting institutions?

The Creation of Money

Since chartered-bank deposits are considered to be money, it is actually possible for the chartered banking system to create money. *The banking system can create deposits through loans—and thus create money.* This process works in the following manner. Assume that you deposit $1000 in a demand deposit at a chartered bank. Assume that the chartered bank keeps 10 percent of the deposit, or $100, as a reserve against the deposit. The bank can lend out $900. When the $900 is taken out of the bank in the form of a loan, money has been created. The person who took out the loan can spend the $900, and you can spend the $1000 that you have in your deposit. Therefore, money has been created.

The changes that these transactions would have on bank A's balance sheet are as follows:

Chartered bank A

ASSETS	LIABILITIES
Reserves + $1000	Demand deposits + $1000

After keeping $100 back for reserves, the bank has $900 worth of excess reserves. If the $900 were loaned out, the balance sheet would read as follows:

Chartered bank A

ASSETS	LIABILITIES
Reserves + $100	Demand deposits + $1000
Loans + $900	

It is likely that the $900 loan will be spent. Once this is done, it may find its way back into a chartered bank. Assume that the $900 goes toward the purchase of a new couch. The furniture-store owner would deposit the $900 in chartered bank B. Assume that chartered bank B also keeps a

10-percent reserve against deposits. The changes to bank B's balance sheet are as follows:

Chartered bank B

ASSETS	LIABILITIES
Reserves + $900	Demand deposits + $900

Chartered bank B

ASSETS	LIABILITIES
Reserves + $90 Loans + $810	Demand deposits + $900

If bank B lends out the $810 in excess reserves, more money has been created. This process of deposits and loans continues until there are no excess reserves to be loaned out. The amount of money created as a result of your initial deposit of $1000 is as follows:

$900   (first loan)
+$810   (second loan)
+$729   (third loan)
+$...   (subsequent loans)

If this process were to continue uninterrupted, the amount of money created from the $1000 deposit would be $9000. A short formula allows for the calculation of the change in the money supply:

$$\Delta M = \frac{\text{excess reserves}}{\text{reserve ratio}}$$

where ΔM represents the change in the money supply

The change in the money supply from our example can be written as follows:

$$\Delta M = \frac{\$900}{0.10} \quad \text{(assumed reserve ratio)}$$

$$\Delta M = \$9000$$

The money supply would increase by $9000 if all the money taken out in loans were put back in demand deposits. If some of the money were deposited into savings deposits, the reserve might change. Assume that the reserve is only 2 percent on savings deposits. With a lower reserve requirement, more money could be loaned out. If more money were loaned out, then more money would be created. If your $1000 was initially deposited in a savings account, the potential increase in the money supply would be:

$$\Delta M = \frac{\$980}{0.02} \quad \text{(assumed reserve ratio for savings deposits)}$$

$$\Delta M = \$49\ 000$$

Several assumptions have to be made when using this formula. The first assumption is that all loans will eventually be redeposited in savings accounts. This also assumes that savings deposits are included in the definition of the money supply. In order for the money supply to expand by the maximum amount, other conditions must be present. If banks decide to hold back more money for reserves, then less money will be created. People also have to be willing to borrow money. It is also assumed that all the money that is loaned out eventually finds its way back into a chartered bank. If some of the loan money moves in hand-to-hand circulation and is not redeposited in a bank, less new money will be created.

The example of money creation refers to chartered banks only. There is a difference between the money-creating power of the chartered banks and that of other financial institutions. First, the official Bank of Canada definition of the money supply includes only chartered bank deposits. Second, the majority of deposits in Canada are with chartered banks. There is a greater likelihood that money will be redeposited into a chartered bank than into another deposit-accepting institution. The money-creating potential of other institutions is further restricted by some legal controls on their ability to make loans.

REVIEW

7.8 Assume that $500 is put into a demand deposit. What is the potential effect on the money supply assuming a reserve ratio of 10 percent? What conditions are necessary for the money supply to expand by this amount?

7.9 If chartered banks decide to keep more reserves, the potential of the banking system in creating money is reduced. Are banks likely to keep much money in reserves? Why or why not?

Money: Demand and Supply

Since money is a commodity, there is a market for it. There are individuals who are willing to buy (borrow) money and there are those individuals who are willing to supply (lend) money. These groups represent the demand and supply sides of the money market.

The Demand for Money

Individual demand for money can be divided into the following categories:

Transactions: It is necessary to have money in order to carry on day-to-day business. People need money in order to purchase food, clothing, recreation, and other items. The business sector needs money in order to pay for the services it requires. This need for money is referred to as the *transactions demand.*

There are a number of factors that influence the transactions demand for money. One factor, from an individual's point of view, is the size of family to be supported. There is a greater demand for money on the part of individuals who support families than among single persons. The financial needs of a family are clearly greater than those of a person who is responsible solely for himself or herself.

The consumer's decision to pay cash or to buy on credit influences the demand for money. The recent increase in the number of credit cards for gasoline, department stores, and other goods and services has probably reduced the amount of money needed to carry out transactions. The ability to readily transfer money from a savings deposit to a demand deposit by using an ATM reduces the need to keep money in demand deposits. The rate of inflation also influences the amount of money held for transactions purposes. If the general level of prices increases by 5 percent, you need 5 percent more money to purchase the items that you normally purchase.

Finally, the amount of money held for transaction purposes depends on the *level of income.* The higher the level of individual income, the more money that can be kept on hand for transaction purposes. It follows that the higher the level of GDP, or national income, the more money Canadians will hold for transactions purposes.

Precaution: Money is also held by individuals in case of an emergency or in order to meet unexpected situations. For example, a major household repair may require attention immediately. In these situations, money is needed at once. The precautionary demand for money simply represents a desire to be ready for unexpected circumstances.

The amount of money held for precautionary purposes depends on the level of income. As individuals' incomes increase, they have more money to keep on hand for emergencies. Individuals in lower income brackets will probably use most of their income for transactions and have little left over for precautionary purposes.

Speculation: Holding money involves a cost. This is the opportunity cost of the interest that is lost by not putting this money into an interest-earning asset. For example, if you buy a $1000 Canada Savings Bond, you earn interest on your money. If you keep $1000 in your pocket or in a demand deposit, you earn nothing. The speculative demand for money depends on the rate of interest. If the interest rate is relatively low, the opportunity cost of holding money is low. If the cost of holding money is low, there is a greater quantity of money demanded. At low interest rates, individuals are also willing to borrow more money. Expectations about the future also influence the speculative demand for money. If there is the expectation that interest rates will increase in the near future, individuals may be unwilling to put their money into an interest-bearing asset at the present time and will instead hold on to their money. At high interest rates, the speculative demand for money is low. Individuals may find it too expensive to hold money in terms of the opportunity costs. They will not be willing to borrow and will want to earn interest on any extra money that they have available. Money will be transferred into interest-earning assets. Therefore, the demand for money is lower at high interest rates.

The demand for money is referred to as *liquidity preference*. It represents a willingness to make assets liquid. A **liquid asset** is one that can be converted into money quickly, and the most liquid asset is money itself. The liquidity-preference curve is shown in Figure 7.1. In the diagram, D_M represents the liquidity preference, or demand-for-money curve. As interest rates (i) fall from i_1 to i_2 the quantity (Q) of money that individuals want to hold increases from Q_1 to Q_2. The interest rates that are measured on the vertical

A liquid asset **is one that can be readily converted into money.**

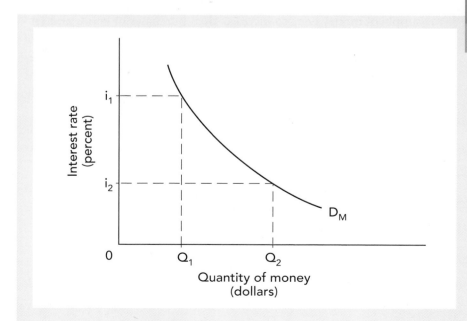

Figure 7.1

The demand for money

The quantity of money demanded is inversely related to the interest rate.

axis of this graph can be considered to be the price of money. If you want to borrow money, the interest rate is the price that you pay. When the interest rate is considered to be the price of money, the D_M curve in Figure 7.1 becomes similar to the demand curves introduced in Chapter 2. The lower the interest rate, the greater the quantity of money demanded.

A change in the interest rate, or the price of money, results in a movement along the D_M curve. Shifts in the demand curve for money occur in a manner similar to the shifting of the demand curve discussed in Chapter 2. When there is a change in a factor that influences the demand for money, other than the interest rate, there is a shift in the demand curve for money. For example, an increase in the level of GDP will result in the demand curve for money shifting to the right.

REVIEW

7.10 Why do people hold money instead of some other asset?

7.11 Divide the money that you have available into transactions, precautionary, and speculative amounts.

The Supply of Money

The supply of money in our economy is an important determinant of economic conditions. It represents the amount of *purchasing power* available. If the supply of money were to increase, then purchases of goods and services would increase as well. The increased spending would mean more jobs and possibly higher prices.

Early economists believed that the relationship between the supply of money and the price level was a direct one. Changes in the money supply would cause changes in the price level. Economists believed that the relationship between money and prices was also constant, and that no other variables affected the price level. The relationship put forth by these economists is known as the **crude-quantity theory of money:**

The crude-quantity theory of money is a mathematical identity that states that the price level is directly related to the amount of money in circulation (P = KM).

$$P = KM$$

where
P = average level of prices
M = money supply
K = a constant value

Assume that the value of the constant, K, is 2.0. If the money supply (M) doubled, then the price level (P) would increase four times. The task of the classical economists was to discover the value of the constant, K.

This relationship proved to be much too simple, but represented a good starting point for further study. Later a more sophisticated relationship between prices and money was developed. This is referred to as the **Fisher equation of exchange,** named after Irving Fisher, the American economist who developed it. The equation states that:

MV = PT

where
M = money supply
V = average velocity of circulation of money per period of time
P = average price level
T = number of market transaction or exchanges per period of time

> The Fisher equation of exchange states that the money supply multiplied by the velocity of money is equal to the number of transactions that take place in the economy multiplied by the average price level (MV = PT).

Two variables, V and T, were added to the earlier theory. The velocity of money (V) can be defined as the average number of times that each unit of the money supply changes hands during a given period. The variable T represents the number of business transactions that take place in a certain period of time. This provides an indication of the level of business activity. The right-hand side of the equation, PT, represents the value of all final transactions that took place in the economy. In other words, the right-hand side of the equation is equivalent to nominal GDP. The equation could therefore be rewritten as follows:

MV = GDP

If the money supply (M) increases, then GDP should increase as well:

↑   ↑
MV = GDP

If the velocity of money (V) increases, the level of GDP should also increase:

↑   ↑
MV = GDP

The velocity of money is the key to this equation. Increases in V would cause GDP to increase even if the money supply (M) remained constant. If the velocity of money does not change, then only changes in the money supply will result in changes in GDP.

The significance of the velocity of money will be discussed further in Chapter 8. If the velocity of money can be proved to be stable, then changes in the money supply would be an effective way to control the level of economic activity.

Let us assume that the velocity of money is stable and the money supply doubles in size. According to the Fisher equation of exchange, the level of GDP would also double. This would increase the number of jobs available as well as the price level. If the money supply were to be cut in half, the level of GDP would be halved as well. If the velocity of money does not remain constant, then it will be difficult to determine the impact on GDP of any change in the money supply.

REVIEW

7.12 What changes did Fisher make to the crude-quantity theory of money?

7.13 Why is the velocity of money important?

The Money Market

The demand for and the supply of money make up the money market, shown in Figure 7.2. The intersection of the liquidity-preference curve (D_M) with the supply of money ($S_M{}^1$) will give an equilibrium price, or interest rate (i_1). The supply-of-money curve in this diagram is shown as a vertical line since the supply of money is constant at any point in time and

Figure 7.2

The money market

An increase in the supply of money lowers the equilibrium interest rate.

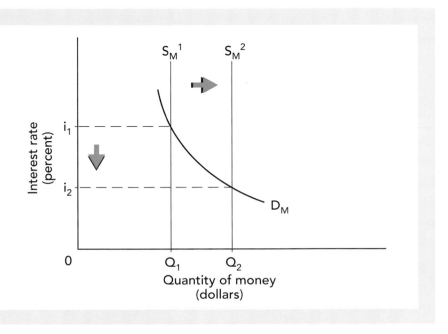

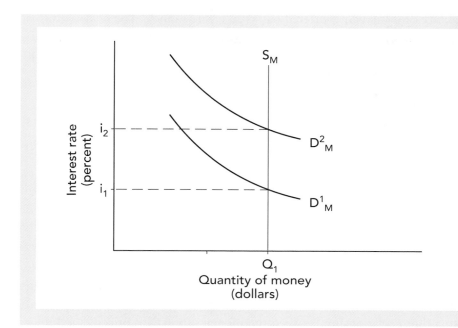

Figure 7.3

The money market

An increase in the demand for money increases the equilibrium interest rate.

is not dependent on the interest rate. Any changes in the demand for or the supply of money will cause the rate of interest to change. For example, in the diagram, an increase in the supply of money has lowered the interest rate to i_2.

The diagram in Figure 7.2 helps explain more fully the impact that changes in the money supply would have on the level of GDP. Any increase in the money supply would result in lower interest rates. Lower rates would encourage more borrowing and less saving on the part of the public. The increase in spending would cause the level of economic activity, GDP, to increase.

$$\Delta M \rightarrow \Delta i \rightarrow \Delta spending \rightarrow \Delta GDP \text{ (where } \Delta \text{ means "change in")}$$

Changes in the interest rate also come from shifts in the demand curve for money. As shown in Figure 7.3, an increase in the demand from D^1_M to D^2_M increases the interest rate from i_1 to i_2.

The Bank of Canada

The amount of money in circulation influences the levels of unemployment, inflation, and economic growth. In Canada the banking system has the ability to expand the money supply. This gives the banking system the ability to influence economic conditions. Are there any controls over the ability of Canadian chartered banks to create money? The answer to this question is yes. The control of the Canadian money supply rests with an independent institution, the Bank of Canada. The Bank of Canada is not a chartered bank but a central bank. Its responsibilities are outlined in the preamble to the Bank of Canada Act.

> ... it is desirable to establish a central bank in Canada to regulate credit and currency in the best interests of the economic life of the nation, to control and protect the external value of the national monetary unit and to mitigate by its influence fluctuations in the general level of production, trade, prices and employment, so far as may be possible within the scope of monetary action, and generally to promote the economic and financial welfare of the Dominion... The primary responsibility of the Bank of Canada is to regulate the money supply in order to promote the economic and financial welfare of the country.

We discussed earlier in the chapter how changes in the money supply can influence economic conditions. The crude-quantity theory of money pointed to a direct relationship between the money supply and prices. The Fisher equation of exchange showed the relationship between the money supply and the level of GDP. It is the Bank's responsibility to control the growth of the money supply in order to influence unemployment and inflation.

The Bank of Canada is an independent institution and is not under the direct authority of the federal government. The independence of the Bank, however, can cause some difficulties. It is possible that policies followed by the Bank may conflict with those followed by the federal government. For example, if the federal government were to see unemployment as the most serious problem facing Canadians, it would undertake steps to increase the level of spending in the economy. These steps might include an increase in government spending and possibly a tax cut. If the Bank of Canada saw inflation as a more serious problem, it would take steps to reduce the money supply and would try to reduce spending. It has been agreed that where policies differ, the federal government has the responsibility of directing the Bank toward policies it would like to see carried out. The Bank of Canada is, therefore, an independent institution making its own economic policy, unless the federal government disagrees with its decision!

The relationship between the Bank of Canada and the government is a close one. The Bank holds some of the government's bank deposits. The Bank provides the federal government with economic advice and lends it money on occasion. The Bank of Canada acts as an agent for the federal government and manages the government's borrowing requirements. It sells government bonds to the public. As part of its role in handling government bond issues, the Bank conducts the weekly auction of treasury bills (see Everyday Economics 7.3).

The Bank also serves as a banker's bank, in that it holds deposits for chartered banks. Part of the legal reserves that chartered banks must have are kept in the form of deposits at the Bank of Canada. The Bank has $398 million in chartered bank deposits (Table 7.4) and can also make loans or advances to the chartered banks. The Bank is referred to as a lender of last resort. The interest rate that the Bank of Canada charges is referred to as the *bank rate.* Chartered banks do not borrow a significant amount of money from the Bank of Canada; however, the bank rate serves as an indicator of what is going to happen to interest rates.

The Bank is also part of the Canadian Payments Association. In 1980, this association was created in order to establish and operate a *national*

Table 7.4 *Bank of Canada, assets and liabilities, end of February 2003*

ASSETS	($ MILLIONS)
Government of Canada direct and guaranteed securities	39 698
Advances to members of Canadian Payments Association	399
Foreign-currency deposits	313
Other investments	3
All other assets	687
Total assets	41 101

LIABILITIES	($ MILLIONS)
Notes in circulation	38 109
Canadian-dollar deposits	
Government of Canada	1 754
chartered banks	398
other members of the Canadian Payments Association	51
other	308
Foreign-currency liabilities	155
All other liabilities	325
Total liabilities	41 101

SOURCE: www.bank-banque-canada.ca (March 2003). Published with the permission of the Bank of Canada.

clearings and settlement system for cheques and other payment orders. Any financial institution that offers accounts on which a customer can write cheques payable to someone else is eligible for membership in the Canadian Payments Association. What is a clearings and settlements system? When someone at a financial institution cashes a cheque that was drawn on an account at another institution, an exchange of funds must take place between the institutions. The drawer's account must be debited and the institution where the cheque was cashed must be reimbursed. The physical exchange of paper items and magnetic tapes between different institutions, and the accounting and balancing involved, make up the clearings and settlements system. Millions of such transactions occur each day.

What role does the Bank of Canada play? Most members of the Canadian Payments Association have settlement accounts and lines of credit at the Bank of Canada. The Bank effects the final settlement of accounts between institutions each day by crediting and debiting member accounts accordingly.

One final responsibility of the Bank of Canada deserves mention: it is responsible for the external value of the Canadian dollar. That is, it is responsible for the value of the Canadian dollar in terms of the currencies of other countries. A further discussion of the Bank of Canada's role in influencing the foreign-exchange value of the Canadian dollar is contained in Chapter 9.

Monetary Policy

Changes in the rate of growth of Canada's money supply influence economic conditions. The Bank of Canada monitors changes in the money supply on a regular basis and takes steps to alter the growth in the money supply when necessary. The action taken by the Bank of Canada to alter the money supply, and ultimately economic conditions, is referred to as *monetary policy*.

Which definition of the money supply should the Bank of Canada concentrate on? Canada's money supply has been growing at a variety of rates depending on which definition of money is chosen. Figure 7.4 shows the annual percentage change in M1 from 1976–2002. In 1990, M1 (currency and demand deposits) decreased by 0.8 percent, while M2 (M1 plus personal savings deposits) increased by 11.2 percent. For the previous year, 1989, M1 increased by only 3.9 percent whereas M2 increased by 13.8 percent.

The selection of a money-supply definition to act as the focus of the Bank of Canada's actions is a difficult decision. Traditionally, changes in

Figure 7.4

Annual percentage change in Canada's money supply (M1), 1976–2002

SOURCE: *Bank of Canada Review.* Published with the permission of the Bank of Canada.

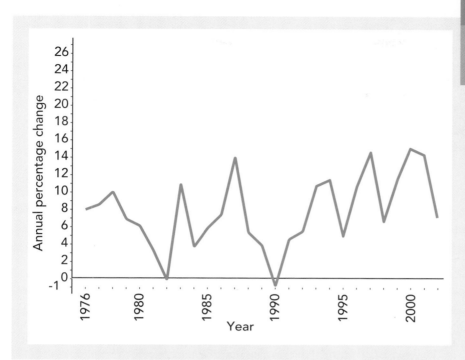

M1 have been the focus of the Bank's activities. However, depositors may transfer money out of demand deposits into other deposits that pay interest and also have chequing privileges. By paying attention to M1 only, the Bank may underestimate the purchasing power in the economy. Regardless of the money-supply definition chosen, how does the Bank of Canada influence the rate of growth of the money supply?

EVERYDAY ECONOMICS 7.3

Treasury Bills

Treasury bills (also called T-bills) are short-term, non–interest-bearing promissory notes issued by the Government of Canada. They are sold by way of an auction conducted by the Bank of Canada every Tuesday. Treasury bills are issued in 91-day, 182-day, and 364-day terms, with the 91-day term being the most common. The bills are sold on a discount basis. That is, the government offers to pay the face value of the treasury bill at maturity. Bills come in varied denominations: $1000, $5000, $25 000, $100 000, and $1 000 000. No interest is paid, but the return for the investor is the difference between the purchase price and the face value. For example, it may be possible to purchase a $100 000 treasury bill for $96 000. On the maturity date, the holder of the treasury bill receives $100 000.

The Bank of Canada acts as the federal government's agent in issuing these bills. It conducts a weekly auction of treasury bills on Tuesdays. The size of the weekly issue varies and depends on the financial needs of the government and the state of the market. Each week the Bank sends out a notice of the amount of maturities of the current week's auction. Chartered banks and investment dealers are referred to as primary distributors and are asked to submit bids on their own behalf and on behalf of their clients.

The Bank receives the bids in the form of sealed tenders. At noon on Tuesday, the sealed tenders are opened. The tenders are arranged in descending order. They are first offered to the highest bidder, and then to the next highest, and so on, until the entire weekly issue has been allocated. The tenders give the price per $100 to three decimal places. For example, a bid of $98.426 on a $100 000 treasury bill means that the bidder would pay $98 426 and receive $100 000 at maturity. Primary distributors may submit multiple bids, and there is clearly no advantage to being the highest bidder since everyone receives the face value at maturity.

The Bank of Canada also bids on treasury bills. First, it submits a competitive bid similar to other primary distributors. It then submits a reserve bid, which is usually not successful. The reserve bid is to ensure that the government receives its money if the bids are not enough to buy up the entire issue. The reserve bid also ensures that the government borrows the money at a reasonable cost. If the reserve bid were not there, it would be possible for all the primary distributors to submit very low bids.

How do financial institutions determine how much to bid for a treasury bill? The bid is calculated using the present-value formula associated with simple interest.

$$P = \frac{S}{1 + rt}$$

where P = present value
S = maturity value
r = annual interest rate
t = time (in years)

If a financial institution wanted to earn 6 percent annually on its money, the bid on a $100 000 182-day treasury bill would be calculated as follows:

$$P = \frac{\$100\ 000}{1 + (0.06)\ (182/365)} = \$97\ 095.13$$

The bid on the treasury bill would be $97 095.

The Bank of Canada calculates the average price and the average rate of return and usually makes the information available at about 2 p.m. on the day of the auction. Information on the highest and lowest bids is also made available.

Questions

1. What would be the reason to bid on a treasury bill?
2. Could a treasury bill be considered a liquid asset?
3. Could the Bank of Canada influence the average yield on treasury bills?
4. What factors could influence the bids that are submitted at the weekly auction of treasury bills?

The Bank Rate

The bank rate is the rate of interest paid by chartered banks on money borrowed from the Bank of Canada.

The **bank rate** is the rate of interest that the Bank of Canada charges the chartered banks when they borrow from it. The bank rate is used as a signal for the direction that interest rates are taking. When it increases, other interest rates follow. Chartered banks usually increase their prime lending rate. The prime lending rate is the rate that a bank charges its most creditworthy customer on loans. When interest rates go up, people are less likely to borrow money. They are also more likely to want to save money, since the return for savings is greater. Increases in the interest rate are likely to decrease the amount of spending, and can be used to fight demand-pull inflation. Conversely, decreases in the bank rate would lead to lower interest rates. The overall spending in the economy would likely increase, which would decrease the level of demand-deficient unemployment.

In September 2000, the Bank of Canada announced a change in the way the bank rate is established. Starting in January 2001, the bank rate is changed at regularly scheduled policy meetings held eight times a year. By establishing fixed dates for bank rate changes, the Bank of Canada hopes to reduce the uncertainty in financial markets associated with not knowing when interest-rate announcements were likely to occur.

Open-Market Operations

Open-market operations are the buying and selling of government bonds on the money market by the Bank of Canada. If the Bank wants to reduce the size of the money supply, it will sell government bonds on the open market. The open market simply means that selling is not restricted to certain groups. By selling bonds, spendable money is removed from circulation. Individuals or institutions who purchase government bonds from the Bank of Canada give up money in return for a non-spendable asset (the bond). If the Bank wants to increase the amount of money in circulation, it will buy bonds back from the public, giving individuals and institutions money in return for bonds. This will increase both the money supply and the purchasing power in the economy.

> Open-market operations refer to the buying and selling of government bonds by the Bank of Canada in order to influence the money supply.

Suppose that the bank sells a $100 000 government bond to the Whitby Life Insurance Company. The balance-sheet transactions of the life insurance company, the chartered bank where the life insurance company has its deposit, and the Bank of Canada are presented in Figure 7.5. The assets of the insurance company will be transferred from a bank deposit to a $100 000 government bond. In order to pay for the bond, the company had to reduce the amount of money in its bank deposit. The reduction in chartered-bank deposits by $100 000 means that the money supply has decreased by this amount.

What does the Bank of Canada do with the cheque from the life insurance company? Since the cheque was written against an account with a chartered bank, the Bank of Canada will present the cheque to the chartered bank for payment. The chartered bank has a deposit at the Bank of Canada and, therefore, this deposit will be reduced by the amount of the cheque. In Figure 7.5, the assets of the chartered bank have been reduced by $100 000 (the reduction in its deposit at the Bank of Canada). The liabilities of the

Figure 7.5

The impact of the Bank of Canada selling a bond to a life insurance company

Bank of Canada		Chartered Bank	
Assets	Liabilities	Assets	Liabilities
Bonds − $100 000	Chartered bank Deposit − $100 000	Deposit at Bank of Canada − $100 000	Deposits − $100 000

Whitby Life Insurance Company	
Assets	Liabilities
Bonds + $100 000 Deposit at chartered bank − $100 000	

Bank of Canada have also been reduced by $100 000 with the reduction in the chartered-bank deposit.

What is the effect on the money supply if the $100 000 bond is sold to a chartered bank? The bank would purchase the bond by taking the money out of its deposit at the Bank of Canada (see Figure 7.6). The bank exchanges one asset for another. There is actually no change in the money supply because deposits in chartered banks have not changed. Although the money supply has not been directly affected, the ability of the chartered bank to lend

Figure 7.6

The impact of the Bank of Canada selling a bond to a chartered bank

Bank of Canada		Chartered Bank	
Assets	Liabilities	Assets	Liabilities
Bonds − $100 000	Chartered bank Deposit − $100 000	Deposit at Bank of Canada − $100 000 bonds + $100 000	

money has been reduced because the reserves (deposits at the Bank of Canada) of the chartered bank have been reduced. If the Bank of Canada wanted to expand the money supply, it would buy government bonds in the open market. This would provide the chartered banks with more reserves to be loaned out. The expansion of the money supply would lead to increased spending and increased gross domestic product.

Other Influences

Prior to 1992, the Bank Act imposed a reserve requirement on chartered bank deposits. That is, chartered banks were required to keep a certain percentage of deposits on reserve. Changing the reserve requirement was one way to influence the growth of the money supply. An increase in the reserve ratio reduced the amount of money banks could lend out, thus limiting the growth of the money supply. A reduction in the reserve ratio made more money available for loans and thus provided for monetary growth.

The Bank of Canada could also influence the money supply by transferring federal government deposits from the Bank of Canada to the chartered banks or from the chartered banks to the Bank of Canada. If federal government deposits are transferred from the Bank of Canada to the chartered banks, the chartered banks will have more reserves and can lend more money. If the federal government deposits are transferred back to the Bank of Canada, chartered banks lose reserves, thus limiting their ability to lend money.

R E V I E W

7.14 Work through the balance-sheet approach for a situation in which the Bank of Canada buys a government bond back from the public. What will be the effect on the money supply?

7.15 Identify two things that the Bank of Canada could do in order to reduce the money supply in Canada. Would this action be undertaken to counteract inflation or unemployment? Explain.

Summary

The existence of money removes our reliance on a barter system. The main function of money is to facilitate transactions between individuals. Apart from acting as a medium of exchange, money also performs other functions. Money serves as a common denominator for prices, which are expressed in terms of a country's currency. Money is also a means whereby individuals can store their wealth.

Throughout history, many commodities have served as money. Regardless of what item is used as money, it must possess certain characteristics. It must be divisible into smaller amounts, easily recognizable, durable, easy to carry, and not easily copied. However, above all else, if an item is to circulate as money it must be seen as having value.

There is a market for money similar to the market for other products. Individuals demand money primarily for carrying out day-to-day business transactions. Money is also demanded for speculative and precautionary reasons. The supply of money in Canada is composed of coins, Bank of Canada notes, and deposits at chartered banks. The interaction of the demand for and the supply of money determines the interest rate, which in turn influences economic conditions. When the level of business and consumer spending responds to changes in the interest rate, the level of GDP is altered.

Since chartered bank deposits are considered to be money, it is possible for the chartered banking system to create money. When banks lend out their reserves, money is created. When loans are redeposited into other banks, it is possible for more money to be created. The banks create money in the sense that they can create deposits.

The Bank of Canada is responsible for the regulation of the money supply in Canada. When the Bank of Canada regulates the money supply in order to influence economic conditions, this is referred to as monetary policy. The tools of monetary policy include changes in the bank rate and open-market operations.

Questions for Review and Discussion

1. What effect do credit cards have on the demand for money? Will credit cards ever replace money?
2. What are some liquid assets with which you are familiar? What type of assets cannot be classified as liquid?
3. Why aren't 1967 Canadian silver dollars circulating in our economy as money?
4. Apart from making exchanges easier, what other uses does money have?
5. Are traveller's cheques considered to be money? Are credit cards money?
6. What makes money a valuable commodity?
7. Can life insurance companies be referred to as financial intermediaries? Explain.
8. Why would chartered banks pay a higher rate of interest on specified term deposits than on personal savings deposits?
9. Would you expect the rate of interest paid on a one-year term deposit to be greater than the rate of interest paid on a three-month term deposit? Why or why not?

10. Examine the following balance sheet for Bank A:

ASSETS		LIABILITIES	
Reserves	$25 000	Demand deposits	$50 000
Loans	$25 000		

  a) If this bank were to lend out its excess reserves, what potential impact would this have on the money supply? Assume a reserve ratio of 10 percent.

  b) If a depositor withdrew $10 000 from a demand deposit, how would this affect the assets or liabilities of Bank A? How would it impact on money creation by the banking system?

11. What limits the Canadian banking system's ability to expand the money supply?

12. Previously, banks were required to keep a certain amount of reserves. Why would a legal reserve requirement be considered a penalty for chartered banks?

13. The chartered banks in Canada are perfectly safe places in which to put your money. Discuss this statement.

14. Can you explain why chartered bank profits increase when interest rates are decreasing?

15. Some analysts have suggested that deposit insurance be scrapped. Would the elimination of deposit insurance change the lending practices of chartered banks? How would it change the decisions of depositors with regard to where they choose to put their money?

16. If the velocity of money remains constant, does it make the Bank of Canada's task of regulating the economy easier? Explain.

17. Show the impact on a bank's assets and liabilities of the bank purchasing a $20 000 government bond from the Bank of Canada.

18. What impact will an increase in the money supply have on
  a) interest rates
  b) business investment
  c) aggregate demand
  d) employment in Canada
  e) prices?

19. Should the coverage limit for Canada deposit insurance, currently at $60 000, be adjusted for inflation? Explain.

20. In 2003, consumer debt (non-mortgage debt) represented 31 percent of household debt compared to 25 percent of household debt in 1994. In 2003, the Bank of Canada increased interest rates in order to reduce the rate of inflation. Would higher interest rates in 2003 have impacted households more than higher interest rates in previous years? Explain.

Suggested Readings

Bank of Canada Annual Report 2002. Ottawa: Bank of Canada, 2003. The report covers the Bank's activities, including attempts to reduce counterfeiting and meeting the demand for bank notes.

Bank of Canada Monetary Policy Report. Ottawa: Bank of Canada. This quarterly publication explains the Bank of Canada's approach to monetary policy.

Canadian Bank Facts. Canadian Bankers Association, May 2000. The annual guide to Canada's banking industry.

Freedman, Charles. *The Canadian Banking System.* Technical Report No. 81. Ottawa: Bank of Canada, 1998. This report provides a good summary of the historical changes in the Bank Act and in the operation of Canadian banks.

MacIntosh, Robert. *Different Drummers: Banking and Politics in Canada.* Toronto: MacMillan, 1991. This book contains an excellent history of banking in Canada, including the history of the Bank of Canada.

McCullough, A.B. "Funny Money." *Horizon Canada* 4, no. 43 (December 1985). Quebec: Centre for the Study of Teaching Canada Inc. This is a brief account, with pictures, of some of the earliest forms of money in Canada.

Pope, William Henry. *All You Must Know About Economics.* Second Edition. Toronto: Bergendal, 1997. A short book on Canada's economic problems with a good chapter on money.

Powell, James. *A History of the Canadian Dollar.* Ottawa: The Bank of Canada. An excellent small book on the history of money in Canada.

Rabbior, Gary. *Money and Monetary Policy in Canada.* Toronto: Canadian Foundation for Economic Education, 1994. This is an easy-to-read book on the history of money, monetary policy, and exchange rates in Canada.

Shearer, Ronald A., John F. Chant, and David E. Bond. *Economics of the Canadian Financial System.* Third Edition. Toronto: Prentice-Hall, 1995. This is a good reference text for teachers of introductory money and banking.

Selected Websites

www.bankofcanada.ca The site for the Bank of Canada. There is access to history, monetary policy, and central bank services.
www.ny.frb.org The website for the Federal Reserve Bank in New York. The site presents information on banking, monetary policy, and money supply statistics.
www.cba.ca The website for the Canadian Bankers Association providing FAQs, statistics, publications, and general information about banking in Canada.

CHAPTER 8

Stabilization Policy

Key Terms

fiscal policy

Phillips curve

stagflation

automatic stabilizer

discretionary fiscal policy

public debt

monetary policy

supply-side economics

Laffer curve

wage and price controls

human resources policies

Chapter Objectives

After successfully completing this chapter, you will be able to:

- explain the unemployment/inflation trade-off
- describe the shortcomings of both fiscal and monetary policies in regulating the economy
- explain the supply-side approach to economic stabilization
- understand the possible problems of large amounts of government borrowing
- relate the shortcomings of long-term wage and price control policies
- explain how human resources policies can be used as economic stabilization policies

Core Concept Building

This chapter summarizes much of the material introduced in Chapters 5 to 7. Ensure that you can distinguish between monetary policy and fiscal policy; focus on the advantages and disadvantages of both types of policy. The chapter also discusses the impact on the Canadian economy of a large public debt.

PRODUCTIVITY GROWTH AND INTEREST RATES

There are many definitions and measures of productivity. In general terms, productivity can be defined as the amount of output produced per worker per hour worked. Several factors influence the productivity of workers. They include the skill level and training of the workers, management techniques, and the quantity and quality of machinery and equipment that the workers use. The productivity of their employees is likely to increase when firms keep pace with the latest technology by investing in the latest machinery, computers, and equipment. The gains in productivity may lag behind the introduction of new equipment as employees need time to adjust to the new technology.

As discussed in Chapter 7, interest rates are determined in the money market through the demand for and the supply of money. The Bank of Canada influences the interest rate through its regulation of the supply of money. The Bank of Canada uses increases in the interest rate to reduce the amount of inflation in the economy. What is the relationship between productivity changes in the economy and the interest rate?

If firms are able to achieve increases in productivity, they can hold the line on price increases. If the output per employee increases, production costs should decrease even taking into consideration the cost of the new machinery and equipment. If prices are increasing slowly in the economy, the Bank of Canada will not be forced to reduce the supply of money and, as a result, interest rates will not increase—at least, interest rates will not increase because of pressure from the supply side of the market. It is always possible that increases in the demand for money could lead to higher interest rates.

It is possible that Canadian businesses can duplicate the results of companies in the United States that have invested heavily in machinery and equipment, especially in computers and information technology. Unfortunately, Canadian productivity growth continues to lag that in the United States.

Approaches to Stabilization Policy

The constant flow of injections and leakages associated with the circular flow of money (see Chapter 6) results in changes in the level of gross domestic product (GDP). Changes in GDP have an influence on the levels of inflation and unemployment in Canada. When the level of GDP is increasing, the demand for goods and services is increasing as well. Employers need workers, and, as more jobs are created, unemployment is reduced. The reduction in unemployment caused by increased spending will, however, lead to higher prices. On the other hand, when the level of GDP is falling, the opposite results occur. The decreases in spending cause unemployment to rise and inflation to be reduced. A comparison of rates of inflation and unemployment from 1966 to 1999 is presented in Figure 8.1.

The federal and provincial governments are concerned about high levels of unemployment and inflation. Both levels of government continually introduce programs aimed at influencing GDP in order to ensure that jobs are being created and that prices do not rise too rapidly. Programs that are introduced to regulate unemployment and inflation are referred to as *economic stabilization* programs. We have seen economic stabilization policies at work earlier in the text: in Chapter 6, the effects of government spending and taxation (fiscal policy) on GDP were analyzed. At the federal government level, **fiscal policy** is the responsibility of the Department of Finance. Similar departments responsible for fiscal policy exist within each provincial government.

How does fiscal policy act as economic stabilization policy? If unemployment were seen as the major economic problem in Canada, governments would endeavour to increase their spending and/or reduce the level of taxation. The subsequent increase in spending by government or by households would create new jobs. One example of increased spending would be an initiative by the government to modernize or expand an existing airport. The money spent on design and construction would have a multiplier effect on the economy. An example of an initiative by government in the area of taxation would be the lowering of personal income tax rates.

Fiscal policies employ changes to the level of government spending and taxation with the goal of influencing economic conditions.

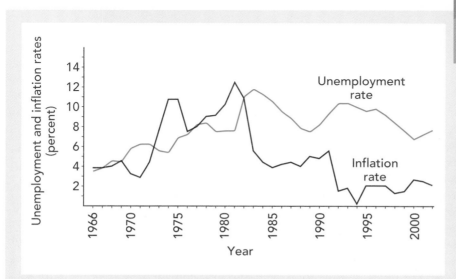

Figure 8.1

Rates of inflation and unemployment

Unemployment and inflation rates from 1966 to 2002

SOURCE: Adapted from the Statistics Canada CANSIM database, Table 326-0002, Series v2461224, and from the Statistics Canada publication *Historical Statistics of Canada*, Catalogue 11-516, 1983, Series D233.

As shown in Chapter 6, both increased spending and lower taxes lead to increases in GDP.

If inflation were the country's main economic concern, the opposite steps would be undertaken. Government spending would be reduced and/or the level of taxation increased. Government spending could be reduced in a number of ways. For example, governments could reduce expenditures in the areas of social services, health, and education. These areas represent the bulk of government spending. Plans for new government office buildings could be put on hold. Intergovernmental transfers could also be reduced. These steps, along with taxation increases, would reduce the overall amount of spending in the economy. This would put less demand pressure on prices and would consequently lower the inflation rate.

An alternate approach to economic stabilization was introduced in Chapter 7. Monetary policy relies on changes in the money supply and is conducted by the Bank of Canada. Changes in the money supply are directly related to changes in spending. The Bank of Canada can alter the money supply by changing the bank rate, changing secondary reserve requirements, and conducting open market operations.

The fiscal and monetary policies presented in previous chapters are being used continually in Canada as solutions to the problems of unemployment and inflation. Yet the problems continue to exist, because fiscal and monetary policies have certain shortcomings in their fight against unemployment and inflation. This chapter discusses the shortcomings of these policies and introduces some alternative approaches to economic stabilization.

Unemployment/Inflation Trade-off

One of the shortcomings of traditional monetary and fiscal policies is their inability to deal simultaneously with unemployment and inflation. For example, if unemployment is seen as the more serious problem, steps will be taken to increase the level of spending. Increased spending in the economy creates a demand for more workers, which reduces the level of unemployment. The increase in spending will also cause prices to rise as the demand for goods and services begins to outstrip the supply. On the other hand, attempts to reduce the rate of inflation by cutting back on spending will also reduce the demand for workers. Spending cuts will, therefore, result in higher levels of unemployment. *There is an inverse relationship between unemployment and inflation: when one increases, the other decreases.* Recent trends in unemployment and inflation are presented in Figure 8.1.

This inverse relationship has been referred to as a *trade-off*. In order to achieve lower levels of inflation, it is necessary to accept, or trade off, higher rates of unemployment. A diagrammatic representation of this trade-off appears in Figure 8.2. According to the P^1 curve in the diagram, a 10-percent rate of inflation is associated with a 3-percent rate of unemployment. If it is desirable to reduce the rate of inflation to 5 percent per annum, then a 5-percent unemployment rate has to be accepted. The reverse is also true, and although these numbers are arbitrarily chosen for the graph they point out the nature of the relationship. This trade-off relationship is often referred to as the **Phillips curve,** named after a British economist who studied the relationship between unemployment and wage increases in the 1950s. It was Phillips' work with wage increases and unemployment that led other economists to believe that there may be an inverse relationship between price increases (inflation) and unemployment.

During the 1960s, several studies were undertaken to determine the exact nature of this trade-off. That is, if it is desirable to reduce the unemployment rate by 2 percent, what rate of inflation must we be prepared to accept? The studies failed to come to a conclusion because the relationship

The Phillips curve is a graphical representation of the negative relationship between rates of unemployment and rates of inflation.

Figure 8.2

Unemployment/inflation trade-off (Phillips curve)

The curve (P) shows the inverse relationships between inflation and unemployment.

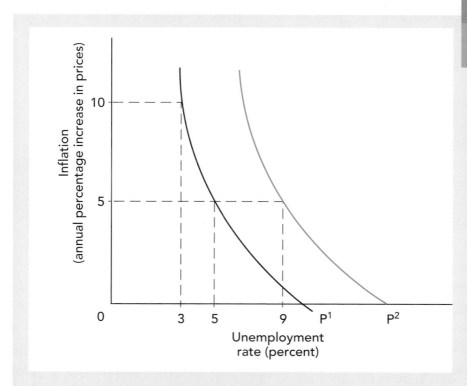

The term stagflation was
coined to describe a
situation of depressed
levels of real output in the
economy combined with
rising prices.

between unemployment and inflation is constantly changing. There is no reason to assume that the trade-off that existed in the 1960s is the same as the trade-off that exists at the start of the twenty-first century. Each year, changes take place in our economy that alter the exact nature of this relationship. Still, a trade-off continues to exist, and any fiscal and monetary policy that attempts to improve one problem tends to make the other problem worse.

During the 1970s, both the unemployment rate and the rate of inflation were steadily increasing. This led some economists to believe that the trade-off failed to exist. In fact, the term **stagflation** was introduced to describe the economic conditions of that period. Stagflation comes from the words *stagnant* and *inflation*. The word stagnant referred to the state of economic activity. During this time period, real GDP was growing very slowly and was associated with high levels of unemployment as the labour force continued to grow. Inflation was also a problem in the 1970s. In fact, it was the inability of government to manage inflation by traditional means that led to the enactment of the Anti-Inflation Program in 1975. This program established legal limits for wages, prices, and profit increases, and is discussed more fully later in this chapter.

The increases in inflation and unemployment during the 1970s and early 1980s did not disprove the existence of a trade-off, but indicated that the trade-off had worsened. That is, in order to reduce inflation to the same level as earlier a higher rate of unemployment had to be accepted. As shown in Figure 8.2, a 5 percent rate of inflation was previously associated with a 5 percent unemployment rate under the conditions described by P^1. If conditions have changed, so that the trade-off is now described by P^2, then a 5 percent inflation rate is associated with a 9 percent unemployment rate.

The trade-off between unemployment and inflation as depicted by the Phillips curve has led to the concept of NAIRU (non-accelerating-inflation rate of unemployment). This term refers to a rate of unemployment that corresponds to a stable (possibly zero) rate of inflation. If the actual rate of unemployment is less than the NAIRU, the rate of inflation increases. If the rate of unemployment is greater than the NAIRU, the rate of inflation decreases. The rate of unemployment consistent with a stable rate of inflation has not yet been determined. Some economists argue that this rate of unemployment will not be determined accurately since the relationship between unemployment and inflation is not stable. The instability in the relationship between unemployment and inflation has resulted in an increase in the NAIRU. Why has the NAIRU been increasing? The following factors account for the increase.

Changing composition of the labour force: As shown in Chapter 5, significant changes have taken place in the Canadian labour force, including the increased participation rate for women and the increase in the number of young labour-force participants. This has resulted in an increase in the overall participation rate and means that a greater percentage of Canadians are working or looking for work than was previously the case. Unfortunately, the demand for workers has not kept pace with the increased supply of workers, and the level of unemployment has increased. As a result of changes in the labour force, the composition of the unemployed is also changing. Among the unemployed are many labour-force participants who want to work only on a part-time basis or who are in the labour force only temporarily. The changing composition of the labour force has increased the measured unemployment rate at any given rate of inflation. The changing composition of the labour force has led to higher labour turnover rates and to higher unemployment rates. The proportions of youth and women in the labour force are increasing. The highest turnover rates in the labour force are found in these two groups of labour-force participants. Youth also have a higher unemployment rate than the labour-force average. As the participation of these groups in the labour force increases, the overall unemployment rate will increase.

Employment insurance: In 1971, Canada revamped its employment insurance program. The new program not only made it easier for unemployed people to qualify for benefits, but also increased the amount of these benefits. These changes have discouraged some unemployed persons from seeking employment, and have increased the unemployment rate (see Chapter 5). Changes in the employment insurance program have also affected the geographic mobility of workers. Unemployed persons who are receiving benefits many not be as willing to relocate to other parts of the country as they would be if they were not receiving the benefits. Prior to the changes in the employment insurance program, workers were more mobile and the unemployment rate was lowered when mobile workers found new employment. When workers are less mobile, employers are not as reluctant to lay off employees. With a reduction in worker mobility, workers can be rehired when needed.

The employment insurance program can also increase the unemployment rate by attracting additional workers into the labour force. These workers are likely to come from demographic groups that traditionally experience higher unemployment rates.

An increase in payroll taxes: Governments in Canada have resorted to payroll taxes in order to finance their spending and to pay for social programs such as health care, pensions, and employment insurance. Payroll taxes have been referred to as "job killers" by making it more expensive to hire employees.

Industrial restructuring: Increases in foreign trade and deregulation of certain industries have changed the competitive nature of many of Canada's industries. Some industries are expanding, while others are contracting. It may not be easy for workers to shift employment from one industry to another. Older workers, in particular, may find the move to a new industry or occupation more difficult than would younger workers. The increased importance of the service sector and the relative decline in importance of the manufacturing and agriculture sectors have also forced a change in employment for many workers.

Low productivity growth: Productivity is generally defined as the amount of output each worker can produce. If worker productivity can increase, then workers can get wage increases without an accompanying increase in the price of the good or service that they produce. If wage increases are granted without productivity improvements, then price increases are inevitable.

Lower production costs and lower prices are only one aspect of productivity. Increases in productivity can lead to higher wages for employees and higher real incomes for business. The prospect of higher real incomes is the incentive for business to invest in expanding facilities or in new ventures. Productivity increases can also lead to better-quality goods and services. Thus a higher standard of living for Canadians is tied to productivity improvements. In addition, the conservation of scarce resources may be a by-product of improved productivity.

Productivity can be measured in a number of ways. One measure is to compute manufacturing output per worker-hour. Another is to calculate real GDP per employed worker. For international comparisons, productivity measures using total hours worked is a more accurate measure of labour production since the average weekly hours may vary between countries. Also, increases in the number of part-time workers is taken into account when using total hours as a measure of productivity as opposed to the number of persons employed.

Regardless of which measure is chosen, Canada's productivity growth rate has been poor by international standards. Since 1973, labour productivity growth in Canada has been slower than in previous years. From 1946 to 1973, labour productivity increased at an average annual rate of 4.1 percent. During the 1980s and 1990s the average growth in productivity was less than one percent. The reasons for the decline in productivity growth are varied. The pre-1973 period was characterized by a major movement of workers from the low-productivity farm sector to higher-productivity activities in the non–farm sector part of the economy. Employment in agriculture has stabilized since 1973, so the gains in productivity arising from the movement of workers from one sector to another have slowed down. Second, labour productivity depends on the amount of capital available to each worker. Since 1973, there has been slower growth in the capital–labour ratio and, as a result, productivity increases have slowed as well. Third, increases in productivity can come from increases in business production. As output expands, productivity advances come from longer production runs and the efficiency associated with learning as the same tasks are repeated. In recessions, productivity declines as output drops off. If companies decrease production but do not lay off employees, output per employee will go down. Other explanations have been put forth to explain the slowdown in labour productivity growth. Some analysts argue that the rapid increases in oil prices after 1973 contributed to the decline in labour productivity growth since less energy was used with each worker. Others argue that the increases in inflation, especially the increases in natural resource prices since 1973, have resulted in fewer resources for labour to work with. Finally, some analysts argue that the quality of labour has deteriorated in recent years.

Declining foreign-exchange value of the Canadian dollar: Through the first half of the 1970s, the value of the Canadian dollar was close to the value of the U.S. dollar in foreign-exchange markets. Beginning in 1976, the foreign-exchange value of the Canadian dollar declined rapidly. By 1978, a Canadian dollar could be purchased for approximately 84 cents in U.S. currency. During the late 1990s and into this century, the Canadian dollar traded in the 66- to 69-cent (U.S.) range.

The falling dollar has led to increases in consumer prices. When the Canadian dollar drops in value on world foreign-exchange markets, it takes more Canadian dollars to buy the same amount of imported goods. Prices of imported goods rise. Since the Canadian demand for imports is relatively inelastic, the higher prices do not substantially decrease the quantity demanded. Canadians continued to purchase imports and to pay higher prices for them.

A lower value for the Canadian dollar makes Canadian-made products cheaper from a foreign point of view. This should increase the demand for Canadian products; however, foreign demand for Canadian products is also relatively inelastic. Lower prices do not result in a large increase in the quantity demanded. Hence, a lower value of the Canadian dollar has not resulted in a significant increase in employment of Canadian workers. A further discussion of foreign-exchange rates appears in Chapter 9.

Fiscal Policy

The use of fiscal policy as an economic stabilization tool involves changes in the level of government spending and taxation. Fiscal policy in Canada can be divided into two types: automatic and discretionary. Automatic policies, or automatic stabilizers, are programs that are already in operation and help to stabilize the economy when economic conditions change. These programs are referred to as automatic because no government decision is taken in order for the programs to become effective. Discretionary fiscal policy refers to a situation in which government is deciding what economic stabilization programs to introduce.

Automatic Stabilizers

Automatic stabilizers are government programs currently in operation that react automatically to help adjust the level of aggregate demand when economic conditions change.

Programs classified as **automatic stabilizers** were not originally introduced as part of an economic stabilization policy. They were introduced to meet other objectives, yet their nature is such that they can influence economic conditions. Two of the most recognized automatic stabilizers are employment insurance and the progressive income tax.

Employment insurance: When individuals become unemployed, their income is reduced to zero. When their spending decreases, the multiplier effect starts to take hold and overall spending in the economy declines. This leads to lower levels of income for other individuals, which in turn decreases their spending. The existence of an employment insurance program may retard this overall spending decline and ultimate income loss. If, while unemployed, individuals can receive some money in the form of employment insurance benefits, they will be more willing and able to spend and the negative consequences of unemployment on the economy will be reduced. Once back to work, individuals are required to contribute part of their earnings to the employment insurance fund. Money is taken out of their paycheque in the good times and returned to workers in periods of unemployment. *In this way, employment insurance tends to stabilize the level of spending.*

Progressive income tax: As mentioned in Chapter 4, the Canadian income tax structure is progressive in nature. Those individuals in the higher income tax brackets pay a higher percentage of their income in taxes than individuals with lower incomes. A progressive income tax has a stabilizing effect on the economy. When an individual's income increases, a higher percentage of income is being paid out in taxes. This reduces the potential increase in spending and dampens inflationary pressures. When an individual's income falls, possibly because of job termination or layoff, he or she pays a lower percentage of income in taxes. The reduction in the income tax rate provides the individual with a greater proportion of his or her income to spend and, in doing so, helps to maintain the overall level of spending.

The automatic stabilizers are not meant to be cures for economic problems. The programs were introduced for reasons of social welfare and equity and not for economic stabilization. The employment insurance program is an income maintenance program and the progressive income tax format is seen as the most equitable way of collecting this tax. It just so happens that the structure of these programs allows them to play an economic stabilization role as well.

Discretionary Fiscal Policy

Discretionary fiscal policy describes a situation in which government is forced to make policy decisions on how best to tackle unemployment or inflation. The process of determining the appropriate combination of government spending and taxes is not that easy. A major difficulty with fiscal policy is the time lag involved before the policy begins to influence economic activity. The first step is identifying, or recognizing, that a problem exists.

For example, price increases may have to be monitored for several months before it is determined that inflation is a problem. That is, it takes time before the data relating to price increases become available. It may also be some time before the evidence of a problem becomes apparent. This time lag is referred to as the *recognition lag.* Once the problem has been identified, a decision on what action needs to be taken must be made. This involves consultation between public servants (lawyers, economists, accountants, etc.) and members of the government—a process that takes time. Before some programs are introduced, they have to be approved by Parliament. Legislation covering the program has to become law through its passage in the House of Commons. This process also takes time and may result in fiscal policy being slow to react to changing economic conditions. This planning and implementation stage is referred to as the *decision lag.* The recognition and decision lags are "inside" lags. There may be a further time lag before the program, once implemented, begins to affect overall

> A discretionary fiscal policy is one aimed at improving economic conditions by changing the level of government spending and taxation.

spending and the reduction in inflation is noticeable. This period of time before the private sector responds to the changes in policy is known as the "outside" lag. Thus, a major drawback to fiscal policy is the time lags in various areas associated with implementing it.

A second drawback to the effectiveness of fiscal policy is the political nature of the policy itself. The final decision on what program to introduce is made by the politicians. Their choice of an economic stabilization program may be influenced by the impact that the program will have on their chances for re-election. For example, tax increases may be the recommended course of action to fight inflation. If an election is just around the corner, the tax increase may be delayed by the present government in favour of another option, since it is obvious that Canadians do not want their taxes increased and may react negatively to such action at the polls. Members of Parliament will not want to infuriate their constituents by increasing taxes just before an election. The same applies to cut-backs in government spending. Since someone is always on the receiving end of government spending, politicians may be reluctant to reduce spending for fear of alienating voters. Both policies—tax increases and cuts in government spending—can be used in order to reduce the level of inflation; however, if political considerations are important, fiscal policy will not be used to fight inflation. On the other hand, fiscal policy may be an effective tool in lessening the burden of unemployment. It is easy for government to increase spending and reduce taxes in order to gain voter approval.

REVIEW

8.4 What are automatic stabilizers? How do they differ from discretionary policies?

The Public Debt

In order to increase the level of government spending above the amount of tax revenue, it may be necessary for the government to borrow money and incur a deficit. The total amount of money owed by all levels of government is referred to as the **public debt**. In recent years, Canadians have become increasingly concerned about the size and cost of this debt. Since borrowing is greatest at the federal level, the federal debt picture will be reviewed.

The net debt of the Canadian governments is equal to the gross public debt minus recorded assets. The net debt in 2001 was more than $803 billion, an amount equal to approximately 73 percent of GDP (down from 102.1 percent of GDP in 1996). The net debt per capita was almost

The public debt comprises the money owed by all levels of government in Canada.

$26 000. In terms of federal government spending, public-debt interest charges amount to approximately 15 percent of total expenditures. For years, the net debt continued to rise for two major reasons. First, the federal government was not able to reduce substantially the level of its spending and second, higher interest rates raised the cost of borrowing money.

The federal government operated with a large deficit until 1996. Starting in 1997, however, the federal government began showing a budgetary surplus. That is, since 1997 government revenue has exceeded government expenditure.

Through borrowing, the government can finance large-scale capital projects such as airports, office complexes, and electricity-generating stations. It would be impractical to finance these projects out of tax revenues in a single year. Since the final product, for example the airport, will be in use for years to come, it makes sense to finance it over a number of years. Borrowing allows the government to do this.

During a recession, it is better to finance government expenditures through borrowing than through taxes. In a recession, people must be encouraged to spend money. Removing money from the circular flow by raising taxes reduces the ability of the public to spend money. When individuals lend money to the government through their purchase of bonds and other securities, they also have less money to spend. Money lent to the government is money that individuals plan on saving and was destined to be spent. Therefore, borrowing from the public does not decrease the overall level of spending to the same extent as taxation. Further, if the federal government borrows money from the Bank of Canada, there will be no negative impact on spending.

To some economists, the size of the public debt is not a major concern because we owe the money to ourselves. That is, the federal government, which represents Canadians, borrows most of its money from Canadians. The majority of all federal government bonds are held by Canadians. An advantage to having a public debt is that it provides a basis for Bank of Canada open-market operations. The Bank of Canada can buy and sell government securities on the open market in order to influence the money supply (see Chapter 7). Not all economists agree, however, that the public debt is beneficial to Canadians; some of the negative aspects of the public debt are listed below.

Inflationary impact: Concern over the increasing public debt in Canada coincides with concern over rising prices. Increased borrowing by all levels of government and the subsequent increase in government spending pushes up prices by creating increased demand for goods and services. Further, in order to borrow money, the government has to compete for funds with anyone else who also wants to borrow. This competition for available money increases the interest rate, and ultimately increases the cost of borrowing for everyone. *If borrowing costs go up for business, prices will increase as a result.*

Crowding out: The competition for funds increases interest rates and pushes up borrowing costs. If borrowing gets too expensive, some companies and individuals may refuse (or be unable) to borrow. These potential borrowers are thus crowded out of the money market. *A reduction in borrowing would lead to a drop in business investment, and any decline in investment decreases our ability to produce goods and services.* It also decreases the efficiency of Canadian companies and makes it more difficult for them to compete in world markets. The impact of crowding out is lessened by the fact that governments can borrow money from sources outside Canada. However, the inflow of money from foreign borrowing increases the foreign-exchange value of the Canadian dollar and may reduce Canada's exports.

Burden on future generations: When the government borrows money, it may pay off the debt over a long period of time (e.g., over 25 years). Some economists argue that the burden of paying off the debt is then shifted to those people who will be living in Canada 25 years from now. The debt has been shifted to a future generation. The politicians who were responsible for the borrowing will no longer be in office when the debt has to be repaid. Is it fair to ask people to pay off the interest and principal on a debt that they did not incur?

The answer to this question lies in the use made of the borrowed funds. If the money was used wisely, it could provide benefits for future generations (e.g., airports, hospitals, etc.) If future generations are going to benefit from present borrowing and spending, perhaps they should help pay for it. If they are not going to benefit from current spending, it seems unfair to make them accept responsibility for the debt.

Externally held debt: Money borrowed in other countries represents a special problem. The cost of this borrowing depends not only on interest rates, but also on fluctuations in the external value of the Canadian dollar. If, during the payback period of the loan, the value of the Canadian dollar declines on foreign-exchange markets, then more Canadian dollars will be required to pay back the loan. The cost of the debt will increase. Assume that the Canadian government borrowed money in the United States at a time when the Canadian dollar had a value equal to the U.S. dollar. Assume also that the yearly interest payments on this borrowing totalled $1 million in U.S. currency. If the value of the Canadian dollar fell to $0.67 U.S., then it would take 1 492 537 current Canadian dollars to make the interest payment to the citizens of the United States. In recent years, the proportion of government debt owed to non-residents of Canada has increased.

Income redistribution: Since governments in Canada borrow primarily from Canadians, it has been said that "we owe the money to ourselves." Yet not all Canadians lend money to the government. Only those who can afford to lend the money do so. If taxes have to be increased to pay off, or service, the debt, all Canadians will be taxed and a redistribution of income may occur. Everyone will be taxed in order to pay off the debt to those who could afford to lend money to the government in the first place. These individuals are more than likely in the higher income categories, and this is seen as a *transfer of income* from all Canadians to higher-income Canadians. This is opposite to the usual direction of income redistribution. When income is redistributed by government, it is more socially acceptable to transfer money from high-income persons to low-income persons.

In order to assess this argument properly, two points must be made. The second largest category of federal government spending is social welfare. Low-income groups are the primary recipients of this spending and are receiving the benefits of government borrowing. Further, if taxes are increased in order to finance the debt, a progressive income tax structure ensures that higher-income groups will pay more of the tax. Therefore, it does not appear that the public debt will significantly redistribute income to higher-income individuals.

Tax disincentives: If taxes have to be increased in order to finance government borrowing, then the resulting high marginal tax rates may act as a disincentive. Individuals may be discouraged from earning higher incomes. With lower incomes, there would be less spending and a lower level of GDP. High taxes and a large public debt may also undermine public confidence in government.

Possible conflict with monetary policy: Anyone who borrows money would like to do so at the lowest possible cost. The same is true for government. The desire of the federal government to borrow at low interest rates may conflict with the Bank of Canada's monetary policy. In an inflationary period, the Bank of Canada may want high interest rates in order to discourage spending. When the government borrows under these conditions, it will have to pay the high interest rate as well. This raises the overall cost of borrowing for Canadians. On the other hand, in a recessionary period, some stimulus to the economy is required. Heavy government borrowing will push up interest rates, and possibly discourage the needed private-sector spending that is required in order to bring the economy out of recession.

In order to evaluate the impact of the public debt, it is necessary to compare the size of the public debt to the level of national income. Your ability to pay back your loans depends on your income. Similarly, the ability of the government to pay back loans depends on the level of national income

International Comparisons 8.1

Projected government deficits as a percentage of GDP, 2004

United States	4.2%
Japan	7.8%
Germany	3.3%
France	3.3%
Italy	2.8 %
United Kingdom	2.2%
Canada	1.0% (surplus)

(GDP or GNP). If one looks back into history, the federal government net debt as a percentage of GNP has not remained constant. A great deal of debt was accumulated during the Second World War, and by 1946 net debt was 113.1 percent of GNP. In the years after the war, net debt as a percentage of GNP began to decline, reaching a low of 13.1 percent of GNP in 1975. After 1975, the percentage began to climb, and by 1996 net government debt represented more than 100 percent of GDP. Many Canadians have expressed concern over the rapid increase in government debt in relation to the public's ability to finance it. The net debt currently represents approximately 70 percent of GDP.

REVIEW

8.5 Why could large amounts of government borrowing lead to higher interest rates?

8.6 How could government borrowing and monetary policy conflict?

Monetary Policy Review

The Bank of Canada's **monetary policy** employs regulation of the money supply in order to influence economic conditions.

Monetary policy is an economic stabilization tool that operates through changes in the money supply. When the money supply changes, the interest rate changes as well—which influences consumer and business spending. A decrease in the money supply increases interest rates, which has a negative influence on spending. Increases in the money supply ultimately lead to increased spending through lower interest rates. The effectiveness of monetary policy as an economic stabilizer is, however, limited by its short-comings, which include:

Timing: As with fiscal policy, there are time lags associated with monetary policy. The inside lag may be somewhat shorter than that for fiscal policy, since parliamentary approval is not required for the Bank of Canada to adjust the money supply. The Bank of Canada is independent of the government. There is also an outside lag before the impact of money-supply changes can have an effect on the economy. That is, increases in the interest rate are not likely to reduce individual and business spending immediately. Many projects that have been in the planning stage for a while will go ahead in spite of increases in the cost of borrowing. The projects that might be curtailed because of the increased cost of borrowing will be those scheduled to come on-stream sometime in the future. Determining the exact moment when money-supply changes will show their impact on economic conditions is difficult. The outside lag associated with monetary policy is longer than that for fiscal policy.

Velocity: The Fisher equation of exchange, $MV = GDP$ (see Chapter 7), showed the relationship between the money supply and the level of economic activity. An important factor in this relationship is the velocity of circulation money (V). Adjustments in the money supply aimed at influencing gross domestic product (GDP) assume that the velocity of money remains unchanged. If the velocity of circulation fluctuates, then the impact of money-supply changes will be more difficult to forecast. For example, if the money supply were reduced, and the velocity of money increased, there could be very little ultimate impact on GDP. If the velocity of money is stable, then the Bank of Canada has more control over economic activity, because changes in the money supply will lead directly to changes in GDP.

The critics of monetary policy as a stabilization tool stress the *variability of velocity* as a major drawback in the use of monetary policy. They argue that changes in the velocity of money could counteract any changes that the Bank of Canada might make to the money supply. If the velocity of money is not stable, then monetary policy is not an effective stabilization policy.

Interest rate inelasticity: In order for monetary policy to be effective, the overall level of spending in the economy has to respond to changes in the interest rate. Consumers and businesses have to see the interest rate as a major factor in their spending decisions. If other factors are more important, then interest-rate changes will not produce the desired effect; that is, interest-rate changes will not affect spending decisions. Some spending decisions are inelastic when it comes to the interest rate. In terms of business investment spending, interest rates have a greater impact on small businesses than on large businesses. Farmers, fishers, and other sole proprietors have to rely more on borrowing as a source of funds. Larger businesses, such as multinational corporations, often have other sources of money (they issue shares in the company) and need not rely as much on borrowed funds. Thus, interest-rate changes influence various parts of the business community in different ways.

It is possible that within a given range of interest rates monetary policy may be ineffective. Assume that the Bank of Canada has been lowering interest rates in order to stimulate economic activity. If interest rates have been lowered substantially and increases in spending have not come about, then lowering the rate further is unlikely to encourage spending. When this situation occurs it is referred to as a liquidity trap.

Expectations: Changing expectations on the part of the public can also determine the effectiveness of monetary policy. In an attempt to curb spending, the Bank of Canada may increase interest rates. Under most circumstances, this increase in the cost of borrowing money would cause spending to decrease. However, what would be the impact on spending if people believed that interest rates were going to go even higher? They may borrow the money at once rather than wait until later, and the high-interest-rate policy would not produce the desired reduction in spending. Expectations about future interest rates may also come into play when interest rates are falling. The Bank of Canada may lower interest rates in order to encourage spending; however, if people assume that rates will fall even further, they may postpone spending until a later date.

Inflation vs. unemployment: It has been suggested that monetary policy may be better suited for fighting inflation than for reducing unemployment. Increases in the interest rate may restrict spending by making it too expensive to borrow. Yet, decreases in the interest rate may not be enough to encourage spending. You cannot force people to borrow money in order to increase overall spending, but you can make it too expensive for them to borrow money. Therefore, monetary policy may not be an appropriate solution for all economic problems.

External value of the Canadian dollar: An in-depth discussion of the value of the Canadian dollar on world markets appears in Chapter 9. It is necessary here, however, to point out the relationship between interest rates and the exchange rate of our currency. If interest rates increase, foreign money may be attracted into Canada in order to take advantage of the high rates. This will increase the demand for Canadian dollars and push up the value of the Canadian dollar relative to other currencies in foreign-exchange markets.

The Bank of Canada is responsible for controlling the external value of the dollar, as well as controlling the Canadian money supply. The Bank often uses the interest rate as part of its stabilization policy and also uses interest rates to influence the foreign-exchange rate. The use of the interest rate to achieve two goals may result in some conflicts. High interest rates may prop up the value of our dollar on world foreign-exchange markets, yet at the same time may lead to reduced spending and higher unemployment at home.

Despite its shortcomings, monetary policy is constantly in use as a stabilization policy, since it is agreed that the amount of money in circulation does influence economic activity. By itself, however, monetary policy may not be effective in solving both unemployment and inflation. It will be most effective when used in conjunction with appropriate fiscal policies.

REVIEW

8.7   Discuss how changes in the velocity of circulation of money can influence the effectiveness of monetary policy.

8.8   What is meant by interest-rate inelasticity?

EVERYDAY ECONOMICS 8.1

Zero Inflation: The Goal of Price Stability

The goal of monetary policy in Canada is stability in the general price level. This is not a recent policy. Several governors of the Bank of Canada have stated that maintaining confidence in the money that we use in Canada is the Bank's main objective. This confidence is sustained when prices are stable.

Monetary policy controls the rate of expansion of the money supply. Monetary policy is transmitted to the economy through changes in the interest rate, which in turn influence aggregate demand. If aggregate demand is increased without a corresponding increase in aggregate supply, the result is inflation. If aggregate demand increases in proportion with increases in aggregate supply, there is price stability.

Is price stability desirable? We can best answer this question by referring to the costs associated with inflation. There are certain costs associated with unanticipated inflation. Income and wealth are distributed from those who cannot protect themselves from inflation to those who can protect themselves. For example, those on fixed incomes suffer while those with indexed salaries can survive in an inflationary setting. Inflation pushes up real interest rates as lenders demand greater protection against unanticipated inflation when lending money. Also, during inflationary times, individuals engage in less productive activities trying to protect themselves from the impact of rising prices. Short-term profits become more important than longer-term returns when businesses are unsure about future price levels. Changes in prices are the signals that cause resources to be allocated in a market system. During inflationary periods, making decisions regarding the allocation of resources is more difficult. Are the price increases temporary or permanent? Are the price changes the result of changes in the marketplace, or are the changes the result of inflationary pressure in the economy? Due to this uncertainty, incorrect decisions can be made in resource allocation if price signals are misread. This was the case during the 1970s when the expectation of permanently high inflation became entrenched in our economy. For example, individuals purchased more real estate than they otherwise would have with the expectation that real estate prices would continue to rise. By 1981, it was realized that inflationary real estate prices were not to continue.

Do individuals adequately protect themselves from inflation? In spite of persistent inflation, most pensions are not indexed to the rate of inflation. At a 5-percent annual rate of inflation individuals on fixed incomes experience a 50-percent reduction in purchasing power in just 14 years. The tax system has also not completely adapted to inflation. The personal income tax is only partially indexed. It is difficult to write contracts for the future when the rate of future inflation is uncertain. Price stability would help individuals make adequate preparation for the future.

Why not just learn to live with a specified, moderate inflation rate? Why not accept the costs of resource misallocation, lost productivity, and income redistribution that accompany inflation? If one is to argue for inflation, one must believe that the costs of fighting inflation are too high compared to those costs of living with inflation. If the perceived benefits of lowering inflation appear small in relation to the costs of reducing it, then there is the risk that individuals will begin to expect inflation. What will stop inflation from getting progressively higher over time?

Do we not need some inflation in order to reduce the level of unemployment? The answer appears to be negative. Countries that have been characterized as low-inflation countries are also characterized by higher levels of economic growth. A reduction of one percentage point in the inflation rate appears to be associated with a one-tenth of a percentage increase in the annual rate of economic growth.

An appropriate monetary policy is necessary to fight inflation. This does not mean, however, that we should not try to improve the way monetary policy is carried out. It should also be noted that the success of monetary policy in fighting inflation will depend in part on the credibility of the monetary authorities.

The Bank of Canada with the cooperation of the federal government has established inflation targets. The Bank wants to keep consumer price increases at 2 percent per year. The Bank has established an acceptable range of 1 to 3 percent for the rate of inflation, and 2 percent falls at the midpoint of this range.

SOURCE: "The Goal of Price Stability," *Bank of Canada Review*, July 1990, pp. 3–7.

Questions

1. If prices were stable from year to year, how would your life change? How would this influence your decisions about your future?
2. How could the Bank of Canada convince Canadians that it is serious about reducing inflation?
3. How would union–management negotiations be altered in an environment of price stability?

Supply-Side Economics

Both monetary and fiscal policy operate on the demand side of the market by influencing the level of spending in the economy. Reductions in spending reduce the rate of inflation, but increase the number of unemployed. If spending increases, the demand for workers goes up and unemployment drops. Spending increases, however, pull up prices because demand for goods and services may outstrip supply. Operating on the demand side of markets accentuates the inverse relationship between unemployment and inflation. Yet the demand side represents only one-half of any market. In order for transactions to take place and prices to be established, the supply side of the market has to be involved. An alternative approach to combatting the problems of unemployment and inflation is to introduce policies that increase the supply of goods and services. If supply increased, prices would fall, or at least rise more slowly, thereby reducing the rate of inflation. More workers would be required to increase the supply of goods, and unemployment would consequently also be reduced.

This approach to economic stabilization is referred to as **supply-side economics.** It is believed that the best supply-side policies are to cut taxes and reduce the government regulations that restrict the supply of products and increase the cost of doing business. Emphasizing productivity improvements is also part of the supply-side approach to policy-making.

Tax cuts would affect supply in the following manner: they would provide businesses with more money for investments, which could be used for modernization of equipment, for repairing equipment, for new construction, or for more research and development. All of these lead to an increased ability on the part of businesses to provide goods and services, and to be more competitive at the same time. A tax cut would also provide an incentive for individuals to earn more money and increase spending. Some economists believe that high taxes can have a negative effect on individual incentives. With a progressive income tax structure, higher-income individuals pay a higher percentage of their income in taxes, and higher tax rates could discourage individuals from earning more money. If they are discouraged from earning money, then they are also discouraged from providing more goods and services. This has a negative impact on gross domestic product.

A reduction in the number of government regulations would also help to increase the supply of goods and services. *First, fewer regulations would reduce business costs, and therefore reduce prices.* As pointed out in an Economic Council of Canada study, present government regulations greatly increase the cost of doing business. Consumers would respond to lower prices by purchasing more.

Second, the lifting of certain legal restrictions would allow more goods and services to be produced. Freed from these restrictions, businesses would be able to expand output. There are, however, certain difficulties in removing these regulations. Many were put in place not for the purpose of restricting output, but to solve another problem of concern to society. For example, certain government regulations, such as pollution controls, are related to concerns about the environment. A relaxation of pollution controls may lead

> **Supply-side economics** describes a stabilization policy that stresses increasing the supply of goods and services in order to reduce the level of prices and to create jobs.

to increased production, but at what cost? The devastation that acid rain has brought to Canadian lakes and farmland points out that pollution is a serious problem for society. It does not make sense to remove environmental controls solely for the purpose of increasing output. Occupational health and safety requirements may also inadvertently restrict the output of goods and services, even though their main objective is worker safety.

An interesting example of unintentionally conflicting government regulation is provided in the following quotation, which refers to the United States (see Davidson, *The Squeeze*, p. 255):

> *The Department of Agriculture requires that temperatures in packing houses be kept low. A packing house which violates the regulation is subject to severe penalties. The result of the low temperatures, however, is that water freezes on the floor. The Occupational Health and Safety Administration says that ice on the floor creates unsafe conditions and must be treated with salt. Packing houses that violate the regulation are also subject to severe penalties. The Environmental Protection Agency says that the salt on the floor contributes to pollution. Packing houses that allow salt on the floor are subject to still additional penalties.*

Supply-side economics emphasizes increased production in order to stimulate employment and take some of the pressure off price increases. The economists who propose this approach to economic stabilization believe that the supply-side approach eliminates the trade-off associated with traditional monetary and fiscal policies. If production is encouraged employment will increase, and the increased supply of goods and services will also help reduce inflation.

Tax cuts may have an additional advantage, according to U.S. economist Arthur Laffer. He postulated that there is a certain tax rate at which government receives the maximum amount of tax revenue. If the tax rate falls below this rate, or rises above this rate, tax revenue will decline. Laffer argued that high marginal tax rates reduce incentives, so individuals do not try to earn more money. In the face of high marginal tax rates, individuals may also seek ways to avoid paying taxes. If tax rates were reduced, not only would individuals have more money to spend, but also government would receive more money through tax revenues.

The Laffer curve is a graphical representation indicating the relationship between the tax rate and the amount of money collected in taxes.

A diagrammatic representation of Laffer's ideas, the **Laffer curve,** is presented in Figure 8.3. The graph shows the relationship between the tax rate and the revenue collected from taxes. At tax rates of 0 percent and 100 percent, no revenue is collected. At point A on the graph, the maximum amount of tax revenue (R_1) is collected. As the tax rate increases the amount of revenue collected in taxes increases, up to a tax rate of r_1. At higher tax

Figure 8.3

The Laffer curve

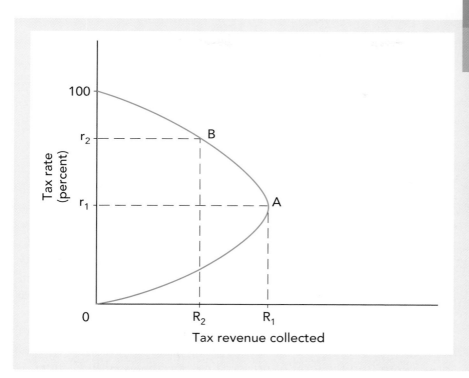

The tax revenue collected is at a maximum (R_1) when the tax rate is at a level of r_1. An increase in the tax rate to r_2 would lead to a drop (to R_2) in tax revenue collected.

rates, the disincentives to earn more money set in and tax revenue actually falls. At a higher tax rate (r_2), less revenue is collected (R_2). Laffer believed that the American economy was in a position identified by point B on the graph, and that a tax cut would improve economic conditions.

Supply-side economics and the Laffer curve have fallen out of favour with economists. Many economists argue that tax cuts, especially when combined with spending increases, do not have the impact on the economy that the supply-siders would predict. The critics of the supply-side approach to economic policy point to the Reagan administration in the United States in the 1980s, when tax cuts did not bring about the economic growth that was predicted. Much of the criticism of the Laffer curve centres on the location of point B. If point B is below point A on the curve, then tax cuts will not have the impact that Laffer predicted. In spite of the criticism directed toward the supply-side approach to economics, the supply-side proponents did remind us that markets are made up of both demand and supply forces. Not all of government's economic initiatives should be focused on the demand side of the marketplace.

interactive
graphics

REVIEW

8.9 How can supply-side stabilization policies help reduce the rate of inflation?

8.10 Analyze the combined impact of the tax rate and the demand for greater earnings on net government revenue, as predicted by the Laffer curve.

Wage and Price Controls

If fiscal and monetary policies cannot prevent excessive price increases, why not pass a law that makes price increases illegal? If it is illegal to raise prices, then inflation will be reduced to zero percent per year. The law prohibiting price increases may also be extended to make wage and salary increases illegal. This approach to stabilizing prices appears simple and straightforward. If it is so simple, why does the government not introduce **wage and price controls**?

In order to answer this question, it is necessary to analyze the impact of a government program that controls wage and price increases. The effect of price controls in the form of price ceilings was discussed in Chapter 3. Price ceilings, if in effect for any length of time, would result in shortages in the marketplace. The demand for goods and services would increase over time, while suppliers would be reluctant to supply more products to the market. A state of *disequilibrium* (quantity demanded exceeding quantity supplied) would remain until some further changes were made.

Shortages are likely to lead to black-market dealings, in which products are sold illegally for a price above the price ceiling. In shortage situations, the quality of the product could also suffer. If businesspeople find their product in great demand, and are not allowed to increase prices, then they might cut back on product quality in an attempt to earn more money. Neither is a desirable outcome of a price ceiling.

Price changes are an important aspect of the free-market system. Changes in the price of a product provide information that helps both buyers and sellers make decisions. If the price increases, buyers may respond by cutting back on their purchases. Suppliers, on the other hand, may see price increases as a signal that more of the product should be offered to the marketplace. *Price changes make the free-market system function effectively.* For example, under normal market conditions an increased demand for restaurant meals would result in higher prices. These price increases would be a signal to potential restaurateurs that the industry is thriving

A government anti-inflationary policy, wage and price controls **are legal limits on the amount of wage and price increases.**

and the number of restaurants would then increase. With more restaurants in operation, the pressure on price increases would diminish. As the supply of meals increases, the price of meals would fall. If prices are initially prohibited from increasing, this information is not being transmitted to the marketplace. How would potential restaurateurs know that there is an increased demand for restaurant meals? What would make them want to open a restaurant? Further, why would they want to open a restaurant if their prices were controlled?

Price changes also assist in the allocation of labour resources. They encourage people to enter certain businesses. They encourage workers to seek the best possible employment. Workers want to work at a job that pays more money than their present job. If wages are not allowed to increase, the movement of workers from job to job will stop. Employers who need more workers in order to supply their product would not be able to raise wages in order to attract those workers. The inability to attract workers could lead to product shortages.

The introduction of wage and price controls would be unfair to some groups of people. Regardless of when the controls are introduced, some workers will have just received a wage increase. Other workers may be about to negotiate a wage increase with their employers. Since the latter group of workers will be prevented from receiving a pay increase, the timing of the controls program is very important. It is also relevant to price increases, as some companies will be prevented from increasing prices while other price increases will be allowed to remain in effect. Undoubtedly the timing of the introduction of any control program will be a political decision.

A wage and price control program would apply only to Canadian-made goods and services. Laws passed in Canada have no impact on the prices of products produced in foreign countries. Canada imports many of these products, including rubber, coffee, tea, bananas, oil, and machinery. There is little that the Canadian government can do to control the price of imports. If we do not want to pay higher prices, we will have to do without many of these products. The foreign-exchange value of the Canadian dollar will also affect the price of imports. If the value of the Canadian dollar falls in foreign-exchange markets, then it will take more Canadian dollars to buy the same amount of imports. This will cause the prices of imported products to increase for Canadians.

Under any controls program, it is easier to control some wages and prices more than others. Some workers have their wage rate written down in a collective agreement with management. These wages are easy to control. Some prices are recorded on the tag accompanying the product, and these prices are also easy to control. The wages and prices that are difficult to control are those of professional services. Some groups of professionals (e.g., dentists) are not allowed to advertise their prices and, as a result, their prices are unknown. In these situations, it would be difficult to monitor price increases.

If wages are controlled, workers will insist that company profits be controlled as well. The control of profits raises some policy questions. Profits may increase not only through price increases but also because the company has become more efficient. When prices are frozen, or restricted, the desire for increased profits may force companies to look for cost-saving options. If profits are controlled, cost-saving measures will not necessarily be introduced. Should the government discourage companies from becoming more efficient? Profits may also increase if sales increase. If this happens, even though prices have not increased, should the company be punished? Profits are also necessary for investment; therefore, if profits are restricted, investment will be reduced and the level of GDP will decline. The level of unemployment also would increase and Canada's ability to produce goods and services would decrease with a reduction in investment. Therefore, if profits are controlled, there could be several negative consequences for the Canadian economy.

In addition to wages, prices, and profits, interest rates need to be controlled under any program of price controls. The control of interest rates is extremely difficult because interest rates are influenced by the international flow of money and cannot be controlled entirely within the geographic boundaries of one nation. If interest rates are kept artificially low in Canada, individuals with money to invest will invest outside Canada, where the rate of return is greater. The resulting shortage of investment funds in Canada would put pressure on the Canadian authorities to raise interest rates to prevent the loss of important investment dollars.

Wage and price control measures have been introduced in various countries, but on only a temporary basis because of the problems associated with such programs. Temporary controls simply postpone wage and price increases, and the eventual removal of controls may lead to rapid wage and price increases in order to make up for lost ground. These increases may also take into consideration the possibility of controls being reintroduced, and could be greater than they otherwise would be. Since wage and price control programs are temporary in nature, they should be accompanied by appropriate monetary and fiscal policies if they are to be effective in controlling prices.

R E V I E W

8.11 Why are wage and price controls used as only a temporary stabilization measure?

8.12 Are some wages and prices easier to control than others? Explain.

Human Resources Policies

Structural unemployment is defined as unemployment that results from a mismatching of the demand for and the supply of workers. The concern over structural unemployment began in the early 1960s, when it was feared that automation in the workplace would eliminate a lot of unskilled jobs. At the same time, it was believed that automation would create new skilled and semi-skilled jobs. The problem for government was to improve the matching process by training the displaced workers for the new jobs that were being created.

Government attempts to deal with structural unemployment are referred to as **human resources policy**. In 1960, the federal government passed the Technical and Vocational Training Assistance Act (TVTA) to meet two objectives. The first objective was to increase employment; the second was to stimulate and broaden the scope of technical and vocational training throughout Canada. The act emphasized training and provided money for improved training at the high-school level, for training in cooperation with industry in the form of skill training and retraining, and for training of the unemployed.

Government human resources policy is a stabilization policy aimed at lessening the amount of structural unemployment in the economy.

The TVTA programs ran until 1965. The federal government then assessed the program in light of various criticisms and started to prepare new legislation. In 1967, the Adult Occupational Training Act (AOTA) was passed. This act committed the federal government to the training and retraining of adults. The provinces were to remain in control of youth and in-school training.

Under the AOTA, the federal government purchased training for individuals from the provincial governments. The federal government would also pay a training allowance to individuals who undertook training. In order to qualify for training, an individual had to be older than the school-leaving age. Training allowances, however, would be paid only to those who had been in the labour force for three years or who had dependents. This was to ensure that students would not leave high school in order to take advantage of training allowances.

In 1985, the federal government introduced the Canadian Job Strategy as the primary instrument in Canada's human resources policy. The Canadian Job Strategy is aimed at coordinating the efforts of the federal and provincial governments in the areas of skill training and job placement. The strategy was also designed to rely on input from business, labour, and community groups in determining priorities. Four distinct groups in the labour market—women, Native peoples, visible minorities, and persons with disabilities—have been identified as requiring special assistance. Other labour-market groups, however, can benefit from the strategy.

Human resources policies in Canada are currently the responsibility of Human Resources Development Canada. The emphasis is on assisting individuals to prepare for, obtain, and maintain employment or self-employment. Not only will achieving this goal result in savings to the employment insurance program and to other social assistance programs, it will add to tax revenues through increased employment.

Human Resources Development Canada is prepared to take several measures in order to reduce the amount of unemployment in Canada. Wage subsidies are available to help employers hire individuals who would not normally be hired in the absence of a subsidy. Assistance in the form of technical assistance, coaching, income support, and advice concerning access to capital is available to those wishing to become self-employed. Training purchases may be undertaken on behalf of individuals, and job-creation partnerships may be established with communities. Finally, the department has a number of measures designed to remove the barriers to returning to work. These include diagnostic assistance, providing job-search skills, group counselling, transportation, and special needs for persons with disabilities.

Canada's immigration policy is also part of our human resources policy. If immigration can help to fill job vacancies that cannot be filled by Canadians, it helps to improve the matching of workers and jobs. Canada's immigration policy is discussed more fully in the next section.

REVIEW

8.13 What type of unemployment is most closely associated with human resources policies?

8.14 How can a better matching of workers and jobs help fight inflation as well as unemployment?

Immigration

Canada's immigration policy is, in part, a human resources program. Included among the goals of our immigration policy is the objective of recruiting qualified workers for Canadian employers. Canada encourages workers with needed skills to immigrate here in order to better match the supply of labour with the demand. In contrast, Canada has been restricting the entry of unskilled workers and the ability of visitors to Canada to seek employment here. Immigrants are also encouraged to settle in areas that are underpopulated and short of needed human resources. This is aimed at reducing the geographic dimension of structural unemployment.

Individuals wishing to migrate to Canada must qualify for entry on the basis of a point system. They have the opportunity of scoring 100 points, with 75 points being the minimum number required in order to be allowed into the country as a landed immigrant. Points are allocated on the basis of certain criteria. The various criteria and the maximum points (units of assessment) are listed below.

CRITERION	MAXIMUM POINTS
Education	25
Work experience	21
Arranged employment	10
Age	10
Knowledge of English and French languages	24
Adaptability	10

Canada's immigration policy for independent immigrants is a major part of Canada's human resources policy. Only applicants who can adapt to our labour market or who meet a certain occupational requirement are allowed to enter the country. Canada also has criteria for allowing entrepreneurs and investors to enter Canada as landed immigrants.

Apart from labour-market considerations, Canada's immigration policy also focuses on reuniting families through sponsorships for immediate family members. Other relatives may be awarded up to ten points, if required, when applying to enter Canada as independent applicants. Finally, Canada's immigration policy has certain conditions for those coming to Canada as refugees.

Table 8.1 shows the number of immigrants to Canada in 2002 by country of last permanent residence. As shown in the table, Asia was the largest source of immigrants to Canada in 2002. Asia has been the largest source of immigrants to Canada since 1979.

Table 8.1 *Top 10 source countries for immigration to Canada, 2002*

COUNTRY	NUMBER	PERCENTAGE
China	33 231	14.51
India	28 815	12.58
Pakistan	14 164	6.18
Philippines	11 000	4.80
Iran	7 742	3.38
Korea, Republic of	7 326	3.20
Romania	5 692	2.48
United States	5 288	2.31
Sri Lanka	4 961	2.17
United Kingdom	4 720	2.06
Total all countries	229 091	

SOURCE: *Facts and Figures*, Citizenship and Immigration Canada, 2002, www.cic.gc.ca. Adapted with the permission of the Minister of Public Works and Government Services Canada, 2003.

EVERYDAY ECONOMICS 8.2

The Economy and Immigration

Proponents of large-scale immigration into Canada argue that immigrants are needed because of the aging population in Canada. As more workers retire, the dependency ratio (workers to non-workers) is reduced. In order to maintain this ratio, it is argued that Canada should allow the entry of more immigrants. There are other economic arguments that favour immigration. Some argue that the larger population would allow Canadian companies to achieve economies associated with mass production and lower prices. Other analysts state that increasing immigration levels would lead to higher per-capita incomes for those Canadians who are already here.

There is some doubt about the validity of these arguments. Reports from different federal government departments have stated that the doubling or tripling of immigration levels would have little impact on the dependency ratio. The fastest rates of growth in real incomes in Canada have occurred in years when net immigration was low.

If the arguments for higher levels of immigration are economic in nature, new entrants to Canada should adapt readily to the labour market. Under Canada's current immigration policy, only one in five new immigrants enters Canada on the basis of labour-market qualifications. The focus of Canada's immigration policy has been family reunification and refugees. Immigrants who come to Canada because of family or humanitarian concerns must be in good health and must not have a criminal record. Thus, many new entrants into the labour force lack the necessary language and job skills to make an immediate contribution to the economy. Further, the proportion of new immigrants who are over age 65 is roughly the same as the proportion of

Canadians over age 65. These immigrants will not be entering the labour force. As a result, there has been a decline in the overall earnings of immigrants and an increase in the level of poverty among new arrivals. Immigrants who came to Canada in the 1990s also came during a recessionary period. Economic conditions during that period help explain the decline in earnings for new immigrants.

Is Canada's population shrinking? The birth rate is declining, but Canada's rate of population growth is higher than for many industrialized countries. Annual immigration of about 80 000 persons (about one-half of the average annual intake in the 1990s) should help Canada's population grow until 2026.

Questions

1. Should the focus of Canada's immigration policy be the reuniting of families or the economy? Can our immigration policy achieve both?

2. Should new immigrants be forced to move to areas of Canada that are experiencing labour shortages? Can Canada force new immigrants to settle in specific parts of Canada and not force other Canadians (e.g., doctors) to do the same?

3. If Canada focuses on immigrants with strong labour-market qualifications, are countries from whence the immigrants came going to be harmed? Explain.

4. Would a focus on improving the productivity of Canadian workers ease concerns about the dependency ratio? Explain.

Summary

One of the shortcomings of traditional monetary and fiscal policies is their inability to simultaneously control unemployment and inflation. When policies are introduced in order to stimulate spending and create jobs, one of the results is higher prices. When steps are taken to control spending and reduce inflation, the rate of unemployment increases. This trade-off between unemployment and inflation can be depicted by means of a Phillips curve.

Both monetary and fiscal policy operate on the demand side of markets, trying to encourage or discourage spending. Both policies suffer from a number of shortcomings; the most notable is that of timing. It takes time for policies to be developed and for the effects of those policies to be realized. The shortcomings of these traditional policies have led some economists to emphasize a supply-side approach to economic stabilization. Rather than regulate demand, they propose policies that would increase the supply of goods and services.

A consequence of past fiscal policy has been increasing public debt. As the size of the debt increases, there is more concern over the negative aspects of such a debt. Some of these aspects are increased inflation, higher interest rates, the burden that is passed on to future generations, possible income redistribution, and the consequences of externally held debt.

Two additional approaches to economic stabilization were discussed in this chapter: wage and price controls, and human resources policies. The first attempts to control inflation by imposing legal limits on wage and price increases. The second attempts to reduce the level of structural unemployment by improving the matching of the demand for, and the supply of, workers.

Questions for Review and Discussion

1. If you were Canada's minister of finance, what programs would you introduce in order to reduce the level of unemployment?
2. Could inappropriate monetary and fiscal policies have a negative impact on the economy? Explain.
3. Discuss the strengths and weaknesses of monetary and fiscal policy in terms of their respective approaches to unemployment.
4. Which of the following programs would you consider to be automatic stabilizers in our economy? Discuss.
   a) general welfare assistance
   b) subsidies to farmers in years when the crop is poor
   c) government military spending
5. How can people's expectations affect the Bank of Canada's attempts to change economic conditions?
6. The increased use of credit cards could lead to inflationary pressure in the economy in spite of the efforts of the Bank of Canada. Discuss this statement.
7. If prices were to remain stable, how would it affect the way you conduct your personal financial affairs?
8. What difference would it make if the majority of Canada's public debt were owed to foreigners as opposed to Canadians?
9. Explain why a supply-side approach to economic stabilization, if successful, would reduce the rate of inflation and the level of unemployment at the same time.
10. The Laffer curve assumes that a tax rate of 100 percent would not bring in any revenue to the government. Explain.
11. There is a geographic dimension to structural unemployment. Unemployed skilled workers and job vacancies may not be in the same location. Should the federal government provide financial assistance to Canadians who want to travel to other parts of the country in search of employment? What are the advantages and disadvantages of such a program?
12. How is Canada's immigration policy related to our human resources policy?

13. What impact would immigration have on the unemployment rate? The price level?

Suggested Readings

Currie, Stephanie. *Economic Opportunities in a Multicultural Society.* Toronto: Canadian Foundation for Economic Education, 1993.

Davidson, James Dale. *The Squeeze.* New York: Pocket Books, 1980. This book discusses changes in the structure of the economy that would improve the lot of the average citizen.

Galarneau, Diane, and Cecile Dumas. "About Productivity." *Perspectives,* Spring 1993, Catalogue 75-001E, Statistics Canada, p. 44.

Humpage, Owen F. "Do Deficits Matter?" *Economic Commentary.* Cleveland: Federal Reserve Bank of Cleveland, June 15, 1993. A short article from the Federal Reserve Bank of Cleveland that addresses government's approach to fighting the deficit.

Rugman, Alan M., and Joseph R. D'Cruz. *Fast Forward: Improving Canada's International Competitiveness.* Commissioned by Kodak Canada Inc., 1991.

Strick, John C. *The Economics of Government Regulation: Theory and Canadian Practice.* Toronto: Thompson, 1990. This is a well-written, 220-page text on government regulation in Canada.

Tremblay, Miville. *A Country Held Hostage: How the World Finances Canada's Debt.* Stoddart: Toronto 1997. The author is a financial writer with *La Presse.* He explains several terms, including Eurobonds and yield curves.

Selected Websites

http://william-king.www.drexel.edu/top/prin/txt/EcoToC.html A Drexel University economics course, including multiple-choice questions.
http://william-king.www.drexel.edu/top/prin/txt/Asapp/cider1.html A lecture by a professor at Drexel on supply-side economics.
www.hrdc-drhc.gc.ca This is the site for Human Resources Development Canada. Information is provided on the department's programs. Links are available to sites with labour market information.
www.conferenceboard.ca At this site, you can search newspaper articles on various topics from the Conference Board of Canada.
www.public-policy.org This site provides links to Canadian and U.S. public policy websites.
www.wanniski.com/ssu.asp This site, labelled Supply-Side University, provides information on supply-side economics and the Laffer curve.
www.cic.gc.ca The website for Citizenship and Immigration Canada. Information is available on coming to Canada as an immigrant.

International Economics

Key Terms

law of comparative advantage
tariff
countervailing duties
non-tariff barriers
infant industry
dumping
General Agreement on Tariffs and
    Trade (GATT)
Canada–United States Automobile
    Agreement
international balance of payments
current account
capital account
foreign-exchange rate
arbitrage
appreciation/depreciation
devalued currency
International Monetary Fund
adjustable-peg system
stabilization fund

Core Concept Building

Canadians trade a great deal with individuals and businesses of other countries. This chapter introduces you to the topic of international economics. Previously introduced concepts such as opportunity costs, production-posssibilities curves, demand and supply, and the Bank of Canada all appear in this chapter.

Chapter Objectives

After successfully completing this chapter, you will be able to:

- appreciate Canada's major trading partners and trading commodities
- explain the law of comparative advantage and use it in a numerical example
- describe the impact of international trade on resource and product prices and on resource allocation
- relate the arguments for and against tariff protection
- discuss the advantages and disadvantages of Canada entering into a free-trade agreement with the United States and Mexico
- relate the objectives of the WTO
- differentiate between the current and capital accounts in the balance of payments
- relate deficits and surpluses in the balance of payments to changes in the foreign-exchange value of the Canadian dollar
- describe how foreign-exchange rates are fixed

WHAT IS A CANADIAN DOLLAR WORTH?

It is possible to view the value of the Canadian dollar in three ways. First, the value of a Canadian dollar is defined by what it can purchase. If a Canadian dollar spent in Canada will buy a toasted bagel, it can be stated that its value is equal to that of a toasted bagel. If a Canadian dollar can purchase two postage stamps, then its value is equal to that of two postage stamps. Changes in the value of a Canadian dollar measured in this fashion are determined by the rate of inflation. When prices increase, the value of the dollar decreases.

A second measure of the value of the Canadian dollar relates to how many units of a foreign currency can be obtained by a Canadian dollar. Although the Canadian dollar is exchanged for many other currencies around the globe, the foreign currency that a Canadian dollar is most compared with is the United States dollar. There have been times when the Canadian dollar was worth more than a U.S. dollar on foreign-exchange markets. However, since 1976 the value of a Canadian dollar on foreign-exchange markets has been less than that of a U.S. dollar. Over the last 20 years, the value of the Canadian dollar has fluctuated from a high of 89 cents U.S. to a low of 63 cents in U.S. currency. The value of a Canadian dollar compared to a U.S. dollar fluctuates daily on foreign-exchange markets. As will be explained fully in this chapter, the foreign-exchange value of the Canadian dollar is influenced by the flow of money into and out of Canada.

The value of a Canadian dollar is also compared to foreign currencies in terms of its purchasing power. Basically, this method compares the value of two currencies by focusing on the amount of goods and services each currency can buy. For example, if a Canadian spends $10 Canadian in Greece and he or she gets about $10 worth of goods and services had they been purchased in Canada, we could say that there is purchasing-power parity between the Greek and Canadian currencies. Ten Canadian dollars spent in Turkey would acquire $15.60 worth of goods and services had they been purchased in Canada. This indicates that the Canadian dollar has more purchasing power than the Turkish currency. Ten Canadian dollars spent in Norway or Denmark would acquire only $6.20 worth, had the goods been purchased in Canada. Our currency does not have a purchasing power equal to those currencies of Norway and Denmark.

A theory explaining the changes in the foreign-exchange values of currencies focuses on the purchasing power of different currencies. The purchasing-power parity theory of exchange rates asserts that exchange rates between currencies will fluctuate toward a situation where the prices of similar goods in different countries are the same. If a certain item costs $10 U.S. in the United States and the exchange rate is 1 dollar = 0.65 U.S. dollar, the value of the item in Canada should be ($10/0.65), or $15.38. If the item sells for more than $15.38 in Canada, then individuals would buy the item in the United States. Purchases of this item in the United States by Canadians would increase the value of the U.S. dollar relative to the Canadian dollar. If the item sold for less than $15.38 in Canada, Americans would find it cheaper to buy the item in Canada. Purchases of the item in Canada by residents of the United States would increase the demand for the Canadian dollar on foreign-exchange markets. The purchasing-power parity theory states that the exchange rate between the two countries will continue to fluctuate until the exchange rate equalizes the purchasing power between the two currencies.

What about the purchasing power of a Canadian dollar compared to a U.S. dollar? The measure of purchasing power between the two countries determines what it costs to buy a basket of 3000 items in Canada compared to what it costs Americans to buy the same basket of 3000 items. Over the last 20 years, the Canadian dollar has fluctuated in a range from 81 to 86 cents U.S. This value is the exchange rate that would equate the purchasing powers of the two currencies given the current prices in each country. Even at times when the official exchange rate between the two currencies was 1 Cdn dollar = 0.64 U.S. dollar, the value of the Canadian dollar in purchasing-power terms was in excess of 85 cents (U.S.). This is an indication that the Canadian dollar is undervalued on foreign-exchange markets.

Canada's Trade Abroad

Canadians carry on business not only with other Canadians, but also with residents of other countries. We buy foreign products such as oranges, cameras, automobiles, clothing, cheese, and wine; we travel in foreign countries, buy foreign bonds and deposit money in foreign banks, hire foreign engineers, and transport products on foreign ships. Residents of other countries purchase Canadian products such as wheat, automobiles, minerals, and lumber, travel in Canada, and carry on a wide variety of business transactions with Canadians.

Market transactions with foreign countries have some unique characteristics, which is why we study them separately from other transactions. First, each country has its own currency. In order for an exchange to take place, an acceptable medium of exchange, or currency, must be found. Individuals and companies who are selling products in international markets prefer to be paid in their own currency in order to pay taxes, rent, the wages of their employees, and the other costs of being in business. If, for example, Canadians are buying products from Great Britain, it will be necessary for Canadians to obtain British pounds in order to pay for the products. British pounds are purchased in the foreign-exchange market (discussed later in this chapter).

Second, international trade brings different languages and customs together. Canadians who hope to conduct business with residents of other countries must attempt to understand different and unfamiliar behaviour patterns. For example, the treatment of time varies around the globe. North Americans tend to react quickly to business requests, whereas Latin Americans are generally more casual about time and are in less of a hurry. In some African countries, the amount of time required to make a decision is directly proportional to the importance of the decision. If Canadians try to speed up the process, those people may see it as an attempt to downgrade their work.

Third, political considerations are extremely important in international dealings. In Canada, there are very few barriers to trading across provincial boundaries. A businessperson in Quebec City may telephone another businessperson in Winnipeg to order some equipment. Most products can be shipped across provincial boundaries easily. However, this is not the case with international boundaries. *National governments may choose to restrict certain products from entering or leaving their countries.* Canada also has some restrictions about what can be allowed into or out of the country. For example, we have had a quota on the amount of shoes and clothes that can be brought into Canada each year. The Canadian government has also restricted the amount of foreign investment into Canada on an annual basis. In addition, Canada has restricted the amount of a product that can leave the country. In recent years, the export of natural gas, for example, has been regulated by the government.

Political differences can also severely restrict or stop trade in certain areas. The racially discriminatory policies of the former government of South Africa led to certain restrictions on trade with that nation. When Argentina invaded the Falkland Islands in 1982, the European Economic Community (EEC) imposed restrictions on imports into Europe from Argentina. When Iraq took over Kuwait in 1990, the United Nations imposed sanctions on trade with Iraq.

The movement of workers from job to job in Canada is basically not restricted by provincial borders. If a worker in Regina, Saskatchewan, sees a good job possibility in Victoria, British Columbia, that person is free to apply for the job, and, if successful, to relocate. Workers are not, however, free to move across international borders. Canadians cannot work in other countries without a work permit. These permits, issued by the foreign country, may not be easy to obtain—just as work permits for non-Canadians may not be easy to obtain in Canada.

For these reasons, international trade must be treated as a separate topic. In Chapter 6, international trade was first introduced during the discussion of the circular flow of income. Exports were regarded as an addition to the circular flow, while imports were seen as a leakage. The importance of these items to the Canadian economy can be seen by pointing out that Canada produces about one-third of its GDP for export. Therefore, any fluctuations in the amount we sell to foreigners will have a definite impact on our economy.

What products do Canadians sell abroad? A list of exports for 2002 is presented in Table 9.1. Our biggest export in terms of dollars is passenger

Table 9.1 *Major merchandise exports and imports by commodity, Canada, 2002*

EXPORTS		
COMMODITY	$ (MILLIONS)	PERCENTAGE
Passenger autos and chassis	49 824.2	12.1
Motor vehicle parts	29 288.6	7.1
Chemicals, plastics, and fertilizers	23 918.8	5.8
Metals and alloys	22 158.9	5.4
Aircraft and other transportation equipment	22 144.7	5.4
Industrial and agricultural machinery	19 517.5	4.8
Natural gas	19 162.5	4.7
Crude petroleum	18 925.2	4.6
Trucks and other motor vehicles	17 968.3	4.4
Lumber and sawmill products	17 514.5	4.3
Newsprint and other paper and paperboard products	12 897.7	3.1
Wood pulp and other wood products	6 238.1	1.5
Metals and metal ores	5 747.3	1.4
Wheat	3 057.6	0.7
Total exports	410 686.5	

IMPORTS		
COMMODITY	$ (MILLIONS)	PERCENTAGE
Motor vehicle parts	43 452.2	12.2
Industrial and agricultural machinery	27 535.9	7.7
Passenger autos and chassis	26 265.1	7.4
Chemicals and plastics	25 720.5	7.2
Agricultural and fishing products	21 777.5	6.1
Metals and metal ores	16 470.2	4.6
Office machines and equipment	15 654.7	4.4
Aircraft and other transportation equipment	14 691.1	4.1
Crude petroleum	11 730.8	3.3
Trucks and other motor vehicles	11 728.9	3.3
Apparel and footwear	8 598.0	2.4
Total imports	356 109.3	

SOURCE: Adapted from Statistics Canada website, www.statcan.ca/english/pgdb/cit.htm (April 2003).

automobiles. Most of our motor vehicles are destined for the United States and fall under the North American Free Trade Agreement. Automotive exports, including cars, trucks, car parts, and engines, account for approximately one-quarter of the dollar value of our exports. The forest industry is also a major part of the export scene, with three products—newsprint, wood pulp, and lumber—comprising almost 9 percent of export sales. Apart from automotive products, Canada's major exports are derived from the resource industries.

Imports into Canada are also listed in Table 9.1. Our biggest import item is motor vehicles and parts, again due to the Automobile Agreement, which allows for specialization of production in each country and duty-free access of automobiles and new parts into each country. Automotive imports accounted for approximately 25 percent of all imports in 2002. Canada's other major imports are basically manufactured products. In fact, Canada is regarded as an exporter of primary or unfinished products and an importer of finished or manufactured products.

What countries does Canada trade with? Canadians trade with countries all over the globe, but some countries are more important *trading partners* than others. As shown in Tables 9.2 and 9.3, our biggest customer is the United States, which imports approximately 87 percent of all our exports. We, in turn, receive 63 percent of our imports from that country. As a result, economic conditions in the United States have a significant impact on Canada's economy. If total spending drops in the United States, spending on Canadian products will also drop. Since the United States is our biggest customer, our exports would be severely affected. Inflation in the United States is also of concern to Canada. If prices in the U.S. are rising, the prices of products imported into Canada will also rise. This could result in a higher inflation rate for Canada.

Canada's second-largest trading partner is Japan. In 2002, our exports to Japan represented 2.1 percent of total exports, while imports from Japan were 4.4 percent of total imports. In Canada's very early years, its major trading partner was the United Kingdom. But as early as the 1880s, the United States replaced the United Kingdom as the major source of our imports. Canada imported mainly manufactured products, and the United States was a cheaper source of these products. Still, the United Kingdom remained the main destination of our exports until the Second World War. It was an importer of the primary products in which Canada specialized, whereas the United States was more self-sufficient in these products.

Table 9.2 *Canada's total exports by destination, 2002*

COUNTRY	TOTAL EXPORTS $ (MILLIONS)	PERCENTAGE
United States	346 457	87.4
Japan	8 287	2.1
United Kingdom	4 385	1.1
China	4 020	1.0
Germany	2 907	0.7
Mexico	2 395	0.6
South Korea	1 970	0.5
France	1 963	0.5
Belgium	1 750	0.4
Netherlands	1 729	0.4
Italy	1 443	0.4
Hong Kong	1 171	0.3
Australia	1 124	0.3
Total exports	396 298	

SOURCE: Adapted from the Statistics Canada publication *Exports by Commodity*, Catalogue no. 65-004, December 2002, pp. 1–4.

Table 9.3 *Canada's imports by country of origin, 2002*

COUNTRY	TOTAL IMPORTS $ (MILLIONS)	PERCENTAGE
United States	218 163	62.6
China	15 976	4.6
Japan	15 406	4.4
Mexico	12 703	3.6
United Kingdom	9 726	2.8
Germany	8 280	2.4
France	5 844	1.7
South Korea	4 856	1.4
Italy	4 434	1.3
Taiwan	4 240	1.2
Norway	3 933	1.1
Malaysia	2 018	0.6
Brazil	1 906	0.5
Total imports	348 445	

SOURCE: Adapted from the Statistics Canada publication *Imports by Commodity*, Catalogue no. 65-007, December 2002, pp. 1–3.

International Trade Theory

Why is it necessary for Canadians to trade with foreign countries? The main reason is that Canadians want goods that are not available in this country. If Canadians want orange juice for breakfast, it must be brought in from outside Canada. If we want to drink tea or coffee, again, these must be imported. Different countries have different climates and different geographical make-ups; some are good for growing certain products but not others.

Even though we may be able to buy a certain product in Canada, some Canadians may prefer the uniqueness of a foreign item. For example, wines from different countries have different characteristics and tastes. French and German wines are popular in Canada, but so are wines from Italy, Spain, Portugal, and Australia. In Canada we produce automobiles, yet some Canadians prefer imports. Certain luxury automobiles, such as those built by Rolls-Royce and Mercedes-Benz, must be imported. The uniqueness of certain products means we must import Cuban cigars, Swiss watches, Scotch whiskey, English china, and other special products.

A second major reason for buying a foreign product is that the import may be cheaper or of better quality. The resources available to a certain country may make it efficient at certain types of production. Canada is very abundant in farmland, and therefore we can specialize in certain agricultural products, such as wheat. We are also surrounded by water and have a fishing industry that exports around the world. Some countries, for example Japan, are not blessed with a large land mass but have a skilled labour force and a great deal of technological innovation taking place. This makes certain products cheaper to produce in such a country than in Canada. Buyers look for the best bargain for their money, whether they buy a domestic product or a foreign one.

Canadians will buy imported products when they are cheaper than Canadian products and of comparable quality. Foreigners will buy Canadian products when they are cheaper than those produced elsewhere. Under this market situation, Canadians would profit by specializing in developing products that they do best, and by having foreigners do likewise. Through trade, each country could receive products at the lowest possible price.

It makes economic sense to specialize in the development and creation of products that you do best. What if a country cannot produce anything more efficiently than another country? Will such a country be able to trade? The answer would appear to be no, yet a theory addressing this question was developed in 1817 by David Ricardo, an English economist and stockbroker. He suggested that even though one country may not be efficient at producing anything, it can still participate in trade. This is because countries that are more efficient at producing everything can still benefit from trading with others. This theory is referred to as the **law of comparative advantage**.

An example may best explain this law. Assume that we are considering two countries: Canada and Mexico. Assume further that we are talking about only two products: wheat and radios. In order to show that trade in these two products can benefit both Canada and Mexico, let us assume that Canada produces both of these products more efficiently than Mexico. In order to compare *efficiencies,* the production of one worker in one week will be used. One worker in Canada can produce either 10 bushels of wheat or 30 radios in one week. In Mexico, one worker can produce either 2 bushels of wheat or 10 radios in a week. It is necessary to assume that all workers are equal within each country in terms of what can be produced. Also, these production levels have to remain the same regardless of how much is produced.

As shown in Table 9.4, Canada is more efficient than Mexico at producing both wheat and radios (five times more efficient at producing wheat, and three times more efficient at producing radios). Would it pay Canada to trade with Mexico in these two products? If a Canadian were to work in the fields growing wheat, he or she could produce ten bushels a week. In order to do this, the Canadian worker gives up the opportunity of producing 30 radios. The opportunity cost of ten bushels of wheat is, therefore, 30 radios. The opportunity cost of one bushel of wheat is therefore three radios.

In Mexico, if a worker produces wheat he or she must sacrifice radios as well. In order to produce two bushels of wheat, ten radios must be sacrificed. The opportunity cost of one bushel of wheat is five radios. Consequently, in Mexico one bushel of wheat is more costly than in Canada

The **law of comparative advantage** is a theory of international trade that states that a country should specialize in and trade those items that it can produce relatively more efficiently than other countries.

Table 9.4 *Production of one worker in one week*

PRODUCT	CANADA	MEXICO
Wheat	10 bushels	2 bushels
Radios	30	10

since more radios have to be sacrificed. If wheat is cheaper in Canada, why not try to exchange Mexican-made radios for Canadian wheat? If Canada were to send one bushel of wheat to Mexico, how many radios would they want in return? In Canada, if one worker produces one bushel of wheat, three radios must be given up. If we can get more than three radios by sending a bushel of wheat to Mexico, it would be a good deal. In order to produce a bushel of wheat, Mexico has to sacrifice five radios. If Mexico can get a bushel of wheat from Canada for less than five radios, it would be better off.

According to these figures, both countries can benefit from trade. The terms of trade are difficult to predict with any accuracy; however, it is likely that Canada will send one bushel of wheat to Mexico for more than three radios, but less than five radios.

This example does not take into consideration transportation costs or the value of each country's currency. Yet it shows that even when one country is more efficient at producing both products, it can still benefit from trade with a less-efficient country. Both countries get more wheat and radios than they would have without trade. Both countries will benefit from trade as long as a comparative advantage exists.

R E V I E W

9.5 Do Canadians trade with foreigners only because of our comparative advantage?

9.6 What does opportunity cost have to do with comparative advantage?

Effects of International Trade

What are the effects of international trade on Canada and Mexico? The potential effects of trade involve three important factors: resource allocation, product prices, and resource prices.

Resource Allocation

The advent of international trade and specialization may result in changes in the ways that resources such as land and labour are used in any country. Resources will move out of industries in which the country has a *comparative disadvantage*, and into industries where the country has a *comparative advantage*. In Mexico, workers will move from wheat production to the radio factories. Land will no longer be used for wheat but may be taken over by a radio factory. In Canada, the results would be opposite. Workers would leave the radio factories in order to work in the wheat fields. More land would be turned over to wheat production.

The shift that takes place in resource allocation due to *specialization* will have an additional effect. The total output of wheat and radios produced in the two countries will increase. With specialization, more output is achieved from the same amount of resources. It follows from our example that if all countries in the world engaged in foreign trade and specialized more in production, then the total output of goods and services would increase.

The impact of international trade on a country's ability to consume is shown in Figure 9.1. The curves for Canada and Mexico show the possible production of one worker in one week for each country. Assuming that the terms of trade are one bushel of wheat for four radios, the consumption possibilities for both countries have shifted to the right after trade. One worker in Canada could produce either 10 bushels of wheat or 30 radios in one week before trade. If the Canadian worker produced only wheat, the possibility exists of trading 10 bushels of wheat to Mexico for 40 radios. For Mexico, the option is 2.5 bushels of wheat or 10 radios after trade. The consumption possibilities for both countries have been enhanced by trade.

Product Prices

The prices of wheat and radios will also be affected by international trade. The demand for wheat produced in Canada will go up. The demand for wheat produced in Mexico will decrease. This will cause the price of Canadian wheat to increase as a result of increased demand, and the price of wheat in Mexico to decrease because of an increased supply from Canada. International trade will bring the prices for wheat in the two countries closer together. This example assumes that transportation costs are zero. In reality, transportation costs are not zero and will have some impact on the price. The relative prices will also be affected by the exchange values of the Mexican peso and the Canadian dollar.

The *relative price* of radios in Canada and Mexico will also change.

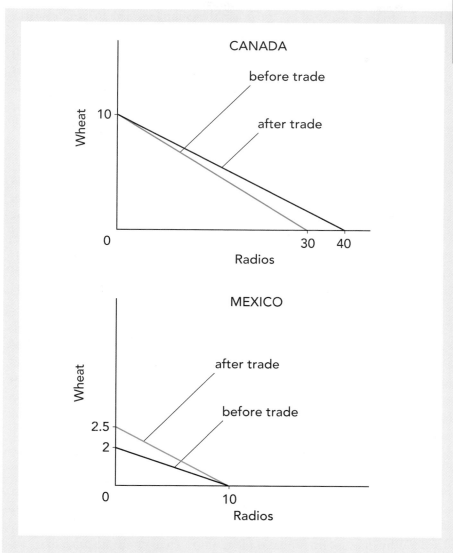

Figure 9.1

International trade and consumption possibilities

The impact of international trade on consumption possibilities for Canada and Mexico. Trade has permitted the consumption of both products to increase.

The demand for Canadian-made radios will decrease and the demand for Mexican-made radios will increase. The price of radios in Canada will decrease because of increased supply, and the price of radios in Mexico will increase because of increased demand. Again, international trade will bring the relative price of radios in Canada and Mexico closer together. If this analysis is extended around the globe, we can assume that international trade will bring prices for all products in different countries closer together.

Resource Prices

Foreign trade will also affect the prices that suppliers have to pay for workers, land, and so on. In Canada the demand for land will increase since wheat is a *land-intensive product.* The demand for land in Mexico will decrease. This will result in higher prices for land in Canada and lower prices for land in Mexico. Radios, in contrast, are a *labour-intensive product.* The demand for workers will be reduced in Canada and will increase in Mexico. Some Canadian workers displaced from the radio factories will find work in the wheat fields. Since wheat growing relies more heavily on land than on workers, not all workers will be re-employed producing wheat. The unemployment among Canadian radio workers will tend to lower the wage rate among radio workers as supply exceeds demand. In Mexico, workers who leave the wheat fields should find new employment in the radio factories because the total demand for workers has increased, and thus would increase the *wage rate* in Mexico.

Assume that workers were allowed to move freely across international borders. What difference would this make? Prior to international trading, wages for radio workers would be higher in Canada than in Mexico. This circumstance would encourage Mexican radio workers to move to Canada. There would now be a greater supply of radio workers in Canada, resulting in lower wages for radio workers in Canada. In Mexico, the reduced supply of radio workers would force up wage rates. The results are similar to those achieved through trading. Wages in Canada are lowered, and wages in Mexico are increased. *International trade is a substitute for the movement of resources.*

R E V I E W

9.7 Why does international trade result in a more efficient allocation of the world's resources?

9.8 Why does international trade result in changes in the price of Canadian resources?

Barriers to International Trade

In spite of the advantages of international trade, all countries have erected some barriers to trade. These barriers are aimed at restricting the amount of foreign products that can be imported. Barriers come in one of two forms. **Tariffs** are the most common trade restriction and represent a tax on the imported product. This tax may be imposed as a source of revenue for

A tariff is a tax imposed on imported products.

the government, but more than likely it is for the protection of domestic suppliers. If the tax raises the price of the import, the domestic supplier will be more competitive.

Countervailing duties are a type of tariff. If the product being imported into Canada has received government financial assistance in the exporting country, it may be subject to a countervailing duty. Canada may argue that the imported product has an unfair advantage in the competition with Canadian-made products. The countervailing duty may be applied in order to allow Canadian products to compete in price. In 1986, Canada and the United States exchanged countervailing duties. The United States imposed a duty on imports of Canadian lumber, and Canada imposed a duty on the importation of American corn. In 1989, the United States imposed a countervailing duty on steel rails exported to the U.S. by Sydney Steel Corporation of Nova Scotia. This duty was imposed as a result of the subsidies that the company had been receiving from both the federal and provincial governments.

The impact of a tariff on hockey sticks is shown in Figure 9.2. The supply curve S_d represents the domestic supply of hockey sticks. The supply curve S_{d+f} represents the total supply, domestic and foreign, of hockey sticks on the market. The addition of foreign suppliers drops the price

A **countervailing duty** is an additional tariff placed on an imported item that has received government financial assistance during production in the exporting country.

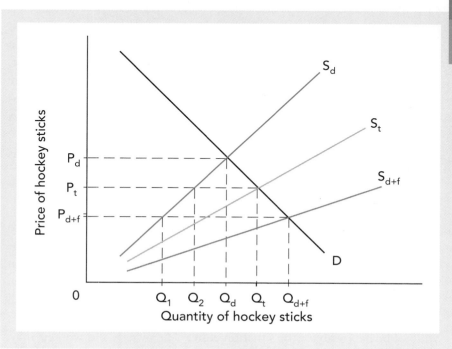

Figure 9.2

The impact of a tariff on hockey-stick sales

As a result of the tariff, the price has increased and the quantity of hockey sticks exchanged in the market has decreased.

from P_d to P_{d+f}. The share of the market held by domestic suppliers also drops, from Q_d to Q_1. If a tariff is imposed on imported hockey sticks, the new supply curve is S_t. The new price is P_t and the new quantity is Q_t. As a result of the tariff, the price has increased and the quantity of hockey sticks exchanged in the market has decreased ($Q_{d+f} - Q_t$). Consumers get fewer hockey sticks. The amount of the market supplied by domestic firms has increased from Q_1 to Q_2. The increase in market share awarded to domestic suppliers is referred to as the *protection effect* of the tariff.

Non-tariff barriers (NTBs) also impose restrictions on international trade. The most common form of NTB is the quantitative import restriction, or quota, which places a limit on the value or quantity of an import. Voluntary export restraints are agreements between importing and exporting countries on the maximum value or number of items to be exported during a set period. This type of NTB became better known as a result of the restrictions on Japanese car sales to the United States in the 1980s.

Various rules and regulations in the importing country can also restrict trade. For example, the importing country may ban a certain type of food additive. Any imports containing the additive will not be allowed to enter the country. Non-tariff barriers have expanded as nations agree to reduce tariffs. In a sense, they have replaced tariffs as a form of protectionism.

Until recently, Canada exported approximately $200 million worth of canola to the European Union (EU). The EU imposed a ban on genetically modified (GM) foods and, since 60 percent of Canada's canola crop is genetically modified, exports of canola to Europe have almost stopped. The EU imposed the ban on GM foods for consumer safety reasons. Canada argues that there is no evidence that GM foods are a safety risk. In fact, since GM crops are grown from scientifically engineered seeds, they require fewer chemicals to combat pests. European Union farmers are heavily subsidized by their governments and, in the case of canola, are protected from competition by a non-tariff barrier.

Why are countries motivated to construct trade barriers? The reasons for this protection are numerous and are listed below.

Unequal Benefits from Trade

Although there are overall benefits from international trade between two countries, certain groups within one country may be hurt by trade. In our example, Canada would have found it advantageous to import radios from Mexico. This would result in the unemployment of radio workers in Canada. Although some of the workers may go to work in the wheat fields, not all will be able or willing to do so. The owners of Canadian radio companies will not be happy about the situation either. The owners and workers may,

Non-tariff barriers impede the flow of international trade through the use of quotas, restrictive rules, and regulations.

therefore, approach the federal government and ask for some protection against the importation of Mexican radios. The federal government may respond by erecting a barrier to trade, such as a quota on the import of Mexican radios. This would reduce the competition for Canadian radios. Both owners and workers would benefit. Many industries in Canada have formed national associations representing their manufacturers. These associations have their offices in Ottawa so that they can lobby the federal government for assistance to their industry; the erection of trade barriers is one such type of assistance.

It should be pointed out that the erection of trade barriers is not without costs. These costs are primarily borne by the consumer, who will pay a higher price and receive less of the product after the barrier is in place. Tariffs add a cost to the product that will show up in higher prices. Quotas and other non-tariff barriers reduce the supply of the product and thus increase the price. Also, in our example, Mexico may retaliate by limiting the importation of Canadian wheat. This would hurt Canadian farmland owners and farm workers who would have sold the wheat to Mexico. Trade barriers, therefore, help some Canadians while hurting others.

Protection of Domestic Living Standards

For numerous reasons, workers around the world do not receive the same wage or salary. These *wage differences* between countries may prompt governments to adjust the differences through trade barriers. For example, if the average wage in Bolivia were 50 cents per hour and the average wage in Canada were $7 per hour, products leaving Bolivia for Canada would be much cheaper due to the difference in wages and would therefore have a definite labour-cost advantage. In order to protect the high wages and living standards in Canada, and to allow Canadian companies to compete for the consumer's dollar, the federal government may place a tariff on all products imported from Bolivia. The argument for the tariff would be that if Canadian companies had to compete directly with cheaper products from Bolivia, Canadian wages would have to be lowered and our standard of living would fall.

This argument overlooks the fact that the wages paid to workers are not the only cost of production and also that wages are tied to *worker productivity*. In industries where workers are paid more, the costs of production may not be any higher than in comparable industries where they are paid less.

If the more highly paid workers produce more than the workers receiving a lower wage, the high-paying company could have even lower per-unit costs. Workers in Canada may be paid more and may be able to produce more because they are more skilled or because they have more sophisticated machinery and equipment to work with. Higher wages do not necessarily produce a higher price for an item, nor do they necessarily reflect a competitive disadvantage.

Trade barriers increase the price of the product to the consumer. It is hard to imagine how higher prices can improve domestic living standards.

Infant Industry

When a company is starting out in an industry, it faces tough competition from existing companies in the industry. The existing firms will already have a clientele established and will be producing on a large enough scale to have lower per-unit costs. In many cases the new company will not survive unless it receives some type of *government assistance.*

At times, government may be anxious to see a new domestic company or a new industry develop. New companies and industries create jobs and increase gross domestic product. It may be difficult for a new industry to get started if it has to compete with those companies that are already established around the world. The newcomer is referred to as an **infant industry.** In order to help the infant industry get on its feet, governments may impose a tariff or quota on the foreign competition. It is argued that as soon as the industry is large enough and competitive in the world markets, the trade barrier will be dropped.

Suppose that some Canadians wanted to cultivate a banana industry in Canada. They may approach the government for assistance. One of the steps taken to promote this industry would be the imposition of a high tariff on all imported bananas. It would be hoped that the Canadian banana industry, producing costly bananas at first, would grow, achieving *economies of scale.* This would make the industry internationally competitive within a number of years. At that time, it might be expected that the tariff on imported bananas could be removed.

There are several difficulties with the argument for imposing a trade barrier in this situation. First, how do we know if the industry will ever become internationally competitive? In the case of bananas, it is highly unlikely. Consumers would continue to pay higher prices for bananas than they would if there were no tariff on imported bananas. Second, if an industry grows up under the protection of a tariff, it may not be forced to develop its efficiency. If it remains inefficient, the tariff is not likely to be removed. Finally, if this industry is eventually going to be successful, why would private individuals not invest in it? Individuals are continually taking risks by putting their money into business ventures with an uncertain future. What rationale is there to treat the infant industry differently from other industries?

A newly established industry is referred to as an infant industry.

Another reason for promoting infant industry is that the economies of some countries are very specialized, relying basically on one product. Fluctuating international markets affect the incomes that these countries receive. In order to add some stability to their economy, these nations would like to develop other industries. To develop these industries, protection must be provided in the form of tariffs and quotas. The argument is that the result—a more diversified economy—would provide economic stability for the country over the long run and that this would override the high costs of the trade barriers.

Military Self-Sufficiency

Trade barriers may be imposed for *strategic reasons*. Some industries may be important for military purposes and, as a result, should not be subject to import competition. The automobile industry would be an example. If military conflict broke out, the automobile industry would be required for vehicle production. The textile industry would be required for uniform production, and so on. The difficulty with this argument is that in times of military conflict *all* industries are likely to be important. Special trade barriers cannot be set up for all of them.

Reaction to Dumping and Foreign Assistance

Charging different prices in different markets is referred to in international trade as **dumping**. It refers to a situation in which a product sells for a lower price in the foreign market than it does in the domestic market. In 2000, Bingo Press & Specialty Ltd. of St. Catharines, Ontario complained that bingo cards imported from Arrow International Inc. of Cleveland, Ohio were being dumped onto the Canadian market. Canada Customs and Revenue Agency has stated that there was evidence of dumping. Importing countries are concerned about dumping because the products dumped are often in competition with domestically produced products. There is a fear that once an import becomes established and has possibly driven some domestic producers out of business, the prices will be increased. When it can be shown that dumping exists, the importing countries usually respond with special tariffs in order to raise the price and protect domestic manufacturers.

Trade barriers in the form of tariffs are also imposed when it is discovered that an imported product was produced with the aid of government assistance in the exporting country. If this assistance leads to lower prices and unfair competition, then the importing country may impose a countervailing duty or tariff on the import. An example in which a countervailing duty was applied was Michelin's decision to export tires to the

Dumping is the practice of selling a product in a foreign market at a lower price than is charged in the domestic market.

United States. The Canadian government had given the Michelin Tire Company financial assistance to locate in Nova Scotia. The Americans argued that giving financial assistance to Michelin gave that company an unfair advantage in the American automobile tire market, and they imposed an additional tariff on Michelin tires.

Diffusion of Technology

In order to be competitive in international markets, companies are forced to spend significant amounts of money on *research and development.* Government assistance is often available to companies that are improving their technology. Once the technology is developed, however, there is no guarantee that it will always benefit the country that helped to finance it. Many companies are multinational in nature and can transfer their technology across international boundaries. It is not possible for countries to duplicate another country's climate or natural resources, yet it is possible to duplicate technology.

Assume that Canada were to give some financial assistance to a multinational company in Canada in order to help the company develop a new computer disk. Once the disk is developed, the company may decide to have the disk produced not in Canada but in another country. The disk would then be imported into Canada from abroad. Such a situation would not be beneficial to Canada. The federal or provincial government in this case helped finance the technological advance, yet Canadians would not have received any of the benefits. In this case, a heavy tariff could be placed on the importation of this disk to encourage the company to produce it in Canada.

Increase in Domestic Employment

As discussed in earlier chapters, economic conditions are continually fluctuating. At times, the economy may be in a recession with high levels of unemployment. A possible cure for unemployment may be to raise trade barriers on imports and force Canadians to buy domestically made products. This argument appears to make sense, because if money is spent on Canadian-made products the money stays in Canada and creates employment here. One problem that may arise with this approach, however, is that Canadian exports may be affected.

If foreign countries cannot sell their products in Canada, they will not have money to spend on Canadian products. If our exports decline, then jobs may be lost. *The trade barrier may protect some jobs, while sacrificing others.* In our earlier Canada–Mexico example, any attempt to protect Canadian radio manufacturers would hurt Canadian wheat producers. What would happen if all countries imposed trade barriers simultaneously in order to increase domestic employment? World trade would be drastically reduced, and all the benefits from trade would be lost. Further, it is unlikely that the overall level of employment would increase.

Trade barriers may be imposed for any of the above reasons. In each instance, the level of international trade is reduced. When trade is reduced, the total output of goods and services that could be achieved is not reached. Prices also remain higher than need be for certain products. Therefore, any decision to erect a trade barrier should take into consideration all of the positive and negative aspects of such a move.

REVIEW

9.9 Explain some of the problems with the infant-industry argument to trade restrictions.

9.10 What do we mean when we say that the benefits from international trade are not spread equally throughout the population?

9.11 Why may higher tariffs not help a country out of a recession?

9.12 Find out how tariffs on foreign imports change the supply of hockey sticks on the market.

Canada and Freer Trade

As early as 1854, a free-trade area existed that encompassed Upper and Lower Canada, New Brunswick, Prince Edward Island, Newfoundland, Nova Scotia, and the United States. Not long after, however, John A. Macdonald's National Policy of 1879 established a series of tariffs on imports in order to encourage Canadian manufacturing. In 1911, the federal election was fought over the idea of free trade with the United States. Robert Borden's Conservative Party, which campaigned on an anti–free-trade platform, defeated Wilfrid Laurier's policy on reciprocity. In 1988, the main issue in the federal election was again free trade with the United States. In that election, the pro–free-trade policies of Brian Mulroney's Progressive Conservatives defeated the parties that were opposed to freer trade with the United States.

Canada's desire for freer trade began to grow after the Second World War with the signing of the **General Agreement on Tariffs and Trade (GATT)**. In 1965, the Canada–United States Automobile Agreement was signed, and in 1989, the Canada–United States Free Trade Agreement came into

An international agreement called the General Agreement on Tariffs and Trade (GATT) **is aimed at reducing the barriers to international trade.**

effect. The latest step in Canada's advance toward freer trade is the North American Free Trade Agreement (NAFTA), which came into effect on January 1, 1994.

GATT and the World Trade Organization

In order to profit from the advantages of international trade, 23 countries signed the GATT in 1947. The agreement was aimed at removing the barriers to international trade. *If international trade flourished, specialization would result in improved standards of living.* GATT became effective in January 1948. Since that time, the number of signatories has increased from the original 23 to the present 145 signatories. GATT was based on a few fundamental principles:

Non-discrimination: The contracting parties agreed that trade between nations should be conducted on a non-discriminating basis. Each nation was to apply any tariffs or trade policy equally to all countries. There were exceptions to this rule only in unusual circumstances. Existing preferential trading arrangements such as the British Commonwealth preferences were allowed to continue. That is, products entering Britain from Commonwealth countries were subject to lower tariff rates than products from other nations.

Multilateral negotiations: GATT provided a mechanism for the discussion of trade problems and for the reduction of trade barriers. Reductions in tariffs were to be undertaken by multilateral negotiations. These are negotiations in which all GATT signatories take part. GATT also established a review panel to examine trade disputes.

Quantitative restrictions: GATT hoped to have countries use only tariffs as a barrier to trade. Quantitative restrictions, such as quotas, were to be prohibited. Although quantitative restrictions have not been eliminated, the use of quotas has been reduced. GATT did provide for the use of quantitative restrictions in situations in which the country was having persistent balance of payments problems.

GATT has assisted in reducing the level of tariffs between trading nations. Tariffs are reduced through multilateral negotiations. The Kennedy Round of negotiations (1964–67) was named after U.S. President John F. Kennedy. The tariff reductions negotiated at this time were phased in from 1967 to 1972. The Tokyo Round (1973–79) focused a great deal of attention on non-tariff barriers. The tariff reductions negotiated during the Kennedy Round had forced countries to look for other types of protection. Non-tariff barriers in the form of rules and regulations began to spring up.

In many ways, non-tariff barriers are more effective than tariffs. Whereas tariffs simply increase the price of the imported article, non-tariff barriers can effectively prevent the article from being imported. Many non-tariff barriers are hard to identify. Non-tariff barriers that were a major concern of the Tokyo Round negotiations can be classified into three types: technical barriers to trade, government procurement practices, and customs valuation.

The eighth round of GATT negotiations got underway in Uruguay in September 1986. Non-tariff barriers were still a concern for countries associated with GATT; however, the emphasis in the latest round of talks shifted to subsidies and market-sharing agreements. Food-exporting countries were upset over the subsidies given to farmers in the European Economic Community (EEC) and the United States. Market-sharing agreements, such as voluntary export-restraint agreements, are at odds with GATT's principle on non-discriminatory behaviour. That is, if action is taken against one country, it should be taken against them all. Many developing countries wanted the topics of increased trade in financial information and investment services discussed at these talks. The Uruguay Round of trade talks was also concerned about intellectual property rights and performance requirements set on foreign investment.

A new GATT agreement was reached in December 1993 and came into effect on January 1, 1995. The agreement gave the world's poorer countries greater access to textile and garment markets in the developed nations. The agreement also reduced domestic agricultural subsidies and lowered tariffs on a wide range of products. The new GATT also resulted in a name change. As of January 1995, GATT was transformed into the World Trade Organization (WTO). Countries wanting entrance into the WTO must agree to liberalizing trade in services, opening up their market to agricultural imports, protecting intellectual property rights, and giving fair treatment to foreign investment. The WTO entrance requirements make it difficult for state-run economies to join.

WTO members take their disputes to an independent disputes-settlement panel that allows the winning country to punish the losing country with trade sanctions unless the losing country changes its ways and complies with international trade rules. There have been complaints against Canadian trade practices by other WTO members. WTO decisions that have gone against Canada recently include:

1997—A WTO ruling rejected Canada's attempt to stop *Sports Illustrated* from selling a split-run edition of its magazine in Canada. A split-run magazine has American content and Canadian advertisements. Canada was imposing an 80-percent excise tax on split-run magazines. Canada was also providing postal subsidies for Canadian magazines. The WTO ruled against both practices. Canada appealed the decision, but in July 1997 the appeal was rejected.

1999—The WTO ruled that Canada's Technology Partnerships and the Canada Account are prohibited subsidies under WTO rules. The Technology Partnerships program was designed to advance research in the aerospace, defence, and environmental industries. Money given to companies under the program was to be paid back from the profits of sales of the products. The WTO ruled that the program offered exports subsidies for Canadian products. The Canada Account offered concessional financing to buyers of Canadian exports.

1999—The WTO ruled that Canada's dairy export system breaks international trade rules. Canada was offering a lower price for milk to companies that processed milk for export. Canadian dairy farmers sell their milk to a marketing board that pays them different prices depending on the end use for the milk. The quantity of domestic milk is set by a quota, but farmers were able to export excess milk for a lower price. The WTO ruled against this two-tiered pricing system. On a related issue, the WTO ruled that Canada could limit dairy imports but cannot restrict imports to the amount that Canadians can carry across the border with them in their shopping bags. Canada must also allow commercial operations to send their dairy products to Canada.

1999—The WTO ruled that the Canada–United States Automobile Agreement discriminated unfairly against automobile imports into Canada from every country except the United States. The Auto-Pact allows three automobile manufacturers—General Motors, Ford, and Daimler-Chrysler—to import cars duty-free into Canada from anywhere in the world. Other companies pay a 6.1-percent duty on imports.

2000—The WTO supported France in a ban on imports of chrysolite asbestos from Canada, agreeing that asbestos poses a risk to human health.

2000—The WTO dismissed Canada's appeal of an earlier ruling that Canada's patent-protection laws violated international trading rules.

2001—Canada lost its appeal against the WTO decision upholding France's ban on Canadian products containing asbestos (see above).

2002—Canada's appeal of the 1999 WTO decision on dairy exports (see above) was denied. Canada's system of subsidizing dairy exports must meet WTO-approved levels of subsidization.

2002—Canada wanted the WTO to rule that the United States must refund softwood duties if the WTO rules in Canada's favour in a complaint by Canada that the United States is illegally putting countervailing duties on Canadian softwood lumber coming into its country. The WTO ruled that the United States does not have to refund the duties to Canadians.

2003—The WTO appointed a panel to investigate whether Canada is illegally subsidizing wheat exports.

Canada has complained to the WTO about trade practices in other countries. Recent decisions by the WTO in Canada's favour include:

1997—In response to a WTO ruling, Japan will scrap all tax discrimination for gin and vodka and narrow the tax differential on whiskey and cognac to 3 percent from 600 percent. Japan agreed to increase the tax on *shochu,* a Japanese liquor, while lowering the tax on foreign liquor.

1997—A WTO decision ruled against Europe's ban on hormone-treated Canadian beef. The ruling stated that it is not possible for countries to act preventively if they suspect something to be harmful. In order to ban a product, there must be scientific proof that environmental or health concerns outweigh trade concerns.

1997—An agreement reached by 70 WTO countries allowed Canadian banks, insurance companies, and securities firms to have greater access to financial-services markets around the world.

1999—It was decided that Canadian exports of beef to the United States are not to be subsidized.

2000—The WTO upheld Canada's patent rules that allow manufacturers of generic drugs to develop and get approval for copies of brand-name drugs that are under patent protection. However, the WTO ruled against Canadian policy that allowed generic drug manufacturers to stockpile "copycat" products in anticipation of the patent expiry date. Generic firms must wait until the patent expires before copying special formulas and undertaking the drug trials required for government approval.

2002—The WTO ruled against the manner in which the United States calculated temporary countervailing duties on Canadian softwood lumber.

2003—A panel of the WTO stated that provincial arrangements for cutting trees are a financial contribution to lumber companies. The panel ruled, however, that this did not prove that lumber companies are getting their wood at a lower price than they would pay were they to get the wood from a private woodlot.

In November 2001 a new round of multilateral trade talks began in Doha, Qatar. This round of talks, known as the Doha Round, is expected to be completed by January 2005. The issues to be discussed in this round of talks include:

Domestic and export subsidies for farmers: The European Union and Japan are strong proponents of farm subsidies. New Zealand, Australia, the United States, and Canada want to eliminate subsidies despite the fact that Canada wants to preserve the system of agricultural marketing boards.

Developing countries: These countries are asking for more time to live up to their trade liberalization promises, especially on intellectual property protection. Also, they do not believe that developed countries have lived up to their WTO obligations. There is a possibility that some less-developed countries will pull out of the WTO.

Anti-dumping: Developing countries see anti-dumping rules as another form of trade barrier. The United States, a country that imposes duties on dumped products, refuses to discuss its anti-dumping rules. Canada is willing to adjust its anti-dumping regulations.

Genetically modified foods: Canada wants these foods banned only when they have been proven to be unsafe. The European Union does not want to have to prove foods unsafe before banning them.

Environment and labour: Canada, the United States, and the European Union want the WTO to establish links with other world organizations to ensure that labour and environmental standards are upheld in the face of increased trade liberalization. Many developing countries see the insistence on labour standards and environmental standards as disguised trade barriers.

Transparency: Canada and others want the WTO to be more open in its negotiations and decision making.

Investment and competition rules: There is interest in setting up rules to protect foreign investors and to harmonize antitrust policies.

Size of the round: The United States wants a smaller, more manageable round of trade talks. The European Union and developing countries want large rounds of multilateral talks to allow for more trade-offs and an agreement where every country can come out ahead.

Services: Canada does not want to open up health or education industries to trade liberalization.

Culture: Canada wants cultural industries declared unique and proposes that the special treatment of culture should be written into the trade rules. The United States is opposed to special trade status for cultural industries.

REVIEW

9.13 What were the original objectives of GATT?

9.14 What were the main issues of the Uruguay Round of negotiations?

EVERYDAY ECONOMICS 9.1

The Jet Wars: Canada versus Brazil

In 1997, Brazil complained to the WTO about illegal subsidies the Canadian government was giving to Bombardier, a Canadian company that designs, manufactures, and markets aerospace transportation equipment as well as recreational products like the SkiDoo and the SeaDoo. Brazil argued that the Canadian company had received subsidies, loan guarantees, and interest-free loans to promote the sale of the Canadair Regional Jet and other aircraft. Canada had previously complained to the WTO about illegal subsidies being given to Embraer, a Brazilian aerospace company, by the Brazilian government under the export financing program Pro-ex. Embraer builds turboprop and jet aircraft that compete directly with Bombardier jets. Specifically, Brazil objected to a number of illegal subsidies including:

- Low-interest-rate loans provided by the Export Development Corporation to Bombardier
- An $87-million loan to Bombardier by the Canadian federal government
- A $57-million payment to Bombardier under the Technology Partnership program
- A $147-million payment to the Quebec company Pratt & Whitney to develop jet engines for the Bombardier aircraft

Regional jets are defined as aircraft having between 30 and 100 seats. The Canadair aircraft is a 50-seat jet selling for about $20 million. Its main competitor is a jet made by Embraer that sells for about $15 million. Canada argued to the WTO that illegal Brazilian export subsidies reduced the above price by more than $2.5 million.

Until 1996, Bombardier had a monopoly in the regional jet market. At that time, Embraer reorganized and began manufacturing 50-seat and 70-seat jets to compete with Bombardier. In 1998, Bombardier had 55 percent of the regional jet market and Embraer had 45 percent. Bombardier employs about 53 000 people, and the Canadian aerospace industry employs approximately 67 000 people; industry sales exceed $15 billion annually. The industry spends approximately $880 million a year on research and development. In Brazil, Embraer employs about 7000 people. Both nations are anxious to support their aerospace industries since they employ thousands of skilled workers and are a major source of exports. Brazil argues that export-financing programs such as Pro-ex are necessary to help Embraer's clients because of the difficulty clients would have getting financing to deal with a Brazilian company.

In March 1999, the WTO ruled that both Canada and Brazil were using illegal subsidies to support their aerospace industries. It ruled that Canada's Technology Partnership program and the export financing program Canada Account were both prohibited under WTO rules. It also ruled that Brazil's export financing program, Pro-ex, was prohibited. Both parties appealed the ruling but the decision was upheld.

After the appeal was turned down, both countries restructured their export-assistance programs. In April 2000, the WTO approved of Canada's changes to the Technology Partnerships program but condemned Brazil for failing to fix its financing for regional jet exports. The WTO also ruled that Pro-ex is out of line only when it acts improperly in financing sales for Embraer. The WTO stated the conditions under which the offer of financing to potential customers could be made. In 2002, the WTO ruled that Canada must withdraw financing from five transactions, including $1.7 billion for an Air Wisconsin purchase of Bombardier aircraft.

As a result of the various WTO rulings, Canada can apply $341 million worth of sanctions annually against imports from Brazil. Canada has not imposed these sanctions, which could be placed on the importation of Brazilian meat, vegetables, coffee, fruit, leather goods, steel, wood, textiles, shoes, wigs, and machinery. Both countries hope that an agreement on subsidies can be reached.

There is some concern that the failure to agree on the aircraft dispute could jeopardize any movement toward a free-trade area covering all of the Americas. If two countries in this geographic region cannot agree on this dispute, the probability of an overall agreement being signed is very small.

Questions

1. Is Canada committing an unfair trade practice by providing financing to Bombardier?
2. Would Canadian consumers benefit from a ban on Brazilian products?
3. What is the opportunity cost to the Canadian government with respect to the subsidization of Bombardier?

The Road to NAFTA

The Canadian government was anxious to develop the domestic automobile industry, which was in decline. There was concern that the population of Canada was not large enough to support the large-scale manufacture of cars. Therefore, in order for the industry to grow it was necessary to increase the export market.

In 1965, Canada and the United States signed an agreement regarding automobile production and trade. The **Canada–United States Automobile Agreement** allowed for the duty-free movement of most vehicles and parts between the two countries. Canada had several objectives in signing the agreement. It wanted to increase automobile production in Canada. It also wanted to increase the productivity of the Canadian automobile worker. This strategy would lead to lower prices for cars and higher wages for workers.

American automobile manufacturers also benefited from the agreement. They did not have to pay the tariff on exports to Canada. They could organize their production in order to make the most efficient use of their factories in both Canada and the United States. Canadian subsidiaries of American companies began to specialize in certain lines of cars, rather than to produce a wide range of cars for the entire market.

In certain respects, the automobile agreement has been a success. Employment and output in the industry have increased since the agreement was signed. Much of this increase would likely have occurred anyway because of a larger and wealthier population. Price differentials that

The Canada–United States Automobile Agreement **allows for the duty-free movement of most vehicles and parts between the two countries.**

existed between cars sold in Canada and those sold in the United States have been reduced. Longer production runs in the Canadian industry since 1965 have increased efficiency. However, since population increases would have brought about more automobile production in spite of the agreement, it is difficult to attribute all increases in efficiency to the agreement alone.

There are some negative aspects of the agreement, however. Canada has continually had a *deficit* in the trade of automobile parts. That is, we have imported more automobiles and parts from the United States than we have exported to that country. Under the agreement, replacement parts were not permitted duty-free access to either country. Canadian parts manufacturers face tariffs when trying to sell in the United States. This has led to an overall deficit in automobile trade for Canada and, in recent years, the deficit has been getting larger.

The Canada–United States Automobile Agreement was altered slightly with the signing of the Free Trade Agreement (FTA) between Canada and the United States. The FTA recognized and incorporated the automobile agreement. The WTO ruled that the auto pact violated numerous international trade regulations, and as a result the pact came to an end in February 2001.

R E V I E W

9.15 Explain why both countries would benefit from signing the automobile agreement.

9.16 How is it possible that wage rates for auto workers could increase and the price of cars relative to that in the United States decrease as a result of the automobile agreement?

In 1986, Canada and the United States began negotiations on a bilateral free-trade agreement. A Canada–U.S. trade agreement was signed on January 2, 1988, and the agreement came into effect on January 1, 1989. The objectives of the agreement are as follows:

a) to eliminate barriers to trade in goods and services between the territories of the parties;

b) to facilitate conditions of fair competition within the free-trade area;

c) to liberalize significantly conditions for investment within this free-trade area;

d) to establish effective procedures for the joint administration of this Agreement and the resolution of disputes; and

e) to lay the foundation for further bilateral and multilateral cooperation to expand and enhance the benefits of the Agreement.

The reduction of tariffs between Canada and the United States is a major part of the agreement. Tariff cuts began on January 1, 1989; after that date, no existing tariff could be increased unless specifically provided for in the agreement.

What are the possible advantages and disadvantages of freer trade with the United States from Canada's point of view? The perceived advantages of freer trade are many. The removal of barriers to the U.S. market provides Canadian producers with duty-free access to approximately 300 million people. This change allows Canadian companies to become more efficient by producing on a larger scale. Canada is producing fewer product lines now than before the signing of the FTA. Greater efficiency leads to lower prices and higher wages for Canadian workers. Duty-free access to a larger market increases employment in Canada. The removal of tariffs protecting Canadian manufacturers also has an impact. Canadian companies are forced to become more efficient if they want to compete. This circumstance should lead to lower prices.

The direction of trade changes with freer trade. Some Canadian cities are in close proximity to major U.S. markets. Atlantic Canada and Quebec are very close to the heavily populated northeastern portion of the United States. British Columbia is closer to west-coast markets than many U.S. cities. Under these circumstances, Canadian manufacturers have a cost advantage in terms of transportation costs.

By making Canada economically stronger, freer trade is likely to make Canada politically stronger as well, by strengthening Canadian unity. Provinces will be eager to remain part of the free-trade area, and therefore would also be interested in remaining part of a united Canada. If a province were to separate from Canada, it would face tariff barriers from both Canada and the United States.

Freer trade also brings other advantages to Canada. First, it stimulates *research and development activity.* This type of activity is essential if Canada is to remain competitive in world markets, and will also help to increase employment. Second, some economists argue that more processing of our raw materials will be done in Canada as access to foreign markets is made easier. More processing of raw materials creates more jobs. Third, our manufacturers are in a better position to handle non-tariff barriers that are being imposed in many countries.

It was hoped that the signing of a bilateral trade agreement between Canada and the United States would protect Canadian industry from sudden protectionist forces arising in the United States. Unfortunately that has not been the case, as the United States has imposed duties on Canadian softwood lumber and wheat.

If access to the U.S. market remains secure, business should be more willing to invest in Canada. Business is more willing to undertake the long-term investment in plants, technology, and human resources that is required in order to successfully compete in a larger market. Firms are unlikely to make major investment commitments in an uncertain trading environment.

Certain disadvantages for Canada accompany freer trade. If Canadian companies are not able to compete, they may be forced out of business. Unemployment in those sectors of the economy may increase. In order to reduce the negative impact of freer trade, tariff reductions were phased in over a number of years.

If the major markets are south of the border, Canadian companies will locate close to their markets. Some American companies closed their Canadian subsidiaries and located closer to these major markets. Further, some economists argue that tariffs are no longer the major impediment to trade. The main barriers to trade are *non-tariff barriers* such as the "buy American" laws that have been passed in a number of U.S. states. The removal of tariffs does not tackle the problem of non-tariff barriers. Even when Canadian companies are efficient, they may be prohibited from competing.

REVIEW

9.17 Discuss the potential advantages to Canada that may result from the FTA.

9.18 The branch plants of many American-controlled companies are located in Canada. How would this influence the consequences for Canada of the Free Trade Agreement?

Mexico

To many Canadians, Mexico is the unknown partner in NAFTA. This brief section is designed to provide some information about the political and economic structure of this country of almost 100 million people. To begin, some quick comparisons: Canada's land mass is about five times that of Mexico, while our population is less than one-third of Mexico's. The Mexican birth rate and fertility rate are about twice the Canadian rate, but life expectancy is lower for Mexicans. Canadian GDP per capita is approximately five times the Mexican GDP per capita.

Politically, Mexico claimed its independence from Spain in 1810. In 1824 a republic was established, but it was not until 1917 that Mexico adopted a constitution. The country is comprised of 31 states and a federal district. The chief executive is the president, who is elected for a six-year term. The president is allowed to hold office for only one term. There are two legislative bodies: the Senate and the Chamber of Deputies. Senators are elected for six-year terms and deputies are elected for three-year terms. The main political parties are the Institutional Revolutionary Party (PRI), which was in power for 71 years until the July 2000 election; the National Action Party (PAN), which currently is the ruling party; the Party of the Democratic Revolution (PRD); the Green Ecological Party (PVEM); and the Labour Party (PT). In 1996, control by the PRI over the election commission was ended, and its supervision turned over to an independent council representing all parties. Citizens are given the right to vote at 18 years of age.

The components of the Mexican economy, and the major parts of those components, are as follows:

Manufacturing (employment): food and beverages, transportation equipment, electrical equipment, clothing, fabricated metals, chemicals, and textiles.

Agriculture (earnings): cattle, dairy products, hogs, wheat, and chickens.

Fishing (size of catch): tuna, mojarra, sardines, and shrimp.

Mining (employment): nonmetallic minerals, crude petroleum, and natural gas. Mexico has the world's sixth largest oil company, PEMEX, which is government-owned and has a monopoly over exploration and extraction of hydrocarbons.

In an attempt to get foreign firms to locate in Mexico, the Mexican government introduced the Maquiladora-9802 program in the 1970s. Under this program, components and raw materials are imported duty-free into Maquiladora designated areas in Mexico. The components and raw materials are held in bond by the manufacturer while further processing takes place. When the resulting final product is exported, and it has to be exported, only the value-added portion of the final product is subject to Mexican taxes. The goal of the program is to get foreign capital into Mexico, because the Mexican government wanted foreign firms to build factories and train workers for manufacturing. The lower wages paid to Mexican workers would also be an attraction for foreign firms wanting to locate in another country. Most of the areas designated as Maquiladora areas were located in the states just south of the U.S. border. By 1996, employment in Maquiladora areas of Mexico reached 750 000 workers. Since the signing of NAFTA, exports from the Maquiladora areas have represented a declining percentage of overall Mexican exports. NAFTA extended duty-free status to all of Mexico and thus non-Maquiladora areas have seen a boost in economic activity and in exports from those areas. NAFTA also allows for the gradual selling of Maquiladora-manufactured products within Mexico.

The Mexican labour market also differs from that of Canada and the United States. There are wide discrepancies in wages and benefits between the workers in big cities and those in small towns. Similar discrepancies exist between workers employed by the government and large companies, versus those in small companies. Many small Mexican companies are part of what is referred to as the "informal" economy. In this economy, the technology and labour practices are not those of a modern industrial economy. Many businesses in the informal economy are family businesses, and master–apprentice relationships are common. There are also wage and benefit differences between employees in the manufacturing areas of the north and the agrarian areas of the south. The unemployment rate in Mexico is about half of the rate in Canada.

Questions

1. Why do Canadians know less about Mexico than about many European nations?
2. Do the lower wage rates paid by Mexican firms pose a threat to Canadian exports?
3. As shown in Tables 9.2 and 9.3, Canada imports more from Mexico than it sells to Mexico. What products are involved in trade between Canada and Mexico?

North American Free Trade Agreement

On January 1, 1994, the North American Free Trade Agreement (NAFTA) came into effect. This agreement provided for freer trade between Canada, the United States, and Mexico. The North American Free Trade Agreement superseded the Canada–United States Free Trade Agreement (FTA). NAFTA's objectives, as stated in Article 102, are to:

a) eliminate barriers to trade in, and facilitate the cross-border movement of, goods and services between the territories of the parties;
b) promote conditions of fair competition in the free-trade area;
c) increase substantially investment opportunities in the territories of the parties;
d) provide adequate and effective protection and enforcement of intellectual property rights in each party's territory;
e) create effective procedures for the implementation and application of this Agreement, for its joint administration and for the resolution of disputes; and
f) establish a framework for further trilateral, regional, and multilateral cooperation to expand and enhance the benefits of this Agreement.

As a result of NAFTA, tariffs on about 9000 products are to be eliminated over a 15-year period. About one-half of the tariffs were eliminated immediately, and by 1999 about 65 percent of the products traded free of tariffs. Cars assembled in North America must have 62.5 percent of the value of the car produced in North America. This regulation prevented offshore manufacturers from gaining duty-free access to the Canadian and U.S. markets.

Mexico is opening up its markets in such areas as telecommunications, agriculture, financial services, and trucking. Clothing from Mexico will have easier access to both Canada and the United States as long as the clothes are made from North American yarns and fabrics.

Many of the concerns surrounding the FTA were expressed with regard to NAFTA. For those Canadians opposed to NAFTA, the low wages in Mexico pose a threat to Canadian business and ultimately to Canadian jobs. A 1992 study by the World Bank found that wage rates in Mexico were approximately one-fifth of the wages in Canada and the United States. However, if wages were the only factor involved in trade Mexican goods would have flooded the Canadian market earlier, because Canadian tariffs on Mexican products were already low (5 percent to 10 percent) prior to the signing of NAFTA. The lower wages paid to workers in Mexico are due to insufficient capitalization, weak management, and the lower productivity of Mexican workers. The same World Bank study found that labour productivity in Mexico was approximately one-quarter of that in Canada and the United States. Changes in the relative values of the currencies can also affect trade even where wage differences may appear to favour one country. For example, if the value of the peso increased relative to the Canadian dollar, Mexican exports could be hurt in spite of a wage-differential advantage.

Opponents of NAFTA focused on the concern that Mexican pollution controls were not as stringent as Canadian pollution controls. Others argued that Mexico has a poor record on human rights and is, thus, not a suitable trading partner. Some opponents to NAFTA argued that the trade agreement would infringe on provincial responsibilities. That is, provincial governments would no longer be able to give preferential treatment to local business. There is also concern for the workers who lose their jobs as a result of NAFTA. Will they be able to obtain employment in the industries that benefit from NAFTA?

Those Canadians in favour of NAFTA argue that Mexican products had easier access to Canada than Canadian products had to Mexico prior to NAFTA. Mexico is an expanding market of more than 80 million people, and since the Canadian market alone is not large enough to support globally competitive large-scale production, Canadian business needs access to larger markets. Work done in other less-developed countries will likely be transferred to Mexico because of the duty-free access it enjoys to both Canada and the United States. Rather than Canadian jobs being transferred to Mexico, it is likely that jobs in other less-developed countries will move to Mexico. Further, if Canada did not get duty-free access to Mexico, then the United States would be the only country with duty-free access to both markets.

Opinions differ on the success of NAFTA to date. A main source of disagreement is the measurement of success. Is success to be determined by job creation, income growth, or the amount of cross-border trade? Although the success of NAFTA has not been established, some trends have emerged. First, Canada and Mexico are gaining market share in the United States at the expense of nations that are not part of NAFTA. In particular, the economies of certain Asian and Caribbean nations have been hurt since NAFTA came into effect. Second, the agreement has not stopped cross-border trade disputes. The United States wants Canada to limit exports of wheat and lumber. Canadian producers want greater access to the U.S. sugar market. Certain Canadian industries, such as apparel and furniture, have increased exports south of the border. It is not clear, however, whether the increase in exports came from freer trade or a lower foreign-exchange value for the Canadian dollar.

EVERYDAY ECONOMICS 9.3

Softwood Lumber

In spite of trade agreements such as NAFTA and the WTO, trade disputes continue to arise between other nations. One of the longest-standing unresolved disputes concerns shipments of Canadian softwood lumber (construction lumber) to the United States. The Americans argue that Canadian softwood lumber destined for the United States is subsidized by the Canadian taxpayer and thus sells for a much lower price than would otherwise be the case. The United States argues that provincial governments in Canada who own the land from which the lumber is taken do not charge the lumber companies a fair stumpage fee. In the United States, cutting rights are auctioned off to the highest bidder.

The dispute goes back a long way. The first duty levied by the United States on the importation of Canadian lumber was in 1930. In 1986, the government of Canada levied an export tax on Canadian lumber shipments to the United States. The tax increased the price of Canadian lumber for export, with the result that the tax dollars remained in Canada. In 1996, with Canadian imports representing 33 percent of the U.S. lumber market, a new agreement was signed with the United States.

As part of the agreement, an export tax on Canadian softwood lumber shipments to the United States was imposed by the Canadian government. The tax was to last five years. In addition, duty-free exports to the United States were capped at $14.7 billion annually. Exports in excess of that amount were subject to duties starting at $50 per thousand board feet. For its part, the United States agreed to suspend countervailing duties until 2001.

Lumber exports from the Atlantic provinces to the United States were exempt from the 1996 agreement. Since 75 percent of lumber from those provinces came from privately owned land, the United States believed that it was not unfairly subsidized. The provinces affected the most by the 1996 agreement were British Columbia, Alberta, Ontario, and Quebec. In British Columbia, forestry represents about 48 percent of manufacturing shipments and about 15 percent of GDP. Any reduction in forestry shipments has a big impact on the province's economy. British Columbia was also affected by the reduction in sales of lumber to Japan and other Asian countries because of the economic slowdown in those nations.

In 2001, the United States imposed a 19.3-percent duty on Canadian softwood lumber. The United States also argued that Canada was dumping softwood lumber on the American market. It claimed that lumber was selling for as much as 36 percent below cost. As a result, it imposed an additional 12.6-percent duty on Canadian softwood lumber. In March 2002, the overall rate was set at 29 percent.

In 2002, Canada asked that a panel under NAFTA be established to rule on the U.S. duties. It also appealed to the WTO to investigate U.S. charges that Canada is dumping lumber on the American market. A July 2002 ruling by the WTO found that the United States erred in the way it calculated the 19.3-percent countervailing duty. The WTO also ruled that Canada had made financial contributions to companies selling lumber to the United States.

The duties imposed by the United States have forced Canadian lumber mills to become more efficient in order to reduce the average cost of lumber. Improvements in efficiency have come from investments in new equipment and concessions granted by the unions to eliminate wage premiums on the operation of a third shift. Mills are also trying to operate at peak capacity. In spite of the duties, lumber prices are falling and U.S. mills are in trouble. Also, the attempt to keep prices high for lumber has attracted imports from other countries into the U.S. market.

In May 2003, the WTO panel stated that provincial lumber arrangements do not necessarily mean that firms are buying lumber at a lower price than the price charged by a private woodlot. The NAFTA ruling was scheduled for July 2003 and was not available at the time of writing.

Questions

1. Canada is the main source of energy imports into the United States. Should Canada reduce exports of energy south of the border in order to gain reductions in countervailing duties on lumber? Explain.
2. Do all American citizens benefit from the countervailing duties imposed on lumber?
3. Using demand and supply curves, show the impact of the decision to impose import duties on softwood lumber. Show the impact in Canada and in the United States.
4. Under what conditions are trade unions likely to make concessions and change the contents of collective agreements already signed?
5. In October 2002, the federal government offered an aid package to workers and communities affected by the U.S. duties. Should the Canadian government offer financial assistance to all groups who are negatively impacted by international trade? Explain.

International Balance of Payments

The international balance of payments **documents all financial transactions between residents of one country and residents of the rest of the world.**

In order to assist with economic planning, the federal government records Canadian foreign trade. Statistics Canada maintains a record of all economic transactions between residents of Canada and the residents of foreign countries. This is referred to as the **international balance of payments.** Essentially, the balance of payments is a record of the amount of money entering Canada and the amount of money leaving Canada. Money enters Canada for a variety of reasons. Some foreigners want to buy our products, such as newsprint and wheat. Others want to travel in Canada or invest in Canadian companies. Some foreigners purchase bonds that are issued by our various levels of government. Money leaves the country for many of the same reasons. Canadians buy foreign products and travel in foreign countries. Others send money to relatives elsewhere. All of these transactions, and more, make up the balance of payments.

Statistics Canada divides the balance of payments into two sections: the **current account** and the **capital account**. The current account records trade in goods and services. Purchases of merchandise as well as payment for services are included in this account. The merchandise part of the account includes those items that are commonly referred to as exports and imports. These are visible or physical items. The service part includes payment for such services as travel, the use of borrowed money, and freight and shipping.

A breakdown of Canada's current account for 2002 appears in Table 9.5, which shows that Canada had a negative balance, or *deficit*, in the current account for that year. More money entered the country (receipts) than left the country (payments) for the items in the current account. This balance amounted to $17 311 million. Further investigation of the table reveals some of the reasons for the positive balance. The goods section of the current account showed a positive balance, or *surplus*, in 2002. Exports exceeded imports by $54 221 million. The surplus was countered by deficits in the services and investment-income sections. In 2002, Canadians paid out more in interest payments and dividends than they received from foreigners. Canadians and Canadian governments have borrowed money in foreign countries. The interest payments on these loans are recorded in the service sector of the current account. Foreigners also invest in Canada by purchasing shares in Canadian corporations. When these corporations make a profit, they distribute part of those profits to shareholders in other countries in the form of dividends. Canadians also have a significant deficit in travel ($1655 million), which appears in the services category in the current account. The role that the foreign-exchange value of the Canadian dollar plays in the determination of these figures is discussed later in this chapter.

The current account is the section of the international balance of payments that records the inflows and outflows of money for merchandise and service items.

The section that records the inflow and outflow of investment dollars is the capital account.

Table 9.5 *Current accounts, Canadian balance of international payments, 2002*

ITEM	RECEIPTS	PAYMENTS	BALANCE
All items	505 140	487 830	17 311
Goods	410 330	356 109	54 221
Services	58 216	66 149	–7 931
Investment income	29 918	60 269	–30 350

SOURCE: Adapted from the Statistics Canada website, www.statcan.ca/english/Pgdb/econ01a.htm (April 2003).

Figure 9.3 presents a historical perspective of Canada's current account balance. There are large fluctuations in the annual current account balance.

As the name implies, the long-term capital account records money flows of a long-term nature. For example, if a foreign company that operates a factory in Canada puts money into the expansion of that factory, the money is included in the long-term capital account and represents a flow of money into Canada. In contrast, if a resident of Canada buys shares in an American company, the purchase represents an outflow of money and is also recorded in the long-term section. International purchases of long-term bonds are also recorded here. In 2002, Canada had a net capital outflow of $4808 million.

R E V I E W

9.19 What is the difference between the current and capital accounts in the balance of payments?

Figure 9.3

Current account balance, 1976–2002

SOURCE: Adapted fom the Statistics Canada CANSIM database, Table 376-0001.

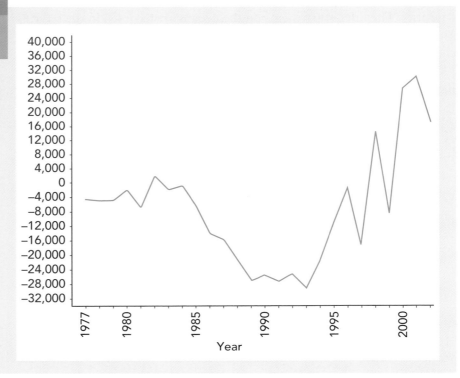

Foreign-Exchange Rates

In order for an economic transaction to take place, a *medium of exchange* is necessary. In Canada, this medium of exchange is the Canadian dollar. Our currency is used to buy food, travel, household articles, and other goods and services. What currency, or medium of exchange, is used if Canadians wish to purchase an article outside of Canada? Since the Canadian dollar is not considered legal tender outside Canada, a new medium of exchange must be found.

Assume that a Canadian company wants to import cheese from a company in France. Since Canadian dollars are not legal tender in France, the French company will want payment for the cheese in French francs. In order to complete the transaction, the Canadian company must acquire French francs. It does this by going to a market where French francs are sold. This is called the *foreign-exchange market*. The Canadian company offers to trade Canadian dollars for French francs. Before the exchange in this market can take place, a price or **foreign-exchange rate** has to be established. How is this exchange rate determined?

When Canadians want to purchase French francs, they increase the demand for francs on the foreign-exchange market. This increase in demand tends to put upward pressure on the price of French francs. Canadian dollars are offered in exchange for the francs. As a result, the supply of Canadian dollars on foreign-exchange markets is increased. When the supply of Canadian dollars increases, there is a tendency for the price to fall. If nothing else changes, this foreign-exchange transaction would increase the price, or *value,* of the French franc and lower the value of the Canadian dollar. If a French company were buying Canadian steel, the opposite would occur. The demand for Canadian dollars would increase and so would the foreign-exchange value of the Canadian dollar. The supply of French francs on the market would increase, and the price of francs would tend to fall.

Each day, thousands of purchases of foreign currencies take place; therefore, the values of these currencies are constantly changing. Each day the Canadian dollar is exchanged for a new price on foreign-exchange markets. These fluctuations in price are a result of constantly changing demand and supply conditions. Still, regardless of what happens to the value of the Canadian dollar on world money markets, it maintains its value within Canada. A dollar is still a dollar, and the only factor that influences the value of the Canadian dollar domestically is the rate of price increases. When prices increase in Canada, the dollar purchases fewer goods and services than before.

Where is the foreign-exchange market located? There is not just one foreign-exchange market, there are many. Any place in which foreign

The foreign-exchange rate is the value of a nation's currency in terms of another nation's currency.

Arbitrage, a system based on international communications, keeps the foreign-exchange value of a currency approximately equal in all markets.

currencies are exchanged can be classified as a foreign-exchange market. In Canada, chartered banks and foreign-exchange dealers are the major participants in this market. If there are many markets, then there can be many prices. The Canadian dollar may trade for a different price in London, England, than in New York. Nevertheless, prices for the Canadian dollar and other currencies are not likely to vary much from market to market. They are kept close together through a system called **arbitrage**. This system, based on good international communications, works in the following manner. Assume that the Canadian dollar was trading at a higher price in London than in New York. Individuals could buy Canadian dollars in New York and sell them in London at a higher price. If many people did this, the demand for Canadian dollars would increase in New York and so would the price. The supply of Canadian dollars would increase in London and the price there would come down. Since these transactions can be made by telephone, they can be made quickly—as soon as any major price differences appear in the two markets. This system of arbitrage, in which currencies are bought "low" in one market and sold "high" in another, tends to keep the value of the Canadian dollar the same in all markets around the world.

Since the Canadian dollar's foreign-exchange value is determined in the marketplace, it is possible to analyze changes in the value of the dollar through demand and supply curves. These curves are presented in Figures 9.4A and 9.4B. The price of the Canadian dollar is presented on the vertical axis in terms of U.S. dollars. The price of the Canadian dollar has to be presented in terms of another currency, and the U.S. dollar is commonly used for this purpose. The quantity of Canadian dollars is presented on the horizontal axis. The demand and supply curves take on their traditional shapes. The demand curve slopes down to the right. As the price of the Canadian dollar falls, a greater quantity of Canadian dollars will be demanded. A cheaper Canadian dollar makes Canadian products and services less expensive for foreigners. The supply curve slopes up to the right. As the value of the Canadian dollar rises, more dollars will be offered to the foreign-exchange market. Canadians can now buy more foreign products with the same amount of our currency. As the value of the Canadian dollar increases, Canadians are more likely to travel outside Canada, buy imported wine, hire foreign architects, and so on.

Any economic transaction that causes money to enter Canada will cause the demand for Canadian dollars to increase. This is represented in Figure 9.4A. If Canada exports more natural gas, the demand for Canadian dollars increases because foreigners need Canadian currency to buy the Canadian natural gas they want. This is shown by a shift in the demand curve from D^1 to D^2 in Figure 9.4A. The price of the Canadian dollar

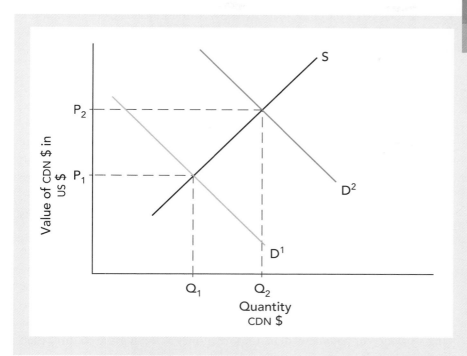

Figure 9.4A

The foreign-exchange market

An increase in the demand for the Canadian dollar increases its value.

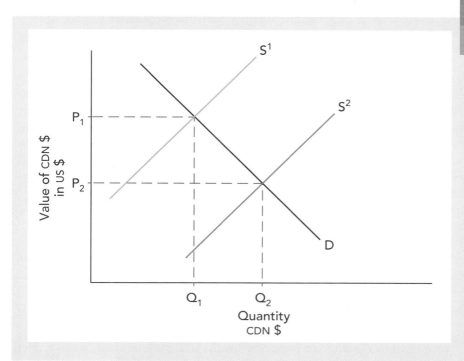

Figure 9.4B

The foreign-exchange market

An increase in the supply of the Canadian dollar on foreign-exchange markets decreases its value.

would increase from P_1 to P_2. The same result would be achieved if foreigners decided to purchase Canadian government bonds or to travel more in Canada. Any transaction that increases the demand for Canadian dollars on foreign-exchange markets will also increase the price, or value, of the Canadian dollar.

The results of more Canadians travelling abroad are shown in Figure 9.4B. In order to travel outside Canada, Canadian dollars must be exchanged for other currencies. This exchange increases the supply of Canadian dollars on foreign-exchange markets. The foreign-exchange value of the Canadian dollar will fall from P_1 to P_2 as the supply curve shifts from S^1 to S^2. The same result would occur if Canadians purchased more foreign products or sent money to relatives in other countries. Any transaction that increases the supply of Canadian dollars on foreign-exchange markets decreases the value of the Canadian dollar.

The foreign-exchange value of the Canadian dollar is directly related to the balance of payments. If Canada has a surplus in the balance of payments, then more money is coming into Canada than is going out. The demand for Canadian dollars on foreign-exchange markets is greater than the supply. This increases the *exchange rate* of the dollar. If Canada is incurring a balance-of-payments deficit, more money is leaving the country than is coming in. The supply of Canadian dollars on foreign-exchange markets is greater than the demand. Thus, the value of the dollar falls.

Any activity or government policy that affects Canada's balance of payments will affect the foreign-exchange rate of the dollar. Canadian trade policies, in the form of tariffs, quotas, and non-tariff barriers, directly influence the flow of money out of and into Canada. Canada's participation in the WTO and NAFTA are also important. In addition to these international policies, domestic policies and activities can influence the dollar's foreign-exchange value. For example, if the federal government decides to stimulate economic activity through increased spending, one of the consequences may be inflation. If the prices of Canadian products begin to rise, foreigners may stop buying them in favour of competing products. If our exports go down, less money comes into Canada and the foreign-exchange value of the dollar drops. Canadian government policy on gasoline prices will also affect the dollar. The decision by the federal government in the 1970s to keep Canadian gasoline prices below world levels attracted tourists from south of the border. Higher gasoline prices in recent years have discouraged tourists from vacationing in Canada.

Private-sector activity may also influence the dollar. A new discovery of oil reserves off Newfoundland may cause investment money to flow into the country. The development of a new tourist attraction in Canada will attract more visitors to our country and increase the value of the dollar, as well as increasing GDP. A Canadian architect, musician, engineer, or other professional who attracts international attention could also bring money into the country. *Again, any transaction that has an influence on the balance of payments has an influence on the foreign-exchange value of the dollar.*

A history of Canadian dollar exchange rates from 1973 to 2002 is presented in Figure 9.5. The Canadian dollar value is given by referring to the number of Canadian dollars required to purchase a U.S. dollar and a British pound. In 1973, the Canadian dollar was virtually at par with the U.S. dollar. In 1974 and 1976, it was worth more than a U.S. dollar, but it has declined in value since then. In other words, it has required more Canadian dollars to purchase a U.S. dollar since 1976 than before that year. The value of various foreign currencies in Canadian dollars for 2003 is presented in International Comparisons 9.1.

REVIEW

9.20 Using graphs in your answer, show the impact of the following:
- a) Japanese tourists visit British Columbia
- b) a Canadian company hires an American architect to design its new office building
- c) a Canadian citizen buys a U.S. government bond
- d) a rich uncle in Europe sends money to relatives living in Canada

Figure 9.5

Canadian dollars required to purchase U.S. dollar and British pound, 1973–2002

SOURCE: Published with the permission of the Bank of Canada.

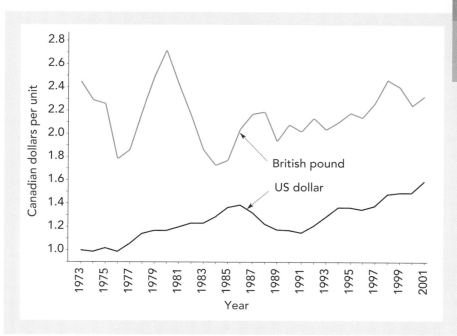

International Comparisons 9.1

Value of foreign currencies in Canadian dollars, October 28, 2003*

Country	Monetary unit	Value in Canadian dollars
Argentina	peso	0.4629
Australia	dollar	0.924
Chile	peso	0.00205
China	yuan	0.1582
Hong Kong	dollar	0.1688
India	rupee	0.0291
Israel	shekel	0.2944
Japan	yen	0.012089
Mexico	peso	0.1184
New Zealand	dollar	0.8037
Norway	krone	0.1858
Russia	rouble	0.0438
South Africa	rand	0.189
South Korea	won	0.0011
United Kingdom	pound	2.225
United States	dollar	1.31
European Monetary Union	Euro	1.528

*Calculated according to market rates as of this date.

Flexible versus Fixed Exchange Rates

Appreciation describes an increase in the value of the currency in relation to another currency under the conditions of a flexible exchange-rate system.

Depreciation is the term used to describe a reduction in the value of the currency in relation to another currency.

The foreign-exchange value of the Canadian dollar fluctuates on a daily basis depending on the demand and supply conditions in the market. The exchange rate is said to be *flexible* or *floating*. When the value of the Canadian dollar increases, the increase is called an **appreciation**. When it falls, the decrease is a **depreciation**.

At one time, the Canadian dollar was fixed in value in relation to other currencies. Regardless of the changes in demand and supply that took place in international foreign-exchange markets, the Canadian dollar kept the same exchange rate. How was this possible, since changes in demand and supply would cause the value of the dollar to change? Under a fixed exchange-rate system, it is necessary for the Bank of Canada to influence market conditions in order to keep the value of the dollar at its fixed rate.

In 1962, the Canadian government set the value of the Canadian dollar at $0.925 U.S. How did the Bank of Canada ensure that the rate remained at this level? If market forces were acting to raise or lower the value of the dollar, it would be necessary for the Bank of Canada to influence the market in such a way that the value of the dollar returned to $0.925 U.S. First, the Bank could purchase or sell Canadian dollars on foreign-exchange markets. If the Bank were to buy Canadian dollars in the foreign-exchange market, the demand for Canadian dollars would increase. This would cause the exchange rate of the Canadian dollar to rise. How would the Bank buy Canadian dollars? It would purchase Canadian dollars with foreign currencies that it has at its disposal. For example, the Bank could offer to sell Japanese yen or British pounds for Canadian dollars. What happens if the Bank does not have any foreign currencies available? If this happens, then it will be necessary for the Bank to borrow foreign currencies from other countries.

If the foreign-exchange value of the Canadian dollar rose above $0.925 U.S. as a result of market forces, then it would be necessary for the Bank of Canada to sell Canadian dollars on the foreign-exchange market. This action would lower the exchange value of the dollar, by increasing the supply of Canadian dollars on the market.

A second method of influencing the foreign-exchange value of the dollar would be to change the level of *interest rates* in Canada. If the value of the Canadian dollar were lower than the desired value, an increase in Canadian interest rates would increase the demand for Canadian dollars. People with money to lend would want to lend it in Canada in order to get a high return. The inflow of money into Canada would increase the demand for Canadian dollars. This would, in turn, increase the value of the dollar. If the value of the Canadian dollar were too high, interest rates would be reduced. Lower interest rates in Canada than in other countries would result in money leaving Canada for a better return elsewhere. With money leaving Canada, the supply of Canadian dollars on foreign-exchange markets would increase and the value of the dollar would fall.

A third option for influencing the value of the dollar would be *foreign-exchange controls.* The Canadian government could regulate the amount of money that Canadians would be able to take outside the country. If there is a limit on the number of dollars that Canadians can supply to foreign-exchange markets, the value of the dollar will remain at a higher level. In past years, Great Britain and Jamaica have had foreign-exchange controls.

What is the ideal value for the dollar? This is a very difficult question to answer. If the dollar is increasing in value, foreign products and foreign vacations are cheaper for Canadians. Our products become more expensive to residents of other countries. With a Canadian dollar decreasing in value, the reverse is true. The ideal value of the Canadian dollar depends on the elasticity of demand for Canadian and foreign products. If we continue to purchase foreign products regardless of the price (inelastic demand), a cheap dollar means that our import costs will increase. Such an increase will cause prices to be higher for products that we use. If foreigners also have an inelastic demand for our products, then we receive less total revenue for our products when the dollar is low. The ideal exchange rate depends on how Canadians and others react to changes in the exchange rate.

Is it better to have a fixed or a flexible exchange-rate system? There is still considerable debate on this point. The primary advantage of the flexible exchange-rate system is that it is automatic. It operates according to demand and supply forces. The Bank of Canada need not interfere with a flexible exchange-rate system. However, the disadvantage of this system is that it creates uncertainty. The exchange rate changes on a daily basis and businesses are less certain about what the costs of foreign purchases will be. This uncertainty may interfere with trade.

Having a fixed exchange rate solves the problem of uncertainty. Fixed rates, however, create other problems. How do you decide what the exchange rate should be? How do you adjust the rate when it needs to be changed? A fixed exchange-rate system requires that the Bank of Canada play an active role in determining the value of the dollar on a daily basis.

We use a combination of the two systems. The rate fluctuates daily, yet these fluctuations are influenced by the Bank of Canada. The Bank uses interest rates and Canadian-dollar purchases to influence the value of the dollar. If the value of the Canadian dollar is falling too quickly on foreign-exchange markets, the Bank will increase interest rates and increase its purchases of the dollar in order to boost its value. If the value of the Canadian dollar is increasing too rapidly, the Bank will lower interest rates and sell Canadian dollars. *Our present foreign-exchange system is flexible, yet the fluctuations are managed by the Bank of Canada.*

REVIEW

9.21 Explain how the Bank of Canada could participate in maintaining a fixed value for the Canadian dollar in foreign-exchange markets.

The International Monetary Fund

During the depression years of the 1930s, many countries **devalued** their currency in order to stimulate exports. A cheaper currency was aimed at making domestic products less expensive to foreigners, and imports more expensive. If exports increased and imports were reduced, then domestic employment would increase as well. With many countries devaluing their currency, international trade became a confusing business. The uncertainty about exchange rates reduced, rather than stimulated, foreign trade.

A devalued currency is one that has decreased in value in relation to another currency under the conditions of a fixed exchange rate system.

In 1944, an international conference was held in Bretton Woods, New Hampshire, in order to find a solution to trade problems. The conference proposed a system of fixed exchange rates aimed at providing stability in the international scene. The **International Monetary Fund (IMF)** was created to oversee the new exchange-rate system and to ensure that the system worked. The purposes of the IMF, as set out in Article 1 of the Articles of Agreement, are as follows:

The International Monetary Fund (IMF) is an international agency established in 1944 with the objective of stabilizing foreign-exchange rates.

a) to promote international monetary cooperation through a permanent institution which provides the machinery for consultation and collaboration on international monetary problems;

b) to facilitate the expansion and balanced growth of international trade, and to contribute thereby to the promotion and maintenance of high levels of employment and real income and to the development of the productive resources of all members as primary objectives of economic policy;

c) to promote exchange stability, to maintain orderly exchange arrangements among members, and to avoid competitive exchange depreciation;

d) to assist in the establishment of a multilateral system of payments in respect of current transactions between members and in the elimination of foreign-exchange restrictions which hamper the growth of world trade;

e) to give confidence to members by making the general resources of the Fund temporarily available to them under adequate safeguards, thus providing them with the opportunity to correct maladjustments in their balance of payments without resorting to measures destructive of national or international prosperity;

f) in accordance with the above, to shorten the duration and lessen the degree of disequilibrium in the international balances of payments of members.

An adjustable-peg system is a system of fixed foreign-exchange rates that can be adjusted if necessary.

The exchange-rate system was called an **adjustable-peg system**. Exchange rates were pegged at a certain par value, but could be adjusted when conditions warranted a change. Nations agreed to maintain a certain par value for their currency in terms of gold or U.S. dollars. The Canadian dollar was set at par with the U.S. dollar. The value of a country's foreign-exchange rate was allowed to vary by only one percent above or below the par value. If a country was experiencing persistent balance-of-payments problems, it could adjust its par value by 10 percent without approval from the IMF. Any larger adjustments required IMF approval. In 1949, Canada dropped its exchange rate to $.909 U.S.

Stabilization funds were established in support of the adjustable-peg system. Each country maintained a fund of domestic and foreign currencies and gold that allowed the country to purchase its currency on world markets to keep the exchange rate at the par value.

In order for the adjustable-peg system to work, it was necessary for each country to maintain a **stabilization fund**. This fund, affiliated with the nation's central bank, was comprised of domestic and foreign currencies and gold. The currencies in the fund were to be used to buy that nation's currency on world markets in order to keep the exchange rate at the par value. For example, if the value of the Canadian dollar fell below the par value, it would be necessary for the Bank of Canada to use some of the currencies in the stabilization fund to buy Canadian dollars in the foreign-exchange market. This action would raise the value of the dollar to its par value. In case a country's stabilization fund became too small, the IMF was empowered to make loans to countries with short-term balance-of-payments problems.

The need to maintain adequate reserves was a serious problem for the adjustable-peg system. If a country were experiencing a continuous balance of payments deficit, it would not have sufficient reserves with which to buy back its currency. It could borrow money from the IMF, but if the balance-of-payments deficit continued, it would soon run out of reserves again. It would be necessary to borrow more reserves from the IMF. Borrowing could not continue indefinitely, and eventually the country's currency would have to be devalued in order to correct the deficit.

The second problem with the adjustable-peg system was that an adequate scheme for adjusting exchange rates was not set up. A country's international balance of payments is constantly changing. Since the exchange rate of its currency is closely tied to the balance of payments, the exchange rate should also change. In actual fact, the exchange rate was rarely adjusted and the rates remained fixed. When the rates did change, they were usually adjusted by a very large amount.

The problems of the IMF and the system of adjustable pegs reached a climax in the early 1970s. Many countries began to put their currencies on a flexible-exchange system. The final straw that broke the adjustable-peg system came when the United States decided to float its dollar. From the beginning of the IMF, the U.S. dollar had been pegged to gold: it took

$35 U.S. to buy an ounce of gold. Today, the flexible exchange-rate system is predominant. However, foreign-exchange rates are not totally free to move according to the forces of demand and supply, as the central banks of most countries are taking steps to manage or influence the foreign-exchange value of their currency.

In recent years the focus of the IMF has changed. It is now a vital lending institution for debtor countries. Since the resources of the IMF are limited, the Fund may not actually lend money to countries in need of assistance but may help them gain access to other sources of finance. A precondition of receiving aid from the IMF is usually an agreement permitting the IMF to play a major role in the development of the country's monetary and fiscal policies. Whereas in the 1970s few conditions were attached to IMF financial assistance, the situation reversed in the 1990s. The Fund now takes an active role in the economic management of many of its developing-country members.

In late 1997, the IMF provided $35 billion (U.S.) in financial assistance to South Korea, Indonesia, and Thailand. The IMF financial assistance provided support for programs aimed at dealing with each country's economic problems, especially where the problems posed a threat to the international monetary system. Financial assistance for these Asian countries came not only from the IMF but from the World Bank, the Asian Development Bank, and other individual nations.

R E V I E W

9.22 What is a stabilization fund? Why is it necessary to the system of adjustable-pegged rates established by the IMF?

EVERYDAY ECONOMICS 9.4

Should Canada Adopt the U.S. Dollar?

In recent years, there has been much discussion about a common currency for the countries in North and South America. Panama and Ecuador have adopted the U.S. dollar as their currency. Argentina and Peru have strong ties to the U.S. dollar. Should Canada peg the Canadian dollar at a fixed value in relation to the U.S. dollar? Should Canada go a step further and abandon the Canadian dollar in favour of the U.S. dollar?

The opponents of adopting the U.S. dollar for Canada argue that Canada would lose political and economic sovereignty. They argue that the floating value of our currency in relation to the U.S. dollar has provided benefits to Canada. If we had pegged our currency at a specific rate in terms of a U.S. dollar, interest rates would have increased in recent years to maintain the fixed exchange rate. Higher interest rates would have hampered the increase in economic activity. They argue that Canadian exports were aided by the decline in the foreign-exchange value of the Canadian dollar during the Asian crisis of the 1990s. The assistance given to Canadian exports through a cheaper dollar has kept the unemployment rate lower than it would otherwise have been. A common currency would not mean a common market for workers. Canadians would not be free to cross the border to accept employment. In Canada at the present time, monetary policy is linked to the rate of inflation in Canada. If Canada adopted the U.S. dollar, monetary policy would be based on the rate of inflation in the United States.

The proponents of a single currency claim that the cheap Canadian dollar in relation to the U.S. dollar makes Canadian exporters lazy. That is, they can rely on a low value for the Canadian dollar to maintain sales to other countries. It is also stated that a low value for the Canadian dollar makes Canadian companies easy takeover targets for foreign multinational firms. A common currency would eliminate the costs associated with foreign-exchange trading and hedging since most of our trade is with the United States. Proponents of a common currency argue that a common currency would lower interest rates since the Bank of Canada would not be forced to raise interest rates in order to prop up the foreign-exchange value of the dollar. Lower interest rates would lead to a reduction in the cost of servicing the public debt. Lower rates would

provide an incentive for more business investment, leading to an increase in productivity, and would assist borrowers, especially homeowners. A common currency would reduce one of the barriers to more foreign investment in Canada. That is, if foreigners did not have to worry about foreign-exchange fluctuations, they would be more likely to invest in Canada.

How would a common currency come about? Clearly this has not been decided, since there is no official decision to adopt the U.S. dollar. One possibility is to disband the Bank of Canada and use the Bank's foreign-exchange reserves to purchase U.S. dollars and coins. All Canadian money would then be replaced with U.S. currency.

Questions

1. In order for a currency to function as a medium of exchange, it must be accepted by the population. Would Canadians accept the U.S. dollar as the official currency?

2. Would use of the U.S. dollar in Canada limit the impact of the government of Canada's fiscal policy? Explain.

3. Explain how a floating exchange rate for the Canadian dollar could reduce the number of unemployed workers in Canada. Why would the situation be different if Canadians used the U.S. dollar? Explain.

Summary

Canadians trade not only with each other but also with residents of other countries. For several reasons, international trade is treated as a separate topic in the study of economics. International trade involves currencies, languages, and customs that are different from our own, and trade is also heavily influenced by political considerations. Because workers are not free to cross national borders in the same way that they cross provincial borders in Canada, international economics has a different context from domestic economics.

Canada's major trading partner is the United States. Approximately 87 percent of our exports are sent to the United States, while about 67 percent of our imports are from that country. Our major export items are motor vehicles and automotive parts. Apart from these manufactured items, many of Canada's export items are primary products requiring very little processing in Canada. Our major import items are also motor vehicles and parts, machinery, and chemicals.

It is beneficial for all countries to participate in international trade. The law of comparative advantage proves that even in a situation where a country is efficient at producing all items, it can still benefit from trade. In spite of the benefits from trade, countries still erect barriers to imports. These barriers are in the form of tariffs or non-tariff barriers.

Recognition of the value of freer international trade led to the development of GATT, the Canada–United States Automobile Agreement, the FTA, and NAFTA.

A record of all financial transactions between residents of Canada and residents of other countries is called the balance of payments. Canada's deficit and surplus in international trade transactions are recorded in the balance of payments. Whether a deficit or surplus exists determines the change in the value of the Canadian dollar. If the balance of payments is in a deficit position, the exchange value of the Canadian dollar is falling. If a surplus exists, the value of the dollar is rising.

Questions for Review and Discussion

1. Many Canadian companies are subsidiaries of foreign companies. What impact do you believe this situation has on Canada's imports? Exports?
2. What effect would international trade have on a country's production-possibilities curve?
3. If Canada were divided into four regions—West, Ontario, Quebec, and East—with no free trade between the regions, what would happen to the standard of living of Canadians? Explain.
4. Identify the comparative advantage and the terms of trade in the following example. The numbers represent the production of one worker in one week.

PRODUCT	NORWAY	SWEDEN
Skis	20 pairs	10 pairs
Snow tires	16 tires	4 tires

5. In past years, Canada has asked the Japanese to put voluntary quotas on the shipment of automobiles to Canada. Who benefits from these quotas? Who loses due to the imposition of quotas?

6. In 1986 the United States placed countervailing duties on a number of Canadian lumber products. Why would American consumers want to pay more for Canadian lumber?

7. In 1986, in response to a U.S. countervailing duty on Canadian softwood lumber, the Canadian government imposed a 15-percent export tax on this product. The United States agreed to drop the countervailing duty. What are the advantages for Canada of an export tax? What are the disadvantages? What would have happened to the price of softwood lumber in the United States? in Canada?

8. Using a graph in your answer, show the impact of the Canadian government imposing a $1 per bottle tariff on imported wine.

9. The Canada–United States Automobile Agreement provided for free trade in automobiles between the two countries. Would you like to see a similar agreement extended to other products? Explain.

10. Replacement parts were not included in the automobile agreement. Why might Canadian parts manufacturers be more concerned about this than American parts manufacturers?

11. What impact does a decline in the foreign-exchange value of the Canadian dollar have on Canada's exports? on imports?

12. Explain the impact that higher interest rates in Canada may have on the foreign-exchange value of the Canadian dollar.

13. What are the advantages of flexible as opposed to fixed foreign-exchange rates?

14. The Toronto Blue Jays and the Montreal Expos pay their players' salaries in U.S. dollars. In order to protect their payroll costs from fluctuations in the foreign-exchange value of the Canadian dollar, the teams buy futures contracts in U.S. dollars. From the information provided on futures contracts in Chapter 2, explain how buying futures contracts in foreign currencies works.

15. In April 2003, the World Health Organization warned travellers not to go to Toronto because of the SARS outbreak. Use a graph to show and discuss the impact of this announcement on the foreign-exchange value of the Canadian dollar.

16. In 2003, Canada imposed new tariffs on imported steel. Why would auto parts companies be opposed to tariffs on imported steel? Would any other groups in Canada be opposed to these tariffs? Explain.

Suggested Readings

Creameans, John E., Ed. *Handbook of North American Industry: NAFTA and the Economies of Member Nations.* First Edition. Lanham, MD: Bernan Press, 1998. An excellent source of material on NAFTA and on the industrial composition of Canada, the United States, and Mexico.

Crosbie, John C. *No Holds Barred: My Life in Politics.* Toronto: McClelland & Stewart Inc., 1997. John Crosbie's memoirs include a discussion about the negotiations surrounding the Free Trade Agreement.

Curtis, Christopher. "The Free-Trade Free-for-all." *Horizon Canada* 7, no. 83 (1986): 1969–77. This is the story of the 1911 federal election fought on the issue of free trade with the United States.

Globerman, Steven, and Michael Walker, Eds. *Assessing NAFTA: A Trinational Analysis.* Vancouver: The Fraser Institute, 1993. An assessment of NAFTA examining environmental provisions, the dispute settlement mechanism, the impact on the financial sector, and the implications for other areas of the economy.

Rabbior, Gary. *The Canadian Economy: Adjusting to Global Change.* Toronto: Canadian Foundation for Economic Education, 1990. This 80-page publication provides trade data as well as a discussion of Canadian trade relationships.

Selected Websites

www.imf.org The website for the International Monetary Fund, with links to a database that includes financial statistics and balance of payments.

www.oecd.org The website for the Organization for Economic Co-operation and Development. Canada is a member of this organization.

www.wto.org The site for the World Trade Organization. Information is available on trade topics, dispute settlement, press releases, and misconceptions about the WTO. The site provides links to trade data for member nations.

www.ftaa-alca.org The website for the Free Trade Association of the Americas.

www.intracen.org The website for the International Trade Centre, which is a technical cooperation agency between the UN and the WTO. The site contains data on trade for many countries.

www.sice.oas.org This site provides trade information for the Organization of American States.

www.fin.gc.ca/LINKS/ITFE.html This site has a list of many trade-related links.

www.dfait-maeci.gc.ca The website for Canada's Department of Foreign Affairs and International Trade.

Industrial Organization in Canada

Key Terms

microeconomics
sole proprietorship
partnership
corporations
perfect competition
monopoly
oligopoly
many differentiated sellers
concentration
foreign ownership

Chapter Objectives

After successfully completing this chapter, you will be able to:

- differentiate among the types of business ownership
- describe the characteristics of the competitive groupings
- define concentration ratios
- discuss the impact of foreign investment on the Canadian economy

Core Concept Building

Different firms face different types of competition. Economists have summarized the various competitive situations into four categories: perfect competition; monopoly; oligopoly; and many differentiated sellers. You will need to understand the differences between these types of competition in order to appreciate Chapters 12 and 13.

SASKPOWER

The sale of electricity in Saskatchewan in the 1920s was undertaken by many small, independent private companies. There were 119 generating stations supplying approximately 44 000 customers. The eight largest generating stations supplied almost 32 000 customers, leaving 111 generating stations serving an average of 108 customers each. Not everyone could get electricity and the prices varied greatly. Operating costs were high for generating stations located in isolated areas of the province. High operating costs led to high prices and limited service.

In 1929, the government of Saskatchewan established the Saskatchewan Power Commission to institute and operate a provincial power system under public control and, at the same time, to regulate the production and transmission of electricity by private and municipally operated generating stations. The commission began purchasing private and municipal generating stations and limited the expansion of existing private companies. At the end of its first year in operation, the commission added 1852 kilometres of transmission and distribution lines. In some situations, electricity was purchased from privately owned plants. The commission provided increased electrical service to the province during the 1930s, and during the Second World War focused on supplying electricity to military camps and air training fields. Communities located close to military bases benefited from the greater availability of electricity.

By 1948, the commission owned 35 generating stations and had more than 8800 kilometres of transmission lines. More than 1500 farms were being provided with electricity compared to 10 in 1929. To ensure that the provision of electricity was improved to rural areas, the government converted the commission to a Crown corporation in 1950. The name became SaskPower. Its mandate was to bring the same service to rural residents as was being received by urban residents. By 1961, rural electrification was complete. By this time, 58 000 farms were receiving electricity through SaskPower transmission lines.

SaskPower built a number of thermal power stations and hydroelectric stations. In 1985, SaskPower became the first utility to control a hydroelectric plant by satellite. When natural gas was discovered in western Saskatchewan, SaskPower became a natural-gas utility and built a pipeline and distribution system. In 1988, another Crown corporation, SaskEnergy, was given responsibility for natural-gas energy.

The website for SaskPower is **www. saskpower.com**.

Introduction to Microeconomics

The first part of this textbook introduced the idea of economic decision-making. It concentrated on the decisions that must be made by Canadians regarding the use of their resources. The issues discussed earlier were those affecting the entire country: unemployment, inflation, economic growth, money and banking, and international trade. That area of economics is called macroeconomics, which is derived from the Greek word "macro," meaning large. In this part of the book, we switch to economic decision-making on a smaller scale. We will discuss the area of **microeconomics**, which emphasizes smaller decision-making units, such as business firms and individual consumers and workers. The term microeconomics is derived from the Greek word *micro*, meaning small.

Types of Business Enterprises

Discussions in the text thus far have made reference to business without defining what we mean by the term. In the Canadian economy, types of businesses vary, ranging from a corner convenience store to a telephone company, from a farmer to an automobile manufacturer, from a self-employed barber to a mining company.

Sole proprietorship: **Sole proprietorships** are the simplest form of business enterprise and are well suited to the small business. Examples of proprietorships are businesses run by doctors, dentists, store owners, farmers, insurance agents, restaurateurs, painters, garage operators, and other self-employed people. Apart from its simplicity, the sole proprietorship has several other advantages. This type of business has no separate existence in legal terms, and all the income earned by the business goes to the single owner. The management of the business is flexible, since the owner need not consult with anyone else on business decisions.

Proprietorships have certain disadvantages as well. First, the owner is liable for the business, and personal assets may have to be used to meet business obligations. Second, the amount of money available to the business is limited to what the owner can provide or borrow. Finally, the owner does not necessarily have the expertise to solve all the problems that may arise in the course of trying to operate a business. If the owner is not skilled in various aspects of business, such as accounting, finance, or marketing, and cannot employ extra people who are skilled to assist in these matters, the business may well fail.

Partnerships: **Partnerships** are similar to proprietorships except that there is more than one owner. Professionals such as accountants and lawyers often use partnerships as a form of business enterprise. The Income Tax Act does not recognize the existence of partnerships, and each partner is taxed individually on the basis of his or her income.

With a partnership, the skills of a number of people are brought into the business. The partnership will also be able to attract more financial resources than a sole proprietorship. It may be easier for a partnership to get a loan from the bank. Liability under a partnership must be determined by

Microeconomics is the area of economics that emphasizes smaller decision-making units, such as business firms, consumers, and workers.

Sole proprietorship is the simplest form of business organization with one owner, usually a small business.

A partnership is a form of business enterprise in which two or more persons own and operate the business firm and are liable for its debts.

the partners involved. It may be that one partner is liable for something that another partner did. Partnerships cannot sue or be sued, so any legal action will have to be undertaken in the name of (or against) one of the partners. Decision-making may take longer in a partnership than in a sole proprietorship, since all partners will want to have their say.

Corporations: **Corporations** are created in Canada only by permission of the government. Both federal and provincial governments have the legal authority to grant charters to corporations. If the business is to be conducted solely within one province, a provincial charter will suffice. If the corporation is formed under a federal charter, it can do business in any part of the country.

The owners of the corporation are referred to as the *shareholders.* They are entitled to attend corporation meetings and share in corporation profits by receiving dividends.

There are several advantages to the corporate form of business enterprise. For one thing, it is easier to acquire large amounts of money than in other forms of business. It addition, lawsuits can be undertaken in the corporation's name, which means that individual shareholders are not responsible for the corporation liabilities. Finally, the death of one of the shareholders does not end the corporation.

The main disadvantage of the corporation lies in the rules and regulations that have to be followed. This makes it a more expensive form of business enterprise. Also, depending on earnings, the level of taxation on corporation income may be quite high. Finally, the management complexities of many corporations slow down decision-making.

Crown corporation: All levels of government in Canada make use of Crown, or government-owned, corporations. There are in excess of 300 Crown corporations at the federal government level and more than 100 at the provincial government level. The shares of Crown corporations are owned by the government, and the directors are appointed by the Governor-in-Council. These corporations are set up with both economic and social objectives in mind. Some control the distribution of certain products; others are used to obtain financing for capital projects.

Crown corporations at the federal government level are divided into three main categories based on their administration and their method of financing. *Departmental corporations* are similar to government departments and perform a variety of administrative, regulatory, and supervisory functions. Most of the employees of these Crown corporations are civil servants; each corporation reports annually to a cabinet minister who is directly responsible to Parliament. Examples of departmental corporations are the National Research Council, the Atomic Energy Control Board, the

A corporation is a business organization created by law that is owned by its shareholders.

Canada Employment Insurance Commission, and the Canadian Polar Commission.

Agency corporations perform a variety of commercial and management functions for the government. They hire their own employees, as a private corporation would. Agency corporations have more financial and administrative independence from government than do departmental corporations. Although their budgets are separate from general department budgets, they must be approved by the appropriate Cabinet minister, the president of the Treasury Board, and Parliament. They get money from parliamentary appropriation, statutory grants, and operational income. Examples of agency corporations are the Canada Deposit Insurance Corporation, Canada Mortgage and Housing Corporation, Farm Credit Corporation, the National Capital Commission, and the National Gallery of Canada.

Corporations in the final category, *proprietary corporations,* are not associated with any government department. Many of these corporations are in direct competition with privately owned companies, and they are expected to finance themselves from their operating revenue. Unlike private companies, however, any deficits that these corporations may have will likely be covered by the taxpayer. Examples are the Royal Canadian Mint and Canada Post.

Several other Crown corporations have been established by special legislation and do not fall into any of the above categories. These corporations perform certain functions that require independence from government control and include the Bank of Canada, the Canadian Wheat Board, the Canadian Broadcasting Corporation, and the Canada Council. In addition to Crown corporations, the federal government has partial ownership in a number of corporations, such as Petro-Canada Limited.

Crown corporations get funding by borrowing money from the government, by parliamentary appropriations, or by borrowing in the money market. The capital budgets for Crown corporations must be approved by the Cabinet, since these corporations are owned by the government.

Provincial and local governments also make use of Crown corporations to achieve their goals. The first major Crown corporation was created in Ontario in 1906 to generate and distribute electricity. Electric utilities are the largest Crown corporations and supply energy in most provinces. All provinces except Nova Scotia have a Crown corporation responsible for developing and operating public housing. All provinces with the exception of Alberta have commissions responsible for the distribution and sale of liquor. Municipal corporations are usually set up to operate water systems, transit systems, and housing authorities.

There are large differences in the structure of these types of businesses, but for our purposes the structure of the individual business is not as important as the *market power* that it possesses. Market power is represented by the ability of the business to control the price of the product.

> ## REVIEW
>
> **10.1** What are the advantages of a partnership in comparison to a sole proprietorship? What are some disadvantages?
>
> **10.2** Which type of Crown corporation is most similar to a privately owned corporation. Why?

Types of Competition

The type of competition that a firm faces will influence the price that is charged for the product. It will also affect the amount of the product available on the market. Grouping Canadian industries according to four competitive models allows for a clearer discussion on the nature of competition faced by businesses in Canada. These groupings are established for discussion purposes only, and it is not expected that a certain industry will be exactly described by the characteristics of the group with which it is associated. The models are intended as aids in analyzing the *price and quantity decisions* of business firms.

The four competitive models are *perfect competition, monopoly, oligopoly,* and *many differentiated sellers.* Each model is reviewed under the following headings:

a) the number of firms in the industry
b) the type of product
c) ease of entry into the industry
d) the firm's control over price
e) the firm's use of non-price competition

Perfect Competition

In industries characterized by **perfect competition**, there are many firms, each one producing only a small percentage of the total output. With a large number of firms, no individual firm has any control over the price of its product and must accept the *market price.* The firm's control over the price of its product is further reduced by the fact that each firm produces an identical product. It is not possible to identify one firm's products from among the products of other firms in the industry. This eliminates the need for non-price competition, such as advertising.

Perfect competition **is a competitive situation in which there are many thousands of firms, each selling an identical product.**

An important aspect of perfectly competitive industries is the relative ease with which new firms are able to enter the industry. Entrance into any industry is going to require a certain amount of money; however, in perfect competition, the financial barriers to entry are less restrictive than in other industries. There are virtually no other barriers to entry.

Entry into an industry is considered easy when certain conditions exist. Established firms must have no price advantage or other advantages when purchasing the necessary resources for production. Further, there can be no advantages for established firms resulting from buyer preference for brand-name products. Finally, it is relatively easy to enter an industry when the production-cost advantages that come from mass production are negligible.

Canadian agriculture is an industry closely associated with perfect competition, with many farmers each producing an identical product. That is, you cannot tell one farmer's beans from another's. Entry into the agricultural business can be costly for new farmers, the major expense being the price of good farmland. It is easier for existing farmers to enter another line of agriculture than it is for new farmers to enter the industry. For example, once a farmer owns the land, he or she can switch from one crop to another, depending on market conditions. In some areas of agriculture, marketing boards restrict the entry of new firms; therefore, these products cannot be considered perfectly competitive. A detailed discussion of Canadian agriculture is presented in Chapter 12.

Monopoly

A monopoly occurs when only one seller of a good or service exists in a given industry.

Monopoly is the extreme opposite of perfect competition. In a monopoly industry there is only one firm. Since it is the only company in the industry, it has control over the price of the product. Industries remain in a monopoly position because there are significant barriers to the entry of new firms.

Government is normally involved in monopolies. Government agencies regulate the pricing practices of telephone, natural gas, and cable television companies. Monopolies like public utilities and the post office are operated by the government itself.

Even though there is only one firm in a monopoly, that firm still may have competition. It competes with all other industries for the consumer dollar. The monopoly also faces competition from close substitutes. For example, natural gas companies have been granted monopolies in specific geographic areas. These companies may be the only ones supplying natural gas in the area, but people do not have to heat their homes with natural gas, because good substitutes are available.

Monopolies do not engage in a great deal of advertising. The advertising done by monopolies is mainly of an informative or public-relations nature. For example, the Bell Telephone System, a monopoly in local telephone service, has advertisements focusing on the quality of telephone service provided to Canadians. One such ad ends with the statement "Bell Canada—one of the best anywhere."

Oligopoly

In an **oligopoly,** there are a few firms. Unfortunately, it is difficult to determine the exact number that makes up "a few." The number of firms is small enough that each firm must consider the reaction of the others when it changes its price. This is referred to as *mutual interdependence.*

The product in an oligopolistic industry can be identical or differentiated. When products are classified as identical, there are no distinguishing characteristics of each product that would allow the manufacturer of the product to be identified. Steel is an example of an identical product. In contrast, differentiated products are readily identified by the manufacturer. Examples of differentiated products in an oligopolistic setting are automobiles, beer, and Canadian chartered banks.

The reason why there are only a few firms in the industry is that barriers limit the entry of new firms. These barriers include such things as brand names and the advantages of large-scale production. Even though barriers exist, they are not as strong as in a monopoly and the entry of new firms is not blocked completely.

Firms in oligopolistic industries use various types of *non-price competition.* These include advertising, sales promotion, product quality, product warranties, and service.

> An oligopoly is a competitive situation characterized by an industry that is comprised of only a few firms.

Many Differentiated Sellers

The competitive group called **many differentiated sellers** is similar in some respects to perfect competition. There are a large number of sellers in the same industry and entry into the industry is relatively easy. However, there are significant differences in relation to the model of perfect competition. First, the products are not identical. It is possible to distinguish the products of one seller from another. The differences may be in terms of product quality, brand name, product design, and so on. Second, each firm in the industry has some control over the price of the product. Finally, firms in this competitive structure make extensive use of non-price competition, especially *advertising.* Through advertising, individual firms hope to differentiate their product from that of their competitors. The more its product is different, the more control that the firm has over the price that it charges.

> Many differentiated sellers describes a competitive situation with many sellers of a similar, but slightly different, product.

Examples of many differentiated sellers are numerous. They include men's and women's clothing, retail stores, restaurants, laundries, barbers and hairdressers, and similar business operations.

REVIEW

10.3 Explain the difference between perfect competition and many differentiated sellers.

10.4 Why would industries characterized by oligopoly and many differentiated sellers use non-price competition like advertising, whereas perfect competitors would not?

10.5 Under what types of competitive structure would you classify the record industry, the furniture industry, and the cable television industry?

Qualifications to Competitive Groupings

The competitive categories that we have defined are meant to serve only as a broad outline. Under certain conditions an industry may be classified as an oligopoly and under other circumstances it may be a monopoly. In many instances, grocery stores are in an oligopolistic situation. In a small town with one grocery store, however, a monopoly situation exists. The competitive nature of an industry may also change over time. For example, at one time there were many more automobile manufacturers than there are today. Let us consider these qualifications further.

Geographic

Depending on geographic boundaries, the competitive grouping of an industry may change. We do not normally consider restaurants and gas stations to be monopolies, yet in a rural area or a small town, a restaurant may well be the only one around. In this situation, the restaurant will behave more like a monopoly than a firm under the conditions of many differentiated sellers. If there are two restaurants, they will act like firms in an oligopolistic setting. Therefore, geographic boundaries have to be taken into consideration when discussing the nature of competition.

International Competition

Imports are an important aspect of many industries. In order to assess the competitive nature of the kinds of industries we've been talking about, foreign companies must be taken into consideration. During the 1960s, the automobile industry was dominated by General Motors, Ford, and Chrysler. Imports have since gained a significant share of the North American market. When General Motors is assessing the competition, it has to consider more firms than just Ford or Chrysler. It is now possible for consumers to purchase cars made in Japan, Britain, Germany, France, and other countries. This means more competition for all the North American automobile manufacturers.

Inter-Industry Competition

All firms, regardless of the kind of industry, are in competition for the consumer's dollar. Not only must they consider other competitors in the same industry, but also they have to take into account all other firms vying for consumer attention. There may only be a few companies manufacturing home computers, yet these products have to compete with thousands of other products for sales.

EVERYDAY ECONOMICS 10.1

The Canadian Wheat Board

In recent years the most controversial Crown corporation has been the Canadian Wheat Board (CWB). Established in 1935, the board is the sole legal marketer of wheat in Canada. The CWB is the 33rd largest firm in Canada and is Canada's fifth largest exporter. What was the rationale for selling wheat through the board? It was assumed that the board would be a counterbalance to large national and international grain companies that were looking to purchase wheat. During the Second World War, the board was given the exclusive authority to buy western grain and sell it to the United Kingdom at favourable prices. The selling of wheat at favourable prices was part of Canada's war policy.

The board buys the grain directly from the farmers and then sells it where it can get the highest price. In effect, the CWB is both a *monopoly* (single seller) and a *monopsony* (single buyer). Interestingly, wheat sold for domestic animal consumption can be sold outside the board, but wheat for domestic human consumption cannot.

Farmers are obligated to sell their wheat to the board, and this is the source of the controversy. Should farmers be allowed to sell their wheat to whomever they wish? At one time, the CWB was the single buyer and single seller of wheat, barley, and oats. Farmers are no longer obligated to sell their oats to the board. Since the marketing of oats was freed from the CWB, the farm-gate price of oats has risen compared to the U.S. price and marketing costs have fallen. There have also been discussions about removing barley from the CWB.

Some studies have concluded that the CWB has a beneficial impact on the incomes of wheat farmers as a result of its dominant position in world grain markets. Nonetheless, some farmers want the freedom to sell their crops to whomever they wish.

Farm groups in the United States have argued that the Canadian Wheat Board's monopoly in selling the wheat of Canadian farmers represents an unfair trade practice.

The board is making some changes. In 1998, the board switched from government control to farmer control. That is, of the 15-member board, 10 members are elected by farmers. In 2000, the board introduced some flexibility in pricing options. Farmers can opt for a fixed return before the beginning of the crop year by taking a contract based on the U.S. future price. In the futures market, buyers and sellers get together to establish a price for a delivery date sometime in the future. Farmers who do not select the fixed-price option can follow the board's current practice of providing farmers with a price for their wheat based on the price that the board gets when it sells the wheat.

Questions

1. Does the CWB represent a monopoly in international grain markets? Explain.
2. Farmers who grow corn and other crops can sell to whomever they wish. Why are wheat growers in a different legal position?
3. Would it be possible for a Canadian Automotive Board to operate in a manner similar to the Canadian Wheat Board? Explain.

In addition, products in different industries may be substitutes for each other. For example, companies that sell natural gas have a monopoly in a certain region. Yet natural gas is not the only available source of home heat: wood, oil, and electricity are different industries but acceptable substitutes. The post office has a monopoly of postal service in Canada, yet this is not the only form of communication available to the consumer. Airlines must compete with other modes of transportation including trains, buses, and automobiles. There may be only a handful of large grocery-store chains, but the consumer does not have to purchase food at one of the chain stores.

Food can be purchased at convenience stores, bulk-food stores, farmers' markets, and so on. Restaurants also provide competition for grocery stores. Therefore, the analysis of competition within an industry has to take into consideration the inter-industry competition.

Technological Change

Over time, the competitive nature of an industry is likely to change. Technological advances cause change to take place and can result in brand-new industries as well as in changes to existing industries. Pocket and "credit-card" calculators have replaced larger, less-sophisticated calculating equipment. Foreign expertise in the production of small cars has permitted foreign automobile manufacturers to make great progress in the North American market. Cotton and wool now share a market with a variety of synthetic fibres. Companies are now selling kits with which you can assemble your own computer. Monopolies and oligopolies may not remain that way forever unless the barriers to the entry of new firms are substantial.

REVIEW

10.6 Why may the nature of competition change as a result of techno-logical improvements?

10.7 Why must geography be considered when determining types of competition?

10.8 Welcome to the 9-Hints Competition Game: decide which type of competition applies to a given situation.

Measures of Concentration

In attempting to categorize industries into one of four competitive types, the measure of competition that we used was the number of firms in the industry. If there was only one firm, the industry was a monopoly. If there were a few firms in the industry, it was an oligopoly, and so on. The number of firms in an industry is not a precise measure of competition. It tells us nothing about either the size of the firms in the industry or the percentage of the industry's business each firm commands. Knowing that there were 11 breweries in Canada in 1985 tells us something about the competition in that industry at the time. Knowing that four of those firms controlled 98 percent of the business tells us more about the competitive nature of the industry.

Economists have developed measures of concentration in order to determine the *competitive nature* of an industry. **Concentration** refers to the degree to which business activity in an industry is dominated by a few firms. One measure of concentration is the proportion of total *industry sales* or output that can be attributed to the industry's four largest firms.

Concentration ratios improve our knowledge of the competitive conditions in certain industries. Yet these ratios do have their shortcomings. The ratios published by Statistics Canada do not contain information on foreign suppliers who compete in the Canadian market. As pointed out in Chapter 9, imports are an important part of certain industries. When imports are not included in concentration ratios, industries will appear to be more concentrated than they actually are.

In addition, concentration figures refer only to national markets, counting the number of firms on a Canada-wide basis. For some industries, it may be more appropriate to calculate regional or local concentration ratios. *Transportation costs* may make it impractical for firms in one part of Canada to compete with firms thousands of kilometers away. Transportation costs

The measure of concentration within an industry indicates the degree to which the industry is dominated by a few firms.

in many industries are significant. In the cement industry, for example, it has been estimated that transportation costs account for more than 34 percent of every dollar of sales. Other industries in which transportation costs are significant are glass bottles, beer, petroleum products, and steel. If transportation costs restrict competition, then concentration measures on a regional or local basis will be higher than on a national basis. Unfortunately, concentration measures on a regional basis are not readily available.

Relying on concentration ratios as a measure of the competitive nature of an industry is complicated by the difficulty in defining an industry. For example, should the provision of energy be considered an industry, or should the various forms of energy—hydroelectric, atomic, natural gas, oil, solar—each be considered to be an industry? In the fast-food market, should all fast-food establishments be lumped together in the same industry, or should each type of fast food constitute its own industry? In some industries, products may be very similar; in other industries, there may be great differentiation in products. The degree of product differentiation impacts on competition.

A further criticism of the concentration ratios refers to the method by which the data were collected. The data on value of shipments are gathered at the individual plant or factory level and all output at the plant is allocated to one industry. If 80 percent of the output at a certain factory was for industry A and the remaining 20 percent of the plant's output was for industry B, the total output of the plant would be listed under industry A. This overstates the value of shipments for industry A and understates the value of shipments for industry B.

If we are to interpret correctly the competitive nature of an industry, we must know whether the industry is expanding or contracting. If the industry is expanding, then it is likely to become more competitive in the future, and increased competition will cause the measure of concentration to decrease. If the industry is contracting, it will become less competitive and concentration measures will increase. Whether or not an industry becomes more competitive depends on the *barriers to entry* for new firms. If major barriers are present, the industry is not likely to become more competitive in the future. Barriers can take several forms. Established firms may be able to take advantage of large-scale production and produce at a lower cost. They may also be able to get a discount if materials are purchased in large quantities. Existing companies may also have an advantage in terms of buyer preference (people prefer to buy a product with which they are familiar).

R E V I E W

10.9   What do we mean by industry concentration?

10.10 Why is the number of firms in an industry not a sufficient measure of the competition that exists in an industry?

Foreign Ownership of Canadian Industry

A unique aspect of Canadian industry is the large degree of **foreign ownership**. The largest company in Canada, General Motors, is completely owned by the parent company in the United States. Of the 50 largest industrial companies in Canada, 25 have some degree of foreign ownership. Canadian dependence on foreign capital is not a recent occurrence, as Canada has traditionally relied on foreigners for much of its investment. The British initially supplied most of the foreign investment. In 1900, approximately 85 percent of foreign investment in Canada came from the United Kingdom. The situation has now changed; the major source of foreign investment in Canada is now the United States, which accounts for approximately 70 percent of the direct foreign investment in this country.

> **Foreign ownership** occurs when foreign residents invest in Canadian assets and financial securities.

Foreign investment in Canada is divided into two categories. *Foreign direct investment* implies managerial control of a business by persons in a foreign country. Under this type of investment, residents abroad will own the factory or other assets established in Canada. *Foreign portfolio investment* refers to the ownership of debt instruments, such as loans and debentures. It may also apply to minority holdings of shares in Canadian companies. Portfolio investment is not accompanied by any managerial control.

This section discusses the benefits and costs of foreign investment in Canada. Reference will be to direct investment where control over business assets in Canada is exercised by persons in another country.

What are the benefits of foreign investment in Canada? They can be summarized as follows:

outward orientation: Foreign-controlled companies tend to be more oriented to world markets than Canadian-owned firms.

market access: Foreign-owned companies locate in Canada in order to have access to the United States and Mexican markets. Other companies make use of Canada's natural resources to make products here for their home market. The increased exports that result from foreign-owned firms strengthen the foreign-exchange value of the Canadian dollar.

access to capital: Foreign-owned firms bring investment dollars to Canada. This investment may not otherwise be undertaken.

technology transfer: Canadian firms gain access to innovative technologies through foreign firms investing in Canada.

research and development: Numerous examples exist of foreign-controlled companies expanding their research capabilities in Canada.

employment: It is estimated that one-tenth of all jobs in Canada are directly dependent on foreign investment.

increased competition: Foreign-owned companies operating in Canada provide competition for Canadian-controlled companies. More competition results in lower prices and better-quality products. Canadian-owned firms are forced to adopt the latest technology and management techniques in order to stay competitive.

improved productivity: There is a direct relationship between foreign ownership and improvements in technology. These improvements lead to lower prices and higher wages.

The benefits of foreign investment, however, are accompanied by certain costs. Those who argue against foreign ownership claim that it results in lower productivity for Canadian workers. They argue that branch plants are not usually large enough to achieve the cost advantages associated with mass production. With the increased competition, Canadian companies also remain small and unable to achieve production economies. Others argue that foreign investment does not cause GDP to increase. If foreign investment is simply a substitute for the Canadian investment that would have taken place, the total level of investment spending, and hence GDP, is not any higher.

Foreign-owned companies may be subjected to some restrictions imposed by their parent country. Some subsidiaries of foreign companies located in Canada are not permitted to export to certain countries. The United States has often forbidden subsidiaries of American companies to sell products to countries it considers to be enemies of the United States. This extraterritoriality of American law was more of a problem in the past than it is now, but problems like these led to the development of the Committee for an Independent Canada in the early 1970s. This non-political committee was interested in restricting the foreign ownership of Canadian industry. Pressure by this committee and others resulted in the formation by the federal government in 1974 of the Foreign Investment Review Agency (FIRA). FIRA had the authority to approve or reject new foreign investment in Canada and foreign purchases of Canadian companies. Foreign investment in Canada had to represent a significant benefit to Canada in order to be approved.

Although foreign investment continued to flow into Canada after FIRA was established, some new investment was discouraged. A survey undertaken in 1983 by the Conference Board of Canada revealed that some foreigners did not invest in Canada because of the added costs, uncertainty, secrecy, and long delays associated with the FIRA process. Other potential investors were unhappy with the political interference in relation to the decision on new investment. They were also worried that in the future more restrictive changes would appear in Canada's legislation regarding foreign ownership and investment. Foreign dissatisfaction with FIRA and an economic recession in Canada led the Progressive Conservative government to scrap FIRA when it came to power in 1984. FIRA was replaced by a new agency, Investment Canada, whose mandate was to attract new investment to Canada.

Foreign subsidiaries are often set up to serve the Canadian market only. The subsidiary is not established for purposes of exporting to other countries. If subsidiaries of foreign firms are not exporting, they will not improve our international balance of payments. Canada is a country that relies on foreign trade, especially exports. Subsidiary companies may be established only in order to perform certain functions. Very little product research and development is done by the subsidiary. This function is usually handled by the parent company. With a limited range of activities performed in Canada, there is only a limited range of jobs available. The more skilled jobs are likely to remain with the parent company. Canada has a good supply of educated and skilled workers and needs more employment opportunities than subsidiary companies are often able to provide.

Foreign ownership of many of our resource industries has created a unique problem. These resources are often exported to the parent country to be used in manufacturing. As a result, Canada has become a major exporter of raw materials but has not developed a strong manufacturing sector geared toward using these resources. Evidence of this was shown in Chapter 9, where Canada's trade statistics were discussed.

Foreign investment in Canada has provided Canadians with a variety of benefits and costs, which vary according to economic conditions. When the economy is good and employment is up, concerns about the ownership of our industry are more abundant. When the level of unemployment is high, and jobs are scarce, there is less concern over who owns the companies that provide employment. Tables 10.1 and 10.2 show the amount of direct investment in Canada by country and industry for 2001.

Table 10.1 *Foreign direct investment in Canada from abroad by country, 2001*

COUNTRY	DIRECT INVESTMENT ($ MILLIONS)	PERCENTAGE
United States	214 960	72.2
United Kingdom	24 713	5.9
Japan	8 285	2.7
Other EU countries	51 551	12.9
Other OECD countries	12 469	3.2
All other countries	8 953	3.1
Total	320 931	100.0

SOURCE: Adapted from the Statistics Canada publication *Canada's International Investment Position*, 2001, Catalogue 67-202, March 2002, page 64.

Table 10.2 *Foreign direct investment in Canada from abroad by industry, 2001*

INDUSTRY	DIRECT INVESTMENT ($ MILLIONS)	PERCENTAGE
Finance and insurance	45 515	20.9
Energy and metallic minerals	67 232	16.3
Machinery and transportation equipment	47 917	11.3
Services and retailing	26 031	8.1
Wood and paper	18 301	7.7
Other industries	115 935	35.7
Total	320 931	100.0

SOURCE: Adapted from the Statistics Canada publication *Canada's International Investment Position*, 2001, Catalogue 67-202, March 2002, page 64.

A 1994 study on the impact of multinationals by Investment Canada concluded that foreign-owned manufacturers operating in Canada are more productive and more export-oriented than Canadian manufacturers. Multinationals added an average of 19 percent more value to the economy per employee and were 73 percent more likely to export. The study concluded that Canada benefits from the technology and management techniques brought to the Canadian subsidiary. The biggest gaps between

Canadian and foreign-owned manufacturers occurred in industries where high tariffs made import competition difficult.

Much of the discussion about foreign investment centres on foreign investment in Canada. Canadians also invest in other nations. In most years the amount of direct foreign investment coming into Canada has exceeded the direct investment by Canadians in other countries. Since 1996, the reverse is true: Canadians have been investing more in foreign countries than foreigners have been investing in Canada (see Figure 10.1).

REVIEW

10.11 List some of the benefits and costs of foreign investment in Canada.

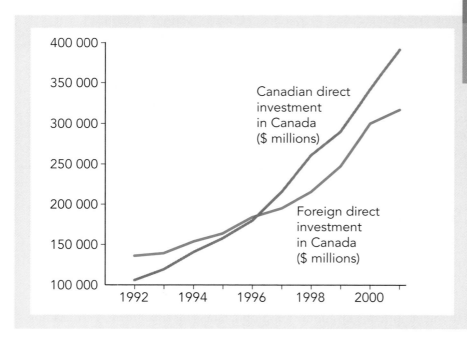

Figure 10.1

Foreign direct investment in Canada and Canadian direct investment abroad, 1992–2001

Source: Adapted from the Statistics Canada publication *Canada's International Investment Position*, 1999, Catalogue 67-202, March 2000, pp 30, 40.

Foreign Ownership of Canadian Newspapers

The ownership of Canada's newspapers is concentrated in a very few companies. The main players in the newspaper business include Thomson Publishing, Hollinger, Quebecor, and Torstar. The newspapers of one company, Hollinger, account for about 45 percent of newspaper circulation in the country. Why is this industry so concentrated?

One reason for the high concentration of ownership involves the high fixed costs that are present in the industry—costs that do not vary with the number of newspapers produced. Every company needs presses, journalists, and so on. Papers with a larger circulation are able to spread these fixed costs over a greater number of papers.

Another reason for the high concentration is the federal government's restriction upon foreign ownership of newspapers. Foreign companies can own up to 25 percent of a Canadian newspaper without any restrictions being placed on the paper. If foreign ownership exceeds this amount, advertisers who advertise in the newspaper will not be able to deduct their advertising expense as a business cost. This regulation is a strong disincentive to advertise in foreign-owned newspapers. Since newspapers rely heavily on advertising revenue, the regulation makes foreign ownership of a Canadian newspaper almost an impossibility.

Two newspaper companies announced their desire to sell some of their Canadian daily papers. Hollinger wants to sell most of its community newspapers and some of its larger metropolitan newspapers. Thomson wants to sell all of its newspapers with the exception of *The Globe and Mail*. With the restriction on foreign ownership in place, the number of potential buyers is reduced.

Questions

1. Canadian companies own newspapers in the United States and other countries. Should foreign companies be permitted to operate newspapers in Canada without restriction?
2. Canada's heritage minister has stated that newspapers are a cornerstone of our cultural industry. Do you agree?
3. Could restrictions on foreign ownership of newspapers lead to more monopolies in the newspaper business? Explain.

Summary

Microeconomics is a section of economics that studies the decision-making process of business firms and individuals. There are various types of business firms operating in Canada. Sole proprietorship is the simplest form of business enterprise and is well-suited to the small firm. Partnerships are similar to sole proprietorships in their appropriateness for small firms. Partnerships differ from sole proprietorships in that they have more than one owner. The corporation is a business firm owned by shareholders. It is suitable for businesses of all sizes, but is especially appropriate for large firms. Canada also has a significant number of Crown corporations. These corporations are divided into three categories, depending on their financial and reporting structure. Proprietary Crown corporations compete directly with corporations in the private sector.

From an economic point of view, the ownership of the business firm is not as important as the competition that the firm faces. The nature of the competition has a direct impact on the decisions made by the firm. Four competitive models are discussed in this chapter. In perfect competition, there are many sellers, each producing an identical product. Monopolies are characterized by one seller, and oligopolies have a few sellers. In the final type of competition there are many sellers of similar but differentiated products.

Concentration refers to the degree to which business activity in an industry is dominated by a few firms. Concentration measures are described in terms of the percentage of the total business activity in an industry that is undertaken by the four largest firms. Those industries having a high percentage of business activity centred on four firms are described as highly concentrated. For example, in the tobacco-products industry, more than 99 percent of the value of all shipments is concentrated in the four largest firms.

Canadian industry is characterized by a high degree of foreign ownership. Canada has traditionally depended on foreign companies for much of its investment. Foreign ownership of Canadian business has brought with it some costs as well as benefits, and the desirability of foreign investment in Canada seems to depend on the state of the Canadian economy.

Questions for Review and Discussion

1. Into what competitive grouping would you put the following businesses in your community?
   a) a restaurant
   b) a hotel
   c) a dentist
   d) garbage pick-up services
2. Concentration and competition are the same thing. Discuss the merit of this statement.
3. Would Canadians be as well off if we were without foreign investment in our country?
4. Name five Canadian companies owned by a company in a foreign country. Name the parent company.
5. Is foreign investment more prominent in some provinces of Canada than in others? Discuss.
6. Why does criticism about foreign ownership decline when unemployment is high?

7. Which form of business enterprise (sole proprietorship, partnership, or corporation) is most likely for each of the following businesses?
   a) automobile manufacturer
   b) law firm with three lawyers
   c) corn farmer
   d) variety store
   e) international courier
   f) electrical contractor

Suggested Readings

Beck, Nuala. *Shifting Gears: Thriving in the New Economy.* Toronto: HarperCollins, 1992. The book discusses those industries that are fading and those that are going to dominate in the years to come.

Berman, Paul D. *Small Business and Entrepreneurship.* Scarborough: Prentice Hall, 1997. As the name implies, this short, easy-to-read text focuses on small business.

FP 500. Toronto: *National Post,* June 2003. This annual issue is an interesting read as well as a good source of business data.

Green, Christopher. *Canadian Industrial Organization and Policy,* 3rd ed. Toronto: McGraw-Hill Ryerson, 1990. This text contains a good discussion of market concentration.

Report on Business Magazine: The Top 1000. Vol 17, No. 1. Toronto: *The Globe and Mail,* July 2003.

 ## Selected Websites

www.bdc.ca The website for the Business Development Bank of Canada. Information is available on assistance to small business.

http://strategis.ic.gc.ca The website for Industry Canada. Links are available to other sites including government support for small business and microanalysis research. The site also contains information on Canada's foreign-investment policy.

www.theglobeandmail.com/robmagazine The Globe and Mail's *Report on Business* magazine makes articles available. The Top 1000 publication is available at this site.

Production Costs

Key Terms

explicit costs
implicit costs
economic profit
short run
long run
production function
division of labour
marginal product
productivity
multifactor productivity measures
fixed costs
variable costs
marginal cost
economies of scale
minimum efficient scale
economies of scope
diseconomies of scale
cluster
marginal revenue

Chapter Objectives

After successfully completing this chapter, you will be able to:

- define explicit and implicit costs
- define average and marginal costs
- distinguish between the short run and the long run
- graph average variable cost, average total cost, and marginal cost
- discuss the impact of the law of diminishing returns on the production function
- describe how long-run average costs are derived
- distinguish between economies and diseconomies of scale

Core Concept Building

We assume that the goal of firms is to maximize profit. Profit is defined as the difference between revenues and costs. The definition of revenue is straightforward, but the definition of cost requires some analysis. Pay particular attention to the definition of profit and to the discussion of cost curves—these curves appear again in Chapters 12 and 13.

THE BRAIN DRAIN

Canada experiences both the immigration of skilled workers and the emigration of skilled workers. In the last half of the 1800s, emigration numbers exceeded immigration numbers. From 1851 to 1901, 2.2 million people emigrated from Canada while only 1.9 million people immigrated to Canada. Emigration numbers remained high until 1931 when the Great Depression and the Second World War significantly reduced emigration totals.

In recent years, immigration numbers have exceeded emigration numbers. Nonetheless, there is concern about the skill set of the people emigrating from Canada and the impact that this emigration will have on our economy and on the productivity of our labour force. Canadians are concerned not only about the loss of individual workers, but also with the loss of entrepreneurial workers who may create hundreds of other jobs in other countries, most notably the United States. Those jobs could have been created in Canada. There is also concern about the loss of investment made in their education by Canadian taxpayers.

The largest groups of skilled emigrants include physicians and nurses. Scientists, engineers, and high-tech workers also represent a large number of emigrants. When compared to the Canadian labour force, the U.S. labour force has a greater proportion of scientists and engineers with masters and doctoral qualifications. Relative to its population, the United States has 50 percent more electrical and computer engineers than does Canada.

Between 1990 and 1996, about 22 000 people a year left for the United States. In 1997, 27 000 people emigrated to the United States. The loss of skilled workers to the United States accelerated during the 1990s, but so did the immigration of skilled workers to Canada from other nations. The impacts of emigration and immigration do not, however, balance out. Canadians who move to the United States readily adapt to conditions there. It takes a longer time for new immigrants to Canada from countries other than the United States to adapt to our society and job market.

Why do skilled Canadians move to the United States? There appear to be several employment-related reasons. First, the tax rate on earned income is higher in Canada. One estimate is that 6 percent fewer Canadians would have emigrated if our taxes were comparable to U.S. taxes. Second, Canadian salaries are below U.S. salaries for similar work. Third, there appear to be more opportunities for skilled workers in the United States.

Elements of Production

In this chapter, we begin to analyze the *supply side* of individual markets first introduced in Chapter 2. The focus of our attention will be on the costs that are faced by individual business firms. As mentioned in Chapter 2, these costs are major determinants of the quantity and price of a product that any firm puts on the market. A change in production costs results in a change in the supply curve.

The business firm was defined in Chapter 10. It is an organization that combines various resources into a final product. It can be a sole proprietorship, a partnership, or a corporation. The objective of the owners of the firm is to earn a profit, which is defined as the difference between the total revenue received by the firm and the total costs incurred.

profit = total revenue − total costs

The concept of total revenue is straightforward. It represents the total amount of money received from sales. In order to calculate total revenue, we multiply the quantity sold by the price.

total revenue (TR) = price (P) × quantity (Q)

The concept of production costs is not as straightforward as that of revenue. First of all, it is necessary to differentiate between explicit and implicit costs. **Explicit costs** are those payments for resources that the firm must purchase. These resources include labour, materials, transportation, rent, and energy. Since these resources are not owned by the firm itself, they must be purchased from outside.

Implicit costs, in contrast, are payments to resources that the firm already owns. The firm may own the building from which it operates. It may also own a certain amount of machinery and equipment. It could own some land. The firm may also have some money that it is planning to invest in the business. Finally, the talents and time of the owner(s) can be considered resources that the firm owns. How does the firm pay for something that it already owns?

An opportunity cost is associated with each of these resources. If the firm uses its own building, the opportunity cost is the money that it could have received had it rented the building to someone else. The opportunity cost of any money invested in the firm is the interest lost by not putting this money into an interest-earning asset, such as a savings account. Finally, the opportunity cost of the owner's time is the money that he or she could have earned elsewhere. Implicit costs represent the sum of the opportunity costs of those resources owned by the firm.

Why are implicit costs included as costs? Opportunity costs represent the value of what was given up in order to operate the business. If the firm does not earn enough money to cover these costs, then it would be better off to enter another line of business or to do something else with the resources that it owns. Since it is desirable to cover these opportunity costs, they are included in the firm's total costs.

total costs = explicit costs + implicit costs

Payments for productive resources that the firm does not own and must purchase are called explicit costs.

Payments for productive resources that the firm already owns are called implicit costs.

Since the total costs of a business firm include both explicit and implicit costs, a profit will be earned only when total revenue exceeds these costs. This is referred to as **economic profit**—the amount of money that comes into the firm over and above the amount necessary to pay off all costs. It can also be regarded as an amount of money over and above that necessary to keep the firm in business.

Economic profit is the excess of total revenue over total costs.

$$\text{economic profit} = \text{total revenue} - \text{total costs}$$

REVIEW

11.1 Why is it necessary that the firm consider opportunity costs when determining whether an economic profit has been made?

EVERYDAY ECONOMICS 11.1

Numerical Calculation of Profit

Accountants and economists may look at profits from different points of view. A numerical example highlights these differences.

Mr. Doolittle was employed at Dawson's Garage as a mechanic. Though he enjoyed his job, he always wanted to operate his own automotive repair shop. He believed that by working on his own he could earn more money than he could working for someone else. He also liked the idea of being his own boss. One day Mr. Doolittle saw an opportunity to start his own business, so he left Dawson's Garage.

While employed at Dawson's Garage, he had been earning $40 000 per year. He had managed to accumulate $20 000 in savings, which he needed to launch his business. This money had been deposited in a savings account at a chartered bank and was earning 5-percent interest annually.

There were certain costs associated with going into business. Mr. Doolittle had to rent a garage, buy machinery and tools, advertise, and hire other mechanics. At the end of one year in the auto-repair business, Mr. Doolittle's costs were as follows:

rent (garage)	$10 000
wages to mechanics	$60 000
advertising	$ 2 000
tools	$ 4 000
electricity	$ 2 000
Total costs	$78 000

During the first year of operation, Mr. Doolittle's garage brought in $130 000 in sales. Did he earn a profit? The traditional calculation of profit is to subtract total costs from total revenue.

$$\begin{aligned} \text{profit} &= \text{total revenue} - \text{total costs} \\ &= \$130\ 000 - \$78\ 000 \\ &= \$52\ 000 \end{aligned}$$

The traditional accounting definition of profit would be that Mr. Doolittle had earned a profit of $52 000 in the first year of operation.

Economists would not agree that Mr. Doolittle's profit was this high. From an economist's point of view, certain costs were not included in the calculation of total costs. These are the implicit costs. Mr. Doolittle gave up a job paying $40 000 per year in order to start his own business. If he did not earn at least $40 000 with his own business, he would be better off working for someone else. Mr. Doolittle also took $20 000 out of his savings account for the new business. At an interest rate of 5 percent, he would have earned an additional $1000 if this money had remained in the bank. In fact, Mr. Doolittle sacrificed $41 000 ($40 000 + $1000) in order to go into business for himself. This amount represents his implicit costs.

In order to calculate profit, the economist believes that explicit and implicit costs should be added together.

explicit costs	= $ 78 000
+ implicit	= $ 41 000
= total costs	= $119 000

economic profit = total revenue − total costs
= $130 000 − $119 000
= $11 000

From an economic point of view, Mr. Doolittle earned $11 000 profit in his first year of operation. He earned $11 000 more than necessary to keep him in business.

What if Mr. Doolittle owned the garage? If so, he would not pay $10 000 in rent. Yet, he would have an opportunity cost if he chose to use the garage for his business. The opportunity cost would be the lost rent from not renting it out to someone else. If he owned the garage, Mr. Doolittle would face the possibility of another cost, namely economic depreciation. The difference between the market value of an asset at the beginning and end of a period is referred to as *economic depreciation*. It is possible that the garage would have gone down in market value over the year.

Questions

1. If Mr. Doolittle's garage earned $110 000 in revenue, what would his accounting profit be? His economic profit?

2. Calculate his economic profit if he had been earning $44 000 a year at Dawson's Garage, and if total revenue brought in by his new business was $130 000 per year.

3. Calculate his economic profit in our original example if the interest rate on his savings account was 10 percent annually.

4. Do you think that Mr. Doolittle would be willing to stay in business for himself even if he was earning less than he did at Dawson's Garage? Why or why not?

5. Do you think that company profits reported in the newspaper are accounting or economic profits? Why?

The Production Function

The production function is the relationship between the number of inputs into the production process and the maximum output attainable from this process. This section discusses the production function under a number of headings. It first discusses the time periods associated with this relationship: the short run and the long run. Also reviewed is the impact of specialization and diminishing returns on the production function and the factors that influence productivity.

Time Periods

Production costs tend to change over time. When analyzing the cost picture of a firm, it is necessary to distinguish between the short run and the long run. The **short run** is defined as a period of time when at least one resource used in the production process remains unchanged. For example, on a farm the amount of land available is usually fixed. For any business there is a period of time when the ability to produce more is constrained by the size of the factory or store. It is impossible to say whether the short run is one month, three months, one year, or five years. This evaluation depends on the nature of the business and the resources that are used. Because firms are always faced with constraints or resources that cannot be changed immediately, they are always producing in the short run.

The **long run** is a period of time when no resources can be called fixed. It is a period of time long enough for the firm to be able to adjust all of its inputs in the production process. All resources, or inputs, that the firm has access to are variable. The firm can buy more machinery, hire more workers, build a new factory, or buy more land. The long run is seen as a planning period, since it is impossible to actually produce in the long run. Production will always take place in the short run because companies are always faced with certain resource constraints that they cannot change.

Because a firm is always operating in a short-run situation, the production costs of the firm will be analyzed in this short-run time frame. The ability of the firm to increase production in the short run will be constrained by the fact that at least one resource, or input, will remain fixed. The example of a furniture factory will help to describe the relationship between production levels and production costs in the short run. Assume that the Pinewood Furniture Company has rented a building for a year. This is a short-run cost because one resource, the building, cannot be changed for at least one year. Assume further that the factory contains all the raw material and machinery necessary to make chairs. The only input to the production process that can be changed is the number of workers. Changing the number of workers in order to change output is referred to as the **production function**. It represents the relationship between changes in inputs, or resources, and changes in output.

The short run is a period of time in the production process during which at least one resource cannot be altered.

The period of time in the production process during which all resources are variable is termed the long run.

The production function refers to the relationship between the amount of resources used and the level of output.

REVIEW

11.2 Why is it not possible for a firm to be actually producing in the long run?

Specialization

As more workers are hired to make chairs, the number of chairs produced will increase. As the labour force is increased, a division of labour will take place. Pinewood Furniture Company will have workers who specialize in certain aspects of chair-making: some workers will be employed in measuring and cutting; some will specialize in lathe work; others will specialize in chair assembly, and so on. *This specialization of labour should permit greater efficiency and greater production.* If one person, working alone, could produce five chairs in a day, two workers should be able to make more than ten chairs in a day if the workers specialize in certain tasks. Consequently, the company would be in a situation of doubling its labour resource and more than doubling its output of chairs.

Why does a **division of labour** result in greater efficiency and more output? Performing the same task over and over would allow the worker to become more proficient at it. If someone's specialty was making chair legs on a wood lathe, the person would develop a certain skill at this job. By continually performing the same task, the worker is likely to find a better way to do the job. Specialization also saves time as workers do not have to move to different work stations and use different tools.

Specialization, however, is not without its costs. These are related to the worker's job satisfaction. The worker may develop a sense of boredom as the same task is repeated over and over again. An individual may also lack a sense of fulfillment in that this task is only one of several other tasks. One worker does not make an entire chair in our Pinewood example. Making a complete chair by oneself might be more satisfying.

In terms of production, the benefits of specialization seem to outweigh the costs. Without specialization, more hours in a day would be required to achieve the same output. As we will show later, lack of specialization can lead to higher production costs and lower wages for workers.

The division of labour refers to the specialization in the performance of tasks by workers in order to permit greater efficiency and greater production.

Diminishing Returns

Would increases in output through increased specialization continue forever? No. At a certain level of output the advantages of specialization would cease. The ability of the Pinewood Furniture Company to produce chairs is limited by the size of the factory. Beyond some point, if more workers are hired their contributions to the daily output of chairs would decrease. They would have less and less of the fixed resources to work with. If each additional worker has less of the fixed resources to work with, that worker will contribute less to the total output than the previous worker.

This situation is known as the *law of diminishing returns.* The idea of diminishing returns was first introduced in Chapter 1 in connection with Malthus' theory of population. It applies equally well to the production situation of a firm. The law states that when increasing amounts of a variable resource are added to a fixed amount of another resource, after a certain point the additions to total output will become fewer and fewer. In our example, the variable resource was workers and the fixed resource was the factory. Since the law of diminishing returns involves a fixed resource, the situation occurs only in the short run.

The production function of our company that demonstrates the concept of diminishing returns appears in Table 11.1. As the number of workers hired increases, the total number of chairs produced increases. Yet, starting with the fourth worker hired, the additions to the total number of chairs produced become fewer and fewer. The third worker added nine chairs to the total output, increasing the output from 13 to 22. The fourth worker added only eight chairs to the total. Each successive worker adds fewer chairs because each successive worker has less space to work in, less material to work with, and so on. The addition to the total output of each extra worker is called the **marginal product** of labour and is shown in the

Marginal product (MP) is the addition to total output as a result of adding one more unit of a productive resource.

Table 11.1 *Production function for Pinewood Furniture Company*

NO. OF WORKERS	TOTAL NO. OF CHAIRS PRODUCED PER DAY	MARGINAL PRODUCT	AVERAGE NO. OF CHAIRS PER WORKER (AVERAGE PRODUCT)
0	0		
1	5	5	5.0
2	13	8	6.5
3	22	9	7.3
4	30	8	7.5
5	37	7	7.4
6	43	6	7.2
7	48	5	6.9
8	52	4	6.5
9	54	2	6.0
10	55	1	5.5
11	55	0	5.0
12	54	−1	4.5

third column of the table. The word "marginal" means extra or additional. Looking at the marginal-product column, we can see that diminishing returns set in with the addition of the fourth worker.

This information is shown graphically in Figure 11.1. The marginal-product curve increases as a result of worker specialization, but starting with the fourth worker, diminishing returns set in and marginal product starts to decline. Is it possible for the marginal product of labour to be zero? Yes; since the size of the factory is fixed, there may be a point at which one more worker does not add anything to the total output of chairs. This is the case with the eleventh worker in Table 11.1. It may even be possible to have too many workers and have total output fall. In our example, the marginal product for the twelfth worker is -1. This is shown on the graph by having the marginal-product (MP) line fall below the horizontal axis.

In the case of the Pinewood Furniture Company, we theorized that diminishing returns set in after the fourth worker was hired. However, in many production situations, diminishing returns do not occur this soon, and they depend on the size of the firm and the type of operation it is engaged in. A company may have hundreds, or even thousands, of workers before experiencing diminishing returns.

The law of diminishing returns is important in our discussions for two reasons. First, it affects the costs of the firm in the short run. If each

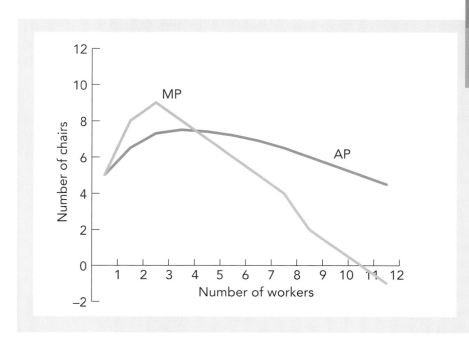

Figure 11.1

Marginal and average products for the Pinewood Furniture Company

MP = Marginal product
AP = Average product

successive worker contributes less and less to the daily output of chairs, the cost of making the chairs is going to increase. Second, the contribution of each worker to the total output influences the company's willingness to hire more workers, and the demand for workers strongly affects the wages that workers will earn. Chapter 14 is devoted to a discussion of how wages are determined. The concept of diminishing returns will reappear there.

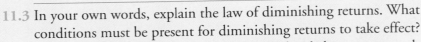

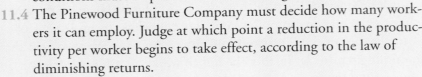

R E V I E W

11.3 In your own words, explain the law of diminishing returns. What conditions must be present for diminishing returns to take effect?

11.4 The Pinewood Furniture Company must decide how many workers it can employ. Judge at which point a reduction in the productivity per worker begins to take effect, according to the law of diminishing returns.

Productivity

Productivity **refers to the amount of output produced by a unit of a certain resource during a specified period of time.**

The amount of output produced by a unit of a certain input during a specified period of time is referred to as **productivity.** Although productivity can be discussed in terms of any input, or resource, it is most often mentioned in reference to *labour*. It is measured in terms such as output per worker-hour or output per person employed. Other measures of labour productivity are also used, yet none is considered to be the most definitive or accurate.

Why is the concept of productivity important? It is closely related to our standard of living. If productivity is increasing, it means that more goods and services are being provided from the same amount of resources. If productivity is increasing, then production costs can be lower and potential price increases can be held back. This means that increases in labour productivity can be associated with higher incomes for workers without the accompanying increase in prices. Productivity is directly related to one of Canada's economic objectives: a reduced rate of inflation.

Productivity is also an important issue in union/management negotiations. Management is willing to increase wages only if the output per worker increases. In this way, production costs will be kept down. Unions try to show how labour productivity has increased in order to justify their demands for higher wages.

What influences labour productivity? Several factors are important and can be broken down into three groups. Factors in the first group influence the productivity of the economy as a whole and are referred to as *macro* influences on productivity. They are as follows:

the structure of the economy: The industrial composition of the economy is changing and, as it changes, it impacts on measures of productivity. The agricultural and manufacturing sectors of the economy represent a declining proportion of the labour force. It is in these two sectors where improvements in machinery and equipment have resulted in increases in productivity. The service sector is growing in terms of employment, but it is more difficult to achieve productivity increases in these industries.

economic conditions: When the economy slows down, employees rarely work overtime and often have their hours of work reduced. If productivity is measured in terms of output per employee, then productivity decreases. Since the demand for goods is more variable than the demand for services, the drop in productivity affects the manufacturing sector more than the service sector.

government policies: Governments can influence productivity by promoting education and training. They can also influence productivity through their policies on competition. Do they promote international trade? Do they support monopolies in their jurisdictions? More competition is likely to lead to higher productivity. A government that is supportive of business may encourage investment in new machinery and equipment.

Factors in the second group influence productivity at the firm level. These are referred to as *micro* influences on productivity.

scale of business operations: As will be discussed later in this chapter, larger firms can take advantage of more efficient machinery and equipment. Workers can also become more specialized in the tasks they perform.

management techniques: Management can influence worker productivity by encouraging the introduction of innovative techniques and by fostering a positive attitude in the workplace.

The third set of factors that influence productivity impact on both the micro and macro level in the economy.

quantity and quality of capital: Workers that use more capital and better-quality capital (machinery and equipment) are more productive. A worker with an automatic sander can finish more wood than a worker sanding by hand. A farmer working 200 hectares of land can produce more than a farmer working 100 hectares of land of comparable quality. The quantity of other resources that labour has to work with is related to the law of diminishing returns. In the short run, as production increases each successive worker has less and less fixed resource to work with. As a result, a point is reached beyond which each successive worker produces less than the previous one hired. Due to the law of diminishing returns, labour productivity declines.

labour force: The characteristics of the labour force, including age, education, and health, influence productivity. As the labour force gets older, the level of experience increases but the average level of education usually decreases. Immigration and emigration also impact on the labour force and on the level of productivity of the labour force.

Multifactor productivity measures indicate the level of productivity in an industry by taking into consideration all relevant resources, not only labour resources.

The conventional measure of productivity is *labour productivity,* which shows the level of output per employee. In 1990, Statistics Canada introduced new measures of productivity called **multifactor productivity measures.** The first measure takes into account all changes in factors of production. The second measure includes not only the productivity gains in the industry itself, but also those in the industries supplying it with energy, materials, and services. This latter measure allows for better international comparisons of productivity change, since there are different levels of vertical integration in different countries. For example, does a steel company own the mines that supply it with iron ore, or does the company purchase the iron ore from someone else? Differences in the level of vertical integration can affect productivity calculations. Apart from improving international comparisons, the interindustry productivity measure can identify an industry that is not achieving major productivity gains itself but is using materials from industries in which productivity gains have been significant.

From 1981 to 2000, labour productivity in the Canadian business sector increased at an average growth rate of 1.4 percent per year. Statistics Canada estimates that 0.6 percentage points of the increase were a result of improved technology and equipment (mainly information technology) being used by workers. Another 0.5 percentage points were attributed to a shift in the labour force to more skilled occupations. More skilled workers are more productive. Finally, 0.3 percentage points were the result of increases in multifactor productivity.

A further discussion of labour productivity and its influence on wage rates appears in Chapter 14.

Short-Run Costs

Fixed costs are production costs that do not vary with the amount produced.

The costs faced by a firm can be divided into two groups, based on production levels. **Fixed costs** are costs that remain the same regardless of the level of output. Even if nothing is produced, these costs are present. Examples of fixed costs are rent, real estate taxes, insurance, and interest payments on any loans. **Variable costs,** on the other hand, vary with the level of output. As output increases, more labour, raw materials, and energy are used. If the amount of resources used increases, costs will increase. The total cost faced by the firm in order to produce a given level of output is the sum of the fixed and the variable costs.

Variable costs **are production costs that vary with the amount of output.**

total costs (TC) = total fixed cost (TFC) + total variable cost (TVC)

More important than total cost for our purposes will be cost per unit produced. This is called the *average total cost.* In order to calculate average total cost (ATC), the total cost (TC) is divided by the level of output (Q).

$$ATC = \frac{TC}{Q}$$

Remember that TC = TFC + TVC. Therefore,

$$\frac{TC}{Q} = \frac{TFC}{Q} + \frac{TVC}{Q}$$

and,

average total cost (ATC) = average fixed cost (AFC)
+ average variable cost (AVC)

How do the shape of the production function and the law of diminishing returns influence costs? As previously stated, only variable costs will be affected, since fixed costs remain the same regardless of the level of output. As the furniture firm in our example starts to increase the level of chair production by hiring more workers, total costs will increase while average total costs fall. If workers can specialize in certain tasks to increase output, the cost per unit (average total cost) will fall. Look back at the figures in Table 11.1. Three workers produced a total of 22 chairs for an average of 7.3 chairs per worker. One worker alone was able to produce only five chairs. Through specialization, the average number of chairs produced per worker increases and the average cost of producing chairs will decrease. After diminishing returns have set in, the average number of chairs produced per worker starts to fall. Diminishing returns set in with the hiring of the fourth worker. The average number of chairs produced per worker falls from a high of 7.5 to 5.5 by the tenth worker. Diminishing returns force the costs associated with producing each chair to rise, assuming that each worker is paid the same wage.

The effects of worker specialization and the law of diminishing returns on a firm's costs are shown in Table 11.2. It is assumed that the fixed costs

Table 11.2 *Production costs and level of output, Pinewood Furniture Company*

LEVEL OF OUTPUT (CHAIRS)	TOTAL FIXED COSTS $	TOTAL VARIABLE COSTS $	TOTAL COST $	MARGINAL COST $	AVERAGE FIXED COST $	AVERAGE VARIABLE COST $	AVERAGE TOTAL COST $
0	50	0	50		–	0.00	–
				30			
1	50	30	80		50.00	30.00	80.00
				24			
2	50	54	104		25.00	27.00	52.00
				22			
3	50	76	126		16.67	25.33	42.00
				20			
4	50	96	146		12.50	24.00	36.50
				26			
5	50	122	172		10.00	24.40	34.40
				28			
6	50	150	200		8.33	25.00	33.33
				40			
7	50	190	240		7.14	27.14	34.28
				50			
8	50	240	290		6.25	30.00	36.25
				60			
9	50	300	350		5.55	33.33	38.89
				70			
10	50	370	420		5.00	37.00	42.00

Marginal cost (MC) is the addition to the total cost of producing one more unit of output.

faced by the furniture company are $50. Fixed costs include rent, insurance premiums, and interest payments on loans. Variable costs include labour, raw materials, energy, and transportation. As shown in the table, average variable costs begin to fall until they are affected by diminishing returns. That is, average variable costs decline until a level of output of five units is reached. The extra cost of producing one more unit begins to rise with the fifth unit produced. The addition to the total cost of producing one more unit is known as the **marginal cost**, and is presented in the fifth column in the table. The impact of diminishing returns is to cause marginal costs to increase. If marginal costs are starting to increase, then average costs will eventually increase as well.

The data in Table 11.2 are plotted in Figures 11.2 and 11.3. In Figure 11.2, the total cost data are presented. The total-cost (TC) curve is the summation of the total fixed-cost (TFC) curve and the total variable-cost (TVC) curve. In Figure 11.3, the average and marginal costs are presented. The average total-cost (ATC) curve is the sum of the average fixed-cost (AFC) curve and the average variable-cost (AVC) curve. The marginal-cost (MC) curve initially declines because of worker specialization, but eventually begins to rise when diminishing returns set in. Marginal costs begin to rise with the fifth unit produced. Eventually the increase in marginal costs begins to influence average variable costs, which also start to increase.

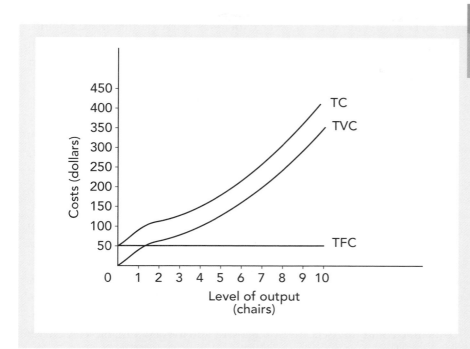

Figure 11.2

Production costs for Pinewood Furniture Company

TC = total costs
TVC = total variable costs
TFC = total fixed costs

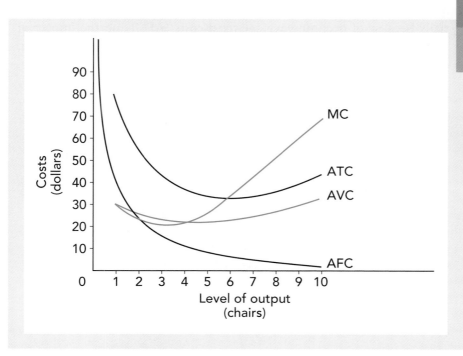

Figure 11.3

Production costs for Pinewood Furniture Company

ATC = average total costs
AVC = average variable costs
AFC = average fixed costs
MC = marginal costs

It should be noted that the marginal-cost curve will always intersect the average variable-cost and average total-cost curves at their lowest points. As long as the marginal cost of producing one extra unit of output is less than the average cost, it will bring the average down. As soon as the marginal cost becomes greater than the average, it begins to bring the average up. Therefore, the only point where the two curves can intersect is at the lowest point on the average curve.

In order to better explain the intersection of the curves in the diagram, an analogy can be made to college test marks. Assume that on two tests you had an average mark of 70 percent. If you obtained a mark of 60 on the third test, what would happen to your average? Since 60 is less than 70, your new average would be less than 70. In fact, it would be 66.7 percent. Similarly, when the cost of producing one more unit of output is less than the average cost of the preceding units, the average cost has to decline. The opposite would have occurred had you scored 80 on your third test. Your average would then increase to 73.3 percent for the three tests. *Again, if the marginal cost of producing one more unit is greater than the average cost, then the average cost has to increase.* The only possible point where the marginal-cost curve could intersect the average-cost and average variable-cost curves is at their lowest points.

It is useful to summarize the discussion of short-run cost curves. The average total cost (ATC) curve is U-shaped. Average total costs decline initially because of declining average fixed costs (AFC) and the impact of specialization on average variable costs (AVC). Eventually in the short run, diminishing returns set in and average variable costs begin to increase, pushing up the average total costs.

REVIEW

11.5 Explain why diminishing returns would cause marginal costs to increase.

11.6 Why must MC intersect AVC and ATC at the lowest points on the AVC and ATC curves?

11.7 The Pinewood Furniture Company is trying to reduce its marginal production costs. Determine at what level of output its average fixed, variable, and total costs are the lowest.

Long-Run Costs

In the long run, a firm is not constrained by one factory size. It can expand and build as many factories as necessary. It can hire more workers. It can purchase more equipment. As sales increase, an increase in all resources will be required. In the long run, the law of diminishing returns does not affect costs since no resources that are used in the production process remain fixed. All resources, or inputs, are variable.

EVERYDAY ECONOMICS 11.2

Sunk Costs Are Irrelevant

To the economist, one type of cost, called a *sunk cost*, is irrelevant to decision making, as there are no opportunity costs associated with sunk costs. Further, economists tend to look to the future when confronted with decisions rather than looking back to the past. Still, what are sunk costs? An example is the best way to explain this concept.

Assume that Garson Manufacturing purchased a metal lathe three years ago for $10 000. At the time of purchase there was an opportunity cost involved in the decision to buy the lathe. What else could the company do with $10 000? Having taken the alternatives into consideration, the company purchased the lathe. There are now newer and more efficient metal lathes on the market. The lathe purchased three years ago needs repairs in order to perform efficiently. Should Garson Manufacturing purchase a new, more efficient lathe, or should the old lathe be repaired? What costs are relevant to the company's decision?

The cost of the new lathe is relevant. What else could be done with the money? The cost of fixing up the old lathe is also relevant. If it is possible to trade in the old lathe or sell it as a second-hand lathe, this, too, is relevant to the decision. If the old lathe could be sold for $4000, there is an opportunity cost to not selling it. What about the original $10 000 spent on the lathe? Where does this cost enter into the decision-making process? The answer is that it does not. The irrelevant factor in this decision-

making process is the difference between the original cost of the lathe ($10 000) and the resale value ($4000). This difference ($6000) is called a *sunk cost*. There is no opportunity cost associated with this cost.

Garson Manufacturing may argue that it cannot afford to sell the old machine for less than it paid for it. The company may argue that it cannot afford to take the loss. But the company has already taken the loss on the old lathe. The purchase of the lathe three years ago is in the past and is no longer relevant to today's decision-making. It is a sunk cost. As far as the old lathe is concerned, the only relevant cost is the opportunity cost of the resale.

Was the cost of the old lathe ever relevant? Yes. Before the purchase of the old lathe, the cost was an important factor in making the decision. Once the decision had been made, however, the cost of the lathe was no longer relevant.

Questions

1. Can you reflect on any sunk costs associated with your personal finances?
2. In the 1970s, CN introduced a new train, the *Turbo,* to run between Toronto and Montreal. (This train was eventually taken out of operation.) Were the costs associated with the development of the *Turbo* part of the cost of running it between these two cities? Explain.

The long run can be seen as a planning period. It is composed of a series of short-run situations. It is not possible for the firm to produce in the long run, since the firm will always be constrained by at least one resource that cannot be changed. Therefore we string a series of short-run situations together in order to determine long-run costs. What happens to costs in the long run? As the firm grows in size, its average total costs are likely to fall. Several factors will cause this. First, the firm may take increased advantage of specialization in the use of labour. A larger factory and a larger production run will allow even greater specialization to take place. Second, larger-scale production may permit some cost saving in terms of management. A doubling of the production staff may not require a doubling of managerial staff as well. One supervisor may be able to supervise two, four, six, or even more employees. Third, larger firms may be better able to take advantage of more efficient production equipment. Certain machines may be too impractical and costly for small operations, but may be well-suited to large production runs. Fourth, larger firms may be able to purchase materials in large quantities at a discount. When inputs are shipped in bulk, there may be savings in transportation costs. Fifth, large firms may be able to borrow money at a lower interest rate or obtain money by issuing more shares. Finally, marketing economies may be achieved by spreading the cost of advertising across a larger output.

An example relating to transportation and warehouse costs helps explain the input cost advantage available to large firms. Many Canadian companies use steel in the manufacturing or construction process. Much of the steel produced in Canada is shipped to a warehouse where it is stored until required by a customer. It is then shipped to the various users in the quantities required. For companies such as automobile manufacturers, which use a large quantity of steel, the warehouse stage of the transportation process can be bypassed. Steel can be shipped directly to the automobile manufacturer from the steel mill. Even though the company that owns the warehouse may handle the transaction, the steel is not delivered to the warehouse, unloaded at the warehouse, stored in the warehouse, and finally, shipped from the warehouse. If the warehouse stage of the process can be bypassed, considerable savings can occur. The cost savings are available only to large users of steel, because smaller companies cannot accept a full truckload of steel all at once.

All of these factors tend to reduce average costs. These are referred to as *economies of large-scale production*, or **economies of scale**, and are more easily attainable in the long run. Economies of scale are present when the firm experiences a more-than-proportionate increase in its output as a result of increasing all its inputs. For example, economies of scale would result if

Economies of scale are decreases in long-run average costs resulting from the efficiencies of large-scale production.

the firm doubled all of its inputs and experienced a more-than-double increase in output. Therefore, in the long run, average costs will decrease as the level of output increases as a result of economies of scale.

The delivery business is one example of economies of scale at work. As a delivery company expands its business, it may replace its smaller delivery van with a larger vehicle, likely a truck. The larger vehicle will cost more to own and operate, but the increase in costs is not in proportion with the increase in carrying capacity. A vehicle twice as large does not cost twice as much to operate. Both vehicles need a driver and licence plates. Both vehicles need to be insured and need maintenance. The larger vehicle will allow the company to operate just one vehicle instead of two vehicles. It will allow the company to transport more parcels in a day without hiring another driver, paying for another licence plate, insuring another vehicle, and so on. The average cost per delivered parcel should decrease.

Economists have determined that economies of scale may be associated with the product, the plant, and the firm. Economies of scale at the product level are associated with the use of more specialized capital equipment. By concentrating on a relatively small number of products, production processes that are well-suited to those products can be set up. While specialized equipment is often expensive, it is usually capable of achieving a greater volume of output for a given level of costs. By focusing on a narrow range of products, the learning, or experience, curve comes into play. As more of a product is produced, costs per unit tend to decline as a result of "learning by doing" on the part of the workers.

Economies of scale at the plant level refer to the effects of a larger plant on per-unit costs of production. The reduction in per-unit costs is associated mainly with the increased specialization of workers and equipment that is a result of larger volumes of output. Economists have tried to identify **minimum efficient scale (MES)** plants for various industries. The minimum efficient scale is the smallest level of output that will allow the firm to reach the lowest average costs possible in the industry. Many Canadian plants are below the MES size. The reasons for the less-than-efficient plant sizes in Canada are the small size of the domestic market and the large geographic area. High transportation costs occur in Canada because of the long distances involved in serving a relatively small market. The high transportation costs encourage companies to build a larger number of small plants, rather than a few large ones.

The concept of a MES is related to the competitive nature of the industry. If the MES is very large, the industry is likely to be a natural monopoly. Where the MES is large, the industry is likely to be an oligopoly. Finally, if the MES is relatively small, the industry will be competitive.

> **The** minimum efficient scale **is the smallest level of output that will allow a firm to reach the lowest average costs possible.**

Costs and the Software Industry

The cost curves developed in this chapter may not reflect the costs faced by all firms. For firms that develop computer software, fixed costs are very high. Fixed costs, which can run to millions of dollars, include research, programmers salaries, technological equipment, the cost of a patent, and, possibly, marketing. Recall that fixed costs do not vary with the number of units sold and, therefore, salaries and marketing can be considered fixed costs. It takes a long time to develop and test new software. The fixed costs may be high but what about variable costs? What is the marginal cost of producing one more unit? The marginal cost is virtually zero since much software is obtained electronically. Consumers can download the programme. The programme may not even appear on a CD. Apart from the extra costs associated with customer support, there are almost no extra costs incurred in selling one more unit.

Initially, revenue from the sale of the programme is used to pay fixed costs and then it goes directly to profit. Does profit just continue to grow? Profit is not likely to be maintained indefinitely. The software will soon face competition in the marketplace and must be improved. New fixed costs will be incurred in developing an improved version of the software. There is a cycle of periodically incurring fixed costs.

Questions

1. Draw ATC and AFC curves for a typical software developer.
2. Are fixed costs in the software industry a barrier to the entry of new firms? Explain.
3. Are economies of scale present in this industry? Explain.

Firm-level economies of scale occur as a result of a number of factors. These include administrative economies that spread overhead, finance, advertising, and research and development costs over a larger output. Larger firms may be willing to take risks more readily if they are more diversified and can fall back on other products. Such firms may also have dealer networks that provide distribution economies.

In Canada, the small domestic market may not allow all firms in the industry to achieve economies of scale. These economies may be achieved only if there are fewer firms in the industry. In other instances, economies of scale may be achieved by specializing in the production of a single product rather than having the firm produce a number of products. Studies that compared production costs in both Canada and the United States have concluded that the smaller plant size in Canada was not as important as the length of the production run. Canadian companies, producing a variety of products, had higher production costs as a result of their shorter production runs. The relatively small size of the Canadian market dictated that firms produce more than one product. Product diversification is especially true for Canadian companies that are subsidiaries of foreign companies. The shifting of production from one product to another involves costs, particularly in terms of downtime when no products are being made. Shorter production runs also reduce the possibility of learning by doing.

Increased specialization may lead to longer production runs. Multinational corporations can give the Canadian subsidiary exclusive control over one of its products. Instead of producing a number of products for the Canadian market, the subsidiary could focus on the production of a single product. As the production levels of this product increase, lower average costs should result. The rationalization of production in the automobile industry between Canada and the United States has allowed Canadian subsidiaries to achieve economies of scale comparable to plants in the United States. One of Canada's objectives in signing the Canada-United States Free Trade Agreement was to allow Canadian companies to specialize to a greater extent and achieve lower production costs.

A concern associated with increased specialization in production is the loss of **economies of scope**. These economies exist when the cost of producing two products (or services) by one firm is less costly than having the two products produced separately by different firms. Two products may be produced at a lower cost by one firm if there are common fixed costs, or overhead expenses, involved in the production of both products. For example, a sales representative can pass on information about two products, not only one, to a potential customer. A limited number of products may be a disadvantage to the sales representative when visiting customers. Research and development activities may also be a source of economies of scope since research into one area may have applications in another area.

Economies of scope **exist when it is less costly for one firm to produce two products than for two firms to produce the products separately.**

Can average costs fall indefinitely as production increases? It is unlikely that this will happen. The firm may get so large that certain inefficiencies set in. For example, a large firm may have too many managerial levels between the person who makes a decision and the person who finally puts the decision into operation. Such a situation can result in poorer communication, less efficiency, and higher costs. Larger firms often take more time to make decisions.

There is also a high correlation between the size of plants and the degree of labour disputes, labour turnover, and other manifestations of worker dissatisfaction. (Larger firms are more likely to be unionized firms.) This correlation is referred to as **diseconomies of scale** and causes average costs to increase. Thus, at a certain level of output, average total costs will begin to rise when diseconomies of scale set in. Just *when* diseconomies of scale will begin to affect costs is difficult to determine. In some firms,

Diseconomies of scale **are increases in long-run average costs resulting from the inefficiencies associated with large-scale operations.**

diseconomies of scale will take effect at lower levels of output than in other firms. The generalized trends in long-run costs are shown in Figure 11.4, which shows the composition of the long-run average cost curve. The long-run cost curve (LAC) is derived from a series of short-run cost curves (SAC₁, SAC₂, etc.). Each SAC curve relates to a certain factory size. At every possible level of output, there exists a point on a short-run average cost curve (SAC) at which this output can be produced. The long-run average cost curve includes those points at which a certain level of output can be produced for the lowest average cost. It should be noted that these points are not necessarily the minimum average cost for each factory size. If a larger factory can achieve lower average costs for a certain level of output, then it makes sense to expand rather than to try to use a smaller factory more efficiently. That is, it is not necessary to include the minimum point of each SAC curve in the LAC curve.

Do firms automatically move from a point where economies of scale are achieved to a point of diseconomies of scale? No-there is likely to be a range of output where long-run average costs remain constant. Over this range of output, the firm is said to be achieving constant returns to scale. This situation is depicted in Figure 11.5.

Figure 11.4

Generalized diagram of long-run costs

The long-run cost curve (LAC) is derived from a series of short-run cost curves (SAC).

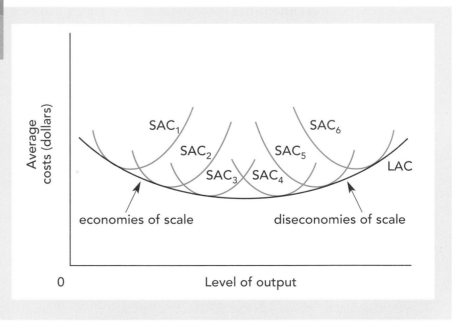

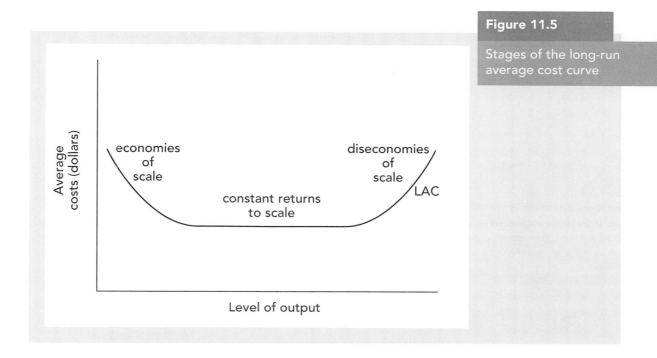

Figure 11.5

Stages of the long-run average cost curve

Economists distinguish between internal economies and diseconomies of scale and external economies and diseconomies of scale. Internal economies and diseconomies of scale are found within the firm and are the economies of scale referred to so far in this chapter. External economies and diseconomies are experienced as the industry expands; that is, as companies increase their output or as new firms enter the industry. If external economies of scale exist, then cost savings are present as the industry expands. The presence of external economies helps explain why firms in the same industry tend to be located in the same geographic area. For example, much of the textbook publishing industry is located in the east end of Metropolitan Toronto. Many firms in the software industry are located in Kanata, Ontario. Many pharmaceutical firms are located in Montreal, and many call centres are in Moncton. One advantage of this close proximity of similar firms is the availability of a trained labour force. External economies can also be realized through trade associations. These associations promote the entire industry, thus reducing advertising and promotional costs.

External diseconomies of scale occur when industry expansion increases costs for all firms in the industry. For example, assume Canada experienced a population boom and there was an increased demand for houses. The increased demand for houses would increase the demand for construction materials required to build houses. Prices for materials such as lumber would increase. The increase in lumber costs would impact all firms in the industry. If the firms in the industry are geographically close, an expansion by all firms will increase labour and land costs. Transportation costs may also increase if traffic congestion becomes a problem.

When a number of similar firms, their customers and suppliers, and training institutions are located in close proximity, it is referred to as a **cluster**. Clusters are a source of external economies and diseconomies of scale. An example of a cluster is the entertainment industry located in and around Toronto. Following New York and Los Angeles, Toronto is third in terms of the number of people employed in this industry. The presence of a cluster means more competition for existing firms. Since all firms in the industry face the same regulations, compete for the same labour pool, have similar taxes, and use the same infrastructure, they must compete by being innovative. Suppliers to firms in the entertainment business must also compete. For example, catering companies must meet the needs of this industry in order to compete. Educational institutions begin to offer programs and courses to prepare students for work in this industry once the cluster is established. The presence of a cluster can also lead to higher costs. The increased demand for workers with specific skills, and for other resources needed by firms in the cluster, pushes up prices and increases costs.

A cluster occurs when a number of similar firms, their customers and suppliers, and training institutions are located in close proximity; clusters are a source of external economies and diseconomies of scale.

REVIEW

11.8 Do diminishing returns affect costs in the long run? Explain.
11.9 What are diseconomies of scale?

Making Decisions

Economics is the study of how people go about making decisions regarding the use of scarce resources. In order for a firm to make decisions about the price of its product and the amount produced, it must have a certain objective in mind. Let us assume that all firms attempt to maximize profits as their main objective. They may have other objectives, but it is generally agreed that the assumption of profit maximization is a good predictor of individual firm behaviour.

As discussed earlier in this chapter,

economic profit = total revenue − total costs

In order to maximize profits, the difference between total revenue and total cost has to be maximized. Another way to view this objective is in terms of marginal revenue and marginal cost. **Marginal revenue** is defined as the addition to total revenue resulting from selling one more unit of output. Marginal cost is defined as the total cost of producing one more unit of output. In order to maximize profits, the firm will continue to expand output up to the point at which

Marginal revenue (MR) is the addition to total revenue as a result of selling one more unit of output.

marginal revenue = marginal costs

If at a certain level of output marginal revenue exceeded marginal cost, it would pay the firm to expand output. There would be more revenue gained from selling the additional output than there would be costs in producing it. As a result, profits would increase. If the cost of producing more output exceeded the revenue that would be acquired from selling it, then it would not make sense to increase production. In this case, if more units of output were produced, then profits would decrease. Only at the level of output at which marginal revenue is equal to marginal cost will profits be maximized.

The numerical example in Table 11.3 explains why equating marginal revenue and marginal cost results in the maximum profit. The price of the product is $5. At quantities less than 4 units, the marginal revenue exceeds marginal cost, and profit increases as the quantity increases from nothing to 4 units. Increasing the output from 4 units to 5 units adds nothing to profit since the marginal revenue and the marginal cost are both $5. At quantities beyond 5 units, marginal cost exceeds marginal revenue and profit starts to decline.

It should be noted that when looking at a firm's maximum profit level of output, the cost per unit (average total cost) is not considered. We are not looking for the maximum profit per unit but the maximum profit overall. However, the *average total cost* of output does enter into the firm's decision-making. The average revenue from the sale of the product must equal the average total cost or else the firm will consider closing down. The average total cost is an important statistic, but not in terms of determining the maximum profit level of output.

Table 11.3 *Total revenue, total cost, and profit for a hypothetical firm (in dollars)*

QUANTITY	TOTAL REVENUE	MARGINAL REVENUE	TOTAL COST	MARGINAL COST	PROFIT
0	0		4		−4
		5		3	
1	5		7		−2
		5		2	
2	10		9		1
		5		3	
3	15		12		3
		5		4	
4	20		16		4
		5		5	
5	25		21		4
		5		6	
6	30		27		3
		5		7	
7	35		34		1
		5		8	
8	40		42		−2
		5		9	
9	45		51		−6
		5		10	
10	50		61		−11

EVERYDAY ECONOMICS 11.4

Do Firms Attempt to Maximize Profits?

In order to study the behaviour of business firms in subsequent chapters, we have assumed that the primary objective of each firm is to maximize profits. We assume that, when a firm is making decisions on price and level of output, the objective of profit maximization is of foremost importance. It should be noted that not all economists agree that firms act in a manner that will maximize profits. Some believe that other objectives are more important. One such objective is to achieve a satisfactory level of profit.

The chief criticism of profit maximization as the sole objective of a business firm is that it is too difficult to achieve. In order to pursue this objective, a firm would have to have perfect knowledge about the demand for its product. This is simply not possible. It is also difficult for this objective to be used in guiding such business decisions as marketing strategy, the direction of future research, and the choice of product line. It is argued that these decisions are too complex and cannot be made by taking into consideration only one objective.

Some economists argue that profit maximization is useful as an objective for the less-complex type of decisions. Shall a certain piece of equipment be purchased? How shall production be scheduled? Other economists believe that the objective holds for analyzing the long-run behaviour of a firm but not the short-run. They argue that the goal of profit maximization does not give a prescription for making a decision when the future is unknown. The firm's decision will be based on the assessment of future probabilities. In the long run, profit maximization makes more sense as a goal of business behaviour. In the long run, only certain firms in an industry will remain in business. These firms must have been able to earn sufficient profits in order to continue in business.

If there are so many criticisms of the profit maximization objective, why is it still used? There are two reasons. First, the objective can be readily defined. It is an attempt to maximize the difference between total revenue and total costs. This definition provides economists with a basis for analyzing firm behaviour. Second, the objective of profit maximization has proved to be a good predictor of firm behaviour.

Questions

1. Can you identify any other possible objectives of a firm besides profit maximization?
2. Can you define what is meant by satisfactory profits?
3. If firms are trying to maximize profits, why do they donate money to various charities?

There are several constraints on the ability of firms to maximize profits. The most significant constraint is that firms may not have all the information necessary to be able to maximize profits. Their information about the purchasing plans of consumers and the production plans of their competitors may not be accurate. Also, firms may overestimate the abilities of their employees or their suppliers to produce products on time at the right cost.

The marketplace may also place a constraint on the ability of a firm to maximize profits. If consumers are not responding in a way the firm estimated they would, more money may be spent on advertising and promotion than was planned. Changes in the market may also affect the ability of the firm to raise money needed for investments.

REVIEW

11.10 The Pinewood Furniture Company tries to produce up to the quantity where their marginal revenue equals their marginal costs. Decide, according to the numbers given, at what level of production their profit is the greatest.

interactive
graphics

Summary

In order to better understand business-firm behaviour, it is essential to know something about production costs and profit. Production costs are divided into two categories: explicit and implicit. Explicit costs are payments for resources that the firm must purchase. Implicit costs are payments to resources that the firm already owns. The total costs of a firm in producing a product are the sum of its explicit and implicit costs.

Profit is defined as the difference between total revenue and total costs. When the total revenue exceeds the sum of explicit and implicit production costs, it is referred to as economic profit.

The production schedule can be divided into short-run and long-run time periods. In the short run, at least one resource remains fixed. This is the reason that the law of diminishing returns begins to influence output and production costs. Since each of the variable resources will have less of the fixed resource to work with as production increases, marginal costs begin to rise.

In the long run, all production resources are variable. Costs are influenced by economies and diseconomies of scale. While economies of large-scale production result in a decrease in average costs, the eventual presence of diseconomies of scale cause long-run average costs to increase.

All business firms are required to make decisions. In order to make decisions, an objective must be present. It is assumed that the objective of all firms is to maximize profits, or the difference between total revenue and total costs. In order to do this, it is necessary for a firm to continue to produce as long as the marginal revenue from increased production exceeds the marginal cost. At the level of production where marginal revenue and marginal costs are equal, profit is maximized.

Questions for Review and Discussion

1. It doesn't matter whether you are an accountant or an economist, profits are profits. Discuss.
2. Fred Quiche had always wanted to get into the restaurant business. He had been working as a restaurant supply salesman and believed that he knew the business well enough to start out on his own. Fred was earning $44 000 per year as a salesman and had accumulated $30 000 in savings. Several years ago Fred had the foresight to purchase a building in the downtown area. He believed that this would make an ideal location for his restaurant. Eventually Fred quit his job and started his own restaurant. He took his savings and purchased the restaurant supplies. At the end of one year in operation his cost structure was as follows:

labour (waiters)	$40 000
food	$10 000
miscellaneous	$ 2 000
depreciation of building	$ 2 000
hydro	$ 1 500
total cost	$55 500

a) Are these explicit or implicit costs?

b) Would you include any other costs in calculating Fred Quiche's total costs for the year?

c) How much money would Fred have had to make in sales in order to break even? (If you included any additional costs under (b), estimate them.)

3. Do accounting statements for a firm reflect opportunity costs? Explain.

4. Is there an opportunity cost associated with owning a patent? Explain.

5. Is it always true that the more workers you have, the more you produce? Discuss.

6. As soon as diminishing returns set in, average costs will begin to increase. Discuss this statement using the curves in Figure 11.3.

7. In what respect does the law of diminishing returns apply to the number of people who can receive swimming lessons at a swimming pool at any one time?

8. Why might two people be able to dig a hole three times as fast as one person? Why might five people need almost as much time as two people to dig the same hole? Assume that all of the people are of equal strength and ability.

9. To what economic principle are all the following sayings related?
   — Too many cooks spoil the broth
   — The straw that breaks the camel's back
   — Too much of a good thing
   Explain this principle.

10. a) Copy and complete the following table, then graph the marginal product and average number of bushels of eggplant against labour (days).

LABOUR (DAYS)	BUSHELS OF EGGPLANT	MARGINAL PRODUCT	AVERAGE NUMBER OF BUSHELS
0	0		
1	3		
2	8		
3	20		
4	29		
5	36		
6	42		
7	46		
8	48		
9	48		
10	45		

b) Insert the data into the spreadsheet as described in review question 11.4.

interactive graphics

11. The accountant at Chipchase Candy Company is trying to determine which costs faced by her firm can be altered and which cannot. From the following list that she has prepared, identify which costs are variable and which costs are fixed.
    a) purchase of paper wrappers for candy
    b) wages of night watchman
    c) vehicle maintenance costs
    d) printing of company's annual report
    e) purchase of sugar
    f) postage
    g) interest on bank loan

12. Identify the following business costs as either fixed or variable:
    a) salaries
    b) property taxes
    c) fire insurance
    d) raw materials
    e) transportation
    f) energy

13. a) Copy and complete the following table, then graph the average costs (fixed, variable, and total) and the marginal cost.

OUTPUT	TOTAL FIXED COSTS $	TOTAL VARIABLE COSTS $	TOTAL COST $	MARGINAL COST $	AVERAGE FIXED COST $	AVERAGE VARIABLE COST $	AVERAGE TOTAL COST $
0	20	0					
1	20	10					
2	20	18					
3	20	24					
4	20	28					
5	20	34					
6	20	42					
7	20	52					
8	20	68					
9	20	88					
10	20	118					

b) Insert the data into the spreadsheet as described in review question 11.10.

14. Much has been written about the differences between Japanese and North American firms. Two of these differences are that:
    a) Japanese firms tend to borrow money rather than raise money through issuing shares in the company;

b) Japanese employees tend to remain employed by the same firm until retirement rather than be subject to layoffs and recalls, as is the case in many North American industries.

How would these differences influence the shape of the ATC, AFC, and AVC curves for both Japanese and North American firms?

15. You have rented a rug cleaner from the local grocery store and have purchased the cleaning solution that accompanies the cleaner. After you are finished, the person in the apartment across the hall wants to use the machine before you return it. She offers to pay you for use of the machine. You have just finished taking an economics course and want to decide how much to ask for based on the concepts of cost. What should you charge her for use of the machine?

16. You are in the grocery store and an announcement is made that for the next ten minutes bottles of cola, regularly $2.00 a bottle, will be sold on a "two for the price of one" basis. Since you are having company that night you take advantage of the sale and buy two bottles to take home. When you arrive home your neighbour asks to buy one of the bottles from you. What price should you charge? (Hint: Think about the various types of cost discussed in this chapter.)

17. In the long run, we need not distinguish between fixed and variable costs. Explain why in the long run all costs are variable.

18. If a firm is making no economic profit, will it remain in business? Explain.

19. Can the law of diminishing returns be applied to growing flowers in a flowerpot? Explain. If so, what are the variable resources? the fixed resource?

20. In 2000, Honda announced that it wanted to make its Alliston, Ontario assembly plant more flexible. One change introduced by Honda was to replace jigs that held welding guns with a general welder. There were separate jigs for each side of the car and separate jigs for three-door and four-door models of the Honda Civic. It took about 15 minutes to switch jigs if necessary. With a general welder, all the welding can be done without the delay. The general welder can also adapt to different models of Honda vehicles within minutes. Honda plans to install the same general welder technology in all of its North American plants. Once this change has been completed, the company will be able to switch production more easily between plants and will also save money (estimated savings are $1.4 billion).

If the new technology can be used with more than one type of vehicle, what is the impact on fixed costs? variable costs?

21. Differentiate between diminishing returns and diseconomies of scale. In what respect are they similar? In what respect are they different?
22. Would a firm want to continue producing if total variable cost exceeded total revenue? Explain.
23. Is the auto parts industry in Southern Ontario an example of a cluster? Explain.
24. Researchers have found a link between the presence of clusters and higher-than-average wage rates. Explain.

Suggested Readings

Eaton, Curtis B., Diane F. Eaton, and Douglas W. Allen. *Microeconomics*. 4th ed. Scarborough: Prentice Hall Canada, 1999. A microeconomics text for those who wish to pursue the topics presented in this chapter in more detail.

Peters, Thomas J., and Robert H. Waterman, Jr. *In Search of Excellence: Lessons from America's Best-Run Companies*. New York: Warner Books, 1984. This book contains interesting accounts of some of the best companies in the United States.

Wright, J. Patrick. *On a Clear Day You Can See General Motors*. New York: Avon Books, 1979. This is the story of John DeLorean's days at General Motors.

 ## Selected Websites

www-bcf.usc.edu/~bpeter/203/Lecture%20Folders/lect9/index.htm A lecture on production and supply.

www.internationalecon.com/v1.0/ch80/80c020.html A note on economics of scale and increasing returns to scale.

http://devicelink.com/mddi/archive/99/08/007.html An article on economies of scale in the electronics manufacturing services industry.

http://abiworld.org/newslet/F2898whyte.html An article on economies of scale.

http://ecedweb.unomaha.edu/lessons/euse1.html A good explanation of fixed costs, with examples.

Perfect Competition: Theory and Practice

Key Terms

marginal revenue curve
break-even point
shut-down point
cobweb theorem
crop restrictions
offer-to-purchase
deficiency payment
marketing boards

Core Concept Building

This chapter discusses the profit-maximizing approach of firms in perfect competition. The chapter also discusses the agriculture sector, the best example of perfect competition. Pay close attention to the method by which firms maximize profit. You will also use the concepts of demand and supply, price elasticity, and cost curves extensively in this chapter.

Chapter Objectives

After successfully completing this chapter, you will be able to:

- describe how the price is determined for a firm in perfect competition
- graphically show the profit-maximizing point for a perfectly competitive firm
- describe the long-run profit position of a perfectly competitive firm
- relate the trends in Canadian agriculture
- describe the short-run and long-run problems of Canadian agriculture
- describe and graph the cobweb theorem
- describe and graph the attempts at price supports in agriculture
- relate the objectives of marketing boards and the possible methods of achieving these objectives

CHANGES IN CANADIAN FARMING

Many changes have taken place in recent years that have impacted directly on farmers. First, scientific and technological change has resulted in more output from the same amount of resources. Hybrid crops, improved farm machinery, pesticides and herbicides, and better irrigation methods are just some of the changes that have resulted in an increased supply of agricultural products. Other advances have altered our food products, such as chicken feed that will help in producing low-fat chickens with high nutritional value. Second, agricultural subsidies given to farmers in the United States and Europe have increased supply to the point that prices for farm commodities have declined drastically. Third, the World Trade Organization is putting pressure on Canada to change its system of supply management.

Also, there are changes taking place in the use of farm products. Corn, for example, is used in the manufacture of wallboard, antibiotics, toothpaste, spark plugs, road de-icer, insecticides, plastics, disposable diapers, airbags, and ethanol. Flax is used in building insulation.

There are changes in the types of products grown. British Columbia is devoting more land to ginseng and to grapes. Framers in the prairies are planting less wheat and more hay, oilseeds, lentils, soybeans, and field dry peas. There are more farms raising bison, llamas, and alpacas. Sheep production is higher in all provinces. In Quebec, deer farming is growing in popularity. Fruit growing, especially blueberries, is more popular in New Brunswick. Finally, more farmers across Canada are turning to organic farming practices.

After the Second World War, 1.2 million Canadians worked on farms. In 2001, that number had dropped to 313 000 Canadians. In addition to farm employment, farm incomes are declining.

In 1975, net farm income in Canada was $11.1 billion. In 2000, net farm income adjusted for inflation was only $2.6 billion.

A look at the province of Saskatchewan gives us a picture of the magnitude of the impact of these changes. Saskatchewan is known as a province driven by agriculture. Its economic picture is changing: in 1959, income from farming represented almost one-half of the total provincial income. By 1998, farm income represented less than 2 percent of total income. Wages from employment now comprise about 60 percent of total income in Saskatchewan, compared to only 30 percent in 1959. Only 5 percent of the Saskatchewan population is employed in agriculture. Small towns that relied on farming are disappearing, and grain elevators are being torn down. As farm economies of scale dictate larger operations, smaller farms are being replaced by larger farms that are more capital intensive than the smaller farms.

Will unemployed farmers find work in other areas? The ability of Saskatchewan farmers to find alternate employment is hampered by the low levels of education in the province. Saskatchewan has the lowest proportion of employed workers with a high-school diploma in Canada. Without a strong educational background the transition to other types of employment for many of these workers will be difficult.

This chapter discusses the characteristics of perfect competition. Since many areas of agriculture are the best examples of perfect competition in our economy, the chapter will also discuss price and income issues related to the Canadian agricultural industry. As you read the chapter, think of the changes that are taking place in this industry.

Characteristics of Perfect Competition

Chapter 10 introduced the characteristics of perfect competition. This chapter discusses the attempt by perfectly competitive firms to maximize profits and the resource allocation implications of perfect competition.

Profit Maximization

One of the competitive models introduced in Chapter 10 was perfect competition, which describes a competitive situation in which many sellers each produce an identical product. As a result of this, no individual seller has any control over the price of the product. The price is determined by demand and supply in the marketplace and, consequently, each seller in the industry is faced with deciding how much to produce. This chapter discusses how an individual seller, or firm, goes about making this decision.

The objective of each firm in an industry is to maximize profits. In order to determine how a firm goes about reaching this objective, it is necessary to have some information on the firm's revenue and costs. Since the price of the product is determined in the marketplace, we will begin by reviewing the demand and supply curves for a perfectly competitive industry. These are shown in Figure 12.1A. The curves intersect at an equilibrium price of P_1.

The demand curve for each individual firm is shown in Figure 12.1B. This demand curve is perfectly elastic, since there is virtually an endless demand for this firm's products at a price P_1. The firm can put as much of this product on the market as it wants without affecting the price. It will not be able to sell this product at a price above P_1, and there is obviously no reason to sell the product at a price below P_1. Because the price is determined in the marketplace, any change in the market price will mean a new demand curve for the firm. The demand curve represents the revenue side of the profit picture for the firm.

In order to maximize profits, it is necessary to maximize the difference between total revenue and total costs (see Chapter 11). Profits will continue to increase as long as the extra revenue from increased production exceeds the extra costs. In other words, the firm will continue to produce as long as marginal revenue exceeds marginal costs.

The short-run cost side of the picture will be similar to that described in Chapter 11. Over a certain range of output, average costs will decline because of increased efficiency. Eventually, average costs will increase as diminishing returns begin to influence the costs. This situation is shown in Figure 12.2. Also included in this figure is the demand curve for the firm.

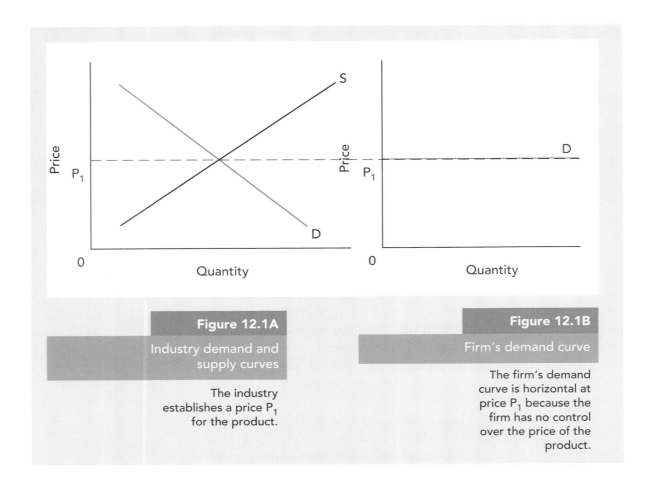

Figure 12.1A

Industry demand and supply curves

The industry establishes a price P_1 for the product.

Figure 12.1B

Firm's demand curve

The firm's demand curve is horizontal at price P_1 because the firm has no control over the price of the product.

A curve relating extra revenue to the quantity of output is called a marginal revenue curve.

The demand curve in Figure 12.2 can be shown to be the **marginal revenue curve** for the firm. The marginal revenue refers to the addition to total revenue from selling one more unit of output. Remember that the price is determined in the marketplace, and does not change regardless of how much of its product the firm supplies to the market. With the price already determined, the firm has only to decide how much to produce. Profits will be maximized by producing at a level of output where the marginal revenue is equal to the marginal cost (or where the price is equal to the marginal cost, since price and marginal revenue are identical). The intersection of these two curves in the diagram occurs at a level of output, q_1.

Is the firm making a profit under the conditions described in Figure 12.2? For each unit that the firm produces, it receives a price P_1. The average cost of producing each of the q_1 units of output is P_{ac}, which is less than P_1. Therefore, the firm is making a profit. This firm is making an economic profit because economic profit = total revenue – total costs. The

Figure 12.2

Revenue and cost curves for a perfectly competitive firm

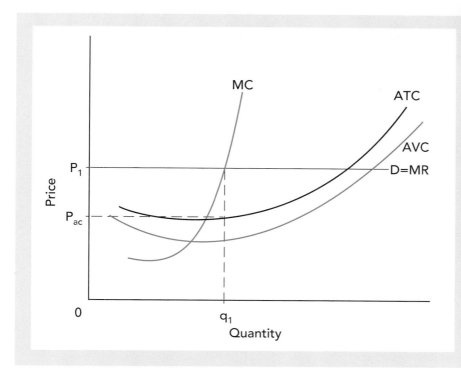

In order to maximize profits, the firm will produce a level of output (q_1) where marginal cost (MC) is equal to the price (P_1). The firm in this diagram is making an economic profit since the price (P_1) is greater than the average cost (P_{ac}) at this level of output.

economic profit made on each unit produced is $P_1 - P_{ac}$. The total economic profit as a result of producing q_1 units is $(P_1 - P_{ac})\, q_1$.

Will this firm continue to make economic profits? The answer is no. Since it is easy for new firms to get into the industry, the presence of economic profits will attract new firms. When new firms enter the industry, the supply of this product on the market will increase and the price will fall. This situation is shown in Figure 12.3A. A shift in the supply curve from S^1 to S^2 has forced a reduction in the price of the product from P_1 to P_2. Our firm now faces a new demand curve (Figure 12.3B), which is perfectly horizontal at price P_2. It will produce where marginal cost (MC) equals marginal revenue (MR_2) in order to maximize its profits, yet its profits have been reduced. Production will fall to a level q_2.

In fact, new firms may continue to enter this industry until the price falls so low that all economic profits disappear. This situation is shown in Figure 12.4. If the price had fallen to P_3 the firm would produce a level of output as shown by q_3. At this level of output, P_3 is just equal to the average costs of production. This is a **break-even situation**, in which the firm is covering explicit and implicit costs but is not earning any economic profits.

The break-even point is the level of production for a firm at which price equals the minimum average cost.

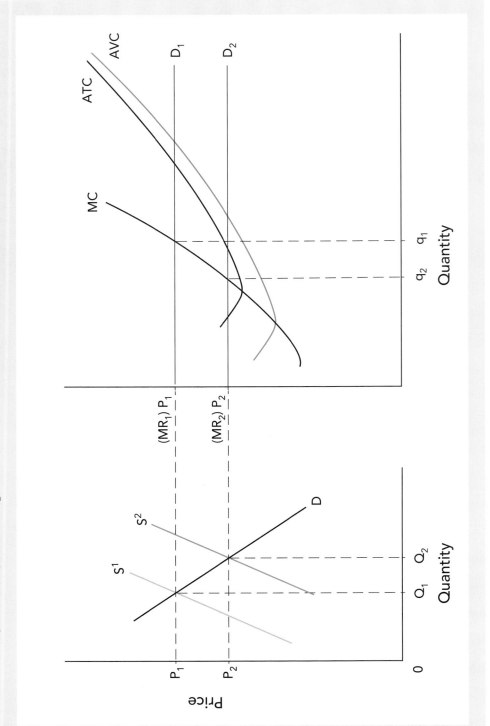

Figure 12.3A

Shift in industry supply curve

When new firms enter the industry the supply curve shifts to S^2. This lowers the price of the product to P_2.

Figure 12.3B

New demand curve

At the new price P_2, the firm's demand curve becomes D_2. The level of output that will maximize profits is q_2.

Figure 12.4

Break-even and shut-down points

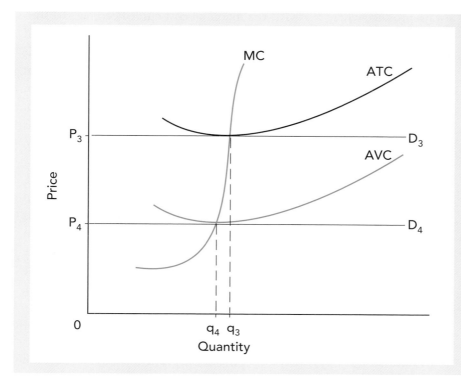

If the price of the product fell to P_3, the new demand curve would be D_3 and q_3 units of output would be produced. At this level of output the firm would break even. If the price fell to P_4, an amount q_4 would be produced. This is known as the shut-down point, since the price is equal to the average variable cost.

break-even point: price = minimum average cost

Will the firm remain in business if the price falls below P_3? Yes, as long as the price remains above *average variable cost* (AVC). Even at a price between P_3 and P_1 (see Figure 12.4), the firm will continue to produce at a loss because it will cost the firm more money to shut down. If the firm shuts down, it will have to pay fixed costs anyway, since fixed costs do not disappear when it shuts down. Fixed costs remain in the short run even if production is not taking place.

If the price is greater than the minimum average variable costs, the firm would be better off to remain in business. It will be able to cover variable costs and will have some money left over to put toward fixed costs. If the price falls to minimum AVC, as shown by P_4, the firm may as well shut down, since it is not paying off any fixed costs anyway. When this happens, the firm is said to have reached the **shut-down point**.

The shut-down point is the level of production at which the average variable cost of each unit of output is equal to the price of the product.

shut-down point: price = minimum average variable cost

Since a firm in perfect competition that is trying to maximize profits will always produce where P = MC, the marginal cost curve becomes the supply curve for the firm. In order to determine how much the firm would produce at any price, simply refer to the MC curve. Not all of the MC curve, however, would be considered to be the supply curve. Since the firm will not produce any amount when the price falls below average variable cost, only the MC above the AVC curve represents the supply curve for the firm.

What happens to the profit picture of the firm in the long run? As noted earlier, if economic profits are being made by firms in the industry, new firms are likely to enter. With more firms in the industry, the supply of the product will increase. This will cause the price of the product to fall. As the price falls, the amount of economic profits made by firms will begin to decrease, and some firms may even be operating at a loss. If some firms in the industry continue to lose money, they will consequently shut down in the long run. Their exit from the industry will cause the industry supply to decrease and the price to increase. A higher price will, however, enable some firms who were losing money to then break even. In fact, in the long run, there is a tendency for firms in this industry to just break even. Since there are no barriers to the entry of new firms, existing firms cannot continue to earn economic profits in the long run.

A numerical example may help explain the profit-maximizing position of a firm in perfect competition. Assume that you own a farm and grow carrots. This year you grew 8000 kilos of carrots that sold for 10 cents per kilo in the marketplace. The average cost of production for you was eight cents per kilo. You made an economic profit of two cents per kilo.

You believe that the price of carrots will remain at 10 cents per kilo next year. Should you increase your carrot production? This decision depends on the marginal cost of producing more carrots. If the marginal cost at your current level of production is eight cents per kilo, you should grow more carrots. As long as the price is greater than the extra cost of growing more carrots, you should grow more carrots—and continue to grow them until the marginal cost reaches 10 cents per kilo. At this level of production, you are maximizing profits. Any increase in production beyond this level would reduce profits because the extra cost of growing more carrots would rise above 10 cents—the market price.

What if the price does not remain at 10 cents per kilo? If economic profits are being made from carrot growing, new suppliers are likely to enter the market. This increase in supply will reduce the market price. If the market price falls below 10 cents per kilo, your carrot production should still be determined by producing at a level where MC = P. If the price falls to eight cents per kilo, you should produce 8000 kilos of carrots. At this level of output, the price is equal to marginal cost and is also equal to your average cost. Here you are just breaking even and earning no economic profit. If the price drops below eight cents per kilo, you must decide whether to continue growing carrots. Your decision will be based on your average variable costs. If the price is still above AVC, then you may continue in the business for the short run, anyway. If the price drops below your AVC, you would be wiser to stop producing carrots.

A summary of the above discussion is presented below:

if P > MC: increase production up to quantity where P = MC
if AVC < P < MC: continue producing at the quantity where P = MC
if P < AVC: shut down

REVIEW

12.1 Why does the firm maximize profits by producing a level of output where the price equals the marginal cost?

12.2 Is it possible for a firm in perfect competition to earn economic profits in the long run?

12.3 See how the market price, and a firm's cost curves, interact to determine the firm's level of profit, and locate the break-even and shut-down prices of their product.

Resource Allocation

Is perfect competition an ideal type of competitive structure for Canadian industry? This is a difficult question to answer. In an industry characterized by a large number of firms, no one firm is likely to be large enough to take advantage of economies of scale, and firms may not be taking advantage of low-cost production techniques. Firms in such an industry are not likely to channel money into product research and development. Also, consumers may not be content with identical, or homogeneous, products and may prefer some variety.

Conversely, there are certain advantages of perfect competition from society's point of view. Perfectly competitive firms tend to be efficient in their use of Canadian resources and will continue to produce a product until the marginal cost is just equal to the price. The marginal cost represents the value of our resources that are being used up in order to produce the product. It includes the labour, land, and capital, which, if not used to make this product, could be used for making something else. By allocating resources for the manufacture of this product, Canadian society acquires the opportunity cost of not being able to use the resources for other products.

What significance is there in the fact that a perfectly competitive firm keeps expanding output as long as the marginal cost is less than the price? In order to answer this, we have to examine what the price of the product represents. Since the price of a product represents how much people are willing to pay for it, the price represents the *value* that consumers get from the product. It can also be seen as representing the benefit of the product to Canadians. The advantage of perfect competition is that each firm expands output to the point at which the benefit that consumers are getting from the product (P) is just equal to the cost of producing it (MC). It should be emphasized that the individual firm is not attempting to equalize benefits and costs from society's viewpoint. The firm is interested in maximizing profits in a manner seen as beneficial to society.

Why will the firm not produce beyond the level of output that equates marginal cost and price? Because if it does, it loses profits. Also, if the marginal cost is greater than the price, the cost of making the additional output (MC) is greater than the value of the output (P). This is not an ideal situation either for the firm or for society. As well, if the firm were to restrict output to a level at which the price exceeded the marginal cost, the firm's profits would be less than they could be. The firm benefits by expanding output. Canadians would also want to receive more output of this product because the benefit (P) is greater than the cost of producing it (MC).

A firm in perfect competition allocates resources efficiently by producing a level of output where P = MC. This is exactly the way society would like to see resources used. However, the firm is not producing this level of output in order to please the rest of society but in order to maximize profits. Thus, perfect competition is seen as an ideal way to allocate resources because firms will produce at a level where the benefits from the additional output are equal to the cost of making the product. The P = MC rule does not consider negative third-party effects, however. The costs associated with negative third-party effects are not included in the marginal costs calculated by the firm. Since possible third-party costs are not included, a firm in perfect competition may produce at a higher level of output than is considered socially optimum.

R E V I E W

12.4 Why is perfect competition seen as an ideal way to allocate scarce resources? Despite this benefit, why would it not be desirable if all industries were perfectly competitive? (Hint: Think of the characteristics of perfect competition.)

An Example of Perfect Competition: Canadian Agriculture

Agriculture is the best example of a perfectly competitive industry even though the characteristic of easy entry into the industry does not apply to all aspects of Canadian agriculture. This section discusses trends in the industry and the various types of government involvement in agricultural markets.

Trends in Canadian Agriculture

At the turn of the century, the major industry in Canada was farming. In fact, government immigration policy encouraged newcomers to Canada to begin farming the available land, particularly in western Canada. At this time, farms were primarily small, self-sufficient enterprises. Farmers raised a variety of crops and livestock, mainly for their own consumption.

The number of farms in Canada has been steadily decreasing. In 1941, the peak year for farms, there were 733 000 farms in Canada; by 2001 this figure had decreased to 246 923 farms (see Table 12.1). The decline in the number of farms has been accompanied by an increase in the average farm

Table 12.1 *Total number of farms by province, Canada, 1951, 1971, 2001*

| PROVINCE | NUMBER OF FARMS | | |
	1951	1971	2001
Newfoundland and Labrador	3 626	1 042	643
Prince Edward Island	10 137	4 543	1 845
Nova Scotia	23 515	6 008	3 923
New Brunswick	26 431	5 485	3 034
Quebec	134 366	61 257	32 139
Ontario	149 920	94 722	59 728
Manitoba	52 383	34 981	21 071
Saskatchewan	112 018	76 970	50 598
Alberta	84 315	62 702	53 652
British Columbia	26 406	18 400	20 290
Canada	623 087	366 110	246 923

SOURCES: Figures for 1951 and 1971 are from the *Census of Agriculture,* Agriculture Census Canada 1986 publication no. 96-102 (Ottawa: Statistics Canada, December 1987), pp. 1–1,1–2. Figures for 2001 adapted from Statistics Canada, 2001 *Census for Agriculture,* www.statcan.ca/english/freepub/95F0301XIE/index.htm.

size. In 1901, the average farm was 50 hectares. In 2001, the average farm was 273 hectares. The number of Canadians employed in agriculture has also declined. One hundred years ago, 60 percent of all families were farm families, whereas today only 3 to 4 percent of all families are farm families. Small, self-sufficient farms are giving way to larger, more specialized, and more capitalized farms. Yet, in spite of the reduction in farms and farm workers, agricultural production is increasing.

What has accounted for these trends? Farms have been increasing in size mainly because farming is becoming more mechanized. The introduction of the tractor and other farm machinery has enabled the farmer to handle larger tracts of land. In order to make the new equipment more economical and efficient, larger farms are required. Farms are also becoming more specialized in order to spread the increased costs of farm operation over a larger volume of output.

Along with changes in farm size have come changes in farm incomes. The net income of farm operators has generally been declining as a percentage of the total income earned in Canada. Agricultural output has represented a smaller proportion of GDP in recent years. Incomes received by farm operators also fluctuate a great deal from year to year. The following sections in the text analyze the reasons for declining and unstable farm incomes.

EVERYDAY ECONOMICS 12.1

Aquaculture

Aquaculture refers to establishments engaged primarily in farm-raising finfish and shellfish. This industry is growing in Canada. From 1991 to 1997, receipts from the aquaculture business doubled. In 1997, revenue from aquaculture totalled $387.9 million.

The industry is concentrated in the provinces on Canada's coasts. In New Brunswick, where Atlantic salmon is farmed in the Bay of Fundy, 46 percent of the province's farm receipts in 1997 were from aquaculture. Aquaculture provided more than double the farm receipts of potatoes in that province. In British Columbia, both shellfish and finfish are farmed. Pacific oysters, Manila clams, and scallops are the shellfish crop and chinook and coho salmon comprise the finfish crop. Aquaculture

in British Columbia employs 4000 people and represents approximately 10 percent of farm receipts. Prince Edward Island farms shellfish. In Newfoundland, the aquaculture crop includes both shellfish (mussels, scallops, soft shell clams, and sea urchins) and finfish (Atlantic salmon, steelhead trout, brook trout Arctic char, wolffish, halibut, yellowtail flounder, and cod). The remaining maritime province, Nova Scotia, and also Quebec, are developing an aquaculture industry.

The most popular cultivated fish is Atlantic salmon. All varieties of salmon account for 83 percent of the farmed fish in Canada. In 1997, 44 000 tonnes of salmon were shipped to the United States, our biggest customer for fish, for a total value of $333 million. Mussels represent 4 percent of farmed fish production and, in 1997, the United States bought 5000 tonnes of mussels valued at $12 million. Oysters represent 3 percent of aquaculture output, with other finfish and other shellfish representing 9 percent and 1 percent respectively.

Aquaculture is not confined to the coastal provinces. Alberta farms rainbow trout. Ontario sold 4000 tonnes of rainbow trout in 1999 worth $17 million. Ontario also farms book trout, largemouth bass, brown trout, Atlantic salmon, Arctic char, tilapia, koi, carp, yellow perch, and walleye.

Question

1. Does aquaculture have the characteristics of perfect competition? Discuss.

Reasons for Low Farm Incomes

Declining farm incomes are a result of the various markets for agricultural products. In these markets, the ability of farmers to supply food has increased faster than increases in the demand for food. As Figure 12.5 shows, when the supply increases more than the demand for a product the price falls. The shift of the supply curve to S^1 and of the demand curve to D^1 has lowered the price of the product to P_1. When the prices of agricultural products decline, farm incomes decline as well. In actual fact, prices of agricultural products have not been declining but have been increasing less rapidly than other prices.

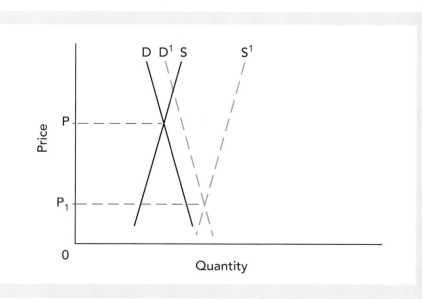

Figure 12.5

Shifts in demand and supply in agriculture

When supply (S^1) increases more than demand (D^1), the price falls.

Instability of Agricultural Prices

Not only have relative farm prices and incomes been declining, they have also been very unstable. This instability, which can also be traced to market forces, is a result of two factors: 1) the inelastic demand and supply in agricultural markets; and 2) fluctuations in the supply of agricultural commodities.

The inelasticity of the demand and supply for food causes farm prices to be unstable. Since food is a necessity, the demand for farm products is relatively inelastic. Price changes do not drastically influence the quantity of food purchased. On the supply side of the market, the curve is relatively inelastic as well, because once farmers have planted their crops, there is very little they can do about the volume of output until next year. Also, in farming, fixed costs are a high percentage of total costs. Since a large portion of total costs are composed of fixed costs, farmers would save very little by cutting back on output when prices drop. Therefore, within a short period of time, the supply of agricultural output is inelastic, because it does not respond significantly to price changes.

How does the inelasticity of demand and supply affect prices? Figure 12.6 shows the effect of inelastic demand and supply curves on market prices. In the figure, two demand curves are drawn intersecting the supply curve S^1 at the same point. This provides an equilibrium market price of P.

Figure 12.6

Comparison of price changes with elastic and inelastic demand curves

With any shift in the supply curve, the price changes more with an inelastic demand curve (D^1) than with an elastic demand curve (D^2).

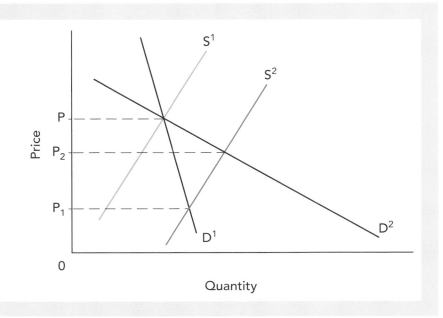

The demand curve D^1 is relatively inelastic, while the demand curve D^2 is relatively elastic. Assume that the supply increases to S^2. Under the conditions of an inelastic demand D^1, the price falls to P_1. Under the conditions of an elastic demand D^2, the price falls to P_2. Given any shift in the supply curve, an inelastic demand will result in a greater change in price than will an elastic demand curve. Since the demand for agricultural products is relatively inelastic, any change in the supply causes food prices to fluctuate greatly. If farm prices fluctuate a great deal, then farm incomes will fluctuate as well.

The curves in Figure 12.6 point out another interesting aspect of farm prices. A good crop can depress farm prices and farm incomes, while a poor crop may increase farm income. A large crop will shift the supply curve to the right, causing a drop in price. Under conditions of an inelastic demand, any drop in price results in less total revenue or less money being spent on the product (see Chapter 2). A poor crop will cause the supply curve to shift to the left, causing a higher price. Any increase in price because of a bad crop raises total revenue as well as farm incomes, because of the inelastic nature of the demand curve.

R E V I E W

12.5 What has accounted for the trend toward larger farms?

12.6 Why have farm incomes been declining in relation to non-farm incomes?

12.7 Does an inelastic demand curve cause farm prices to fluctuate more in response to supply changes than if the demand were elastic? Explain.

12.8 What would be the effect on farm-product prices if one farmer were to withhold his crop from the market? If all farmers were to withhold their crops from the market?

The Cobweb Theorem

In addition to market inelasticities, price fluctuations in agriculture are due to fluctuations in the supply of agricultural products on the market. Some of these fluctuations are due to changes in weather conditions; however, the main cause of supply variation lies with the farmers themselves. A possible explanation of farmer reaction to changing farm prices is provided by the **cobweb theorem**. This theorem, which has been used to explain changes in hog prices, assumes that farmers determine the size of next year's crop, or number of livestock, on the basis of this year's price. If prices are

The cobweb theorem, an explanation of price fluctuations in agriculture, assumes that farmers determine the size of next year's crop on the basis of this year's price.

high this year, farmers will plan to increase their output next year. On the other hand, if prices are low this year, next year's output will be reduced.

An example of the cobweb theorem is presented in Figure 12.7. In the diagram, S represents the short-run supply curve for the product. The other supply curves, S^1, S^2, S^3, and S^4, represent the supply curves of the product on the market in Years 1, 2, 3, and 4. The amount of crop supplied next year is determined by relating this year's price to the short-run supply curve. When next year's crop is harvested, it becomes the basis for the supply curve for that year. The yearly supply curves determine the price for each year, depending on where they intersect the demand curve. In the diagram, it is assumed that the elasticities of demand (D) and supply (S) are equal.

Assume that the quantity of this product put on the market in the first year is equal to Q_1. With this supply curve (S^1), the price of the product in Year 1 will be P_1. If the price P_1 prevailed in the market in Year 1, then farmers will want to supply Q_2 to the market in the second year. This result is determined by relating P_1 to the short-run supply curve. This increase in supply (S^2) will depress the market price to P_2 in Year 2. The lower price

Figure 12.7

The cobweb theorem

S represents the short-run supply curve for the industry. S^1, S^2, S^3, and S^4 represent the yearly supply curves. The intersection of the yearly supply curves and the demand curve (D) establishes the price.

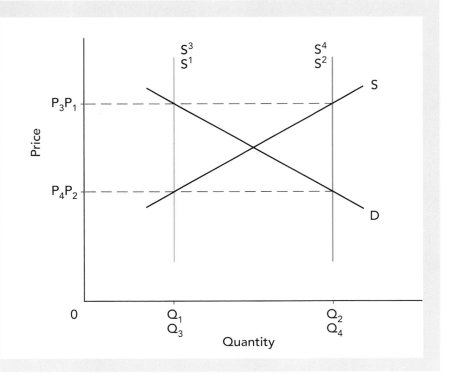

in Year 2 will convince some farmers to get out of this crop, and supply will drop to Q_3 in Year 3. This change shifts the supply curve to S^3 and a higher price (P_3). In subsequent years, the trend continues.

The cobweb theorem explains why farm prices fluctuate. It also explains why prices may never reach an equilibrium level. If the demand and supply elasticities for the product are identical, the price will continue to fluctuate around the equilibrium point.

What if demand and supply elasticities are not equal? If the price elasticity of demand is greater than the price elasticity of supply, the price fluctuations associated with the cobweb theorem will get smaller and smaller. The price gets closer and closer to the equilibrium price. In this situation, the consumer is responding more to price changes than the supplier is. The smaller response to price changes on the supply side of the market dampens the fluctuations in price. If the price elasticity of supply exceeds that of demand, the price fluctuations get bigger and bigger. The price gets further and further away from equilibrium. In this situation, the suppliers react to price changes more than the consumers, causing the large changes in supply from year to year.

REVIEW

12.9 What is the cobweb theorem trying to explain?

12.10 In order for the cobweb theorem to be an accurate description of agricultural prices, what assumption has to be made?

Price Supports

From the preceding discussion, it can be determined that the problem of agricultural incomes is twofold: 1) they are generally lower than non-farm incomes; and 2) they fluctuate more than non-farm incomes. In order to overcome these difficulties, a number of government-assisted programs have been introduced.

Crop Restriction

One possible solution to low and fluctuating incomes is to limit the amount of a product that a farmer can produce. This means imposing a quota, or **crop restriction,** on each farmer's output. The effect of this restriction is shown in Figure 12.8. As shown in the graph, a shift in the supply curve from S^1 to S^2 raises the price of the product from P_1 to P_2. If the demand for the product is inelastic, then an increase in price will result in an increase in the total revenue that farmers receive.

A crop restriction is a government quota designed to reduce the quantity of an agricultural product on the market.

Figure 12.8

A crop-restriction program

A restriction of the supply from S^1 to S^2 raises the price from P_1 to P_2.

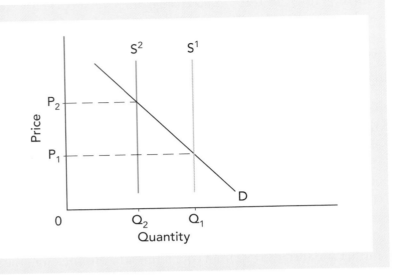

It should also be noted that any quota system will also prevent wide fluctuations in supply and will limit price-and-income fluctuations as well. A quota system has been introduced in Canada for many agricultural products, including tobacco, milk, and eggs. As a result, consumers are forced to pay a higher price for less output than before the quota was introduced.

Offer-to-Purchase

In the offer-to-purchase program of agricultural price support, the government establishes a price floor and then offers to buy any surplus product not sold in the marketplace.

The **offer-to-purchase** type of program establishes a minimum price for which the product can be sold. The minimum price results in a *surplus*, which government offers to purchase from farmers at the minimum price. In Figure 12.9, the minimum price is designated by P_m. At this price, consumers are willing to purchase only Q_d, while suppliers are willing to supply Q_s. The surplus ($Q_s - Q_d$) is purchased by government. The problem then becomes one of disposing of the surplus, or storing it. The size of the surplus will partially depend on the elasticity of demand for the product. The more inelastic the demand, the smaller the surplus. If the demand is inelastic, increases in the price are not going to reduce quantity demanded to a significant degree.

Who pays for the offer-to-purchase price-support program? Consumers pay increased prices for farm products compared to the free-market price. Taxpayers pay for buying up the surplus and possibly for storing it.

Figure 12.9

The offer-to-purchase program

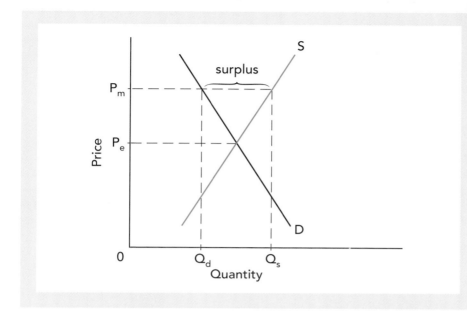

The imposition of a
price floor (P_m) results
in a surplus ($Q_s - Q_d$).

Deficiency Payment

The deficiency-payment price-support system solves the problem of a surplus. Under this system, no minimum price is set. Instead, the government guarantees to pay farmers the difference between the average market price and a specified support price. All farmers receive the same **deficiency payment** per unit regardless of the market price received for their product. This scheme is depicted in Figure 12.10. In the graph, P_s is the support price and Q_1 the amount that farmers are willing to produce at this price. However, in order to sell Q_1 on the market, a price of P_m is established. The deficiency payment is then $(P_s - P_m) Q_1$.

Apart from solving the problem of storing and disposing of a surplus, the deficiency-payment price support ensures a lower price for the consumer. One possible disadvantage is that this type of price support could be more expensive than the offer-to-purchase system. If the demand for the product is highly inelastic, it is possible that the cost to government from the deficiency-payments program would be higher than under the offer-to-purchase program.

The Organization for Economic Co-operation and Development estimates that the government was the source of 19 percent of Canadian farm income in 2001. The percentages in the United States, the European Union, and Japan were 22, 38, and 64 percent respectively. The 19-percent figure quoted for Canada may be lower than it should be as it does not take into

The **deficiency-payment**
system is an agricultural
price support program
whereby the government
pays the farmer the
difference between the
average market price for a
product and the support
price.

Figure 12.10

The deficiency-payment schedule

At the support price P_s, farmers decide to produce an amount Q_1. This brings about a price P_m in the marketplace. Government will pay to the farmer the difference between P_s and P_m for Q_1 units of output.

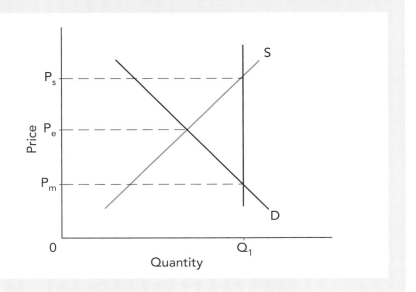

consideration the benefit that farmers receive from supply quotas. As pointed out in this chapter, supply restrictions increase the price. The higher prices can be seen as an indirect subsidy.

It is also estimated that governments in Canada provide $3.53 in subsidies for every dollar earned by farmers. These subsidies come in three forms. First, there are direct payments from the government to farmers. These payments are primarily aimed at lowering the price of crops destined for export. Second, supply restrictions in some sectors of agriculture increase the price received for the product. Third, the taxpayer assists groups who support the agriculture industry such as those involved in research and development and those who lobby governments on behalf of farmers.

REVIEW

12.11 Why, under an offer-to-purchase system, may quotas on farm production be necessary?

12.12 How does the deficiency-payment scheme differ from the offer-to-purchase scheme?

12.13 The government is thinking of implementing a price support for sandwiches. Examine the effects on the market when price supports are in effect, and what this costs the government, depending on the elasticity of demand for sandwiches.

Marketing Boards

Because individual farm operators have no control over agricultural prices, they have been encouraged to cooperate with one another to influence market conditions. Through joint action, farmers have tried to influence the supply of the product on the market, its distribution, the demand for the product, and ultimately its price. One attempt at joint action has been the creation of **marketing boards**. A marketing board is a compulsory marketing organization for primary or processed agricultural products. The compulsory nature of the board means that a specified commodity is subject to the rules and regulations of the marketing board. The authority that marketing boards possess over the supply and marketing of a specific agricultural commodity can come from either the federal or the provincial government.

A marketing board **is a compulsory marketing organization for primary or processed agricultural products.**

Marketing boards have been established in Canada since 1929. At present, there are more than 100 producer-marketing boards in Canada. The primary purposes of these boards are 1) to maintain or increase incomes of the producers of a particular product; 2) to stabilize income from the sale of the product; and 3) to standardize the terms of sale of the product.

Not all marketing boards have exactly the same objectives and methods of operation. A number of powers and procedures are available to them:

- *Pooling:* All of the proceeds from sales of the product are pooled so that each producer receives the same average price after adjustments for such items as grade.
- *Price setting:* A board may have the authority to set wholesale, consumer, or producer prices.
- *Quotas:* Marketing and/or producer quotas can be set for each producer.
- *Licensing:* Licences may be required for growers, producers, processors, dealers, or any other person involved in any way with the marketing process.
- *Seizure and disposal:* Any product marketed contrary to board orders may be seized and disposed of.
- *Trade regulation:* Both export and interprovincial trade may be regulated.
- *Purchase and sell:* The product may be purchased by the board and sold through the board.
- *Market information and development:* Producers can be supplied with market information, leading to a development of domestic and foreign markets.

Each marketing board operates under a different mandate, with somewhat different goals and methods of operation.

> ## REVIEW
> 12.14 What are the objectives of marketing boards in Canada?

EVERYDAY ECONOMICS 12.2

The Canadian Egg Marketing Agency

The development of provincial marketing boards enabled farm organizations to better control the volume of production. Provincial control over agricultural output, however, is not sufficient control in light of interprovincial trade. As egg producers in each province began to develop control over the supply of eggs, they began to recognize the need for a national egg-marketing plan. The passage of the Farm Products Marketing Agencies Act in 1971 permitted national marketing agencies in eggs and poultry. The Canadian Egg Marketing Agency (CEMA) became fully operational in June 1973.

Provincial egg-marketing boards divide up their provincial share of the national market by allocating quotas to individual producers. The CEMA determines the market share for each province. Quotas were originally based on the number of eggs but are now based on the number of hens that each producer is allowed to have. With a restriction on hens, but not eggs, there is some incentive for farmers to try to produce more eggs from the same number of hens. The main exemption from the quota system is for small egg-producing operations (defined as having fewer than 100 to 500 hens, depending on the province). The federal government has also imposed a tariff on the importation of eggs and egg products in compliance with the World Trade Organization (WTO). The tariff has been reduced from its initial level.

Prices for table eggs are determined at the provincial level and are based on a national survey of egg farmers. The survey collects information on the costs involved in producing eggs and determines the weight that each cost factor should have in the pricing formula. The costs taken into consideration are the cost of pullets (laying hens); the cost of feed and the cost to transport it; labour costs; overhead; depreciation; and producer return. On the basis of these production costs, egg prices are established on a monthly basis. Prices are also adjusted to reflect seasonal variation in demand.

The CEMA stimulates egg consumption through advertising and promotion. It has developed advertising slogans such as "Get Cracking," "Have Eggs Instead," "Eggs, Nature's Comfort Food," and "Eggs, Grade A Goodness." Finally, the CEMA attempts to improve egg quality and productivity in the egg industry.

Questions

1. Why was it necessary to establish a national egg-marketing agency in addition to provincial egg-marketing boards?

2. Using demand and supply curves in your answer, show the impact of the following:
   a) CEMA setting a minimum price for eggs;
   b) CEMA imposing a quota on egg production in Canada; and
   c) the federal government imposing a tariff on the importation of eggs into Canada.

3. Why would the CEMA find it necessary to advertise in order to increase egg consumption?

A Defence of Supply Management

Canada's system of restricting the output of some agricultural products has received some criticism in recent years as the world discusses freer trade in agriculture. It is argued that this system of supply management restricts competition and increases prices to the consumer. The Consumers' Association of Canada has asked that marketing boards be replaced by a market-driven system that would charge consumers the world price for poultry, eggs, and milk. How do the proponents of supply management defend the restrictions placed on eggs, chicken, milk, and other products?

The defence begins by asserting that supply management sets only the "farmgate" price—the price received by the farmer. This price is based on a formula that reflects the costs of production. The retail prices are set by the grocery stores. Prices to the consumer are determined not by supply conditions alone but by the interaction of demand and supply. The quantity of product that is produced is determined not by farmers themselves but by a committee with representatives from processors, consumers, restaurants, and government as well as farmers. The price to the consumer also depends on processing costs. Agricultural representatives have argued that processors should increase their productivity levels and help to keep costs down instead of focusing on supply management as the source of their difficulties. Supply management also results in less price fluctuation in the market.

If supply management keeps Canadian farmers in business, people are kept on the land and rural communities can prosper. Proponents of supply management point to the United States, where large corporations control the production and processing of chicken. They argue that the same scenario will occur in Canada. Without supply management, there is a fear that cheaper foreign products would take over the market. Do Canadians want to depend on foreign sources for food? Supply management prevents the spread of corporate farming, ensures the survival of independent farmers with a commitment to the environment, and provides Canadians with healthy food. Even under the supply-management system, farmers leave the industry. There is no guarantee that all farmers will be financially well-off within the supply-management system.

If agriculture were to compete on an international basis, foreign exchange rates would play a role in the success of the Canadian industry. Do we want the success of an industry as important as agriculture to be subject to the fluctuations in foreign-exchange rates?

Finally, commodity producers under supply management do not receive government stabilization payments, as do farmers in other sectors of agriculture.

Questions

1. Do you agree with the arguments put forward by the proponents of supply management? Explain.
2. Why are consumers generally opposed to supply management?
3. Why are price fluctuations smaller under a system of supply management?

Summary

Perfect competition is a competitive situation in which many firms are producing and selling an identical product. The price of the product is determined by the marketplace; no individual firm has any control over the price. The demand curve for each firm is perfectly horizontal at the market price. Because the price is determined by the market, each firm must decide how much of the product to produce. A firm maximizes profit by producing at a level of output at which the price is equal to the marginal cost.

There is no guarantee that a firm will earn economic profits, or even remain in an industry. If the price of its product falls below the average variable cost, the firm may shut down. If the price is equal to the average total cost, the firm is breaking even. If the price is greater than the average total cost, an economic profit is being made. When economic profits are being made, new firms are attracted into the industry and the market price falls. The decline in price leads to a decline in economic profit. In the long run, firms in perfect competition tend to break even.

The industry most resembling the perfect competition model in Canada is agriculture. Farm prices have been increasing less rapidly than non-farm prices because advances in agricultural technology have allowed the supply of farm products to increase faster than the demand for them. Farm prices also tend to fluctuate a great deal because of the inelastic demand and supply conditions in agricultural markets and fluctuations in the supply of farm products. In order to assist farmers, governments have introduced a variety of crop restriction, offer-to-purchase, and deficiency-payment programs. Marketing boards have also been established in order to raise and stabilize farm incomes.

Questions for Review and Discussion

1. Do you think that most of the costs facing a farmer are fixed or variable? List various costs of production in agriculture, and state whether they are fixed or variable.
2. Much of the increase in the supply of agricultural products has been attributed to improvements in technology. Does the farmer develop these improvements? Where is most of the research and development related to agriculture undertaken?
3. How can you account for the fact that in Canada the supply of food is increasing faster than the demand, while in many other parts of the world a shortage of food is the major problem?
4. Should the government undertake programs to encourage people to stay on the farm?

5. Is it fair to offer income and price programs to farmers and not to other businesses?

6. It is likely that price-support programs assist the operators of small farms more than the operators of large farms. Discuss this statement.

7. Using your knowledge of demand and supply curves, discuss the different impacts of the price-support programs considered in this chapter, depending on whether the demand for the product is elastic or inelastic.

8. If the supply of farm products were to decrease, prices would increase. The supply would decrease if a number of farmers decided to leave the industry. Why would some farmers be reluctant to give up farming in spite of low incomes?

9. How would the cobweb theorem apply to livestock? Would prices fluctuate from year to year, or could the cycle be extended over a couple of years?

10. Economist: "What crop have you planted this year?"
    Farmer: "Barley."
    Economist: "Why? Was the price of barley high last year?"
    Farmer: "No. The price of corn was low."
    Explain this conversation, relying on your knowledge of the cobweb theorem.

11. In this chapter, we described a cobweb-theorem situation in which the elasticities of demand and supply were the same. The theorem also applies to situations in which the elasticities of demand and supply are not the same. Draw cobweb-theorem graphs for the following situations:
    a) the elasticity of demand is greater than the elasticity of supply; and
    b) the elasticity of supply is greater than the elasticity of demand.

12. Why do marketing boards find it necessary to promote the demand for the product as well as to regulate the supply? Use demand and supply curves in your answer.

13. Why do marketing boards require that all producers adhere to the regulations of the board?

14. The presence of economic profits in an industry will attract new suppliers into the industry. With new suppliers entering the market, what will happen to the demand for the resources required to make this product? What might happen to the price of these resources? What might happen to the cost curves in this industry as a result of the expansion of the industry?

15. In professional sports, the fixed cost associated with operating a franchise represents a large percentage of total costs. Does this fact help

explain why many sports teams may continue to operate even though they are claiming to lose money?

16. Why is the government more concerned about providing income support for farmers than for other groups, such as service-station owners?

17. It has been stated that Japanese firms have higher fixed costs than North American firms. Does this help explain why Japanese firms may produce large quantities of output? Does it help explain why their prices may be lower than for comparable North American firms?

18. The imposition of quotas in milk farming has had an impact on the cheese industry in Canada. Cheese producers who were unable to acquire sufficient milk have been forced to shut down. Using demand and supply curves, show the impact of milk quotas on the milk and cheese markets.

19. Assume that the federal government gives a 20-cent-per-kilogram subsidy to Canadian grape growers. Show the impact of this subsidy on the marginal cost, average variable cost, and average total cost curves for an individual grape grower. Would the impact on the curves be different if the subsidy were given in a lump sum as opposed to a per-kilogram subsidy? Explain.

Suggested Readings

Borcherding, Thomas, with Gary W. Dorosh. *The Egg Marketing Board: A Case Study of Monopoly and Its Social Costs.* Vancouver: Fraser Institute, 1981.

Grubel, Herbert G., and Richard W. Schwindt. *The Real Cost Of the B.C. Milk Board: A Case Study in Canadian Agricultural Policy.* Vancouver: Fraser Institute, 1977.

Farming Facts 1999. Catalogue no. 21-522-XPE. Ottawa: Statistics Canada. February 2000. A short pamphlet on farm issues.

Canadian Agriculture at a Glance. Catalogue no. 96-325-XPB. Ottawa: Statistics Canada. December 1999. An excellent source book on Canadian agriculture including readings and data.

 ## Selected Websites

www.cwb.ca The site for the Canadian Wheat Board. Information is available on marketing, grain movement, and publications.
www.canadaegg.ca The website for the Canadian Egg Marketing Agency. Market information, recipes, nutrition, and media releases are available on this site.
www.canswine.ca/comp.html The site for the Canadian Pork Council. More information can be found at www.canpork.ca.
www.agr.gc.ca/cal/calweb_e.html A library of agricultural documents.
www.cfa-fca.ca The website for the Canadian Federation of Agriculture.

How Imperfect Competition Functions

Key Terms

natural monopoly
predatory pricing
socially optimum price
fair-return price
consumer surplus
price discrimination
horizontal merger
vertical merger
conglomerate merger
kinked demand curve
price leadership
cartel
retail price maintenance
misleading price advertising
Competition Act

Core Concept Building

This chapter reviews the profit-maximizing approach taken in three types of imperfect competition: monopoly, oligopoly, and many differentiated sellers. Before tackling the concepts in this chapter, review the concepts of demand and supply, price elasticity, and cost curves.

Chapter Objectives

After successfully completing this chapter, you will be able to:

- describe the barriers to entry into a monopoly
- graph the profit-maximizing point for a monopoly
- differentiate between the socially optimum and fair-return approaches to monopoly regulation
- describe the conditions necessary for price discrimination to exist
- describe how oligopolies come into existence
- graph the kinked demand curve and describe the assumptions behind the curve
- relate illegal activities under the Competition Act
- graph the profit-maximizing position for a firm in many differentiated sellers
- discuss the advantages and disadvantages of advertising on the economy
- describe the long-run position of a firm in many differentiated sellers

TO COMPETE OR NOT TO COMPETE?

It was stated in Chapter 3 that government intervention in the free market may be necessary in order to ensure that competition in the provision of goods and services exits. Competition results in lower prices and better-quality products. The federal government has legislated the Competition Act with the objective of maintaining competition in the marketplace. This act is discussed in this chapter. Apart from enacting the legislation, what is the attitude of Canadian governments toward competition? The answer is not entirely clear.

In 1999, the government of Canada prohibited a merger of two of Canada's major banks, Royal Bank and the Bank of Montreal, arguing that increased concentration of Canada's banking industry was not in the interest of the consumer. It then permitted the merger of a chartered bank, the Toronto-Dominion Bank, with a large trust company, Canada Trust. In the same year, the federal government suspended the application of its own Competition Act when faced with the possibility of an airline monopoly in Canada. Eventually a monopoly was created when Air Canada merged with Canadian Airlines. A concern expressed by the policy-makers in the discussions regarding the airlines was foreign ownership of Canadian Airlines. Does it matter who owns the airlines that fly over Canada's air space? Is a Canadian monopoly better than competition involving foreign firms?

What is the attitude toward competition in the book publishing and book selling industries? Mergers over the last 20 years have significantly reduced the number of textbook publishers in Canada. Canada has legislation specifying who can own a book publishing company in Canada. There are also restrictions on foreign book sellers setting up shop in Canada. Would foreign booksellers not carry Canadian books if there were a market for them?

The federal government took away the monopoly that the Bell companies had over long-distance telephone service. Yet, the federal government continues to grant monopolies to cable television companies. Provincial governments permit monopolies in certain areas of the economy and encourage competition in others. For example, in Ontario, Ontario Hydro no longer has a monopoly over electricity generation, and natural-gas suppliers no longer have geographic monopolies. Some provinces have monopolized the sale of beer and alcoholic beverages, and quotas have been applied to certain agricultural products. Why can you not raise chickens for sale if you think you can make a profit doing it? Why do farmers need permission to grow tobacco?

This chapter discusses various types of competition, beginning with monopoly. While reading the chapter, take note of the reasons for the presence of monopoly.

What Is Imperfect Competition?

The types of competition described by *monopoly, oligopoly,* and *many differentiated sellers* are examples of imperfect competition. In contrast to the circumstance of perfect competition, in a situation of imperfect competition each firm has some control over the price that it charges for its product. This means that in order to sell more, the firm must lower its price. The firm, therefore, deals with a demand curve that is downward-sloping to the right. Although each firm has some control over the price, the extent of that control is determined by the exact nature of the competition in that industry.

Characteristics of a Monopoly

An industry that is referred to as a monopoly is one in which there is only a single producer of the product (see Chapter 10). The product is one for which there are generally no close substitutes. Examples of monopolies are public utilities, daily newspapers, the post office, natural gas, and the telephone service. Although there may not be any close substitutes for the product, monopolies do, in fact, have competition because they must compete along with every other product for the consumer's dollar. In addition, other products may be substituted for the monopoly product in a pinch. For example, there may be only one supplier of telephone service in your area, but you do not have to use the telephone in order to communicate with other people. The post office and courier services provide competition for the telephone company through alternative methods of communication.

Barriers to Entry

The major characteristic of a monopoly from an economist's point of view is that barriers prevent the entry of new firms into the industry. If the monopoly is profitable, new firms should be encouraged to start up. If the industry remains a monopoly, there must be a reason. What are these barriers?

Economies of Scale

In some cases, the existing firm that represents the monopoly may be producing on such a large scale that it is realizing *economies of scale,* and producing with lower average costs. It may not be possible for new firms to enter the industry and to compete on the basis of price. Economies of scale, then, become a barrier to the entry of new firms. Where this is the case, the monopoly situation most likely developed over time. As the industry expanded, those firms that began to realize economies of large-scale production drove their competitors out of business. Eventually, only one competitor remained.

An example of this type of monopoly can be found in the newspaper industry. In many cities, there remains only one daily afternoon newspaper. As a newspaper's circulation increases, it starts to achieve economies of scale. The newspaper can then charge a lower price to customers. Also, newspapers whose circulation increases will find it easier to attract advertisers. The newspapers with lower circulation will find it more difficult to compete, and eventually will drop out of the industry.

Advantages to Being Established

In addition to economies of scale, there are certain advantages to being already established in the industry. For example, consumers are familiar with an established company's name and may be reluctant to try a new product. Established companies may find it easier to borrow money, as they are seen to be better risks, and may be able to borrow at lower interest rates. The advantages associated with already established firms provide another barrier to new firms.

Natural Monopolies

A natural monopoly describes an industry in which it is more efficient to have only one seller of a good or service since average costs decline as output increases.

As we discussed in Chapter 3, in some industries competition may be impractical. It may be more efficient to have only one supplier of a product. With only one supplier, the company will be able to achieve economies of scale and provide the product or service for the lowest possible price. This is known as a **natural monopoly**. Examples of natural monopolies are local telephone service, natural gas, and public utilities. In the case of natural monopolies, government either regulates or operates the company in the industry. Government ownership or regulation of the industry is the barrier preventing competition.

In Canada, certain companies are granted a monopoly to provide cable television service within a defined geographic area. Competition is not permitted in this market. In the United States, cable television companies face competitors in some markets. Technological developments have undermined the label of natural monopoly that has been applied to the cable television industry. These technologies include private cable, wireless cable, direct-broadcast satellite, and the use of common carrier lines. In spite of these advances, government regulation maintains a monopoly on the cable television industry in Canada.

Ownership of Raw Materials

In some industries, the company is a monopoly because it owns or controls the raw materials that the industry requires. An example of this is the DeBeers company, which controls the distribution of diamonds worldwide although it does not own all the diamonds. In order to compete with DeBeers, a company must either own a mine or sign a marketing agreement with a mine owner. In Canada, the International Nickel Company (INCO) has a virtual monopoly in the ownership of that mineral. INCO is the major supplier of nickel in the world. Its position in the industry is maintained because it owns the natural resources that provide its product. However, in recent years other nations have brought nickel mines into production, threatening INCO's dominance in the industry. If certain raw materials necessary to an industry are difficult to acquire or if their supply is scarce, it may be impossible for new firms to enter that industry.

Patents

Patents are another way of maintaining a monopoly. When the inventor of a product takes out a patent, there is a monopoly on the production of that product. This monopoly remains throughout the life of the patent. In Canada, patents last for a period of 17 years (except on some products such as pharmaceuticals).

In some situations it may be possible for potential competitors to circumvent the barrier of a patent. The development of new technology and the creating of new product designs may permit the production of competing products. An example of how a patent may not ensure a monopoly is the case of the ball-point pen. Milton Reynolds took out a patent on the ball-point pen in 1945. He started producing the pens, and sold them for $12.50 each. Reynolds was earning high profits, which attracted competition. The new firms were able to get around the patent and began to compete with Reynolds. Within one year, the price of the pen had been reduced to $2.98. In later years the price of the pen was reduced even further. The competition reduced Reynolds' profits.

This story points out that monopolies will be able to earn high profits only if the barriers to the entry of new firms are invincible. If the barriers can be circumvented, then new firms will compete away much of the economic profit.

EVERYDAY ECONOMICS 13.1

Drug Patent Legislation

In recent years, a vigorous debate has taken place in Canada on the length of time that a patent should exist for new drugs. For how many years should a company retain a monopoly over the sale of a new drug before generic competitors can enter the market? In 1923 it became legal to sell generic drugs in Canada as long as they were manufactured in Canada. Because the Canadian market was so small at the time, very few generic drugs were manufactured here. In 1969, companies were allowed to sell generic drugs before the patent expired as long as they paid a royalty (4 percent) to the holder of the patent. This practice is known as compulsory licensing. The 1969 amendments also permitted the sale of imported generics. Even though the generic drug was processed in Canada, the ingredients were usually manufactured elsewhere.

The length of patent protection was shorter in Canada than in other countries, and this prompted complaints from brand-name manufacturers. For example, in the United States drug patents ran for 17 years. Canada was the only country that permitted compulsory licensing. The argument against compulsory licensing was that it discouraged pharmaceutical manufacturers from undertaking research and development in Canada. In 1987 Canada passed the Drug Patent Law, which extended drug patent protection to ten years, during which time generic producers cannot make copies of the drug. The patent protection period could be reduced to seven years if the generic components were made in Canada. In return for better patent protection, the brand-name manufacturers promised to increase spending on research and development in Canada.

Lengthening of the time that a patent is protected could lead to higher drug prices. The prospect of higher drug prices was a concern for individuals and for provincial health plans that covered prescription drugs. In order to monitor drug prices, the 1987 legislation also established the Patented Medicine Prices Review Board. From 1987 to 1991, drug prices increased at a slower rate than the overall Consumer Price Index. Also, research and development expenditures increased in the industry from 4.2 percent of sales to 9.2 percent. Employment in the industry increased, especially in the province of Quebec.

In 1993, Canada increased the length of a patent on new drugs to 20 years. The change brings Canada's drug patent protection more in line with other industrialized countries (the EEC has 25 years for drug patent protection). Since it takes about ten years from the time a patent is filed until production begins, the new legislation gives brand-name manufacturers approximately a ten-year monopoly on selling. The legislation also prohibited the exporting of generic drugs from Canada that are under patent protection in this country.

In 1998, the European Union (EU) challenged Canada's drug-patent legislation before the WTO. The EU argued that the legislation did not provide for the full protection of patented pharmaceutical inventions for the entire duration of the term of protection. The Patent Act gives brand-name companies 20-year patent protection, but during that time generic drug companies can develop and test copies of brand-name products. They can also apply for government approval of the generic drug. Six months before the expiry date of the patent, the generic companies can begin producing and stockpiling the drugs. The EU argued that the rights given to the generic drug manufacturers may permit the drugs to come on the market before the patent expires.

The WTO ruled that generic companies should be allowed to develop copies of brand-name drugs while the patent protection is still in place. The WTO also ruled that the generic companies should not be permitted to stockpile drugs in anticipation of the expiry of the patent. In another ruling, on a U.S. complaint against Canada, the WTO stated that Canada must extend patent protection on 66 000 different drugs, inventions, and high-technology innovations. Canada appealed the WTO ruling, but in September 2000 the appeal was dismissed. As a result of the WTO ruling, Canada passed an amendment to the patent legislation bringing Canada in line with international drug patent standards. The issue of developing countries' access to cheap copies of patented drugs is one of the items to be settled in the Doha Round of WTO negotiations.

Questions

1. Those in favour of extending drug-patent protection argue that Canadians will now have earlier access to new medicine. Explain their reasoning.

2. A reduction in the length of time that a patent is protected would reduce the profits for the inventor of the new drug. Would companies be willing to undertake research and development if potential profits were reduced?

3. Some drugs are very expensive. The price of yearly AZT treatment for AIDS was $10 000. Pressure from the AIDS lobby forced AZT's manufacturer, Wellcome PLC of Britain, to reduce the cost. Should companies be allowed to profit from disease? Explain.

Unfair Competition

Large firms may be able to prevent the entry of new firms into the industry through measures that can be considered unfair. For example, a company may purposely reduce the price of its product in order to eliminate the competition. Once the competition has been eliminated, the company is free to increase its prices. This is referred to as **predatory pricing**; although illegal, it is often difficult to prove. For example, it may be difficult to determine whether low prices are aimed at eliminating competition or are a result of lower average costs. If lower prices are a reflection of lower costs, then the charge of unfair competition is not applicable. On the other hand, a monopolist company may argue that low prices are necessary in order to compete effectively.

The *legal barriers* imposed by government are the most formidable of all. If it is illegal to get into the industry, the monopoly situation is ensured. Other barriers may be eliminated over time. For example, product research and development is one way of getting around the barriers that maintain a monopoly. If new products can be developed by others, they may effectively compete with the monopolist.

Predatory pricing entails the lowering of prices, usually below the costs of production, in order to eliminate the competition.

R E V I E W

13.1 Explain how economies of scale provide a barrier to the entry of new firms.

EVERYDAY ECONOMICS 13.2

Diamonds Are Forever

The majority of the world's diamonds are mined in the Republic of South Africa, other sub-Saharan countries, and Siberia. Smaller diamond deposits have been found in South America, the United States, Australia, and Canada. In Canada, diamonds have been found in the Northwest Territories.

One company, DeBeers, has a virtual monopoly in the diamond market. The company, originally based in Johannesburg and now in London, has about 70 percent of the market in diamonds. DeBeers tries to control the supply of diamonds by mining as many as possible and also by buying up

nearly all of the available rough-cut diamonds available on the open market. The company has agreements with Botswana and Namibia that require each country to sell all its diamonds to the DeBeers-controlled Central Selling Organization, although Namibia is considering terminating this agreement. DeBeers has also focused on the demand side of the market by aggressively promoting the purchase of diamonds through advertising.

Cutting firms buy diamonds from DeBeers in sessions called "sights" several times a year. Diamond dealers from all over the world buy the diamonds from the cutters. Jewellers buy their diamonds from the dealers and then sell them to the public.

Can this virtual monopoly last forever? Diamonds that originate in countries such as Sierra Leone, Angola, and the Democratic Republic of the Congo are being sold to fund armed conflict. These diamonds have been referred to as "conflict diamonds" and have given the gem a bad name. New mines are opening up in countries like Canada, and diamonds are now being extracted from the ocean floor. New ways are also being developed to create synthetic diamonds. As a result, DeBeers is finding it more difficult to control the supply side of the diamond market. In addition Russia, the world's second largest producer of diamonds, has given a monopoly to Almazy Rossil-Sakha for the distribution of its diamonds. It will no longer sell all its diamonds to DeBeers.

Since DeBeers has close to a monopoly in the diamond market, it has been barred from doing business directly in the United States since the Second World War. There is currently a belief that the United States will change this policy and allow direct market access to DeBeers. Since the United States represents a large market for diamonds, easier access to this market can only benefit the company.

In 2000, DeBeers announced that it will no longer try to control the world's diamond supply. It will focus its efforts on creating a demand for diamonds.

Questions

1. What does DeBeers have to do to maintain the virtual monopoly in the diamond market?
2. Can you think of any other markets that operate in a similar way to the diamond market?

Profit Maximization

If a monopoly is interested in maximizing profits, the company must attempt to produce at a level that equates marginal revenue and marginal costs. We can assume that the cost structure of the company is similar to the one developed in Chapter 11. That is, in the short run the average costs will initially decline because of specialization, but will later increase as a result of diminishing returns. What does the revenue side of the picture look like for a monopoly?

In order to answer this question, it is necessary to know something about the demand for the product. Since a monopoly is the only seller in an industry, the demand curve for the monopoly's product is the same as the demand curve for the industry. For most products the demand curve slopes downward to the right, and we will assume that it does for the monopoly in our example—the only bakery in a small town. The demand schedule for the bakery's cakes is shown in Table 13.1.

In order to sell more cakes, it is necessary for the bakery to lower the price. Since it is very difficult to sell similar cakes for different prices to different customers, the bakery must lower the price for all customers. Doing so affects the marginal revenue that the bakery receives for selling more cakes. For example, at a price of $10 the bakery would sell only one cake per week. If the price were reduced to $9, the bakery could sell two

Table 13.1 *Demand schedule for cakes per week*

PRICE ($)	QUANTITY DEMANDED	TOTAL REVENUE ($)	MARGINAL REVENUE ($)
11	0	0	
10	1	10	10
9	2	18	8
8	3	24	6
7	4	28	4
6	5	30	2
5	6	30	0
4	7	28	−2
3	8	24	−4

cakes per week, which would increase the bakery's total revenue to $18. The marginal revenue from selling the additional cake is $8. The information in Table 13.1 is graphically demonstrated in Figure 13.1. The demand curve is plotted from the first two columns in the table, while the marginal revenue curve is plotted from the second and fourth columns. As shown in the diagram, the marginal revenue curve lies below the demand curve.

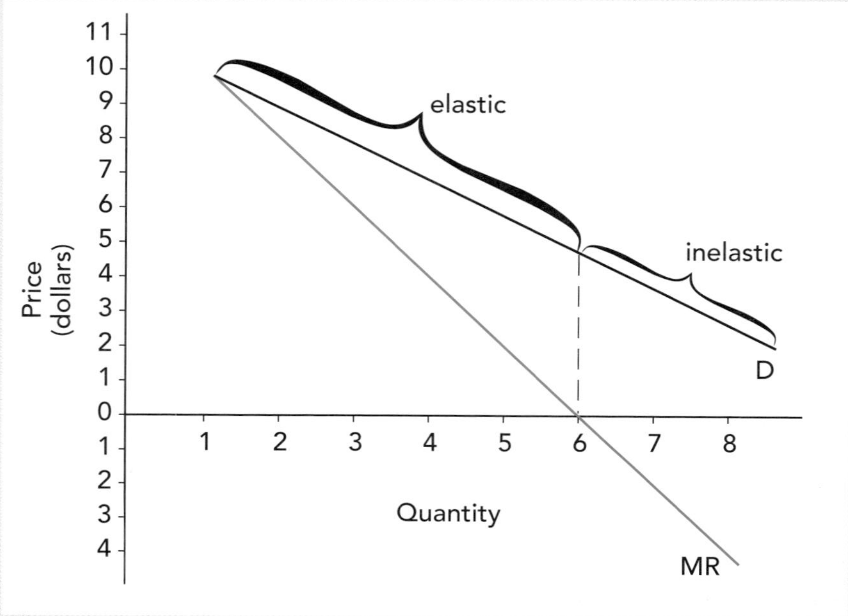

Figure 13.1

Demand (D) and marginal-revenue (MR) curves for a monopoly

The marginal-revenue curve is derived from the demand curve for a product and refers to the addition to total revenue of selling one more unit of output.

The table provides some information about the *price elasticity of demand* for cakes. In the price range $6–$10, any decrease in the price increases the total revenue received by the bakery. This fact indicates that the demand in this price range is elastic. In the price range $3–$4, any reduction in price leads to a decline in total revenue, indicating an inelastic demand. Finally, in the price range $5–$6, the drop in price leaves total revenue unchanged, indicating unitary elastic demand. It is possible for the marginal revenue to be negative. If the price of cakes were lowered to $4 from $5, there would be a reduction in total revenue. If total revenue declines, then marginal revenue must be negative. This occurs in the inelastic portion of the demand curve.

Since the demand curve slopes down to the right, the firm has some control over the price that it charges. In order to determine that price, the revenue and cost situation for this company have to be reviewed together (see Figure 13.2).

In order to maximize profits, the firm will produce at a level of output at which marginal revenue and marginal cost are equal (see Chapter 11). For our bakery, this occurs at five cakes. Beyond this point, marginal costs exceed marginal revenue. To produce more than five cakes would be to

Figure 13.2

Profit maximizing position for a monopoly

In order to maximize profits, the firm produces a level of output at which marginal cost is equal to marginal revenue. This occurs at five units.

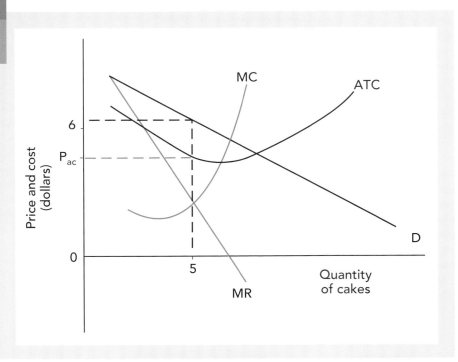

reduce profits: the extra cost (MC) of making more cakes is greater than the extra revenue (MR) gained from selling those cakes. If five cakes were produced, the price of the cakes would be $6 each, as indicated by the demand curve.

The monopoly does not charge the highest price possible for its product. The firm is interested in maximizing profits, so it charges a price consistent with that objective. At too high a price no one would purchase the product.

Simply because a firm has a monopoly in a certain area does not guarantee that a profit is earned. The product may not be in demand by consumers, or costs of production may be too high. In either case, it is quite possible that a loss could occur, and eventually the firm could go out of business unless conditions were to change.

The bakery whose cost and revenue position is shown in Figure 13.2 is making an economic profit. The average cost of producing five cakes (P_{ac}) is less than the price ($6). Will the bakery continue to earn an economic profit? The ability to earn an economic profit over a long period of time depends on the barriers to entry. If it is relatively easy for new firms to enter the industry, the initial firm's economic profits will be competed away. If the barriers to entry are formidable, then new firms will not enter and economic profits will continue to be earned. In most monopoly situations, the barriers to entry prevent the establishment of new firms and permit economic profits to exist in the long run.

The monopoly does not produce a level of output in the inelastic portion of the demand curve (see Figure 13.1). In the elastic portion of the demand curve, any increase in output (and subsequent drop in prices) will lead to increases in total revenue. In the inelastic portion of the demand curve, reductions in price lead to lower total revenue because marginal revenue is negative in this section of the demand curve.

R E V I E W

13.2 Why does the demand curve for a monopoly slope down to the right?

13.3 Why could a monopoly continue to earn economic profits in the long run when a firm in perfect competition cannot?

13.4 Measure the effects of varying demand on monopoly profit.

interactive graphics

Economic Effects of a Monopoly

When perfect competition was discussed in Chapter 12, we learned that each firm maximizes profits by producing at a level of output at which price equals the marginal cost. *Profit maximization* at this level of output is seen as desirable, since the firm continues to produce more output as long as price exceeds marginal cost. Because the price of the product is representative of its value (or benefit) to society, the firm continues to produce as long as the value (price) exceeds the costs of production (marginal cost). This is an ideal situation from society's point of view, and it is said that perfect competition results in an efficient allocation of resources.

How do monopolies rate according to this criterion? At the level of output at which a monopoly maximizes profit, the price is greater than the marginal cost (see Figure 13.2). This circumstance indicates that the value of this product to society is greater than the extra costs of producing more of it. We are willing to pay the price in order to receive more of this product, yet we do not receive any more. If this is so, why does the monopoly not expand production? The answer to this question lies in the monopoly's attempt to maximize profits. If more of the product were produced, it could be sold only by lowering the price, and monopoly profits would drop. The monopoly is withholding some of this product from the market in order to keep up the price and maximize profits.

It can be argued that the actions of a monopoly lead to misallocation of our nation's resources. Consumers are eager to receive more of this product and want more resources devoted to its production. They are even willing to pay more than the extra cost of producing it. Yet the monopoly withholds some of this product from the market in an attempt to maximize profits. In order to improve the allocation of resources, government often regulates the price that the monopoly can charge. If the government does not like the price that a monopoly charges while trying to maximize profits, then the government must select an appropriate price. Two approaches to monopoly price regulation are discussed below and displayed in Figure 13.3.

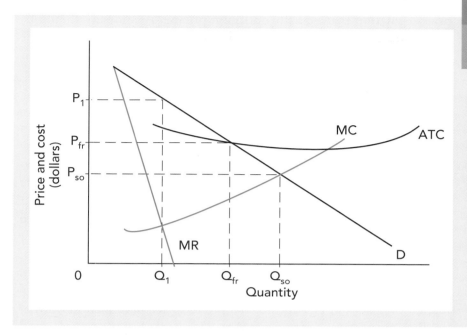

Figure 13.3

Socially optimum and fair-return pricing

The socially optimum price (P_{so}) occurs where the demand and marginal-cost curves intersect. The fair-return price (P_{fr}) occurs where the demand and average-cost curves intersect.

The first approach is called the **socially optimum price.** It is patterned after the results obtained in perfect competition. If government were concerned over the price and the resource allocation effects of monopolies, then it could legislate a price that would be equal to the marginal cost. The monopoly would continue to expand output up to the point at which the benefits from additional output (the price) were just equal to the costs of producing it (the marginal cost). This price would be where the demand curve intersects the marginal-cost curve. This would lower the price to P_{so} and more of the product would be put on the market (Q_{so}). One difficulty with this approach would be the possibility of the monopoly not receiving a high enough price to cover costs. If the average-cost curve were above the P = MC point, as it is in Figure 13.3, the monopoly would operate at a loss. This is not desirable, because the company would go out of business.

Socially optimum pricing, an approach to monopoly price regulation, sets the price at a level equal to the marginal cost.

The second approach to monopoly price regulation is called **fair-return pricing** and requires that the price be set equal to the average cost. This principle would permit the company to break even. Since implicit costs are included in the average-cost calculation, the firm would be willing to stay in business. Figure 13.3 shows P_{fr} as the point at which the demand curve intersects the average-cost (AC) curve. The quantity that would be produced is Q_{fr}.

The fair-return price, a price used in the regulation of a monopoly, is equal to the average cost of production.

Fair-return pricing seems to be a more practical approach to monopoly price regulation than socially optimum pricing. A company should be allowed to break even and cover implicit costs as well as explicit costs. The difficulty with this approach lies in determining the exact level of implicit costs. These costs are the sum of the opportunity costs of the resources owned by the firm (see Chapter 11). It may be difficult to determine opportunity costs. If a monopoly invests money in a business, what return on this money should be considered an opportunity cost? For example, if the firm expands its main offices at a cost of $6 million, what is the opportunity cost of this expenditure? Should it be equal to the interest paid on a savings account in a chartered bank? Should it be more because there is more risk attached to investing in your business than in getting a safe return on your money in a bank? Should extra money be made available for product research and development? How should implicit costs be adjusted for inflation? Prior to establishing a fair-return price, these questions must be answered.

Government regulation of a monopoly, although often logical in theory, has some very practical problems, the first of which concerns the estimation of costs and demand for the product. We have mentioned that implicit cost estimates may be hard to determine. Estimates of demand may also be difficult to obtain. A second problem has to do with encouraging efficiency on the part of the company, once regulated. Would the monopoly be interested in lowered costs of production? The answer may be no, if lower costs mean a lower regulated price. In contrast, the company may be willing to accept additional costs as long as these increase the regulated price. Money may be spent on luxuries like new office furniture in order to ensure that costs remain high. This system of price regulation by government may lead to a certain amount of inefficiency. Product quality may also suffer in an attempt by the firm to realize more money. If the firm can charge the same price for a lower-quality product, then profits should increase.

The third problem relates to spillovers, or third-party effects. Additional costs may be present in the case of negative third-party effects. These may inadvertently not be considered in the regulation of the monopoly price. The use of nuclear energy provides a good example. The storage problems and possible nuclear radiation leaks are third-party costs that are difficult to assess. These third-party costs may not be reflected in the product price.

Regardless of whether socially optimum or fair-return pricing is used, the consumer receives more of the product for a lower price than would be the case if the monopoly were not regulated. In Figure 13.3, both P_{so} and P_{fr} are below the profit-maximizing price (P_1).

The economic effects of a monopoly can also be seen by looking at the impact of monopoly on consumer surplus. Consider the market in

Figure 13.4. The equilibrium price is P_0. All consumers can purchase the product for P_0. Some consumers are willing to pay more than P_0, yet they only pay P_0. The difference between the price consumers would be willing to pay for a given quantity of a product and the price that they actually pay is referred to as **consumer surplus**.

The concept of producer surplus is also shown in Figure 13.4. Producer surplus is the difference between the price that producers get for a product (P_0) and the marginal cost of making more of it. Under the conditions of perfect competition shown in the diagram, the sum of the consumer and producer surpluses is maximized.

What impact does a monopoly have on consumer and producer surplus? By determining output where MC = MR, the monopoly restricts the amount of the product on the market and increases the price. The increase in price reduces the consumer surplus (see Figure 13.5). Part of the reduction in consumer surplus goes to the monopoly and part results in a "deadweight loss," which is of no benefit to any party. Part of the deadweight loss is a loss of consumer surplus and part is a loss of producer surplus.

Under conditions of perfect competition, the sum of the consumer and producer surpluses is maximized. Under conditions of monopoly, the sum of the consumer and producer surpluses is reduced from that which would exist in perfect competition. The difference in the sums is referred to as "deadweight loss."

Consumer surplus is the difference between the price consumers would be willing to pay for a given quantity of a product and the price that they actually pay.

Figure 13.4

Consumer and producer surpluses under perfect competition

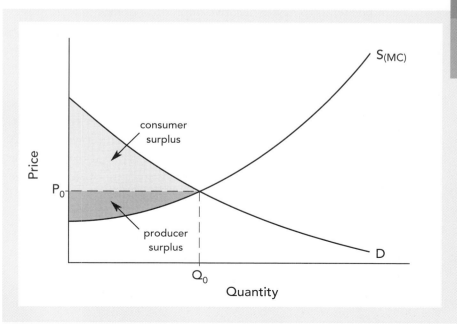

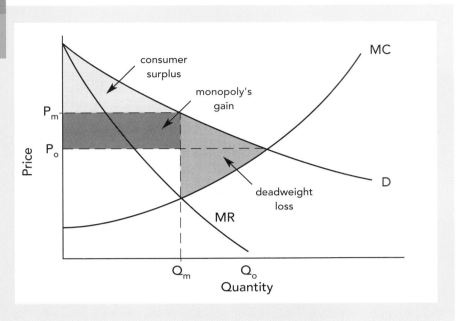

The monopoly suffers a loss of some producer surplus, yet it takes away some of the consumer surplus from the consumer. The monopoly gains at the expense of the consumer.

The public tends to have a negative impression of monopolies. It sees the monopoly as a company charging the highest possible price and "ripping off" the consumer. When we compare monopolies to perfect competition, we see that they do lead to a misallocation of resources. Yet this is not the only basis on which to judge a monopoly. Monopolies may have certain advantages compared to other types of competition. They may be large enough to achieve economies of scale and produce at a lower average cost. The consumer may then be able to obtain products at a lower price. A major disadvantage of a perfectly competitive firm is that it may never be large enough to achieve economies of scale. If a firm cannot take advantage of economies of large-scale production, its costs will not be reduced. If costs are not reduced, then prices will not be reduced.

There is a tendency for firms in perfectly competitive industries to break even in the long run. Breaking even leaves no money for modernization and product research and development. The ability of a monopoly to earn economic profits, unless regulated by government, enables the company to undertake product research and development from which the consumer ultimately benefits in the form of new and better products.

Some economists argue that a monopoly will not commit money to product research and development. They believe that there is no incentive to do this, because the firm is already in a monopoly position. Others argue that the monopoly needs to undertake research to assist in reducing costs and to increase economic profits. However, if it is a government-regulated monopoly, it may be forced to lower prices if costs are reduced, and this may reduce the incentive to be innovative. A monopoly may be interested in developing new products if that will allow the company to maintain its monopoly position. If the company does not develop new products, some other company will. Monopolies cannot be expected to last forever.

R E V I E W

13.5 Does fair-return pricing allow the monopoly to earn a profit? Discuss.

Price Discrimination

The demand curve for a monopoly's product slopes down to the right. This means that if the company wants to sell more of its product, it is necessary for it to lower the price. All consumers benefit from the lower price, even those who were willing to pay a higher price.

Knowing that some buyers would purchase the product at higher prices than others, the monopoly may be tempted to divide up the market and sell to different buyers at different prices, even though the costs of providing the good or the service are the same. This is known as **price discrimination,** and, if successful, will increase monopoly profits. Certain conditions must be present in order for price discrimination to exist.

First, the monopoly must be able to identify separate markets for the product, and they must be kept separate. It must be made impossible for those who purchase the product at the lower price to sell it to those who are willing to pay the higher price. The second condition is that the buyers in each market must have a different reaction to price changes. Those who are able to purchase the product for the lower price will be those with the more elastic demand curve. They may be unwilling to buy the product at the higher price.

Bus tickets provide an example of price discrimination. Local transit companies usually have different prices for adult and student passengers. Students usually pay the lower price, because they are more sensitive to price increases. Different-coloured tickets make it impossible for a student to purchase bus tickets and sell them to an adult. Some companies may

> **Price discrimination is the practice of charging different prices to different consumers for an item produced under similar cost conditions.**

even have special rates for senior citizens and children. The different-coloured tickets effectively keep the markets separate. Other examples of price discrimination include theatre tickets, business and residential telephone rates, luncheon specials at restaurants, and excursion air flights.

Professional persons are also in a good position to charge different prices to different customers. Dentists, for example, may charge a lower price for their services to clients who are not in a financial position to pay the regular fees. It is easy to keep the markets separate in this case. Individuals cannot sell their dental work to others. Also, there are different price elasticities of demand for dental services, depending on the patient's income.

Price discrimination also may occur on an international basis. This is referred to as *dumping*. If a Canadian product sells for a lower price in a foreign country than in Canada, we say that it has been dumped abroad. The lower foreign price is usually a result of a more elastic demand for the product in the foreign country. In order to sell the product, its price has to be reduced abroad. Although the foreign country may appear to benefit because it gets the product for a lower price, most countries prohibit the dumping of products on their markets. The prohibition usually comes when the product competes with a domestically produced item. Otherwise, foreign nations would be happy to receive products at the lowest possible price.

R E V I E W

13.6 Why are monopolies in a better position to practise price discrimination than firms in other types of competition?

13.7 Are different ticket prices to a sporting event (e.g., a hockey game) an example of price discrimination?

13.8 Find out how a company can use discriminatory pricing to maximize its profit.

Degrees of Price Discrimination

Since not every customer is willing to pay the same price for a product, firms must devise a pricing strategy. The price the consumer is willing to pay for a product depends on the factors listed in Chapter 2 when the demand curve was discussed. Individual tastes and preferences, individual incomes, and the prices of related products all influence the willingness of an individual consumer to purchase a product. In order to maximize profits, firms would like to get consumers to pay the actual maximum amount they would be willing to pay for a product.

If a firm can get each customer to pay the maximum amount he or she would be willing to pay for a product, it has practised first-degree price discrimination. Only under certain circumstances can this be done. One such circumstance is an auction, preferably an auction where the bids are sealed. In this manner, the seller is extracting the maximum amount out of each customer. The seller receives the highest possible revenue from the sale of the product. Only certain products can be sold at an auction such as this. This type of sale is limited to items that are in scarce supply where all buyers have the same access to information about the product. It also must be impossible for buyers to cooperate among themselves in fixing the bids.

If it is not possible for a firm to practise first-degree price discrimination, second-degree price discrimination may be possible. Under this form of price discrimination, customers are able to pay a lower price for volume purchases. This form of pricing is based on the concept of diminishing marginal utility. It is assumed that the consumer gains less utility, or satisfaction, from each successive unit of a product. For example, on a hot day a cold soft drink may provide a great deal of satisfaction. A second soft drink may be satisfying, but less so than the first. The consumer may therefore be willing to pay a high price for the first soft drink but not the same price for the second soft drink. In order to get the consumer to purchase more than one soft drink, the price needs to be lowered. Firms offer a lower price to those who purchase larger quantities. If you

are willing to buy a six-pack of soft drinks, you will get a lower price per drink. If you are willing to buy 24 cans at once, you will get an even lower price per can. By offering quantity discounts, the firm retains the customer who wants only one item and is willing to pay for it, and also attracts those customers who would buy more items if the price were lowered.

Third-degree price discrimination involves pricing based on the characteristics of the consumer. For example, students and senior citizens are charged a lower price for theatre tickets, bus tickets, newspaper subscriptions, and so on. Under this form of price discrimination, it is necessary to keep the two groups separate. Those who can receive the product or service for a lower price must not be able to resell the product or service to someone else. This form of pricing can work only in markets where brand names are important, where products have a great deal of differentiation, or where there are cost savings associated with large-scale production.

Questions

1. Is the selling of treasury bills (see Chapter 7) an example of first-degree price discrimination? Explain.
2. Are yearly passes to amusement parks, such as Canada's Wonderland in southern Ontario, examples of second-degree price discrimination? Explain.

Oligopoly

In a competitive situation described as an *oligopoly*, there are only a few firms. When one firm establishes its price, it has to take into consideration the reaction of the other firms. The products in oligopolistic industries can be either homogeneous or differentiated. Examples of homogeneous, or identical, products are steel, sugar, and aluminum. Examples of differentiated products where an oligopoly exists are automobiles and grocery stores. There are two major reasons why there are only a few firms in oligopolistic industries:

Economies of scale: As mentioned in Chapter 11 and earlier in this chapter, economies of scale are cost advantages associated with large-scale production. These cost advantages arise from quantity discounts, increased specialization, and the use of more efficient machinery and equipment. Technological improvements have been the major factor behind increased economies of scale. As some firms in an industry expand, they are able to achieve economies of scale and lower-cost production. This gives them an advantage over their rivals. Eventually some rivals drop out of the industry. Not only do economies of scale result in only a few firms being left in the industry, they also prevent new firms from starting up. In order to be able to compete, a new firm would have to start out with large-scale production, which is very difficult for a new company to do. Economies of scale could be considered a barrier to entry into oligopolistic industries, as well as entry into a monopoly industry.

Mergers: A merger can be defined as a circumstance in which one firm acquires another, or in which two or more firms amalgamate in order to make one single firm. The purpose of a merger is usually to increase the share of the market. The newly combined firm may have more control over setting the price for its product. It may also be able to better achieve economies of scale through quantity purchases of materials and increased specialization.

> The combination of two firms engaged in the same activity is called a horizontal merger.

Mergers may be of different types. A **horizontal merger** is a combination of two firms engaged in the same activity, usually in the same geographic market. For example, two grocery stores that operate in the same city may be merged. A **vertical merger** is one in which firms that engage in different levels of activity are combined. An example of a vertical merger, or integration, would be an automobile company merging with a tire manufacturer. Tires are one product of the automobile manufacturing process. Finally, a **conglomerate merger** is one in which a firm acquires another firm that is engaged in a different business. For example, a railroad company may purchase a paper mill. Of the three types, horizontal mergers result in fewer firms in an industry and can be a major reason for the existence of oligopolies.

> The combination of two firms engaged in different levels of the same activity describes a vertical merger.
>
> A conglomerate merger is one in which a firm acquires another firm that is engaged in a different business.

REVIEW

13.9 How do oligopolies come about?

The Beer Oligopoly

Canada's beer industry is clearly an oligopoly. The top two breweries— Molson Companies Ltd. and John Labatt Ltd.—have sales that account for approximately 90 percent of total Canadian beer sales. Imported beer and several smaller Canadian breweries account for the remainder. Why is the Canadian beer industry so concentrated?

A major reason for the high degree of concentration is mergers and acquisitions. Larger companies have acquired smaller breweries, while others have merged to form one company. In the mid 1800s there were 165 breweries in Canada. In Quebec prior to the First World War there were 16 breweries in operation. National Breweries Ltd. of Quebec, over a period of time, consolidated 14 of them into one firm. The large Quebec breweries had fewer brands, higher volume, and better advertising than the smaller Ontario breweries. The Quebec breweries had acquired 12 percent of the Ontario market by 1928.

At this time there were 37 small breweries in Ontario. Most were not operating at capacity. Profits were low and the breweries needed modernization. E.P. Taylor studied the Ontario situation and began a process of mergers and acquisitions using Brading Breweries Ltd. as the starting point. His initial targets were breweries that produced half of the total sales of beer in Ontario. These breweries were Kuntz Brewery in Kitchener; O'Keefe, Canada Bud, Dominion, and Cosgrave's in Toronto; Regal in Hamilton; Carling in London; Taylor & Bate in St. Catharines; British American in Windsor; Kakabeka Falls in Fort Frances;and the Sudbury Brewery in Sudbury. Taylor also wanted to acquire and close breweries that accounted for about 20 percent of Ontario beer sales: Budweiser, Copland, City Club, Heather, Reinhardt, Rock Springs, Grant's, Cronmiller and White, Bixel, Perth, Walkerville, Riverside, Hofer, Tecumseh, Formosa Spring, Gold Belt, Port Arthur, Soo Falls, Lake-of-the-Woods, Fort Frances, and Welland. In 1937 the name of the brewery that amalgamated the smaller firms was Canadian Breweries Ltd. (later Carling O'Keefe Ltd., and now a part of Molson Breweries).[1]

The beer industry in Canada can be described as a duopoly (a market with two sellers). Labatt Brewing Company Ltd. and Molson Breweries each have about 45 percent of the market. A characteristic of oligopolies is price wars, and the beer industry is no exception. In the summer, both companies often offer reductions on cases of 24 bottles (or cans) of beer. The price war is undertaken when beer sales are at a peak: 75 percent of all beer is sold in the months of May to August.

Industry barriers restrict the entry of new firms. The large advertising expenditures of the two firms restrict competition: each company spends approximately $200 million annually on advertising and promotions. In some provinces, higher sorting fees are imposed on companies that use distinctive bottles. These higher fees can amount to thousands of dollars a year and represent a barrier to innovative firms. There are barriers to transporting beer between the provinces and between Canada and the United States. Steps are being taken, however, to remove these barriers. Any reduction in trade barriers should open the door to more competition in the industry.

Although two companies still dominate the beer industry in Canada, the barriers to entry are breaking down. There is more selection in beer stores than in the past as smaller breweries are making inroads in the market.

[1] Rohmer, *E.P. Taylor*, pp. 50–76.

Questions

1. In what sense would advertising expenditures be a barrier to the entry of new firms?
2. Do you think that beer companies should be allowed to compete on the basis of price?
3. Why might the two major beer companies want some of the smaller Canadian breweries to remain in operation?

Pricing Policies

In an oligopolistic situation each firm must consider the reaction of competitors when setting the price. Although firms may not be certain how their rivals will react, they have to keep possible reactions in mind. For example, if one firm lowers its price and its rivals follow with the price cuts, it is possible that no firm will benefit. Depending on the overall demand for the product, firms may sell approximately the same amount of the product, even after the price cut. In the case of an inelastic demand, price cuts do not lead to large increases in the quantity demanded.

If a firm in an oligopoly does not know how its competitors will respond to changes in its price, then it is impossible to know the shape of the demand curve that it is facing. The firm does not know if its sales will increase as a result of a price reduction, since other firms may lower their prices as well. If the firm raises its price, it is not certain if others will follow. If rivals do not respond with higher prices, then the firm could lose a significant amount of business. If it is, therefore, impossible to describe the demand curve for a firm in an oligopoly, then it is impossible to describe the marginal-revenue curve. If the firm is interested in maximizing profits by equating marginal revenue and marginal costs, the appropriate level of output is more difficult to determine. Observers of oligopolistic industries have noted two characteristics of prices in these industries. The first is that prices tend to be inflexible, meaning that they do not change very often. Second, when prices do change, all firms tend to change them. A good example of this is the automobile industry. At the same time each year, prices for the new-model cars are announced. During the year, if price reductions are required, they appear to happen simultaneously. These characteristics have led to a theory of oligopolistic pricing called the **kinked demand curve** (see Figure 13.6), which is an attempt to draw a demand curve for a firm in an oligopolistic setting. The demand curve for an oligopoly appears to be composed of two sections: one elastic and one inelastic. Why does the demand curve in Figure 13.6 have a bend, or kink, dividing it into two sections?

The kinked demand curve represents a situation in which the firm is uncertain about the reaction of its rivals to price changes. If the price is at P_1 the firm may be reluctant to raise the price. If the section of demand curve above P_1 is elastic, any increase in price will result in a drop in total revenue. This will happen if other firms do not follow the price increase. The firm may also be reluctant to lower its prices if it believes that its rivals will not lower their prices. It may perceive the lower portion of the demand curve as being inelastic, and will be unwilling to lower its price if total revenue will fall.

The kinked demand curve is a demand curve that is composed of two sections—elastic and inelastic—separated by a bend, or kink, and is an attempt to explain price rigidity in oligopolistic industries.

Figure 13.6

The kinked demand curve

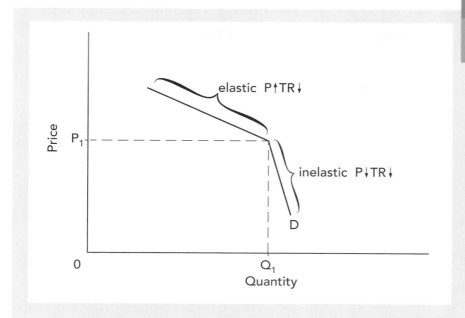

If the firm raises the price above P_1 and other firms in the industry do not, it will lose sales and total revenue will fall. If the firm lowers the price below P_1 and other firms follow, then it may not increase sales substantially and total revenue will decline. Since total revenue declines with either option, the price remains at P_1.

If the firm raises the price above P_1 and other firms in the industry do not, it will lose sales and total revenue will fall. If the firm lowers the price below P_1 and other firms follow, then it may not increase sales substantially and total revenue will decline. Since total revenue declines with either option, the price remains at P_1.

This perception explains why the firm may keep the price at the kink for some time. It does not explain, however, the way in which P_1 was arrived at. The theory of the kinked demand curve also does not explain how the price would change and for these reasons, it is not a totally acceptable theory of oligopoly pricing.

The theory of the kinked demand curve assumes that the firm does not know how rivals will react to price changes. The firm is operating in an atmosphere of uncertainty. In order to eliminate this uncertainty, the firm may try to co-ordinate its pricing policies with its rivals. This activity is referred to as *collusion*. Collusion is easier in an oligopoly than in other types of competition because of the small number of firms. However, its practice is illegal in Canada, and is prohibited under the Competition Act, along with certain other business practices. Even if outright collusion does not take place, oligopolies are often characterized by **price leadership**, which serves to avoid competition. Price leadership is a situation in which one firm raises its price and the other firms in the industry follow with

Price leadership **occurs in an oligopoly when one firm raises its price and other firms in the industry follow with their own price increases.**

price increases. The price leader may be a dominant firm in the industry. If one firm accounts for a large percentage of industry sales, it may be able to set its price in order to maximize profits. The remaining firms are likely to accept this price for their product. The price leader need not be the largest firm in the industry. It may simply be a firm that has been a good judge of market conditions in the past.

EVERYDAY ECONOMICS 13.5

Gasoline Prices

Anyone who drives a car has been puzzled by fluctuations in the price of gasoline. Prices can change as much as 15 percent from day to day. Automobile drivers also notice that when one station changes its price, others follow. Why do gasoline prices fluctuate so much?

As we know, prices are determined by the interaction of demand and supply. The demand for gasoline at the pumps is fairly steady during the week, except for Friday and at the start of long weekends. On the cost side, most of the costs associated with bringing gasoline to the market remain fairly steady. Crude oil, from which gasoline is made, has seen significant price increases in recent years. Crude oil is purchased in advance under long-term contracts with refineries. Because of these contracts, there is not much fluctuation in the price of gasoline from day to day. Other expenses associated with gasoline retailing, such as marketing and payroll, also remain steady from day to day or from week to week.

If the cost side of the market does not fluctuate a great deal and the demand is steady, why the fluctuations in price? Part of the answer lies in the cost components of a litre of gasoline and the portion of the price determined by the retailer.

For example, assume that gasoline sells for 62.9 cents a litre in Vancouver. The cost breakdown is as follows:

Crude cost	20.1 cents (approx.)
Federal Tax	14.1 cents
Provincial Tax	15.0 cents
Refining/Marketing costs and profit	10.7 cents
Retail margin	3.0 cents

Provincial taxes and the retail margin vary across the country. The retail margin varies from a low of approximately 3 cents to a high of 4.7 cents. The fluctuations in gasoline prices are mainly a result of changes in the retail margin. In order to maintain market share, retailers will reduce their profit margin or even operate at a loss for a short period of time. If one station is willing to reduce its margin and reduce the price, other stations will follow. The result may be a price war. Consumers are happy to see price wars but are not so happy to see all stations increase their prices together. When prices rise in unison, consumers cry that there has been some collusion on the part of the major oil companies. Investigations by Canada's Bureau of Competition Policy have not uncovered any evidence of collusion among the oil companies.

Why are gasoline prices usually lower in the United States? The main reason is taxes. In 1996, government taxes in Canada were 29 cents per litre compared to 14 cents in the United States. Transportation costs are also higher in Canada as refineries are located farther from the stations. In

Canada, there are twice as many stations per capita as in the United States. Canadian retailers must have a higher retail margin in order to meet costs.

Questions

1. What characteristics of gasoline retailing are typical of an oligopoly?
2. What steps can gasoline retailers take to differentiate their product from their competitors' products?

The concept of the kinked demand curve also explains why firms in an oligopolistic situation resort to advertising and new-product development in order to compete. If firms are reluctant to change prices, other forms of competition are essential. Through advertising, it is hoped that the upper portion of the demand curve will become more inelastic. When it becomes necessary for prices to rise (under substantial cost increases), the firm would not lose as many sales if advertising is successful in altering the demand curve.

R E V I E W

13.10 Why is the price rigid at the kink in Figure 13.6?

Cartels

A **cartel** can be described as a formal arrangement, either written or verbal, among producers to regulate the price and total output of a product. Instead of competing, the firms form a monopoly in the sense that they have *sole control* over the market. In Canada cartels are illegal, yet they have been established for many products on an international scale. These products include oil, bauxite, copper, tin, uranium, coffee, sugar, cocoa, aluminum, and rubber. Cartels tend to be found in the resource industries or in those that have identical products.

In order to succeed, a cartel must possess certain characteristics. The firms in the cartel must control a major amount of the total output of the product. That is, if strong competition exists from other producers, the cartel is not likely to be successful. The demand for the cartel's product must be growing or at least remain steady. If demand starts to fall, some producers will want to lower prices in order to stimulate sales. It may be difficult to reach agreement on price cuts. Also, close substitutes cannot be readily available; the demand for the product should be inelastic. The final

A cartel is a formal arrangement, written or verbal, among producers that regulates the price and total output of a product.

criterion for success is the willingness of individual firms to abide by the decisions of the group. If some firms are unwilling to restrict the amount of the product that they put on the market, or are unwilling to maintain a high price, the agreement will break down.

A look at a real-world cartel points out how difficult it is for a cartel to survive. Possibly the best-known cartel is the Organization of Petroleum Exporting Countries (OPEC). This 13-nation (now 11-nation) group received international recognition in 1973 as a result of the sharp increases in world oil prices. In fact, oil prices quadrupled in 1973–74 in the wake of a Middle East war. Oil prices increased drastically again later in the decade and prices tripled between the years 1978 and 1980. The OPEC cartel was given much of the credit for these price increases. Beginning in 1981, however, oil prices started to fall.

EVERYDAY ECONOMICS 13.6

The Coffee Cartel

In 1993, The Association of Coffee Producing Countries (ACPC) was formed representing 29 coffee producing nations in Africa, Asia, and Central and South America.

The aims and objectives of the association are as follows:

- securing stable markets in terms of demand and supply. The coffee market has experienced periods of product shortages and surpluses. These situations where the market is not in equilibrium have produced fluctuations in coffee prices and in the incomes of coffee producers. APAC hopes to regulate supply to reduce price swings.

- contributing to the economic and social development of coffee-producing countries. Coffee production impacts the lives of 25 million people. In order for the supply of coffee to be managed, a trained labour force is needed along with productive land and a domestic infrastructure that will support the industry.

- improving the quality of coffee. Consumers are conscious of coffee quality. The association aims to assist its members in quality improvement and control.

- coordinating coffee policies among member countries. Unless members of the association (cartel) cooperate, the cartel will not achieve its goals. Cooperation in a cartel can be difficult since each member country has its own priorities.

- promoting coffee consumption. APAC realizes that, for a cartel to be successful, a steady increase in the demand for the product is required. APAC hopes to introduce coffee to new markets.

Previous agreements between producing countries to control coffee production and prices had collapsed. Since the collapse of the last agreement, coffee prices had fallen from a high of $130 per quintal to $50 per quintal in 1993. The creation of APAC was to reverse the downward spiral of coffee prices and to stabilize coffee prices at a level that was fair to producers. APAC members realized that the price should be set at a level that would also encourage consumption.

By 2000, it was obvious that the association's attempts to halt the skid in coffee prices were not successful. The price of raw coffee beans had fallen to 69 cents (U.S.) per pound. Since coffee producers claim they need 92 cents (U.S.) per pound in order to break even, in 2000 the association established the minimum price at 95 cents (U.S.) per pound. The association stated that it would purchase any surplus coffee on the market in order to reduce supplies and keep the price up. If the price reaches $1.05 (U.S.) per pound, any surplus coffee will be sold on the open market. ACPC argued that its pricing policy would not only increase the price of coffee but would reduce the volatility of coffee prices.

In 2001 ACPC shut down when coffee prices reached their lowest level in three decades. Many decisions made by the cartel were not binding and members did not comply with the cartel's production levels. Brazil, Costa Rica, and Colombia initially withheld coffee from the market but returned to their original supply levels once they discovered that others were not reducing supply.

From what countries do Canadians get their coffee? Approximately 23 percent of the coffee imported into Canada comes from Brazil and 22 percent comes from Colombia. Guatemala provides 14 percent, Mexico provides 7 percent, 5 percent comes from Peru, and Vietnam and Costa Rica supply 4 percent each. A variety of other countries supply the remainder of our coffee imports.

Questions

1. The coffee cartel is setting a price floor for coffee. Use demand and supply curves in your answer to show the impact that this price floor will have on the market for coffee.
2. In order for a cartel to be successful, certain conditions must be present. Are these conditions present in the coffee market?
3. Is it easier to maintain a cartel when prices are rising or when prices are falling? Explain.

Was OPEC a successful cartel during these years? There is no doubt that the OPEC nations controlled the majority of the world's oil supplies. It is estimated that they had 80 percent of the non–communist-world's oil reserves. In order to push up prices, the OPEC nations needed only reduce their oil production. Yet during the 1970s these countries did not impose production quotas on each other. Many OPEC nations actually increased oil production in response to the higher oil prices. It was only when prices started falling in 1981 that OPEC tried to get its members to agree on production quotas. Agreement on production quotas among members of a cartel is not easily obtained, and such was the case with OPEC. Some nations, like Saudi Arabia, have vast oil reserves and want to take a long-term view of oil prices. Others, like Algeria, have small reserves of oil and are more interested in the short-term price for this resource.

If high prices were not achieved by reductions in supply, they must have been achieved by increases in demand. During the 1970s the demand for oil was steadily increasing. Also during this decade, many governments were printing money and rapidly expanding the money supply. This led to inflation in certain countries and to increases in the price of oil. When the brakes were put on the expansion of the money supply, and the rate of inflation was reduced, oil prices began to fall. A recession in the Western world in the early 1980s also led to a reduction in the demand for energy. Consumers had also reacted to high energy prices by buying more fuel-efficient cars and living in more fuel-efficient homes.

A cartel will remain successful only if there are no substitutes for its product. The oil price increases during the 1970s were possible because there were few substitutes for oil. By the 1980s, other non-OPEC nations had increased their exploration for sources of oil. Canada, along with the United States, Britain, and Norway, became increasingly self-sufficient in oil. Norway is currently the second-largest oil exporter after Saudi Arabia. Only three of the ten largest oil-producing nations in the world are members of OPEC. Progress was also being made in the development of other sources of energy, such as solar and nuclear. In the 1990s, the OPEC nations adhered to quotas and, as a result, the price of a barrel of oil increased. In mid-2000, some OPEC members increased production in order to reduce the magnitude of the price increase.

Competition Act

Since 1889, Canada has passed legislation aimed at protecting the consumer from unfair business practices. The early legislation was primarily *anti-monopoly* legislation. It was directed not only at single-firm monopolies, but also at those monopolies that result when companies collude to set prices and divide the market.

In 1910, the Combines Investigation Act was passed by the federal government. The act was passed in order to prohibit practices that would unduly restrict competition, including combinations aimed at price fixing, misleading advertising, and price discrimination.

A major difficulty of the legislation was the interpretation given to the word "unduly." How much did competition have to be reduced in order for it to be unduly lessened? Changing economic conditions may bring about changes in the interpretation of the word, which has been defined as "improperly, excessively, and inordinately." It has also been defined as detrimental to the public interest. *Basically, it is illegal for companies to restrict competition to the point at which these companies can pursue their activities as if they did not have any competition.*

Amendments to the Early Legislation

Several amendments have been made to the 1910 legislation—changes directed at preserving competition in Canadian industry. The legislation in its present form prohibits the following business practices:

Mergers and monopolies: A merger is defined in the act as the acquisition or control over the business of a competitor whereby competition is likely to be lessened to the detriment of the public interest.

Mergers are prohibited where it can be shown that competition is unduly lessened. One such merger to attract public attention was the acquisition of Simpsons department stores by the Hudson's Bay Company. The Thomson newspaper chain then purchased a controlling interest in the Hudson's Bay Company. Neither merger was denied under the act and, in fact, very few mergers have ever been denied under its provisions. The merger of Molson and Carling breweries in 1989 was allowed to proceed. The merger of Imperial Oil and Texaco was allowed to proceed only after the Competition Tribunal ordered Imperial to divest itself of 600 gas stations, a Nova Scotia oil refinery, and other facilities. In 1991, a proposed merger of the flour and flour-related businesses of Canada Packers Inc. and John Labatt Ltd. was denied by the Bureau of Competition Policy. The bureau refused to approve the merger on the grounds that competition would be excessively reduced in Montreal and in the West. In 1995, the merger of SmithBooks and Coles was approved. Both companies agreed to eliminate covenants in leases that prevented other book retailers from opening in direct competition with SmithBooks and Coles. In 1998, the Royal Bank of Canada and the Bank of Montreal, and the Canadian Imperial Bank of Commerce and the Toronto Dominion Bank, announced respective plans to merge.

The bank mergers were not approved. In 1999, the Loblaws purchase of Provigo and the Atlantic assets of the Oshawa Group was approved by the Competition Bureau under certain conditions. Loblaws was required to sell a number of stores in order to reduce the company's position in the market. In 2000, the federal government approved the merger of Air Canada and Canadian Airlines. In the same year, the Competition Bureau objected to the proposed purchase of Cadbury Schweppes soft drink business by Coca-Cola. The Bureau was concerned that Coca-Cola would have a dominant position in the industry. It was also concerned about the impact on independent bottlers who bottle soft drinks for the major companies. Because of arrangements that existed between the bottlers and the companies, Coca-Cola would have had control over Pepsi-Cola suppliers.

In 2000, a number of merger announcements prompted examination by both the Competition Bureau and the Canada Radio and Tele-communications Commission (CRTC). The proposed mergers involved BCE and CTV and BCE and *The Globe and Mail.* Also under review are Quebecor's purchase of Groupe Videotron and CanWest Global's purchase of 200 publications from Hollinger. The boundaries between companies that operate in the print media, in broadcasting, and via the internet and telecommunications are becoming blurred. In order to determine if competition is maintained in an industry, it will be necessary to define the boundaries of the industry. In 2001, the merger of Indigo Books & Music and Chapters was approved on the condition that the new company sell 23 of its stores. In 2002, the Competition Bureau blocked the acquisition of 17 radio stations by Astral Media Inc. even though the CRTC had approved the sale.

Monopolies that come into being through legal means are not prohibited. For example, government-owned and regulated monopolies are not illegal. Also monopolies created because of patent legislation are acceptable. The monopoly itself is not illegal, but the abuse of monopoly power is illegal. In 1990, a Competition Tribunal ruled that NutraSweet had effectively maintained monopoly powers over the aspartame market at the expense of potential competitors. Under the tribunal's order, NutraSweet can no longer sign contracts that make it the exclusive aspartame supplier to domestic companies. In 1994, an agreement was reached that would open up Canada's banking machine network to more companies. Up to that point, Interac had virtual control over this industry.

In 2000, the Competition Bureau forced H. J. Heinz Co. of Canada to change its anticompetitive practices that allowed it to maintain a virtual monopoly in the baby-food market. Heinz was in a monopoly position in the market because the federal government had placed high anti-dumping duties on Gerber products forcing Gerber to pull out of the Canadian market. Heinz had been paying retailers lump sums of money to agree not to carry the products of competitors. Retailers who carried only Heinz products were also given special discounts. The Competition Bureau stated that these practices created a barrier to entry for competitors that lessened competition in the market.

Agreements that would restrict competition: Agreements between companies that would restrict the entry of new firms, fix prices, or limit the production and distribution of goods and services are prohibited. Generally, anyone who restrains or limits trade is guilty of an offence. The act applies to transporting, producing, manufacturing, supplying, storing, or dealing in any product.

Four Quebec cement companies were fined $5.8 million in 1996. In the same year, five companies were found guilty of conspiracy to limit sales of oxygen, nitrogen, hydrogen, and carbon dioxide. The fines were $6.46 million. In 1997 four Toronto-area electrical contractors were fined $2.5 million for conspiring to rig bids at major building projects. In 1998, Archer-Daniels-Midland Co. pleaded guilty to fixing prices of a food additive for chicken and pigs called lysine, and citric acid, which is used in food products and drinks. The fine was $16 million.

In September 1999, five vitamin manufacturers were fined a total of $88.5 million after they pleaded guilty to a conspiracy to fix prices for bulk vitamins (A, B2, B6, C, E, and beta carotene) and food additives. The largest fine in the group, $50.9 million, was levied against Swiss-based Hoffman-LaRoche, which has 40 percent of the world's animal and human vitamin market. The price fixing resulted in increased prices for many consumer products, including breakfast cereal and hamburger, as well as animal feed and pharmaceuticals. The other companies fined were BASF (Germany), Rhone-Poulenc (France), Daiichi Pharmaceutical (Japan), and Eisai (Japan).

In 2001, Fujisawa Pharmaceutical and Pfizer Inc. were found guilty of fixing prices on sodium erythorbate, a food preservative used to maintain the colour and flavour of meat and other processed foods. Investigations into Noranda's involvement in controlling the price and supply of sulphuric acid, and price fixing among office and commercial paper suppliers, are not finished. In 2003, gasoline sellers were found not guilty of collusion to set gasoline prices.

Not all agreements between companies are illegal. Companies can agree to exchange statistics and credit information, define trade terms and product standards, and co-operate in research and development.

Retail price maintenance: It is illegal for a manufacturer to set the retail price at which the product must be sold. Manufacturers may be interested in maintaining a certain image of their product and may resent price lowering by retailers. In the past, some manufacturers have refused to sell to retailers who lowered the price below the suggested retail price. This practice is also prohibited by the Act: companies cannot discriminate against retailers who use the product as a "loss-leader."

The largest fine ever imposed for **retail price maintenance** was $150 000. The guilty party was Levi-Strauss of Canada. The company took advantage of world denim shortages between 1972 and 1975 to select the retailers that it sold to. These were retailers who sold the company's jeans at prices that the company had set. In 1989, Chrysler Canada Ltd. was ordered to recommence supplying automobile parts to a Montreal trading house. The trading house exported parts to Europe, South America, and the Middle East, and Chrysler wanted the operation to expand. When the trading house did not expand, Chrysler refused to supply it with parts. Prosecutions under this section of the act are numerous.

In 2002, Stroh's brewery paid a $250 000 fine for attempting to exert influence over the price at which its beer was sold. In March 2003, GlaxoSmithKline Inc. was found not guilty of an allegation that it had refused to supply its products to Internet pharmacies that sell them to customers in the United States.

Retail price maintenance, **whereby a manufacturer insists that a product be sold at a specified price, contravenes the Competition Act.**

Misleading price advertising, **an illegal activity, occurs when the prices actually charged are higher than those advertised.**

Misleading advertising: The act prohibits misleading the public by charging prices higher than advertised prices, a practice called **misleading price advertising.** The largest fine under this section of the act was imposed on Simpson-Sears in 1983 for misrepresenting the value of diamond rings. The fine was $1 million. Misleading the consumer on matters other than price is also illegal. Popsicle Industries was fined $200 000 for running short of Nintendo game cartridges offered as prizes in a promotion. Remington was fined $75 000 for making a false claim about its electric razors. In 2000, a Montreal direct-mail company was fined $500 000 for misleading advertising in relation to weight-loss products and a get-rich-quick book. The Competition Bureau is investigating a complaint that Bernard Haldane Associates, which sells services to job seekers, is guilty of misleading advertising. Those who complained to the Competition Bureau stated that for a fee of $5000 to $8000 they received little more than help writing a résumé. In 2003, Toyota agreed to pay $2.3 million to charity to settle an investigation into its "Access Toyota" program. Customers complained that Toyota dealers were prevented from selling cars below advertised prices, contrary to what was stated on the company's website.

Price discrimination: It is illegal to discriminate between buyers who are buying similar quantities and qualities of a product. It is legal to give quantity discounts on bulk purchases, and price reductions for special events such as clearance sales are also acceptable.

Predatory price cutting: Predatory pricing is an attempt to monopolize, or substantially reduce, competition by selling at an unreasonably low price, or at a price that is below cost. In theory, once the competition has been eliminated, prices would increase.

Of the hundreds of complaints involving predatory pricing, only a small number are formally investigated. An even smaller number end up in court. The result was only one conviction. In order to acquire a conviction, the court needs to be convinced that the company had an explicit policy of predatory pricing aimed at eliminating the competition. The guidelines for prosecutions under this legislation state that companies with less than 35 percent of the market share are not likely to engage in predatory pricing in order to monopolize the market. The guidelines also focus on the ability of the firm to recover the short-term losses through higher prices. If the recovery of losses is not possible, the prosecution is not likely to be successful.

Is predatory pricing legislation necessary? Price is only one element in a competitive environment. Firms can also compete on the basis of quality and service. By not permitting some types of low-price competition, the consumer is forced to pay higher prices. Does predatory pricing legislation discourage companies from engaging in price wars, offering rebates, or participating in other schemes to lower the price of products? Rather than compete effectively, could one firm accuse a competitor of predatory pricing? The accusation alone may be enough to get the competitor to cease the price-reduction policy.

Would a firm attempt to monopolize the market by continuing to sell below cost? If low prices were the only barrier to entry, new firms would enter once the prices were increased. Low prices cannot be maintained indefinitely in order to reduce competition. It is also possible that competitors may cut back production in the face of extremely low-price competition. If so, the price-cutting firm may be forced to increase output in order to meet the increased demand. This action may result in more losses than were originally anticipated.

Hoffman-La Roche Ltd., a major manufacturer of pharmaceutical drugs, was convicted of predatory pricing in 1980. The company manufactures two tranquilizers, Valium and Librium. It was convicted of selling Valium at unreasonably low prices. The court decision also charged that the practice of discounting and giveaways was in violation of the Act. In fact, the company gave away 82 million pills worth $2.6 million in a 12-month period. Hospitals and governments received drugs at prices substantially below cost.

In 2002, a Competition Tribunal began investigating a complaint by WestJet Airlines that its rival, Air Canada, practised predatory pricing with respect to air service from Hamilton, Ontario to Moncton, New Brunswick. WestJet claimed that Air Canada offered fares below operating costs; the tribunal's task is to determine how airlines should calculate the cost of operating a flight.

Changes in Competition Law

As economic conditions change, the objectives of legislation designed to ensure competition may change as well. In 1977, several amendments to the Combines Investigation Act came into effect. The act was extended to cover business practices in the service sector of our economy. This sector was exempt from coverage under the previous legislation. Other changes prohibited pyramid selling, bait and switch selling, misleading advertising, and the repricing of goods in stock.

Further changes were deemed necessary in order to ensure that legislation guaranteed competition in our economy. The Combines Investigation Act was enacted under the criminal-code powers of the federal government, making the burden of proof on the part of the government more difficult. The government is required to prove beyond any reasonable doubt that companies colluded in order to fix prices or divide up the market. The government must also prove that the actions of companies unduly lessened competition. These changes make convictions more difficult to achieve. If the legislation were to be placed under civil law instead of criminal law, it would be more effective in preserving competition in the marketplace.

To be effective, competition law should cover areas not currently covered. One area is agriculture. Marketing boards have the legal authority to fix prices, set quotas, and basically to divide up the market. These practices are illegal in all other segments of our economy, and many economists argue that they should be illegal in agriculture as well. Trade unions and professional organizations are also exempt from competition law. In some instances these groups have been able to restrict entry into their occupation with the effect of keeping the price for their services high. Often these groups argue that restrictions on entry into their area are necessary for public safety and protection. Further discussion of the effects of unions on labour markets is contained in Chapter 14. Crown corporations also need to be covered in the legislation because many of these corporations compete with private corporations in the marketplace.

Changes to Canada's competition law were passed in June 1986. The new act is known as the **Competition Act.** The purpose of the Act is to maintain and encourage competition in Canada in order to:

a) promote the efficiency and adaptability of the Canadian economy;
b) expand opportunities for Canadian participation in world markets while at the same time recognizing the role of foreign competition in Canada;
c) ensure that small and medium-sized enterprises have an equitable opportunity to participate in the Canadian economy; and
d) provide consumers with competitive prices and product choices.

The major changes from the previous legislation are in the area of mergers and acquisitions. Companies are now required to notify the government before large mergers and acquisitions take place. The new law also gives the competition regulatory authorities a say in bank mergers in addition to the role of the minister of finance in this area. Under the old legislation, mergers were illegal if they were proven to be detrimental to the public interest. Under the new legislation, mergers are illegal if they have substantially lessened competition. The interpretation of the word "substantial" will be very important in these situations. It is not certain if the regulatory authorities will review and consider the competition that continues to exist after the merger in determining whether a merger was illegal.

The Competition Act is federal government legislation prohibiting business practices that substantially restrict competition.

Two other significant changes were introduced under the Competition Act. The old criminal-law standard was replaced with a new civil-law review. A competition tribunal is to be established to replace the courts in the adjudication process. This should speed up the decision-making process. In 1990, the constitutionality of the Competition Act was challenged. A Federal Court of Appeal stripped the tribunal of the power to enforce its own orders. A Quebec Superior Court justice ruled the tribunal unconstitutional because its members do not meet the test of impartiality demanded of judges. However, in April 1991 the Nova Scotia Court of Appeal reversed a lower court decision and found the Competition Act to be constitutional; in 1992, the Supreme Court of Canada ruled the Competition Act to be constitutional.

In April 2000, the federal government announced its intention to overhaul the Competition Act. The proposed changes would give more power to the Competition Bureau and would also allow citizens to take action against the Competition tribunal. These changes were announced after a study by the London-based Global Competition Review gave Canada's Competition Bureau only two stars out of a possible five in its international rankings. The low ranking came as a result of perceived political interference in the decision making by the Competition Bureau and the lengthy delays before a decision is made. Canada's Competition Bureau responded to the report by saying the methodology was flawed and the authors of the report relied too much on anecdotal information.

EVERYDAY ECONOMICS 13.7

The Microsoft Case

The Federal Trade Commission in the United States began investigating Microsoft in June 1990. In 1993 the United States Justice Department took over the investigation, and in 1994 the Justice Department and Microsoft signed a consent decree stating that Microsoft cannot require computer makers that license its operating system to license any other software products. In other words, if a computer manufacturer installed a Microsoft operating system, the manufacturer would not be required to install any other Microsoft software, such as an internet browser. In 1997, the Justice Department stated that Microsoft had violated the decree by bundling Internet Explorer with Windows 95. The defence given by Microsoft was that internet browsers are an integrated part of the operating system. Microsoft was required to separate the internet browser from the operating system. In 1998, Microsoft agreed that computer makers could install Windows 98 without the Internet Explorer icon.

In 1998, a new charge against Microsoft was investigated. The charge stated that the company used its monopoly power to thwart competition. In November 1999, a judge ruled that Microsoft had monopoly power with its Windows operating system for personal computers and this power was used to the detriment of consumers, computer makers, and other companies. A mediator was appointed to reach an agreement with Microsoft to settle this case. By April 1999, it was deemed that mediation had failed and Judge Jackson brought down a decision: he stated that Microsoft had maintained its monopoly power by anti-competitive means and had violated the Sherman Antitrust Act by tying its internet browser to its operating system. Consequently, Jackson ruled that Microsoft should be split into two companies: one company would be for the Windows operating system and the other company would be for applications software such as Excel, Word, and Internet Explorer. Appeals could delay the implementation of this order for several years.

There is precedence in the United States for splitting monopolies into various sections. Standard Oil and AT&T were split after being found guilty of monopoly charges. Standard Oil was split into 34 regional monopolies and AT&T was divided into seven local phone companies and a long-distance company.

Questions

1. Do you believe that Microsoft acts as a monopoly in Canada?
2. Is Microsoft a natural monopoly?
3. The United States Justice Department ruled that Microsoft abused its monopoly power. How did Microsoft maintain its monopoly in the face of competition?

EVERYDAY ECONOMICS 13.8

Price Fixing

Section 45 of the Competition Act states that it is an offence to conspire with another person to "unduly" prevent or lessen competition. Competition can be lessened through price fixing, restricting supply, customer and geographic market allocation, and group boycotts. Here, we will concentrate on price fixing.

With reference to section 45, the word *unduly* has been interpreted as "significantly." In other words, if the attempt to fix prices has, for example, a significant economic impact, it is unlawful. Because the word creates some uncertainty about what constitutes a significant lessening of competition, critics argue that even lawful agreements between companies are discouraged. For example, three furniture stores may want to send out a joint flyer advertising their geographic location, or a special sale. Should this type of cooperation be illegal? On the other hand, others complain that it is too difficult to prove price fixing and, thus, too difficult to prosecute offenders. Companies that have engaged

in price fixing can argue that competition was not unduly lessened since the price did not increase very much. Does the legislation need changing? Can anything be done to change the legislation?

The Competition Bureau states that prosecutions do occur under the legislation, and a substantial amount of money has been collected in fines. Section 45 allows the government to prosecute those who try to restrict competition. In order to obtain better evidence for prosecutions, the Competition Bureau has introduced an immunity policy. Under this policy, cartel participants who cooperate with the Bureau in an investigation receive immunity from prosecution. The Supreme Court of Canada has also ruled that the determination of whether competition has been unduly lessened depends on the presence of market power and the behaviour of the accused. In order to convict a firm, or firms, of price fixing, it is necessary to prove that the firm, or firms, had the *ability* to increase the price (i.e., market power). It may be difficult to prove the presence of market power—and, if so, to get convictions.

Several recommendations for changes to section 45 have been submitted to the government. At the time of writing, no changes have been made.

Questions

1. The Supreme Court states that firms must have market power to be guilty of price fixing. In your opinion, what is meant by *market power*?

2. Should all agreements between firms be submitted to the government for approval? Why or why not?

3. One suggestion is to prosecute only those arrangements that have a negative social impact. Discuss this suggestion.

Many Differentiated Sellers

In this type of competitive situation, there is a relatively large number of sellers. As with an oligopolistic structure, the exact number of sellers is difficult to determine. The large number of firms makes it difficult for any collusion to take place on prices. In fact, it can be assumed that the firms in the industry make price and output decisions without regard to the reactions of other firms. Entry into the industry is relatively easy, as is evidenced by the large number of firms. Industries characterized by many differentiated sellers have low concentration ratios.

Each seller offers a similar, yet not identical, product. The products may be differentiated in any number of ways. The differences may be real or simply imagined on the part of the consumer. For example, a consumer may believe one shirt to be of better quality than another, even though their construction is identical. These imagined differences are often created in the mind of the consumer by such things as brand names, trade marks, and advertising.

For other products a real difference may be present: the workmanship, design, materials, and quality of the products could differ. The location of a store or outlet may be another difference. This could be the only advantage that many firms have over other firms. Another difference in products could be the availability of credit. If one store permits payments over time, it may have an advantage over one insisting on cash.

What is the significance of the fact that product differentiation exists? It means that firms have some control over the price of their product. In perfect competition, because of identical products, each firm is forced to accept the market price. In an atmosphere of many differentiated sellers, *product distinction allows for price variation:* in fact, the more that a firm is able to distinguish its products from its competitors, the more control it will have over price.

The second feature of a differentiated market is that there is room for non-price competition. Firms may offer better service or product warranties, or they may get involved in advertising their product. As with other types of competition, firms in industries characterized by many differentiated sellers will try to maximize profits. This will require that they produce a level of output where marginal cost (MC) is equal to marginal revenue (MR).

We can assume that the short-run cost structure of a firm is similar to other firms. What does the revenue side look like? The demand curve for a firm under these competitive conditions is very elastic. The more substitutes for the product, the more elastic the curve is likely to be. The profit-maximizing position of the firm is shown in Figure 13.7.

The diagram is similar to that of a monopoly. The basic difference is the shape of the demand and marginal revenue curves. The curve is more elastic than that of a monopoly. By equating MC and MR, the firm will maximize profits. This will occur at a price of P_1 and a level of output of Q_1. In our diagram the firm is making an economic profit since P_1 is greater than the average cost of production (P_{ac}). If economic profits are being earned in the industry, new firms are likely to enter. In this competitive society, there are relatively few barriers to the entry of new firms. As new firms enter, the demand curve for existing firms shifts to the left. The curve also becomes a little more elastic because there are now more competitors and more sub-

Figure 13.7

Profit maximization for a firm in many differentiated sellers

In order to maximize profits, the firm produces a quantity of output (Q_1) where marginal revenue (MR) and marginal cost (MC) are equal. The profit-maximizing price is P_1. In the diagram opposite, economic profits are being made, since the price (P_1) is greater than the average cost of production (P_{ac}).

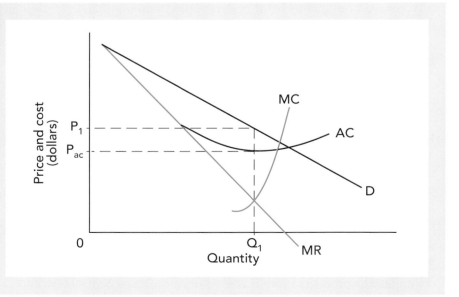

stitutes for the product. The shift to the left in the demand curve reduces the economic profits to the firm. In fact, as long as economic profits are being made, new firms will enter. The tendency in this industry is for firms to break even in the long run.

Even though there is a tendency to break even, some firms may continue to make economic profits, if they can sufficiently differentiate their product from that of their competitors. This differentiation can result from better quality, better styling, or simply better location. It may be hard to compete away the profits earned as a result of superior location.

REVIEW

13.11 Would you expect the demand curve for a firm in this type of competition to be elastic or inelastic? Why?

13.12 Observe how the elasticity of demand affects total profits in a marketplace of many differentiated sellers.

Non-Price Competition

In order to further differentiate its products from those of its competitors, a firm is likely to resort to various types of non-price competition. Improvements in product quality and design may be undertaken in order to improve the firm's position in the market. Some changes in the product may be simply in packaging. The main type of non-price competition is *advertising*. In addition to providing information, advertising may try to persuade the consumer to buy the product.

Advantages of Advertising

The primary advantage of advertising is that it provides *information* to the consumer. As indicated in Chapter 3, better information allows the market system to function more effectively. Advertising can inform a consumer about the ingredients in a product, its safety features, and other favourable attributes. Since fuel efficiency is more important to consumers than it used to be, automobile manufacturers have included kilometres per litre in their product promotion.

Advertising also helps in supporting our communications industry. It pays for television and radio programs as well as for a major part of our newspapers and magazines. In the case of the latter two products, the consumer does pay for part of the product. However, this amount is less than it would be in the absence of advertising.

Some argue that advertising may lead to lower-priced products. If advertising can convince consumers to spend money, the firm may be able to increase production. If economies of scale can be achieved, then lower costs will result and possibly lower prices. If advertising can keep up the level of consumer spending, then employment in the community will be at a higher level. If people are buying products, then workers are needed to produce the products. If foreign firms advertise, then domestic firms will also have to advertise in order to maintain sales. It can also be argued that jobs are created in the advertising business.

Finally, it can be argued that advertising leads to better-quality products. In order to have successful advertising, it is necessary that the firm have something to advertise. The demands of advertising could stimulate product research and development.

Arguments against Advertising

The main argument against advertising is that it increases the cost of making and selling a product. This raises the price to the consumer. In spite of the claims that advertising informs the consumer, much advertising is solely aimed at persuading, not informing. Beer advertising provides a good example. Very little information is provided about the product. The ads simply show people having a good time and suggest that the consumer associate good times with the product.

Advertising support for the communications industry may not be a definite advantage. It may lead to some bias in reporting. If one company spends a great deal of advertising money at a radio station, the station may not report any negative stories about that company. It can be argued that advertising diverts resources away from more productive uses. Advertising expenditures do not result in the production of any goods or services, only the promotion of them. Advertising may lead to social costs, such as visual pollution in the form of billboards and neon lights.

Will advertising get the country out of a high unemployment situation by encouraging spending? Advertising tends to be *pro-cyclical* and not *counter-cyclical*. This means that companies traditionally increase their advertising spending in times of high economic activity and cut their spending in poor times. If advertising spending is lower in times of recession, then how can it stimulate employment?

Privately produced goods, such as television sets and automobiles, are advertised, whereas public goods such as hospitals and roads are not. Does the variation in the use of advertising distort people's ideas about the relative value of these products? Should government advertise these services and solicit funds?

Advertising may, under certain circumstances, be considered a barrier to entry into a market and thus help to reduce competition (see Everyday Economics 13.4, on the beer oligopoly). If large companies in the industry have large advertising budgets, they may make it difficult for new firms to capture a sizable portion of the market.

R E V I E W

13.13 From your point of view, what is the most important advantage of advertising? The major disadvantage?

The Function of Profits

The discussion of *pricing behaviour* in this chapter sheds some light on the function of profits in our economy. Profits represent the excess of a firm's revenue over its costs. In one sense, profits are a return to the firm for the effort put forth in producing and selling a product or service. In the case of a sole proprietorship, any economic profit goes to the individual owner. In the case of a limited company, the shareholders are the recipients of profits. It is not necessarily true, however, that the shareholders receive all of the economic profit that a firm earns. Corporate income taxes, both federal and provincial, are based on profit. Much of the remaining profit after taxes is used for business investment. In order to remain competitive, it is necessary for businesses to purchase improved machinery and facilities. The existence of economic profit allows a firm to undertake the research and development of new products.

From an economist's point of view, profits are more than simply a return to the owners of the business. *Profits serve as a signal in the determination of what goods and services Canadians should produce.* If firms in an industry are earning an economic profit, the industry is likely to attract new competitors. The entrance of new firms will reduce the economic profit of existing firms. The existence of an economic profit in an industry indicates that consumers are interested in purchasing this product or service. If new firms enter the industry and survive, it will be because consumers continue to want this product. If firms in an industry are not earning an economic profit, new firms are not attracted to the industry. Also, existing firms will drop out of the industry. The supply of this product on the market will decrease.

Can profits be too high or too low? If the industry is competitive and new firms are free to enter, then it cannot be said that profits are too high or too low. If they are too high, new firms will enter the industry. If profits are not high, then new firms will not be eager to enter the industry. The existence of profits provides a signal that consumers value this product and want more of it to be produced.

If there are significant barriers to the entry of new firms, then economic profits will not be competed away. For example, one firm may have taken out a patent on a new product. While the patent is in effect, it is illegal for others to produce the product.

In a case like this, the firm with the patent may continue to earn economic profits over a long period of time. If this firm is earning economic profits, there will be an incentive for others to develop products of their own. The consumer will benefit from improved products and more choice in the marketplace. The toughest barriers to break down in entering an industry are imposed by government. In some industries, firms have continued to earn economic profits as a result of government barriers that reduce competition.

REVIEW

13.14 What role do profits play in our economy?

Summary

Imperfect competition refers to a competitive situation in which each firm has some control over the price of the product that it produces. The demand curve for each firm in the circumstances of imperfect competition is downward sloping to the right. In order to sell more output, the firm has to lower the price to all buyers.

An industry in which there is only one seller is referred to as a monopoly. The barriers to entering the monopoly industry are substantial enough to prevent the entry of new firms. These barriers include government legislation, patents, economies of scale, and ownership of raw materials. The presence of barriers to entry ensures that a monopoly that is earning economic profits will continue to do so.

In order to maximize profits, the monopoly produces a level of output at which marginal revenue is equal to marginal cost. At this level of output, the monopoly is producing less than the socially desirable amount. In order to improve the allocation of resources, government often steps in to regulate the price that the monopoly can charge. This can be done through socially optimum pricing or fair-return pricing. Whichever method is selected, the consumer receives more of the product for a lower price.

In an oligopoly, there are a few sellers of an identical or a differentiated product. The presence of only a few sellers in these industries attests to the fact that there are also strong barriers to entry, as is the case with monopoly. Each firm in an oligopolistic setting has to be concerned about the possible reaction of its competitors to any change in its price. The inability to predict the reaction of competitors means that the construction of a demand curve for an oligopolistic firm is very difficult. One attempt to construct a demand curve is demonstrated by the kinked demand curve. This curve is composed of an elastic portion and an inelastic portion, separated by a kink. The curve is drawn under the assumption that other firms do not follow a price increase but do follow a price decrease.

In order to reduce the level of uncertainty in their industry, firms in an oligopoly may collude on prices and output. Any agreement aimed at fixing prices is illegal in Canada under the Competition Act. Other illegal activities under this act include retail price maintenance, misleading advertising, price discrimination, predatory price cutting, and mergers that would unduly lessen competition.

In the many differentiated sellers situation, there is a relatively large number of sellers. Each firm offers a similar yet differentiated product. Since entry into the industry is relatively easy, new firms will start up whenever economic profits are present. The entry of new firms reduces the economic profit of existing firms and in the long run, firms tend to break even.

Advertising is used as a means of competition in situations of oligopoly and of many differentiated sellers. From an economic point of view, there are several disadvantages to advertising. The main advantage is that it provides information and promotes the more efficient functioning of markets. The main disadvantage is that it leads to higher product costs.

Questions for Review and Discussion

1. Explain why different prices for the same meal at lunchtime and at dinnertime is an example of price discrimination. Does this situation meet the conditions necessary for price discrimination?
2. The CRTC grants cable TV companies a monopoly in a specific geographic area. How much profit should cable TV firms be allowed to make?
3. Is it possible for a monopoly to lose money? If so, use a graph to describe this situation.
4. During the recession year of 1990, Canadian hotels offered lower room rates to attract customers. One hotel executive was quoted as saying that his hotel chain did not want any rooms to remain empty. In light of

your knowledge of costs and pricing, what is the lowest rate that a hotel could offer a customer?

5. Would you want hospitals to advertise? Why or why not?

6. In an attempt to increase attendance, the Toronto Blue Jays announced that ticket prices for the same seats would vary for the 2003 season. Early in the season and late in the season, tickets will be less expensive than in the summer months. The Toronto Blue Jays spokesperson announcing the pricing policy indicated that other sports are in competition with the Blue Jays in the spring and in the fall. Is this an example of price discrimination? Explain. How do the price changes relate to the perceived price elasticity of demand for the product offered to the fans by the Blue Jays?

7. Firms in an oligopolistic situation have advertising expenditure as a larger percentage of their products' selling price than do firms in other types of competition. Explain why this is so.

8. Why might it be tempting for firms in an oligopolistic setting to collude on prices?

9. During the 1970s, oil prices increased substantially. Much of the credit for these increases was attributed to OPEC, the oil cartel. What conditions must be present in order for a cartel to be successful? Why did oil prices start to fall in the early 1980s? Relate your answer to the success of OPEC as a cartel.

10. The kinked demand curve is an attempt to explain the demand curve for a firm in an oligopolistic situation. Explain the assumptions behind the curve. What are some of the drawbacks in using this curve to explain oligopolistic behaviour?

11. Does the kinked demand curve help explain why price wars occur in oligopolies?

12. Cocoa producers have formed the Cocoa Producers Alliance in an attempt to raise the price of cocoa. The goal of the cartel is to take low-grade cocoa off the market in order to increase the price of the remaining beans. Using demand and supply curves in your answer, show the impact of this strategy on the cocoa market.

13. In response to lower maple syrup prices, Quebec producers have discussed a supply management system for maple syrup. Would Quebec maple-syrup producers be successful in establishing a cartel? Discuss.

14. Explain how the easy entry into an industry of many differentiated sellers affects the elasticity of the demand curve that each firm has to deal with.

15. The primary difference between perfect competition and many differentiated sellers is the product differentiation that exists in the latter. What implications does this have (a) for the firm's ability to set the

price of the product, and (b) for the firm's need to use non-price competition?

16. Restrictions on advertising are being lifted for veterinarians. What form of advertising are veterinary clinics likely to use? Will this lead to increased competition among clinics?

17. The New Democratic Party of Ontario proposed in the mid 1990s to introduce government-owned car insurance in the province with the objective to lower car-insurance premiums and to ensure access to fair settlement of claims. At present, there are 80 companies selling car insurance in Ontario. Is it possible for these companies to form a cartel in order to increase car-insurance premiums? Discuss.

18. The major difference between many differentiated sellers and perfect competition is that in the former type of competition, the products are differentiated. Are differentiated products a benefit to society?

19. What do we mean by saying that advertising expenditures are pro-cyclical rather than counter-cyclical?

20. In 2003, in an attempt to win back customers and boost sales, fast-food chains like McDonald's and Burger King lowered prices. Burger prices dropped below $2.00, and in some cases below $1.00, in an attempt to increase sales. The discounts cut into profit margins. Industry executives complained that when prices are drastically discounted, sales must increase substantially in order to break even. However, in spite of the lower prices, some restaurants had lower sales than before the drop in prices.
    a) Is the demand for Burger King's food elastic or inelastic? Explain.
    b) If sales have decreased after the price cut, what can we say about the demand curve for that product?
    c) Are fast-food restaurants an example of an oligopoly? Explain.

Suggested Readings

Armstrong, Donald. *Competition Versus Monopoly: Combines Policy in Perspective.* Vancouver: Fraser Institute, 1982. This book contains a lengthy discussion of the nature of competition.

Consumer and Corporate Affairs Canada. Annual Reports of the Director of Investigation and Research, Competition Act. The annual reports provide information about the operation of the various sections in the Competition Act.

Moskowitz, Milton, Michael Katz, and Robert Levering (eds.). *Everybody's Business: An Almanac.* New York: Harper and Row, 1980. This thick softcover book contains interesting histories of many well-known companies.

Rohmer, Richard. *E.P. Taylor: The Biography of Edward Plunket Taylor.* Toronto: McClelland and Stewart, 1978. This biography contains a good discussion of Taylor's attempt to purchase many independent beer companies in the 1930s.

Selected Websites

www.crtc.gc.ca The website for the CRTC; includes rules of procedure, news releases, and the CRTC's mandate.

http://canada.justice.gc.ca/en/index.html The Competition Act and the Competition Tribunal Act can be accessed from this site.

www.ct-tc.gc.ca/english/casetype.html Information is available at this site on Competition Tribunal cases.

The Pricing of Resources

Key Terms

derived demand
value of marginal product
marginal-revenue product
monopsony
marginal-resource cost
featherbedding
craft unions
industrial unions
collective bargaining
certification
bargaining unit
arbitration
equalizing differences
economic rent
transfer earnings
present value

Chapter Objectives

After successfully completing this chapter, you will be able to:

- graph and describe both the value-of-marginal-product curve and the marginal-revenue-product curve
- discuss the factors that will cause the demand curve for labour to shift
- discuss the determinants of the elasticity of demand for labour
- describe graphically how wages are determined
- describe union attempts to increase wages
- discuss the various barriers to labour-market mobility
- define equalizing differences

Core Concept Building

The setting of wage rates in the labour marquet is the focus of this chapter. Note that businesses are not the suppliers in labour markets—they want employees, so they represent the demand side of the market. You will use the following concepts in this chapter: law of diminishing returns, opportunity cost, demand and supply, and price floors.

EDUCATION AND EARNINGS

There is a direct relationship between the level of education and earnings. For all age groups, the higher the level of education, the higher the earnings. Why does more education lead to higher earnings? Unfortunately, the answer to that question is not clear.

Some economists argue that more education makes a worker more productive. That is, a college graduate is more productive than a high-school graduate and thus is paid a higher salary to reflect the difference in productivity.

Other economists disagree. They argue that education levels are used as a screening mechanism to select potential employees. A degree, a diploma, or a certificate signals to an employer that this individual has the potential to be a productive employee. The educational system sorts out productive employees. When employers use the educational system to sort out prospective employees, the process is known as signalling. If employers continue to use education as a signal of one's productivity, then there must be a relationship between productivity on the job and level of education.

It is possible that higher levels of education do not make a person more productive; rather, they may be a proxy for individual characteristics that are associated with labour-market success. That is, in order to succeed at school, one needs to have intelligence, discipline, and perseverance. A graduate is also likely to have good communication skills, a trait that businesses desire in their employees.

If more education makes a person more productive, an argument could be made for large government expenditures in education since a better-educated labour force would be more productive. On the other hand, if education is simply a signal that saves employers time and effort in sorting out employees, the argument for government funding of higher education is not as strong. What do you think?

Analyzing Resource Markets

In Chapter 5, we introduced the concept of the circular flow of income (refer to Figure 5.1). The upper loop of the diagram illustrated the product markets. In these markets, households exchange money for a variety of goods and services. Households represent the demand side of the market and businesses represent the supply side. The lower loop of the diagram showed the resource markets. In these markets, businesses purchase the resources necessary for manufacturing a product or supplying a service. In the lower loop of the circular flow, households represent the supply side of the market and businesses represent the demand side. Up to this point in the text, our focus has been on the product markets. In this chapter, we will analyze the *resource markets*.

Resources: Demand and Supply

In our analysis of resource markets, we should first review the demand side of these markets. Since the easiest resource to relate to is labour, let us initially focus our discussion on the demand for labour. However, the theory developed in this section also applies to the markets for the other resources—land and capital.

The Demand for Labour

The primary feature of the demand for any resource is that it is **derived demand**; that is, the demand for the resource depends on the demand for the final product that the resource is used to produce. For example, the demand for automobile workers depends on the demand for cars. The demand for construction workers depends on the demand for new buildings. The demand for other resources such as uranium, nickel, zinc, and fertile land depends on the demand for the final products that these resources are used to produce.

The demand for each resource also depends on the *productivity* of that resource. The term "productivity" was introduced in Chapter 11. It refers to the amount of the final product that the resource can produce. Productivity depends on a number of factors. In the case of labour, it depends on education and training, management techniques, and the quality of other resources with which labour works. In the short run, labour productivity also depends on the law of diminishing returns. As more and more workers are hired in the short run, each successive worker has less and less capital to work with. Thus, the productivity of each additional worker is less than the productivity of the preceding worker.

The relationship between a firm's production function and the law of diminishing returns was first introduced in Chapter 11. Table 11.1 related the number of workers to the number of chairs that could be produced in a day. The productivity of labour is shown in the table: the productivity of each worker is represented by the *marginal product* of labour. After a certain point, the addition to total output (the marginal product) brought on by hiring one more worker becomes less and less. This is because each additional worker has less and less of the fixed resources to work with.

Since each successive worker starts to contribute less than the previous worker to the total output, each successive worker brings in less value to the company. In fact, if we know the price that chairs will sell for, we can calculate the value of the additional output that each worker contributes to the firm. Assume that each chair sells for $20. The value that each worker adds to the firm is referred to as the **value of marginal product** and can

Derived demand is the demand for a resource based on the demand for the good or service that the resource helps to produce.

The value of marginal product is an increase in total revenue resulting from employing one more unit of a productive resource in a perfectly competitive industry.

be determined by multiplying $20 times the marginal product associated with that worker.

value of marginal product (VMP) = price × marginal product

Using the data presented in Table 11.2, we can calculate the value of the marginal product for each worker. This information is presented in Table 14.1, and plotted in Figure 14.1.

The value-of-marginal-product (VMP) curve represents the demand curve for labour in a situation in which the price of the chairs does not change as more chairs are sold. In other words, in the situation of perfect competition, the VMP curve is the demand curve for workers. Why is it the demand curve?

A demand curve indicates what quantity of a certain product will be demanded at all possible prices. Assume that the price of labour, or the wage rate, is $100 per day. How many workers would the firm be willing to hire at this wage rate? The answer is seven. The firm would not hire the eighth worker since that worker contributes only $80 worth of output, while being paid $100. As long as the value of the marginal product exceeds the wage rate, the worker would be hired. If the wage rate were to change,

Table 14.1 *Value of marginal product, Pinewood Furniture Company*

NO. OF WORKERS	TOTAL NO. OF CHAIRS PRODUCED PER DAY	MARGINAL PRODUCT	VALUE OF MARGINAL PRODUCT ($20 × MARGINAL PRODUCT)
0	0		
1	5	5	$100
2	13	8	$160
3	22	9	$180
4	30	8	$160
5	37	7	$140
6	43	6	$120
7	48	5	$100
8	52	4	$ 80
9	54	2	$ 40
10	55	1	$ 20
11	55	0	$ 0
12	54	−1	$−20

Figure 14.1

The value-of-marginal-product curve

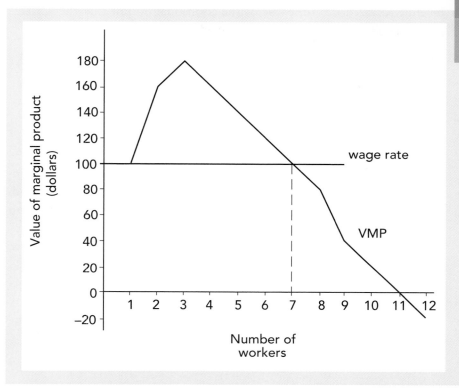

The value of marginal product (VMP) represents the demand curve for a certain type of worker. The number of workers hired depends on the intersection of the wage rate and the VMP curve.

the company would equate the wage rate with the value of the marginal product in determining how many workers should be hired.

For example, if the wage rate were to increase to $140 per day, only five workers would be hired. Because the number of workers hired depends on the VMP, this curve represents the demand curve for this type of worker.

A firm in perfect competition will hire workers to the point at which

wage rate = value of marginal product

This assumes that the wage rate remains the same for each worker regardless of how many workers are hired.

If the firm operates in an imperfectly competitive market, then a change has to be made in the derivation of the demand curve for labour. In an imperfectly competitive market, the demand curve for the product produced by each firm slopes down to the right. In order to increase sales, the firm has to lower the price. The contribution that each worker makes to the firm cannot be determined by multiplying the price by the marginal product, since the price is constantly changing as more of the product is sold.

Marginal-revenue product (MRP) **is the increase in total revenue as a result of employing one more unit of a productive resource (MP × MR).**

Instead, the marginal product of the worker is multiplied by the marginal revenue received from the sale of the additional output that the worker produces. This is called the **marginal-revenue product** (**MRP**).

marginal-revenue product = marginal revenue × marginal product

The MRP curve represents the demand curve for labour for an imperfectly competitive firm. If an imperfect competitor is interested in maximizing profits, then the firm will hire workers up to the point at which

wage rate = marginal-revenue product

The VMP and MRP curves represent the demand curve for a certain type of worker for a single firm. In order to determine the overall demand curve for this type of labour, it is necessary to add up the demand curves of each individual firm. This is referred to as the *market demand curve*. In most cases, a given firm will have more than one demand curve for labour; there would be a different demand curve for each type of worker hired, because the productivity of different types of workers varies.

REVIEW

14.1 What does the value of the marginal product represent? How do you calculate it?

14.2 Why does the value of the marginal product represent the demand curve for labour for a firm in perfect competition?

Changes in the Demand for Labour

What will cause the demand curve for labour to shift? In Chapter 2, demand curves were drawn assuming that the other factors influencing demand remained unchanged. The same holds true when drawing the demand curve for labour. If these factors change, then the demand for labour will also change. What factors are held constant in drawing the demand curve for labour?

The first factor held constant is the *price* of the product that the worker helps to produce. If the price of the product changes, then the demand for labour will change as well. For example, assume that there was an increase in the demand for solar-heating units for houses. This would increase the price of these units in the marketplace. The increased demand and price for solar-heating units would increase the demand for workers needed to manufacture and install these units. The demand for labour is derived directly from the demand for product.

Second, changes in the *productivity* of the worker will cause the demand for these workers to change and the marginal-product curve to shift. Since the demand curve for labour is derived by multiplying the marginal product of the worker by the marginal revenue, any change in the marginal product will cause the demand curve to shift. As workers become more productive, the demand for their services will increase. What would cause the productivity of labour to increase? Changes in productivity were discussed in Chapter 11; they are often associated with the equipment that the worker uses. For example, the introduction of word-processing equipment has made secretaries more productive. Alterations to documents and manuscripts can be made more easily and quickly on a word processor than on a typewriter. Changes in productivity can also come from improvements in the quality of the worker. Additional education and training allow workers to increase their output of goods and services. The more a worker can produce, the more the worker is in demand.

A third factor that could influence the demand for labour is a change in the price of a resource that is used along with labour, or that is a substitute for labour. In many situations, labour and another resource are complementary. For example, jewellery makers use gold, silver, and precious stones in their craft. If the price of gold or silver increases, it will affect the price of the jewellery. As a result of increases in the price of jewellery, consumers may decide to reduce the quantity they wish to buy (demand). This decision will have an impact on the demand for jewellery workers, and fewer workers will be needed. A change in the price of a complementary resource will therefore cause a shift in the demand for labour.

In other situations, resources may be substitutes for each other. The introduction of robots in some manufacturing establishments is an example of machinery being substituted for workers. If the price of machinery is attractive, companies could be encouraged to substitute machines for workers. A reduction in the price of a substitute resource shifts the demand curve for labour to the left. The introduction of new machinery may not always result in a reduced demand for labour. The new machinery may help reduce production costs and, therefore, reduce the selling price of the product. If prices are reduced, the quantity demanded of the product will increase, and the demand for workers will increase as well.

Wage-Rate Determination

In order to determine the equilibrium wage rate for a certain type of worker, it is necessary to put the demand and supply sides of the market together. In many instances, firms can demand more workers without having an impact on the market wage rate. These firms each represent a small proportion of the total demand for this type of worker. If the firm can hire as many workers as it needs at a constant wage rate, it will hire workers up to the point where the wage rate equals the value of marginal product (or marginal-revenue product). In this situation, the wage-rate line (see Figure 14.1) becomes the labour-supply curve for this firm in relation to that particular occupation. The supply curve is perfectly elastic, indicating that at this wage rate ($100 in Figure 14.1) the supply of workers to the firm is virtually unlimited. In some cases, the firm may not be able to hire an unlimited number of workers at the same wage rate. In this situation, the supply curve for labour to the firm is upward sloping to the right, as shown in Figure 14.2. There is a positive relationship between the wage rate and the quantity of workers supplied.

In order to attract workers, the firm may be forced to increase the wage rate. The firm's demand for this type of worker may represent a large proportion of the total demand for this type of worker. Any increase in the demand for workers by the firm will mean an increase in the market demand for this type of worker. Economists use the term **monopsony** (single buyer) to refer to a situation where only one firm hires a specific type of worker. When this firm increases its demand for workers, the overall demand for this type of worker increases. Increases in the demand lead to increases in the wage rate. If it becomes necessary to increase wages in order to attract new workers, existing workers will want to receive the wage increases as well. Thus, the cost to the firm of hiring one more worker may be greater than the wage rate paid to that worker, as the firm will have to compensate exist-

Monopsony **refers to a situation where only one firm hires a specific type of worker.**

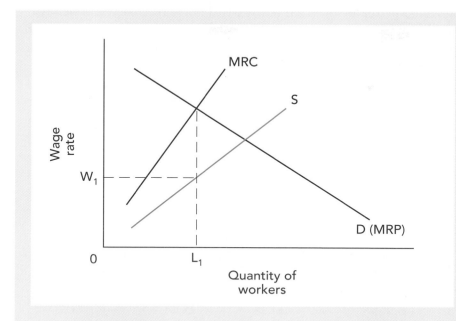

Figure 14.2

Wage-rate determination in the firm

The number of workers hired (L_1) is determined by the intersection of the marginal-resource cost (MRC) and the marginal-revenue-product (MRP) curves. The wage rate paid to these workers is determined by reference to the supply curve.

ing employees. The extra cost of hiring one more worker is known as the **marginal-resource cost (MRC)**.

An example may help the explanation of this process. Assume that the Direct Current Electric Company employs five electricians at a wage of $15 per hour. The company is interested in hiring an additional electrician, although there are no electricians in the local labour market who are unemployed. In order to attract an employee to the company, it will be necessary to increase the wage rate and hire the electrician away from another firm. Assume that $16 per hour is sufficient to attract a new employee.

What is the cost of hiring this employee? It is $16 per hour plus the money necessary to bring existing employees up to the new rate. Each of the five electricians will receive an additional $1 per hour. This brings the marginal-resource cost of hiring another electrician to $21 per hour. The determination of whether or not to hire this worker depends on the contribution that this worker can make to the firm (the marginal-revenue product). The company will hire the worker as long as the marginal-revenue product exceeds the marginal-resource cost.

A diagram representing the determination of wage rates under these conditions is shown in Figure 14.2. If it is necessary to increase wages as more workers are hired, then the marginal-resource-cost curve (MRC) will be

Marginal-resource cost (MRC) is the addition to total cost as a result of adding one more unit of a productive resource.

upward sloping to the right. The firm will hire the number of workers represented by the intersection of the MRP and MRC curves, which is L_1 workers. Once it is determined that L_1 workers are to be hired, the wage rate is set by referring to the supply curve. As shown in Figure 14.2, L_1 workers will be willing to work at this job for a wage rate of W_1.

A short numerical example helps to explain the shape of the marginal-resource-cost curve. In Table 14.2, the supply schedule for a certain type of worker appears in the first two columns. As the wage rate increases, the number of workers supplied to the market increases as well. The total-resource-cost column shows the cost to the firm of hiring workers at that wage rate. The marginal-resource cost represents the addition to total-resource cost of hiring one more worker. Notice that the marginal-resource cost is greater than the wage rate in every case.

Table 14.2 *Derivation of the marginal-resource-cost curve*

WAGE RATE ($ PER HOUR)	NUMBER OF WORKERS SUPPLIED	TOTAL RESOURCE COST ($)	MARGINAL RESOURCE COST ($)
15	5	75	
			21
16	6	96	
			23
17	7	119	
			25
18	8	144	
			27
19	9	171	
			29
20	10	200	

REVIEW

14.5 Why is the marginal-resource cost (MRC) of hiring one more worker not always equal to the wage rate paid to that worker?

Equilibrium in the Labour Market

The sum of all the marginal-revenue-product curves for all the firms that require a certain type of labour is known as the market-demand curve for that occupation. The interaction of the market-demand curve and the market-supply curve determines the equilibrium wage rate for the occupation (see Figure 14.3). Any factors that result in a shift of the firm's MRP curve will cause the market-demand curve for the occupation to shift as well. For example, an increase in the demand for the final product will cause

Figure 14.3

The equilibrium wage rate in the labour market

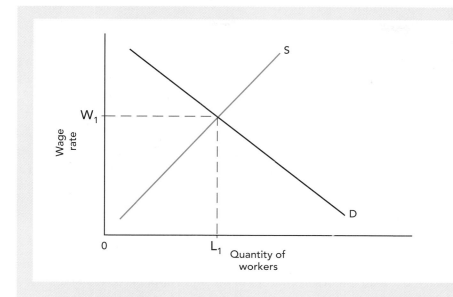

The equilibrium wage rate for a certain type of worker (W_1) is found at the intersection of the demand and supply curves.

the demand for the labour required to make that product to shift to the right. Any change in worker productivity will also shift the demand curve for labour.

An introduction to the supply of labour appeared in Chapter 5. The Labour Force Survey calculates the *participation rate,* as well as the unemployment rate, on a monthly basis. The participation rate is defined as the percentage of the population who are in the labour force—in other words, the percentage of the population who either have a job or would like to have a job. A detailed discussion of changes in Canada's participation rate appeared in Chapter 5.

In this chapter, we are concerned not about the overall supply of labour, but about the supply of labour to a specific job. The short-run supply of labour identifies the quantity of labour that will be offered to a specific job, depending on the wage rate. In general, the higher the wage rate, the greater the number of people who would be willing to do the job. At very low wage rates, the number of workers willing to do a job is also low. Their time could be better spent working at another job or participating in a leisure activity. As the wage rate increases, the number of workers willing to do the job increases as well. The opportunity cost of not working at this job increases along with the wage rate. The supply curve for workers to most jobs, therefore, is upward sloping to the right (line S in Figure 14.3).

Any change in the demand for or the supply of labour will result in a new equilibrium wage rate. If the demand for a certain type of labour increases, then the wage rate will increase as well. If the supply of a certain type of labour increases, everything else remaining the same, then the wage rate will fall. It should be remembered that the demand and supply curves in Figure 14.3 are *market curves*. That is, they represent the total demand for this type of worker and the total supply of workers available.

REVIEW

14.6 Learn about how the demand for a product influences the demand for labour, and the cost of labour.

The Elasticity of Demand for Labour

The price elasticity of demand for consumer products, introduced in Chapter 2, is an important concept in the study of markets. The price elasticity of demand indicates exactly how consumers respond to price changes in terms of the quantity that they are willing to buy. The price elasticity of demand for labour is also important in a discussion of resource markets. The more elastic the demand for labour, the more it is likely that employers will respond to changes in wage rates in terms of the number of workers demanded. If the demand for labour is elastic, then a reduction in the wage rate will substantially increase the number of workers demanded. An increase in the wage rate will significantly reduce the number of workers hired. Conversely, if the demand for labour is relatively inelastic, then changes in the wage rate will not affect the quantity of labour demanded to any great extent.

Knowledge of the elasticity of demand for labour is an important aspect in union/management negotiations. If the demand for labour is inelastic, union leaders will be anxious to achieve substantial wage increases for their members. Large wage increases will not greatly reduce the demand for union workers. In contrast, if the demand for labour is elastic, then wage increases may result in reduced employment for union members. The possibility of high unemployment among union members may temper the demand for wage increases. The elasticity of demand for workers clearly influences union demands when bargaining with management.

The government has similar concerns about the elasticity of demand for labour when contemplating minimum-wage increases. Minimum-wage increases will result in a greater decrease in employment if the demand for labour is elastic. That is, the higher the minimum-wage rate, the fewer workers employers will be likely to hire. Increases in the legal minimum wage are meant to be a benefit for workers. Yet if these increases lead to many workers losing their jobs, the increase will have negative rather than beneficial results.

What determines the elasticity of demand for labour? First, it depends on the elasticity of demand for the product that labour produces. *The more elastic the demand for the product, the more elastic the demand for the workers.* If consumers respond to price increases by substantially reducing the quantity of the product demanded, then employers will be forced to reduce their demand for workers when faced with wage increases. For example, the demand for airline tickets is elastic. If the price of airline tickets were to rise, the quantity of tickets demanded would decrease significantly, which would cause a decrease in the number of airline employees required. Since an increase in wages paid to airline employees will lead to an increase in airline ticket prices, the company has to be concerned about the size of the wage increase granted. A sizeable wage increase may lead to reduction in staff in order to keep costs, and ultimately prices, down.

Second, elasticity depends on the number of substitutes for labour. If there are few substitutes, the demand is inelastic. If there are several substitutes, the demand tends to be elastic. Where substitutes are available, employers can substitute for workers when faced with wage increases. For example, robots that can paint a car on the production line have long been available. As the wages paid to workers on the line increased, it made more sense economically for the company to use robots instead of workers.

Not only is the elasticity of demand influenced by the number of substitutes for labour, it is influenced by the elasticity of supply of those substitutes. If the supply of the substitute for labour, for example robots, is very elastic, an increase in the demand for robots will not substantially increase the price of robots. If the price of the substitute does not increase significantly when the demand for it increases, it will continue to be a good substitute for labour. Employers can continue to switch to this substitute when the wage rate for labour increases. The demand for labour under these circumstances will be elastic.

On the other hand, if the supply of robots is inelastic, any increase in the demand for robots will increase their price. As the price of robots increases, employers will be less willing to substitute robots for labour. This will result in the demand for labour being less elastic than in the situation described in the previous paragraph.

Third, the elasticity of demand for labour is greater in the long run. Over time employers will be better able to adjust to wage increases. Over time, consumers will be able to purchase substitutes for the products that may not be available in the short run, making the demand for those products more elastic. If the demand for those products is more elastic, the demand for labour to make those products is also more elastic.

Fourth, the elasticity of demand for labour depends on the percentage of total costs that labour costs comprise. If labour costs represent only a small portion of total costs, then the demand for labour will be inelastic. Wage increases may not greatly affect the firm's total costs and as a result, wage increases may not affect employment. If labour costs are a large portion of total costs, firms will be forced to respond to wage increases by reducing the number of workers employed. Under these conditions, the demand for labour is elastic.

The final condition influencing the elasticity of demand for labour is the shape of the marginal-product curve. This curve shows how fast the productivity of each successive worker declines. If the productivity of each successive worker declines rapidly as new workers are hired, then the demand for labour is likely to be inelastic. If the productivity of each successive worker declines slowly as new employees are hired, the demand for labour is likely to be elastic. In the first case, the marginal-product curve has a steep slope; in the second case, it has a gradual slope.

R E V I E W

14.7 Why is some idea of the elasticity of demand for labour important in union/management negotiations?

The Backward-Bending Supply Curve

The theory behind the supply curve for labour focuses on the decision to work. The theory can be summarized as the work–leisure trade-off. In order to explain the work–leisure trade-off, we assume that an individual has only two choices regarding the use of his or her time. The choice is work or leisure. Clearly, some time must be spent sleeping, eating, and performing other essential duties. However, the choice in using discretionary time boils down to working for pay or participating in a leisure activity.

The work–leisure trade-off theory treats leisure as a commodity that can be purchased. The demand for this commodity depends on its price. What is the price of leisure? The price of leisure is the opportunity cost of not working for pay. If you have the opportunity to work for $10 an hour and you choose not to work, the price of leisure is $10 per hour. As the price of leisure increases, less leisure will be demanded. That is, as one's hourly wage rate increases, the opportunity cost of not working increases. As the wage rate increases, the quantity of leisure demanded should decrease and individuals are encouraged to work more. This desire for less leisure in the face of an increase in the price for leisure is called the substitution effect.

The demand for a commodity is also a function of one's income. As income increases, more leisure can be purchased. Increases in hourly wage rates should result in increases in income if hours of work remain the same. Therefore, as the hourly wage rate increases, an individual should demand more leisure. This increased demand for leisure is called the income effect.

The income and substitution effects work in opposite directions in response to a wage rate increase. The income effect encourages one to purchase more leisure while the substitution effect encourages one to work more hours. Which effect dominates? Discussion surrounding the income and substitution effects has led economists to propose a backward-bending supply curve for labour (see Figure 14.4). At low wage rates, it is assumed that the substitution effect will dominate as individuals may not believe that their income is high enough to purchase more leisure. At some higher wage rate (W_1), the income effect begins to dominate. Individuals have enough income to demand more leisure.

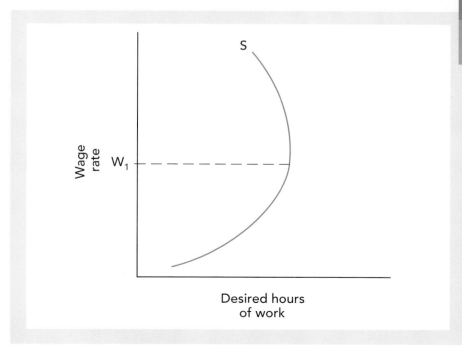

Figure 14.4

The backward-bending supply curve for labour

The desired hours of work are reduced at higher wage rates.

Payroll Taxes: Job Killers

The Canada Pension Plan (CPP) and the Employment Insurance program (EI) are examples of payroll taxes currently in place in Canada. Both employers and employees contribute to both CPP and EI. What impact do payroll taxes have on the labour market? Assume that the payroll tax is stated as $0.25 per hour per employee. The imposition of the payroll tax reduces the employee's MRP by $0.25. The MRP curve that represents the demand curve for a specific type of worker will shift down by $0.25. The market demand curve will also shift down by $0.25. The impact of this shift is shown in Figure 14.5.

Prior to the imposition of the payroll tax, L_1 workers were employed at the wage rate, W_1. After the imposition of the tax, the wage rate is W_2 and only L_2 workers were employed. The payroll tax has resulted in a lower wage rate for those still employed

and a loss of employment for others. Note that in this example the equilibrium wage rate does not fall by the full amount of the tax.

Some employers may be unable to reduce the wages of their employees because of contractual obligations such as a collective agreement. In such cases, future wage increases may be delayed or, if possible, some employment benefits reduced. Other employers may not be able to reduce the wage rate below the minimum wage. If the wage rate cannot be reduced, the number of workers on the payroll will be.

The impact of payroll taxes on employment levels may be greater for small businesses than for large businesses. For small businesses, payroll taxes constitute a greater proportion of total taxes, and small businesses have higher compliance and administrative costs. Small businesses tend to be

Figure 14.5

The impact of a payroll tax

The imposition of the payroll tax has shifted the demand for labour from D^1 to D^2.

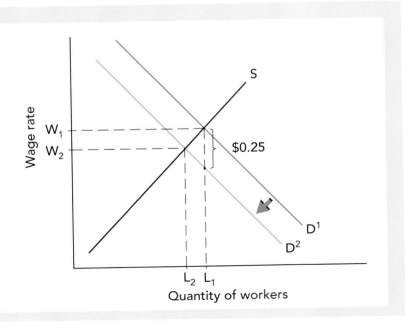

labour-intensive and hire more low-wage, low-skilled workers. Payroll taxes have more of an impact on the cash flow of small businesses. Finally, small businesses are less likely to be unionized and thus the impact of payroll taxes is more likely to be felt by the employees.

Questions

1. Use demand and supply curves to show the impact of a payroll tax where the supply curve is vertical. What impact is there on the wage rate in this situation?

2. What impact does the elasticity of demand for labour have on the impact of a payroll tax?

3. The federal government has announced that CPP premiums on eligible earnings will increase from the current rate of 6 percent to 9.9 percent in 2003. Why might CPP premiums be considered to be a regressive tax?

The Impact of Labour Unions on Wage Rates

One of the main objectives that workers have in joining labour unions is to increase wages. If a union is to be successful at increasing wages, it has the option of trying to increase the demand for its members, or of trying to restrict the supply of workers who can do the job. Let us first analyze the attempts by unions to increase the demand for labour.

Increasing the Demand for Labour

The demand for labour is derived from the demand for the product and the productivity of the worker. If the labour union is to increase the demand for workers, it must increase either of these two factors. Workers do not usually promote the products that they produce. Such promoting is left up to the employer. Yet if unions can increase the demand for the products that they produce, the demand for their services will increase. If the demand for their services increases, the wage rate will increase as well. The International Ladies Garment Workers' Union is one labour organization that has tried to promote the sales of domestically produced women's clothes. This union has advertised on television and has set up booths at shows and exhibitions. The Canadian Automobile Workers has also tried to promote the purchase of domestically produced cars. In Ontario, contractors and the electricians' union (IBEW) have jointly promoted their services on the radio.

There are other ways whereby unions can increase the demand for labour. They can press the federal government to introduce tariffs and quotas on imports. The introduction of these trade barriers should increase the demand for domestically produced goods. Labour unions may also negotiate make-work projects with employers. This procedure, known as

**Featherbedding refers to
practices or work rules that
may set unreasonable
limits on the amount of
work employees may
perform in a given period
of time, or may result in
payment for unneeded
workers doing jobs that
duplicate others' efforts.**

**A trade union whose
members all possess a
particular skill is called a
craft union.**

**A trade union that
attempts to organize all the
workers in a particular
industry is called an
industrial union.**

featherbedding, retains jobs for workers whose jobs have become redundant. Featherbedding, used mainly in the construction and railway industries, maintains the demand for labour, rather than increasing it. Still, featherbedding prevents a drop in wages for certain groups of workers.

Labour unions can also take steps to increase the productivity of workers. This effect can be accomplished by providing training and skill development for union members. Encouraging management to introduce better machinery and equipment may also improve productivity. Increases in productivity will lead to increases in the demand for workers.

Influencing the Supply of Labour

The ability of a labour union to influence the supply side of the labour market depends on the type of union in question. There are basically two types of unions: craft and industrial. **Craft unions** are made up of workers who have a common skill or craft. Examples of craft unions are electricians, plumbers, and printers. **Industrial unions** organize workers by industry, for example automobile, steel, chemical. Members of industrial unions include all workers in the industry, including unskilled, semi-skilled, and skilled workers.

Craft labour unions try to increase the wages paid to their members by reducing the supply of labour. If they can cause the supply curve to shift to the left, the equilibrium wage rate will increase (see Figure 14.6). How can unions reduce the supply of labour? This reduction can be accomplished by several means. The unions could press employers to hire only union members. They could insist on long apprenticeships for workers before they are qualified to work at the trade. Craft unions could press government for compulsory retirement programs, for restrictions on hours of work, and for tougher regulations on the immigration of workers.

Industrial unions are not in the same position as craft unions to reduce the supply of labour. They cannot insist on long apprenticeships since many of their members work at unskilled jobs that do not require apprenticeship training. It is also more difficult for industrial unions to restrict membership. In fact, industrial unions are interested in including all the workers in their industry in their membership. Industrial unions must increase wages by ensuring that no members agree to work for less than a certain minimum, or base, wage. In effect, the industrial union tries to establish a wage (price) floor. The setting of a price floor will only work if all members agree and are willing to go out on strike in order to achieve their goal. The difficulty with price floors is that unemployment results among some members (see Chapter 3). The greater the elasticity of demand for

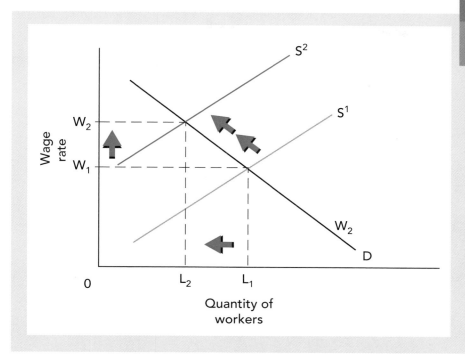

Figure 14.6

Restricting the supply of labour

A decrease in the supply of labour from S^1 to S^2 increases the equilibrium wage rate from W_1 to W_2.

workers, the more likely it is that some workers will lose their jobs as a result of the wage increase.

The impact of an industrial union on wages and employment is shown in Figure 14.7. The equilibrium wage rate before the union pushes for a wage increase is W_1. The number of workers hired at this wage is L_1. If the union insists on a minimum wage rate of W_2, the number of workers hired will fall to L_2. The decline in employment will be greater the more elastic the demand curve. The establishment of a new base rate, W_2, means that a new supply curve for labour is created. The new supply curve is W_2aS, since no one can be employed for a wage below W_2.

R E V I E W

14.8   How could trade unions increase the demand for the workers whom they represent?

14.9   How can craft unions restrict the number of members in the union?

14.10 Discover how variations in the minimum wage rate affect the unemployment rate.

Figure 14.7

Figure 14.7

Establishing a minimum rate for union members

Industrial unions try to set a wage rate (W$_2$) above the existing equilibrium wage (W$_1$). This results in a decline in employment from L$_1$ to L$_2$.

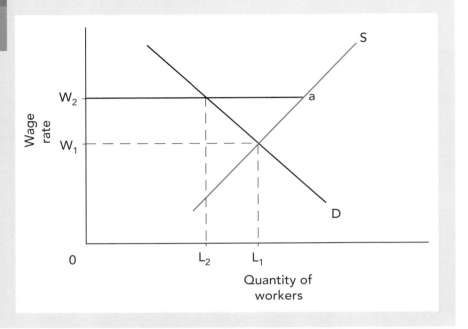

EVERYDAY ECONOMICS 14.2

Do Unions Raise Wages?

One of the reasons that workers join unions is to increase their hourly wage rates. Through collective action rather than individual action, workers hope to force the employer to pay higher wages. The threat of a strike hangs over the employer's head in the face of union wage demands.

Do unions in fact succeed in raising wages? The answer is not clear. Those who argue that unions do raise wages point to the wage differential that exists between union and non-union workers. Especially in the case of skilled jobs, workers who are union members have a higher hourly wage rate. Those who argue that unions do not raise wages point to the fact that union workers who are highly paid now were highly paid prior to joining the union. They argue that it is not the union but the industry that determines the wage rate. If the industry that

employs the workers can afford to pay high wages, then the workers will receive them.

Union membership is no guarantee of a wage increase. During the recession years of the 1980s and 1990s, many union members were forced to settle for wage freezes or wage reductions. These concessions on the part of workers occurred in such industries as airlines, railways, mining, and automotive. Large unions such as the Teamsters and United Steelworkers have, at times, been unable to negotiate wage increases for their members.

Numerous studies have attempted to measure the impact of unions on wage rates. The studies have been concerned with different industries and have been undertaken at different times. The general conclusion is that unions account for a wage differential of at least 10 percent when compared with the wages of non-union workers. These studies also point out that unions can have an impact on the wages of non-union workers. Employers may grant larger than required wage increases to non-union employees in order to avoid having the employees join a union. Workers who are members of a union tend to receive better benefits than non-union workers.

There is some evidence that unionized workplaces occur in industries with less desirable working conditions. That is, the health and safety hazards of the industry may be greater than those in largely non-unionized industries. Some of the wage rate differential attributed to unions may be compensation for undesirable situations.

Questions

1. If unions do raise wages, why did unionized workers at Canadian Airlines accept a pay cut?
2. What do you believe is the most important factor in the determination of wage rates?
3. If it was unlikely that a union would improve wage rates in a certain industry, why would workers still want to join a union?
4. What is the association between wage-rate increases or decreases and the elasticity of the demand for labour?

Collective Bargaining in Canada

Collective bargaining is the process whereby employees negotiate with an employer as a group, rather than individually, regarding the terms of their employment. Individuals acting alone have very little bargaining power in negotiations with an employer. When employees negotiate with an employer collectively, they are more likely to achieve improvements in working conditions. If a single employee walks away from his or her job because of a dispute over working conditions, the production process is not likely to be adversely affected. If all the employees of a company walk away from their jobs, production will cease.

Governments in Canada have tried to promote the process of collective bargaining between employees and their employers. Legislation requires that an employer negotiate with a certified trade union or group of employees. Legislation also permits compulsory union membership and the compulsory deduction of union dues from the employee's paycheque. Most employees in Canada are covered by provincial legislation in matters pertaining to collective bargaining. Employees in industries such as banking, communications, and transportation are covered by federal government legislation.

Collective bargaining **involves the negotiating of an employment contract between management and the union representing the employees.**

Certification

If an employer must negotiate with employees on a collective basis, it first must be determined that the employees want to negotiate their working

The process by which a labour union acquires the bargaining rights for a group of employees is called certification.

A bargaining unit defines those jobs or positions represented in the collective agreement between the employer and the representative of the employees, the union.

conditions in this manner. It also has to be determined which employees at the company will be grouped together for bargaining purposes. This process is referred to as **certification**.

Employees who do not currently negotiate with their employer over working conditions, but who wish to do so, must determine if the majority of employees wants to bargain collectively. One procedure to follow is to ask employees to join a labour union. Those employees who want to join the union must sign a membership card and pay a small fee. If enough employees agree to join the union, the union can approach the Labour Relations Board about becoming the certified bargaining agent for the employees of this particular firm.

What number constitutes enough employees? It may be impossible to contact all the employees in the company. It may also be impossible to get all the employees to agree to union membership. In some provinces, when 40 percent of the employees have signed union cards, this percentage is sufficient evidence for holding a representation vote. If as many as 55 percent of the employees have signed union cards, the Labour Relations Board may declare that the union represents the employees and can approach the employer regarding negotiations about working conditions. If a vote is held, the union must get the support of just over 50 percent of the employees in order to represent the **bargaining unit** in negotiations.

What is the bargaining unit? Not all employees of a company are in the union and negotiate collectively with the employer. Persons in supervisory positions such as managers and supervisors are not in the bargaining unit. Security guards are not in the bargaining unit. Other employees such as student workers and part-time workers may be omitted. Office and plant employees are often in separate units and negotiate separately with the employer. Professional engineers often have their own bargaining unit. *The certification process determines which employees are in the bargaining unit.* The determination is made by the Labour Relations Board if the employer and the union cannot agree on the composition of the unit. The representation vote cannot be taken until the bargaining unit is established.

Negotiating a Collective Agreement

Once certified as the bargaining agent for the employees, the union must approach the employer about negotiating a contract of employment conditions. Although the employer must negotiate with the union, the employer does not have to agree to union demands in regard to working conditions. If agreement cannot be reached, a work stoppage may result in order to speed up the process of agreement. A strike occurs when the employees walk off the job in order to put pressure on the employer to accept their demands. A lockout occurs when the employer refuses to allow the employees to enter company premises until an agreement is reached.

The focus of Canada's collective-bargaining legislation has been to prevent work stoppages. In many jurisdictions a third party, brought in to attempt *conciliation,* is made available to assist both parties in achieving an agreement before a work stoppage takes place. The conciliator attempts to persuade both sides to soften their positions before a strike or lockout occurs. It is common for the legislation to insist that the conciliation procedure be exhausted before a work stoppage can occur. The term *mediation* is also used in connection with third-party intervention. Mediation is similar to conciliation.

When the union and employer agree on a set of working conditions, a contract, or collective agreement, is drawn up. Once both sides have signed the agreement, they must adhere to its provisions. There cannot be a strike or a lockout during the term of agreement. Any disputes during the term of the agreement must be settled by **arbitration** if the parties cannot settle the agreement themselves.

Because all firms face different competitive conditions and have varying degrees of control over the price of their products, working conditions for their employees will also vary. Some companies operate in a monopoly situation. Others face tough competition from foreign competitors. The ability of labour unions to improve the working conditions for their members depends on the firm's ability to provide those conditions and still remain competitive.

Arbitration is a procedure whereby an independent third party settles disputes between union and management during the life of a collective agreement.

Contents of Collective Agreements

Working conditions contained in collective agreements cannot conflict with minimum-employment standards contained in legislation. That is, if labour legislation sets a minimum wage of $7 per hour, the collective agreement cannot establish wages at less than $7 per hour. The agreement must also adhere to minimum standards concerning statutory holidays, vacations, hours of work, severance pay, and similar employment standards.

All employer/employee agreements contain three articles. The employer must recognize the union as the bargaining agent for employees in the bargaining unit. The bargaining unit is also defined. There must be no strike or lockout during the life of the agreement. Finally, the company and the union agree to settle any alleged violation of the agreement by arbitration. In the arbitration process, a neutral third party studies the agreement and makes a decision regarding the alleged violation.

Other articles included in collective agreements are:

Wages: This article sets out the rate of pay for each job covered by the agreement.

Hours of work: The standard hours of work, either on a daily or weekly basis, are specified.

Overtime pay provisions: The rate of pay for hours worked in excess of standard hours or for hours worked on a holiday is set out.

Vacations with pay: The amount of vacation with pay to which an employee is entitled is set out. In many agreements, the number of weeks of vacation may increase with the number of years of service.

Seniority: This article establishes the rules by which seniority is recorded. The years of service in the bargaining unit are referred to as an employee's seniority.

Grievance procedure: This is the procedure for settling alleged violations of the agreement. In most agreements there are several stages set out by which the dispute may be settled before it goes to arbitration.

Union security: This article defines the relationship between the union and the members of the bargaining unit. Under a closed-shop form of union security, the company agrees to hire and employ only members of the union. Under a union shop, all members of the bargaining unit must join the union. A Rand-formula shop requires that all members of the bargaining unit pay union dues whether or not they are union members.

Rights of management: The rights of management are set out in this article. In most agreements, many decisions rest with management except those specifically given up in the agreement.

Glossary of Collective-Bargaining Terms

The following terms are associated with the practice of collective bargaining in Canada.

accreditation: In the construction industry, employers may join an association in order to negotiate a collective agreement with a trade union. Accreditation of an employers' association as a bargaining agent is similar to certification of a labour union as a bargaining agent.

Canadian Labour Congress (CLC): The largest federation of independent unions in Canada. The CLC has been compared to a "union of unions."

COLA: Cost-of-living allowance (or adjustment). An allowance paid, or an adjustment made, to wages set out in the collective agreement in order to compensate for increases in the Consumer Price Index.

contracting out: The practice of having certain stages in the production process or other work functions performed by outside contractors and not by members of the bargaining unit.

decertification: The process of decertification removes the rights of the bargaining agent for members of a bargaining unit.

final-offer selection: This is a form of arbitration whereby the arbitrator selects either the company's last offer or the union's last proposal. One proposal only is selected in its entirety. The purpose of such a procedure is to force the parties to submit reasonable proposals.

ratification: The process by which members of the bargaining unit vote on and accept a proposed collective agreement.

unfair labour practices: Acts undertaken by the company or the union to thwart the other party's attempt to bargain "in good faith." These include such activities as discriminating against an employee for engaging in union activity and interfering with an employee's right to join a union.

picketing: The act of workers gathering outside the plant or office and carrying placards announcing that they are on strike.

secondary boycott: The union, during a strike, will try to put pressure on a third party in order to influence the company against which they are striking. The third party may be a supplier or a customer of the company.

EVERYDAY ECONOMICS 14.3

Should Civil Servants Be Given the Right to Strike?

Civil servants are employees of the government. In some Canadian jurisdictions, government employees are not permitted to go on strike; in other jurisdictions they have been given the right to strike. Should civil servants be treated in a different manner from other employees in terms of the right to go on strike in order to press for improved working conditions?

There is one major difference between the collective-agreement negotiation process that takes place in the private sector and that which takes place in the public sector involving government employees. The difference concerns the ability of the employer to pay for any improvement in working conditions that the employees receive. In the private sector of our economy, an employer is constrained in the presentation of an offer to employees on working conditions by the realities of the marketplace. Any improvement in working conditions that increases costs must be translated into higher prices for the product or service. Can the company afford to raise prices? An increase in price may result in a loss of sales to a competitor or in a reduction of the quantity demanded by consumers. The ability of a company to raise the price will depend on the competitive environment that it faces.

In the public sector, ability to pay is not as much of a concern. Taxes can always be increased in order to pay for the improvement in employee working conditions. The federal government could borrow from the Bank of Canada in order to meet an increase in costs. Services provided by government are rarely in competition with similar services in the marketplace. It is less likely that business will be lost to a competitor. The government need not make a profit in order to continue to operate, and will not shut down if it finds itself operating in a deficit position.

Once the government has assumed the responsibility for a service, it also has the responsibility to continue to provide the service. Government services are often in a monopoly position in the marketplace. The consumer has no alternative when these services are interrupted by a strike. In cases such as Canada Post, the government has declared it illegal to establish another post office in Canada. Does the government not have the responsibility to provide this service?

The nature of employment in the public sector is also different from that in the private sector. Employment in the public sector is more stable and not subject to swings in the business cycle. That is, civil servants are not usually subject to the series of layoffs and rehiring that occur in the private sector.

These distinctions between public- and private-sector employment lend support to the belief that there can be differences in labour legislation affecting the two groups of workers. These differences could extend to denying the right to strike to civil servants.

In contrast, some arguments can be made in favour of giving civil servants the right to strike. Should civil servants not have their employment rights protected in the same manner as other employees? If the right to strike is taken away from civil servants, what bargaining power do they have available in their negotiations with the employer? In the private sector, employees can threaten to go on strike if their demands are not met. What can civil servants do? If government employees are not allowed to strike, government may not be sincere in the negotiation process. The government may not be too anxious to reach a settlement because the employees will continue working even without a contract.

Restrictions have already been placed on civil servants and their right to negotiate. For example, changing some working conditions, such as pension plans, would require changes in legislation to implement and, therefore, cannot be negotiated. Removing the right to strike gives civil servants even less control over their working conditions.

In situations in which government employees are not permitted to strike, disputes over the content of the collective agreement are sent to a third party for a decision. The third party, referred to as an arbitrator, makes a decision that is final and binding on the parties involved. Relegating the decision to an arbitrator is not without its difficulties. Who should be selected as an arbitrator? What criteria should be used in arriving at a decision? Should government be permitted to abdicate its responsibility in this area of government spending?

Questions

1. If strikes are illegal for a certain category of civil servants, what action should government take in the case of an illegal strike? What problems does government face in taking this action?

2. In some cases, civil servants are permitted to go on strike but certain jobs are considered to be essential. Those employees in designated occupations are not permitted to strike. What criteria should determine an essential occupation? Does the classification of essential occupations that are unable to strike reduce the bargaining power of the union?

3. Decisions regarding working conditions for civil servants are often influenced by political considerations. In order to remove politics from the decision-making process, why not hold a referendum of citizens on the proposed collective agreement for civil servants? In your answer discuss some of the advantages and disadvantages of such a proposal.

Wage Differentials

Not everyone earns the same hourly wage rate. Why are there wage differences between occupations? Imagine two occupations with market conditions as shown in Figure 14.8. The market conditions in occupation A result in a higher wage (W_A) than in the market for occupation B (W_B). If there are no restrictions on workers moving between occupations, then workers in occupation B would move over to the market for occupation A. This would increase the supply of workers in occupation A (S_A^2) and lower the equilibrium wage rate (W_E). The reduced supply of workers in occupation B would cause the equilibrium wage rate to rise to W_E. If workers were free to move between occupations, the equilibrium wage in both markets would eventually be the same.

In real life, there are barriers that prevent the movement of workers from occupation B to occupation A. Wage rates, therefore, are different from occupation to occupation. If the flow of workers from occupation B to occupation A is restricted, the wage will not decline very much in occupation A. In occupation B, the workers who cannot go to occupation A will keep the wage rate for B lower than it would be if workers were mobile. As long as barriers to the mobility of workers exist, occupational wage differentials will remain. What are these barriers?

One barrier is simply *a lack of information*. If workers in occupation B do not know that occupation A exists, or do not know the wages paid in A, then they will not be inclined to move. Labour-market information in the real world is seldom perfect; this is the main reason for establishing Canada Employment Centres and other placement agencies.

A second barrier is *skill* or *education requirements*. Occupation A may require a certain degree of training, which those presently in occupation B do not possess. Not everyone is capable of doing every job. For example, not everyone is qualified to be a dentist. Because there are some restrictions on becoming a dentist, the wages of dentists will remain higher than they would without these restrictions. The limited number of vacancies at schools of dentistry ensures that the market will not be flooded with new dentists. The government also assists in maintaining the wage differential between dentists and other occupations by not allowing anyone to practise dentistry unless qualified. Any restriction that reduces the supply of labour to an occupation will maintain higher wage rates in that occupation.

A third restriction may be *geographic location*. Occupation A may be located in another part of the country from occupation B. If workers are reluctant to move, then wage differentials will remain. People often do not wish to relocate. They are unwilling to leave family, friends, and familiar

Figure 14.8

Wage differentials

A wage differential between occupations A and B will cause a flow of workers from the lower-wage occupation to the higher-wage occupation. This movement of workers will tend to equalize the wage rates between occupations.

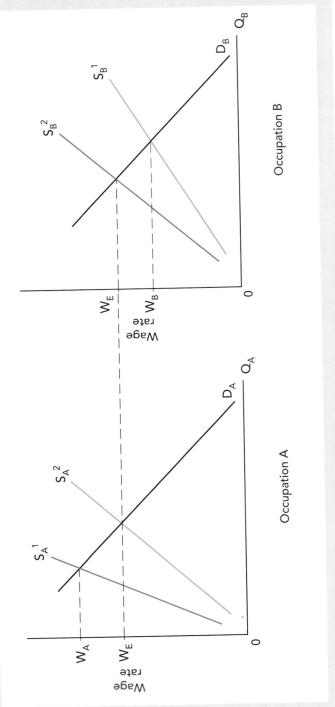

surroundings. In fact, worker mobility has declined in recent years. It is possible that government social welfare programs and the unemployment insurance system have made relocating to other parts of the country less attractive. If workers are not forced to move due to financial reasons, they may not do so. This applies especially to older workers. If workers do not move to where the higher wages are being paid, wage differentials will continue to exist.

Discrimination may also be a barrier to worker mobility. Employers may refuse to hire workers because of their skin colour, sex, marital status, nationality, and so forth. If discrimination can reduce the supply of workers to an occupation, wage differentials between occupations will be maintained.

Labour unions may also restrict mobility. Some unions have negotiated contracts with employers that state that new employees must be union members before being hired. Since only a certain number of people are union members, this condition restricts the number of people that can do the job. This situation is known as a *closed-shop* arrangement. Labour unions may also encourage government to insist on long apprenticeship periods before a person is qualified to work in a trade. The presence of a long training period may discourage some people from entering that occupation. Unions restrict the mobility of workers into certain occupations in order to maintain wage differentials.

Government has assisted in the maintenance of occupational wage differentials by granting certain professions the statutory power to regulate themselves. That is, certain professional associations can license, control, and govern the members of their profession. The justification for self-regulation is that members of the profession are best suited for setting proper standards of competence. This control gives great powers to the members of such a profession. Licences to practise in the profession may only be given to those who pass the licensing examination. Entrance requirements for schools of training may also be established, as well as restrictions on the number of such schools. The fact that these professions have been given complete monopoly over the practice of the profession means that they are likely to restrict supply in order to keep the wage up. They operate in a fashion similar to monopolies in product markets. Examples of such professions are doctors and lawyers.

If there were no barriers to worker mobility, would all wages be the same? The answer is no. Each occupation has certain characteristics that lend themselves to wage differences. For example, some jobs may involve a certain amount of danger or unsafe conditions. Since not everyone is willing to do this type of work, these jobs are likely to pay higher wage rates than

The attractive characteristics of a job, called the equalizing differences, may compensate for lower wages when that job is compared to other jobs.

others. Certain occupations may also pay more because they are unhealthy, dirty, involve unusual working hours, have a greater risk of unemployment, and so on. The attractive aspects of some occupations, on the other hand, may result in lower wage rates. These attractive aspects are called **equalizing differences** and include clean and safe conditions, regular hours, job security, and possibly prestige. The idea of equalizing differences is presented in Figure 14.9. The heights of the two columns for jobs A and B are equal, indicating that they are equally attractive. Job B is able to pay a lower wage because of the attractive features, or equalizing differences, of the job. Job A is less attractive than job B and must offer a higher wage rate in order to attract workers.

Some reasons for wage differentials were introduced by Adam Smith in 1776 in his book *The Wealth of Nations*:

> *The five following are the principal circumstances which, so far as I have been able to observe, make up for a small pecuniary gain in some employments, and counterbalance a great one in others: first, the agreeableness or disagreeableness of the employments themselves; secondly, the easiness and cheapness, or the difficulty and expense of learning them; thirdly, the constancy or inconstancy of employment in them;*

Figure 14.9

Equalizing differences

The presence of equalizing differences in Job B makes it just as attractive as Job A even though the wage rate is lower.

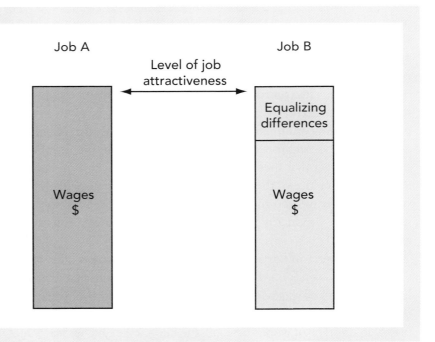

fourthly, the small or great trust which must be reposed in those who exercise them, and fifthly, the probability or improbability of success in them.

Equalizing differences are the attractive aspects of a job that compensate the worker for lower wages. The issue of compensation can be viewed from another angle. How much more money do employees demand in order to work in less desirable working conditions? The increase in the hourly wage rate that is necessary to get employees to work under more hazardous conditions is called a *compensating wage differential.*

R E V I E W

14.11 Identify four barriers to worker mobility between jobs.

14.12 Why would government want to restrict the number of people who could practise a certain trade or profession?

EVERYDAY ECONOMICS 14.4

Paralegals—Make Them Legal?

Does all legal work in the province of Ontario need to be handled by lawyers? Can individuals other than lawyers who have some legal training handle simple legal matters for a fee? If someone other than a lawyer handles a legal issue, how does the consumer know that he or she is qualified? Do lawyers need to have a monopoly in matters involving the law? These questions and others are of concern to the legal profession, the general public, and the government. To help answer these questions, the Ontario government appointed retired Supreme Court of Canada Justice Peter Cory to study the role of paralegals in the provision of legal services in 1999. The Ontario government wanted to ensure that purchasers of legal services received professional advice at the same time ensuring that the justice system remained accessible to ordinary citizens. Justice Cory's report, submitted in June 2000, recommends increased responsibilities for paralegals. Paralegals are defined as non-lawyers who work independently performing legal services before boards, tribunals, or some courts for a fee. Justice Cory's recommendations include the following:

- paralegals could perform some of the family-law and real-estate work now being performed by lawyers such as drawing up simple wills, undertaking uncontested divorce proceedings, and representing vendors in real-estate transactions.

- paralegals should be allowed to swear affidavits and undertake simple incorporations. In the area of criminal law, however, they should not be allowed to handle summary convictions. However, they could perform work in the following areas of the criminal code: vagrancy; using slugs and tokens; defacing coins; falsifying employment records; and public nudity.

- paralegals should be licensed after successful completion of a two-year college program.

- the paralegal industry should be regulated to prevent untrained and irresponsible persons from performing paralegal work. The report recommended an independent body be established to regulate paralegals. Representation on this regulatory body would come from the Attorney General's office, the general public, the Law Society of Upper Canada, and independent paralegals.

Questions

1. Using demand and supply curves in your answer, show the impact on the market for lawyers of an expansion in the responsibilities for paralegals.
2. Using demand and supply curves in your answer, show the impact on the market for paralegals of the requirement that paralegals complete a two-year college program.

EVERYDAY ECONOMICS 14.5

Pay Equity

Research indicates that, on average, women working full time earn less than men who work full time. Is this wage differential a result of discrimination against women in the labour market? Is discrimination preventing women from obtaining more highly paid occupations? The belief that discrimination was present in the labour market led to changes in human rights legislation that were designed to prevent discrimination, and to changes in employment standards legislation that guaranteed equal pay for equal work. According to the equal pay standard, men and women must be paid the same wage if they are performing the same job. Some differences in wages can remain if the wage differential is based on seniority or on the amount of work performed. In spite of these legislative changes, average wages and salaries for women continue to lag behind those of men. Governments across Canada are seeking equality of results and not just equality of opportunity. Equal pay for equal work laws have been criticized as inadequate, since in many cases men and women do not perform the same job. Thus, a series of pay equity laws have been introduced.

Pay equity requires employers to pay men and women the same wage for jobs that are different but are of similar *value*. For example, the secretaries in a company, who are most likely women, may have been earning less than the men working in the warehouse. What are the reasons for the wage differential between secretaries and warehouse employees? Is the secretarial job cleaner, safer, and more pleasant? Is the warehouse job less secure and more subject to layoffs? Do warehouse jobs require more physical effort?

Whatever the reasons, the market has determined that warehouse employees should be paid more than secretarial workers. The equalizing differences associated with secretarial work must therefore be sufficient to compensate for the lower pay. If the equalizing differences did not exist, secretarial workers would seek warehouse jobs in sufficient numbers to equalize the wage rates. Under pay-equity legislation, secretaries need not apply for warehouse jobs in order to receive higher wages. If a government inspector determines that the secretarial and warehouse jobs are of equal value to the firm, the wages for the two jobs must be equalized. How are different jobs to be evaluated and compared? The market takes all aspects of the job into consideration when determining the wage rate. Government inspectors use the criteria of skill, effort, responsibility, and working conditions for job comparisons and evaluation.

The implementation of pay-equity legislation raises a number of issues for students of economics. What will be the impact of pay equity on employment for women? If employers are required to raise wages to a level greater than the current marginal revenue product, the number of employees will likely be reduced. Unemployment for women would then likely increase. Will employers relocate to jurisdictions that do not have pay-equity legislation, resulting in a loss of jobs for both men and women? Private-sector wages are determined to a great extent by what customers are willing to pay for the product. Will consumers be willing to pay more for the product in order to support the goal of pay equity?

Pay-equity legislation is normally applied to the government sector before being extended to the private sector. Public services provided by government usually have no competition in the marketplace. The increases in costs associated with pay equity can therefore be borne more easily by the public sector.

Will pay equity reduce the incentive to train for higher-paying jobs? If pay equity can improve wages without further education and training on the part of the employee, why go to the trouble of acquiring further skills? Some occupations are more highly-paid because of the relative shortage of workers in those occupations. Canadians should be training for these occupations in order to make the most efficient use of our labour resource.

What about wage differentials between two occupations dominated by men, or between two dominated by women? In some cases, these differences are greater than the differences between typical jobs dominated by either men or women. Can wage differences between two occupations dominated by men be the result of discrimination in the labour market? Should legislation be passed to achieve pay equity between jobs typically held by the same sex?

What causes the differential between average men's and women's salaries to exist? One study determined that most of the salary differential can be explained by the impact of marriage on a woman's career and on her attachment to the workplace. In this study, marital status accounted for all but 8 percent of the difference in wages. In fact, in one study, never-married women with university degrees earned 9.8 percent more than comparable men. In another study, these women earned 99.2 percent of what comparable men earned. If a major determinant of wage differentials is a woman's marital status, what role does pay-equity legislation have to play?

Who makes the decision on job comparison? In one U.S. study, similar jobs were ranked according to value by different states. Each state ranked the jobs differently. Which ranking was correct? Also, should pay-equity officers take such factors as the risk of layoffs into consideration? Clearly the wage rates set by pay equity officers are subjective in nature.

Questions

1. Would employers interested in maximizing profits arbitrarily pay men higher wages than women? Discuss.
2. Should legislation be passed to achieve equity between different occupations that are dominated by men? Between those dominated by women?
3. Canadian governments are under spending pressure because of the public debt. In light of the debt, can governments afford to monitor pay equity in the private sector?

The Price of Land

In Chapter 5, rent was included in the calculation of gross domestic product (GDP). *Rent is the income paid to the land resource, and is determined by the interaction of demand and supply in the marketplace.* The demand curve for land for a specific use such as housing is the sum of the marginal revenue product (MRP) curves for the firms that want this resource. As is the case with the labour resource, the demand for land depends on the productivity of the land and the market price for the final product. Although the supply of land in general is fixed, the supply curve for land for a specific purpose slopes upward to the right. For example, when the price of houses increases, the price of land used for housing will also increase. This increase in price results in more land being supplied for housing. Hence, the supply curve for land for this specific purpose has a positive slope. The intersection of the demand and supply curve determines the price of land in the market (see Figure 14.10).

The concept of **economic rent** is also shown in Figure 14.10. Rent means something different to an economist than it does to other people, who

 Economic rent **entails the payment to an economic resource above the amount necessary to attract it to a specified use.**

The return to land is divided into transfer earnings and economic rent.

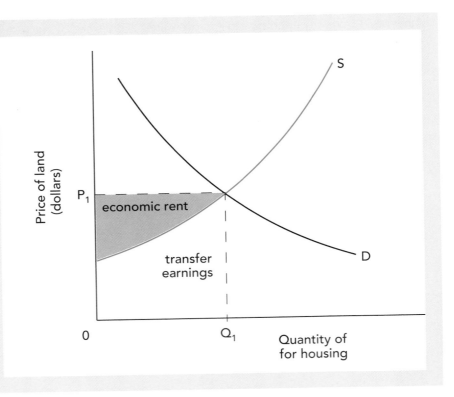

refer to rent as the price paid for using an apartment, a building, a car, or some other object owned by someone else. To an economist, rent is a payment to the land resource above the minimum amount of money necessary to attract this resource into a specific use. The minimum amount of money required to attract land into a specific use is known as **transfer earnings** (see Figure 14.10). The equilibrium price for land in this example is P_1 and all the land receives the same price. Some land would be offered for this use at a lower price than P_1. If that land can attract a price P_1, then it is earning an economic rent.

Transfer earnings are the minimum amount of money required to attract land into a specific use.

An example may help explain the concept of economic rent. Land located in the heart of a major Canadian city may have more than one use. It may be used for housing, agriculture, commercial or industrial development, or parkland. Some land will be offered for housing even at low prices for the land. Other parcels of land will only be offered for housing if the price of housing land goes up. Once the price of land has been established as P_1 (see Figure 14.10), all land used for housing will likely command the same price. The land originally offered for housing at a lower price than P_1 will be earning an economic rent. The economic rent that each parcel of land earns will not be the same.

What happens to economic rent when the supply of land is fixed? When the supply curve for land is perfectly inelastic, the price of land is determined solely by the demand for land (see Figure 14.11). In this case, all the income earned by the land is economic rent. Assume that a certain piece of land is only good for growing tobacco and cannot be used for other purposes. The price of this land is determined by the demand for tobacco. If there were no demand for tobacco, this land would have no market price. Therefore any price that this land receives provides the land with economic rent.

The concept of economic rent has been used in connection with other resources as well. In professional sports, for example, many athletes are earning economic rent. Many professional athletes who love their sport would willingly offer their services to an employer for less money than they are currently earning. Many baseball players in the major leagues would be willing to work for less than $200 000 per year even though the vast majority of them earn more than this figure. The income that they earn over and above the amount that they would be willing to work for is called economic rent. For example, if a certain catcher with the Montreal Expos were willing to play baseball for $200 000 per year and the Expos offered him a salary of $500 000 per year, his economic rent would be $300 000. Why do many baseball players and other athletes receive economic rent? The

Figure 14.11

Equilibrium price of tobacco land

When the supply curve for land is perfectly inelastic, all the income earned from land is economic rent.

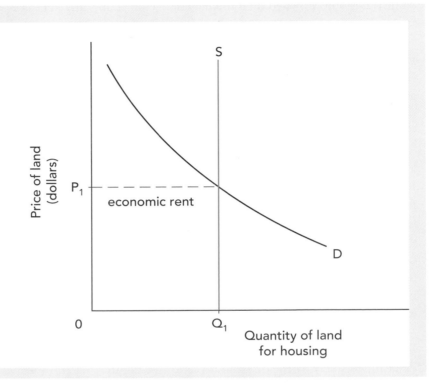

existence of economic rent for athletes is due to the unique ability of the athlete and to the high demand for his or her sport on the part of the viewing public.

REVIEW

14.13 What do we mean by economic rent?

The Market for Capital

Capital goods are manufactured resources such as buildings, machinery, and equipment. Since they are durable they can help to produce goods and services for several years after the initial purchase. Eventually capital goods wear out and must be replaced. A demand for new capital is thus created. Technological changes also create a demand for new capital goods by making current machinery and equipment obsolete. For example, rapid changes in computer design and computer software have forced companies to purchase up-to-date equipment if they want to remain efficient and competitive.

The demand curve for capital goods is influenced by the law of diminishing returns. If both land and labour resources are fixed, then purchases of additional capital goods will eventually contribute less and less to total output. In other words, the marginal productivity of additional capital goods will eventually begin to decline. The firm will only purchase more capital if the price of the capital goes down.

In making the decision to purchase a capital good, the firm must consider the amount of additional output that can be produced in the future with the aid of this capital good. The dollar value of that future output has to be compared to the present dollar cost of the machinery or equipment. In other words, the money that can be earned in the future from the purchase of a capital good must be discounted to the present. It is necessary to calculate the **present value** of these earnings. The formula for discounting a stream of future earnings follows:

The dollar value today of a future sum of money is called the present value.

$$\text{present value (PV)} = \frac{y_1}{1 + i} + \frac{y_2}{(1 + i)^2} + \frac{y_3}{(1 + i)^3} + \cdots + \frac{y_n}{(1 + i)^n}$$

where

y = earnings obtained from the capital good in a given year
i = interest rate
n = year

Assume that a firm is considering the purchase of a new machine at a cost of $3500. In order to determine the feasibility of buying this machine, the firm must determine *the present value of the future earnings* that this machine is likely to bring to the firm. The interest rate is 10 percent per annum and the firm estimates that the yearly earnings derived from this machine will be $1000. The machine is expected to last five years. Is this machine a worthwhile purchase? In order to answer this question, the present value of the stream of future earnings must be calculated.

$$PV = \frac{\$1000}{1 + .10} + \frac{\$1000}{(1 + .10)^2} + \frac{\$1000}{(1 + .10)^3} + \frac{\$1000}{(1 + .10)^4} + \frac{\$1000}{(1 + .10)^5}$$

PV = $909.09 + $862.45 + $751.31 + $683.01 + $620.92

PV = $3790.78

On the basis of this information, the purchase of the machine makes sense. The present value of the machine is $3790.78 and the purchase price of the machine is $3500, creating a net present value of $290.78. If the purchase price of the machine had been greater than $3790.78, it would not have been a wise decision to buy it.

The decision to purchase the machine is dependent on the annual earnings that can be expected from the machine and on the interest rate. In the above example, it was assumed that these annual earnings would be $1000 per year. In reality, this may not be the case. Annual earnings from the machine are likely to decline each year that the machine is in use. The interest rate is also an important factor in this decision. If the interest rate were 14 percent in the above example instead of 10 percent, the present value would be $3433.08. Under these conditions, the firm would not purchase the machine for $3500.

Why is the interest rate so important in making an investment decision? If the firm had to borrow the money in order to purchase this machine, the cost of borrowing would be an important consideration in making the decision. If money could be borrowed at 10 percent, then it would be advisable to purchase the machine. However, if money can only be borrowed at 14 percent or more, the present value of this machine is below the purchase price. The machine should not be purchased at this rate of interest. Even if the money does not have to be borrowed in order to make the purchase, the interest rate is significant. The firm must consider the opportunity cost associated with the use of available funds. In our example, if the firm could invest its money in some other manner than by buying the machine, and could get at least 14-percent interest, then it should proceed in that direction. If the firm can get a return of only 10 percent on invested funds, then it would be advisable to purchase the machine. *Therefore, the demand for both money and capital goods will be greater at lower interest rates.*

The interest rate also influences the supply of money available to be borrowed. At higher interest rates, more money will be made available. At lower interest rates, less money is made available for borrowing. As discussed in Chapter 7, the intersection of the demand for and the supply of money will determine the equilibrium interest rate.

REVIEW

14.14 Why is the interest rate important in making the decision to purchase capital equipment?

Summary

Labour markets are a good example of how resource markets operate in our economy. Since there are various markets for labour, or workers, the interplay of demand and supply determines wage rates and levels of employment. The demand for labour is referred to as a derived demand, since it is dependent on the demand for the product that labour helps to produce. The demand for labour is also influenced by the productivity of the worker. The greater the productivity, the greater the demand.

Changes in the demand for labour come about as a result of changes in the price of the product that labour helps to produce, and in changes in worker productivity. A change in the price of a substitute for labour would also influence demand. If the price of highly technical equipment falls, employers may be encouraged to substitute that equipment for workers. Finally, any change in the price of a resource that labour works with will affect demand.

The elasticity of demand for labour is an important concept in such areas as union/management bargaining and government wage policy. The greater the elasticity or demand for labour, the more any wage increase will affect employment levels. Elasticity is determined by the following factors: the elasticity of demand for the final product; the percentage of total costs which labour costs comprise; the number of substitutes for labour; and the shape of labour's marginal-product curve.

Wage rates are determined by the interaction of the demand for and the supply of labour. In many instances, the individual firm will have no control over the wage rate paid to certain workers. In other cases, the firm will have an influence on workers' wages, depending on how many are hired. In situations where the firm can influence the wage rate, it has to consider the marginal-resource cost of each worker hired.

Trade unions attempt to increase the wages of their members. They can do this either by increasing the demand for their members or by decreasing the supply of their members able to perform a certain job. Most union activity is directed at the supply side of the labour market. Craft unions try to shift the supply curve to the left, while industrial unions try to reshape the supply curve by imposing a wage (price) floor.

Collective bargaining is the process whereby employees negotiate together with an employer regarding the terms of their employment. In order to ensure that the employer negotiates with employees, a labour union must be certified as the bargaining agent for the employees. The certification procedure establishes that the union has the backing of a majority of employees in the bargaining unit. Once certified, the union approaches the employer to begin the negotiations leading to a collective agreement. If an agreement is reached, the working conditions for the employees are set for the duration of the agreement. If an agreement cannot be reached, a strike or lockout may occur.

Not all occupations pay exactly the same wage. Differences in wage rates are due to two factors: barriers and equalizing differences. Labour-market barriers restrict the flow of workers from one job to another. Equalizing differences are attractive features of certain jobs that make up for lower wage rates.

The income paid to land can be divided into transfer earnings and economic rent. Transfer earnings are the minimum amount of money required to attract land into a specific use. Economic rent is a payment to land above the minimum amount of money necessary to attract this land to a specific use.

The demand for capital is heavily influenced by interest rates. In making a decision to purchase a capital good, the firm must consider the amount of additional output that can be produced in the future with the assistance of this capital good. This future stream of earnings must be discounted to the present, using the interest rate, in order to make the purchase decision.

Questions for Review and Discussion

1. Why do companies hire workers? Based on your answer, what is a major determinant of wage rates?
2. Which of the following activities would result in higher wages for the workers involved?
   a) an increase in the demand for new cars, on autoworkers' wages;
   b) a decrease in the price of Japanese imported cars, on Canadian autoworkers' wages;
   c) an increase in the number of building permits, on the wages of construction workers;
   d) an increase in interest rates, on the wages of construction workers; or
   e) an increase in the graduates from law school, on the salaries for lawyers.
3. Would employers pay all employees the minimum wage if there were no unions? Why or why not?
4. Explain the impact of government imposing a minimum wage on a group of employees in terms of the MRP curve for those workers.
5. Advances in technology have been cited as the main reason for job losses in some industries. Can you think of a way whereby advances in technology could increase the number of jobs in an industry?

6. What effect would restrictions on immigration have on wage rates?

7. From your knowledge of wage differentials, can you offer reasons to explain the wage differential that exists between wage rates for men and women?

8. Certain negative aspects of a job result in higher wages being paid to people who do these jobs. Discuss these negative aspects.

9. An article in *The Globe and Mail* in July 2000 stated that many girls as young as age 13 decide not to study mathematics and physics. What impact may this decision have on wage differentials for men and women?

10. Assume that a union organizes apple pickers in Nova Scotia. What impact will this have on the following?
    a) the wages of apple pickers;
    b) the employment of apple pickers;
    c) the price of apples; and
    d) the possible introduction of equipment that can pick apples.

11. Why are craft unions more interested in reducing the number of workers who can perform a certain job than industrial unions are?

12. If there were no barriers to mobility in the labour market, the wages for all occupations would be identical. Evaluate this statement.

13. During the Second World War, the cost of hiring some employees— for example, domestic servants—increased. Explain why this happened using your knowledge of the labour market.

14. Loblaws announced in May 2000 that it would test cashier-less checkout counters in its grocery stores. Customers will scan their own groceries through the checkout counter. Using demand and supply curves, discuss the impact on the market for cashiers.

15. A section of land in Northern Ontario can be used only for nickel mining. Using demand and supply, show the impact on the price of land of a decrease in the price of nickel.

16. What effect do future interest rates have on the decision to purchase capital equipment?

17. Give an example of a monopsony in the labour market.

Selected Websites

www.ilo.org Information on international labour standards, press releases, and publications from the International Labour Organization.

http://laws.justice.gc.ca/en/L-2/ The Canada Labour Code.

www.clc-ctc.ca The site for the Canadian Labour Congress (CLC).

www.econ.rochester.edu/eco108/ch12/micro12/sld046.htm A series of slides showing the calculation of the marginal product of labour.

The following are websites for labour unions:
www.cupe.ca: Canadian Union of Public Employees
www.cupw-sttp.org: Canadian Union of Postal Workers
http://caw.ca: Canadian Automobile Workers
http://opseu.org: Ontario Public Service Employees Union
www.psac.com: Public Service Alliance of Canada
www.cep.ca: Communications, Energy and Paperworkers Union of Canada

GLOSSARY

ability-to-pay approach Taxation approach that proposes individuals be taxed based on their ability to pay taxes; an alternative approach to taxation theory.

adjustable-peg system A system of fixed foreign-exchange rates that can be adjusted if necessary.

aggregate demand The total demand for goods and services in the economy, including consumption, investment, government spending, and the difference between exports and imports.

aggregate supply The total production of goods and services available in the economy over a certain period of time.

appreciation An increase in the value of a currency in relation to another currency under the conditions of a flexible exchange-rate system.

arbitrage A system based on international communications; keeps the foreign-exchange value of a currency approximately equal in all markets.

arbitration A procedure whereby an independent third party settles disputes between union and management during the life of a collective agreement.

automatic stabilizers Government programs currently in operation that react automatically to help adjust the level of aggregate demand when economic conditions change.

average propensity to consume (APC) The ratio of consumption to income (or gross domestic product).

average propensity to save (APS) The ratio of savings to income (or gross domestic product).

balanced-budget multiplier The amount by which an equal increase in taxes and in government spending increases GDP.

bank rate The rate of interest paid by chartered banks on money borrowed from the Bank of Canada.

bargaining unit The tasks in a company that are covered in the collective agreement between the employer and the union.

barter The process by which goods or services are exchanged without the use of money.

benefits-received approach Taxation approach that proposes individuals be taxed based on the benefits they receive from government programs.

branch banking A system of banking in which a commercial bank is permitted to operate branches of the main bank.

break-even point The level of production for a firm at which price equals the minimum average cost.

caisse populaire Financial institution that is usually organized on the basis of Roman Catholic parish boundaries and that receives funds by selling shares and accepting deposits from members.

Canada–United States Automobile Agreement Allows for the duty-free movement of most vehicles and parts between the two countries.

capital account The section of the international balance of payments that records the inflow and outflow of investment dollars.

cartel A formal arrangement, written or verbal, among producers that regulates the price and total output of a product.

certification The process by which a labour union acquires the bargaining rights for a group of employees.

change in demand A response to a change in a factor previously held constant.

change in quantity supplied A response to a change in the price of a product or service.

change in supply A response to a change in a factor previously held constant.

change in the quantity demanded A response to a change in the price of a product or service.

chartered bank Financial institution operating under the authority of Parliament that accepts deposits and lends money to businesses, government, and households.

circular flow of money The directional flow of money in the economy from the business sector to households and back.

cluster Occurs when a number of similar firms, their customers and suppliers, and training institutions are located in close proximity; clusters are a source of external economies and diseconomies of scale.

cobweb theorem An explanation of price fluctuations in agriculture; assumes that farmers determine the size of next year's crop on the basis of this year's price.

collective bargaining The process of management and the union representing the employees negotiating an employment contract.

command approach A situation in which resources—land, labour, and capital—are jointly or publicly owned.

Competition Act Federal government legislation prohibiting business practices that substantially restrict competition.

concentration The degree to which an industry is dominated by a few firms.

conglomerate merger Occurs when a firm acquires another firm that is engaged in a different business.

Consumer Price Index (CPI) The ratio of current prices of consumer products to the prices of those products in a base year; the percentage change in this index from year to year is referred to as the rate of inflation.

consumer surplus The difference between the price consumers would be willing to pay for a given quantity of a product and the price that they actually do pay.

corporation A business organization created by law that is owned by its shareholders.

cost-push inflation Increases in the general price levels resulting from firms passing on their cost increases to consumers in the form of higher prices.

countervailing duty An additional tariff placed on an imported item that has received government financial assistance during production in the exporting country.

craft union A trade union whose members all possess a particular skill.

credit union Financial institution that sells shares and accepts members' deposits; oriented toward consumer lending.

crop restriction A government quota designed to reduce the quantity of an agricultural product on the market.

crude-quantity theory of money A mathematical identity that states that the price level is directly related to the amount of money in circulation (P = KM).

current account The section of the international balance of payments that records the inflows and outflows of money for merchandise and service items.

deficiency-payment system An agricultural price-support program whereby the government pays the farmer the difference between the average market price for a product and the support price.

demand side Those who are willing to purchase a good or service.

demand-deficient unemployment Unemployment that results from a lack of overall spending in the economy.

demand-pull inflation The increase in the general level of prices that occurs when the aggregate demand for goods and services exceeds the supply.

deposit insurance Insurance on the deposit liabilities of chartered banks and other financial institutions.

depreciation A reduction in the value of a currency in relation to another currency.

derived demand The demand for a resource based on the demand for the good or service that the resource helps to produce.

devalued currency Currency that has decreased in value in relation to another under the conditions of a fixed exchange-rate system.

direct tax A tax imposed on the individual who should pay the tax.

discretionary fiscal policy Aims at improving economic conditions by changing the level of government spending and taxation.

diseconomies of scale Increases in long-run average costs resulting from the inefficiencies associated with large-scale operations.

disposable income The income that remains in the household after taxes have been paid.

dissaving Occurs when spending is greater than disposable income.

division of labour The specialization in the performance of tasks by workers to permit greater efficiency and greater production.

dumping The practice of selling a product in a foreign market at a lower price than is charged in the domestic market.

economic profit The excess of total revenue over total costs.

economic rent Payment to an economic resource above the amount necessary to attract it to a specified use.

economies of scale Decreases in long-run average costs resulting from the efficiencies of large-scale production.

economies of scope Exist when it is less costly for one firm to produce two products than for two firms to produce the products separately.

elasticity The extent to which the quantity of a product demanded responds to a change in price.

employment rate The employment-to-population ratio.

equalization payments Payments to provinces to ensure that the province can provide a reasonable level of public services without resorting to extremely high levels of taxation.

equalizing differences The attractive characteristics of a job that may compensate for lower wages when that job is compared to other jobs.

equilibrium GDP Stable gross domestic product; occurs when savings equal investments.

equilibrium price The price at which the quantity demanded of a product is equal to the quantity supplied.

excise tax A tax levied by government on the suppliers of certain products.

expenditure multiplier The amount by which a change in aggregate demand is multiplied in order to determine the change in GDP.

explicit costs Payments for productive resources that the firm does not own and must purchase.

fair-return price A price used in the regulation of a monopoly that is equal to the average cost of production.

featherbedding Practices or work rules that may set unreasonable limits on the amount of work employees may perform in a given period of time, or that may result in payment for unneeded workers doing jobs that duplicate others' efforts.

federalist system System in which two levels of government have jurisdiction over each citizen.

fiat money The currency issued by a government or a bank that is not matched by holdings of gold or other securities.

fiscal policies Changes to the level of government spending and taxation with the goal of influencing economic conditions.

Fisher equation of exchange States that the money supply multiplied by the velocity of money is equal to the number of transactions that take place in the economy multiplied by the average price level (MV = PT).

fixed costs Production costs that do not vary with the amount produced.

foreign ownership Investment by foreign residents in Canadian assets and financial securities.

foreign-exchange rate The value of a nation's currency in terms of another nation's currency.

foreign-trade multiplier The amount by which a change in aggregate demand is multiplied in order to determine the change in GDP, taking into account the impact of foreign trade.

free-market approach An approach to economic decision making that stresses private ownership of property and resources.

frictional unemployment Short-term unemployment on the part of individuals who have voluntarily left one job and are in the process of looking for another.

full-employment level of GDP The level of aggregate demand in the economy required to ensure that everyone who wants employment has a job.

General Agreement on Tariffs and Trade (GATT) An international agreement aimed at reducing the barriers to international trade.

Gresham's Law States that bad money forces good money out of circulation.

gross domestic product (GDP) The value of all final goods and services produced in a country in a given year.

gross public debt The combination of unmatured bonds, treasury bills, and notes as well as other liabilities.

hidden unemployed Those members of the population who are not actively seeking a job because they do not believe there are suitable jobs available.

horizontal merger The combination of two firms engaged in the same activity.

human resources policies Stabilization policies aimed at lessening the amount of structural unemployment in the economy.

hyperinflation A very rapid increase in the level of prices that leads to a lack of public confidence in the currency.

implicit costs Payments for productive resources that the firm already owns.

indexing Making adjustments to taxes or payments according to changes in the rate of inflation.

indirect tax A tax levied against one individual in the expectation that it will be paid by another individual.

industrial union A trade union that attempts to organize all of the workers in a particular industry.

infant industry A newly established industry.

inflationary gap The decrease in the level of aggregate demand required to bring the equilibrium level of GDP down to the full-employment level of GDP.

insurance-induced unemployment Unemployment that is caused by the level of employment-insurance benefits, which makes looking for work unattractive.

international balance of payments Documents all financial transactions between residents of one country and residents of the rest of the world.

International Monetary Fund (IMF) An international agency established in 1944 with the objective of stabilizing foreign-exchange rates.

inverse relationship A relationship in which an increase in the value of one variable results in a corresponding decrease in the value of the other.

investment Business spending on machines and equipment, new residential construction, and any change in inventories.

invisible hand A term to describe the effect that a free-market economic system has of directing the self-interests of individuals toward a common goal.

Keynesian economics A theory that proposes that government take an active role in the economy, increasing government spending in order to support the demand for goods and services and, therefore, to preserve employment

kinked demand curve A demand curve composed of two sections—elastic and inelastic—separated by a bend, or kink; is an attempt to explain price rigidity in oligopolistic industries.

Labour Force Survey A monthly measure of the number of unemployed in Canada; provides an indication of the country's economic condition.

Laffer curve A graphical representation indicating the relationship between the tax rate and the amount of money collected in taxes.

law of comparative advantage States that a country should specialize in and trade items it can produce relatively more efficiently than other countries.

law of diminishing returns States that when a fixed resource is combined with increasing amounts of a variable resource increases in total output will eventually become smaller and smaller.

legal tender That part of the money supply that is acceptable for purchases and for repayment of debt.

liquid asset An asset that can be readily converted into money.

long run The period in the production process during which all resources are variable.

macroeconomics The area of economics concerned with the overall view of an economy rather than with individual markets.

many differentiated sellers A competitive situation with many sellers of a similar but slightly different product.

marginal cost (MC) The addition to the total cost of producing one more unit of output.

marginal product (MP) The addition to total output as a result of adding one more unit of a productive resource.

marginal propensity to consume (MPC) The proportion of any increase in income that is used for consumption.

marginal propensity to save (MPS) Relates changes in the level of savings to changes in the level of income.

marginal revenue (MR) The addition to total revenue as a result of selling one more unit of output.

marginal revenue curve A curve relating extra revenue to the quantity of output.

marginal tax rate Rate that defines the percentage of any additional income that is paid in taxes.

marginal-resource cost (MRC) The addition to total cost as a result of adding one more unit of a productive resource.

marginal-revenue product (MRP) The increase in total revenue as a result of employing one more unit of a productive resource (MP x MR).

market The interaction of buyers and sellers for the purpose of making an exchange of goods or services and establishing a price for them.

marketing board A compulsory marketing organization for primary or processed agricultural products.

microeconomics The area of economics that emphasizes smaller decision-making units, such as business firms, consumers, and workers.

minimum efficient scale The smallest level of output that will allow a firm to reach the lowest average costs possible.

misleading price advertising Occurs when the prices actually charged are higher than those advertised; an illegal activity.

monetary policy The Bank of Canada's regulation of the money supply in order to influence economic conditions.

monopoly Occurs when only one seller of a good or service exists in a given industry.

monopsony A situation where only one firm hires a specific type of worker.

multifactor productivity measures Indicate the level of productivity in an industry by taking into consideration all relevant resources, not only labour resources.

National Accounts Data compiled by Statistics Canada that measure the overall level of business activity in Canada.

natural monopoly An industry in which it is more efficient to have only one seller of a good or service since average costs decline as output increases.

natural rate of unemployment The unemployment rate present when the economy is operating at full capacity.

net debt Gross debt minus recorded assets.

net domestic product (NDP) The value of final goods and services produced in a country in a given year, minus an allowance for capital consumption and indirect business taxes.

non-tariff barriers Impediments to the flow of international trade in the form of quotas, restrictive rules, and regulations.

offer-to-purchase A program of agricultural price support in which the government establishes a price floor and then offers to buy any surplus product not sold in the marketplace.

oligopoly A competitive situation characterized by an industry that comprises only a few firms.

open-market operations The buying and selling of government bonds by the Bank of Canada in order to influence the money supply.

opportunity cost The value of the best possible alternative that is given up in the decision to use a resource.

paradox of thrift States that an increase in the level of savings in the economy can lead to lower levels of income and ultimately to lower levels of savings.

participation rate The percentage of the population that is employed or actively seeking employment.

partnership A form of business enterprise in which two or more persons own and operate the business firm and are liable for its debts.

perfect competition A competitive situation in which there are many thousands of firms, each selling an identical product.

personal disposable income (PDI) The level of personal income that remains after income taxes have been paid.

personal income (PI) The total of consumption spending and savings in the economy.

Phillips curve A graphical representation of the negative relationship between rates of unemployment and rates of inflation.

positive relationship A relationship in which an increase or a decrease in one variable results in a corresponding increase or decrease in the other variable.

predatory pricing The lowering of prices, usually below the costs of production, in order to eliminate the competition.

present value The dollar value today of a future sum of money.

price ceiling A government-imposed maximum price.

price discrimination The practice of charging different prices to different consumers for an item produced under similar cost conditions.

price elasticity of demand The extent to which the quantity of a product demanded responds to a change in price.

price floor A government-imposed minimum price.

price leadership In an oligopoly, occurs when one firm raises its price and other firms in the industry follow with their own price increases.

price system The technique by which scarce resources are allocated to the production of those products and services that provide the greatest return to the resource owner. In this way, the system of prices, rents, wages, and interest organizes economic activity.

privatization The transfer of control of a company from government to private ownership.

production function The relationship between the amount of resources used and the level of output.

production-possibilities curve The maximum amount of two products that can be produced using all available resources efficiently.

productivity The amount of output produced by a unit of a certain resource during a specified period of time.

progressive tax Tax approach in which the percentage of income an individual pays in taxes increases as the individual's level of income increases.

proportional tax Tax approach in which the percentage of income paid in taxes remains constant regardless of an individual's level of income.

public debt Money owed by all levels of government in Canada.

real GDP The level of gross domestic product adjusted for increases in the average price level.

recessionary gap The amount that aggregate demand must increase in order to bring the equilibrium level of GDP up to a full-employment level.

regressive tax Tax approach in which the percentage of income paid in taxes decreases as the level of income increases.

retail price maintenance Occurs when a manufacturer insists that a product be sold at a specified price; contravenes the Competition Act.

Say's Law States that the supply of products creates its own demand, since all production creates income for households that can be spent on goods and services.

scarcity Anything that is available in only a limited supply.

seasonal unemployment Results from the seasonal nature of some industries, such as agriculture, construction, tourism, and recreation.

short run A period in the production process during which at least one resource cannot be altered.

shut-down point The level of production at which the average variable cost of each unit of output is equal to the price of the product.

socially optimum pricing An approach to monopoly price regulation that sets the price at a level equal to the marginal cost.

sole proprietorship The simplest form of business organization, with one owner; usually a small business.

stabilization funds Funds established in support of the adjustable-peg system; each country maintained a fund of domestic and foreign currencies and gold that allowed the country to purchase its currency on world markets to keep the exchange rate at the par value.

stabilization payments Payments to ensure that provincial taxation revenues do not decline substantially from one year to the next.

stagflation A situation of depressed levels of real output in the economy combined with rising prices.

structural unemployment Results from a mismatching of the demand for, and the supply of, workers on an occupational or geographic basis.

supply Those who are willing to sell a good or service.

supply-side economics A stabilization policy that stresses increasing the supply of goods and services in order to reduce the level of prices and to create jobs.

tariff A tax imposed on imported products.

tax multiplier The amount by which any change in the level of taxation must be multiplied in order to determine the impact on GDP.

third-party effects The results of a transaction between two parties that may also have an impact on others, positive or negative.

transfer earnings The minimum amount of money required to attract land into a specific use.

treasury bills (T-bills) Short-term, non–interest-bearing promissory notes issued by the Government of Canada.

trust company Financial institution that acts as a trustee for property interests and conducts other confidential business.

underemployment The term used to describe a situation in which individuals are employed but not at jobs that fully utilize their skills.

unemployment rate The percentage of the labour force that is not employed yet is seeking employment.

unit banking The system in which commercial banks are either not permitted to operate branches or permitted to operate only a limited number.

unmet public goods Those goods and services not provided by the free-market system due to the difficulty of charging a fee to the beneficiaries of the good or service.

value of marginal product An increase in total revenue resulting from employing one more unit of a productive resource in a perfectly competitive industry.

variable costs Production costs that vary with the amount of output.

vertical merger The combination of two firms engaged in different levels of the same activity.

wage and price controls Legal limits on the amount of wage and price increases.

Wagner's law of increasing state activity Postulates that in industrialized economies government spending can be expected to grow at a faster rate than the total output of goods and services.

INDEX